THE THEORY AND PRACTICE OF VOCATIONAL GUIDANCE

THE THEORY AND PRACTICE OF VOCATIONAL GUIDANCE

A Selection of Readings

BARRIE HOPSON AND JOHN HAYES

Vocational Guidance Research Unit

"To fill up a work with these scraps may, indeed, be considered as a downright cheat on the learned world, who are by such means imposed upon to buy a second time in fragments and by retail, what they have already in gross, if not in their memories, upon their shelves."

HENRY FIELDING, *Tom Jones*

PERGAMON PRESS

OXFORD · LONDON · EDINBURGH · NEW YORK

TORONTO · SYDNEY · PARIS · BRAUNSCHWEIG

Pergamon Press Ltd., Headington Hill Hall, Oxford
4 & 5 Fitzroy Square, London W.1
Pergamon Press (Scotland) Ltd., 2 & 3 Teviot Place, Edinburgh 1
Pergamon Press Inc., 44–01 21st Street, Long Island City, New York 11101
Pergamon of Canada Ltd., 207 Oueen's Quay West, Toronto 1
Pergamon Press (Aust.) Pty. Ltd., 19a Boundary Street, Rushcutters Bay, N.S.W. 2011, Australia
Pergamon Press S.A.R.L., 24 rue des Écoles, Paris 5e
Vieweg & Sohn GmbH, Burgplatz 1, Braunschweig

First edition 1968

Library of Congress Catalog Card No. 68–23973

08 013284 7

Contents

Foreword

PATRICK MEREDITH

THE editors of this compilation of readings in The Theory and Practice of Vocational Guidance have performed an important service. Even a cursory glance at the scope of its contents will reveal that this is a service not only to psychologists professionally engaged in vocational guidance but to a great many other potential readers, in fields as diverse as economics, education, sociology, psychiatry, industrial relations, demography, government, human geography, and even philosophy. These readings also carry important implications for statistics, information-theory, computer-science and decision-theory. And the emphatic stress on the central role of the "self-concept" points to deep considerations of ethics and ontology.

This volume serves both to display the wide range of considerations which have dominated the thinking of workers in the vocational field, but at the same time to suggest, by the implication of topics omitted, some of the further problems to which their attention should be drawn. In particular we have a very far-reaching problem to solve which lies at the very roots of the prevailing educational concept of the relation between school and occupation. Some twenty years ago in a little book now out of print (*Visual Education and the New Teacher*, 1946, Visual Education Centre, Exeter) I made the following comments on the relevance of occupational films to the school curriculum:

"Vocational Guidance . . . has been conceived and developed hitherto mainly in terms of tests and evaluations of the child's potentialities. But there is something more fundamental than guidance by tests. It is the individual's *dominant interest* which largely determines his success and helps him overcome his limitations. And interest in a job depends, in turn, on a clear mental picture of the job. A keen interest based on a misconception of the nature of the job may lead to bitter disillusionment and failure. It is therefore the business of the schools to acquaint their pupils with *the way the world works*, in all its occupational diversity. '*The Occupational Life of Man*' *should be an integral feature of all curricula for at least the last two years of school life when interests are crystallizing and vocational decisions are being made*. Now it is exactly here that the technique of the documentary film can ideally fulfil its function. But it should not merely provide a sporadic film show to focus attention on one particular occupation. A long-term programme is needed, based on consultations between the industrialist, the educational and visual experts, the vocational psychologist and the Ministry of Labour. The programme must obviously take account of the national situation. Any good film depicting a job is *ipso facto* propaganda for that job, and if that job is likely to be overcrowded in the near future such propaganda is in nobody's interest. Effort should be directed where it is most needed. We thus require collections of occupational films, books, etc.; lists of typical factories, offices, farms, etc., suitable for school visits; conferences to bring together those concerned in this work; and arrangements for supplying the schools with all the necessary information and material.

"In this way we can bridge a gap which ought never to have existed, the gap between the school-world and the work-a-day world. Naturally the attempt will meet with opposition from those who prefer to see education as a 'spiritual' process having nothing in common with the solid material activities of the workshop and the market-place.

"What defeatist cynicism is this which would carefully wrap up education in cotton-wool while treating industry as something dirty, commercial and (by implication) immoral? Is the child then to be carefully nurtured by other-wordly religion until the age of fifteen or sixteen and then cynically pushed into a world which recognizes none of the principles of his education and encourages him to forget them as quickly as possible? This absurdity can be quickly disposed of. Are all teachers, administrators, inspectors and ministers of education so spiritually minded that they spend their time loving one another and the children, never thinking for one moment about their salaries, never struggling for position, or prestige, but devoting themselves single-mindedly to one thing and one thing only, the spiritual welfare of the children? What of industry on the other hand, or to take a wider term, the occupational world? In this world do we never see a struggle for ideals, a consideration of human values, a loyalty to fellow-workers, a disinterested pursuit of patriotic aims, bravery in the face of extreme occupational hazard and many other values which, if we are to use the term at all, can only be described as spiritual? These things have only to be stated to blast sky-high the sickly pretentiousness of this exclusive claim for the spirituality of education. This is one world and we are all in it together, children, teachers, workers, and the rest, all showing a blend of aspirations and imperfections. It is essential for the health of industry and education alike for the two to be organically related, all accepting the hard claims of material and economic fact, all struggling by their own nature to achieve a life which triumphs over those facts."

My impression is that today the concept of the curriculum as a microcosm of *this* world, rather than of the abstract fictitious world of the academic imagination still haunted by Plato, is as far as ever from realization. And children are still deprived of an adequate picture of the solid occupational world in which they will find their destiny and for which they need guidance in making their own choice, though as John Hayes shows in his paper on the role of occupational information, there is no shortage of techniques for bringing occupational knowledge into the school. It may be, however, that vocational guidance has set itself a task whose information requirements are too complex even for computer-aided techniques, a task which should properly be regarded as the responsibility of the educational system as a whole rather than of a specialist corps within the system. If the curriculum could be redesigned so as to make it mirror our actual culture as it is, and as it is tending, so that the information-handling process became part and parcel of curriculum-design, taking advantage of all modern aids, the specialist counsellor could be left with a more manageable "client-oriented" job. His would be the task of helping the uncertain individual to find his way among conflicting choices, in which the uncertainty would not be due to ignorance of the occupational world (for the curriculum would have remedied this) but to uncertainty in his own self-concept.

This brings us back to the fundamental importance of the individual self, and it is a pleasure to read the opening contribution by Donald Super (whom I once had the privilege of instructing in English constitutional history and elementary Greek at a school in Switzerland some thirty years ago. I wonder who could have guided him then to his subsequent career?). The self-concept is implicit in his phrase "work as a way of life". It would be very wide of the mark to suppose that a curriculum which mirrors the occupational world would simply replace academic training by vocational training. It would redefine the academic task in truer terms which would accept life as it is, a process in which man's attainment and self-discovery is through *occupation* (including the occupation of parenthood).

An important medium for bringing the reality of the occupational world into the field of awareness of the school-child is the "occupational visit", as Barrie Hopson demonstrates in his paper on the subject, so long as it is competently planned and executed, with all necessary safeguards. And he rightly points to the opportunity which such a visit offers not only to grasp the occupational reality but to deepen the child's self-awareness in response to a challenging experience.

One of the problems wide open for a fresh approach is that of the economics of guidance, counselling and selection, not merely in a financial sense but in terms of effort, information and expert manpower. Cronbach and Gleser have made a pioneering contribution to this problem (Cronbach, L. J., and Gleser, G. C. *Psychological Testing and Personnel Decisions*, 2nd ed., University of Illinois Press, Urbana, 1965) and it has important implications for the traning of the counsellors themselves. *Quis custodet ipsos custodes?* A viable career depends upon a reasonable economy in the disposition of one's time and resources. Peter Daws, the Director of the Vocational Guidance Research Unit in the Psychology Department at Leeds, under whose leadership the compilation of this volume was made possible, shows a sensible awareness of the oft-neglected need to avoid "biting off more than one can chew". In his contributions on "What will the school counsellor do" he advises that, in this country at any rate, "Our own counsellors will need to accept a more modest definition of their role." I would suggest that this is not merely prudent parsimony dictated by national economic stringency, but an indication of wide application in many other professions. Perhaps most of us tend to interpret our professional roles too ambitiously and do too much inadequately instead of a reasonable amount adequately. Economy is not parsimony but effectiveness and elegance of performance. An overworked counsellor, stretched beyond his resources, is going to give less than his best to those whom he counsels.

And this brings an overlong Foreword to a provocative conclusion. Rightly the many contributors are exploring the theoretical foundations of vocational guidance in all directions and offer an impressive array of findings and concepts. But the practitioner has a job to do and some one must tackle the task of taking the perplexing implications of theory down to a manageable set of elemental principles. It was the merit of Alec Rodger, who must surely be regarded as the founding father of vocational guidance in this country, to perceive the need for an essentially simple and manageable taxonomy of guidance-objectives into which a great mass of early theory was unobtrusively packed. Theory has moved on a long way but it is right and proper that his famous "Seven-point Plan" should find a place in this selection, and not merely for its historic interest. It embodies an implicit uneconomic and pedagogic principle of direct relevance to the training of counsellors however modern their techniques. If they become over-elaborate in their daily practice they will no longer see the wood for the trees and their advice will be anxious, uncertain and confused. We may need a few more than seven points, but we must not have so many points that they become a blur. And it is here precisely that the effective use of the computer, in relieving the human brain of the necessity for handling vast areas of information, will be seen at its true value. It is significant that Loughary, Friesen and Hurst, in their paper on "Autocoun" conclude with the need to assure ourselves, "That automated systems contribute to, rather than inhibit, the freedom of the individual".

Equally significant is their finding that of the two counsellors involved in the experiment the one whose statements and decisions were "more like the machine" was the one whose additional data "were based on a knowledge of the pupils". This is reassuring and affords a valuable footnote to Alec Rodger's remark that "Neither the Seven-point Plan nor any other is likely to turn a bad judge of people into a good one".

A word of acknowledgement and appreciation of those who make possible the establishment of our Vocational Guidance Research Unit at Leeds University is due here. For without the resources of the Unit the production of this volume might never have been undertaken. Our thanks are due to the Calouste Gulbenkian Foundation and to the Department of Scientific and Industrial Research (as it was then styled at the time of the award of their grant three years ago). And lastly a tribute to Mr. Hans Hoxter whose persistent devotion to the cause of vocational guidance in this country prodded us all into action.

Preface

IN BRITAIN there has been a resurgence of interest in vocational guidance over the past few years. Several universities have established post-graduate courses to train school counsellors, and many others are beginning to introduce courses dealing with some aspect of vocational theory into their undergraduate psychology, sociology, and education syllabuses. Courses in careers work have also been introduced by a number of teacher training colleges.

Students, teachers and practitioners in this field are faced with a common problem: a paucity of available literature. British research has been limited and although a great deal of basic work on the theory and practice of vocational guidance has been done, and is well documented in the U.S.A., its existence is not widely known in this country. Those who are aware of some of this work are frustrated by the long delays in obtaining the material they require, especially since many of the relevant journals are not taken by British libraries. Most of the material has to be obtained direct from the U.S.A. and not only is this an expensive process but it is also very time-consuming.

It was this situation that encouraged us to prepare this collection of material. We have selected contributions from amongst the best American literature supplemented, wherever possible, by British work relevant to vocational guidance in this country.

We would like to express our sincere appreciation to Peter P. Daws, Director of the Vocational Guidance Research Unit in the University of Leeds, for his active support and encouragement and for his invaluable comments and criticisms. The work on this collection began when both the editors were members of the Vocational Guidance Research Unit. The work of the Vocational Guidance Research Unit is supported by the Gulbenkian Foundation and by the Social Science Research Council, but neither of these organizations necessarily shares the views expressed in this book.

Our thanks are due to F. P. G. Whitaker, Director of the Department of Management Studies in the University of Leeds, who has also given this enterprise enthusiastic support.

Finally we would like to express our appreciation to Miss W. Bee, Mrs. A. V. Riddell and Miss C. L. Slater for efficiently preparing the manuscript in the best traditions of "crisis" typing.

BARRIE HOPSON
JOHN HAYES

Part I. THEORY

"Every man's work, whether it be literature or music or pictures or architecture or anything else, is always a portrait of himself."

SAMUEL BUTLER

Introduction

THE subject of Part I of the book is occupational choice. The major points of emphasis are two: "why" people choose one job in preference to another, and "how" this is accomplished.

People can always provide ready-to-wear answers to describe how they came to choose a particular job, but subjective evaluation is notorious for its attractive "red herrings". It is, therefore, most disappointing when we look for objective investigations into the phenomenon of occupational choice to discover that until quite recently the cupboards were depressingly bare. Psychology, in the form of Mrs. Hubbard, did not really have a change of heart until the early nineteen-fifties. As it transpired, the provider was not a psychologist, but the economist Eli Ginzberg and his associates (1951), who were to bring to the attention of psychologists and sociologists the paucity of empirical information and theoretical interest existing at the time.

Prior to Ginzberg's book, *Occupational Choice: An Approach to a General Theory*, three generalized approaches to occupational choice can be elicited. Part I of this book is concerned with theories of occupational choice and decision-making; none of the following three approaches can justify the title of "theory".

ACCIDENT HYPOTHESIS

This may be described as the "St. Paul on the road to Damascus" approach. With a blinding flash of insight, a person suddenly "hits" on the idea of being, for example, a plumber, by watching one at work on the sink in his house. The anthropologist Malinowski explained his transference of interest from chemistry to anthropology following the experience of reading Frazer's *Golden Bough* during a convalescence from tuberculosis. Whistler relates how, if he had not failed a military examination, he would have lived out his life as an army officer. These examples illustrating some of the ways in which people describe the discovery of their *raison d'être*, are, in reality, emphasizing the role of chance occurrences in life decision-making processes. This explanation of occupational choice sees chance as the important operating factor.

No one doubts the substantial element of chance operating in these examples, but all that they illustrate is that chance was an important factor reinforcing trends already existing at that point in time. The accident factor is seen as the iceberg trip above the submerged mass of earlier experiences and individual dispositions. Many people observe plumbers at work in their kitchens but they are not all motivated to rush out to seek employment as a plumber. Many American young men fail their West Point examinations, but they do not all become artists like Whistler. Thousands of people must have read Frazer's *Golden Bough*, and some of these could also have been recovering from tuberculosis, yet they were not all converted to anthropology as a career.

In explaining their occupational choices as accidents—"I was walking down the High Street, saw this advert in the window, went in and got the job"—most people mean that they were affected by an unplanned exposure to a powerful stimulus. But there are countless such occurrences in everyone's life, and the important question is why are some of these stimuli responded to while others are ignored. The "accident" hypothesis does not tell us.

An attempt to deal with the problem of the selection/non-selection of stimuli in the occupational choise process has been made by the developmental theorists like Super (Chapter 1), Tiedeman (Chapter 4), Blau (Chapter 5), and the *decision-making theorists* (Chapter 6 and 7).

IMPULSE HYPOTHESIS

This approach has been stressed in particular by the psychoanalysts who emphasize the importance of unconscious motivations in everyday life. Ernest Jones quotes the case of the child who showed an unnaturally strong interest in micturition who became a well-known engineer of bridges and canals. We have all heard stories of the sadist who becomes a surgeon or a butcher, and the homosexual who becomes a barber. Again, however, a few examples do not substantiate an all-embracing theory. As the accident hypothesis attributes all occupational choice to the responses of an individual to external forces, so the impulse hypothesis stresses the all-importance of internal factors, that is, the emotional forces. Many surgeons can be shown not to have had abnormal sadistic urges during childhood, and all engineers involved in the construction of bridges and canals do not exhibit childish fascination with micturition. Also, occupational choices other than surgery are made by persons with strong sadistic impulses, and even if this category of occupations were broadened to include butchers, dentists, prison officers, etc., it would still be too narrow to include all occupations permitting expression of so pervasive an impulse.

An attempt to substitute a more sophisticated approach to the question of "impulses" and their effects on occupational choice has been made by "need theorists" like Anne Roe (Chapter 11) and psychoanalytic theorists like Bordin, Segal and Nachman (1963).

TALENT-MATCHING APPROACH

This approach grew up from the needs of the vocational guidance practitioners—professionals working privately, within a youth employment service, guidance agency, or some branch of the educational system. Their work, fundamentally, is to find a suitable occupation for an individual sitting in front of them. The essentials of this approach are contained in the directions of Frank Parsons (1908), the pioneer of the American vocational guidance movement, half a century ago, with his assertion that the choice of a vocation consists of three phases, "... (1) a clear understanding of yourself, your aptitudes, abilities, interests, ambitions, resources, limitations, and their causes; (2) a knowledge of the requirements and conditions of success, advantages and disadvantages, compensations, opportunities, and prospects in different lines of work; (3) true reasoning on the relations of these two groups of facts." As Calia (1966) points out, this, to many modern practitioners, still sounds very contemporary.

This approach to occupational choice is typified in practice by the work of Strong (1955) in the field of vocational interest measurement. By this, the likes and dislikes of various occupational groups are ascertained, and individuals are ranged against these measures to see which of the occupational interest profiles is most like their own profile. If a man's profile emerges more like that of a civil engineer than of any other occupational group, he is told that here is a job that will suit him as far as interests are concerned. By a similar process, his aptitudes and attainments may be assessed objectively to discover if he could succeed in the job as well as being interested in it.

Hull (1928) saw clearly that vocational guidance viewed from this position did not even require a counsellor. The entire process could be mechanized, and he designed a machine that would accomplish the matching process. Our modern computors would make even shorter work of such a task (Loughary *et al.*, Chapter 31).

This approach is, of course, primarily atheoretical and therein lies its major deficiencies. It overlooks the vital question of the needs of the individual and the satisfactions he requires from life and work. In a word, it overlooks his self-concept. It does not really tell us "why" a person chooses one job in preference to another or "how" he makes a choice. It only informs us of the probabilities of success having once chosen an occupation, and many theorists would quarrel with this assumption. In Chapter 17 Donald Super points out the difficulty of defining occupational success.

If generalized approaches suggested by the layman and the vocational counsellor for their respective ends are primarily atheoretical or do not under investigation hold water, what can the social scientists offer?

For many years the scientific basis of the psychology of occupations had been that of the psychology of individual differences typified by Strong's library of career profiles. This resulted in a neglect of other possible approaches as the questions formulated by this approach placed false limits on the subject. The sorts of questions being asked may be designated "snapshot" questions—what type of person will do well in this type of job? What differentiates this occupational group of workers from any other occupational group? What are the range of occupations open to a person with these aptitudes and interests? What abilities are essential to successful participation in this occupation?

"Cinematographic" questions did not readly emerge until the early forties with Carter's (1944) emphasis on the developmental aspect of a person's vocational life. A youth was not to be viewed as at one instant a non-vocational being who suddenly at the age of fourteen or fifteen becomes vocationally oriented. Vocational interests were emphasized by Carter as being part of the general developmental process of the social organism, as integral a part as physical, emotional, social, and intellectual development. The European studies of Buehler (1933) and Lazarsfeld (1931) were also concerned with this aspect of the problem of occupational choice, but their work was largely unknown to American psychologists reared in esoteric schools of psychology in the twenties and thirties, and is largely still unknown in Britain today.

Developmental studies themselves, when initiated, tended to take one of two forms. Perhaps the most important empirically and theoretically speaking has been what Super (1957) calls the *life stages studies.* For example, Miller and Form (1951) in their book on industrial sociology describe life as consisting of a number of periods through which most people pass: there is an "initial work period", in which part-time work and temporary jobs predominate and during which the subject is in school or is receiving higher education. This is succeeded by the "trial work period", in which there is a succession of relatively short-lived part-time jobs. Then comes the "stable work period" with a small number of long-term jobs, followed finally by a "retirement period" in which people typically hold no jobs at all, or jobs with much less responsibility. Miller and Form then analysed the job sequences of men at various socio-economic levels and found that the patterning of careers differed from level to level.

The "great leap forward" in vocational psychology, stemming from the life stages approach, was the publication of the first serious attempt at a comprehensive theory of vocational development through a number of clearly defined stages of physical, intellectual, social, and emotional growth, by Eli Ginzberg and his associates (1951). Ginzberg's theory is described and discussed by Donald Super in Chapter 1.

The essential point made by Ginzberg was that the vocational process was largely irreversible the further one proceeds due to such irrevocable decisions as the choice between educational alternatives, mainly due to the time factor, but also to the personal development of interests, values and life style.

The *life patterns* approach is slightly different from the *life stages studies.* By this, an individual's behaviour and role playing is analysed over a period of time to ascertain persistent and recurrent themes or trends. Thus a life pattern is isolated. This method has been used in the cross-sectional technique, e.g. by Hollingshead (1949) in his study of *Elmtown's Youth*, and by Dennis, Henriques and Slaughter (1956) in their study of a Yorkshire mining town.

There is also the longitudinal approach as used by Douglas (1964) in his study which should provide a great deal of valuable information on the determinants of occupational choice and existing patterns of choice. Nelson (1964) gives a clear account of the problems to be studied by this project regarding occupational choice.

No practitioner can afford to ignore research progress into the explanation of the occupational choice process. If he does he will most likely be making implicit assumptions about the process that could have unforeseen consequences for the counselling situation. At first glance, the theoretical scene may look so complex, and at times contradictory, that the counsellor might be tempted to retreat to the ramparts of his own *common-sense*. But his *common-sense* must be analysed carefully, as each counsellor will carry around with him a set of behavioural hypotheses whose real essence is likely to be hidden by the *obvious naturalness* of the beliefs. It may only be *common-sense* to some observers that people are engaged in work in order to define their identity, to provide existential meaning in an abjectly meaningless world. To others it is *common-sense* for work to be seen as a means to obtaining other, more mundane, ends. To sway towards one extreme or the other is to redefine one's entire set of attitudes towards work, life, vocational guidance and personal counselling. The theoretical bases for a counsellor's actions must always be systematically explored and laid bare by his own introspections. The vocational theorist can help in this process of self-revelation.

REFERENCES

BORDIN, E. S., NACHMANN, B., and SEGAL, S. (1963) An articulated framework for vocational development. *Journal of Counseling Psychology*, **10**, 107–116.

BUEHLER, CHARLOTTE (1933) *Der menschliche Lebenslauf als psychologisches Problem.* Leipzig, Hirzel.

CALIA, V. (1966) Vocational guidance: after the fall. *Personnel and Guidance Journal*, **45**, 320–327.

CARTER, H. D. (1944) *Vocational Interest and Job Orientation*. Stanford University Press.

DENNIS, N., HENRIQUES, F., and SLAUGHTER, C. (1956) *Coal is Our Life*. London, Eyre & Spottiswoode.

DOUGLAS, J. W. B. (1964) *The Home and the School*. London, McGibbon & Kee.

GINZBERG, E., GINSBURG, S. W., AXELRAD, S., and HERMA, J. L. (1951) *Occupational Choice: An Approach to a General Theory*. New York, Columbia University Press.

HOLLINGSHEAD, A. B. (1949) *Elmtown's Youth*. New York, Wiley.

HULL, C. (1928) *Aptitude Testing*. New York, World Book Co.

LAZARSFELD, P. (ed.) (1931) *Jugend und Beruf*. Jena, C. Fischer.

MILLER, D. C., and FORM, W. H. (1951 *Industrial Sociology*. New York, Harper.

NELSON, D. (1964) Studying the employment and training of a national sample of 17-year-olds. *Occupational Psychology*, **38**, 183 –190.

PARSONS, F. (1908) *Choosing a Vocation*. Boston, Houghton-Mifflin.

STRONG, E. K., JR. (1955) *Vocational Interests 18 Years after College*. Minneapolis, University of Minnesota Press.

SUPER, D., CRITES, J., HUMMEL, R., MOSER, H., OVERSTREET, P., and WARNATH, C. (1957) *Vocational Development: A Framework for Research.* New York, Teachers College Press.

ADDITIONAL READING

For accounts of the growth of the vocational guidance movement in the U.S.A., see:

BOROW, H. (1964) Notable Events in the History of Vocational Guidance. Chapter 3, *Man in a World at Work*, ed. H. Borrow. Boston, Houghton-Mifflin.
BREWER, J. M. (1942) *History of Vocational Guidance.* New York, Harper.
WILLIAMSON, E. G. (1964) An historical perspective of the vocational guidance movement. *Personnel and Guidance Journal*, **52**, 854–859.

For accounts of the beginnings of me vocational guidance movement in the United Kingdom, see:

MACRAE, A. (1934) *The Case for Vocational Guidance.* London, Pitman.
DAWS, P. P. (1968) *A Good Start in Life.* Leeds, Vocational Guidance Research Unit; Careers Research Advisory Centre, Cambridge.

For discussions on significant social and philosophical issues surrounding vocational guidance, see:

BECK, C. E. (1965) *Philosophical Foundations of Guidance.* New York, Prentice-Hall.
MILLER, C. H. (1961) *Foundations of Guidance.* New York, Harper.
STEFFLRE, B. (ed.) (1965) *Theories of Counselling.* New York, McGraw-Hill.
WILLIAMSON, E. G. (1961) *Vocational Counselling: a Reappraisal in Honour of Donald G. Patterson.* Minnesota Studies in Student Personnel Work No. 11. University of Minnesota Press.
WILLIAMSON, E. G. (1965) *Vocational Counselling.* New York, McGraw-Hill.

SECTION 1

Theories of Vocational Choice and Decision-making

"If you want to understand a man, find out what he takes for granted."

LOUIS WIRTH

THIS section opens with Donald Super's theory of vocational development. Since 1951, Super and his colleagues working on the Career Patterns Study at Teachers College, Columbia University, have exerted considerable influence on the thinking concerned with vocational development. Super begins by outlining Ginzberg's theory and eliciting some of its deficiencies. Using the concepts of life stages and career patterns, he describes vocational development as a process of implementation of the self-concept in an occupational setting. He emphasizes the compromise process that occurs between the individual and the social factors operating on him, and between the self-concept and reality, which is essentially a process of role-playing in fantasy or in the real world.

Taking the self-concept as the linchpin of vocational development, Starishevsky and Matlin have devised a model to illustrate how people translate their self-concepts into occupational terms. They distinguish between "occtalk" and "psychtalk", which consist, respectively, of statements made by an individual about occupations and himself. Within the limits of this system, they suggest that the degree to which the self-concept is incorporated into occtalk can be ascertained.

Holland defines vocational choice as the preference for, or employment in, one of six broad occupational categories. An individual searches for "work environments" which are congruent with his preferred ways of coping with environmental tasks generally. Within a given class of occupations the level of choice is defined as a function of intelligence and self-evaluation.

Tiedeman is primarily concerned with the role of decision in vocational development, and, like Super, has as his ultimate goal the prediction and understanding of an individual's career pattern. Vocational development is defined as a process of decision-making where each decision to be made has two basic characteristics, a period of anticipation, and a period of implementation or adjustment.

Blau and his colleagues are concerned with all the possible variables that influence occupational choice and entry. Occupational choice is seen as a compromise between preferences for and expectations of being able to enter a particular occupational field. They emphasize that the decisions of selection can be just as important as the individual's preferences in determining which occupation he will enter. This restricting factor on the freedom of choice is often underemphasized by the developmental theorists' concern with basic needs, patterns of personal orientations, and the occupational implementation of the self-concept.

For Ziller, occupational choice is fundamentally a decision-making situation in which risk-taking plays the major role, and therefore he believes that individual differences in risk-taking tendencies should be considered to be an important determinant of occupational choice.

Hilton is preoccupied with the same problem. He sees career development as "the accretion of a chain of decisions", so that the ability to make decisions becomes of key importance. This suggests that decision-making is a skill that can be taught, which is exactly what Tiedeman is attempting to do in his current research programme.

To conclude this section, Stefflre outlines ten propositions in an effort to work towards a unifying theory of vocational development under the aegis of role theory. He outlines four models illustrating the relationships between the self, self-concept, occupational persona, and occupational role expectations.

The role of decision-making in occupational choice has been particularly stressed in this section, as too often the factors leading up to the actual choice situation are investigated fully but what happens in the real process of making a decision is less well understood.

References are given after each contribution where research has been stimulated by that theoretical approach. The lists are not fully comprehensive, but are selected from research that is felt to be of greatest relevance to the ideas expressed in the preceding article.

1. A Theory of Vocational Development*

Donald E. Super

Two and one-half years ago a colleague of mine at Columbia, Dr. Eli Ginzberg, an economist, shocked and even unintentionally annoyed many members of the National Vocational Guidance Association by stating, at the annual convention, that vocational counselors attempt to counsel concerning vocational choice without any theory as to how vocational choices are made. A year later Dr. Ginzberg published his monograph on *Occupational Choice*, in which he stated:

> Vocational counselors are busy practitioners anxious to improve their counseling techniques ... the research-minded among them devote what time they can to devising better techniques. They are not theoreticians working on the problem of how individuals make their occupational choices, for, though they have no bias against theory, they have little time to invest in developing one [ref. 10. p.7].

Ginzberg continues, apropos of the fields of psychology and economics:

> there are good reasons why the problem [of how occupational choices are made] has not been a focus of investigation for psychology or economics 1 ... The process has roots in the interplay of the individual and reality, and this field is only now beginning to be included in the boundaries of psychological inquiry. The obverse formulation applies to economics, which as a discipline concentrates on a detailed analysis of reality forces and satisfies itself with a few simplified assumptions about individual behavior [ref. 10. p. 7].

These conclusions were based partly on a review of the research literature which I did at his request, and partly on a number of discussions in which he, his research team, and I participated. Consequently, I have a feeling of responsibility, not for the conclusions which he drew, but for drawing my own conclusions and for sharing them with my colleagues in psychology and guidance.

Basis of Ginzberg's criticisms. It may help to point out that Ginzberg's conclusions were based on a review of the research literature which was designed to provide answers to specific questions asked by his research

* Presidential address at the annual meeting of the Division of Counseling and Guidance, American Psychological Association, Washington, D.C., September 1, 1952.

(Reprinted from *American Psychologist,* vol. 8, No. 4 (May 1953), pp. 185–90, by permission of the publisher and author.)

team in order to help them plan their own research project. What synthesizing of results I did was undertaken to answer these questions. I did not attempt to answer the question "What theories underlie the principles of vocational guidance now generally accepted by practitioners?"

But I do agree with his analysis of the situation with regard to theory construction: we have done relatively little of it, and for the reasons he has suggested. However, this does not mean that we have operated without theory. It is the principal purpose of this paper to set forth a theory of vocational development, a theory inherent in and emergent from the research and philosophy of psychologists and counselors during the past two decades. But first I should like, as a help in formulating a more adequate theory, briefly to present the theory of occupational choice put forth by Ginzberg and his associates, to show how each of its elements had already been set forth by psychologists doing research in this field, and to point out some of its limitations.

THE GINZBERG THEORY

As Ginzberg, Ginsburg, Axelrad, and Herma summarize their theory of occupational choice, it contains four elements:

1. *Occupational choice is a developmental process which typically takes place over a period of some ten years.* This theory of Ginzberg's, it should be noted, is one of the points made by the official statement of the *Principles and Practices of Vocational Guidance*,[33] first formulated by the National Vocational Guidance Association 25 years ago; it is a point stressed by Kitson in his *Psychology of Vocational Adjustment*,[14] published in 1925; and, in 1942, in my own *Dynamics of Vocational Adjustment*[28] several pages are devoted to a discussion of the fact that "choosing an occupation ... is a process which ... may go on over a long period."

2. *The process is largely irreversible:* experience cannot be undone, for it results in investments of time, of money, and of ego; it produces changes in the individual. This second theory of Ginzberg's is clearly implied in Charlotte Buehler's 20-year-old theory of life stages,[5] in Lehman and Witty's equally old studies of play interest,[15] in Pressey, Janney, and Kuhlen's 13-year-old discussion of adolescent and adult development,[20] and in my own 10-year-old text on vocational adjustment.[28]

3. *The process of occupational choice ends in a compromise between interests, capacities, values, and opportunities.* This third theory of Ginzberg's is well illustrated in the practices of individual diagnosis developed by the Minnesota Employment Stabilization Research Institute 20 years ago and described by Paterson and Darley;[19] it was further demonstrated and described by the Adjustment Service experiment 17 years ago;[2] and it is basic to presentations of the use of diagnostic techniques in texts such as Bingham's[3] and mine,[29] both of which appeared before the completion

of Ginzberg's study. In fact, Frank Parsons,[18] in 1909, discussed vocational counseling as a process of helping the individual to study both himself and possible occupational opportunities, and to work out a compromise between his abilities, interests, and opportunities. He called this last process "true reasoning."

4. Ginzberg's final theoretical formulation is that *there are three periods of occupational choice*: the period of *fantasy* choice, governed largely by the wish to be an adult; the period of *tentative* choices beginning at about age 11 and determined largely by interests, then by capacities, and then by values; and the period of *realistic* choices, beginning at about age 17, in which exploratory, crystallization, and specification phases succeed each other. Those who are acquainted with Lehman and Witty's early research in the change of interest with age,[15] with Strong's more searching work[25] in the same area, with Sisson's research in the increasing realism of choice with increasing age,[23] with Charlotte Buehler's research in life stages,[5] and with the use made of these data by Pressey[20] or by me,[28] will find these three choice periods familiar. The special contribution of Ginzberg and his associates is the postulation of the successive dominance of interests, capacities, and values as determinants of choice before reality begins to play a major role.

It is easy, and perhaps even rather petty, thus to take a theoretical contribution and demonstrate its ancestry, showing that there is nothing particularly original about it. This is, undoubtedly, the normal reaction to claims of originality. But originality is more generally the result of a rearrangement of the old than the actual creation of something new: the rearrangement is original because it brings out details or relationships which have been missed or points up new applications. Ginzberg's theory is indeed an important contribution, this seems clear to me, at least, as I recollect the struggle I had in writing parts of my *Dynamics of Vocational Adjustment* (a struggle which resulted from the lack of a theoretical structure and from inadequate research), and as I work on its revision in the light, among other things, of Ginzberg's theoretical formulation and the thinking which it has stimulated. I have used this critical approach to Ginzberg's work in order to demonstrate that we have not entirely lacked a theoretical basis for our work in vocational guidance, and to show that the elements of theory on which we have based our practice have been sound, at least in that they have foreshadowed the elements which one group of theorists used when they went about constructing a theory of occupational choice.

Limitations of Ginzberg's Theory

But this is not the whole story. Ginzberg's theory is likely to be harmful because of its limitations, limitations other than those of research design and numbers in his basic study.

First, it does not build adequately on previous work: for example, the extensive literature on the nature, development, and predictive value of inventoried interests is rather lightly dismissed.

Second, "choice" is defined as preference rather than as entry or some other implementation of choice, and hence means different things at different age levels. To the 14-year-old it means nothing more than preference, because at that age the need for realism is minimized by the fact that the preference does not need to be acted upon until the remote future. To the 21-year-old student of engineering, on the other hand, "choice" means a preference which has already been acted upon in entering engineering school, although the final action will come only with graduation and entry into a job. No wonder that reality plays a larger part in choice at age 21, when, unlike choice at age 14, it is by definition a reality-tested choice!

A third defect in Ginzberg's theory emerges from these different meanings of the term "choice" at different ages: it is the falseness of the distinction between "choice" and "adjustment" which he and his research team make. The very fact that choice is a continuous process going on over a period of time, a process rather far removed from reality in early youth but involving reality in increasing degrees with increasing age, should make it clear that there is no sharp distinction between choice and adjustment. Instead, they blend in adolescence, with now the need to make a choice and now the need to make an adjustment predominating in the occupational or life situation.

Finally, a fourth limitation in the work of the Ginzberg team lies in the fact that, although they set out to study the process of occupational choice, and although they properly concluded that it is one of compromise between interests, capacities, values, and opportunities, they did not study or describe the compromise process. Surely this is the crux of the problem of occupational choice and adjustment: the nature of the compromise between self and reality, the degree to which and the conditions under which one yields to the other, and the way in which this compromise is effected. For the counseling psychologist's function is to help the individual to effect this compromise. He must not only know the factors which must be compromised and how these have been compromised in the experience of others, but also the dynamics of the compromising process, so that he may facilitate this process in his counselee with constructive results.

ELEMENTS OF AN ADEQUATE THEORY OF VOCATIONAL DEVELOPMENT

An adequate theory of vocational choice and adjustment would synthesize the results of previous research insofar as they lend themselves to synthesis; it would take into account the continuity of the development of preferences and of the differences in the stages, choices, entry, and adjustment; it would explain the process through which interest, capacities, values, and opportunities are compromised. The second part of this paper will be devoted to a sketch of the main elements of such a theory of vocational development as they appear in the literature, and the third and final part will consist of an attempt to synthesize these elements in an adequate theory. The term "development" is used rather than "choice," because it comprehends the concepts of preference, choice, entry, and adjustment. There seem to be a dozen elements to a theory of vocational development: they are taken up in sequence.

Individual Differences

One of the basic elements of a theory of vocational development has been the theory of individual differences, a cornerstone of modern educational and vocational psychology. Kitson based much of his early *Psychology of Vocational Adjustment*(14) on this theory and on the findings on which it was based. It was essential to the work of the Minnesota Employment Stabilization Research Institute.(19) It is surely unnecessary to document the fact of individual differences in aptitudes, interests, and values, or the significance of these differences for vocational development.

Multipotentiality

A second basic element of theory has been the concept of the occupational multipotentiality of the individual. It was first documented for intelligence by Army psychologists in World War I, and was stressed by Kitson in his early textbook. It was documented for interests by Strong's work on the classification of occupational interests.(26) It is a well-established fact and a basic assumption of vocational counseling that each person has the potential for success and satisfaction in a number of occupations.

Occupational Ability Patterns

The existence of occupational ability patterns, that is, the fact that abilities and interests fall into patterns which distinguish one occupation from another, was established by the Minnesota Employment Stabilization Research Institute(19) and has been confirmed in other studies, particularly those of the United States Employment Service.(8) People have been found to prefer, enter, remain in, like, and succeed most consistently in occupations for which they have appropriate patterns of traits. The theory of the patterning of aptitudes and interests within individuals and within occupational families and the significance of this patterning for choice, entry, and adjustment are widely accepted and applied by counselors and psychologists today.

Identification and the Role of Models

Much has been made of the importance of identification with parents and other adults in individual development by psychoanalytically oriented writers, and this concept is widely used by counseling psychologists regardless of orientation. It has been little documented, however, in psychological research in the vocational choice and adjustment process. The work of Friend and Haggard[9] and a study by Stewart[1] do, however, provide some objective basis for the theory that the childhood and adolescent identifications play a part in shaping vocational interests, and also provide role models which facilitate the development and implementation of a self-concept, provided that the required abilities and opportunities are present.

Continuity of Adjustment

The continuity of the adjustment process was stressed by Kitson in his 1925 textbook as a result of his analysis of the careers of men whose success was attested to by being listed in *Who's Who in America.* The fact that adolescents and adults face a succession of emerging problems as they go through life, and that some of these problems are peculiar to the various life stages, was brought out by the studies of life stages made by Charlotte Buehler[5] and by those of occupational mobility conducted by Davidson and Anderson,[7] Strong,[26] and Miller and Form.[16] And theories of the development of interests have been formulated by Carter[6] and by Bordin,[4] theories which I modified slightly in my book on testing and upon which I drew in describing the process of vocational choice and adjustment in a speech first made at Ft. Collins, Colorado, in 1949, revised several times, and later published in the journal *Occupations*, under the title of "Vocational Adjustment: Implementing a Self-Concept".[30] These formulations are drawn on again as the cement for the various elements which need to be brought together in a theory of vocational development and as an explanation of the process of compromise between self and reality.

Life Stages

The work of psychologists and sociologists in describing the stages through which growth and development proceed, and in showing how these stages bear on the process of vocational choice and adjustment, has already been referred to. It was drawn on heavily in the text by Pressey, Janney, and Kuhlen,[20] in my own first text,[28] in Ginzberg's research,[10] and in a recent text on *Industrial Sociology* by Miller and Form[16] which is as important for its original contribution and synthesis as it is annoying for its bias against anything that does not conform to sociology as they conceive of it. Buehler's theory of development through the exploratory, establishment, maintenance, and decline stages is translated into occupational terminology by Miller and Form, who also documented the theory for American careers, while Ginzberg, Ginsburg, Axelrad, and Herma have developed in more detail the phases of the exploratory stage. This latter theory needs confirmation with a larger sample and more objective procedures, in view of Small's[24] recent failure to confirm it with a somewhat different adolescent sample, but the general theory of life stages is basic to vocational guidance and will be drawn on heavily in my attempt at synthesis.

Career Patterns

The formulation of a theory of career patterns resulted from the occupational manifestations of life stages first documented by Davidson and Anderson,[7] added to for a select group by Terman's genetic studies of gifted persons[31] and then pointed up by Ginzberg and his associates[10] and by Miller and Form.[16] Career pattern theory appears to be a key element in the theoretical basis of vocational guidance, for it gives the counselor basic assumptions concerning the social, educational, and occupational mobility of his counselees, and it enables him to foresee types of problems which a given client is likely to encounter in establishing a career.

Development Can Be Guided

Another basic element in a theory of vocational development is the theory that development through the life stages can be guided. Although there is ample evidence that ability is to some extent inherited, and that personality too has its roots in inherited neural and endocrine make-up, there is also good evidence that manifested aptitudes and functioning personality are the result of the interaction of the organism and the environment. It is a basic theory of guidance as we know it today that the development of the individual can be aided and guided by the provision of adequate opportunities for the utilization of aptitudes and for the development of interests and personality traits.

Development the Result of Interaction

That the nature of the interaction between the individual and his environment is by no means simple has been brought out by a variety of investigations ranging from studies of the effects of foster homes and of education on intelligence[17] to evaluations of the effects of occupational information and of test interpretation on vocational plans and on self-understanding.[13] The realization of this fact and the acceptance of this principle have led to a greater humility in our claims for counseling and to a greater degree of sophistication in our use of guidance techniques.

The Dynamics of Career Patterns

The interaction of the individual and his environment during the growth and early exploratory stages, little understood though the process actually is, has been much more adequately investigated than has this same process during the late exploratory, establishment, and maintenance stages. We still know relatively little about the dynamics of career patterns. Terman's work[31] tells us something about the role of intelligence, Strong's[26] about interests, and Hollingshead's[11] about social status, but no adequate studies have been made of the interaction of these and other factors in determining whether the individual in question will have a career pattern which is typical or atypical of his parental socioeconomic group. It was partly with this objective that an investigation known as the Career Pattern Study was launched in Middletown, New York, last year.

Job Satisfaction: Individual Differences, Status, and Role

Early theories of job satisfaction stressed the role of intelligence and interest in adjustment to the occupation or to the job, building on studies of the relationships between these traits and occupational stability such as those made by Scott [ref. 22, ch. 26] and by Strong.(26) More recently other investigations such as the Hawthorne(21) and Yankee City studies,(32) anticipated in this respect by Hoppock's work(12) and by a minor study of mine(27) in job satisfaction, have played up the importance of the status given to the worker by his job, status both in the sense of group membership or belongingness and of prestige.

While researches interested in the role of one kind of factor or another have tended to emphasize the signal importance of that type of factor, there is nothing inherently contradictory or mutually exclusive in these findings. They can all be included in a comprehensive theory of job satisfaction or work adjustment. This is the theory that satisfaction in one's work and on one's job depends on the extent to which the work, the job, and the way of life that goes with them, enable one to play the kind of role that one wants to play. It is, again, the theory that vocational development is the development of a self concept, that the process of vocational adjustment is the process of implementing a self concept, and that the degree of satisfaction attained is proportionate to the degree to which the self concept has been implemented.

Work Is a Way of Life

This leads to a final theory, one that has been more widely accepted and stressed by sociologists than by psychologists, but familiar to most counselors and considered basic by some writers in the field. This is the theory that work is a way of life, and that adequate vocational and personal adjustment are most likely to result when both the nature of the work itself and the way of life that goes with it (this is, the kind of community, home, leisure-time activities, friends, etc.) are congenial to the aptitudes, interests, and values of the person in question. In the estimation of many, this is a basic element in a theory of vocational development.

A THEORY OF VOCATIONAL DEVELOPMENT

Now that we have surveyed the diverse elements of a theory of vocational development, there remains the final task of organizing them into a summary statement of a comprehensive theory. The theory can be stated in a series of ten propositions:

1. People differ in their abilities, interests, and personalities.

2. They are qualified, by virtue of these characteristics, each for a number of occupations.

3. Each of these occupations requires a characteristic pattern of abilities, interests, and personality traits, with tolerances wide enough, however, to allow both some variety of occupations for each individual and some variety of individuals in each occupation.

4. Vocational preferences and competencies, the situations in which people live and work, and hence their self concepts, change with time and experience (although self concepts are generally fairly stable from late adolescence until late maturity), making choice and adjustment a continuous process.

5. This process may be summed up in a series of life stages characterized as those of growth, exploration, establishment, maintenance, and decline, and these stages may in turn be subdivided into (*a*) the fantasy, tentative, and realistic phases of the exploratory stage, and (*b*) the trial and stable phases of the establishment stage.

The Main Stages of Vocational Development Described by Super and Ginzberg

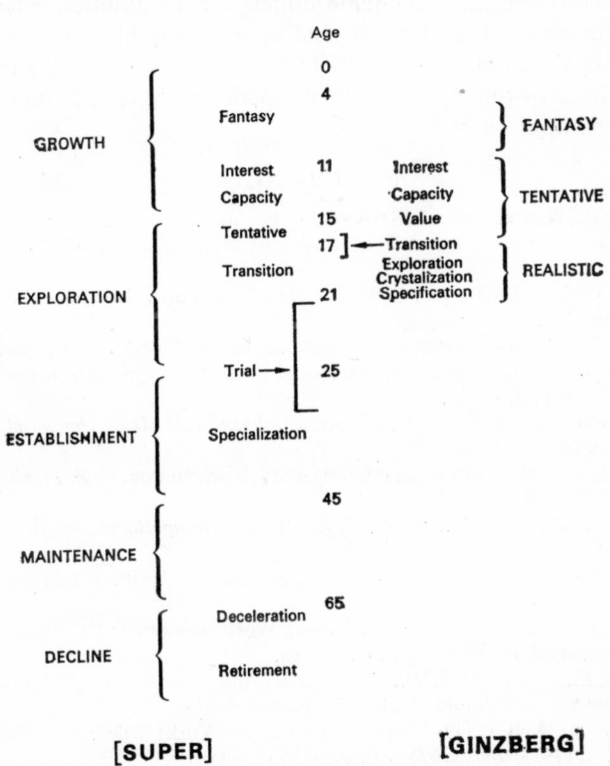

6. The nature of the career pattern (that is, the occupational level attained and the sequence, frequency, and duration of trial and stable jobs) is determined by the individual's parental socioeconomic level, mental ability, and personality characteristics, and by the opportunities to which he is exposed.

7. Development through the life stages can be guided, partly by facilitating the process of maturation of abilities and interests and partly by aiding in reality testing and in the development of the self concept.

8. The process of vocational development is essentially that of developing and implementing a self concept: it is a compromise process in which the self concept is a product of the interaction of inherited aptitudes, neural and endocrine make-up, opportunity to play various roles, and evaluations of the extent to which the results of role playing meet with the approval of superiors and fellows.

9. The process of compromise between individual and social factors, between self concept and reality, is one of role playing, whether the role is played in fantasy, in the counseling interview, or in real life activities such as school classes, clubs, part-time work, and entry jobs.

10. Work satisfactions and life satisfactions depend upon the extent to which the individual finds adequate outlets for his abilities, interests, personality traits, and values; they depend upon his establishment in a type of work, a work situation, and a way of life in which he can play the kind of role which his growth and exploratory experiences have led him to consider congenial and appropriate.

REFERENCES

1. Barnett, G., Handelsman, I., Stewart, L. H., and Super, D. E. (1952) The Occupational Level scale as a measure of drive. *Psychol. Monogr.*, **65**, No. 10 (Whole No. 342).
2. Bentley, J. H. (1935) *The adjustment service*. New York: American Association for Adult Education.
3. Bingham, W. V. (1937) *Aptitudes and aptitude testing*. New York: Harper.
4. Bordin, E. S. (1943) A theory of vocational interests as dynamic phenomena. *Educ. psychol. Measmt.*, **3**, 49–66.
5. Buehler, Charlotte (1933) *Der menschliche Lebenslauf als psychologisches Problem*. Leipzig: Hirzel.
6. Carter, H. D. (1944) Vocational interests and job orientation. *Appl. Psychol. Monogr.*, No. 2.
7. Davidson, P. E., and Anderson, H. D. (1937) *Occupational mobility*. Stanford: Stanford University Press.
8. Dvorak, Beatrice (1947). The new U.S.E.S. General Aptitude Test Battery. *Occupations*, **25**, 42–49.
9. Friend, J. G., and Haggard, E. A. (1948) Work adjustment in relation to family background. *Appl. Psychol. Monogr.*, No. 16.
10. Ginzberg, E., Ginsburg, S. W., Axelrad, S., and Herma, J. L. (1951) *Occupational choice*. New York: Columbia University Press.
11. Hollingshead, A. B. (1949) *Elmtown's youth*. New York: Wiley.
12. Hoppock, R. (1935) *Job satisfaction*. New York: Harper.

13. Johnson, D. G. (1951) The effect of vocational counseling on self-knowledge. Unpublished doctor's dissertation, Teachers College, Columbia University.
14. Kitson, H. D. (1925) *Psychology of vocational adjustment.* Philadelphia: Lippincott.
15. Lehman, H. C., and Witty, P. A. (1927) *Psychology of play activities.* New York: Barnes.
16. Miller, D., and Form, W. (1951) *Industrial sociology.* New York: Harper.
17. National Society for the Study of Education, G. M. Whipple (Ed.) (1940) *Intelligence: its nature and nurture.* Bloomington, Ill.: Public School Publishing Co.
18. Parsons, F. (1909) *Choosing a vocation.* Boston: Houghton Mifflin.
19. Paterson, D. G., and Darley, J. G. (1936) *Men, women, and jobs.* Minneapolis: University of Minnesota Press.
20. Pressey, S. L., Janney, J. E., and Kuhlen, R. G. (1939) *Life: a psychological survey.* New York: Harper.
21. Roethlisberger, F. J., and Dickson, W. J. (1939) *Management and the worker.* Cambridge: Harvard University Press.
22. Scott, W. D., Clothier, R. C., and Mathewson, S. B. (1931) *Personnel management.* New York: McGraw-Hill.
23. Sisson, E. D. (1938) An analysis of the occupational aims of college students. *Occupations*, **17**, 211–215.
24. Small, L. (1952) A theory of vocational choice. *Vocat. Guid. Quart.*, **1**, 29.
25. Strong, E. K., Jr. (1931) *Change of interest with age.* Stanford: Stanford University Press.
26. Strong, E. K., Jr. (1943) *The vocational interests of men and women.* Stanford: Stanford University Press.
27. Super, D. E. (1939) Occupational level and job satisfaction. *J. appl. Psychol.*, **23**, 547–564.
28. Super, D. E. (1942) *Dynamics of vocational adjustment.* New York: Harper.
29. Super, D. E. (1949) *Appraising vocational fitness by means of psychological tests.* New York: Harper.
30. Super, D. E. (1951) Vocational adjustment: implementing a self-concept. *Occupations*, **30**, 88–92.
31. Terman, L. M., and Oden, M. H. (1947) *The gifted child grows up.* Stanford: Stanford University Press.
32. Warner, W. L., and Low, J. D. (1947) *The social system of the modern factory.* New Haven: Yale University Press.
33. *Principles and practices of vocational guidance.* Cambridge, Mass.: National Vocational Guidance Association, 1927.

REFERENCES TO GINZBERG'S THEORY

Ginzberg, E., Ginsburg, S. W., Axelrad, S., and Herma, J. L. (1951) *Occupational Choice: An Approach to a General Theory.* New York, Columbia University Press.

Beilen, H. (1952) Factors in occupational choice. Unpublished Ph. D. Thesis. Teachers College, Columbia University.

Brunken, R. J. (1966) Perceived parental attitudes and parental identification in relation to problems in vocational choice. *Journal of Counseling Psychology*, **13**, 394–402.

Caplow, T. (1952) Review of Ginzberg's theory of occupational choice. *American Journal of Sociology*, **57**, 522–523.

Davis, D. A., Hagen, N., and Strouf, J. (1962) Occupational choice of twelve-year-olds. *Personnel and Guidance Journal*, **40**, 628–629.

GINZBERG, E. (1952) Toward a theory of occupational choice. *Occupations*, **30**, 491–494.

KITSON, H. D. (1951) Review of Ginzberg's theory of occupational choice. *Occupations*, **29**, 611–613.

MEADOW, L. (1955) Toward a theory of vocational choice. *Journal of Counseling Psychology*, **2**, 108–112.

SMALL, L., (1953) Personality determinants of vocational choice. *Psychological Monographs*, **67**, No. 1 (Whole No. 351).

SMALL, L., SWEAT, L. G., and VON ARNOLD, B. (1955) Personality needs as a determinant of vocational choice and their relationship to school and work. New York, Vocational Advisory Service.

WHITLOCK, G. (1962) Passivity of personality and role concepts in vocational choice. *Journal of Counseling Psychology*, **9**, 88–90.

ADDITIONAL REFERENCES TO SUPER'S THEORY

SUPER, D. E. (1957) *The Psychology of Careers*. New York, Harper.

SUPER, D. E., and BACHRACH, P. B. (1957) *Scientific Careers and Vocational Development Theory*. New York, Teachers College, Columbia University.

SUPER, D. E., CRITES, J. O., HUMMEL, R. C., MOSER, H. P., OVERSTREET, P. L., and WARNATH, C. G. (1957) *Vocational Development: A Framework for Research*. New York, Teachers College, Columbia University.

SUPER, D. E., and OVERSTREET, P. L. (1960) *The Vocational Maturity of Ninth-Grade Boys*. New York, Teachers College, Columbia University.

SUPER, D. E., STARISHEVSKY, R., MATLIN, N., and JORDAAN, J. P. (1963) *Career Development: Self-Concept Theory*. Princeton, N.J., College Entrance Examination Board.

GRIBBONS, W. (1962) Changes in readiness for vocational planning from the eigth to the tenth grade. *Personnel and Guidance Journal*, **42**, 908–913.

GRIBBONS, W., and LOHNES, P. (1965) Predicting five years of development in adolescents from readiness for vocational planning scales. *Journal of Educational Psychology*, **56**, 244–253.

KINNANE, J., and GAUBINGER, J. (1963) Life values and work values. *Journal of Counseling Psychology*, **10**, 362–372.

STEPHENSON, R. R. (1961) Occupational choice as a crystallized self-concept. *Journal of Counseling Psychology*, **8**, 211–216.

SUPER, D. E. (1954) Career patterns as a basis for vocational counseling. *Journal of Counseling Psychology*, **1**, 12–20.

SUPER, D. E. (1959) Vocational development: a factor in vocational guidance and counseling. *Youth Employment*, **12**, 6–12.

SUPER, D. E. (1959) Vocational orientation during the school years. *Youth Employment*, **12**, 13–18.

SUPER, D. E. (1960) The critical ninth grade: vocational choice or vocational exploration. *Personnel and Guidance Journal*, **39**, 106–109.

SUPER, D. E. (1961) Consistency and wisdom of vocational preferences as indices of vocational maturity in the ninth grade. *Journal of Educational Psychology*, **52**, 35–43.

SUPER, D. E. (1961) Some unresolved issues on vocational development research. *Personnel and Guidance Journal*, **40**, 11–14.

SUPER, D. E. (1963) The definition and measurement of early career behaviour: a first formulation. *Personnel and Guidance Journal*, **41**, 775–780.

SUPER, D. E. (1964) A developmental approach to vocational guidance: recent theory and results. *Vocational Guidance Quarterly*, **13**, 1–10.

2. *A Model for the Translation of Self Concepts into Vocational Terms*

Reuben Starishevsky and Norman Matlin

Self-concept theory as used by the counseling psychologist is designed to predict the occupation ultimately chosen by the subject. The developing or maturing individual is constantly reacting to environmental stimuli in a manner characteristic of his own formulation of the nature of the environment and of himself. The way in which the person has reacted in the past, constructing his formulation of the world, determines his future and his choice of occupation as part of that future. One can, then, view vocational choice as an expression of self concepts formulated and reformulated throughout the life stages. People differ both in their self concepts and in the ways in which they translate self concepts into occupational terms. Hence, people choose different occupations.

Implicit in the central idea of translation is a recognition, for purposes of analysis, of two realms or languages: an area of psychological statements and an area of occupational terms. Self concepts being expressable in psychological terms, are in the first area. They consist of all statements in psychological terms that the subject is willing to make about himself or others. A person's understanding of himself cannot develop without comparison and contrast with others. Furthermore, to understand a person's description of himself, we will need to know to whom else he applies this description. Suppose a person says: "I am intelligent." This statement will be quite different depending on whether he further says "everyone is intelligent" or "very few people are intelligent." In the first, since he shows no acknowledgment of non-intelligence, his statement may have little meaning, though it could be an index of confused thought. Alternatively, if he gives as the other example of intelligence a person whom he has described with a concatenation of feelings of annoyance and disgust, this data may be necessary to our understanding of what intelligence means to him. The position taken here is that a person's psychological pictures of others are an integral part of his self-concept system.

The self-concept system may be viewed as a person's psychological field, his formulation of the world. This definition departs in a measure from

(Reprinted from *Career Development: Self-Concept Theory*, New York, College Entrance Examination Board, by permission of publisher and authors.)

Sarbin's (1954) definition of the self concept as what a person believes himself to be, the combined self perceptions; the model's definition is more inclusive and self contained: what a person perceives himself and others to be.

Self concepts are verbalized in a series of statements in which the self or another person is the grammatical subject and a psychological variable the predicate, for example, "I am intelligent," "John is lethargic." All of these statements are statements that the person is willing to make. These statements represent, *ipso facto*, a choice. In making the statements in the example above, the person is denying the statements "I am stupid," "John is active." Both the statements asserted and the statements denied, being couched in terms meaningful to the speaker, are part of the language or psychological terminology called, for simplicity's sake, *psychtalk*. Since psychtalk is a sum of all statements whose predicates are dimensions a person habitually uses to differentiate people, the predicates may be aptitudes or interests or other variables in which the psychologist is interested, if these happen to be what the subject uses to differentiate people.

In the area of occupations a parallel situation exists. The statements that a person is willing to make of himself and others, the predicates this time being the names of occupations or their equivalents, constitute his occupational self concept. Similarly, saying "I intend to be a physician" precludes saying "I am going to be a paleontologist."

All possible statements in this form constitute the realm of occupational terminology or *occtalk*. In the realm of occtalk, all statements need not be verbal. Applying to medical school is the equivalent of saying "I am going to be a physician." In the model no distinction is made between the manner of asserting a statement. At certain times one kind of assertion is more appropriate; nonetheless, they are treated as functionally equal.

RELATIONSHIPS OF STATEMENTS

The main assumption of this self-concept theory concerns the relationship between statements in these two realms. First, it is asserted that any statement in occtalk made by a partcular person can be translated into a statement or series of statements in that person's psychtalk, just as a sentence in French can be translated into an equivalent sentence in English. For example, the statement "I want to be a lawyer" might mean "I am socially minded, I am aggressive, I am interested in upholding community values." Alternately, it might mean "I am theory oriented, I am introverted, and I am scholarly." In order to know, we must consult the person's "dictionary." A person's dictionary is a listing of predicates in psychtalk equivalent to predicates in occtalk. For the moment, let us assume that this book of equivalences can be obtained for each person.

The second assumption of this self-concept theory is that the occupational self concept, which is in effect defined as the occupational statements opted is, at least in part, an incorporation of the self concept. In other words, any statement in occtalk that a subject is willing to make implies a translation of a psychtalk statement which is part of his psychological self concept. Of course the occupational self concept may include some parts which are not part of the psychological self concept, for example, a person may take a job which is not entirely satisfying. But the job must have some element in harmony with his self concept or he would not consider it.

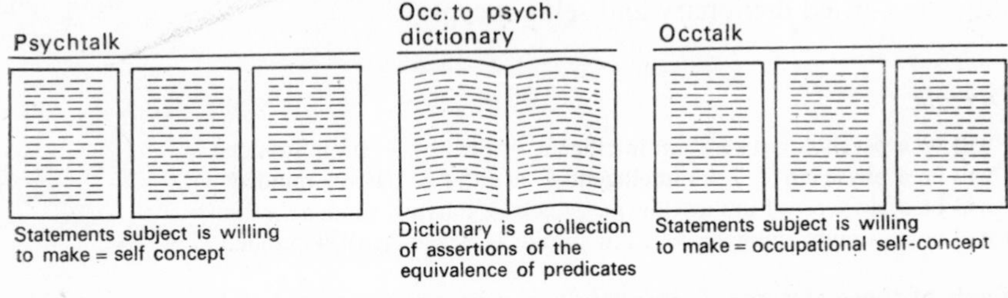

Statements subject is willing to make = self concept

Dictionary is a collection of assertions of the equivalence of predicates

Statements subject is willing to make = occupational self-concept

Not all of a person's self concepts are necessarily incorporated in occtalk. People may differ in the level of incorporation, the degree to which a person's self concepts find expression in his occupational statements. The level is never zero, that is, a person never makes an occupational statement incompatible with his self concepts.

A simple version of the system might look like the diagram above.

Let us assume that our subject has a psychtalk consisting of only three dichotomous dimensions: (1) intelligent—stupid, (2) healthy—sick, and (3) broad-minded—narrow-minded. Further, let us assume that there are only three people with whom the person is familiar enough to make statements: himself, John, and Bob. There would then be 18 possible statements in his psychtalk.

Self is intelligent	John is intelligent	Bob is intelligent
Self is stupid	John is stupid	Bob is stupid
Self is healthy	John is healthy	Bob is healthy
Self is sick	John is sick	Bob is sick
Self is broad-minded	John is broad-minded	Bob is broad-minded
Self is narrow-minded	John is narrow-minded	Bob is narrow-minded

These statements come in pairs whose members are mutually exclusive, since dichotomies have been used in the example. If the dimensions had not been dichotomous, statements would come in sets whose members are mutually exclusive. If our subject says, "John is intelligent" he cannot completely assert "John is stupid." His self concept, therefore, will consist of nine statements. Let us further assume that our subject's self concept consists of the following nine statements:

Self is intelligent	John is intelligent	Bob is stupid
Self is healthy	John is sick	Bob is healthy
Self is broad-minded	John is narrow-minded	Bob is narrow-minded

Let us assume that our subject has four occupations in his occtalk: psychologist, physician, lawyer, and opium smuggler. Let us suppose further that his dictionary is as follows:

intelligent + healthy + broad-minded = psychologist
intelligent + healthy + narrow-minded = physician
intelligent + sick + narrow-minded = lawyer
stupid + sick + narrow-minded = opium smuggler

It would then be possible to make such translations as the following from the above-listed dictionary and self concept:

Occtalk

I will be a psychologist = I am intelligent + healthy + broad-minded
I will be a physician = I am intelligent + healthy + narrow-minded
I will be a lawyer = I am intelligent + sick + narrow-minded
I will be an opium smuggler = I am stupid + sick + narrow-minded

Each of these statements in occtalk can be characterized as having a specific level of incorporation. The statement "I am a psychologist" since it means "I am intelligent, healthy, and broad-minded" agrees completely with the subject's self-concept, that is, has a level of incorporation of 100 per cent. The statement "I am a physician" on translation is found to agree with the subject's self concept on two of the three dimensions, that is, the statement has a level of incorporation of 67 per cent. Similarly the statement "I am a lawyer" has a level of 33 per cent, and "I am an opium smuggler" has a level of 0 per cent. The second postulate asserts that the subject, so long as he maintains his present self concept and dictionary, would not say "I would like to be an opium smuggler."

It can be seen from the formulation that numerous occupations are taken as compatible, in varying degrees, with a person's self concept. In fact, this picture would seem to fit the real world where many, if not most, people seem capable of entering many different occupations. While this has presented a problem of overlap to previous research, the present model seems to accommodate this perverse aspect of reality.

The level of incorporation shows promise of providing an important index. Several hypotheses can be made about statements on different levels of incorporation, for example, the hierarchy of a subject's statements rank-ordered by level of incorporation will correlate highly with his hierarchy of occupational preferences; the higher the level of incorporation the more likely it is the subject will choose that occupation; people leaving occupations will leave for an occupation on a higher level of incorporation; the lower the level of incorporation of one's occupation the more likely one is to pursue an avocation with a high level of incorporation of the self concept.

In a sense, the concept of level of incorporation is here being used in the way in which many researchers use the concept of motivation. Motivation in this model has been assimilated to the degree that the tendency toward greater incorporation is taken as the motivating force in vocational development.

POSTULATES

Two formal postulates constitute the model.

Postulate 1: Every statement in occtalk is translatable into psychtalk.

Definition:

1. *Statement:* a pairing of a specific person with a predicate. No distinction is made between verbal statements, for example, "I am broad-minded," "I am going to be a lawyer," action statements, for example, applying to law school, and mental statements, for example, daydreaming about being a lawyer.
2. *Occtalk:* the totality of all statements whose predicates are the names of occupations.
3. *Translatable into:* equivalent to. The equivalence of any two statements is asserted solely as an equivalence in the mind of a particular person. The translation of a particular statement requires a knowledge of the person's dictionary, that is, series of predicates equivalent in psychtalk and occtalk.
4. *Psychtalk:* the totality of all statements whose predicates are dimensions the person habitually uses to differentiate people.

Postulate 1, being unidirectional, makes no assertion about the translatability of any statement in psychtalk into occtalk, that is, there may be statements in psychtalk which differentiate people, but do not differentiate occupations. Nor does Postulate 1 imply any one-to-one correspondence between statements.

Postulate 2: Every statement in the occupational self concept is at least partly a translation of the self concept.

Definition:

1. *Occupational self concept:* the totality of statements in occtalk the person is willing to make. (Differs from Super's use of the term vocational self concept.)
2. *Self concept:* the totality of statements in psychtalk a person is willing to make.

The degree to which the self concept is translated by a statement in occtalk is the level of incorporation of that statement. Postulate 2 states that the level of incorporation of a statement in the occupational self concept is never zero.

PROCESSES OF INCORPORATION

Up to this point, level of incorporation, a measure of the degree of translation of the self concept occurring in specific occtalk statements, has been discussed without regard to the processes by which a high level occurs. It may be hypothesized that these processes, also called incorporation, will occur to achieve or maintain a high level of incorporation for the statements in the occupational self concept.

In certain cases deliberate incorporation takes place, that is, a person takes stock of some or all of his characteristics and considers various occupations in the light of the degree to which they allow him to exercise personality variables important to him. In general, this would be increasingly likely with greater maturity and sophistication. For example, a person just completing a doctorate in psychology might decide whether to be a therapist or a research person by so articulate a method.

At an earlier age a less deliberate process of incorporation, identification, may occur. The child perceives himself as similar to some important figure in his life. He creates the dictionary definition of the occupation of this figure on the bases of what he takes to be this figure's personality characteristics. Of necessity, the occtalk statement indicating desire to enter this occupation will have a high level of incorporation.

Following naturally from identification, role playing will serve to incorporate the self concept. A child playing a role may discover new aspects of an occupation which fit the picture he has of himself, that is, he may revise his dictionary to give the preferred occtalk statement a higher level of incorporation. He may discover new things about himself, adding to his self concept new statements which, being translated into the preferred occtalk statement, also raise the level of incorporation. Of course he may find the role uncongenial, causing him to seek another occupation to role play, hopefully productive of a higher level of incorporation.

The above processes sample, rather than exhaust, possible methods of incorporation. The model does seem amenable to hypotheses concerned with processes by which incorporation may occur.

METADIMENSIONS

Self-concept theory has been concerned with such dimensions as structure and congruence. These are characterizations by the theorist of the subject's self concept. To keep these distinct from the dimensions forming the predicates of psychtalk, these are referred to as metadimensions.

Of necessity, metadimensions are a nomothetic rather than an idiographic method of understanding; they rank order subjects according to some aspects of their self concept rather than attempt to understand the subject's interrelationships solely in terms of the subject's own system.

Complexity has been defined by Lundy and Berkowitz (1957) as that which distinguishes among a greater number of different aspects of people or situations, employing more functional concepts and showing more variety in the relationship between them.

The number of constructs in use determines the upward limit of the number of people or occupations that can be differentiated. A person whose psychtalk predicates are limited to two dichotomous dimensions can distinguish only four classes of people or occupations; three dichotomous dimensions permit recognition of eight groups. Obviously, the number of possible differentiated groups is X^n, when X is the number of choices along the dimension that are permitted and n the number of functioning dimensions. A subject with two dichotomous dimensions, asked to provide a dictionary of 10 occupations, is forced to make a minimum of six duplicates. He may, in fact, make more duplicates than this, and is likely to if the two dimensions are related in his mind.

Consideration of complexity in this fashion has several advantages. It enables prediction in the model; it identifies complexity with an operation which has shown adequate test-retest reliability on several occasions and which has been shown by Bieri and Blacker (1956) to correlate with behavior in the Rorschach Test; it is amenable to mathematical handling.

It will be noted that complexity can be a metadimension of the self concept or the dictionary, the maximum number of differentiations possible in the self concept serving as the upward limit of the dictionary. The occupational self concept is unidimensional and cannot be ordered by any metadimension which requires more than one dimension. Complexity cannot be applied to a language which contains all possible alternatives; a particular subject's psychtalk can be considered as allowing or not allowing for the possibility of complexity, although in itself it is neither complex nor simple.

Congruence is a measure of the incompatibility of statements, the sole criterion being the canons of logic. As a metadimension, it can be applied only to the self concept. It cannot apply to the languages, for a language being composed of all statements includes all possible contradictions. It cannot apply to the dictionary for no assertion about one occupation can contradict an assertion about another occupation. Nor can the occupational self concept show incongruences. The statements at their face value cannot be contradictory, for the model allows for the possibility that several occupations may be an implementation of the self concept, the assertion of acceptability of several occupations not being considered a contradiction. Nor can two occtalk statements in translation be considered incompatible, for we consider compatibility the compliance with the demand based on the laws of logic, while requiring compatibility in occupational self concept would demand compliance to both the laws of logic and the formulation of the model. Failure of the subject to agree with the model must be considered the theoretician's error, not the subject's. For example, a subject who describes himself as intelligent, healthy, broad-minded; describes physicians as stupid, sick, and narrow-minded; and maintains he wants to be a physician is a problem for the model. It may be that the instruments used were inadequate or the basic postulate may be false. In any event, our subject has not subscribed to the postulate, which purports to predict regularities in his behavior. Accusing the subject of inconsistency when the regularities fail to appear is frowned upon in certain circles. The metadimension is perforce restricted to the self concept.

However, congruence does have use, provided that it is kept in mind that the burden of proof is on the experimenter to demonstrate that the contradiction is existent in the thinking of the subject, and is not merely a paradox. Where incongruence is present to any marked degree, it suggests ambivalence and can be considered an indication of maladjustment.

Structuring, the amount of peakedness in the description of a particular person or occupation, is a metadimension that not only requires several dimensions, but requires the dimensions to be, if not continua, at least separable into several degrees. This formulation is quite compatible with the model and can generate useful hypotheses. The instrument for measuring the self concept will have to be geared to the use of finer breakdowns than dichotomies; but this may well repay the additional effort. Structure is applicable to the self concept and to the dictionary. The occupational self concept is unidimensional.

Realism as a metadimension differs in that it rank orders a subject on the basis of a comparison of the self concept, the dictionary, or the occupational self concept with some standard outside the subject's system; the previous metadimensions rank ordered subjects on the bases of characteristics internal to their systems.

The standard is reality. In practice, we would have to accept the psychologist's evaluation of reality, which, despite objective tests to answer specific questions, remains at this point a matter of judgment. Until we have an understanding of how the psychologist makes his judgment of reality, it will be difficult to know what to do with a ranking of subjects on this basis.

Stability is a metadimension applying to the self concept, the dictionary, and the occupational self concept. It can be operationally defined as a test-retest correlation for any period over a year, the long interval allowing the use of stability as a measurement of the subject rather than the test.

The metadimensions listed above are intended to sample rather than exhaust the universe of possible metadimensions.

OPERATIONS

Kelly's (1955) Role Construct Repertory Test may be used to generate statements in psychtalk. This test presents the subject with a series of role titles, three at a time, and asks him to state in what way two are alike and one is different. The dimensions set forth in the subject's answers may be taken as the dimensions of psychtalk. As part of the repertory test the subject is asked for each of the people named to indicate which end of each dimension is most appropriate. Each cell of this grid may be considered a statement in the subject's self concept.

Since it is basic to the model's understanding of the self concept that it must be mapped along dimensions that a subject himself chooses, it is necessary to forego the convenience of an inventory or adjective checklist. The latter would attempt to plot the subject's self concept in the dimensions of the inventor of the test, which are bound to differ to a greater or lesser degree from those of the subject. The dictionary may be built by asking subjects to rate each of a series of occupations on a seven-point scale for the constructs obtained on his repertory test.

The occupational self concept may be obtained in several ways, depending upon the hypotheses tested. For testing commonality hypotheses, working in a particular job can be taken as the statement of occupational self concept. In other cases the subject may be asked to rank order a series of occupations in terms of attractiveness. The ordering is assumed to represent the order of probability of a statement, the subject as grammatical subject, and the occupation as predicate being included in the occupational self concept.

SUMMARY

A model has been proposed based on a self-concept theory of vocational development. The model postulates that statements in the occupational field are translatable into statements in the psychological field, and that statements of the occupational self concept incorporate statements of the self concept. Some of the metadimensions of the self concept, some hypotheses, and the construct and index of the level of incorporation were discussed in terms of the proposed model.

BIBLIOGRAPHY

Bieri, J., and Blacker, E. (1956) The Generality of Cognitive Complexity. *Journal of Abnormal and Social Psychology*, **53**, 112–117.

Kelly, G. A. (1955) *The Psychology of Personal Constructs*. New York: W. W. Norton & Co., Inc.

Lundy, R. M., and Berkowitz, L. (1957) Cognitive-Complexity and Assimilative Projection. *Journal of Abnormal and Social Psychology*, **55**, 34–37.

Sarbin, T. R. (1954) Role Theory, in Lindzey, G. (ed.) *Handbook of Social Psychology* (Cambridge: Addison-Wesley Publishing Co., Inc.), Chap. 6.

Super, D. E. (1957) *The Psychology of Careers* (New York: Harper Bros.).

ADDITIONAL REFERENCES TO THE STARISHEVSKY–MATLIN MODEL

SUPER, D. E., STARISHEVSKY, R., MATLIN, N., and JORDAAN, J. P. (1963) *Self-Concept Theory*. New York, College Entrance Examination Board.

OPPENHEIMER, E. (1966) Relationship between certain self-constructs and occupational preferences. *Journal of Counseling Psychology*, **13**, 191–197.

3. A Theory of Vocational Choice*

JOHN L. HOLLAND

PREVIOUS theories of vocational choice appear to have two serious deficiencies: they are either too broad or too specialized. Some theories—for example, Ginzberg's theory and Super's theory of vocational development (1951, 1957)—are so general in statement that they are of negligible value for integrating present knowledge or stimulating further research. In contrast, other writers (Bordin, 1943; Hoppock, 1957; Roe, 1957) have concentrated on more limited aspects of vocational choice with more explicit theories, but these are incomplete in that they are self-concept-centered, need-centered, or etiologically-oriented, although there is an extensive literature implying that all of these divergent emphases are probably of importance in vocational choice. The need for more comprehensive theorizing is also indicated in previous papers by Bachrach (1957), Beilin (1955), and Blau *et al.* (1956).

The present paper is an attempt to delineate a theory of vocational choice which is comprehensive enough to integrate existing knowledge and at the same time sufficiently close to observables to stimulate further research. Essentially, the present theory assumes that at the time of vocational choice the person is the product of the interaction of his particular heredity with a variety of cultural and personal forces including peers, parents and significant adults, his social class, American culture, and the physical environment. Out of this experience the person develops a hierarchy of habitual or preferred methods for dealing with environmental tasks. From an ecological standpoint, these habitual methods are associated with different kinds of physical and social environments, and with differential patterns of abilities. The person making a vocational choice in a sense "searches" for situations which satisfy his hierarchy of adjustive orientations. The following sections

* The author wishes to acknowledge the constructive and critial reviews of this paper by Donald L. Thistlethwaite, C. H. Patterson, Junlius Seeman and John W. Gustad. This paper was supported in part by research grants from the National Science Foundation and the old Dominion Foundation.

(Reprinted from *Journal of Counseling Psychology*, vol. 6, No. 1 (1959), pp. 35–43, by permission of publisher and author.)

specify the theory in terms of the occupational environments, the person and his development, and the interactions of the person and the vocational environment.

THE OCCUPATIONAL ENVIRONMENTS

The following environments are the major classes of occupational environments useful in organizing knowledge about vocational choice. The classification, though not exhaustive, is assumed to include all the major kinds of American work environments. Ultimately the classification may include more subcategories; however, in view of the present state of evidence, it seems simpler and more desirable to predict for major occupational areas rather than for specific occupations. The major occupational environments are:

1. *The Motoric Environment.* Illustrative occupations are laborers, machine operators, aviators, farmers, truck drivers, and carpenters.
2. *The Intellectual Environment.* Illustrative occupations are physicists, anthropologists, chemists, mathematicians, and biologists.
3. *The Supportive Environment.* Illustrative occupations are social workers, teachers, interviewers, vocational counselors, and therapists.
4. *The Conforming Environment.* Illustrative occupations are bank tellers, secretaries, bookkeepers, and file clerks.
5. *The Persuasive Environment.* Illustrative occupations are salesmen, politicians, managers, promoters, and business executives.
6. *The Esthetic Environment.* Illustrative occupations are musicians, artists, poets, sculptors, and writers.

THE PERSON AND HIS DEVELOPMENT

The Developmental Hierarchy

At the time of vocational choice the person has a set of adjustive orientations. The adjustive orientations, corresponding to the six occupational environments, are designated as motoric, intellectual, supportive, conforming, persuasive, and esthetic methods or orientations. Each orientation represents a somewhat distinctive life style which is characterized by preferred methods of dealing with daily problems and includes such variables as values and "interests," preferences for playing various roles and avoiding others, interpersonal skills and other personal factors. For every person, the orientations may be ranked, according to their relative strengths, in a quasi-serial order or hierarchy. The life style heading the hierarchy determines the major direction of choice.

This intrapersonal hierarchy can be defined by coded "interest" inventories, though such inventories are incomplete estimates of the hierarchical ordering. "Interest inventories" are conceived here as personality inventories which reveal information such as the person's values, attitudes, needs, self-concept, preferred activities, and sources of threat and dissatisfaction.*

The Modal Personal Orientations

The following formulations are an attempt to integrate and conceptualize the extensive evidence about persons in the major occupational classes. In the main these formulations were derived by reviewing the Strong scoring keys, and a variety of major studies by Strong (1943), Gough (1955), Laurent (1951), Weinstein (1953), Forer (1951), and others. Although admittedly theoretical, these characterizations may help to integrate research and develop theory about occupational classes.

The motoric orientation. Persons with this orientation enjoy activities requiring physical strength, aggressive action, motor coordination and skill; and perhaps above all they wish to play masculine roles. They prefer dealing with concrete, well-defined problems as opposed to abstract, intangible ones. In a sense, they prefer to "act out," rather than to "think through," problems. They avoid situations which require verbal and interpersonal skills, because they lack such skills and are often threatened by close relationships with others. They conceive of themselves as aggressive, strong, masculine persons with conventional political and economic values. Persons of this orientation are typified by their masculinity, their physical strength and skills, their concrete, practical way of dealing with life problems, and their corresponding lack of social skills and sensitivities.

The intellectual orientation. Persons of this orientation appear to be task-oriented people who generally prefer to "think through," rather than to "act out," problems. They have marked needs to organize and understand the world. They enjoy ambiguous work tasks and intraceptive activities and possess somewhat unconventional values and attitudes. They avoid interpersonal problems which require interpersonal relations with groups of people or with new people from day to day.

In general this orientation is designated as intellectuality since the concept seems to subsume the following key variables represented in this classification: (a) Abstraction as opposed to concreteness; (b) Anality as opposed to orality; (c) Intraception as opposed to extraception; (d) Asociality as opposed to sociality. Weinstein's work suggests that this orientation represents the anal retentive character (1953). Stern's concept of the Rational type also resembles the major outline for this orientation (1956). Fromm's Hoarding orientation and Horney's Detached type appear to be similar types (Blum, 1953).

The supportive orientation. Persons of this orientation prefer teaching or therapeutic roles, which may reflect a desire for attention and socialization

* Blau *et al.* (1956) have also indicated the need for a "preference hierarchy". Their conceptualization and definition of this concept are, however, quite dissimilar from the one proposed here.

in a structured, and therefore safe, setting. They possess verbal and interpersonal skills. They are also characterized as responsible, socially oriented and accepting of feminine impulses and roles. Their chief values are humanistic and religious. They are threatened by and avoid situations requiring intellectual problem-solving, physical skills or highly ordered activities, since they prefer to deal with problems through feeling and interpersonal manipulations of others.

Persons of this class are best typified as orally dependent in the sense of being verbal, feminine, and dependent. This orientation corresponds to Fromm's Receptive orientation and Horney's Compliant type (Blum, 1953). Weinstein's study of social workers supports these hypotheses (1953).

The conforming orientation. Persons of this class prefer structured verbal and numerical activities, and subordinate roles. They achieve their goals through conformity. In this fashion, they obtain satisfaction and avoid the conflict and anxiety aroused by ambiguous situations or problems involving interpersonal relationships and physical skills. Their habitual subordination of personal needs appears to make them generally effective in well-structured tasks. Their values and attitudes represent strong identifications with power, externals, and status.

This orientation is perhaps best characterized as extraception: conformity, a whole-hearted acceptance of cultural values and attitudes, a living in the eyes of others with an emphasis on excessive self-control. The latter emphasis reveals a related pattern of adjustment which may develop almost necessarily from the need to conform, the obsessive concern with rules and regulations for living. The stereopathic type as conceptualized by Stern *et al.* (1956) parallels this orientation.

The persuasive orientation. Persons of this class prefer to use their verbal skills in situations which provide opportunities for dominating, selling, or leading others. They conceive of themselves as strong masculine leaders. They avoid well-defined language or work situations as well as situations requiring long periods of intellectual effort. Although they share a common orientation of extraception, they differ from persons of the Conforming orientation in their need for ambiguous verbal tasks and related skills; their sociality; and their greater concern with power, status, and leadership.

This class is best designated as having an "oral aggressive" orientation. Weinstein's study of lawyers supports this conceptualization (1933). Fromm's Marketing orientation and Horney's Aggressive type (Blum, 1953) correspond in general outline.

The esthetic orientation. In general, persons of this orientation prefer indirect relationships with others. They prefer dealing with environmental problems through self-expression in artistic media. They avoid problems requiring interpersonal interaction, a high degree of structuring, or physical skills. They resemble persons with an intellectual orientation in their intraceptiveness and lack of sociability. They differ from the latter group in that they appear to have a greater need for individualistic expression, are more feminine, and perhaps have less ego strength; that is, they appear to have less self-control and a greater need for direct emotional expression, and they probably suffer more from emotional disturbance. Feather (1950), for example, has found that maladjusted students in MMPI terms tend to have high scores on the artistic, literary, and musical scales of the Kuder. The complex person on Barron's complexity-simplicity dimension (1953) reflects this orientation. Segal's findings (1954) for advanced accounting and creative writing students are also consonant with the summaries for the conformity and esthetic environments.

The Level Hierarchy

Within a given class of occupations the level of choice is a function of intelligence and self-evaluation, variables which can be defined by intelligence tests and status scales. Self-evaluation might best be defined by scales of occupational content, such as the OL scale of the Strong or Sim's occupational status scale (1952). The person's score for a status scale of the former type is assumed to represent an estimate of self-evaluation, a general concept which includes one's status needs, and perception of level of competence and potential competence, and the self-estimate of one's worth with respect to others. The most direct evidence for the existence of a self-evaluative disposition is furnished by the *Q*-sort analysis of high and low scores on an MMPI status scale employed by Block and Bailey (1955) in an assessment study of 100 Air Force Officers. The significant *Q*-sort statements for high and low scorers appear congruent with the "self-evaluation" hypothesis, especially since "low scorers" are described by raters as: "... lacks confidence in his own ability, is self-abasing; feels unworthy, guilty, humble; given to self-blame ..." In contrast, the high scorers appear to reflect a very positive self-evaluation: "... is an effective leader, emphasizes success and productive achievement ..." A study by Barnett is also consistent with the self-evaluation hypothesis. Barnett (1952) reports a correlation of −.73 between the OL score and an index of satisfaction with chronic unemployment. "As OL scores increased in magnitude expressed satisfaction with vagrancy declined."

Presumably self-evaluation is a function of the life history in which education, socio-economic origin, and family influences are major determinants. The importance of these factors for determining level of choice is exemplified by Hollingshead's study (1949) of adolescents in a midwestern community, in which level of choice was closely related to student socio-economic status.

The factors of self-evaluation and intelligence are assumed to summate and determine level of choice. Their relative degree of influence is presently unclear, although this theory assumes their equal importance. The following formula indicates the relationship between the more significant factors affecting level of occupational choice.

Occupational Level = (Intelligence + Self-evaluation), where self-evaluation is a function of socio-economic origin, need for status, education, and self-concept.

By categorizing these factors in terms of their implication for approximate level of choice, it may be possible to manipulate them for prediction and exploratory purposes. For example, the intelligence levels developed by Miner (1957) or others could be used in conjunction with status scales categorized for similar levels to make predictions about occupational level. It appears possible to make predictions by averaging the ranks for these variables. The resultant of these variables is designated as the occupational level; the ordering of levels is the level hierarchy. For example, if four intelligence and self-evaluation levels are assumed, then the averaging of levels yields the series of predictions shown below. Presumably the empirical study of these variables should yield an analogous formula for predicting level of choice.

Person	Intelligence level +	Self-evaluation level =	Occupational level
A	1	1	1.0
B	1	2	1.5
C	1	3	2.0
D	1	4	2.5
E	2	3	2.5
F	2	4	3.0
G	3	4	3.5
H	4	4	4.0

THE INTERACTION OF THE PERSON AND THE VOCATIONAL ENVIRONMENTS

Schematically, the vocational choice process may be outlined as follows:

1. The person directs himself toward the major occupational class for which his development has impelled him by selecting the occupational class at the head of his particular hierarchy of classes. This dimension of choice is designated as the range of choice, or the variety of relatively different major choices.

2. Within a major class of occupations, the person's selection of an occupation is a function of his self-evaluation and his ability (intelligence) to perform adequately in his chosen environment.

3. Both of the above processes are mediated by a series of personal factors, including self-knowledge and evaluation, knowledge of occupational classes (range of information and the degree of differentiation between and within occupational environments), the orderliness of the developmental hierarchy; and a series of environmental factors including the range of potential environments, social pressures from family and peers, evaluations

of employers and potential employers, and limitations—arbitrary in terms of the theory—imposed by socio-economic resources and the physical environment.

The Role of the Developmental Hierarchy

In the development of the person, a quasi-serial order is established so that the person has an ordering of preferences for the six major environments. In analytic terms, this ordering appears analogous to the effects of the psycho-sexual history. The orientation heading the hierarchy may represent the highest level of fixation, and the ordering of subsequent orientations may represent the traces of other levels of development in order of their influence in the adult personality. The nature of this ordering affects the person's range of vocational choice in a variety of ways:

1. A well-defined hierarchy (one developmental pattern dominating all others) results in directional choice with minimal conflict or vacillation.

2. An ambiguous hierarchy (two or more competing developmental patterns) results in vacillation in direction of choice, or no choice.

3. Blocking of the hierarchical choice by economic factors, employer evaluation (rejection), or any other factor in a well-defined hierarchy results in the selection of the second developmental pattern if the second pattern dominates the third pattern. If the second and third patterns are of equal strength, then vacillation in direction of choice occurs.

4a. Although persons with the same dominant adjustive pattern may head in the same direction, differences in the ordering of the remaining patterns will result in differences in stability of choice; that is, modal patterns will be associated with stability and atypical patterns with instability. The work of Hoyt, Smith, and Levy (1957) is relevant to the latter hypothesis. They hypothesized that "the greater the integration of an individual's interest pattern, the greater the stability of his SVIB profile." Their re-testing of a sample of 121 students over a four-year period confirmed this hypothesis.

More convincing evidence of the relation of profile patterns and stability of choice has been obtained by Strong (1943, pp. 388–411), and Strong and Tucker (1952). The latter study of military physicians appears to illustrate "drifting" in terms of "range of choice." Strong finds that physicians who have become Army Command and Staff medical officers differ from other service physicians in that they have higher average scores on the SVIB for the following occupational keys: public administrator, office worker, personnel manager, math-science teacher, life insurance salesman. These results suggest that physicians with secondary business and leadership motivation are more apt to "drift" into administrative roles than are physicians with more typical or modal patterns for physicians.

4b. Modal patterning for a particular class of occupations makes for optimal functioning. A useful index of modal patterning can be obtained from the Strong literature. A sample of modal Kuder patterns has been classified by Holland *et al.* (1953) and appears to be more amenable to research than are the Strong patterns. The latter study, in which Barnette's data (1951) were re-examined by the use of modal Kuder patterns, suggests that veterans with modal patterns for a particular occupational class are more apt to be judged "successful" than are veterans with more atypical patterns. Similarly, Terman reports that his "C" group, or the low achievers of his gifted group, were characterized by a "considerable number of men ... whose employment records indicated they were drifters" (1947, p. 325). They were characterized further by having more C's and fewer A's on the SVIB as well as having lower OL scores. His findings suggest that his C group had many individuals without well-defined hierarchies, with negative self-evaluations (low OL), and with a history of vocational indecision, which seems loosely consistent with the present theory.

4c. Patterning may affect the intensity of a particular direction or the resistance to external forces. Persons with a particular adjustive orientation and modal pattern for that particular direction may be expected to have more resistance to external pressures than will persons with the same dominant direction but with an atypical pattern for that direction. Modal patterns as opposed to atypical patterns probably should be regarded as integrated patterns—integrated in the sense that they represent a set of values, attitudes, and adjustive skills consistent with modal profiles found among many people, so that related classes of occupations occur at the top of the hierarchy and unrelated classes occur at the bottom. The examination of Strong's scale matrices and patterns (1943; Darley & Hagenah, 1955), and the classification codes developed by Holland *et al.* for the Kuder (1953), demonstrate the clustering of similar occupations not only in terms of positive values and desired situations, but also in terms of values, problems, and environments which are devaluated or avoided.

Personal and Occupational Knowledge

Self-knowledge operates to increase or decrease the accuracy with which the person makes a choice. Self-knowledge is defined as a person's ability to make discriminations among potential environments in terms of his own attributes. Self-knowledge may or may not be expressed in verbal statements of "insight." Self-evaluation as distinguished from self-knowledge is the worth the person attributes to himself. Self-knowledge refers to the amount of information the person possesses about himself. Over-evaluation leads to the selection of environments beyond the person's adaptive skills (unrealistic aspirations) and under-evaluation leads to the selection of environments below the person's skills.

Hypotheses. This formulation suggests the following hypotheses:

1. Persons with inaccurate self-knowledge make inadequate choices more frequently than do persons with more accurate self-appraisals.

2. Persons with limited self-knowledge, including self-evaluation, may make inadequate choices with respect to both range and level of choice.

3. Persons whose self-knowledge is limited in both range (direction) and level (relative level of intelligence) will represent the extremes of inadequate vocational choice. In contrast, persons with relatively accurate self-knowledge will make more adequate choices.

A person's knowledge of occupational classes sets loose limits on his range of choice. A person's differentiation of the major classes and the specific occupations within classes also affects the accuracy with which he can make adequate and stable choices. If, for example, he thinks only of "laboring jobs" versus "clerical jobs," he can make only crude choices with a relatively low probability of being adequate. The person who can differentiate kinds of clerical and laboring jobs is apt to make choices with a higher probability of adequacy. Since it is assumed that the person learns about occupational environments, it is assumed further that a "selective perception" of environments takes place which results in learning more about some environments than about others, especially of the environments potentially meaningful for the person's developmental hierarchy.

Hypotheses. This formulation suggests hypotheses such as the following:

1. Persons with more information about occupational environments make more adequate choices than do persons with less information.

2. Adequacy of choice is in part a function of age, since time alone provides more learning opportunities for the accumulation of information.

3. Persons with more adequate choices will exhibit greater differentiation and organization of occupational knowledge than will persons with less adequate choices.

4. The amount of occupational knowledge will be positively correlated with the person's developmental hierarchy; that is, the person will know more about the occupations heading his hierarchy than he will about occupations at the bottom of the hierarchy.

The validity of the first hypothesis is suggested by Stone's study of the effects of occupational courses and vocational counseling (1948). In clinical practice, much vocational counseling rests on this assumption, since it is the basis for providing occupational information to clients.

External Influences

A variety of obvious external influences also affects the operation of the developmental hierarchy. Vocational opportunities, for example, limit the range of possible choices; likewise, the social pressures created by significant persons affect both the level and direction of choice. Persons who have a well-ordered hierarchy with a modal pattern for a given class of occupations will be least affected by such forces, while persons with ambiguous hierarchies will be most affected.

The time at which social influence occurs is crucial in affecting choice. In early adolescence, prior to a well-integrated hierarchy, social pressures probably have marked effect. Similarly, the childhood relationships outlined by Roe (1957) undoubtedly are of considerable importance in establishing a particular hierarchy, although parental relationships are only one set of many important environmental influences.* In contrast, social pressures in late adolescence or early adulthood would be less influential.

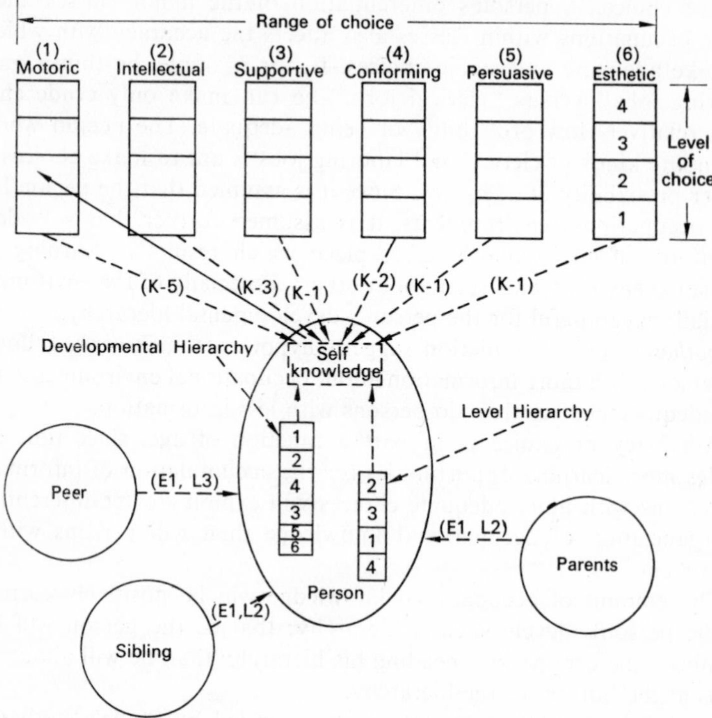

FIG. 1. Constructs and dimensions for the prediction of vocational choice.

In Figure 1 the interactions are diagrammed for a person with a typical Motoric orientation at the second level of choice. The basic dimensions of

* The inherited physical, temperamental, and psychological abilities are probably of equal significance. Likewise, sibling and peer relationships, as well as childhood and adolescent social, educational, and prevocational experiences, are assumed to make significant contributions to the formation of the personal hierarchy. In the present theory it is assumed that vocational interest inventories reflect the end product of this developmental process. This is especially plausible when the individual Strong keys are reviewed clinically. For example, the parental atmospheres suggested by Roe's theorizing may be obtained by inference from the Strong keys. Such inferences, however, are not necessary to implement the present theory and appear of lesser *immediate* value in studying the vocational choice process, although the effects of childhood training practices are required to provide a more complete analysis of vocational choice in an ultimate sense.

the occupational classification shown in this figure are, of course, similar to Roe's (1956). The major differences lie in the rationale for level of choice and the number and definition of the major occupational classes. This classification scheme will be treated more extensively in a separate paper.

The dotted lines from peer, parents, and sibling to the person indicate the social influences exerted for particular occupational environments (E) and the level (L) within a particular environment. The numbers accompanying these symbols refer to the numbered environments and levels. Similarly, the dotted lines from the environments to the person symbolize knowledge (K), including knowledge of barriers, that the person has about the various environments. The magnitude of the accompanying number is an index of the amount of information that the person possesses about each environment. In conjunction with occupational knowledge, self-knowledge operates to facilitate or inhibit the operation of the hierarchies by acting as a screen among these various forces and hierarchies.

SOME POTENTIAL RESEARCH

The present theory suggests a number of research problems. Admittedly in order to execute these studies more explicit definitions and additional clarification of some concepts are required in most instances; however, these difficulties do not appear insurmountable. The following paragraphs summarize some research directions.

1. The value of the concept of a developmental hierarchy appears amenable to study and extension through the use of coded interest inventories. Recent work by Hoyt *et al.* (1957) also provides a method and some evidence for the value of this concept.

2. The determination of level of choice might be explored through the use of intelligence, status, and self-concept measures, in order to define the relationships among these variables and the integrative value of the concept, self-evaluation.

3. Simple occupational knowledge tests might be devised to explore the relationships hypothesized in the theory concerning the amount and selective perception of occupational information as well as the correlations between developmental and level hierarchies, and occupational information.

4. The proposed occupational environment classification might be examined and clarified rationally by reviewing the evidence for a sample of typical occupations for each orientation and at each level, and by the administration of appropriate assessment devices. A systematic review of the evidence relating to major occupations, and an examination of the extent to which the present theory adequately integrates the available data, are the next step in checking the theory. The present classifications are, of course, only a set of preliminary sketches. What is needed is a set of well-

integrated portraits obtained by reviewing the evidence, classifying it, and interpreting it in terms of meaningful patterns and variables.

5. More complex studies of the interaction of the key variables in the theory might be attempted by using the available definitions. Such studies even if done without precise definition may serve to highlight neglected variables and relationships.

REFERENCES

BACHRACH, P. B. (1957) Research notes from here and there. *J. counsel. Psychol.*, **4**, 71–74.

BARNETT, G. J., HANDELSMAN, I., STEWART, L. H., and SUPER, D. E. (1952) The occupational level scale as a measure of drive. *Psychol. Monogr.*, **66**, No. 10 (Whole No. 342).

BARNETTE, W. L., Jr. (1951) Occupational aptitude patterns of selected groups of veterans. *Psychol. Monogr.*, **65**, No. 5 (Whole No. 322).

BARRON, F. (1953) Complexity-simplicity as a personality dimension. *J. abnorm. soc. Psychol.*, **48**, 163–172.

BEILIN, H. (1955) The application of general developmental principles to the vocational area. *J. counsel. Psychol.*, **2**, 53–57.

BLAU, P. M., GUSTAD, J. W., JESSOR, R., PARNES, H. S., and WILCOCK, R. C. (1956) Occupational choice: a conceptual framework. *Industr. Labor Relat. Rev.*, **9**, 531–543.

BLOCK, J., and BAILEY, D. (1955) Q-sort item analysis of a number of MMPI scales. *Tech. Memo.* OERLTM-55-7, AFPTRC

BLUM, C. (1953) *Psychoanalytic theories of personality*. New York: McGraw-Hill.

BORDIN, E. S. (1943) A theory of vocational interests as dynamic phenomena. *Educ. psychol. Measmt*, **3**, 49–65.

DARLEY, J. G., and HAGENAH, THEDA (1955) *Vocational interest measurement*. Minneapolis: Univ. of Minnesota Press.

FEATHER, D. B. (1950) The relation of personality maladjustments of 503 University of Michigan students to their occupational interest. *J. soc. Psychol.*, **32**, 71–78.

FORER, B. R. (1951) Personality dynamics and occupational choice. Paper read at APA convention.

GINZBERG, E., GINSBURG, S. W., AXELRAD, S., and HERMA, J. L. (1951) *Occupational choice: An approach to a general theory*. New York: Columbia Univ. Press.

GOUGH, H. G., MCKEE, M. G., and YANDEL, R. J. (1955) Adjective check lists analyses of a number of selected psychometric and assessment variables. Berkeley: The Institute of Personality Assessment and Research, University of Calif., Mimeo.

HOLLAND, J. L., KRAUSE, A. H., NIXON, M. ELOISE, and TREMBATH, MARY F. (1953) The classification of occupations by means of Kuder interest profiles: I. The development of interest groups. *J. appl. Psychol.*, **37**, 263–269.

HOLLINGSHEAD, A. B. (1949) *Elmtown's youth*. New York: Wiley.

HOPPOCK, R. (1957) *Occupational information*. New York: McGraw-Hill.

HOYT, D. P., SMITH, J. L. Jr., and LEVY, S. (1957) A further study in the prediction of interest stability. *J. counsel. Psychol.*, **4**, 228–233.

LAURENT, H., Jr. (1951) A study of the developmental backgrounds of men to determine by means of the biographical information blank the relationship between factors in their early backgrounds and their choice of professions. Unpublished doctoral dissertation, Western Reserve Univ.

MINER, J. B. (1957) *Intelligence in the United States*. New York: Springer.

ROE, ANNE (1956) *The psychology of occupations.* New York: Wiley.
ROE, ANNE (1957) Early determinants of vocational choice. *J. counsel. Psychol.*, **4**, 212–217.
SEGAL, S. J. (1954) The role of personality factors in vocational choice: A study of accountants and creative writers. Unpublished doctoral dissertation, Univ. of Michigan.
SIMS, V. M. (1952) *Sims SCI Occupational Rating Scale.* New York: World Book.
STERN, G. G., STEIN, M. I., and BLOOM, B. S. (1956) *Methods in personality assessment.* Glencoe, Illinois: The Free Press.

ADDITIONAL REFERENCES TO HOLLAND'S THEORY

HOLLAND, J. L. (1966) *The Psychology of Vocational Choice.* Waltham, Mass., Blaisdell-Ginn.
HOLLAND, J. L. (1958) *Preliminary Manual for Holland Vocational Preference Inventory.* Palo Alto, California, Consulting Psychologists Press. Now published by Educational Research Associates, Iowa City, Iowa.

ASHBY, J. D., WALL, H. W., and OSIPOW, S. W. (1966) Vocational certainty and indecision in college freshmen. *Personnel and Guidance Journal*, **44**, 1037–1041.
ASTIN, A. W. (1963) Further validation of the environmental assessment techniques. *Journal of Educational Psychology*, **54**, 217–226.
ASTIN, A. W., and HOLLAND, J. L. (1961) The environmental assessment technique: a way to measure college environments. *Journal of Educational Psychology*, **52**, 308–316.
BLOCHER, D. H., and SCHULTZ, R. A. (1961) Relationships among self-descriptions, occupational stereotypes, and vocational preference. *Journal of Counseling Psychology*, **8**, 314–317.
BOHN, M. (1966) Psychological needs related to vocational personality types. *Journal of Counseling Psychology*, **13**, 306–309.
GONYEA, G. (1961) Dimensions of job perceptions. *Journal of Counseling Psychology*, **8**, 305–313.
HOLLAND, J. L. (1958) A personality inventory employing occupational titles. *Journal of Applied Psychology*, **42**, 336–342.
HOLLAND, J. L. (1960) The relation of the vocational preference inventory to the sixteen personality factor questionnaire. *Journal of Applied Psychology*, **44**, 291–296.
HOLLAND, J. L. (1962) Some explorations of a theory of vocational choice. I. One and two year longitudinal studies. *Psychological Monographs*, **76**, No. 26 (Whole No. 545).
HOLLAND, J. L. (1963) Exploration of a theory of vocational choice and achievement. II. A four-year prediction study. *Psychological Reports*, **12**, 547–594.
HOLLAND, J. L. (1963/4) Some explorations of a theory of vocational choice. IV. Vocational preferences and their relation to occupational images, daydreams, and personality. *Vocational Guidance Quarterly*, Summer, Autumn, and Winter issues.
HOLLAND, J. L., and NICHOLS, R. C. (1964) Explorations of a theory of vocational choice. III. A longitudinal study of change in major field of study. *Personnel and Guidance Journal*, **43**, 235–242.
OSIPOW, S. H., ASHBY, J. R., and WALL, H. W. (1965) Personality types and vocational choice: a test of Holland's theory. *Harvard Studies in Career Development*, No. 37. Center for Research in Careers, Harvard Graduate School of Education, Cambridge, Mass.
SCHUTZ, R. A., and BLOCHER, D. H. (1961) Self-satisfaction and level of occupational choice. *Personnel and Guidance Journal*, **40**, 595–598.
STOCKIN, B. C. (1964) A test of Holland's occupational level formulation. *Personnel and Guidance Journal*, **42**, 599–602.

4. *Decision and Vocational Development: A Paradigm and Its Implications*

DAVID V. TIEDEMAN

FOR almost 50 years the vocational psychologist has attempted to view vocational development through the keyhole of *success* in educational and vocational endeavors. Career is practically invisible from that angle of vision. The career is more apparent in relation to vocational *interests*. Still more of career is apparent in relation to educational and vocational *choices*. Ultimately, however, we must view career in terms of vocational *development* as Professor Super does in his recent text[1] on the subject.

Super's writings about vocational development[1-3] provide a clear outline of its process and its investigation. However, we still need an explicit statement of the process of *decision* in vocational development. The structure of decision must be specified before investigations of the theory of vocational development can enter new phases.

DECISION AND VOCATIONAL DEVELOPMENT

The compromise inherent in discovering and nourishing the area of congruence of person and society as expressed in an individual's vocational behavior is effected within a set of decisions. The set of decisions and the context of relevance for the anticipation and implementation of each constitutes the essence of vocational development. The purpose of this article is to attempt a formal statement of this proposition, a statement sufficiently specific to make it amenable to investigation.* The structure is represented symbolically in Figure 1, but needs further elaboration.

The analysis of vocational development is oriented by each of several *decisions* with regard to school, work, and life which a person makes as he matures. With regard to *each* decision, the problem of deciding may be profitably divided into two *periods* or aspects, a period of anticipation and a period of implementation or adjustment.

(Reprinted from *Personnel and Guidance Journal*, vol. 40 (Sept. 1961), pp. 15–20, by permission of the publisher and author.)

* It must be remembered that this is merely a paradigm. I believe that the paradigm has important correspondence with the available data of vocational development. Considerable study of this paradigm is still needed before it can be fully accepted, however.

I. The Period of Anticipation

Anticipatory behavior may itself profitably be analyzed into subaspects or *stages.* Relevant stages are those of exploration, crystallization, and choice. During exploration, activities are somewhat random and probably very acquisitive. As *patterns* begin to emerge in the form of alternatives and their consequences, we speak of crystallization. Finally, with clarification and commitment, choice occurs and the person begins to organize or to specify in preparation for the implementation of his choice. More specifically, each stage may be considered as follows:

Stage IA: Exploration. In exploration a number of different alternatives or possible goals (g_{1j}) are considered.* Relevant goals are those which can possibly be attained from the opportunities associated with the decision under consideration. The alternatives or goals *set* the field (f_{1j}) for choice; they specify the context in which choice emerges. The intended image is that of an open mind considering various purposes or goals. Conditions of relevance are given *order and meaning* only in relation to the goal. Hence the high saliency of the goal for understanding of the associated field. At this stage, fields are relatively transitory, highly imaginary (perhaps even fantastic) and not necessarily related one to the other. They are possibly a relatively unassociated set of possibilities and consequence. In exploration, a person probably reflects at least upon his aspiration, opportunity both now and in the future, interest, capability, distasteful requirements that still could be tolerated, and societal context for himself and his dependents. These are relevant aspects of the field set by each goal [*i.e.*, (g_{1j}) (f_{1j})]. In short, a person attempts to take the measure of himself in relation to each alternative as he senses it. The *structural* components of this so-called "measure" and further specification.

Stage IB: Crystallization. The "measures" are probably accessible only in terms of organization or order, 0_1 [g_{1j} (f_{1j})], of all relevant considerations in relation to each of the goals (g_{1j}). This order is an aspect of crystallization. Crystallization is not irreversible, however. Sequences of tentative crystallizations, new explorations, and recrystallizations can be a part of this process.

Parenthetically, it is well to remember that each stage is intended to represent a *discrete* change in the condition of the decision. The *quality* of the decision is different at one stage than at an earlier one. In a sense, a metamorphosis takes place. The former elements are there but the new

* Since we are attempting a fairly explicit notation, two subscripts are necessary to specify the designated goals. The first subscript (1 in this case) refers to all goals of relevance to the first decision problem. The second subscript, *j*, denotes the several (in fact *j* can take values 1 to n_1) possible goals or alternatives conceived in relation to the first problem of decision. A companion symbol will also be used to specify the variability possible with the field (f_j) called to mind by each goal. At a later time we shall wish to note that a *specific* one of the n_1 goals g_{1j} is now relevant. We shall denote that condition by replacing *j* by a dot (.), *i.e.*, $g_{1\cdot}$ ($f_{1\cdot}$).

stage changes the *character* of considerations with regard to a previous stage. These conditions are represented by discrete stages and names in the paradigm. The metamorphosis is neither instantaneous nor irreversible, however. Hence, a representation of this process by double arrows ($\rightleftarrows$).

$$\text{Exploration}\begin{Bmatrix} g_{11}(f_{11}) \\ g_{12}(f_{12}) \\ \vdots \\ g_{1n_1}(f_{1n_1}) \end{Bmatrix} \rightleftarrows \text{Crystallization } \{O_1[g_{1j}(f_{1j})]\} \rightleftarrows \text{Choice } \{g_1.(f_1.)\}$$

$$\rightleftarrows \text{Specification } \{G_1.(F_1.)\} \rightleftarrows \text{Induction } \{[G_1.(F_1.) \subset \eta_1.\zeta(_1.)] \rightarrow G_1'.(F_1'.)\}$$

$$\rightleftarrows \text{Transition } \{[\eta_1.(\zeta_1.) \subset G_1'.(F_1'.)] \rightarrow \eta_1'.(\zeta_1'.)\}$$
$$\rightleftarrows \text{Maintenance } \{O_1'[G_1'.(F_1'.); \eta_1'.(\zeta_1'.)]\}$$

FIG. 1

Advance and retreat is possible at any stage and neither is necessarily limited to contiguous stages. Advance ordinarily eventually predominates, however. Therefore, the advancing is represented as the longer arrow.

Stage IC: Choice. As crystallizations stabilize, choice or decision becomes imminent. With choice, a particular goal, and its relevant field $g_1.(f_1.)$ say, orients the behavioral system of the person of relevance for his vocational development. This goal may be elected with varying degrees of certainty and its motive power will vary as a result. Therefore, the "power" of this orientation is probably a function of the complexity and of the antagonism of alternatives involved in the ultimate crystallization. Furthermore, the degree of "rationality" generally available to the person in the matter of this decision will also affect the motivating power of the resulting resolution of alternatives. Some conditions of emotionality in relation with the decision will strengthen it; others will weaken the decision.

Stage ID: Specification. Choice readies the individual to act upon his decision. In the relative tranquility prior to his initiation, however, the individual has opportunity further to specify his anticipated position. An elaboration and perfection of the image of the future ensues.* Specification probably not only perfects the image of self in position but also dissipates some of the former doubts concerning the decision. Otherwise it will result in a return to a more primitive stage of the process. Such specifications probably create potentials for action in circumstances of high relevance for their realization. Consider, for instance, the college student who has crystallized his college major. His subsequent specifications ordinarily create a potential directing his behavior for quite some time.

* We denote this elaboration by similar but not identical symbols, *i.e.*, $G_1.(F_1.)$.

II. The Period of Implementation and Adjustment

Imaginative concerns come face to face with reality on the day of initiation of implementation; a stage of *induction* begins. Superiors and colleagues associated with the position a person elects to fill start the process of perfecting their expectations for him. Eventually, however, a person ascertains that he is accepted; he "arrives," so to speak. A *transition* or metamorphosis occurs. The primary mode of reaction is no longer responsive; it becomes assertive. As the need for assertiveness subsides, however, a stage of maintenance ensues; status quo reigns as possible. Equilibrium is re-established. These three stages of this period of implementation may be further specified as follows:

Stage IIA: Induction. Eventually experience starts and induction occurs. The individual field organized by the person's goal comes into operating interaction with society's (*i.e.*, school or employer) related but not identical goal and field.* During induction, the person's primary orientation of relevance for his goal is receptive. This condition is represented in Figure 1 by noting that the individual's goal and field *assimilatively* become a part of the region (represented symbolically as $\subset$) of the position the person is electing to fill. This process leads to a further perfection of individual goal and field, $G_1'.\ (F_1'.)$ say. A ready assimilation of individual goal and field into the group purpose of relevance for the position is probably a necessary aspect of "success."

Stage IIB: Transition. With the gaining of confidence that one has been successful, a new phase starts: transition. In transition, the primary orientation of relevance for the goal becomes assertive. The group goal and field $[\eta_1 .\ (\xi_1 .)]$ is attacked in order to make it a part (again represented by $\subset$) of the modified goal and field of the person. If the individual is successful the group goal and field is modified, *i.e.*, becomes $\eta_1' .(\xi_1 .)$.

Stage IIC: Maintenance. With modification of both the individual and group goals and fields, the maintenance phase is initiated. Both partners of the interaction strive to keep the resulting organization (represented as $0_1'[G_1'.(F_1'.); \eta_1'.(\xi_1'.)]$). The individual is satisfied, at least temporarily. The group considers him successful also. Of course, the person is likely to have an image of himself as successful in these circumstances, too. Maintenance is not unalterable; it is merely a condition of dynamic equilibrium. A new member joining the social system, new strivings of existing members of that system, or a quickening of the strivings of the person himself may disturb the status quo at any time. Such disturbances, *as elected by the person* or as forced upon him, contribute either to his vocational development or disintegration.

* Since this goal and field is usually related but not identical, we denote it by the Greek analogues of our Latinized notation, viz. η for G and ξ for F. Thus we write $\eta_1 .\ (\xi_1 .)$ for this aspect of our conception.

DEPENDENT DECISIONS AND VOCATIONAL DEVELOPMENT

The described process of deciding upon a course of action and of implementing that decision in a manner intended to perfect idiosyncratic interests in a collaborative relation of interests is *possible* in each decision of relevance for vocational development. The course of events of relevance to decision may be unfolding with regard to *several* decisions simultaneously, however. Man can reflect these particular matters into systems permitting organization of diverse sets. *It is these systems of secondary* (*or perhaps of more comprehensive*) *order that specify vocational development.* Therefore let us speculate about the structure within which those data may be comprehended.*

Consider, for instance, an embryo physician as a freshman in college. He is probably still in a stage of induction with regard to his college choice, may be specifying his choice of a medical school while tentatively crystallizing with regard to an area of specialization in medicine, and also exploring with regard to a place to practice medicine.

Vocational development then is self-development viewed in relation with choice, entry, and progress in educational and vocational pursuits. It is a process occurring over *time* in man who is capable of anticipation, experience, evaluation, and memory. Man is aware of some of the relevant conditions but not of others although, in the latter case, his behavior may well be quite consistent with another person's suppositions concerning such conditions.

Hence, vocational development not only occurs within the context of a single decision; vocational development ordinarily occurs within the context of several decisions. Man both remembers and imagines. Therefore, crystallization in relation to selection of the first goal which led to organization O_1 can progress in some relation with tentative crystallizations concerning a second goal, g_{2j}, or even of a third, g_{3j}, or later goal. In fact, the discovery of dependencies among the several decisions hinges upon anticipatory behavior emerging in relation with several goals rather than with one alone. Similarly, traces of earlier considerations and evaluations of experience are ever present in any later mode of thought or of action. Hence after-effects of all former stages with regard both to a particular decision and all earlier ones are ever present in a current stage with regard to a special decision.

The *anticipations* at a given time with regard to one or more decisions *can* influence a person's mode of action with regard to: (1) a particular decision now in question; (2) those earlier decisions whose drama is not yet completed; and (3) those later decisions that are as yet either being considered or are not yet fulfilled. Similarly, experience related to a present

* An explicit notational statement of this structure is available upon request.

decision and prior ones influences development of later events. These contingencies of evaluation of experience and of imagining of the future are probably most relevant to the matters of *organizations* of self as represented in the stages of crystallization and maintenance. The organization of self experienced in the maintenance stages of several decisions hopefully improves in quality and in the satisfaction it offers the person as his life progresses.

The aim of vocational counseling is to enhance the operation of reason in this dynamic process of vocational development and to free the person for progress in taking and acting upon a particular decision as well as in viewing decisions in relation with those taken and those possible. In this way, the counselor hopes to bring each client in his responsibility to view his educational and vocational decisions as a means—ends chain; that which is an end at an earlier time is to become a means for a later goal. Behavior is to become purposeful; evaluation is to become more meaningful; and an elaboration of self is to ensue. No goal is to become so compelling that it either destroys judgment in situations of conflicting goals or cannot give way to a later, and more fulfilling, goal.

THE PATTERN OF LIFE AND VOCATIONAL DECISIONS

The study of vocational development requires a specification of the context of decision in relation to the purposes a person hopes to realize in life through the vocational expression of himself. A slight approximation of the *nature* of these decisions is already possible from consideration of the structure of man, school, and work which limits man's vocational development. Such a specification is attempted in Figure 2 where definite physical and social limitations upon career development are represented in relation with the life span.

Figure 2 suggests the validity of the characterization of vocational development which Super[1] has derived. Considerable exploration takes place in adolescence. Taking up work immediately after leaving a school is a major problem in transition. Trial of work (*i.e.*, the failure to pass beyond induction with regard to a series of job decisions) followed by establishment (transition in Figure 1), maintenance, and decline (a phase not considered in Fig. 1) seems a good characterization of the higher order effect of the *inter-dependent* career decisions. First there is mostly exploration, crystallization, choice, and specification. Next there is mostly a series of inductions. Then there may be several transitions. Finally, maintenance may dominate. Of course, there is ultimately disengagement from work in what to Super[1] is decline. If career has been truly consummated, however, this is an earned respite enjoyed in integrity. Man has surmounted his environment rather than the reverse.

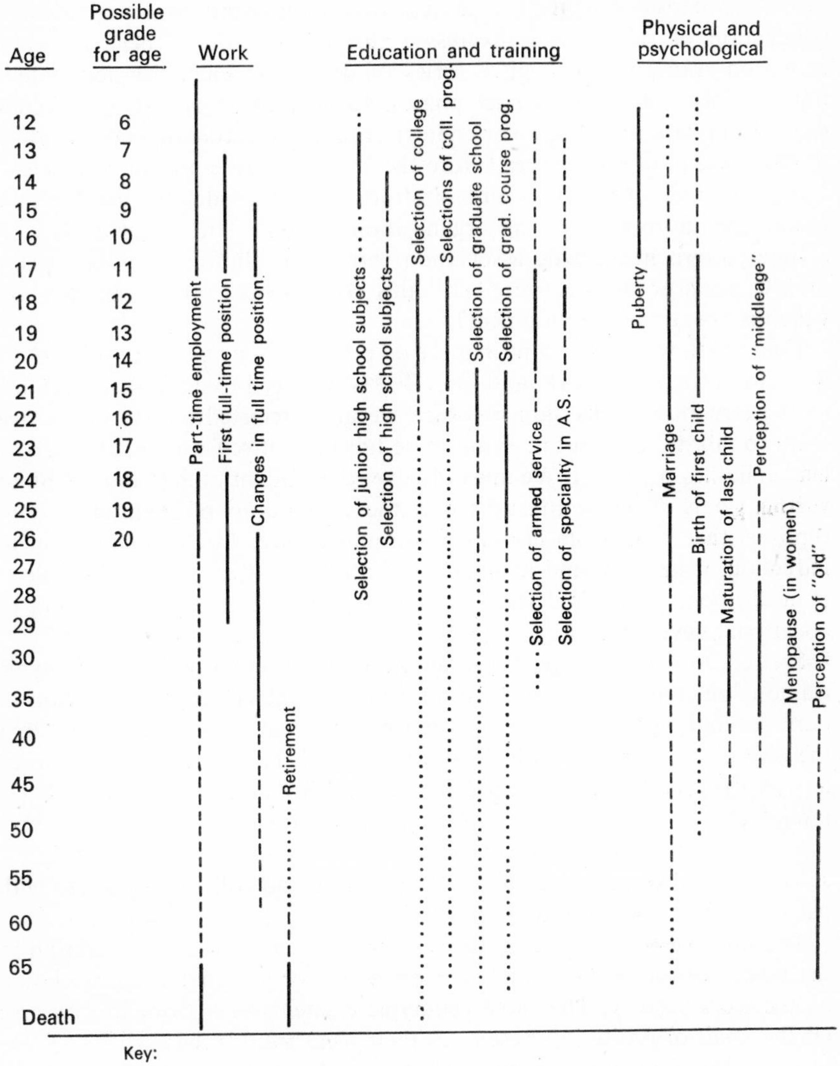

Age	Possible grade for age
12	6
13	7
14	8
15	9
16	10
17	11
18	12
19	13
20	14
21	15
22	16
23	17
24	18
25	19
26	20
27	
28	
29	
30	
35	
40	
45	
50	
55	
60	
65	
Death	

Key:

Solid line ——— Indicates time when a decision must be considered
Broken line – – – – Indicates time when a problem can and may exist
Dotted line ······· Indicates a period when a problem can exist but usually does not

FIG. 2

NEEDED RESEARCH IN VOCATIONAL DEVELOPMENT

We are considering then a process of evolving and of acting upon a conception of self as it is expressed through vocational behavior. The evolution transpires through a series of decisions. Each decision potentially consists of seven distinct phases. Each decision is also to be considered in relation with a wider context of past and future decisions leading to the presentation of career before the world in pride and in confidence. Hence vestiges of previous organizations of self gradually dissolve into newer and more overarching organizations of self. The career evolves in a time pattern in intimate association with the evolution of other aspects of life. So how do we "research" this *second-order* process of decision which is vocational development?

First of all, we need to tune in more on people's *thoughts* about themselves in relation to study, work, and life. That is, we need to address informants to the structure of decision in which we are interested and to encourage them to talk to us about it. From these talks about self we must learn how field solidifies with goal. We must discover the content of field in relation to various goals. Next we must discover the *organization* of exploratory conceptions that precipitate crystallization and choice. Modes of reaction in induction, transition, and maintenance are also matters we should collect, ponder upon, order, and learn to use in anticipating relevant matters of vocational development.

Second, as we study vocational development from an internal, genotypic frame of reference we must do so in a manner that permits verification of our speculations. Our efforts need not embrace empiricism so fiercely that the object of our regard, self, is utterly ignored, however. Rather we must learn to use that "self" in specified ways. Why don't we let the self establish its own classification of occupations for us, for instance? Our predictions of choice would probably be greatly improved by this simple substitution of frame of reference. The result could still be articulated with *our* opinion of the world and thus verified.

The final aspect of my comment is that we must use a new criterion in the investigation of vocational development. For me, that criterion should be the work history. The three genotypic elements of a work history are: (1) the *kinds* of positions chosen; (2) their *sequence*; (3) the *duration of stay* in each. Much of our research on choice, personality, occupational classification, and some of our research on interests needs consideration in relation to the kind of position chosen. The residue of research on interests and all of our research on successful and satisfactory pursuit of educational and vocational endeavors relates to the matter of duration or implementation of choice. Finally, our emerging research on vocational development is of direct relevance to the matter of sequence of choice.

The work history then is the reality with which we must relate the considerations of career as career is understood through dependent decisions about school and work. This spreading of a life across the record of a work history *is* the vocational development about which we must always strive to formulate definite and verifiable propositions.

REFERENCES

1. SUPER, DONALD E. (1957) *The psychology of careers.* New York: Harper and Bros.
2. SUPER, DONALD E., and BACHRACH, PAUL B. (1957) *Scientific careers and vocational development.* New York: Teachers College, Columbia University, Bureau of Publications.
3. SUPER, DONALD E., CRITES, JOHN O., HUMMEL, RAYMOND C., MOSER, HELEN P., OVERSTREET, PHEOBE L., and WARNATH, CHARLES F. (1957) *Vocational development: a framework for research.* Career Pattern Study Monograph 1. New York: Teachers College, Columbia University, Bureau of Publications.
4. TIEDEMAN, DAVID V., O'HARA, ROBERT P., and MATTHEWS, ESTHER (1958) *Position choices and careers: elements of a theory.* Cambridge, Mass.: The Senior Author (13 Kirkland Street). (Mimeographed.)

ADDITIONAL REFERENCES TO TIEDEMAN'S THEORY

FIELD, F. L., KEHAS, C. D., and TIEDEMAN, D. V. (1962) *The Self Construct in Career Development: A Construct in Transition.* Harvard Studies in Career Development, No. 24. Cambridge, Mass., Harvard Graduate School of Education.

TIEDEMAN, D. V., O'HARA, R. P., and BARUCH, R. W. (1963) *Career Development: Choice and Adjustment.* Princeton, N.J., College Entrance Examination Board.

TIEDEMAN, D. V., and O'HARA, R. P. (1960) *The Harvard Studies in Career Development: In Retrospect and Prospect.* Harvard Studies in Career Development, No. 15A. Cambridge, Mass., Harvard Graduate School of Education.

TIEDEMAN, D. V., O'HARA, R. P., and MATHEWS, E. (1958) *Position Choices and Careers: Elements of a Theory.* Harvard Studies in Career Development, No. 8. Cambridge, Mass., Harvard Graduate School of Education.

CASS, J. C., and TIEDEMAN, D. V. (1960) Vocational development and the election of a high school curriculum. *Personnel and Guidance Journal*, **38**, 538–545.

FRENCH, W. L. (1959) Can a man's occupation be predicted? *Journal of Counseling Psychology*, **6**, 95–99.

HARRON, V. A. (1966) The vocational decision making process among college males. *Journal of Counseling Psychology*, **13**, 217–277.

KITRICK, A., and TIEDEMAN, D. V. (1961) Conception of self and perception of role in schools of nursing. *Journal of Counseling Psychology*, **8**, 62–69.

O'HARA, R. P., and TIEDEMAN, D. V. (1959) The vocational self-concept in adolescence. *Journal of Counseling Psychology*, **6**, 292–301.

O'HARA, R. P. (1966) Vocational self concepts and high school achievement. *Vocational Guidance Quarterly*, **15**, 106–112.

5. Occupational Choice: a Conceptual Framework*

PETER M. BLAU, JOHN W. GUSTAD, RICHARD JESSOR, HERBERT S. PARNES and RICHARD C. WILCOCK

WHY do people enter different occupations? The problem of explaining this can be approached from various perspectives. One may investigate, for example, the psychological characteristics of individuals and the processes of motivation that govern their vocational choices and, for this purpose, consider the social and economic structure as given conditions which merely impose limits within which these psychological processes operate. It is also possible to examine the ways in which changes in the wage structure and other economic factors channel the flow of the labor force into different occupations, in which case the psychological motives through which these socioeconomic forces become effective are usually treated as given. Still another approach would focus upon the stratified social structure, rather than upon either the psychological makeup of individuals or the organization of the economy, and would analyze the effects of parental social status upon the occupational opportunities of children. Each of these perspectives, by the very nature of the discipline from which it derives, excludes from consideration some important variables which may affect occupational choice and selection. For this reason, representatives from the three disciplines—psychology, economics, and sociology—have collaborated

* The many, varied factors influencing an individual's selection of an occupation are related in a conceptual framework in this article, which endeavors to tie together in a meaningful pattern the economic, psychological, and sociological aspects of the process of job choice. The article does not present, however, a theory of occupational choice; rather, the purpose of the authors is to set up a systematic pattern for empirical research, out of which it may be possible at a future date to develop a theory.

This article is the result of interdisciplinary collaboration which was initiated in a seminar on occupational choice sponsored by the Social Science Research Council. Peter M. Blau is a sociologist at the University of Chicago. John W. Gustad is a psychologist at the University of Maryland. Richard Jessor is a psychologist at the University of Colorado. Herbert S. Parnes is an economist at the Ohio State University. Richard C. Wilcock is an economist at the Institute of Labor and Industrial Relations, University of Illinois.

(Reprinted from *Industrial and Labour Relations Review*. vol. 9, No. 4 (1956), pp. 531–543, by permission of editor and authors.)

in the development of a more inclusive conceptual framework, which is presented in this paper.*

CONCEPTUAL SCHEME

It should be stressed that we are proposing a conceptual framework, not a theory of occupational choice and selection. A scientific theory must, in our opinion, be derived from systematic empirical research. To be sure, many empirical studies have been carried out in this area, and a variety of antecedents have been found to be associated with occupational position, such as intelligence,† interests,‡ and job-market conditions,** to name but a few. The identification of isolated determinants, however, cannot explain occupational choice; indeed, it may be highly misleading. While it is true that Negroes are less likely to become surgeons than whites, this finding does not mean what it seems to imply (namely, that race determines the capacity to develop surgical skills). To understand this correlation, it is necessary to examine the intervening processes through which skin color affects occupational position, notably the patterns of discrimination in our society and their implications for personality development. In general, theory is concerned with the order among various determinants, that is, the interconnections between direct and more remote ones. The function of a conceptual scheme of occupational choice and selection is to call attention to different kinds of antecedent factors, the exact relationships between which have to be determined by empirical research before a systematic theory can be developed.††

Occupational choice is a developmental process that extends over many years, as several students of the subject have pointed out.‡‡ There is no single time at which young people decide upon one out of all possible careers,

* We gratefully acknowledge the assistance of the Social Science Research Council, which sponsored the interuniversity summer research seminar (1954) that provided the opportunity for our collaboration. Although one member of this seminar, Leonard Reissman, has not joined the rest of us in the authorship of this article, we are indebted to him for his help in formulating many of the ideas in it.

† Naomi Stewart, A.G.C.T. Scores of Army Personnel Grouped by Occupation, *Occupations*, Vol. 26, 1947, pp. 5–41; Carroll D. Clark and Noel P. Gist, Intelligence as a Factor in Occupational Choice, *American Sociological Review*, Vol. 3, 1938, pp. 683–694.

‡ Edward K. Strong, Predictive Value of the Vocational Interest Test, *Journal of Educational Psychology*, Vol. 26, 1935, pp. 331–349.

** Donald E. Super and R. Wright, From School to Work in the Depression Years, *School Review*, Vol. 49, 1940, pp. 123–130.

†† For a discussion of the distinction between conceptual scheme and systematic theory, see Robert K. Merton, *Social Theory and Social Structure* (Glencoe: Free Press, 1949), pp. 83–96.

‡‡ See especially Eli Ginzberg *et al.*, *Occupational Choice* (New York: Columbia University Press, 1951); and Donald E. Super, A Theory of Vocational Development, *American Psychologist*, Vol. 8, 1953, pp. 185–190.

but there are many crossroads at which their lives take decisive turns which narrow the range of future alternatives and thus influence the ultimate choice of an occupation. Throughout, social experiences—interactions with other people—are an essential part of the individual's development. The occupational preferences that finally crystallize do not, however, directly determine occupational entry.* Whether they can be realized, or must be modified or even set aside, depends on the decisions of the selectors, that is, all persons whose actions affect the candidate's chances of obtaining a position at any stage of the selection process (which includes, for instance, acceptance in a teachers college as well as employment as a teacher). Of course, the candidate's qualifications and other characteristics influence the decisions of selectors, but so do other factors which are beyond his control and which may even by unknown to him, such as economic conditions and employment policies. Hence, the process of selection, as well as the process of choice, must be taken into account in order to explain why people end up in different occupations. Moreover, clarification of the selection process requires analysis of historical changes in the social and economic conditions of selection, just as study of the choice process involves analysis of personality developments.

The social structure—the more or less institutionalized patterns of activities, interactions, and ideas among various groups—has a dual significance for occupational choice. On the one hand, it influences the personality development of the choosers; on the other, it defines the socioeconomic conditions in which selection takes place. These two effects, however, do not occur simultaneously. At any choice point in their careers, the interests and skills in terms of which individuals make their decisions have been affected by the past social structure, whereas occupational opportunities and requirements for entry are determined by the present structure. The values that orient a person's efforts and aspirations may have developed in a period of prosperity, but he has to find a way to make a living in a depression.

This twofold effect of the social structure is schematically presented in the chart (page 63). The left side suggests that the molding of biological potentialities by the differentiated social structure (Box 3) results in diverse characteristics of individuals (Box 2), some of which directly determine occupational choice (Box 1). At the same time, as indicated on the right side, the social structure changes (Box III), resulting in a socioeconomic

* Several studies have shown that occupational preferences are "unrealistic," that is, fewer students become professionals than had aspired to do so; for instance, Earl D. Sisson, Vocational Choices of College Students, *School and Society*, Vol. 46, 1937, pp. 763–768. This disproportionate attractiveness of some occupations is, of course, the expected result of the fact that they offer much higher rewards than others. Occupational expectations, on the other hand, are much more realistic than aspirations; see, for example, E. S. Jones, Relation of Ability to Preferred and Probable Occupation, *Educational Administration and Supervision*, Vol. 26, 1940, pp. 220–226.

organization at any point in time (Box II), some aspects of which directly determine occupational selection (Box I).* These two developments, separated only for analytical purposes, must be joined to explain entry into occupations. The explication of the schema may well start with the process of entry, presented at the top of the chart.†

PROCESSES OF CHOICE AND SELECTION

A choice between various possible courses of action can be conceptualized as motivated by two interrelated sets of factors: the individual's valuation of the rewards offered by different alternatives and his appraisal of his chances of being able to realize each of the alternatives.‡ These valuations and appraisals of chances are acquired through and modified by social experience, and both are conceived to be roughly ordered in hierarchical fashion for each person—a hierarchy of preferences (valuations) and a hierarchy of expectancies (appraisals). The course of action upon which an individual decides will reflect a compromise between his preferences and his expectations (an attempt to maximize expected value). Thus, his actual choice will probably not be identical with his first preference if his expectation of reaching the preferred goal is very low.

Before applying this formulation to the study of occupational choice, some possible objections must be met. Katona's distinction between habitual action, which is not preceded by *deliberate* decisions, and problem-solving behavior, which is governed by explicit choices,** raises the question whether some people do not simply drift into jobs without ever having made explicit choices between alternative occupations. Indeed, Reynolds' findings suggest that this is the case for many workers, since they do not have sufficient information about the range of alternative opportunities to make deliberate rational choices in their careers.†† This calls attention to the importance of taking labor market information into account

* The lists of factors in the second and third boxes are illustrative rather than exhaustive.

† The oversimplification involved in treating occupational entry as occurring at a single point in time will be dealt with presently.

‡ This conceptualization constitutes a point of convergence between recent economic and psychological formulations concerning the conduct of individuals in choice situations that involve some risk. See Samuel P. Hayes, Some Psychological Problems of Economics, *Psychological Bulletin*, Vol. 47, 1950, pp. 289–330; John von Neumann and Oskar Morgenstern, *Theory of Games and Economic Behavior* (Princeton: Princeton University Press, 1944); Kurt Lewin *et al.*, Level of Aspiration, in J. McV. Hunt, *Personality and the Behavior Disorders* (New York: Ronald Press, 1944); Julian B. Rotter, *Social Learning and Clinical Psychology* (New York: Prentice Hall, 1954); and Egon Brunswik, *The Conceptual Framework of Psychology* (Chicago: University of Chicago Press, 1952).

** George Katona, Rational Behavior and Economic Behavior, *Psychological Review*, Vol. 60, 1953, pp. 307–318.

†† Lloyd G. Reynolds, *The Structure of Labor Markets* (New York: Harper & Brothers, 1951).

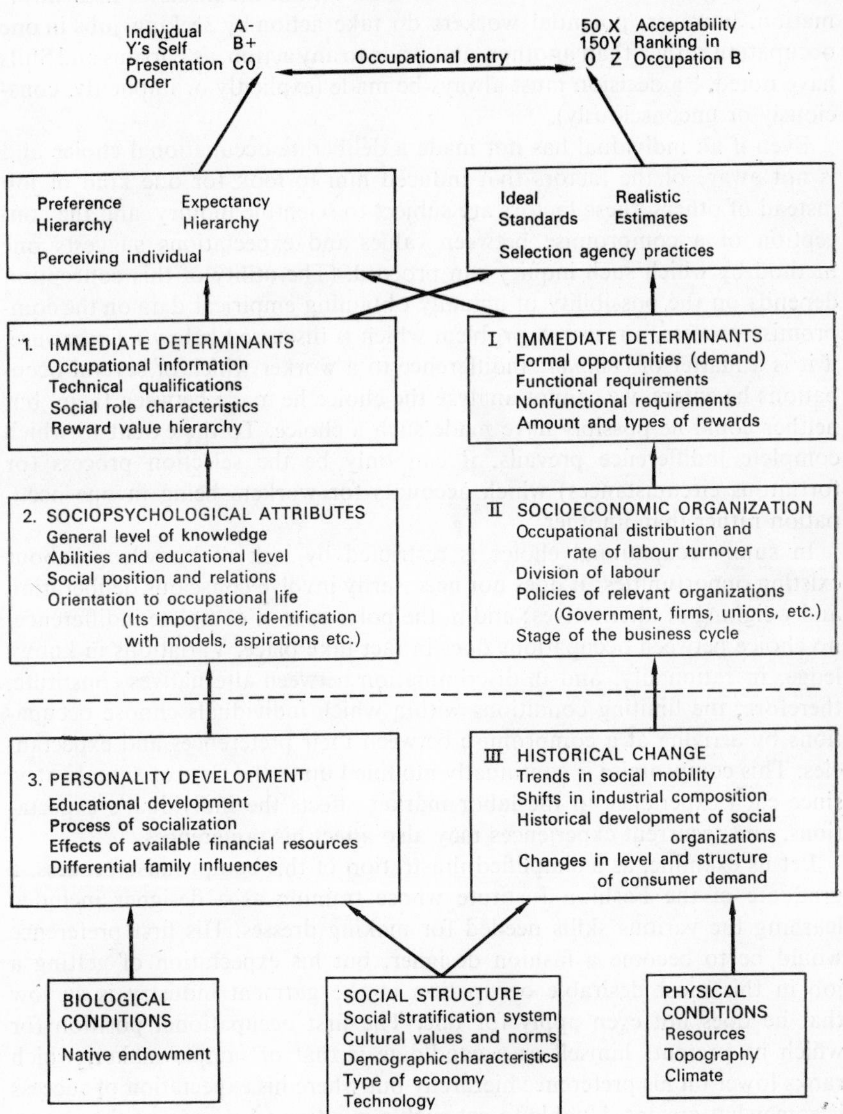

Schema of the process of occupational choice and selection

in the study of occupational choice, because a person can obviously choose only among the alternatives known to him. Within the limits of their information, however, potential workers do take action by seeking jobs in one occupation rather than another, and prior to any action, as Parsons and Shils have noted, "a decision must always be made (explicitly or implicitly, consciously or unconsciously)."*

Even if an individual has not made a deliberate occupational choice and is not aware of the factors that induced him to look for one kind of job instead of others, these factors are subject to scientific inquiry, and the conception of a compromise between values and expectations suggests one method by which such inquiry can proceed. (The utility of this conception depends on the possibility of actually obtaining empirical data on the compromise process, a research problem which is discussed below.) To be sure, if it is a matter of *complete* indifference to a worker which of several occupations he enters, we cannot analyze the choice he made between them, but neither could he possibly have made such a choice. To the extent to which complete indifference prevails, it can only be the selection process (or fortuitous circumstances) which accounts for workers being in one occupation rather than another.

In sum, occupational choice is restricted by lack of knowledge about existing opportunities; it does not necessarily involve conscious deliberation and weighing of alternatives; and in the polar case of complete indifference, no choice between occupations does in fact take place. Variations in knowledge, in rationality, and in discrimination between alternatives constitute, therefore, the limiting conditions within which individuals choose occupations by arriving at a compromise between their preferences and expectancies. This compromise is continually modified up to the time of actual entry, since each experience in the labor market affects the individual's expectations, and recurrent experiences may also affect his preferences.

Let us examine, as a simplified illustration of this compromise process, a graduate of the Fashion Institute whose training as a designer included learning the various skills needed for making dresses. His first preference would be to become a fashion designer, but his expectation of getting a job in this most desirable occupation in the garment industry is so low that he does not even apply for one. The first occupational position for which he presents himself as a candidate is that of sample maker, which ranks lower on his preference hierarchy but where his expectation of success is somewhat greater. Unable to get such a position (A on top of the chart), he tries to find work as a finisher, another skilled trade that may lead to a career as a designer. Since he obtains employment as a finisher (B), what position he would have looked for next (C) is irrelevant; indeed, this third alternative may not have crystallized in his own mind.

* Talcott Parsons and Edward A. Shils, eds., *Toward a General Theory of Action* (Cambridge: Harvard University Press, 1951), p. 89.

This account of why an individual chooses a given occupation must be supplemented by an explanation of why he is selected for it. Let us assume that the employment practices in the industry have the result, whether achieved by deliberate effort or inadvertently, that persons with certain characteristics, including considerable practical experience, have the greatest chance of being hired as finishers. Since only fifty candidates of this type present themselves for two hundred openings (X), employers also accept 150 applicants whom they consider not quite as suitable for the job, such as individuals with more than adequate training but without experience (Y). Having found a sufficient number of workers, employers are not forced to lower their requirements further and hire persons who are not properly trained (Z). There is probably a floor below which employers would not be willing to drop their requirements. The closer the qualifications of applicants approach this floor, the greater is the likelihood that employers will redefine the entry situation by increasing rewards in order to attract better qualified workers.

Occupational choice, then, can be conceptualized as a process involving a series of decisions to present oneself to employers or other selectors as a candidate for a number of more or less related occupations. Each decision is governed by the way in which the individual compromises his ideal preference and his actual expectations of being able to enter a given occupation, the latter being conditioned by previous rejections and other experiences. Occupational selection, on the other hand, consists of successive decisions of employers (or other selectors) about applicants for jobs. The decision concerning each candidate is guided by the employer's ideal standards and by his estimate of the chances that a better qualified candidate than the one under consideration will present himself in the near future. The process of occupational selection involves a regression from ideal standards (or an increase of rewards), the limits of which are defined by the occupational choices of potential workers. Correspondingly, the process of occupational choice involves a descent in a hierarchy of preferences (or the acquisition of new qualifications), which comes to an end, at least temporarily, by being selected for an occupation.

DETERMINANTS OF OCCUPATIONAL ENTRY

Eight factors, four pertaining to occupations (Box I) and four characterizing individuals (Box 1), determine occupational entry. First, the demand for new members in an occupation is indicated by the number of vacancies that exist at any one time, which can be more easily ascertained, of course, for the employed than for the self-employed. The size of the occupational group, its tendency to expand, and its turnover rate will influence the demand for new members. The second factor, functional requirements, refers to the technical qualifications needed for optimum performance of occupational tasks. The third one, nonfunctional requirements, refers to those criteria affecting selection that are not relevant to actual performance, such as veteran status, good looks, or the "proper" religion. Fourth, rewards include not only income, prestige, and power, but also opportunities for advancement, congenial fellow workers, emotional gratifications, and indeed, all employment conditions that are defined as desirable.

Turning now from the attributes of occupations to those of potential workers, a fifth factor that influences occupational entry is the information people have about an occupation—their knowledge about the requirements for entry, the rewards offered, and the opportunities for employment and advancement. Two characteristics of individuals are complementary to the two types of occupational requirements, namely, their technical skills to perform various occupational duties and their other social characteristics that influence hiring decisions, such as a Harvard accent or skin color.* Finally, people's value orientations determine the relative significance of different kinds of rewards and thus the attractive force exerted by them.†

To be sure, many other characteristics of individuals influence their careers—their level of knowledge, ability, and education, their social position and relationships, and their orientation toward occupational life, to cite only the most general ones (Box 2). It may be hypothesized, however, that the effects of all other factors can be traced through the immediate determinants of occupational entry. In other words, unless a social experience or attribute affects the information individuals have about occupations, their technical or social qualifications for entry, or their evaluation of occupations, it is not expected to influence their careers. Similarly, whereas many aspects of the socioeconomic organization (exemplified in Box II) must be examined to explain the four characteristics of occupations outlined in Box I, it is these four (plus the four directly relevant characteristics of individuals) that directly account for occupational entry, according to the hypothesis advanced here.

PROBLEMS FOR RESEARCH

It is evident that the significance of such a conceptual scheme depends entirely on whether the empty categories it supplies can be "filled" through empirical research and, if so, whether theoretical propositions that explain occupational choice and selection can be derived from the data. The conceptual framework merely suggests the variables to be taken into account,

* Discrimination and nepotism illustrate how the relationship between nonfunctional requirements and role characteristics—being a Jew or a nephew, respectively—influences chances of entry.

† Indeed, these values determine which employment conditions constitute rewards; for instance, whether working in a group is more rewarding than working alone.

but the crucial theoretical question concerning the relative influence of these various determinants of occupational entry cannot be answered by conceptual analysis but only on the basis of empirical research. The type of research needed for this purpose may be briefly illustrated.

As a starting point, one could select a town in which most of the labor force is employed by a few large companies. Interviews with a sample of high-school students would be designed to determine the four factors in Box 1; that is, the information they have about working conditions and opportunities in different occupations, their occupational skills and qualifications, their other social characteristics that may influence employment chances, and the value they place upon different kinds of rewards. Since reward is defined as any employment condition that contributes to satisfaction, an important function of the interview would be to identify the various conditions that constitute rewards for different individuals. Three of the four items called for in Box I could be obtained from personnel officers in the various companies: the number and types of vacancies to be filled, the qualifications required to fill each type, and the rewards offered by each position (including under rewards again all working conditions that may contribute to satisfaction). The remaining factor, nonfunctional requirements, would be determined in a follow-up interview with the student respondents after they entered the labor market. By comparing applicants who were rejected with those who were accepted for a given position, it would be possible to discern the social characteristics that do, in fact, govern hiring practices, whether the selectors are aware of it or not. The occupational positions of the respondents, also ascertained, in the follow-up survey, would constitute the criterion for constructing a theoretical model that makes it possible to predict occupational entry on the basis of a knowledge of the eight determinants. To validate this model, the predictions made with it in *other* studies *prior* to obtaining data on occupational entry would have to be confirmed by these data.*

The research outlined does not take into account the social and psychological processes through which the determinants affect occupational entry. An empirical investigation of the process of choice as here conceptualized would have to inquire, first, whether individuals actually rank occupations in a hierarchy of preferences and a hierarchy of expectancies, and, second, what the nature of these hierarchies is. One method for doing this is to administer questionnaires employing paired comparisons of occupations to young people prior to entry into the labor market. The instructions, which would be designed to control one of the two variables while measuring the other, might read, respectively: "If you had an opportunity to get either

* To demonstrate that the model contains all immediate determinants of occupational entry, it would be necessary to show that the correlation between occupational position and any other antecedent factor (not included in the model) disappears if the variables included in the model are controlled.

of these two kinds of jobs, which one would you prefer?" and "Without considering which job you like better , which one of these two would you have the best chance of getting?" Respondents would be permitted to state that they are indifferent to the two alternatives.

Answers to such questions raise problems of validity as well as reliability. Repeating the same procedure after a month or so could furnish a check on its reliability, that is, on whether the answers are meaningful or sheer guesswork. Validation would consist of determining whether the data on preference and expectancies, properly weighted, make it possible to predict the occupational positions for which respondents later actually present themselves as candidates. If this is not possible, improved instruments for measuring preferences and expectancies might be devised. For example, short descriptions of different kinds of work could be substituted for occupational labels, which often have little meaning, particularly for less educated respondents. As a matter of fact, a comparative analysis of the rankings obtained by using occupational labels and different descriptive statements would itself help to clarify the character of preferences and expectancies.

Of course, not all people end up in the first occupation for which they present themselves. Many are not accepted; others quit or are fired after a brief trial period.* The individual's second choice, however, is not likely to be governed by the same preferences and expectancies as his first one, since his experiences in the labor market, and possibly elsewhere, have probably given rise to changes in his expectations and even his preferences.

These socially induced changes in the two hierarchies constitute the core of the compromise process.† To study this process, repeated intensive interviews with entrants into the labor market would have to discern how modifications in occupational expectations and values are produced by various social experiences, such as inability to get a job, expulsion from professional or vocational school, being repelled by unanticipated aspects of the work, and many others. Also of interest would be an analysis of the contigency factors that influence the compromise process. For instance, what is the significance of differences in the tenacity with which an individual adheres to his first choice despite continuing inability to realize it? What difference does it make whether initial expectations are more or less realistic,

* In any research on occupational choice, it has to be decided how long an individual must have remained in an occupation before he is considered to have entered it rather than merely to have tried it out or to have been tried out for it in the process of choice and selection. Various studies have shown that first jobs are not indicative of future careers. See, for example, Reynolds, *op. cit.*, pp. 113–114, 127–133; and Gladys L. Palmer, *Labor Mobility in Six Cities* (New York: Social Science Research Council, 1954), pp. 135–136.

† Super, *loc. cit.*, p. 187, emphasizes the importance of investigating the compromise process and criticizes Ginzberg *et al.*, *op. cit.*, for failing to do so. We are here suggesting some conceptual tools with which the empirical investigation of the compromise process could be carried out.

as indicated by a comparison between an individual's expectations and the actual occupational chances of persons with his qualifications and social characteristics?

Inasmuch as the compromise process is conceived as an intervening variable between various determinants and occupational entry, its relationships to these antecedents raise a host of additional problems for research. What are, for example, the effects of differences in knowledge of employment and working conditions on preferences and expectancies? How does the importance his career assumes in the thinking of an individual influence the compromise process? What differences are there between socioeconomic classes with respect to evaluation of various rewards, preferential ranking of occupations, and discrimination made in these rankings? Do members of the working class generally discriminate less in their occupational preferences, or do they make finer discriminations than middle-class people between different working-class occupations? What is the relative significance of income and education in producing these differences between socioeconomic classes? How is the process of occupational choice affected by other social characteristics, such as ethnic background, rural-urban residence, religious affiliation, and frequency of church attendance?

Empirical investigation of the processes of occupational selection is, perhaps, even more complicated than that of choice processes. At this point, a few illustrations to indicate the range of research problems in this area must suffice. How are selection practices changed in response to a shortage of skilled workers? Specifically, under what conditions does such a shortage result not in increased rewards, but in a reorganization of the production process that makes it possible to employ workers with lesser qualifications? (The answer to this question has far-reaching implications for economic theory as well as for social welfare.) If nonfunctional barriers to occupational entry (such as sex, age, or skin color) are withdrawn during a temporary labor shortage, what determines whether these nonfunctional requirements are reintroduced once the labor shortage subsides? Are the differences in nonfunctional requirements between occupations greater than those between employers within each occupation? (Only if analysis of variance gives an affirmative answer to this question is it permissible to speak of differences in nonfunctional requirements between occupations.)

Research might also test the hypothesis that the greater the rewards offered by an occupation, the more pronounced are the barriers to entry that are unrelated to technical qualifications. Cases of persisting shortages in essential occupations, such as nursing and teaching, could be investigated to determine the political and social factors that prevent the so—called law of supply and demand from increasing rewards sufficiently to overcome the shortages. The impact of bureaucratization on the selection process might be studied by comparing hiring procedures, say, for typists in the federal government, in a large private concern, and in a sample of small firms. Corresponding comparisons could be made to examine the influence of labor unions on occupational selection.

THE HISTORICAL DIMENSION

We must now turn our attention to the developments that precede the period of occupational entry, to which only occasional references have been made so far. On the chart, the time dimension is presented as cut between the second and third boxes. The upper part indicates the social and psychological conditions of choice and selection; the lower part, the developments that produce these conditions. Thus, the family's position in the stratified social structure determines the financial resources available for preparing children for their careers. It is also reflected in the parents' value orientations, their child-rearing practices, the number of children, and the likelihood that the family is organized along authoritarian rather than egalitarian lines. These elements of family structure affect the process of socialization, in which biological potentialities are transformed into personality traits. Of course, the process of socialization is not confined to the home; associations with peers and teachers constitute other important socializing experiences for an individual, but these are not independent of the neighborhood in which his family lives, the attitudes toward people it has instilled in him, and the behavior patterns that it has cultivated and which encourage one kind of person instead of another to befriend him. With advancing specialization, the individual's educational development in school assumes increasing significance as a ladder for occupational mobility or as a barrier against it.* The internal conditions that govern occupational entry are the result of these different processes of personality development (Box 3), and the external conditions that govern entry have their roots in historical changes in the social structure (Box III).†

It is an oversimplification, however, to conceive of occupational choice and selection as occurring at one point in time, even if this is defined as a limited time interval rather than an instant, and even if the effects of earlier developments are taken into consideration. To think of the transition from

* The growing significance of specialized formal education first reduces the family's influence on careers but later enhances it again. At an early stage, it means that the school has become the substitute for parents as the provider of vocational skills. Once this is an accomplished fact, further specialization in the educational system has the consequence that educational decisions made before the child can act independently have crucial implications for his subsequent occupational life.

† Changes in the social structure also affect the course of personality development, as previously mentioned, and basic historical change, in turn, may well be contingent on the emergence of new personality patterns. See on this point Erich Fromm, *Escape from Freedom* (New York: Farrar and Rinehart, 1941).

graduation from medical school to the establishment of a medical practice as the time of occupational choice, and of entry into medical school as merely one of the factors that influenced it, is hardly realistic; but to treat entry into medical school as the point of choice is not a satisfactory procedure either, since not all students become physicians. A series of successive choice periods must be systematically analyzed to show how earlier decisions limit or extend the range of future choices.

This requires the repeated application of the conceptual scheme at crucial stages in the individual's development. Thus, choice of high-school curriculum could be investigated (see Box 1) by examining the information pupils have about each curriculum and its vocational significance, their grades, their role characteristics and relationships with other pupils and teachers in different programs, their value orientation toward education and occupational life, and the social experiences that gave rise to these characteristics, as well as the direct influence parents exerted on choice of curriculum. Of equal relevance would be (see Box I) an analysis of the existing opportunities for entering various high-school programs, the grades needed for acceptance, the other criteria that govern selection, the rewards offered by different programs (including parental resources or scholarships that permit a pupil to anticipate going to college), and the historical trends that produced these conditions in the educational system.* Once the curriculum has been decided upon, the consequent diverse experiences at high school become part of the developments of individuals that affect the immediate determinants of subsequent choices.

The study of the process of occupational entry itself often involves more than one application of the schema. An individual who is not accepted in the first occupation for which he presents himself may have to retrace his steps before he can choose another, by reorienting his thinking or acquiring new skills. Hence, a new choice situation, influenced by the earlier rejection and the actions it stimulated, must be investigated the next time he presents himself as a candidate for an occupation. Indeed, there is no reason to discontinue the analysis with the first full-time job. The schema can be applied again to explain how shifts to new occupations result from the modifications of immediate determinants produced by the experiences during previous employment and the contemporaneous changes in social conditions.† The comparison of choice patterns at successive stages in the life history of individuals will indicate the way in which the relative significance of each determinant changes, and the contrast of patterns under varying socioeconomic conditions will suggest how such conditions affect the relative significance of the determinants. Technical qualifications, for

* For two studies of the significance of social class for the selection process in high school, see A. B. Hollingshead, *Elmtown's Youth* (New York: Wiley, 1949), and W. Lloyd Warner *et al.*, *Who Shall Be Educated?* (New York: Harper & Brothers, 1944).

† The experience can be "negative," such as the absence of expected promotions.

example, may be of decisive importance at one stage or under certain conditions, but relatively unimportant at another stage or under different conditions.*

The study of historical trends in occupational selection also involves analysis of the processes through which the patterns of selection at an earlier period influence those at a later one. For example, interviews with high-school teachers and students could be designed to determine how differences in personality and conduct between natural science and social science instructors—differences which are expressions of earlier selection processes—affect occupational selection in the next generation by attracting different types of youngsters to work in the two fields. Another project might be concerned with the effects that the contrasting social characteristics of the members of various occupations have upon the public image of these occupations and with the implications of differences in public image for occupational entry. A related question is that of the significance of upward mobility into an occupation for subsequent selection. If two professions are compared, one with many members who originated in lower socioeconomic strata and one with only few such members, is there any distinction between the criteria that govern the selection of future colleagues in the two groups? (A parallel problem is posed by the impact of upward mobility on occupational *choice*, which could be examined by contrasting the occupational choices of children whose fathers, although holding similar occupational positions now, had different socioeconomic origins.) As a final illustration of research in this area, a hypothesis may be suggested for investigation: the influence of parental social class on occupational selection is partly due to the fact that the common interests of individuals reared in the same social class affect their chances of being accepted in an occupational group.† Interviews with students in professional schools, repeated at successive stages in their training, could furnish data to test this hypothesis. Confirming evidence would consist of finding that there is a relationship between parental social class and failure to complete professional training, but that this relationship disappears if either degree of acceptance by fellow students or extent of common interests with them is controlled.

SUMMARY AND CONCLUSION

The main points of this paper can be briefly outlined:

1. The conceptual scheme presented is not a substitute for a theory of occupational choice and selection, but merely a framework for systematic

* In addition, variations in the relative significance of determinants exist among occupational groups. Thus, technical qualifications are not equally important for entry into all occupations, and discrimination against ethnic minorities is more prevalent in some than in others.

† On the relationship between occupational entry and having interests in common with the successful members of an occupation, see Edward K. Strong, *Vocational Interests of Men and Women* (Stanford: Stanford University Press 1943).

research which, in due course, will provide the material needed for constructing such a theory.

2. The social structure affects occupational choice in two analytically distinct respects: as the matrix of social experiences which channel the personality development of potential workers, and as the conditions of occupational opportunity which limit the realization of their choices.

3. Although four characteristics of individuals and four of occupations have been specified as determinants of occupational entry, the two crucial questions are: what developments in the lives of potential workers and in the history of the socioeconomic organization determine these characteristics, and what are the processes of choice and selection through which they affect occupational entry?

4. Occupational choice is conceived as a process of compromise between preferences for and expectations of being able to get into various occupations. This compromise is continually modified, since the experiences of individuals in the course of searching for suitable careers affect their expectations and often also their preferences.

5. Lest the complicated and extended developmental process that culminates in occupational choice be oversimplified, it is necessary to consider it as a series of interrelated decisions rather than as a single choice. The repeated application of the suggested framework for analysis at crucial turning points in the lives of individuals makes it possible to trace this development and to show how earlier decisions, by narrowing the range of future possibilities, influence the final choices of occupations.

6. The analysis of the processes by which individuals choose one occupation in preference to others must be complemented by an analysis of the processes by which some individuals, and not others, are selected for a certain occupation. To be sure, it is legitimate scientific procedure to treat the actions of selectors as given conditions in the investigation of occupational choice, and it is equally legitimate to treat the actions of choosers as given conditions in the investigation of occupational selection, but only the combination of both procedures makes it possible to explain why people end up in different occupations.

Although this article is concerned with the determinants of occupational entry, not its consequences, the distinction between the latter and the former breaks down once historical developments are taken into account, since the consequences of earlier occupational choices and selections become determinants of later ones. A labor shortage may result in changes in the wage structure or in technological reorganizations that permit the employment of less skilled workers—new conditions which help determine future occupational entry. When it becomes generally known that dissatisfaction with their career is less prevalent among the members of one occupation than of another, these psychological consequences of occupational entry become one of the rewards the anticipation of which influences the occupational choices of the next generation. Whether a person experiences upward mobility or finds his aspirations frustrated in his career will also find expression in the orientation toward occupational life that he transmits to his children and thus in their occupational choices. At these points where consequences turn into determinants, the study of occupational choice and selection merges into the economic study of labor markets, the psychological study of personality adjustment, and the sociological study of social mobility.

6. *Vocational Choice and Utility for Risk*

ROBERT C. ZILLER*

SINCE vocational selection is a critical individual decision-making situation, the stochastic models of human decision-making behavior developed in recent years should be helpful in the current efforts to formulate a theory of vocational choice (Meadow[4] and Super[6]). In the present report a theory of vocational choice based on a model of individual decision-making behavior under conditions of uncertainty and risk is sketched, and an experiment is described within this framework. Briefly, it is proposed that vocational choice is a decision-making situation in which risk plays a major role, and therefore, individual *risk-taking* tendencies determine, in part, occupational choice.

THEORETICAL BACKGROUND

An idea similar to the hypothesis just presented was first suggested by Friedman and Savage.[2] However, in their discussion the economic aspects of vocational choice were emphasized almost to the exclusion of the psychological aspects of the problem. Yet, their decision-making model may be adapted to accommodate psychological variables.

On the other hand, psychologists have long felt that personality characteristics are related to vocational choice. The classic examples relative to the theory presented here are the flights of individuals into rarely chosen occupations in order to insure success. However, no clear-cut theory has embraced these aspects of vocational choice. Thus, it is suggested that a stochastic model of individual decision-making behavior in a vocational choice situation be developed to admit both economic and psychological variables.

In the process of selecting a vocation,† the vast array of alternatives is reduced enormously as a consequence of individual interests, abilities, economic limitations, and lack of information. The remaining possibilities

* The writer wishes to acknowledge the assistance of Mrs. Kathryn McClay who aided in several stages of the development and completion of this project.

† In general, the terminology used throughout the theoretical presentation follows Preston and Baratta[5] and Coombs and Beardslee.[1]

(Reprinted from *Journal of Counseling Psychology*, vol. 4, No. 1 (1957), pp. 61–64, by permission of publisher and author.)

form the individual's scale of judgment. These alternatives under consideration by the subject vary with regard to prize, price, and possibility of success; it is these factors along with *utility for risk* which determine the final decision.

The *prize* is the object which an individual stands to gain in the event of success. The *price* or *stake* is the object which an individual stands to lose in the event of failure. The probability of success is the ratio of the number of persons who succeed and the number of persons who enter the field. These three variables are regarded as psychological variables and are not necessarily related to *real* properties such as *dollar* values or *objective* probability. Thus, the prize may be a perceived gain in wealth or prestige or an expanded and more acceptable self-concept.

In the decision-making process, the price is compared with the prize under the condition of probability of success. However, the decision is not made on a purely probability basis (Coombs and Beardslee[(1)]). Liking to gamble or willingness to take a risk (utility for risk) may also be a parameter of decision-making under uncertainty. Actually, the latter variable, utility for risk, may be the more fruitful area of inquiry for psychologists and is, in fact, the variable selected for study in the experiment reported here.

Thus, an individual in the process of selecting a vocation may be compared to a gambler who must decide what he is prepared to wager for a given prize under certain expectations of success. However, the variables involved in vocational choice are of a more subjective nature. Furthermore, the value of the prize and price and the probability of success are subject to continuous changes over time with reference to a given vocation, as a result of the decisions of others and a multitude of economic, psychological, and sociological factors.

Continuing with the gambling model, it is proposed that vocations vary with regard to the degree to which the prize is commensurate with the price under the given probability of success (fair-risk). Compare the vocational choices of engineering and engineering sales. The latter in comparison with the former offers a chance of greater gain or income, but the income is also more variable due to the usual commission arrangements. Thus, the choice of engineering sales entails a greater degree of risk, and individual choice may be predicted from a measure of individual utility for risk.

METHOD

Subjects

The subjects for the experiment were 182 Sophomores from the University of Delaware Army ROTC program.

Procedure

During the last period of a three-hour final-testing session for ROTC Sophomores, the measure of utility for risk was administered ostensibly as an achievement test to determine, in part, the course grade for the semester. Following this, the subjects completed a questionnaire supposedly distributed by the Army to gauge the expected flow of Army inductees with various skills, abilities, and interests.

Utility for Risk

The development of the instrument measuring utility for risk is described in detail elsewhere (Torrance and Ziller,[8] Ziller[9]). Essentially, the device is patently a short true-false achievement test. In the present study, the instrument was composed of twenty items pertaining to military terms most of which were at least vaguely familiar to the subjects either from newspaper reports or through ROTC course work. For example:

1. Defilade is the delivery of fire so as to sweep the length of a line of troops.
2. Texas Towers has reference to the radar system of the Air Defense Command.
3. The Army is responsible for NIKE operations.

A valid item in this instrument is that for which the subjects have insufficient information and thus are unable to respond with any great assurance of success. The directions to the test were as follows:

> Knowledge of military terms is an important objective of the military training program. Familiarity with the following terms also indicates an interest in military affairs in general. In the items below, indicate whether the statement is True or False by circling the appropriate symbol. Your score will be determined by subtracting two times the number wrong from the number correct; that is, you will be penalized if you guess incorrectly.

Theoretically, the measure of utility for risk is the ratio of the number of items on which the subject hazards a guess to the number of items not known by the subject. The risk score is derived from the formula:

$$R = \frac{2W}{2WU}$$

where W refers to the number of incorrect responses and U refers to the number of items omitted. In an earlier study (Swineford[8]), the reliability of a similar device was estimated as .796. In the present study, no relation was found between the risk index and intelligence as measured by the total score of the ACE (r = .02).

In general, the device appears to measure the ability to sustain a loss in a decision-making situation under conditions of uncertainty and risk (Ziller[9]).

Vocational Choice

When the vocational questionnaire data were analyzed, eighteen categories developed. However, due to the small number of subjects in accounting, art, general engineering, law, medicine, ministry, armed services, physics, and physical education, these categories were excluded from the analysis. Moreover, the agriculture group was eliminated because of the diversity of positions necessarily included in this category (dairy farmer, plant pathologist, creamery manager, poultry nutritionist, etc.). A separate category labeled *Unknown* was indicated by the responses of nine subjects who wrote that they "did not know" for what vocation they were preparing. In general, these latter students were enrolled in the College of Arts and Sciences and may be referred to as liberal arts students.

RESULTS

The arcsine transformation was applied to the risk scores and the resulting indexes tabulated according to vocational choice. Subsequently, an analysis of variance test was calculated (see Table 1). The results are statistically significant at about the 5 per cent level of confidence. Students selecting sales as a vocation are found to have the highest index of risk preference, and the undecided students tend to show the lowest risk proclivity.

TABLE 1
ANALYSIS OF VARIANCE OF THE UTILITY FOR RISK AMONG VOCATIONS

Vocation	*N*	Mean Utility for Risk
Sales	19	65.5
Mechanical Engineering	14	60.7
Education	12	60.3
Business Administration	15	59.9
Chemical Engineering	33	53.1
Electrical Engineering	8	43.8
Civil Engineering	14	43.6
Undecided	9	40.6

	Mean Variance	d.f.	*F*.*
Between	1154.54	7	2.16
Within	535.56	116	

* *F* required at .05 level 2.08

DISCUSSION OF RESULTS

The study was designed to test the validity of a theory of vocational choice based upon a model of individual decision-making behavior under conditions of uncertainty and risk. The results lend support to the proposal and encourage further testing of various aspects of the theory as it applies to vocational choice.

It is tempting to speculate as to the job characteristics which lead high risk-takers to select the various vocations. For example, what explanation can be offered for the wide differences in the utility for risk between mechanical engineers on the one hand and electrical and civil engineers on the other? Personnel from the University of Delaware's School of Engineering and the Placement Bureau suggest that a greater variety of positions are open to mechanical engineers in comparison to other engineering fields. Thus a college degree in mechanical engineering may not insure success on a specific job to the same extent as a degree in other fields of engineering.

The results with regard to the students who are undecided as to vocational objectives at the end of their sophomore year are also intriguing. These undecided students tend to score low on the risk measure. Abstracting somewhat, it may be hypothesized that indecision and utility for risk are negatively correlated. Now, if this line of reasoning is extended, the measure of utility for risk may be useful in predicting the effectiveness of potential business executives who are continually faced with the necessity of making decisions on the basis of inadequate and incomplete information.

The results with regard to salesmen are in accord with the stereotype of this group. It would be interesting to determine the relation of utility for risk and success within in a sales group of a particular organization.

Finally, it is worth noting the risk-taking tendencies of the three individuals considering a military career. While these data were not included in the statistical analysis due to the small sample involved, it was observed that this group scored higher than the sales group with reference to risk taking. On the other hand, the directions to the test may have encouraged those interested in a military career to guess.

In general, the results are supporting and provocative. However, the study should be cross-validated. Moreover, a larger scale project including both men and women and a larger number of vocational areas will provide additional information upon which a theory of vocational choice based upon an individual decision-making model may be developed in greater detail.

SUMMARY

Recent theoretical developments in the area of individual decision-making behavior were adapted for conditions of vocational choice. A test of the resulting theory was described. The results supported the theory and suggested further investigations relating utility for risk and specific occupational choices.

REFERENCES

1. Coombs, C. H., and Beardslee, D. (1954) On decision-making under uncertainty. In R. M. Thrall, C. H. Coombs and R. L. Davis, *Decision Processes*. New York: John Wiley, pp. 255–282.

2. FRIEDMAN, M., and SAVAGE, L. J. (1948) The utility analysis of choices involving risk. *J. political Econ.*, **56**, 279–304.
3. GINZBERG, E., GINSBURG, J. W., AXELRAD, S., and HERMA, J. L. (1951) *Occupational Choice*. New York: Columbia University Press.
4. MEADOW, L. (1955) Toward a theory of vocational choice. *J. counsel. Psychol.*, **2**, 108–112.
5. PRESTON, M. G., and BARATTA, O. (1955) An experimental study of the auction-value of an uncertain outcome. *Amer. J. Psychol.*, **61**, 183–193.
6. SUPER, D. E. (1953) A theory of vocational development. *Amer. Psychologist*, **8**, 185–190.
7. SWINEFORD, FRANCIS (1938) The measurement of a personality trait. *J. educ. Psychol.*, **29**, 295–300.
8. TORRANCE, E. P., and ZILLER, R. C. Risk and life experience. *Research Bulletin*, Air Force Personnel and Training Research Center, Lackland Air Force Base, San Antonio, Texas, in press.
9. ZILLER, R. C. A measure of the gambling response—set in achievement examinations (submitted to *Educ. psychol. Measmt*).

7. Career Decision-Making

THOMAS L. HILTON*

CAREER decision-making is an imperfect process at best. Precisely what determines its course has received little direct attention, even though the larger problem of career development has been widely studied. In this paper, five possible conceptions of the process will be summarized and a theoretical model resulting from exploratory research by the author will be presented. The model is descriptive, not normative. We are concerned at this point with how individuals typically make career decisions, not with how they might optimally make them. The five different models are not an exhaustive inventory of available models described in the literature; the author has omitted those which represent integrations of the approaches which will be described. Two examples are the excellent models by Blau *et al.* (1956) and Ginzberg *et al.* (1951).

FIVE POSSIBLE MODELS

The Attribute-Matching Model

The approach to career development which has received the most attention in the last fifty years has been referred to by Super and Bachrach as the trait-and-factor theory (1957, p. 9). Being closely associated with psychometric test development and the guidance movement in this country, it emphasizes individual differences and how they should influence the process of occupational choice.

The decision-making model implicit in this trait-and-factor approach might be called *attribute matching*. The assumption is that the individual first takes an inventory of his personal attributes; then he ascertains the

* The author, who formerly was on the faculty at Carnegie Institute of Technology, is indebted to Herbert A. Simon and William R. Dill for valuable criticism of an early draft of this paper, to the dean of the Graduate School of Industrial Administration, Carnegie Institute of Technology, for support of the early stages of the research on which the paper is based, and to the U.S. Office of Education Cooperative Research Program for more recent research support.

(Reprinted from *Journal of Counseling Psychology*, vol. 9, No. 4 (1962), pp. 291–298, by permission of editor and author.)

attributes required for successful adjustment in each of some set of occupations; and lastly he selects that occupation the requirements of which best match his attributes. This is the process in its simplest form.

The Need-Reduction Model

The second model of career decision-making is that which underlies the approach to career development associated with dynamic personality theory. Here the goal of the process is to reduce need tension and this suggests the title given to the model. With varying degrees of awareness of their behavior, individuals seek out or gravitate to those occupations which satisfy their needs. To the extent that conscious decision-making goes on, the individual appraises his own needs and estimates the need-reducing value of some set of alternatives. Teaching may be selected, for example, because the individual perceives it as satisfying his need to nurture young people.

The Probable Gain Model

This is closely related to the various models of rational behavior employed in economics. These assume that the individual is faced with some set of alternatives each of which has certain outcomes which have a certain value to the individual and a certain probability of occurring. In accordance with one of several possible rules (see Arrow, 1951, pp. 404–437) the individual chooses an alternative which will maximize his gain. He can, for example, try to minimize his maximum possible loss, or he can maximize expected value.

The Social Structure Model

This model emphasizes the mobility provided and the limits imposed by the various social structures through which an individual's career carries him. Becker and Strauss (1956) view the maturing individual as a passenger on an escalator. But not an ordinary escalator—it may detour desired positions, its movement may be stopped or accelerated and it may branch into multiple lines, and to be a passenger, there may be stringent requirements. In accordance with this sociological approach the problem of the decision-maker becomes one of deciding which escalator to get on or, if he is already on one, whether he should switch to another.

In the final analysis the decision which Social Man has to make is very similar to that of Economic Man. Choosing an escalator is choosing an alternative. The differences lie in the assumptions which economists and sociologists make about the value of key variables. The sociologist assumes that given certain alternatives, pathways, or careers the probabilities of certain outcomes occurring are very high, so high in fact that they can be regarded as certainties. For example, if one becomes a surgeon it is practically a certainty that he will enjoy high status in the community. The decision problem for the individual becomes one of deciding what outcomes he values the most and, secondly, whether he values these enough to pay the entrance requirements (the cost of training, relinquished income, license fees, etc.).

Also implicit in the sociological literature is the assumption that the number of pathways or escalators which the environment provides may be severely limited, particularly if the individual is a member of a minority group, and that the individual has highly circumscribed power to influence the number. Thus, according to this view, obtaining and handling a large amount of information about a large number of alternatives is not likely to be a major problem for the individual.

The Complex Information Processing Model

A major premise of this model is that the individual is faced with multitudinous behavioral alternatives and that it is his limited capacity to handle information about them which limits the rationality of decision-making. Rather than being an escalator-rider, the career decision-maker is a chess player. Simon has pointed out that "there is a complete lack of evidence that, in actual human choice situations of any complexity, these computations (required by the "classical" concepts of rationality) can be, or are in fact, performed" (1955, p. 104). He then proposes some modifications that simplify the choice process, the principal one being that the individual can search for those outcomes which are satisfactory to him and then search for a behavioral alternative which has outcomes all of which are in the set of satisfactory ones.

The incomparability of different outcomes, which has frequently been cited as a shortcoming of classical economic theory, is particularly critical in career decisionmaking. How do we, for example, compare the intellectual stimulation of a work setting with the pleasantness of the climate of the locale? One solution is provided by Simon's approach: instead of attempting a complete ordering of payoffs, the different values can be thought of as the components of a vector function with a satisfactory payoff being one which has values achieving the satisfactory level of each vector.

THE CHOICE OF A MODEL

Evaluating the possible models of career decision-making is difficult for there has been little direct, deliberate testing of one against another. To the extent that the value of a model rests on the amount of data it explains we, therefore, are circumscribed at this time. There are, however, some general observations which raise questions about the usefulness of certain of the models for the particular problem at hand.

Perhaps the best critique of the attribute-matching model is provided by E. K. Strong in commenting on the limitations of the Vocational Interest

Blank as a predictor of occupational choice. Strong makes a distinction between preference and choice and discusses the factors which cause choice to differ from preference.

> A number may be mentioned: (1) pressure of family or friends of family to enter a given vocation, to live near mother, etc.; (2) desire to marry, which handicaps further preparation for the preferred occupation; (3) an opportunity to become immediately established; (4) lack of necessary finances to finish education; (5) lack of necessary ability; (6) lack of necessary personality; (7) lack of requisite health; (8) lack of information about preferred and competing occupations so that adequate plans cannot be formulated (1943, p. 30).

A study by the author of the developing careers of 300 teachers (1955, 1957, 1960) led to the same conclusions. It was common for members of the sample to be interested in teaching but not interested in being teachers. In some cases this was true even though their interests as measured by the Strong Blank were highly similar to teachers in their field. Thus for the attribute-matching model to be at all adequate it must include a very broad range of personal characteristics, e.g., interests, values, social perceptions, abilities.

Second, the model does not provide for consideration of some questions essential to an understanding of the decision-making process:

> What are the conditions which initiate the matching process? Casual empiricism indicates that individuals do not constantly engage in decision-making.
>
> Which alternatives are considered and in what order? Obviously the individual does not match his attributes against all possible occupational alternatives.
>
> What does the individual do in the absence of accurate information in regard to himself and the alternatives he considers?
>
> Which set of attributes of the individual are matched? Is it the attributes which the individual perceives himself as possessing at the moment? Or the individual's estimate of the attributes he is likely to have in the future? Or the attributes he might have under some ideal conditions?
>
> When does the matching process terminate? Or, put in another way, when is the individual satisfied with the match obtained? Is there some absolute minimum for a satisfactory fit?

The need-reduction model of career decision-making provides a basis for comparing the attractiveness of different alternatives, namely their drive-reducing potential. But most of the limitations of the attribute-matching model are also true of it. Also this model imposes even greater information-gathering requirements on the individual. Estimating the drive-reducing potential of an alternative requires extensive knowledge of it. Even if it is assumed that this information is obtainable, we face the problem of comparability inherent in the economic model. Is an alternative which fully satisfies one's need for recognition but frustrates one's need for nurturance more attractive or less attractive than an alternative for which the reverse is true?

Also there is the effect of those variables which the social structure model is designed to account for, the impact of the individual's social environment on his choice process. How does one incorporate such accidents of birth as race, color, and parental social status into a need-reduction model?

Clearly each of these models of career decision-making has limitations but at the same time each has useful features. The author's previous research indicates that, in accordance with the attribute-matching model, individuals do take an inventory of themselves as part of their decision-making process. Or at least they have a perception of themselves, a self image. Recorded interviews collected by the author are replete with *self-perceptions* such as the following:

I like to work with people.
I am a person who has to look at both sides of questions.

Also there are statements about the *attributes of occupational roles*:

To be a surgeon you have to have good manual dexterity.

In addition we find statements about the S's *needs*:

I have to have a job in which I can be creative.
If I couldn't talk to someone every so often I'd go nuts.

There is *awareness of social structure*:

The good thing about teaching is that anybody can get a job if he's qualified.
There are lots of openings in the government for my people. (From a Negro student.)

Lastly, in the interviews there are many *Economic-Man kind of statements*:

I can make more in industry than in college teaching.

Thus, each of the fields of social science which we have mentioned above is represented in the beliefs or—as they shall be labeled in the balance of this paper—the *premises* which appear in interviews. To complete the inventory, there are premises about the S's *present state of well-being*:

Things seem to be going very well.
I ought to decide what I want to be.

And premises referring to *things* which are *important* to the S:

It is unforgivable to make money by cheating others.
Whatever you decide, you have to leave the way open so you can change your mind.

Obviously some of these statements are misperceptions, but since our interest lies primilarily in their behavioral consequences their veridicality is irrelevant.

ELEMENTS OF A THEORY

It is proposed that premises such as the above are the basic ingredients of career decision-making—the building block of career decisions. The number which enter into a given decision appears to be very limited, usually less than eight.* Since their function is more direct and immediate than the influence of needs, interests, or values, a possible source of error is removed by focusing directly on them.

In regard to the decision-making process itself we find the same absence of precise information, knowledge and ordering of payoffs which Simon points out in his critique of classical economic models. Furthermore, Ss

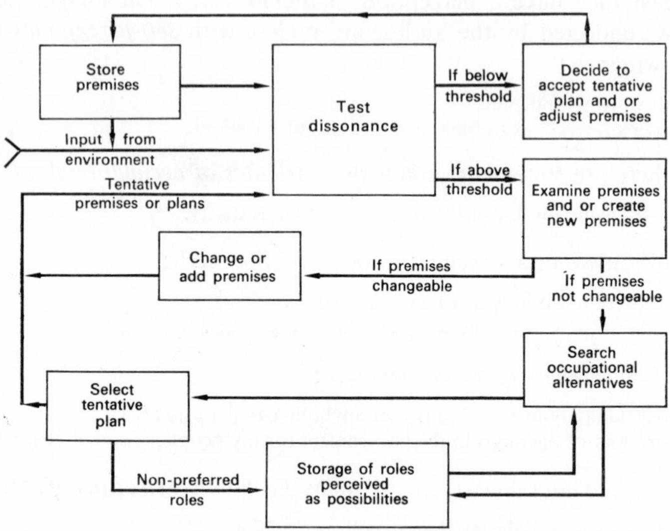

FIG. 1. Flow chart of career decision-making

typically exhibit the simplified payoff functions which he proposes; outcomes tend to be regarded as satisfactory or unsatisfactory. The climate of a particular research laboratory is adequately stimulating or it is not.

In general, the complex information processing approach which Simon has applied to organizational behavior and individual problem solving has proved to be a useful way of conceptualizing career decision-making. Using the language and method of presentation of computer technology, the processes involved in career decision-making can be described with as much precision as is required. The only limits to the exactness of the program are the creativity, insight, and perseverance of the programmer, and the storage capacity of the computer available.

In this way the sequential nature of career decision-making can readily be represented. What appear to be separate decisions usually consist of series of more elemental tests such as the following:

Should I pay attention to information about alternatives in the environment?

* The resemblance of this observation to G. A. Miller's "magical number seven" (1956) is suggestive.

Is it time to reconsider my present course of action or should the reconsideration be postponed?

Have I searched for alternatives long enough?

Cognitive Dissonance in Career Decision-Making

In addition there is the important problem of predicting when decision-making begins, when it is terminated and what the individual does when unable to find a satisfactory alternative. To provide for these questions the author proposes that the motivating factor in career decision-making be regarded as the reduction of what Festinger has labeled cognitive dissonance (1957). This may also be described as the maintenance of internal consistency, or the maintenance of cognitive or structural balance but there are indications that Festinger's term is more appropriate, even though the model proposed here differs in important respects from his formulation. For example, the author perceives efforts to reduce dissonance as preceding and facilitating decision-making rather than following it, as Festinger does.

A flow chart of the author's conception of career decision-making is given in Figure 1. In developing this flow chart the author has been influenced by the models of organizational behavior which March and Simon have outlined (1958).

The decision-making process is initiated by some input from the environment. This input could be, for example, an offer of a new position, a warning that the person should decide on a career, or information to the effect that one's income is not sufficient. If, when dissonance is tested, the input has raised dissonance above the tolerable level, the person examines his premises, i.e., his beliefs and expectations about his environment and himself. If his premises can be changed to accommodate the input, he makes the change, and the revised set of premises are tested for dissonance. Notice also on the diagram the arrows indicating that the revised premises may affect any subsequent inputs from the environment.

If the person finds that his premises cannot be revised, he searches for possible alterations in his behavior, one of which may be implied by the environmental input. He selects an alternative and tests the tentative plan for dissonance. If the dissonance is now below threshold he *makes a decision* to accept the tentative plan and adjusts his premises accordingly. If, when tested, the dissonance is still above threshold, he repeats the process, either revising his premises or trying another behavioral alternative.

In emphasizing the direct role of premises in decision-making, the author is not discounting the role of unconscious factors, i.e., feelings and tendencies which the subject cannot verbalize, even to himself. Casual empiricism suggests that such feelings do influence decision-making. But the influence is indirect. Specifically, feelings appear to influence the order in which alternatives are considered and the energy decision-makers will spend in trying to make certain alternatives less dissonant by revising premises.

IMPLICATIONS OF THE MODEL

Assuming that the author's adaptation of Festinger's concept is appropriate to the problem, several sets of hypotheses can be proposed to account for various aspects of career development. Of major interest are the hypotheses which the model suggests in regard to the difficulty which individuals experience in trying to make certain necessary career decisions. In terms of the model, *high difficulty* can be defined as continued unsuccessful attempts to reduce cognitive dissonance. Thus, the problem becomes one of identifying the causes of dissonance and the ways in which it is reduced. These ways or methods will be referred to as strategies.

Second, there is the problem of identifying the short- and long-term effects of different strategies. Obviously some strategies—postponement, for example—are unsuccessful in reducing dissonance in the long run, but they may hold dissonance to a low level for a short period. Related to this is the question of the appropriateness of the career decisions which result from different strategies. A strategy may be successful in reducing dissonance but its cost in terms of constraints it imposes on individual behavior may be excessive.

Factors Which Increase Dissonance

On the basis of exploratory interviews and the model which has been proposed, it is hypothesized that the following factors tend to increase the likelihood of dissonance.

1. Nearness in time to culturally determined point at which decision must be made, e.g., senior year in college.
2. Exposure to malevolent environment, e.g., excessive demands, threats, withdrawal of support, social rejection.
3. High opportunity for change of career.
4. A high number of perceived occupational alternatives.
   a. Perception of few limits imposed by lack of ability or other role requirements.
   b. Information about extensive range of alternatives.
5. High heterogeneity among perceived alternatives.
6. High demand for certainty of knowledge about alternatives.
7. Elaborate premises in regard to acceptable career decisions.
   a. Requirement that plan be reversible.
   b. Requirement that investment in any one career never be lost.
   c. Long planning horizon, i.e., requirement that decision fulfill long-term criteria.
8. Personal inability to suppress or distort premises.
9. Social pressure not to postpone decision-making.

Dissonance-Reducing Strategies

The two principal strategies for reducing dissonance are incorporated in the diagram presented. These are:

1. The manipulation of premises. For example, a man may convince himself that he "really doesn't want all the headaches which go with executive positions."
2. The search for and selection of a new occupational plan or position.

Frequently the premises which the decision-maker adheres to cannot be manipulated and a decision cannot be made among available alternatives. The author has observed among graduate students indications that the following strategies may be employed in this case:

3. Adoption of a very general career plan which does not irrevocably commit the decision-maker to a specific course of action.
4. Postponement of decision. Evidently dissonance can be reduced for short periods by deciding to postpone decisions until some specified time in the future, e.g., "until I see if I pass the examination."
5. Adoption of a short-term career with consideration only of contemporary characteristics of the occupational role.

Long-Term Effects

Some of the factors creating dissonance are transitory; once a decision is made, once the person commits himself, they no longer operate. But other factors are more enduring, an example being gross lack of congruence between a person's premises about himself and the requirements of the occupational role in question.

As far as long-term effects are concerned, the dependent variable of most interest to the author is role performance. This can be loosely defined as the length of time which the decision-maker continues to enact an occupational role.

In studying specific career decisions one can assume that the environment of the decision-maker remains constant during the period of the decision-making. But in examining the long term effects of a series of decisions it has to be recognized that the individual is engaged in constant transactions with the environment. His actions change the environment and, consequently, the subsequent environmental inputs. In addition there are changes in the environment which are relatively independent of the individual's actions, e.g., changes in the labor market. Blau *et al.* (1956) have conceptualized this area.

Also the individual changes. The contents of his cognitive storage are in flux and he is repeatedly faced with behavioral alternatives. Premises are augmented, re-evaluated, modified, rejected. Thus long-term prediction is exceedingly complex. At present we can only guess about the factors which should decrease the chance of dissonance and thereby increase the likelihood of an individual's remaining in a given occupational role for a long period of time. These are:

1. Conformance with and compatibility of the norms and requirements of the occupational rôle in question. This reduces threats of rejection and other sources of dissonance between an individual's premises and his behavior.
2. Social support of the individual's professional involvement. This augments or reinforces premises consonant with continued role performance.
3. Absence of role alternatives because of
   a. Limited range of abilities and interests.
   b. Lack of professional qualifications.
   c. Absence of competing social roles.

4. Absence of opportunistic, short-run, decision-making strategies.
5. Absence of environmental barriers and restrictions.

There remain many difficult theoretical problems. Three of the most central questions are:

1. What is the cumulative effect of reducing dissonance by postponing decisions?
2. How do you account for the emergence of particular premises in a person's repertoire, and their stability or instability over long time periods?
3. Do premises have differing "truth-values" to the individual? Preliminary observations indicate that they do. If so, how does this influence the subject's method of dissonance reduction?

SUMMARY

Career development can be described as the accretion of a chain of decisions. The ability to make appropriate decisions then becomes of key importance. But precisely how individuals resolve decision-making conflict efficiently is an open question. The process has received little direct attention. Five possible models of the process were examined: the attribute-matching model, the need-reduction model, the probable gain model, the social structure model, and the complex information processing model. Each was found to have some useful emphasis but most of them involved assumptions not consistent with available research findings or informal observations. Drawing mostly from the complex information processing approach to human problem solving and from interviews with Ss in the process of decision-making, the author presented a tentative model of the decision-making process which incorporates Festinger's theory of cognitive dissonance. The author proposes that the reduction of dissonance among a person's beliefs about himself and his environment is the major motivation of career decision-making. The decision-making process is instigated by inputs from the environment which raise dissonance to an intolerable level and terminate when the individual, by one of several means which are outlined, succeeds in reducing dissonance. Three sets of hypotheses which are based on the model are presented.

REFERENCES

ARROW, K. J. (1951) Alternative approaches to the theory of choice in risk-taking situations. *Econometrica*, **19**, 404–437.

BECKER, H. S., and STRAUSS, A. (1956) Careers, personality, and adult socialization. *Amer. J. Sociol.*, 253–263.

BLAU, P. M., *et al.* (1956) Occupational choice: a conceptual framework. *Ind. Labor Rel. Rev.*, **4**, 531–543.

EDWARDS, W. (1954) The theory of decision making, *Psychol. Bull.*, **51**, 380–417.

FESTINGER, L. (1957) *A theory of cognitive dissonance*. Illinois: Peterson & Co.

GINZBERG, E., *et al.* (1951) *Occupational choice: an approach to a general theory*. New York: Columbia Univ. Press.

HILTON, T. L. (1955) Ego-involvement in teaching—its theory and measurement by a word completion technique. Unpublished doctoral dissertation, Harvard Univ.

HILTON, T. L., LEVIN, H., and LEIDERMAN, G. L. (1957) Studies of teacher behavior. *J. exp. Educ.*, **26**, 81–91.

HILTON, T. L. (1960) Alleged acceptance of the occupational role of teaching. *J. appl. Psychol.*, **44**, 210–215.

MARCH, J. G., and SIMON, H. A. (1958) *Organizations*. New York: Wiley.

MILLER, G. A. (1956) The magical number seven, plus or minus two: some limits on our capacity for processing information. *Psychol. Rev.*, **63**, 81–97.

SIMON, H. A. (1955) A behavioral model of rational choice. *Quarterly J. Econ.*, **49**, 99–118.

STRONG, E. K. (1943) Vocational interests of men and women. Stanford: Stanford Univ. Press.

SUPER, D. E., and BACHRACH, B. (1957) *Scientific careers and vocational development theory*. New York: Teachers College.

8. Vocational Development: Ten Propositions in Search of a Theory

BUFORD STEFFLRE

AMONG the problems that a vocational development theory must deal with are those of differential strength of influences and proper recognition of societal and psychological forces. Our zest for power in a theory has led us to all-purpose explanations which purport to elucidate behavior of all people—men, women, lower class, middle class, Western, non-Western. Perhaps attempts to understand the relative importance of various factors in influencing different kinds of people will be more useful in helping us see the significance of work roles in our lives. This article sets out 10 propositions in an effort to work toward a unifying theory which, under the general rubric of role theory, may lead to a better appreciation of the varying significances of occupational membership.

These 10 propositions are as yet more exploratory than explanatory, but they may focus attention on areas needing consideration. The propositions will be followed by a statement of their implications for counselors and some evidence of their heuristic possibilities and value.

1. *An occupation permits an expression of the individual's public personality which is a special instance of differentiation of function.* In our culture we know something about the behavior and status of an individual when we know his age and his sex, but we know much more when we know his occupation. The occupational title has been called our "calling card and price tag." On the job, an individual wears an occupational "persona"—a mask which reveals some of him and hides some of him. Work need not be a complete expression of the person as he sees himself, but rather it is an expression of that part of himself that he wants to reveal publicly on the job. He chooses his occupational persona with the view from both sides of the mask in mind—how the world will look to him and how he will look in the eyes of the world.

2. *The occupational persona represents the individual's choice among those masks he would like to wear and those that society will permit him to wear.* It is a compromise, then, between the image he would like to project and

(Reprinted from *Personnel and Guidance Journal*, vol. 44, No. 6 (1966), Pp. 611–616, by permission of editor and author.)

the one he is permitted to project. Limitations of capacity and limitations of opportunity are here reflected. It gives us a clue to the answer to the question, "How would he like to be seen?" but it does not necessarily supply the answer itself, for it is rare that the individual has complete freedom in this matter just as it is equally rare that he is completely subject to the dictates of society.

3. *An occupational role may represent avoidance reaction as well as, or instead of, approach reaction.* When we study "What makes Sammy run?" we learn as much by studying what he is running away from as we do by studying what he is running toward. When a child tells us that he wants to be a doctor, he may indeed be saying something about his attraction to the life of a physician, but he may also simply be telling us that he wants a life different from his present one. The occupation of doctor may represent a change in social class, security, prestige. It may be a way of telling us what he does not want in his present, rather than what he does want in the future. The individual may not be so much attracted by a given job as repelled by many others.

4. *The importance of the work aspect of the public personality—the occupational persona—varies from being psychologically peripheral to being central.* In Havighurst's phraseology, the occupation may vary from being "ego involving" to being "society maintaining." It would seem that in general the job is of more central importance to men than to women in our present culture. It is of more central importance to the middle class than to the lower class or upper class. Finally, it is more central to the ordinary individual in a work oriented, Protestant ethic culture, such as that represented by Europe and the United States, than it is in a tradition directed society such as may still be found in non-Western, less-developed countries. The peculiarly Western concept of work is too often thought to be universal.

> That free men should be willing to work day after day, even after their vital needs are satisfied, and that work should be seen as a mark of uprightness and manly worth, is not only unparalleled in history but remains more or less incomprehensible to many people outside the Occident. (*The Ordeal of Change*, Eric Hoffer.)

This proposition does not state that this is the way things should be but rather tries to describe the way they are. The selection and maintenance of an occupation may be of great psychological importance to a middle-class man in the United States but will be of less psychological significance to a lower class woman in Guatemala. If she works at all outside the home, she works to make money to support herself and her family. The man described, however, works, at least in part, so that he may know who he is. He secures from his job not only economic and psychological gratification, but also philosophic identification.

> No one will claim that the majority of people in the Western World, be they workers or managers, find fulfillment in their work. But they do find in it a justification of their existence. (*The Ordeal of Change*, Eric Hoffer.)

Although everyone who works wears an occupational persona, it reveals more of some than of others.

5. *The societally limiting forces that determine the occupational persona of any individual vary from the accidental to the essential.* If we agree that it is a rare individual who can choose his occupational persona with complete freedom, we must see what sort of limitations he may encounter from society.

First, unique individual contacts may determine the occupation and so limit what is possible largely through accident. The youth graduating from high school may live across the street from someone who tells him that General Motors is hiring assembly-line workers. The next week he goes down and secures his job. The graduate student getting his doctorate may secure his first job because his major professor has a friend in another university and so learns of an opportunity.

Second, the general economic situation may determine what is possible. In times of severe depression, a student may stay in school and receive training when otherwise he would be at work. In very good times a student may drop out of high school and take a job that he otherwise might not get were it not so readily available. The state of the economy, then, limits the selection of the occupational persona.

Third, the sociological context may determine the occupational level at which one works. The child of a professional family will have difficulty not going to college and not working at a white-collar occupation. The child of a lower-class family may have reverse difficulties. Our family origin does much to determine what we consider an appropriate occupational persona. Do we not tacitly agree that certain jobs are "suitable" and certain jobs "unsuitable" for given families?

Fourth, the psychological makeup of the individual may lead him to choose certain occupations that permit him to express his uniqueness. Although we know relatively little about this relationship, there has been some research and much speculation. The Worker's Trait Study of the Department of Labor would be an example of our belief that psychological factors are important in occupational selection. The theory building of Roe and others suggests that this is a notion that many find compatible.

Finally, the philosophical commitment of the individual may determine the meaning of life and of work and thereby influence his selection of an occupational persona which he feels appropriately expresses his humanness. The concept of an occupation as a "calling" embodies this dimension.

In summary, forces limiting the selection of an occupational persona may be accidental (situational), economic, sociological, psychological, or philosophical. This proposition relates to the previous one because men more than women, middle class more than the other classes, people in work-oriented more than "being"-oriented cultures, are apt to be influenced by the forces near the end rather than the beginning of this list. A woman is more apt to select a job on the basis of accident or the general economic situation rather than her own psychological dynamics or her basic belief about the meaning of life. Men, on the other hand, particularly those of the middle class in Western society, are more apt to view the occupational persona as an expression of their humanness, and their uniqueness.

6. *The expression of the public personality through an occupation—the selection of an occupational persona—must be made on incomplete information.* It has been said that we "choose an occupation as we do a wife, largely on faith." We cannot possibly know all about ourselves when we move into an occupation, nor can we know all about a particular occupational role until we experience it. Some ignorance, then, both personal and social, is inevitable at the time of the selection of an occupational persona.

7. *The stability of the choice of an occupation after additional information about the work role becomes available varies directly with the psychological commitment to the occupation on the part of the chooser.* The lack of information posited by the last proposition may result in a situation where there is a very great difference between the occupational persona and either the self-concept or the occupational role expectation, or a situation where they merge. That is, the mask that we have labeled the occupational persona may so resemble what is behind it that the person looks the same with or without his mask. On the other hand, the mask may fit very badly and the person behind it may be quite different from the one we see on the job. If there is considerable psychological commitment (such as we would expect to find in the middle-class, work-oriented male) and the individual finds that his work role is not precisely what he thought it would be or if the job changes as a result of technological advances, he would be more apt to change to a different job within the same occupation rather than to change occupations. On the other hand, women of the lower class in tradition-directed society would be more apt to change to another occupation. The more central the job is to the individual, the more apt he is to try to accommodate himself to it rather than to move to another one. One obvious reason for this situation is that an individual whose job *is* central is apt to have invested much more time and money in preparation for the occupation than is his less work-oriented counterpart.

8. *As further information about the self comes to light, it is more apt to lead to change within the occupation for those who are psychologically committed to the occupation as opposed to change to a different occupation for others.* The elements of maleness, middle-class status, and work orientation more than the elements of femaleness, lower- or upper-class status, and tradition direction will be associated in this contingency with staying in an occupation rather than moving to another one.

9. *The occupational persona and the self-concept have a symbiotic relationship that moves them toward congruence.* If the individual stays in the occupa-

tion, he will change either himself or the conditions of his employment so that the way he behaves on the job and the way he really is tend to become more harmonious. If the mask does not fit, either the mask will be altered somewhat or the individual, over a period of time, will accommodate so that comfort becomes a function of time. The college professor who is not absent-minded learns to be!

10. *The selection of an occupational persona may express any of four relationships between the self and society.* The first relationship might be called "fitting." In this situation the self (S) is congruent with the self concept (SC), which in turn is congruent with the occupational persona (OP) which was selected on the basis of an accurate occupational role expectation (ORE). ($S \cong SC \cong OP \cong ORE$.) This situation results in a healthy expression of the self and is best explained by self-theory. What we have here is the idealized concept of the selection of an occupation as being the implementation of a self-concept. In those cases when all is well in the world this explanation seems to be a suitable one. Such consummations, however devoutly desired, do not seem to occur with sufficient frequency to be a complete explanation of the selection of work roles.

A second relationship might be called "permitting." In this situation the self-concept is not completely congruent with the self. The occupation persona, however, may be congruent with the self-concept as it is and may have been selected with an accurate occupational role expectation. ($S \neq SC \cong OP \cong ORE$). Such a situation leads to denial of that part of the self which is not recognized in the self-concept and may have either of two possible outcomes. One may result in inadequate job performance, for the job may require characteristics that though present in the self-concept are not present in the self. A person who overestimates his mechanical skills may not be very useful as an auto repairman. A counselor who overestimates his warmth and understanding may not be a successful counselor, even though his selection of counseling as an occupation was an attempt to implement his self-concept because, unfortunately, the self-concept was not congruent with the self. A second possibility may result when the occupational persona permits the expression of those characteristics present in the self but denied awareness in the self-concept. To use an occupational cliché as an example, it might by hypothesized that some prison guards are not completely aware of that part of themselves that enjoys disciplining others. Or perhaps an occasional school teacher is unaware that his control of the impulses of the children is related to the threat that he perceives from his own impulses. This relationship between the individual and the selection of his work role seems best explained by the mechanism of repression as viewed in psychoanalytic theory.

A third relationship might be called "transforming." In this situation the self-concept is congruent with the self but the individual does not wish to idsplay all of his self-concept in an occupation. The occupational persona, therefore, is not completely congruent with the self-concept even though it may be based on an accurate occupational role expectation. ($S \cong SC \neq OP \cong ORE$). Such a situation may lead to guilt. The example for this relationship that occurs to me is that of the rather feminine individual who when faced with a choice at the time of service selects the Marines. It is as though he hopes to magically transform himself by the selection of an occupation. We are all familiar with the neurotic who selects counseling as an occupation. Could it not be that at least some of these people are quite aware of their difficulties and hope through a kind of magical transformation to take on the stability and maturity which is associated in the public mind with members of their occupational reference group—counselors. This situation seems best explained by role theory.

The fourth relationship may be thought of as "binding". In this situation the self-concept is congruent with the self and the occupational persona congruent with the self-concept. However, the occupational persona has been selected on the basis of inaccurate occupational role expectations. ($S \cong SC \cong OP \neq ORE$.) Such a situation often leads to shame. An example would be the individual who desires to be a school counselor and then finds on the job that he is asked to do many things that do not seem to him to be appropriate tasks. He finds that he is not actually counseling very much, but is involved perhaps in attendance matters, discipline enforcement, psychometrics, and other socially valuable activities that he did not realize were part of this occupation in many work settings. It is this situation with which, as counselors, we seem to be most concerned, and it seems to be explained best by a modification of the trait and factor theory or the old "square pegs in square holes" notion. Often we feel that the provision of accurate occupational information will take care of most of the problems of vocational selection, but making such information available is but part of the total problem because, as has been seen, we also need to work on a clarification of the self-concept and a recognition of what the psychodynamics of the selection of an occupational persona constitute for a given individual.

IMPLICATIONS

What are the implications of these 10 propositions for the counselor? One would be that the choices moving the individual toward an occupation are of variable importance depending upon his age, sex, social class, nationality, and other conditions. For some people, vocational development and occupational choice may be a very central and ego-involving personality statement, while for others it may be quite peripheral and have little significance for their identity as persons. A second implication is that the counselor should search for the hidden meaning of a choice. Is it an act which implements a clear self-concept, or does it permit a denial of part of the self? Was his choice made on the basis of accident or the economic situation, or on the basis of clearly worked-out life values and an understanding of his own personality? Finally, as counselors, this theoretical framework suggests that we should aim at helping students to understand themselves and not merely be concerned with their making "wise" choices. The selection of the occupational persona may be a choice of great importance in the life of the individual, or it may be relatively inconsequential. Let us remember that our work values are not necessarily those of our clients.

Finally, do these 10 propositions constitute a basis for a theory of vocational development? They seem to have some of the aspects of a theory. They attempt to explain on a differential basis who will do what in a given situation. They suggest some hypotheses which may be testable:

1. There will be differences between a person's self-concept and his "self as seen on the job"—that is, his occupational persona. These differences will be less for middle-class than for lower- or upper-class workers, less for men than for women, less for Western than for non-Western workers. (Q-sorts leading to correlations of self-concept and occupational persona might be an appropriate technique to test this hypothesis.)

2. Expressions of dislike (avoidance reactions) may predict vocational development. (Longitudinal studies such as those by Strong would seem appropriate in helping us test this hypothesis by working from declarations as well as low interest inventory scores. The stability of "C" ratings on the Strong give some support to this notion.)

3. Crucial variables in vocational development are more apt to be accidental and economic for lower class than for middle class, for females than males, for non-Western than for Western workers. A reverse relationship should be found for psychological and philosophical causation. (Career development studies should be useful in such research.)

4. Perceptions of role expectations and of the self will change after an occupation is entered. (The administration of questionnaires or interviews before and after job experience would test this hypothesis.)

5. Occupational, as opposed to job, stability will be differentially related to class, sex, and culture. (Again, career studies could be used.)

6. Proposition 10 would call for much creativity in testing. Hypotheses generating research might begin with an examination of relationships among (a) the self as seen by others, (b) the self-concept, (c) self as seen on the job, and (d) occupational role expectations. (Would self-descriptions and descriptions by others support the notion of relationships describable as "fitting," "permitting," "transforming," and "binding"?)

The propositions, remember, are in search of a theory, a unifying principle which will relate one proposition to another in such a way that a pattern emerges. Until the pattern is clear they remain 10 notions that some may find provocative and illuminating.

ADDITIONAL REFERENCES TO VOCATIONAL THEORY

For anyone concerned with developments in the theoretical or practical areas of vocational guidance, the following journals should be consulted frequently:

American

Journal of Counseling Psychology and *Personnel and Guidance Journal*, c/o The American Psychological Association, Inc., 1200 Seventeenth Street, N.W., Washington, D.C. 20036.

Vocational Guidance Quarterly, c/o American Personnel and Guidance Association, Inc., 1605 New Hampshire Avenue, N.W., Washington, D.C. 20009.

British

Occupational Psychology, c/o National Institute of Industrial Psychology, 14 Welbeck Street, London, W.1.

British Journal of Educational Psychology, c/o Methuen & Co. Ltd., 11 New Fetter Lane, London, E.C.4.

Educational Research, c/o National Foundation for Educational Research, The Mere, Upton Park, Slough, Bucks.

The following American textbooks should be standard bookshelf acquisitions for anyone interested in vocational theory:

ADAMS, J. F. (ed.) (1964) *Counseling and Guidance*. Macmillan, New York, and Collier-Macmillan, London (Paperback).

BOROW, H. (ed.) (1964) *Man in a World at Work*. Boston, Houghton-Mifflin.

PETERS, H. J., and HANSON, J. C. (eds.) (1964) *Vocational Guidance and Career Development*. Macmillan, New York, and Collier-Macmillan, London (Paperback).

There follows a list of books and articles to which there has as yet been no reference, which provide a wide range sampling of comment, criticism, and review, in vocational theorizing.

CAPLOW, T. (1954) *The Sociology of Work*. Minneapolis, University of Minnesota Press.

CLARK, K. E. (1961) *Vocational Interests of Non-Professional Men*. Minneapolis, University of Minnesota Press.

FLANAGAN, J. C., DARLEY, J. G., SHAYCOFT, M. F., GORHARM, W. A., ORR, D. B., and GOLDBERG, I. (1962) *Design for a Study of American Youth*. Boston, Houghton-Mifflin.

GHISELLI, E. E. (1966) *The Validity of Occupational Aptitude Tests*. New York, Wiley.

GROSS, E. (1958) *Work and Society*. New York, Thomas Crowell.

HERZBERG, F., MAUSNER, B., and SNYDERMAN, B. (1959) *The Motivation to Work*. New York, Wiley.

HOPPOCK, R. (1963) *Occupational Information*. New York, McGraw-Hill.

HUGHES, E. (1958) *Men and Their Work*. Glencoe, Ill., Free Press.

NOSOW, S., and FORM, W. (eds.) (1962) *Man, Work and Society*. New York, Basic Books.

ROE, A., and SIEGELMAN, M. (1964) *The Origin of Interests*. Washington, D.C., American Personnel and Guidance Association.

ROSENBERG, M. (1957) *Occupations and Values*. Glencoe, Ill.

THORNDIKE, R. L., and HAGEN, E. (1959) *10,000 Careers*. New York, Wiley.

VROOM, V. H. (1964) *Work and Motivation*. New York, Wiley.

WYLIE, R. C. (1961) *Self-Concept Theory*. Lincoln, University of Nebraska Press.

BECKER, H. S., and STRAUSS, A. (1956) Careers, personality, and adult socialization. *American Journal of Sociology*, **62**, 253–263.

BECKER, H. S., and CARPER, J. (1956) The development of identification with an occupation. *American Journal of Sociology*, **61**, 289–298.

BORDIN, E. S. (1943) A theory of interests as dynamic phenomena. *Educational and Psychological Measurement*, **3**, 44–66.

BORDIN, E. S., NACHMANN, B., and SEGAL, S. J. (1963) An articulated framework for vocational development. *Journal of Counseling Psychology*, **10**, 107–116.

BOROW, H. (1960) Research programs in career development. *Journal of Counseling Psychology*, **7**, 62–70.

BOROW, H. (1961) Vocational development research: some problems of logical and experimental form. *Personnel and Guidance Journal*, **40**, 21–25.

BOROW, H. (1961) An integral view of occupational theory and research. In *Man in a World at Work, ibid.*

COHEN, A. (1964) Sociological studies of occupations as a "way of life". *Personnel and Guidance Journal*, **63**, 267–272.

CRITES, J. O. (1964) Research on vocational guidance: status and prospect. In Borow, H. (ed.) *Man in a World at Work, ibid.*

CRITES, J. O. (1965) Measurement of vocational maturity in adolescence: I. Attitudes test of the Vocational Development Inventory. *Psychological Monographs*, **79**, No. 595.

DANSKIN, D. G. (1965) Studies in the sociological aspects of specific occupations. *Personnel and Guidance Journal*, **36**, 104–111.

ERIKSON, E. E. (1959) Identity and the life cycle. *Psychological Issues*, **1**, 1–171.

FLETCHER, F. M. (1966) Concepts, curiosity and careers. *Journal of Counseling Psychology*, **13**, 131–138.

FRENCH, W. L. (1959) Can a man's occupation be predicted? *Journal of Counseling Psychology*, **6**, 95–101.

GRIBBONS, W. D., HALPERIN, S., and LOHNES, P. R. (1966) Applications of stochastic models in research on career development. *Journal of Counseling Psychology*, **13**, 403–408.

HACKMAN, R. B. (1965) The problem of vocational choice in vocational guidance. In J. F. Adams (ed.), *Counseling and Guidance*, New York, Macmillan.

HADLEY, R. G., and LEVY, W. V. (1962) Vocational development and reference groups. *Journal of Counseling Psychology*, **9**, 110–114.

HERSHENSON, D. B. (1965) Some personal and social determinants of occupational role-taking in college students. *Journal of Counseling Psychology*, **12**, 206–208.

HEWER, V. H. (1963) What do theories of vocational choice mean to a counselor? *Journal of Counseling Psychology*, **10**, 118–125.

KASSARJIAN, W. M., and KASSARJIAN, H. H. (1965) Occupational interests, social values, and social character. *Journal of Counseling Psychology*, **12**, 48–54.

LARCEBEAU, S. (1958) Étude d'un questionnaire d'intérêts pour garçons de 10 à 12 ans. *Bulletin de l'Institut National d' Étude du Travail et d'Orientation Professionnelle*, **14**, 232–254.

LEVINE, S. (1963) Occupation and personality: relationship between the social factors of the job and human orientation. *Personnel and Guidance Journal*, **41**, 602–605.

MEADOW, L. (1955) Toward a theory of vocational choice. *Journal of Counseling Psychology*, **2**, 108–112.

RODGER, A., and CAVENAGH, P. (1962) Personnel selection and vocational guidance. In *Society: Problems and Methods of Study*, (ed.) A. T. Welford, M. Argyle, D. V. Glass, J. N. Morris. London, Routledge & Kegan Paul.

SIMONS, J. B. (1966) An existential view of vocational development. *Personnel and Guidance Journal*, **44**, 604–610.

SMALL, L. (1952) A theory of vocational choice. *Vocational Guidance Quarterly*, **1**, 29.

STRONG, D. J., and FEDER, D. D. (1961) Measurement of the self-concept: a critique of the literature. *Journal of Counseling Psychology*, **8**, 170–178.

Symposium (1965) A. RODGER, A. THOMPSON, M. H. BROLLY, P. E. VERNON, and W. M. O'NEILL The criterion problem in selection and guidance. *Occupational Psychology*, **39**, 77–101.

TYLER, L. E. (1955) The development of vocational interests. *Journal of Genetic Psychology* **88**, 33–44.

TYLER, L. E. (1961) Research explorations in the realm of choice. *Journal of Counseling Psychology*, **8**, 195–201.

The reader will find it profitable to regularly peruse the following journals:

Sociology of Education Abstracts

This provides a ready acquaintanceship with the results of all British and much European and American research involving all aspects of education, including vocational development and education.

Annual Review of Psychology

Every two or three years a review of the major researches in "counseling psychology" is presented. For example, see A. Brayfield's review in the 1963 edition.

Journal of Counseling Psychology

This journal periodically publishes reviews of the major researches into counseling psychology for a particular year: for example:

MYERS, M. A. (1966) Research in counseling psychology—1964. **13**, 371–379.

CARKHUFF, R. R. (1966) Counseling research, theory and practice—1965. **13**, 467–480.

SECTION 2

The Home and the School

"Hear my son, the instruction of thy father
And forsake not the teaching of thy mother:
For they shall be a chaplet of grace unto thy head,
and chains about thy neck."

PROVERBS 1: 8–10

SECTION 1 concentrated on the total process of vocational development and educational and vocational decision-making. The papers in this present section deal with the influence of home and school factors on vocational development. How does a child's home and his school affect his vocational development? What are the factors in these environments that will help to determine his occupational entry? How important are these socializing agencies in shaping the individual's hierarchy of occupational preferences?

Lipsett examines the social factors that impinge on vocational development. He reviews research on the influence of social class, home environment, type of school, peer group relations, and institutionalized pressure groups. The value of this research for the counsellor is that is enables him to develop a more accurate insight into the role perceptions and expectations of his counsellee. The individual must be viewed against his total social and educational background.

Stacey, though primarily concerned with occupational mobility, reviews researches which describe the influence of social psychological factors on vocational development and occupational entry. He examines the influence of the family, intelligence, achievement motivation, deferral of gratification and other factors.

Roe portrays a theory of vocational choice based upon a child's early interaction with his parents. From three characteristic "family atmospheres" —emotional concentration on the child, avoidance of the child, and acceptance of the child—she predicts the resulting adult orientations and the classes of occupations to which these early childhood experiences will lead. This scheme has produced a large number of research investigations, which are reported in the additional references.

With the influence of society, the family, and psychological factors examined, the final article in this section looks at the effects of sibling associations and birth order on occupational role preferences. Sutton-Smith, Roberts, and Rosenberg provide evidence for the importance of sex status and birth order in the development of dispositions of functional value individually and socially, and which dispose individuals towards certain types of occupation.

9. *Social Factors in Vocational Development*

LAURENCE LIPSETT

AS THE guidance movement developed in its first three or four decades, its progress was marked by refinement of tests and other measuring devices. From the development of intelligence tests, it proceeded to interest inventories, dexterity tests, and a variety of devices purporting to measure various aptitudes and personality traits.

While the counseling and guidance profession was emphasizing tests, sociologists and social psychologists had begun to discover the importance of social factors relevant to vocational development, such as the relationship between social class membership and attending college.[8, 14, 15]. Some results of sociological studies are reflected in the theories of vocational choice or vocational development outlined by Ginzberg,[7] Super,[13] and Beilin.[1] The trend from "vocational guidance" to "counseling psychology" may also represent some implicit leaning toward a broader frame of reference which would give more consideration to social factors. It is the purpose of this paper to (1) bring together some of the published sociological information most relevant for counseling psychology, (2) suggest additional inferences from social factors, and (3) outline specific kinds of social information which counseling psychologists would need in order to incorporate sociological knowledge and theory into their professional practice.

IMPORTANCE OF SOCIAL FACTORS

The dynamics of vocational development and vocational adjustment can be understood only when there is consideration not only of individual factors but also the social influences upon the individual and the interaction between individual and group. As Cottrell[3] has synthesized, "any item of social behavior is understood only as it is seen as a functional part of a situation composed of interacting selves, and in functioning in an interactive system, the organism not only develops the response patterns representing its part in such an interact but actually incorporates the response patterns of the others in its reactive system."

(Reprinted from *The Personnel and Guidance Journal*, vol. 40, No. 5 (January 1962), pp. 432–437, by permission of the publisher and author.)

Lewin[9] points out that "it seems impossible to predict group behavior without taking into account group goals, group standards, group values, and the way a group sees its own situation and that of other groups." It is just as impossible to predict individual behavior without knowing these facts about the individual's reference groups and the strength of his ties to them.

SOCIAL FACTORS AFFECTING VOCATIONAL DEVELOPMENT

Social Class

Probably the broadest and most significant social factor affecting human behavior is social class identification. For many years Americans rejected the notion of social class to a point where this aspect of social living was not studied to any significant extent. However, the investigations of Warner and his associates[14] have identified social stratification in American communities which is not seriously questioned.

Although Ginzberg and associates[7] found that boys from low income families went through the same stages of vocational development as did high income boys, there was considerable difference in the choices and the reasons for them. In the high income group the boys, even at an early age, tended to assume that they would go to college, and as they entered the realistic stage their choices tended to be limited to the professions. Low income boys, on the other hand, thought in terms of a job which would pay more than the father's steady employment, skilled work, and a job without exposure to serious accidents. "For most of this group, to own a business is the outer limit of their expectations." Ginzberg interprets the case material to suggest that one of the major limitations facing the lower income group is their modest level of aspiration. "Their environment obscures the appropriate translations of interests and capacities into realizable occupational choices. ... Boys with mechanical interests and ability are not able to think beyond becoming mechanics or electricians ... they believe that there is little that they can do (about vocational planning) beyond selecting a high school where they can pursue an appropriate vocational course."

Beilin[2] has framed an explanation for the lack of social mobility through education as follows: "These (reasons) appear, for the most part, organized about the attitude that education is not important; the way of life it presents essentially alien, the rewards at the end of the line not worthwhile or not worth the effort, and the goals not achievable. The educational system is seen as hostile and, at the least, offers the minimum of rewards." Havighurst and Rodgers[8] illustrate this point with the case of a boy with an IQ of 139 whose father was a master plumber. The family could afford to send this boy to college, and this was urged by both teachers and parents. But the youth said, "My friends are all going to stay in town; my girl friend is here; I like this place. Why should I leave it?"

On the other hand, Hollinshead[8] points out how individual motivation can surmount obstacles of finances and social class. One boy, whose father was a janitor, whose parents had not gone beyond the eighth grade, wrote at the age of 16, "The worst thing that could happen to me is that I should fail in my plans to go to college and enter a profession." He secured a scholarship and went to college.

In studying the probability that a particular boy or girl will go to college, Havighurst and Rodgers[8] have formulated a proposition in the form of a mathematical equation:

P (probability of attending college) = a (mental ability) plus b (social expectation) plus c (individual motivation) plus d (financial ability) plus e (propinquity).

Carson McGuire[8] applied the same concept set forth in this formula in identifying three groups that have a high probability of attending college:

a. The high-status static—a person from the upper or upper-middle class who has absorbed the educational attitudes of his social group.

b. The climber—a lower-middle or a working-class youth who has a solid and realistic ambition to "get ahead" in life. This person has friends among boys and girls of higher social status, spends time in their homes, and absorbs their educational attitudes. He has a good mind, a strong personality, understands that self-control and hard work will be required of him, and is prepared to make the sacrifices necessary to achieve higher education and consequently social mobility.

c. The strainer—a lower-middle or a working-class youth whose goals in life are mixed and whose personality is vacillating. He wants to "make good" yet is not completely sure what this means. He makes friends with boys and girls higher on the social ladder, but is never quite sure that he desires their way of life. In the end it is something external to him, such as a G.I. Bill of Rights, that decides whether or not he will go on with his education.

In a study of students in the retailing department of a technical institute Wilson[17] found results which would be in line with some of McGuire's formulations. Wilson identified groups of high achievers and low achievers. An index of mobility showed that there was no significant difference between the two groups in total mobility, but there was a difference significant at the one per cent level between the two groups in magnitude of deviation from background status. In the low achievement group there were individuals who had downward mobility as well as individuals with upward mobility. Wilson drew the inference that the high group accepts to a greater extent its status background, while the low achieving group rejects its family status.

In discussing social class factors thus far, the principal distinction has been between those who go to college and those who do not. However, there are important differentiations in social status within each of these groups. Warner's[14] scale for identifying social class membership includes seven ranks of broad occupational groups running somewhat parallel to the *Dictionary of Occupational Titles*. Several studies, all of which correlate highly, have established a further breakdown of specific occupations according to prestige ratings.[4, 5, 16] On the basis of these studies, Sims[10] has developed an occupational rating scale for general use.

Educational motivation is related not only to social class membership in general but also to particular aspects of social class, such as ethnicity and religion, which may often be combined. Stetler reports that in Connecticut 49 per cent of high school graduates of Italian origin applied for college, compared with 57 per cent of Catholics, 63 per cent of Protestants, and 87 per cent of Jews.[8] These data suggest that the ethnic factor may be one of the important elements in social class membership which contribute to vocational choice, although it is recognized that other factors, such as urban residence, may have been contributing to the apparent ethnic differences.

NONCLASS FACTORS

Home

The first social group of which most children are aware is the home, and little documentation is needed to demonstrate the importance of home influences in occupational planning. Parents, regardless of their social class, do a great deal to determine whether a child will be work-orientated or a sluggard, whether he will seek or avoid responsibility. The demonstrated affection and the social skills of the parents contribute much to the affective capacities and skills of the child, which in turn determine the type of society and the type of job in which he will be comfortable. Many of these elements lie in the field of individual psychology, since they contribute to individual personality, but they are derived from the social influences of the home.

Some of the most occupationally helpless young people are the children of self-made men who say, "I don't want my boy to have to work as hard as I did." Shielding a youngster from work is almost certain to render him somewhat incapable of facing work effectively. One of the writer's clients had completed college without ever having earned a cent of his own. At age 22 he was not yet ready to consider what type of occupation would be most suitable because he had not begun to think seriously of the idea of any gainful employment for himself.

The foundations of goals and motivations are also likely to be developed very early in life. Through the example of his parents, a child first learns the values or goals that are considered most important. He quickly senses whether the parents place greatest stress on having a bigger car than the neighbors, on enjoying camping and picnics, on creating and enjoying aesthetic experiences, or in exemplifying their religious beliefs in their daily lives. He is likely to absorb the values of the parents, but even if he rejects them, he will be deeply influenced by them.

Siblings may also have an important influence on the career plans of each other. The oldest child's success and satisfaction in an occupation may influence his younger brothers in that direction. On the other hand, sibling rivalry may induce a younger brother to make a definite effort to avoid following in an older sibling's footsteps. Older siblings are an important source of information about colleges and jobs. To an even greater extent than in the case of parental influences, however, it is difficult to generalize about sibling influences or to make predictions without knowing the quality of relationships in the particular family. For the most part vocational counselors and counseling psychologists tend to operate on the basis of some broad assumptions in this area: (1) that an oldest child tends to be more responsible and a youngest child or only child tends to be less responsible; (2) that there is some tendency for children to follow in the career and social class patterns of their parents and older siblings. It is recognized, however, that such assumptions would need explicit verification in each case.

School

Cutting across class lines, the school may often be an important influence on vocational choice. Children who perform favorably in the school environment are likely to be influenced toward higher education and in turn toward the professions. The previous section on social class influences has cited cases where the class influence was too strong to permit upward mobility in spite of scholastic success. But the constructs of Havighurst and McGuire[8] also take into account the dynamics by which class influences may be overcome. This process is likely to include relationships with peers of a higher social class. The school is usually the medium through which these friendships are initiated.

Apart from specific friendship patterns, a student from a middle class family is more likely to attend college if he attends a school from which a high percentage of graduates go on for higher education. He will hear more discussion of college among his peers and it probably will seem the "thing to do."

Attending a vocational high school has an obvious influence on vocational choice. Although many vocational graduates fail to enter the trades for which they were trained, they fall under the vocational influences of the school. As Hollinshead[8] points out, early entrance into a vocational curriculum tends to inhibit social mobility. The way in which the class system affects curriculum choice has been outlined in the Yankee City study.[15] There is a strong tendency for upper class youth to take college preparatory curriculums and for lower class youth to elect vocational curriculums.

Teachers also exert an influence on the vocational choices of their students. The tendency for the faculty to reward and encourage students who meet faculty expectations is felt in the formal process of guidance and in informal faculty-student contacts. On a questionnaire designed to determine reasons for students' choice of a college, Smith and Lipsett(12) found that 22 per cent first heard about the college through high school teachers or counselors and 10 per cent were most influenced in their decisions by teachers or counselors.

Community

Some aspects of community membership are associated with social class identification. But there are also unique features of community which have an important bearing on vocational choice. As Hollinshead(8) notes, there is a strong tendency for urban youth to attend college in greater numbers than rural youth. In part this may be due to the greater availability of college education in the city, with lower average cost. It is likely that some of this influence is also due to other people in the social milieu.

In communities like the Westchester and Nassau suburbs of New York City, community influences supplement those of the school in conveying the impression that the normal thing is to go from high school to college and then into a profession. In contrast, one might consider a rural community where the high school principal once told the writer. "Very few of our students go to college, even though a reasonable percentage have the ability to profit from it. Their parents are farmers, who want their children to take care of the farms and stay in the community." If this feeling represented only one set of parents, it would have less social significance, but it is an influence which pervades the whole community.

One high school senior who was a counselee of the writer said, when asked about his aspirations, "I just want to graduate and get a job at ———" (the community's largest employer). When asked what he would like to do at this firm, he had no ideas and no real vocational goals except the security of a large, paternalistic employer. Experience with other youth and adults indicates that this feeling is sufficiently widespread to represent a community influence.

Pressure Groups

In the recent periods of labor shortages, there have developed a number of deliberate attempts to persuade young people to enter certain occupations, such as engineering, library work, teaching, and almost all of the professions. Most professions have national organizations which prepare informational material about the profession, including a description of the work, training institutions, and the like. This material is often presented in the form of a "guidance pamphlet" designed to appeal to high school students. The more ethical ones present disadvantages as well as advantages of the profession.

Television and periodical advertisements may be more emotional in content. They may even appeal to a wife on the basis of living conditions.

Going even further in the same direction are the advertisements of certain proprietary schools, with headlines like, "Make money in (name of occupation)". There is no hesitation in using any trick of advertising or propaganda to serve the advertiser's purpose. The continued existence of these schools and their continued use of this type of appeal attests to its influence.

Role Differentiation

Super[13] asserts that "vocational development is essentially that of developing and implementing a self concept." By this he means a role, or a "more or less coherent and unified system of items of interpersonal behavior."[11] A role is meaningful only in some social context. In his early relationships in a primary group an individual may learn to play a role of group sociability, a role of individual prominence, or a role of group goal facilitation. He is likely to seek an occupation which will provide an outlet for the role which gives him the greatest satisfaction. A goal of sociability, for example, might lead a person toward certain selling jobs, but probably would not lead him to the jobs involving particularly high-pressure methods. The person seeking an executive position may be motivated by a desire for dominance, but he might also be motivated more by recognition. In our culture a boy under a dominant feminine influence is likely to seek a passive, or submissive, or ingratiating role. This thesis is presented by Farson[6] in explaining the dynamics of the counselor's role. Although much of the concept of role is explainable in psychoanalytic terms or in terms of other theory regarding individual personality, an individual's role differentiation occurs only within a social group, and it is only through the interaction between individual and group that the role becomes crystallized.

IMPLICATIONS FOR GUIDANCE

If the thesis is accepted that social factors are of great importance in the vocational development and career planning of an individual, it follows that a counselor needs to understand these social factors and their influence upon an individual. This is necessary to help the individual understand himself and to develop plans which will lead to a satisfying career. In light of the foregoing discussion, it would appear appropriate for a guidance counselor or counseling psychologist through interviews or other means to find out and give consideration to the following points:

1. Social Class Membership

The facts that identify the counselee's social class, including occupation and income of parents, education of parents, place and type of residence, and ethnic background.

2. Home Influences

Goals that parents have for the counselee, place among siblings, influence of siblings, role of counselee in the family, family values and counselee's acceptance of them.

3. School

Scholastic achievement, relationships with peers and with faculty, group goals and values in the school, vocational specialization if any.

4. Community

Group goals and values—the "thing to do" in the community, special career opportunities or influences, counselee's identification with the community and desire to stay there and accept its values.

5. Pressure Groups

Has the counselee (or his parents) been exposed to any particular influence that leads him to value one occupation over another? Is this influence compatible with the counselee's abilities, values, and needs?

6. Role Perception

Does the counselee want to be a leader, a follower, an isolate, or just a "good Joe"? Is the counselee's perception of himself and his role in accord with the way others perceive him?

The counselor who has a thorough understanding of these points, as well as the counselee's measured interests, intelligence, special aptitudes, and leisure time activities will be more likely to view his contribution in its proper perspective. He will be unlikely to try to pick an occupational goal for a counselee on the basis of a few tests, and he will be more humble in viewing his own role as a relatively minor one in the complex and long-range process of vocational development, with its ultimate compromise between many different influences.

REFERENCES

1. Beilin, Harry (1955) The application of general development principles in the vocational area. *J. counsel. Psychol.*, **2**, pp. 53–57.
2. Beilin, Harry (1956) The utilization of high level talent in lower socioeconomic groups. *Personnel guid. J.*, **34**, pp. 175–178.
3. Cottrell, L. (1942) The analysis of situational fields in social psychology. *Amer. sociol. Rev.*, **7**, pp. 370–382.
4. Counts, G. (1925) The social status of occupations. *Sch. Rev.*, **32,** 16–27.
5. Deeg, M., and Paterson, D. (1947) Changes in the social status of occupations. *Occupations*, **25**, 206.
6. Farson, R. (1954) The counselor is a woman. *J. counsel. Psychol.*, **1**, 221–223.

7. GINZBERG, E., *et al.* (1951) *Occupational choice*. New York: Columbia University Press.
8. HOLLINSHEAD, B. (1951) *Who should go to college*. New York: Columbia University Press.
9. LEWIN, K. (1947) Subjective and objective elements in the social field. *Frontiers in group dynamics, human relations*, **1**, 5–41.
10. SIMS, V. (1952) *Sims SCI Occupational Rating Scale*. Yonkers: World Book Co.,
11. SLATER, P. (1955) Role differentiation in small groups. *Amer. sociol. Rev.*, **20**, 498.
12. SMITH, L., and LIPSETT, L. (1952) Why students choose a particular college. *Coll.& Univ.*, **27**, 264–269.
13. SUPER, D. E. (1953) A theory of vocational development. *Amer. Psychologist*, **8**, 185–190.
14. WARNER, W., MEEKER, MARCHIA, and EELLS, K. (1949) *Social class in America*. Chicago: Science Research Associates.
15. WARNER, W., HAVIGHURST, R., and LOEB, M. (1944) *Who shall be educated?* New York: Harper.
16. WELCH, MARYON (1949) The ranking of occupations on the basis of social status. *Occupations*, **27**, 240.
17. WILSON, J. (1954) Psycho-social factors related to educational achievement. Unpublished doctoral dissertation, University of Chicago.

10. Some Psychological Aspects of Inter-Generation Occupational Mobility

B. G. STACEY

I. INTRODUCTION

In all industrial societies there is great movement within the occupational hierarchy. The study of occupational mobility involves the analysis of the causes and consequences of this movement. Inter-generation mobility is movement between generations; it is assessed by comparing the occupational levels of father and children. Intra-generation or career mobility is movement during an individual's working life; it is assessed by comparing his occupational levels at different times in his life.

Since the end of the Second World War, there has been a growing concern among sociologists with all aspects of mobility. Many investigations have been carried out and there is a great deal of empirical and observational material available. Sociologists have tended to concentrate on the description of the patterns of mobility and the evaluation of the processes of educational selection in allocating people to various occupations strata. Considerable interest has also been shown in how the changing occupational structure affects mobility and how different fertility rates in the various strata determine the extent to which these strata biologically replenish themselves (Glass, 1954; Lipset and Bendix, 1959; Aaronovitch, 1961; Halsey, Floud and Anderson, 1961; Lockwood, 1962; Young and Gibson, 1963).

Sociologists have attempted to explain the causes of mobility primarily by the changing requirements of the occupational structure, differential fertility rates and the unequal distribution of family income and educational opportunities. In recent years their work has been supplemented by that of psychologists who have attempted to distinguish other factors conducive to mobility. Psychological research has shown that there are certain family influences and personality characteristics related to upward and downward mobility.

The complicated relationships between psychological and social structural factors mean that many diverse factors may contribute to an association between a single factor and occupational mobility. The occupational

(Reprinted from *Brit. J. soc. Psychol.* vol. 4 (1965), pp. 275–286, by permission of the author and publisher.)

experiences of an adult may be the result of (i) his educational and vocational opportunities, (ii) the kind of environment to which he has been exposed, (iii) his abilities, (iv) his personality characteristics including his skills in interpersonal relations, (v) his educational and vocational performance. This raises the question whether any psychological factor can ever be regarded as a determinant of mobility rather than as one of its consequences. Even if a factor can be shown to be an antecedent of mobility, it can be argued that the experience of mobility may influence the operation of the factor. There is no easy answer to this question. One can only critically examine the available empirical data, bearing this problem in mind. Particular attention must be paid to time sequential data, i.e. data from childhood, adolescence and adulthood. If the data from different age groups is consistent then it does provide grounds for concluding that the factor is a determinant of mobility rather than a consequence.

In this paper the aim is to review the psychological investigations relevant to the study of the mechanisms underlying inter-generation occupational mobility. These studies focus upon the influence of the family and the effects of variations in intelligence, motivation, values and interests. The review is not exhaustive but does indicate the trend of research in this field.

2. THE INFLUENCE OF THE FAMILY

The findings from several studies indicate that the better educated and upwardly mobile are likely to come from small families and that the eldest son, irrespective of the number of children, has the greatest chance of upward movement. This applies particularly to the upwardly mobile from the working class (Himmelweit, 1954; Floud, Halsey and Martin, 1956; Jackson and Marsden, 1962; *Higher Education*, 1963; Douglas, 1964). This is important because more than a third of children come from families of four or more children. These findings can be partly explained by variations in the amount of attention and encouragement that children receive in families of different sizes. In addition, the financial problems of bringing up a large family must often lead parents to encourage their children to leave school and start work early. It is also likely that the most ambitious plans are made for the first-born son and a good education is seen as the means of fulfilling these plans.

It can be argued that it is the more intelligent or the more ambitious parents who restrict the size of their family and encourage their children to do well at school and that the "small family" is simply incidental to this. The available data does not support this view. For people with limited incomes, a small family does mean that the children can be better cared for at home and supported at school. But in addition, a small family heightens the interaction between parents and children within the family. This appears to promote a more rapid development of intellectual ability which, in turn, means a greater likelihood of a good educational performance (Nisbet, 1953; Lipset and Bendix, 1959).

There are enormous differences in family circumstances. This is the result of a variety of material, social and cultural factors, including the highly unequal distribution of income and property, varying knowledge of educational and vocational opportunities and different attitudes, values and interests. The differences in family circumstances influence a child's attitudes towards school work and other activities thereby affecting the child's interests, aspirations and performance. To take one example, there is no doubt that children have a considerable advantage when their parents take an interest in their activities and encourage them to do well. Further, this becomes increasingly important as they get older. On the other hand, children are handicapped when their parents take little interest in their activities (Himmelweit, 1955; Floud *et al.*, 1956; Jackson and Marsden, 1962; Douglas, 1964). Interestingly, Douglas (1964) found that in all social classes, parents who give their children most encouragement also give them the best care in infancy.

The upwardly mobile from the working class come predominantly from its "prosperous" sections, though the prosperity may depend upon "high" wages or upon the economy and security of a council house. They usually have strong support from one or both parents. They tend to come from neighbourhoods where the social classes are mixed and go to schools in which the influence of middle-class parents is felt. This provides a favourable learning environment where the children are exposed to values and norms which facilitate upward mobility. In fact, the family influences are partially supported by the wider social structure (*15–18*, 1960; Jackson and Marsden, 1962; Ellis and Clayton, 1963, Douglas, 1964). It has also been found that a substantial minority of the upwardly mobile from the working class comes from families in which one or both parents are of middle-class origin, from "sunken middle-class" families (Young and Willmott, 1957; Lipset and Bendix, 1959; Jackson and Marsden, 1962; Douglas, 1964). This suggests that parents who are downwardly mobile into the working class often compensate for their movement by successfully educating their children in state schools and re-establishing the status of the family. It appears that it is often the downwardly mobile mother who provides the drive and ambition in such families.

There is a great deal of evidence available showing that the family has an important influence upon educational performance and upon occupational aspirations and movement. As children grow up, their abilities, interests and aspirations are progressively affected by their accumulated experience. Typically the family environment of the upwardly mobile is in many ways more favourable than that of the static or the downwardly mobile. The parents of the upwardly mobile tend to have smaller families, to provide above-average home conditions, to take an active interest in their children and to encourage them to work hard. The quality of maternal care also tends to be above-average. In fact, the influence of the mother is as important, and sometimes more important, than that of the father. These factors are mutually supporting and lead the children to attend the better primary and secondary schools and to do well at school. This leads many to go on to some form of higher education or vocational training. An adverse family environment restricts or leads to a deterioration in ability and has an unfortunate influence on interests and aspirations. Bad housing, overcrowding, unemployment, financial difficulties, matrimonial problems, parental apathy, excessive or unrealistic parental ambitions, and emotional problems are examples of factors which have been shown to have a depressive effect on children and young people. Adverse family circumstances are associated with average and below-average educational performance and limited occupational opportunities (Lipset and Bendix, 1959; Jackson and Marsden, 1962; Ellis and Clayton, 1963; *Higher Education*, 1963; Douglas, 1964; Swift, 1964).

The influence of the family in the process of occupational mobility is obviously of tremendous importance. Characteristically, the family trains children for the occupational and social status of their parents. Many of the factors which hinder mobility are connected with the family. But some families, deliberately or unintentionally, train their children for a different occupational and social stratum, influencing the direction and extent of the mobility of their children.

3. THE ROLE OF INTELLIGENCE

In an industrialized economy the educational system functions as a selector and promoter of talent. It becomes the main channel for occupational mobility. A few exceptional people do rise in the social structure without the benefit of educational qualifications but they are usually restricted to the spheres of entertainment, sport, business entrepreneurship and crime. The employment opportunities of most people are determined by their qualifications. In all social classes intelligence (i.e. measured ability) is related more strongly than any other single factor to educational performance. Between 40 and 60 per cent of the variation among students can be accounted for by differences in intelligence (Burt, 1961; Rossi, 1961; *Higher Education*, 1963; Young and Gibson, 1963; Douglas, 1964).

In the British educational system a great emphasis is placed on intelligence testing. Whatever is measured by intelligence tests affects educational placement, hence opportunities for educational achievement. One would like to examine the relationship between intelligence and occupational mobility directly. This is not possible because intelligence-test results are influenced by social factors which influence occupational opportunities. However, it is possible to draw some inferences from the available data.

A comparison of the characteristics of a sample of teenage children from non-manual family backgrounds and a sample of teenage children from manual backgrounds was made by Jayasuriya (1960). He found that the former had higher educational and occupational aspirations, a higher level of achievement motivation and placed more emphasis on values conducive to aspiration and achievement. However, these broad differences were overlaid by differences due to the influence of intelligence. Tendencies toward occupational striving and the correlates of such striving were characteristic of the more rather than the less intelligent children irrespective of social origin in both grammar and modern schools. The evidence indicated that the privileged position of the more intelligent child, the greater social approbation he receives and his own awareness of the advantages open to him, lead him to have a higher level of striving and also enable him to acquire the values appropriate to such striving. The evidence also indicated that "among the determining factors of downward mobility ... low intelligence itself must be regarded as an important contributory influence."

Further data showing a relationship between intelligence and mobility comes from a study of the factors influencing the change of status of women at marriage (Scott, Illsley and Thomson, 1956). These investigators found that women in Aberdeen who move up the occupational hierarchy at marriage (comparing the husband's level with the father's) obtain higher intelligence-test scores than those who marry at the same level. In turn, those who marry at the same level score more highly than those who move down. For example, about 70 per cent of the daughters of manual workers who marry non-manual workers score above average on an intelligence test whereas about 25 per cent of the daughters of manual workers who marry manual workers score above average. The investigators also found that the upwardly mobile daughters of manual workers receive an education better than the average for their group and tend to be in non-manual occupations at the time of marriage. These findings clearly illustrate the interrelations between intelligence, education and occupational mobility.

Though there is a significant correlation of about 0.5 between social origins and intelligence-test scores, a proportion of children from lower-strata families are highly intelligent and a proportion of children from upper-strata families are dull (for detailed information see Burt, 1961). The mean intelligence of the children belonging to each occupational group exhibits a marked regression to the mean and the intelligence of the children within each occupational group varies over a far wider range than that of their parents. Halsey (1958) presented an analysis of a mathematical-genetic model of the distribution of high intelligence and showed that even if high intelligence is assumed to be completely inherited and to be of greater frequency among people in the higher strata, there will be a greater number of people of high intelligence in the lower strata. This information about the distribution of intelligence indicates that pronounced discrepancies in intellectual ability between dull children from higher-strata families and bright children from lower-strata families will promote a certain amount of upward and downward mobility in every generation. Burt (1961) estimated the actual amount of inter-generation mobility which results from the discrepancies at between 20 and 30 per cent of the population, but this is almost certainly an over-estimate.

On the basis of the data presented by Oppenheim (1956); Lipset and Bendix (1959); Jayasuriya (1960); Burt (1961); Halsey *et al.* (1961); and Douglas (1964), a number of hypotheses can be tentatively put forward to explain the complicated relationships between social origins, intelligence, motivation, values and educational performance. They are:

(1) Intelligence is strongly related to educational performance at all occupational and social levels.
(2) High intelligence will tend to increase the capacity of children from the lower strata to comprehend the values and norms held by higher occupational groups. Low intelligence will tend to reduce the capacity of the children from the higher strata to adopt the values and norms of their background.
(3) Parental support will help lower-strata children of high intelligence to accept the need for educational and occupational achievement. This may lead these children to identify with higher occupational groups and to acquire some of the social aspects of the middle-class way of life. Parental pressures often increase the educational difficulties of the higher-strata children of low intelligence.
(4) Intelligent children from the lower strata who are rejected by their class peer group in their home neighbourhood will tend to identify themselves with the middle-class school evironment. Dull children from the higher strata who are not accepted by their peer group in their home neighbourhood will tend to accommodate themselves to their working-class peers at school.
(5) In school, intelligence is related to performance. But the decision to obtain a higher education or professional training is made outside the school, therefore class position will be a significant factor in this decision.
(6) In grammar-type schools education is intertwined with middle-class values, in colleges and universities it is more removed from such values. This means that social origins will be a more important influence on performance at school than at college or university.
(7) Intelligence, combined with relevant motives and values, makes an important contribution to the generation of mobility independently of the system of education.

As long as intelligence tests do not differentiate between inherent ability, motivation, values and social influences, it will be extremely difficult to test these or other hypotheses conclusively. Though the available evidence does not allow a definite statement about the exact role of intelligence in occupational mobility to be made, there can be little doubt that the great individual differences in intelligence are of importance. Discrepancies be-between the intelligence of a proportion of children and the occupational positions of their parents must be a potent factor affecting occupational movement in a society where educational performance is of prime importance in occupational placement.

4. ACHIEVEMENT MOTIVATION

The association between intelligence and mobility is a partial one. There are certainly highly intelligent people born into the lower occupational strata who are not upwardly mobile and dull people born into the higher strata who are not downwardly mobile. This can be partly explained by the different opportunities to which people are exposed but it is also a function of the capacity and willingness of people to take advantage of any opportunities available. This, in turn, depends on intelligence and motivation.

A few empirical studies have been carried out which suggest some of the motivational sources of occupational mobility. Most have focused on the influence of the achievement motive. Achievement motivation is a drive or general behaviour tendency to work hard, to accomplish tasks requiring skill or effort, to do a difficult job well, to excel over others and always to avoid failure (Murray, 1938; McClelland, Atkinson, Clarke and Lowell, 1953; Atkinson, 1958). The results from several investigations indicate that achievement motivation is one of the important motivational sources of occupational movement.

It appears that class differences in achievement motivation and associated values are largely responsible for the greater stress upon upward mobility striving among adolescents in the middle class than in the working class (Douvan, 1956; Rosen, 1956; Jayasuriya, 1960). The meagre evidence available suggests that the middle-class adolescent is more conscious of the need for achievement than the upper-class adolescent (McArthur, 1955; Rosen, 1956). Jayasuriya (1960) found that achievement motivation, achievement orientated values and mobility values are positively related to educational and occupational aspirations among secondary-school children from all social backgrounds, even when intelligence is partialled out. High achievement motivation is positively correlated with high intelligence, indeed academic success is probably both a cause and effect of high achievement motivation.

The Atkinson–McClelland theory of achievement motivation predicts that the strength of achievement motivation will be positively associated with upward mobility and negatively associated with downward mobility (Atkinson, 1958; McClelland, 1961). Crockett (1962) obtained results which supported the theory in relation to the upward mobility of persons reared in the lower strata but which did not support the theory in relation to strength of achievement motivation and downward mobility.

Further evidence is available from Douvan and Adelson (1958) who analysed "some of the psychic accompaniments of upward and downward mobility striving among adolescent boys". They found marked differences between the upward- and downward-"aspiring" boys. The upward aspirers possessed a high degree of available energy for use in all activities; the downward aspirers were less active and more apathetic. The upward aspirers showed a pervasive achievement orientation whilst the downward aspirers were more concerned with security. The downward aspirers were much more dependent on their parents than the upward aspirers, yet showed signs of rebellion against them. The downward aspirers also showed a much lower degree of self-acceptance and self-confidence than the upward aspirers.

Though these studies are highly suggestive, we need to know much more about the relationship between the strength of achievement motivation and educational and occupational performance, particularly among people with equal opportunities.

5. DEFERRAL OF GRATIFICATION

A few investigators have shown that a pattern of values and behaviour called deferral of gratification is associated with occupational aspirations and movement. The deferral of gratification pattern involves a general willingness to give up fairly immediate satisfactions for the sake of future gains. It necessarily entails the exercise of self-restraint. The deferred gratification pattern can be expressed in many ways and is associated with traditional middle-class values (Schneider and Lysgaard, 1953; Oppenheim, 1956; Strauss, 1962). The work of Riesman (1950) and Sears, Maccoby and Levin (1957) throws light on the development of the deferred gratification pattern and on the varying family situations which contribute to it.

Reissman (1953) examined the relationship between the inclination to defer gratifications and occupational aspirations. His method was to ascertain whether considerations such as a demand to give up leisure activities, to move to another district, to work harder, to spend less time with the family or to take greater responsibilities would deter a person from accepting a better job. He found that people with high occupational aspirations allowed relatively few such considerations to interfere with their ambitions. People with low aspirations were governed much more by immediate considerations.

The idea of a relationship between deferred gratification and occupational movement has been examined in the context of sexual behaviour and marriage. Kinsey (1953) presented data which indicated a deferral of heterosexual experience in adolescence on the part of those who were upwardly mobile. Further, he found that persons born into the manual strata who ultimately move into professional jobs show a youthful sexual pattern of behaviour congruent with that of the class into which they move. Similarly, persons born into the higher strata who move into the manual strata show a youthful sexual pattern of behaviour corresponding to that in the strata to which they move. Kinsey considered this a process of "anticipatory sexual socialization." Lindenfeld (1960) found that among single students in a coeducational college both upwardly mobile male and female students were more restrictive in sexual attitudes than the static. This restrictiveness persisted in behaviour as indicated by less frequent engagement in sexual intercourse. It has also been found that the postponement of marriage is an aid to upward mobility (Mukerjee, 1954; Svalastoga, 1959).

Beilin (1956) criticized the use of the concept "deferred gratification" to explain any behaviour because the idea of postponement is introduced by the observer and may not be apparent to the people being observed. To support this view, Beilin described a study of the factors differentiating mobile from static adolescents. He noted that the deferral of various kinds of gratification differentiated the two groups but pointed out that the adolescents concerned were not aware of a deferring process. For example, upwardly mobile adolescents from the lower socio-economic groups saw themselves satisfying their desire to go to college rather than reliquishing or postponing other activities. However, the values associated with the concept of deferred gratification are so common in the middle class that one must be sceptical of Beilin's interpretation.

The research findings suggest that the upwardly mobile come disproportionately from families who teach their children to defer gratifications and satisfactions for future gains. This would involve early training in independence and self-control and the inculcation of a long time perspective expressing itself in activities such as saving money, obtaining a higher education or professional training, postponing sexual gratification and marriage, strictly budgeting time and being persistent in all activities (Oppenheim, 1956). Conversely, the downwardly mobile should come disproportionately from families which have not trained their children in this way.

Strauss (1962) has reported a study in which the deferred gratification pattern was found to be related to achievement motivation. The relationship was not eliminated by controls for intelligence and socio-economic status. He concluded that there is a general pattern of deferred gratification which contributes to the achievement syndrome and that this is functional for mobility.

6. OTHER FACTORS

If a person places a high value on status symbols, or uses status symbols to gain social recognition, or strives for certain positions to obtain prestige, it can be said that the person is greatly concerned with status and its manifestations. The person is exhibiting what various writers have called "status concern", "status anxiety", "status seeking" and "status striving". It has often been asserted that status anxiety, etc., is an important motive in upward mobility. At present there is no empirical evidence to support this view. Knowledge of the influence of status striving and status symbols on behaviour is really at the anecdotal level.

Several investigators have been concerned with the question of upward movement in the large structures of industry and commerce (Riesman, 1950; Mills, 1951; Warner and Abegglen, 1955; Whyte, 1956). These investigators have described the type of personality that thrives in these large, bureaucratic structures and the kind of social skills used to promote advancement.

Social technique or skill in social behaviour is probably a factor in upward mobility. Social technique has many facets but it does involve the ability to assess a situation, to judge other people reasonably accurately, and to react appropriately to situations and people. Social technique defines the manner in which goals are sought and the way intelligence and abilities are used. It is that aspect of personality which is immediately apparent to other people. Inadequacy in social skills is probably a barrier to upward mobility.

It is highly likely that acute physical, mental or social disabilities are an obstacle to upward mobility and often lead to downward mobility. Examples of such disabilities are prolonged illness, physical and mental handicaps of a disabling kind, personality characteristics that result in an inability to make adequate contact with other people and marked insensitivity to interpersonal relations and social pressures. There is evidence available which indicates that schizophrenics tend to be downwardly mobile (Wardle, 1962).

Two studies carried out in Scotland suggest that physical characteristics possibly contribute to occupational mobility. Illsley (1955) reported that the daughters of manual workers who married men at a higher occupational level than their fathers, were superior in physique and health and had more favourable obstetric rates than their static counterparts and the daughters of higher-strata fathers who moved down at marriage. Jahoda (1962) suggested that myopia increases an individual's chances of moving up the occupational scale via a higher intelligence level, whilst other types of ametropia have the opposite effects. Personal physical appearance may also be influential. It has been argued that comely women from the lower strata have a real chance of upward movement at marriage because of their physical attractiveness. However, Lipset and Bendix (1959) were of the opinion that upward mobility through marriage is only the final stage of a long mobility process.

To account for the emotional rationale behind men's desire to improve their status, Lipset and Bendix (1959) put forward a hypothesis based on Veblen's analysis of consumer behaviour. The way a person is evaluated by his fellows determines in large measure his self-evaluation. Hence, if a given pattern of consumption is esteemed in society, a person will try to match that pattern in order to improve his self-evaluation. Occupational advancement is the means of obtaining the wherewithal for consumption, hence the desire for upward mobility.

7. CONCLUSIONS

Occupational mobility is a complex process in which social structural and psychological factors are interrelated. The slowly changing occupational structure provides the setting for a certain amount of upward and downward mobility in each generation. At all social levels, some people realize the existing opportunities and rise in the occupational hierarchy, and some fail to maintain themselves in the position of their families and fall in the hierarchy. The empirical studies reviewed in this paper indicate some of the psychological factors influential in this process.

Intelligence is an important factor, though its influence is modified by the complex interplay between family influences, the educational system and occupational stratification. A variety of studies have provided evidence that motivation is a factor. Values and attitudes, internalized early in life, operate with intelligence and motives as determinants of occupational aspirations and movement. Social skills are probably significant. Some evidence indicates that physical characteristics are associated with mobility. The studies reported suggest that this is a promising line of enquiry. Finally, there is massive evidence that the family plays a crucial role in the mobility process.

The review of the literature indicates several deficiencies in the research. Many investigations have been based on samples of teenage schoolchildren and students. From these studies we obtained information only about the relationship of psychological factors to probable mobility experiences. More information about the relationship of particular psychological factors to the occupational experiences of adults is needed. Further, investigators have been primarily concerned with upward mobility. Downward mobility requires more attention than it has received in the past. There has also been neglect of the occupational aspirations and experiences of women.

In future studies it should be worthwhile for investigators to examine the possible influence of other factors. One example would be the relationship of anxiety to occupational aspirations and experiences. Affiliation, power and acquisitiveness are all motives which may be related to mobility. We also need to know more about the role of marriage in the mobility process, particularly with relation to women.

The results obtained to date demonstrate the fruitfulness of considering the influence of psychological factors in conjunction with social structural factors. By integrating the work of psychologists and sociologists it should be possible to advance considerably our knowledge of the various processes by which people reach their occupational positions in society.

REFERENCES

Aaronovitch, S. (1961) *The Ruling Class*. London: Lawrence and Wishart.

Atkinson, J. W. (ed.) (1958) *Motives in Fantasy, Action and Society*. Princeton: Van Nostrand.

Beilin, H. (1956) The pattern of postponability and its relation to social class mobility. *J. soc. Psychol.* **44**, 33–48.

Burt, C. (1961) Intelligence and social mobility. *Brit. J. statist. Psychol.* **XIV**, 3–24.

Crockett, H. J. (1962) The achievement motive and differential occupational mobility in the United States. *Amer. sociol. Rev.* **27**, 191–204.

Douglas, J. W. B. (1964) *The Home and the School*. London: MacGibbon and Kee.

Douvan, E. (1956) Social status and success strivings. *J. abnorm. (soc.) Psychol.* **52**, 219–223.

Douvan, E., and Adelson, J. (1958) The psychodynamics of social mobility. *J. abnorm. (soc.) Psychol.* **56**, 31–44.

Ellis, R. A., and Clayton, W. (1963) Structural supports for upward mobility. *Amer. sociol. Rev.* **28**, 743–749.

15–18 (1960), vol. 2. London: H.M.S.O.

Floud, J., Halsey, A. H., and Martin, F. M. (1956) *Social Class and Educational Opportunity*. London: Heinemann.

Glass, D. V. (ed.) (1954) *Social Mobility in Britain*. London: Routledge.

Halsey, A. H. (1958) Genetics, social structure and intelligence. *Brit. J. Sociol.* **9**, 15–28.

Halsey, A. H., Floud, J., and Anderson, C. A. (1961) *Education, Economy and Society*. Glencoe, Ill.: The Free Press.

Higher Education (1963) Appendix 1. London: H.M.S.O.

Himmelweit, H. T. (1954) Social status and secondary education since the 1944 Act: Some data for London. In Glass (1954).

Himmelweit, H. T. (1955) Socio-economic background and personality. *Int. Soc. Sc. Bull.* **7**, 29–35.

Illsley, R. (1955) Social class selection and class differences in relation to stillbirths and infant deaths. *Brit. med. J.* 24 Dec., 1520–1524.

Jackson, B., and Marsden, D. (1962) *Education and the Working Class*. London: Routledge.

Jahoda, G. (1962). Refractive errors, intelligence and social mobility. *Brit. J. clin. soc. Psychol.* **1**, 96–106.

Jayasuriya, D. L. (1960) A Study of Adolescent Ambition, Level of Aspiration and Achievement Motivation. Unpublished London Ph.D. thesis.

Kinsey, A. C. (1953) Social level and sexual outlet. In *Class, Status and Power: A Reader in Social Stratification* (eds. Bendix, R. and Lipset, S. M.). Glencoe, Ill.: The Free Press.

Lindenfeld, F. A. (1960) A note on social mobility, religiosity and students' attitudes towards pre-marital sexual relations. *Amer. sociol. Rev.* **25**, 81–84.

Lipset, S. M., and Bendix, R. (1959) *Social Mobility in Industrial Society*. London: Heinemann.

Lockwood, D. (1962) Social mobility. In *Society* (eds. Welford, A. T., Argyle, M., Glass, D. V. and Morris, J. N.). London: Routledge.

McArthur, C. (1955) Personality differences between middle and upper classes. *J. abnorm. (soc.) Psychol.* **50**, 247–258.

McClelland, D. C., Atkinson, J. W., Clark, R. A., and Lowell, E. L. (1953) *The Achievement Motive*. New York: Appleton-Century-Crofts.

McClelland, D. C. (1961) *The Achieving Society*. Princeton: Van Nostrand.

Mills, C. W. (1951) *White Collar*. New York: Oxford Univ. Press.

Mukerjee, R. (1954) Social mobility and age at marriage. In Glass, D. V. (1954).

Murray, H. A. (1938) *Explorations in Personality*. New York: Oxford Univ. Press.

NISBET, J. (1953) Family environment and intelligence, *Eugen. Rev.* **XLV**, 31–42.

OPPENHEIM, A. N. (1956) A Study of Social Attitudes of Adolescents. Unpublished London Ph.D. thesis.

REISSMAN, L. (1953) Levels of aspiration and social class. *Amer. sociol. Rev.* **18**, 233–242.

RIESMAN, D. (1950) *The Lonely Crowd.* New Haven: Yale Univ. Press.

ROSEN, B. C. (1956) The achievement syndrome: a psychocultural dimension of social stratification. *Amer. sociol. Rev.* **21**, 203–211.

ROSSI, P. (1961) Social factors in academic achievement: a brief review. In Halsey *et al.* (1961).

SCHNEIDER, L., and LYSGAARD, S. (1953) The deferred gratification pattern: a preliminary study. *Amer. sociol. Rev.* **18**, 142–149.

SCOTT, E. M., ILLSLEY, R., and THOMSON, A. M. (1956) A psychological investigation of primigravidae II: maternal social class, age, physique and intelligence. *J. obstet. gynaec. Brit. Emp.* **63**, 338–343.

SEARS, R. R., MACCOBY, E. E., and LEVIN, H. (1957) *Patterns of Child Rearing.* Evanston, Ill.: Row, Petersen.

STRAUSS, M. A. (1962) Deferred gratification, social class, and the achievement syndrome. *Amer. sociol. Rev.* **27**, 326–335.

SVALASTOGA, K. (1959) *Prestige, Class and Mobility.* London: Heinemann.

SWIFT, D. F. (1964) Who passes the 11 plus? *New Society*, 5 March, 6–9.

WARDLE, C. J. (1962) Social factors in the major functional psychoses. In Welford *et al.*, *Society.* London: Routledge.

WARNER, W. L., and ABEGGLEN, J. C. (1955) *Big Business Leaders in America.* New York: Harper.

WHYTE, W. H. (1956) *The Organization Man.* New York: Simon and Schuster.

YOUNG, M. and WILLMOTT, P. (1957) *Family and Kinship in East London.* London: Routledge.

YOUNG, M., and GIBSON, J. (1963) In search of an explanation of social mobility. *Brit. J. statist. Psychol.* **XVI**, 27–35.

NISBET, J. (1953) Family environment and intelligence. *Eugen. Rev.* XLV, 31–42.

[illegible] (1950) [illegible] *Social Attitudes of Adolescents.* Unpublished London Ph.D. thesis.

[illegible] (1953) Levels of [illegible] and social class. *Amer. sociol. Rev.* 18, 23[illegible]–242.

[illegible] New Haven: Yale Univ. Press.

[illegible] (1964) The [illegible] a [illegible] dimension of [illegible] *Amer. sociol. Rev.* 29, [illegible]

[illegible] (1961) Social [illegible] a brief review. In HALSEY *et al.* 1961.

[illegible] and [illegible] (1953) The deferred gratification pattern: a preliminary study. *Amer. sociol. Rev.* 18, [illegible]

[illegible] A [illegible] study of [illegible] social class, age, [illegible] *Amer. J. Sociol.* [illegible]

[illegible] and [illegible] H. (1953) [illegible] *Class Status, Power.* [illegible] Free Press.

[illegible] and [illegible] Social [illegible]

[illegible] (1958) [illegible] In [illegible]

[illegible] Routledge.

[illegible] New York [illegible]

[illegible] (1951) The [illegible] and [illegible]

[illegible] and [illegible] (1957) [illegible] and [illegible] London: [illegible]

[illegible] and [illegible] (19[illegible]) [illegible] *Brit. J. Psychol.* XVI, 2[illegible]–43.

11. *Early Determinants of Vocational Choice**

ANNE ROE

THIS paper suggests some hypotheses about the relationships between early experience and attitudes, abilities, interests, and other personality factors which affect the ultimate vocational selection of the individual. Although the writer has drawn heavily upon the general literature, as well as some of the psychoanalytical studies, upon studies of early interest patterns, of parent–child relations, and of personality differences related to parent attitudes and to birth order, data from individual studies are not quoted. This is a speculative paper, and there is little *direct* evidence for the hypotheses which are suggested. However, the writer does not know of any contradictory evidence and believes most of these hypotheses would be relatively easy to check. In a paper of this length only an outline can be given.

These hypotheses have been developed with reference to the present United States culture, including the major variations due to gross socio-economic subdivisions, but the author has not tried to consider alterations which might be introduced by minority positions of one sort or another. Differences between gross cultural subdivisions are primarily differences in percentages of incidence of types of behavior, rather than absolute differences in kind of behavior, and are analogous to the differences in incidence of different bloodgroups in different races. It is to be understood that these hypotheses are intended to indicate major trends, and that other variables not mentioned here can be expected to introduce modifications in specific instances.

Let us first consider some general hypotheses with regard to personality variables as these are expressed in behavior, and particularly in behavior of the sorts that psychologists concern themselves with, for example, intelligence, interests, and special abilities. Some of the individual variation in all of these is undoubtedly due to inheritance, to differences in genetic endowment, but of the extent and precise nature of these genetic differences we know almost nothing certainly. We not only know nothing about

* Paper read at APA Symposium on Theories of Vocational Choice, on September 1, 1956, Chicago, Illinois.

(Reprinted from *Journal of Counseling Psychology*, vol. 4, No. 3 (Fall, 1957), pp. 212–17, by permission of the publisher and author.)

probable genetic differences in the strengths of basic needs or drives, but we have not even begun to consider this problem. Gross hereditary differences in such things as specific sensory capacities and the plasticity and complexity of the central nervous system must greatly affect behavior, but beyond these it is uncertain how far specifically genetic elements are primary factors.

In this connection the author offers five hypotheses.

HYPOTHESES ON RELATION OF EARLY EXPERIENCE TO VOCATIONAL CHOICE

1. *The hereditary bases for intelligence, special abilities, interests, attitudes, and other personality variables seem usually to be nonspecific.* There may be a genetic basis for some "factors" of intelligence or aptitudes, but on this there is no clear evidence. Sex, as genetically determined, also involves some differentiation of abilities. It is, nevertheless, probable that in most instances genetic elements limit the degree of development rather than directly determine the type of expression.

2. *The pattern of development of special abilities is primarily determined by the directions in which psychic energy comes to be expended involuntarily.* The statement applies also to interests, attitudes, and other personality variables. Please note the word *involuntarily.* It is intended to emphasize the fact that the things to which the individual gives automatic attention are keys to his total behavior. The point will not be expanded here, but the relevance of these hypotheses to the relations between personality and perception is clear.

3. *These directions are determined in the first place by the patterning of early satisfactions and frustrations.* This is the developing pattern of need primacies or relative strengths. In the earliest years these are essentially unconscious, and they probably always retain a large unconscious element. As noted before, we know nothing at all about genetic variability in basic needs, but it can be fairly assumed that it exists.

Maslow's hierarchical classification of needs is the most useful for focussing the present discussion (Table 1).

The hierarchical arrangement is important. *Maslow's theory states that higher order needs cannot appear until lower order needs are at least relatively well satisfied.* It seems reasonable to assume that higher order needs are of later evolutionary development in man and some of them may not be well established in terms of species evolution. If this is so, it would follow that they would show greater variability within the species. Lower order needs, on the other hand, are essential for the maintenance of life, and this permits much less variability in their strength. Differences in the degree of variability of these needs are of significance for us, and it is particularly the higher needs with which we are concerned. It would also appear that there is some

TABLE 1
BASIC NEEDS (MASLOW)

1. Physiological needs
2. Safety needs
3. Need for belongingness and love
4. Need for importance, respect, self-esteem, independence
5. Need for information
6. Need for understanding
7. Need for beauty
8. Need for self-actualization*

* The author would place this lower in the hierarchy or handle it as a more generalized need.

difference in the age at which these needs or drives may begin to function. By the time the healthy child is a few months old the first five are probably affecting his behavior, although in widely varying degree.

4. *The eventual pattern of psychic energies, in terms of attention directedness, is the major determinant of the field or fields to which the person will apply himself.* This is revelant not only to vocation, of course, but to the total life pattern of the individual. It determines what sort of special abilities and interests will be predominant.

5. *The intensity of these (primarily) unconscious needs, as well as their organization, is the major determinant of the degree of motivation as expressed in accomplishment.* This implies that all accomplishment is based on unconscious as well as on conscious needs, but it does not imply that these needs are necessarily neurotic. There is accomplishment which is a free expression of capacity, although this may be relatively rare. Accomplishment on this basis can generally be distinguished from accomplishment on other bases. The relevance of this hypothesis to eventual vocational performance is evident.

It may not be so evident how the patterns and intensities of these basic needs are affected in the first place by the early experiences of the child. The following three hypotheses are concerned with this problem.

6. *Needs satisfied routinely as they appear do not develop into unconscious motivators.* Intensity of the need is not a variable, since it is stated that the need is "satisfied." The fact that the satisfaction is gained routinely is important, and it implies the need to distinguish sharply between simple, direct, matter-of-fact need gratification and gratification with fuss and fanfare.

7. *Needs for which even minimum satisfaction is rarely achieved will, if higher order, become in effect expunged, or will, if lower order, prevent the appearance of higher order needs, and will become dominant and restricting motivators.* Lower order needs, of course, require some degree of satisfaction for the maintenance of life. The hypothesis would mean, e.g.,

that a child whose expressions of natural curiosity were thoroughly blocked, would cease to be curious. On the other hand, with less effective blocking, hypothesis 8 would apply.

8. *Needs, the satisfaction of which is delayed but eventually accomplished, will become unconscious motivators, depending largely upon the degree of satisfaction felt. This will depend, among other things, upon the strength of the basic need in the given individual, the length of time elapsing between arousal and satisfaction, and the values ascribed to the satisfaction of this need in the immediate environment.*

The last hypothesis is the most significant for this study. It must be understood that the forms in which need satisfaction will be ultimately sought, in adult life, may not be obviously related to the basic needs referred to in the hypothesis. All of the well-known mechanisms of diplacement, projection, etc., may function here. The problem of tolerance of deferred gratification is linked to such experiences as are implied in this hypothesis.

PATTERNS OF EARLY EXPERIENCE WITH PARENTS

Let us turn now to variations in the early experience of children, and in particular to differences in parental handling of children. We can consider only major variations here, and it must be understood that the classification used is an arbitrary one, intended to delimit, as usefully as possible, nodal areas in a series of essentially continuous distributions. Several levels of classification are suggested, overlapping variously. Major behavioral variations are presented in outline form below, and a figure shows these, together with their relation to basically warm and cold attitudes of parents, and their relation to the outcome in the child in terms of his orientation with regard to persons.

The specific behaviors of the parents are of less importance than their attitudes towards the child. It is impossible here to discuss the relative effect of maternal and paternal attitudes, of similarities or differences in them. The classification used here refers to the dominant pattern in the home, whether shown by one or both parents. The major subdivisions refer to the child's position in the family emotional structure: as the center of attention, as avoided, or as accepted.

A. Emotional Concentration on the Child

This ranges between the extreme of overprotection to that of overdemandingness. Perhaps a sort of mean between these two is the quite typical anxiety of parents over a first child, anxiety which, in the same parents, may be much alleviated for the second child, with resulting considerable differences in the personality pictures of the two children.

1. *Overprotection.* The parent babies the child, encourages its dependence and restricts exploratory behavior. There is often concentration upon physi-

cal characteristics and real or fancied "talents" of the child. The parents maintain primary emotional ties with the child.

2. *Overdemanding.* The parents make heavy demands upon the child in terms of perfection of performance and usually institute quite severe training. In later years they may push the child to high achievement in school and work. In somewhat milder forms we may have the sort of family status "noblesse oblige" pattern, in which development of skills is encouraged but the pattern of skills is a prescribed one. This is very typical of upper class families, with emphasis upon development of conceptual as opposed to motor skills. Severer forms may blend into rejection or may be cover for this.

B. Avoidance of the Child

Here, too, two extremes are suggested—rejection and neglect. Care below the minimum adequate amount has well-documented effects, as studies of orphans have shown. Most other studies have few, if any, children in this group. Parents providing this sort of home do not cooperate in psychological studies. (The author would not suggest that non-cooperation is evidence of this type of care!) Minimal need gratification is provided.

1. *Emotional rejection of the child.* Not necessarily accompanied by overt physical neglect. Lack of gratifications is intentional.

2. *Neglect of the child.* This may, in fact, be less harmful psychologically than emotional rejection accompanied by physical care. It shades into the next classification. Gratification lacks are generally not intentional.

C. Acceptance of the Child

Children in this group are full-fledged members of the family circle, neither concentrated upon, nor overlooked. Parents are noncoercive, nonrestrictive, and, actively or by default, encourage independence. The minimum amount of social interaction is supplied at one extreme (this may be very low) and at the other extreme the group approaches the overprotecting one. The major breakdown in this group is on the basis of the warmth or coldness of the family climate.

1. *Casual acceptance of the child.* Noninterference here is largely by default.

2. *Loving acceptance.* Noninterference and encouragement of the child's own resources and his independence may be intentional, even planned, or a natural reflection of parental attitudes towards others generally.

RELATION OF PARENTAL ATTITUDES AND NEED SATISFACTION

Homes in which children are the center of attention provide pretty full satisfaction of physiological and safety needs, and attention to needs for love and esteem, but gratification is usually not entirely routine. The overprotecting home places great emphasis upon gratification, and generally upon immediacy of gratification, which keeps lower level need satisfaction in the foreground. Belongingness, love, and esteem are often made conditional upon dependency and conformity, and genuine self-actualization may be discouraged. There is likely to be encounragement of any sort of any special or supposedly special capacities, however. The overdemanding parent may make satisfaction of needs for love and esteem conditional upon conformity and achievement, which is frequently oriented to status. Needs for information and understanding may be encouraged, but within prescribed areas, and the same is true for self-actualization needs.

By definition, the next group has major lacks in need gratification. Rejecting parents may provide adequate gratification of psychological and safety needs, but refrain from love and esteem gratification, and frequently seem deliberately to withhold the latter or even to denigrate the child. Neglect of physiological and safety needs, but not beyond necessary minimal gratification is much more tolerable than personal depreciation and deliberate withholding of love. If there is no contrast with attitudes towards others in the immediate group there will be stultification of the child's development in some respects but not distortion of it.

Accepting parents offer reasonable gratification of all needs. This is unlikely to be emphasized in the way in which the first group do it, although the extremes of the loving subgroup may tend in this direction. Gratifications will not be deliberately delayed, but neither will delay be made disturbing. The major difference in the subgroups is probably in the way in which gratifications are supplied, and in the degree of deliberate encouragement and gratification of needs.

PARENTAL HANDLING AND ADULT BEHAVIOR PATTERNS

It has been suggested before that perhaps the earliest subdivision of direction of attention, and one which has significance for the whole life pattern of the individual, is that referring to persons, and that this may be towards persons or towards nonpersons. The author does not say towards persons or away from persons, since away from persons may imply defensiveness; the term *object* is avoided since attention may go to animate or inanimate nonpersons, and because object, in psychoanalytic terminology usually comes out to mean other person. Perhaps primary attention to self should be a separate division, or a subdivision of attention to persons. (The exclusiveness with which one of these attitudes dominates the attention of any individual is, of course, another variable, not taken account of here.)

Possible relationships between these orientations and parent–child interaction are suggested in Fig. 1. The next to the outer segment of the circle indicates the probable orientation of the child in terms of persons or nonpersons. The division is suggested by jagged lines, since it is uncertain. The other subdivisions were set arbitrarily.

This basic orientation with respect to persons later ramifies into patterns of special interests and abilities. The degree of social interests is clearly related, and it is likely that verbal abilities are associated with this, since

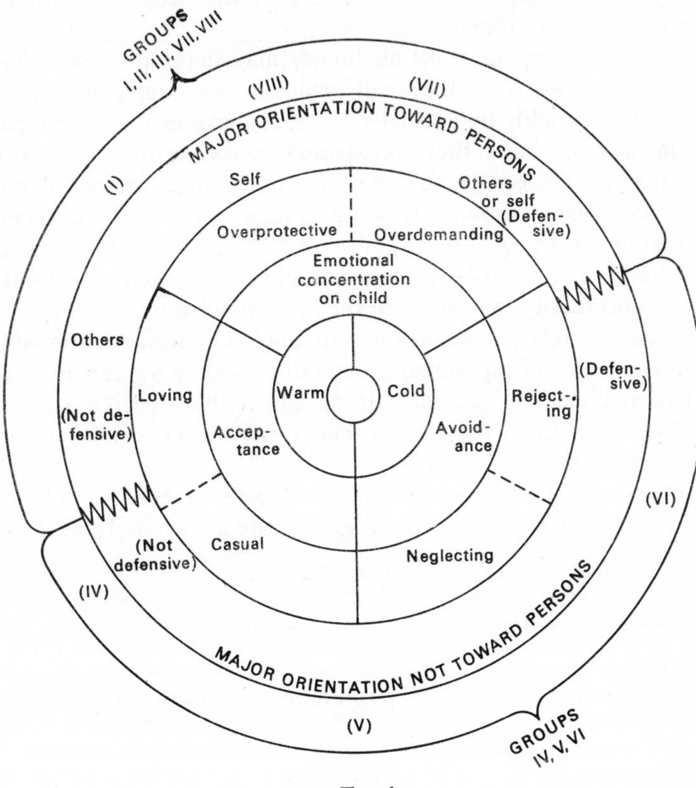

FIG. 1

personal interactions are so largely mediated through words. Scientific and mechanical interests reach their fullest development in those who are concerned with nonpersons.

REFLECTION OF EARLY EXPERIENCE IN VOCATIONAL CHOICE

Depending upon which of the above situations are experienced, there will be developed basic attitudes, interests and capacities which will be given expression in the general pattern of the adult's life, in his personal relations, in his emotional reactions, in his activities, and in his vocational choice. More than any other aspect of life, the occupation usually reflects most clearly the coalescence of the genetic and experiential variables discussed above.*

Persons from child-centered families who do not develop primary self-concentration will still be quite constantly aware of the opinions and attitudes of other persons towards themselves and of the need to maintain self-position in relation to others.

Persons brought up in rejecting homes may develop intense defensive awareness of others; if so they will probably have aggressive tendencies which may most readily find socially acceptable expression in occupational terms. On the other hand, they may strongly reject persons and turn defensively to nonpersons, or they may be unaware of other persons as different from objects in the environment, so far as their own relation to them goes.

Those from accepting homes may have primary interests in persons or in nonpersons; it will not be defensive in either case, and it will not carry the sort of uncertainty that many in the first group show.

It is possible to relate these attitudes quite directly to occupational choice (Roe, 1). The major occupational groups discussed below can, however, be thought of as indicating general patterns rather than specific occupational groups. This strengthens the general theory, but makes its relevance to this symposium less exact.

This classification has two dimensions: focus of activity and level at which the activity is pursued. The categories are shown in Table 2.

TABLE 2
CATEGORIES IN ROE CLASSIFICATION OF OCCUPATIONS

Groups	Levels
I. Service	1. Professional and managerial 1
II. Business Contract	2. Professional and managerial 2
III. Organizations	3. Semiprofessional, small business
IV. Technology	4. Skilled
V. Outdoor	5. Semiskilled
VI. Science	6. Unskilled
VII. General Cultural	
VIII. Arts and Entertainment	

Relationships between group categorization and early experience are suggested in the outer section of Fig. 1.

Although most of this discussion refers to Group rather than Level, Hypothesis 5 has relevance to the latter category. This concerns the degree of motivation. Need intensity may affect, within limits due chiefly to socio-economic background and intelligence, the level at which the mature occu-

* There are clearly exceptions to the usual role of the occupation as a focus for attitudes, capacities, and interests. In these instances, an avocation, or some other aspect of life, serves the same purpose.

P/C

pational life is set; it must definitely affect the relative positions within that level which the individual attains, and even more specifically the position attained within his own occupational group. Most of those selecting occupations in Groups I, II, VII, and VIII have major orientation towards persons as do many, if not most, in Group III. Group IV, V and VI, are chiefly comprised of persons whose major orientation is towards nonpersons. More exact relations cannot be generally indicated. There are, however, some relations which are strongly suggested; these are shown in parentheses in the figure. Indeed, there is some indication that an ordered, counterclockwise arrangement of these groups is not untenable.

REFERENCE

1. ROE, ANNE (1956) *Psychology of occupations.* New York: John Wiley & Sons, Inc.

ADDITIONAL REFERENCES TO ROE'S THEORY

ROE, A. (1953, 1961) *The Making of a Scientist*, New York, Dodd, Mead and Co., 1953; Apollo edition.

ROE, A., and SIEGELMAN, M. (1964) *The Origin of Interests.* Washington, D.C., American Personnel and Guidance Association.

BRUNKEN, R. J., and CRITES, J. O. (1964) A family relations inventory to measure perceived parental attitudes. *Journal of Counseling Psychology*, **11**, 3–12.

CRITES, J. O. (1962) An interpersonal relations scale for occupational groups. *Journal of Applied Psychology*, **46**, 87–90.

GREEN, L. B., and PARKER, H. J. (1965) Parental influence upon adolescents' occupational choice: a test of an aspect of Roe's theory. *Journal of Counseling Psychology*, **12**, 379–383.

GRIGG, A. E. (1959) Childhood experience with parental attitudes: a test of Roe's hypothesis. *Journal of Counseling Psychology*, **6**, 153–155.

HAGEN, D. (1960) Careers and family atmospheres: an empirical test of Roe's theory. *Journal of Counseling Psychology*, **7**, 251–256.

JONES, K. J. (1965) Occupational preference and social orientation. *Personnel and Guidance Journal*, **43**, 574–579.

MOSER, H., DUBIN, W., and SCHELSKY, J. M. (1956) A proposed modification of the Roe occupational classification. *Journal of Counseling Psychology*, **3**, 27–31.

ROE, A. (1961) Personality structure and occupational behaviour. In Borow, H. (ed.), *Man in a World at Work, ibid.*

ROE, A., HUBBARD, W. D., HUTCHINSON, T., and BATEMAN, T. (1964) Studies of occupational history. Part 1: Job changes and the classification of occupations. *Journal of Counseling Psychology*, **13**, 387–393.

SCHAEFER, E. S., and BAYLEY, N. (1960) Consistency of maternal behaviour from infancy to preadolescence. *Journal of Abnormal Social Psychology*, **61**, 1–6.

SWITZER, D. K., GRIGG, A. E., MILLER, J. S., and YOUNG, R. K. (1962) Early experiences and occupational choice: a test of Roe's hypothesis. *Journal of Counseling Psychology*, **9**, 45–48.

UTTON, A. C. (1960) Recalled parent–child relations as determinants of vocational choice. *Vocational Rehabilitation and Education*, **3** and **4**, 20.

UTTON, A. C. (1962) Recalled parent–child relations as determinants of vocational choice. *Journal of Counseling Psychology*, **9**, 49–53.

12. Sibling Associations and Role Involvement*

Brian Sutton-Smith

John M. Roberts

and B. G. Rosenberg

This paper proposes that a person's experience of particular sibling associations may have a lasting effect upon his involvement in adult roles. It reviews the evidence from several earlier investigations dealing with the effects of ordinal position and sibling sex status on role involvement. A first monograph studied the responses of preadolescent children in the eight, two-child ordinal positions and the twenty-four, three-child ordinal positions to anxiety, impulsivity and masculine-feminine inventories (Rosenberg and Sutton-Smith, in press). A second article compared the effects of ordinal position at age 20 years with its effects at ages 10 and 6. In this study use was made of the Minnesota Multiphasic Inventory (MMPI), a device for clinical diagnosis (Sutton-Smith and Rosenberg, MS.). A third article demonstrated that ordinal position affects responses not only on self-report inventories but also on cognitive variables (Rosenberg and Sutton-Smith, 1963). The present paper adds data from the responses of 20-year-olds in the eight, two-child ordinal positions on the Strong Vocational Interest Inventory, the most widely used test for predicting vocational preferences.

In general, it can be said that the studies so far completed indicate that the effects of ordinal position and sibling sex status vary with age and with the nature of the variables being considered. Sex of sibling has stronger effects on adjustment, anxiety and interest inventories, and ordinal position has stronger effects upon mental abilities—with boys affecting girls more than vice versa, and first-borns affecting non-first-borns more than vice versa. In explaining the effects of different ordinal positions and sibling sex status on masculine–feminine role differences, the view has been taken

* This investigation was supported in part by grants MHO4161-03 and MHO7354-01 from the National Institute of Mental Health.

(Reprinted from *Merrill-Palmer Quarterly*, 1964, vol. 10, pp. 25–38, by permission of editor and authors.)

that these positions and statuses are arbitrary phenomena, so that if systematic relationships are found, the problem is to locate the different types of learning experience involved (Sears, 1950). In the recent literature there has been, perhaps, an overstress on primary socialization as the critical learning experience and the reason for the differences which occur between the different ordinal positions (Schacter, 1959). Less attention has been paid to the role of secondary socialization factors. Yet is was assumed traditionally that first-born males, as in the case of cultures stressing primogeniture, received special acculturative pressures throughout their development.

In the explanations that follow it will be assumed similarly that the effects of ordinal position are not due simply to infant patterns of reinforcement, but also to the fact that these continue to be supported by later socialization procedures on the part of adults. A number of investigators have suggested the nature of such procedures (Bossard, 1955; Krout, 1939; Lasko, 1954; Rosen, 1961; Sampson, 1962). Mention has been made, for example, of the higher achievement and responsibility training of first-borns, the greater amount of attention to them and preference for them, and the like. Continuous and changing influences of these sorts on the part of parents are perhaps most appropriately termed *position-typing* influences, to distinguish them from *sex-typing* influences about which relatively more seems to be known (McCandless, 1961, p. 329).

The learning experiences which a child gets in nuclear families as a result of his ordinal position and sibling sex status, however, do not derive solely from the position and sex-typing influence of his parents. The child is, in fact, involved in at least two broad classes of dyadic relationships. The first is with his parents. The second is with his siblings and may be conceptualized partly, at least, in terms of the sex and power of those siblings. In our previous work for example, the all-male dyad of two boys (M1M and MM2)* has been found to be more masculine than the other two-boy ordinal positions (M1F and FM2) at all age levels. The least well adjusted dyad has been the older girl with a younger brother (F1M and FM2). The evidence from these and other studies (Winch, 1962) seems to support the view that girls are more influenced by both their siblings and their parents than are boys. There may even be some respects and some relationships in which the influence of the siblings is more important than that of the parents. While it is impossible to say at this point how strong the respective influences are, it is clear that the matter is now open for debate, and the preponderant attention usually given to parents, called in question.

* The letters M or F denote the sex of the subject or the sibling. The number follows the letter designating the subject and refers to the subject's ordinal position (1 = first-born; 2 = second-born). Thus, "M1M" = first-born boy with younger brother; "FM2" = second-born boy with older sister.

CULTURAL INTERPRETATION

At this juncture in the present program of research it is possible to go in either of two directions. The specific learning experiences that lead to the ordinal position and sibling sex status effects can be directly examined. Or, the general function of such positions and statuses in culture can be studied. This particular paper takes the latter alternative, and subsumes the previous interpretations of the data which were defined narrowly in social learning terms, within a broader cultural paradigm. The system presented is admittedly speculative, but if it serves to force our attention beyond its present theoretical encapsulation within the parent–child interaction, it may serve a useful purpose. The stance taken is that sibling association effects, because they are matters of social learning and not simple facets of nature, will demonstrate systematic relationships to cultural functions on the adult level. And that this occurs because the role differentiations that are learned in childhood lead to the development of interests and competencies which are functional both for the individual and the culture. (The notion of an implicit process of cultural selection and survival of adaptive social characteristics is implied by this statement.)

At the cultural level of analysis the relationships between role differentiation and the informational storage, retrieval, and decision-making processes found in simple and complex cultures has been discussed elsewhere (Roberts, in press). In simple cultures where the average adult controls a substantial portion of the total cultural content, role differentiation is minimal. But in complex cultures where the average adult cannot control more than the smallest fraction of the total cultural content, role differentiation or specialization is extreme. In any complex culture, therefore, role recruitment constitutes a cultural problem. In earlier research it has been suggested that in the case of the Zuni pueblo, differences in child socialization between and within families, variations in adult personalities, differences in value orientations, and a complex array of social roles are functionally related; further, that this totality constitutes a solution to the Zuni problem of using a small number of people to staff a moderately complex role system (Roberts, 1961). Thus, in general, it follows that if a culture is complex and there is considerable role variation in childhood, then the greater the predisposition the child is given by his childhood experience to play a specialized type of role, the more effective will be his subsequent performance in the adult culture.

Since a complex role system taps diverse interests and talents, it is to the advantage of society to socialize its members in such a way that they display diverse interests and talents, favorable to satisfying the diverse cecruitment needs of the role system as a whole. At a general level this rircumstance is dramatically achieved in the differential socialization of boys and girls and their recruitment into different sex roles. In more complex societies the same sex differentiation obtains but it is further varied by the different socialization patterns occurring in distinctive class, occupational, rural, urban, religious, military and other settings. It is our present contention that still another mechanism providing for the differential socialization of children is that provided by the social learning experiences associated with different ordinal positions and sibling sex statuses.

The current literature on ordinal position may be read to contain support for this type of position. Take, for example, the various writings that appear to imply greater affiliation needs in first borns (Schacter, 1959; Sears, 1950; Capra and Dittes, 1962; Sarnoff and Zimbardo, 1961). Hypothetically we may generalize that in the nuclear family of modern industrial society it has been advantageous to have first-born children (on the farm, the eldest son), who were high in affiliation needs so that they would be responsible for the care of their parents and other aged and weak dependents, and younger children low in such needs so that they could easily set up independent lives in distant places. If the position-typing of the parents favored such differences in affiliation needs it would be culturally adaptive.

In order to take the discussion off this more speculative plane, however, we have currently been investigating relationships between different ordinal positions, sibling sex statuses, and occupational preferences. If the position-typing, sex-typing, and sibling association influences follow the lines we have suggested there should be a relationship between these positions and occupational preferences. It is unlikely, of course, that such variation in socialization as occurs regularly among different positions is enough to permit the prediction of specific occupational choices. Nevertheless, if it can be argued that life in a specific position predisposes a person to certain classes of occupation, some cogency will have been added to the general line of argumentation presented above.

METHOD

As a pilot study the Strong Interest Inventory was administered to 137 college sophomores in an elementary psychology class at Bowling Green State University. There were 72 women and 65 men, divided up amongst the eight ordinal positions as follows: F1F = 19; FF2 = 19; F1M = 18; MF2 = 16; M1M = 17; MM2 = 17; M1F = 16; FM2 = 15. The men were administered the 48-item male scale and the women the 29-item female scale.* As 80 per cent of this group were sophomores in education and,

* Table A (3 pages) and Table B (2 pages) giving the mean scores for the 48-item male and the 29-item female scales, respectively, have been deposited as Document No. 7656 with the ADI Auxiliary Publications Project, Photoduplication Service, Library of Congress, Washington 25 D.C. To order a copy of this tabular material, specify Document No. 7656 and remit $ 1.25 for photoprints or $ 1.25 for 35 mm. microfilm. Advance payment is required. Make checks or money orders payable to: Chief, Photoduplication Service, Library of Congress.

therefore, already of homogeneous occupational grouping, it was not expected that many differences would be found between the varying ordinal positions, though it was felt that the directional findings might be of some value. There was no significant difference between groups on a manual/non-manual socioeconomic comparison. The classification of occupations that follows was made on a variety of bases deriving from previous research. The classifications used made sense to these investigators, but must await further research if their reliability and validity is to be maintained, though as will be seen, most of them follow self-evident criteria.

RESULTS

The female groups showed a predominantly premarital career profile with higher scores in the occupations of elementary school teacher, office worker and stenographer secretary. For males the predominant profile in all groups included social science teacher, math and physics teacher, aviator, printer, and music performer. As Tables 1 and 2 indicate, the few differences

TABLE 1
GROUP DIFFERENCES ON THE STRONG INTEREST INVENTORY: MALES

Occupational Category	Sibling Positions	t	P
Psychologist	M1F > FM2	2·28	·05
	{M1F, M1M} > {MM2, FM2}	2·43	·02
Architect	{M1F, M1M} > {MM2, FM2}	1·91	·10
Public Administrator	{M1M, M1F} > {MM2, FM2}	1·89	·10
CPA	{M1M, M1F} > {MM2, FM2}	1·81	·10
Pharmacist	MM2 > FM2	1·94	·10
Specialization Level	M1F > FM2	1·71	·10
	{M1M, M1F} > {MM2, FM2}	2·19	·05

found do not exceed chance expectation for the many possible comparisons involved. As this was an exploratory investigation, however, it was decided to compare the direction of the various scores across the ordinal position categories. In the following analysis, therefore, we will compare the frequencies with which particular ordinal groups have the highest average scores on the occupational categories. As each sex contains four ordinal groups (in a two-child family) it is possible for each group to have either the 1st,

TABLE 2
GROUP DIFFERENCES ON THE STRONG INTEREST INVENTORY: FEMALES

Occupational Category	Sibling Positions	*t*	*P**
Artist	MF2 > FF2	1·95	·10
Author	MF2 > FF2	1·93	·10
Librarian	MF2 > FF2	1·82	·10
	F1M > FF2	1·97	·10
English Teacher	{F1F, F1M} > {FF2, MF2}	1·74	·10
Psychologist	FF2 > MF2	1·83	·10
Lawyer	FF2 > F1F	2·07	·05
Social Science Teacher	F1M > MF2	2·69	·02
YWCA Secretary	{F1M, FF2} > {MF2, MF2}	1·88 1·85	·10 ·10
Life Insurance Sales	MF2 > F1F	1·94	·10
	FF2 > F1F	1·86	·10
	{MF2, FF2} > {F1F, F1M}	2·25	·05
Nurse	F1F > FF2	2·18	·05
	{F1F, F1M} > {FF2, MF2}	1·89	·10
Math-Science Teacher	F1F > MF2	2·40	·05
	F1M > MF2	1·71	·10
	{F1F, F1M} > {MF2, FF2}	2·18	·05
Lab Technician	F1F > FF2	2·03	·05
	F1F > MF2	1·79	·10
	{F1F, F1M} > {MF2, FF2}	1·83	·10
Engineer	F1F > MF2	2·29	·05

* All Tests are two-tailed.

2nd, 3rd, or 4th highest score on a particular occupation. Further, it is possible to compare actual occupancy of the highest two positions (1st and 2nd) with the chance expectancy that high scores will be randomly distributed for each and all occupations across all ordinal groups. No levels of significance are given for this exercise as most of the group differences are not themselves significant, though many of the directional departures from chance distribution would be.

DISCUSSION

In the following discussion it will be assumed that high interest in an occupation disposes a person to ultimately find gratification in that occupation and to persist in it (Tyler, 1962). Which is to say that we are here assuming that occupation preference may be used as an index of role involvement, and that such role involvement may in turn be regarded as an index of suitability for recruitment to the role in question. The findings should be considered in that light.

1. It has been noted that first-borns appear to be higher on need achievement, academic achievement, and affiliation needs. There is research also suggesting that they have higher general responsibility training (Bossard, 1955; Sampson, 1962). They are more often put in charge of other children and of household chores and in general get more extensive experience of playing an adult surrogate role than do non-first-borns. It might be predicted, therefore, that this would predispose them to take up parent surrogate occupational roles, in particular, teaching. On the male and female forms of the Strong Vocational Interest Inventory there are nine teaching occupations (English teacher, social science teacher, elementary school teacher, home economics teacher, math and science teacher, physical education teacher, business education teacher, industrial arts teacher, vocational agricultural teacher), which because of the overlap between the scales present 22 possibilities for scoring in the 1st or 2nd highest positions. While we might expect by chance a distribution of 11 : 11 first- and second-borns in these two highest scoring positions, we find in fact that 18 of the two highest scoring positions are occupied by first-borns. It will be noted that the relevant results in Table 2 are consistent with this direction. First-born girls have higher scores ($p = < .10$) on English teacher, social science teacher, and math and science teacher. Perhaps the surrogate training provided in the family has cultural advantages in predisposing first-borns, in particular first-born girls, to show greater interest in these roles.

2. The foregoing finding suggested the possibility that first-borns would, in general, prefer culturally conservative roles. There was support for this view in earlier work showing first-borns to be more conforming (Becker, 1962), and to have stronger identification with parents (Sears, Maccoby, and Levin, 1957; Storer, 1961). Hypothetically it may have been culturally adaptive to have at least one segment of the population more or less committed to the preservation of the traditional social roles. Our definition of a conservative occupation was derived rather tenuously from Getzels and Jackson's work on creativity (1962, p. 56). They demonstrated that less creative persons were more likely to prefer professional occupations. It has already been demonstrated that first-borns have a higher preference for the academic professions. Results for other professions, were not, however, so striking. There were 32 possible 1st or 2nd highest scoring positions and

21 of these were occupied by first-borns. This is not a sufficiently striking departure from chance expectation to suggest that this particular generalization merits much further consideration—though there is some support for the idea in Table 1, where first-born males show higher scores on Psychology, Public Administration and C.P.A. Results for females are inconclusive.

3. In addition to contrasts between ordinal positions, the present investigators were interested in the effects of particular sibling dyads* on occupational choices. It has already been mentioned that the all-boy dyad (M1M and MM2) was the most masculine in all previous studies, using the MMPI at age 20, the Rosenberg–Sutton-Smith masculinity-femininity play scale at preadolescence (1959), and scores derived from Koch's studies at age 6 (Brim, 1958). This dyad had the most masculine scores on the Strong Interest Inventory. Examination of the occupations for which this dyad shares the highest preferences (1st or 2nd) indicates that they include the activities of producing, buying, and selling—all of which may be ultimately related to standard economic transactions within this culture. These occupations are: life insurance salesman, buyer, real estate salesman, banker, purchasing agent, production manager, farmer, accountant, sales manager, president of manufacturing company. First or second highest positions are occupied by this dyad in 18/20 cases. If masculinity is interpreted in its traditional sense for this culture it may mean that boys who are higher in masculinity show a higher interest in conventional economic types of achievement (Swanson and Miller, 1958; McClelland, 1961).

Throughout previous research the girl with the older brother (MF2) has, in general, been the most masculine girl, even to the extent of having a male cognitive profile with, in general, higher quantitative than verbal scores. On the present female inventory this girl shows the highest interest in the two economic items on that list, life insurance and buyer.

We have been considering the characteristics which the members of the male dyad hold in common. It is also possible to consider the ways in which the members of this dyad are distinct. In a previous series of researches these investigators have been concerned with the development of two styles of achieving, or two success styles as they have been called. One of these is achievement by strategy; another is achievement by physical power. It has been contended that these styles are modelled by games of strategy and physical skill, and various sociometric and ludic correlates have been advanced in support of this position (Roberts, Arth, and Bush, 1959; Roberts and Sutton-Smith, 1962; Sutton-Smith and Roberts, 1963; Sutton-Smith and Roberts, in press; Roberts, Sutton-Smith, Kendon, in press). If particular ordinal positions predispose a person to one or other of these success styles and if it is possible to classify occupations in terms of the

* These are inferred dyads. The complementary ordinal positions were *not* from the same families.

dominant success style involved, then it may be possible to discover a relationship between ordinal position and occupational choice.

Illustrations of physical power as a success style may be found in the application of physical power to persons, animals, and other living things. A case can be made for the presence of this style in eight of the occupations on the male scale: physician, osteopath, dentist, veterinarian, farmer, policeman, mortician (by extension), and YMCA physical director. In the present data for males, first place for all these roles is occupied by second-born male (MM2), except for physician, where the second-born holds 2nd place. In only one instance do the first-born males occupy either of the first two positions on any of these occupations, and that is 2nd place on mortician.

In sum, the second-born boy is always found in either a 1st or 2nd highest scoring position for power occupations; whereas with one exception, the first-born boy (M1M) is always found in a 3rd or 4th position (8 : 0-1 : 7).

A second success style is that of the strategist where outcomes are determined through rational decisions. Several of the studies cited above have shown a relationship between games of strategy and aspects of managing social systems. One can argue that in all the following roles, management of a social system is involved: production manager, personnel director, public administrator, YMCA secretary, city school superintendent, social worker, CPA, senior CPA, accountant, office man, purchasing agent, banker, sales manager, lawyer, president manufacturing concern. In all cases 1st or 2nd position is occupied by an M1M. The second-born boys are distributed randomly across all scoring positions, so that while it is true to say that first-borns are to be found exclusively in strategic occupations, it is not true to say that non-first-born boys are never found in strategic positions. There is slight support in Table 1 for this difference between older and younger boys. First-borns show a greater interest in the strategic occupations of C.P.A. and Public Administrator. Early research (Roberts and Sutton-Smith, 1962) has suggested that differences in child training may help to account for these differences, though the second-born boy's preference for power style may perhaps result from a reaction to dominance by the elder brother (Krout, 1939).

The male dyad then is distinguished by its masculinity and by its interest in conventional economic activities. The older brother shows a consistent preference for a strategic success style and the younger brother shows a preference for a power success style.

4. In general, we would expect the all-girl dyad to have high feminine scores on most inventories (F1F and FF2). But their scores have not been consistently the most feminine across all age levels and all scales, though there is a tendency for that to be the case. This feminine dyad does not, however, differ from other girl's groups in this inconsistency of scoring pattern on masculine-feminine scales. The two girls do have the highest feminine scores on the present inventory. They share additionally the two

highest scoring positions on the occupations of office work and stenographer-secretary. There is a suggestion here, perhaps of some variable of routine-responsibility as a central kernel to the female role. This same dyad is not as clearly differentiated on the success styles as was the case with the male dyad, but such differences as there are, occur in the reverse direction from those found with the boys.

There are three occupations that fit within the definition of the strategic success style (social worker, lawyer and YWCA secretary) and the second-born girl (FF2) is always in one of the two highest scoring positions and the first-born girl (F1F) is never in one of those positions. There are six occupations on the female scale which appear to fit the definition of the power success style. These are: nurse, dentist, laboratory technician, physician, dietitian, and physical therapist. With one exception the highest score is always obtained by F1F. Without exception the second highest score is obtained by F1M. In sum, the power style is quite clearly a first-born girl's monopoly on this scale (11 : 1). First-born girls appear to prefer a power style, which together with their preference for surrogate parent roles, strongly suggests the importance of nurturance and the physical management of resources to the first-born girl. It is not difficult to conjecture that the position typing effect of rewarding older girls for carrying out nurturance and responsibility, would lead to the learning of high need nurturance and would be reflected in an occupational interest in roles allowing the continuance of surrogation and physical care. (We might hazard that this first-born girl, backed up by her mother, needs exercise little deception in the management of her younger siblings. The cultural and adaptive value of having a segment of the population with such an interest is self-evident. We may conjecture similarly, that the second-born girls' development of a strategic style may be reactive to the overpowering pressure of two mothers—the real mother and the older sister.)

5. In earlier work, it has been found that the opposite sex siblings affect the masculinity-femininity scores of the subject in the direction of the sibling's sex. In the present study it was found that the most expressively creative occupations of artist, music performer, author, and architect were preferred most by subjects with opposite sex siblings. All possible 1st and 2nd highest scoring positions were occupied by subjects with opposite sex siblings (14 : 0). The highest scoring positions (1st) are always occupied by the boy with the younger sister (M1F) on the male scale, and the girl with an older brother (MF2) on the female scale. This older brother, younger sister dyad is apparently the most creative. The next most creative dyad is the older sister (F1M) with the younger brother (FM2). The success style of these two dyads (M1F and MF2; F1M and FM2) is presumably that of creating new solutions and new culture. In earlier research with the MMPI it has been shown that the second and less creative of these dyads (F1M and FM2) has also the highest scores on emotional conflict. It is

apparently the cross-sex affect, rather than the emotional conflict which contributes to the interest of these two dyads in the expressive arts. Table 2 offers some partial corroboration of the present directional findings by showing that MF2 has higher scores ($p = < .10$) than FF2 on the occupations of artist and author. It is interesting to note that the girl who is highest on expressive creativity (MF2) is also the girl highest on the earlier conventional economic items.

If the technically creative professions are considered—psychologist, physicist, mathematician, engineer, and chemist on the male scale; psychologist and engineer on the female scale—we find again that all the highest scoring positions are held by boys with a younger sister (M1F 6 : 0). There is not, however, any consistent finding with regard to the younger sister (MF2). That is, M1F shows high interest in both the expressively and technically creative occupations, while MF2 shows consistent interest in only the expressively creative occupations. Similarly though not so markedly for the girls, the older sister with the younger brother (F1M) is always in the two highest positions for both expressive and technical creativity (lawyer and psychologist) but her younger brother (FM2) is not. Thus, both older brother (M1F) and older sister (F1M) are high on expressive and technical creativity, but their younger sister (MF2) and brother (FM2) respectively are high only on expressive items.

Highest scores for the girls on the technically creative items are taken by FF2 and F1M, and for the boys by the M1F just mentioned and MM2. These particular two girl groups also get highest scores on the items mentioned above as involving a strategic success style. Putting the technically creative female items (2) together with the strategy female items (3), these two girl groups occupy all 1st and 2nd positions (10 : 0). There are no similar consistent relationships for these two groups of boys between technical creativity and strategy.

In conclusion, it seems evident that the differences in ordinal position and sibling status may well have a bearing on the staffing, involvement, and recruiting of the members for the complex role system in our society. The precise nature of the interrelationships must await further research. The importance of the study of sibling associations in other than the nuclear and the two-child family is certainly established.

CONCLUSION

Although the present classification of occupations is arbitrary and most of the present data only directional, considerable support has been given to the worthwhileness of a more extensive investigation of the following propositions:

A. That ordinal position and sibling sex status involve distinctive social learnings, deriving from the position-typing and sex-typing influences of the parents and other adults and from the interactive influence of the siblings.

B. That these distinctive social learnings have survived in modern complex culture because they in turn lead to the development of dispositions which are individually and socially of functional value.

C-1. That social learning amongst first-borns includes high surrogate training and strong identification with the parents (conscience, conformity, affiliation, dependency, volunteering, internalization) and leads both to academic success and a readiness to take parent-surrogate roles as exampled by a preference for teaching.

C-2. That the social learning in the male dyad (M1M and MM2), leads to high sex-role masculinity and high interest in conventional economic activities. That within this dyad the first-born male is differentiated from the second-born male by his interest in a strategic success style, and the latter is differentiated by his interest in a power success style.

C-3. That social learning in the female dyad leads to high femininity and an interest in routine occupations. That within this dyad the first-born is distinguished by an interest in a power success style (F1F) and the second-born (FF2) by an interest in a strategic success style. The girl dyad thus reverses the male dyad in its success style interests.

C-4. That the social learning in the opposite sex sibling dyads (M1F and MF2) (F1M and FM2) contributes to an interest in expressive creativity. The older brother and the younger sister comprise the most creative dyads. For both dyads the older members (M1F and F1M) also show interest in technical forms of creativity.

REFERENCES

BECKER, S. W., and CARROLL, J. (1962) Ordinal position and conformity. *J. abnorm. soc. Psychol.*, **65**, 129–131.

BOSSARD, J. H. S. (1955) Personality roles in the large family. *Child Developm.*, **26**, 71–78.

BRIM, O. G., JR. (1958) Family structure and sex-role learning by children: a further analysis of Helen Koch's data. *Sociom.*, **21**, 1–16.

CAPRA, P. C., and DITTES, J. E. (1962) Birth order as a selective factor among volunteer subjects. *J. abnorm. soc. Psychol.*, **64**, 302.

GETZELS, J. W., and JACKSON, P. W. (1962) *Creativity and Intelligence*. New York: Wiley.

KOCH, HELEN L. (1956) Children's work attitudes and sibling characteristics. *Child Developm.*, **27**, 289–310. (a)

KOCH, HELEN L. (1956) Some emotional attitudes of the young child in relation to characteristics of her siblings. *Child Developm.*, **27**, 393–426.

KOCH, HELEN L. (1960) The relation of certain formal attributes of siblings to attitudes held toward each other and toward their parents. *Monogr. Soc. Res. Child Developm.*, **25**, 1–124.

KROUT, M. H. (1939) Typical behavior patterns in twenty-six ordinal positions. *J. genet. Psychol.*, **55**, 3–30.

LASKO, JOAN K. (1954) Parental behavior toward first and second children. *Genet. Psychol. Monogr.*, **49**, 97–137.

McCandless, B. R. (1961) *Children and Adolescents: behavior and development*. New York: Holt, Rinehart & Winston.

McClelland, D. C. (1961) *The Achieving Society*. New York: Van Nostrand.

Miller, D. R., Swanson, Guy E. (1958) *The Changing American Parent*. New York: Wiley.

Roberts, J. M. (1961) The Zuni in *Variations in Value Orientations*, by Florence R. Kluckhohn and Fred L. Strodtbeck. Evanston, Ill.: Row, Peterson, 284–316.

Roberts, J. M. The self-management of cultures in *Explorations in Cultural Anthropology*. Ward Goodenough (ed.), in press.

Roberts, J. M., Arth, M. J., and Bush, R. R. (1959) Games in culture. *Amer. Anthrop.*, **61**, 597–605.

Roberts, J. M., and Sutton-Smith, B. (1962) Game involvement in children. *Ethnology*, **10**, 166–185.

Roberts, J. M., Sutton-Smith, B., and Kendon, A. Strategy in games and folktales. *J. soc. Psychol.*, in press.

Rosen, B. C. (1961) Family structure and achievement motivation. *Amer. Sociol. Review*, **26**, 574–578.

Rosenberg, B. G., and Sutton-Smith, B. (1959) The measurement of masculinity and femininity in children. *Child Developm.*, **30**, 373–378.

Rosenberg, B. G., and Sutton-Smith, B. Ordinal position and sex-role identification. *Psychol. Monogr.*, in press.

Rosenberg, B. G., and Sutton-Smith, B. Relation of birth order, sex-role identification and mental ability. Paper presented at the biennial meeting of Soc. Res. Child Developm., Berkeley, Calif., April 13, 1963.

Sampson, E. E. (1962) Birth order, need achievement and conformity. *J. abnorm. soc. Psychol.*, **64**, 155–159.

Sarnoff, I., and Zimbardo, P. (1961) Anxiety, fear, and social affiliation. *J. abnorm. soc. Psychol.*, **62**, 356–363.

Schacter, S. (1959) *The Psychology of Affiliation*. Stanford, Calif.: Stanford Univ. Press.

Sears, R. R. (1950) Ordinal position in the family as a psychological variable. *Amer. Sociol. Rev.*, **15**, 397–401.

Sears, R. R., Maccoby, Eleanor E., and Levin, H. (1957) *Patterns of Child Rearing*. Evanston: Row, Peterson.

Storer, N. (1961) Ordinal position and the Oedipal complex. Lab. of Soc. Relat., *Harvard Univ. Bull.*, **10**, 18–21.

Sutton-Smith, B., and Rosenberg, B. G. (1960) Play and game list. IBM Form I.T.S. 1100 A 6058. New York.

Sutton-Smith, B., and Roberts, J. M. (1963) Game involvement in adults. *J. soc. Psychol.*, **60**, 15–30.

Sutton-Smith, B., and Roberts, J. M. Rubrics of competitive behavior. *J. genet. Psychol.*, in press.

Sutton-Smith, B., and Rosenberg, B. G. Age changes in the effects of ordinal position on sex role identification. (MS.)

Tyler, L. E. (1962) *The Work of the Counselor*. New York: Appleton-Century.

Winch, R. F. (1962) *Identification and its Familial Determinants*. Indianapolis: Bobbs-Merrill.

ADDITIONAL REFERENCES FOR THE INFLUENCE OF THE HOME AND THE SCHOOL ON VOCATIONAL DEVELOPMENT

Carter, M. P. (1962) *Home, School and Work*. Oxford, Pergamon.

Coleman, J. S. (1961) *The Adolescent Society*. New York, Free Press of Glencoe.

DENT, H. C. (1958) *Secondary Modern Schools: An Interim Report.* London, Routledge & Kegan Paul.

DOUGLAS, J. W. B. (1964) *Home and the School.* London, Macgibbon & Kee.

ERIKSON, E. (1950) *Childhood and Society.* New York, Norton.

FLOUD, J. E., HALSEY, A. H., and MARTIN, F. M. (1957) *Social Class and Educational Opportunity.* London, Heinemann.

FRASER, E. (1959) *Home Environment and the School.* London, University of London Press.

GLASS, D. V. (ed.) (1954) *Social Mobility in Britain.* Glencoe, Ill., Free Press.

GORDON, C. W. (1957) *The Social System of the High School: A Study in the Sociology of Adolescence.* Glencoe, Ill., Free Press.

JACKSON, B., and MARSDEN, D. (1962) *Education and the Working Class.* London, Routledge & Kegan Paul.

MACPHERSON, J. S. (1958) *Eleven Year Olds Grow Up.* London, University of London Press.

MEAD, M. (1951) *The School in American Culture.* Cambridge, Mass., Harvard University Press.

MOGEY, J. M. (1956) *Family and Neighbourhood.* Oxford, Oxford University Press.

TAYLOR, W. (1963) *The Secondary Modern School.* London, Faber.

WISEMANN, S. (1964) *Education and Environment.* Manchester University Press.

YOUNG, M., and WILLMOTT, P. (1957) *Family and Kinship in East London.* London, Routledge & Kegan Paul.

ALLEN, E. A. (1960) Attitudes of children and adolescents in school. *Educational Research*, **3**, 65–80.

BENDIX, R., LIPSET, S. M., and MALM, F. T. (1954) Social origins and occupational career patterns. *Industrial and Labour Relations Review*, **7**, 246–261.

BERNSTEIN, B. (1961) Social class and linguistic development: a theory of social learning. In *Education, Economy and Society*, J. Floud, A. H. Halsey, and C. Arnold Anderson (ed.). Glencoe, Free Press.

BERNSTEIN, B. (1965) A socio-linguistic approach to social learning. In *Penguin Survey of the Social Sciences 1965*. Penguin Books.

COLEMAN, J. S. (1959) Academic achievement and the structure of competition. *Harvard Educational Review*, **29**, 339–351.

DYNES, R. R., CLARKE, A. C., and DINITZ, S. (1956) Levels of occupational aspiration: some aspects of family experience as a variable. *American Sociological Review*, **21**, 212–215.

FLOUD, J., and HALSEY, A. H. (1961) English secondary schools and the supply of labour. In *Education, Economy, and Society, ibid.*

FLOUD, J., and HALSEY, A. H. (1961) Homes and schools: social determinants of educability. *Educational Research*, **3**, 83–88.

GRIBBONS, W. D., and LOHNES, P. R. (1965) Shifts in adolescents' vocational values. *Personnel and Guidance Journal*, **44**, 248–252.

HORROCKS, J. E. (1965) Adolescent attitudes and goals. In *Problems of Youth.* M. Sherif and C. Sherif (ed.). Chicago, Aldine.

HORWITZ, M. (1956) Psychological needs as a function of social environments. In L. D. White (ed.), *The State of the Social Sciences.* Chicago, University of Chicago Press.

KINNANE, J. F., and PABLE, M. W. (1962) Family background and work value orientation. *Journal of Counseling Psychology*, **9**, 320–325.

KRIPPNER, S. (1963) Junior high school students' vocational preferences and their parents occupational levels. *Personnel and Guidance Journal*, **41**, 590–595.

McDILL, E. L., and COLEMAN, J. S. (1965) Family and peer influences in college plans of high school students. *Sociology of Education*, **38**, 112–116.

MOWSESIAN, R., HEALTH, B., and ROTHNEY, J. W. M. (1966) Superior students occupational preferences and their fathers' occupations. *Personnel and Guidance Journal*, **45**, 238–242.

PARSONS, T. (1959) The school class as a social system: some of its functions in American society. *Harvard Educational Review*, **29**, 297–318.

SCHELSKY, H. (1961) Family and school in modern society. In *Education, Economy, and Society, ibid.*

SCHMIDT, J. L., and ROTHNEY, J. W. M. (1955) Variability of vocational choices of high school students. *Personnel and Guidance Journal*, **34**, 142–146.

STRODTBECK, E. L. (1958) Family integration, values, and achievement. In D. McClelland *et al.* (eds.), *Talent and Society*. Princeton, N. J., Von Nostrand.

TURNER, R. H. (1960) Sponsored and contest mobility and the school system. *American Sociological Review*, **25**, 855–867.

SECTION 3

The Transition from School to Work

"I would there were no age between 16 and 23 or that youth would sleep out the rest; for there is nothing in between but getting wenches with child, wronging the ancientry, stealing, fighting."

SHAKESPEARE, *A Winter's Tale*

THE first traumatic interruption to the settled continuity of childhood, occurs at the time of school entry. It is then that the child has to adapt from being a relatively self-centred individual into a socially responsive being. The next major transitional period occurs when he is expected to leave behind the irresponsibilities and indulgencies of childhood and embark upon the tortuous path to adult citizenship. This change of role definition occurs in the transitional period from school to work. Educationalists and industrialists for some time have expressed concern regarding the smoothness of this transition. Evidence exists to support the claim that large numbers of adolescents feel varying amounts of "work shock" on beginning their first job. This period is one of the vital points in the socialization process, and, as such, a real understanding of the variables involved and the difficulties experienced is essential to anyone concerned with preparing youth for the adult world.

Keil, Riddell, and Green examine various theoretical approaches to the question of the adjustment of young people to working life. They define certain inadequacies in these approaches and suggest a theoretical framework to take into account all the factors that could operate during the transitional period. They review much previous research in the light of their framework of "informal" and "formal" influences in the adjustment process.

Maizel's study of the entry of school leavers into work at Willesden, attempted to assess the value of the Youth Employment Service in placing school leavers during the transitional stage and afterwards. 45 per cent of the sample were placed by the Youth Employment Bureau, compared with a national figure of 37 per cent. The public image of the Youth Employment Service is reflected in that vacancies registered with it are concentrated in unskilled and semi-skilled manual work, and that it is predominantly the smaller firms who notify their vacancies to the bureau. The study also suggests that the Service concentrates as much on helping the person seeking a change of employment as it does on the school leaver seeking his first job. These issues have important implications for the Youth Employment Service as a whole regarding its role in the transition from school to work.

Palmer examines the assertion that the transition from school to work *is* a period of stress, difficulty, and dissatisfaction. She found that although real stress exists, it may not be as widespread as is sometimes claimed. Approximately two-thirds of the young workers in her sample had favourable attitudes toward their jobs, but it was the social aspects of the job that provided the biggest adjustment problem for 50 per cent of them.

There is, undoubtedly, a need for a more need-oriented dissemination of occupational information, vocational guidance and counselling, at all levels of education. The studies of Wilson (1952), Jahoda (1953), Chown (1958), and others, emphasize these needs at the secondary modern school level, while Hill's (1965) study of sixth-form grammar-school boys illustrates that too often in Britain the situation arises by which the more intelligent the child the less he knows about the realities of the outside world due to a sheltered programme of academic eclecticism.

13. *Youth and Work: Problems and Perspectives*

E. TERESA KEIL, D. S. RIDDELL, and B. S. R. GREEN

INTRODUCTION

THE literature on the adjustment of young people to working life is large, but lacks coherence.[(1)] Although the subject has become a popular research topic, there have been no thorough surveys of the field. This article, in the light of an extensive survey of the literature, develops a method of approach which differs from those adopted by the small number of previous writers who have found any theoretical interest in the topic.

It should not be forgotten that the provision of full-time education for the whole of the population of Great Britain is less than a hundred years old. While the period of compulsory school attendance has increased, the minimum age of leaving has been fifteen years only since 1947, and fourteen only since 1922. Six out of every ten boys and girls leave school at the minimum age. The same proportion complete their education at secondary modern schools.[(2)] Of fifteen year old male leavers 60 per cent go into unskilled and semi-skilled work, and 35 per cent into apprenticeships. Proportions going into unskilled work decline steeply as the age of leaving increases, but even among seventeen year old leavers, about one out of four goes into unskilled work.[(3)] Because of the large numbers in the age group (the "bulge"), there has been a slight decrease in the proportion entering apprenticeships in the last year or two, although the total number of apprentice entrants has gone up.

Educationalists and administrators have argued for a long time that the transition from school to work involves stress. A departmental committee was set up in 1916 by the President of the Board of Education, which, in its report emphasised the difficulties of the period between leaving school and taking up apprenticeships, as well as those for young workers going into stop-gap and unskilled employment, remarking that,

> "The effect in discouragement, disillusionment and disappointment on the morale and on the health of young people on the threshold of adult life is one of the gravest menaces of the times, and a contributory cause to permanent and intermittent unemployment, and to juvenile delinquency."[(4)]

(Reprinted from *Sociological Review*, vol. 2, 1966, pp. 117–137, by permission of editor and authors.)

The proposals of this committee were to set up compulsory, one day a week, day continuation schools until the age of sixteen; to provide better vocational education; and thus to alleviate the sudden transition. For various reasons they were largely still-born.[5] However, such proposals have been continually reviewed, on the same grounds, and re-appear in the 1944 Education Act, and in the *Crowther Report*, which gives its recommendation for setting up county colleges—the modern version of day continuation schools—a priority second only to that of raising the leaving age to sixteen.[6]

PREVIOUS THEORETICAL APPROACHES

Apart from the recent studies by Carter, Veness, and *Crowther Report* itself,[7] few areas of the general subject of moving from school to work have been carefully investigated, and the material as a whole shows a remarkable lack of systematization, and a failure to consider previous work. With the exception of the topic of occupational choice,[8] which is not considered here, there have been few organized surveys, and much of the literature consists of the impressions of teachers, personnel managers, youth employment officers, etc., which, although valuable in themselves, give only a partial insight into the problems of young people at this period of their lives, and are loaded with moral judgements and evaluations.[9] Some of this material is reconsidered in the later sections of the paper.

The literature on adjustment to work is even less helpful. One of the major features of any adjustment to a worker's rôle or position, however defined, must be the preparation received in school. In peasant societies without formal school systems the introduction to work is a gradual one,[10] whereas in modern industrial societies, a child is separated from the working world for a large part of his day, and his formal contact with work is severely limited by legislation. Noticing this contrast, some writers have been led to suggest that entering work after being a schoolboy involves some sort of a shock, often termed a "culture shock," creating problems of adjustment.[11]

This view has been most fully developed in a long section of Miller and Form's text, *Industrial Sociology*, which is one of the most systematic approaches to the subject.[12] They argue that for the young person entering industry there are two sets of problems—those arising from differences of situation and position; and those arising from differences in orientations.

	School	*Work*
(a) *Situation*	Ages are all very similar, apart from teachers.	Ages vary over a wide range.
(b) *Position*	A boy in his last year is very familiar with the institution, knows how it works, has some weight in it, if not a formal authority position.	A new entrant is a very minor figure, with no experience and no authority.

(c) *Value Orientations*

School	*Work*
1. Enforced permanent group membership.	Freedom of employer and employee to terminate employment.
2. Co-operation.	Self-interest.
3. Morally correct behaviour.	Amorality.
4. Full self-development.	Learning persistence at a job.
5. Valuation by individual characteristics.	Valuation by characteristics of group and class membership.(13)

Furthermore, Miller and Form cite some evidence to show that in the United States, aspirations do not correspond with the possibilities that the labour market offers. 91 per cent of the respondents in a pre-war survey wanted white collar jobs—only one in five got them.(14) The shock which the authors suggest occurs from going to work results from the confrontation of the realities of the work situation with the expectations carried from the school situation.

Some criticism of this approach is fairly self-evident. While it is true that age structures vary in schools and in industry, the implications of this for the psychology of the new entrant are not known. The above list of school value orientations may correspond more to the exhortations of educational philosophy than to the realities of school situations. The list of work values does not correspond in many respects with the findings of industrial sociologists and psychologists who have made systematic studies of worker behaviour in industry. In addition, the presentation of these differences in such a dichotomous fashion does injustice to the actual complexity of the experiences young people undergo in their last years at school and in their first years of work. Miller and Form tend to assume that all school situations and all work situations are the same. There is evidence to suggest that they differ very much according to broad differences in social class, type of school, occupational level and type of work situation, etc.

For instance, work on aspiration suggests that for groups of school children with similar social backgrounds, there are national differences. Among children of broadly working class origin, in France wishes incline to handicrafts and small farming,(15) in the United States they tend to reflect mobility aspirations,(16) in this country, Germany and parts of Poland, they are directed towards a skilled trade—a "trade in one's hands," to use the stereotyped phrase summing up the vocational aspirations of this section of British youth.(17) Additionally, investigators have noted, and sometimes been dismayed by, the realism of the aspirations of some young people in this country:

"Indeed the fantasy choices of these boys are at a distressingly mundane and realistic level; the majority rarely leave their immediate world. We had expected that in their flights of fancy they would select the more exciting occupations such as pilot, professional footballer, explorer, 'pop' singer, or even the old-fashioned engine driver. Instead we have the boy who expects to be a labourer at the brick yard choosing the very same job in fantasy, and the potential rubber moulder, who, when offered the whole world from which to choose, still wants to be a rubber moulder."[18]

However, investigations agree that while knowledge of wages and hours is very accurate, knowledge of work content and training requirements is very slight. Within the limits of manual work, there is a concentration of aspiration towards skilled trades, and, within them, towards certain favoured trades such as printing, hairdressing, which must mean that a considerable proportion of young people are going to be frustrated. There are several studies showing that young people choose unrealistically but within a realistic range, and, in general, it seems that the poorer the school performance, the lower the realism of aspiration.[19]

An alternative approach is that of the French sociologist, de Maupeou. This relates the adjustment of young workers to the conceptions possessed by them of industrial society in its broadest sense.[20] If these conceptions are inadequate—i.e. do not correspond to the present or future realities of the situation, tension will be built up, and frustration or dissatisfaction will occur. De Maupeou outlines the different conceptions young workers have, and the type of response they will make to industrial situations. There are two difficulties about this approach. The first is the virtual impossibility of defining an "accurate" conception of industrial society in its entirety. Thus, various views which de Maupeou characterizes as "unrealistic" may correspond closely to the immediate future of the industry which a young person is in, even if not to that of industrial society as a whole. Secondly, these conceptions, where they are coherently held at all, and the responses inferred from them may, in fact, develop out of general features of upbringing and experience, and it is to this possibility that we should turn if we wish to understand adjustment problems of different social groups.

AN ALTERNATIVE APPROACH

The above approaches offer many valuable insights. However, evidence from a wide range of research suggests that family, neighbourhood, peer groups, education received, influences from mass media, the extent of formal vocational guidance, all need to be considered, and that experience from these sources, as well as the nature of the work undertaken, are relevant to the development of any particular reaction towards working life. This implies that entering the world of work and adjusting to it is a *process*.

An indication of the nature of this process may be given in the following way: (a) *The socialization of the young person to the world of work*, together with (b) *Previous work experience*, and (c) *Wider social influences*, lead on the one hand to (d) *The formulation of a set of attitudes towards, and expectations about, work*. (a), (b) and (c) together, and (d) provide the explanation for (e) *The actual job entry*, and from this, (f) *Experiences as a worker* lead to a situation of (g) *Adjustment/non-adjustment for the young worker* which can be expressed either by a measure of satisfaction, by a re-formulation of (d) above, by ritualized dissatisfaction, or by job change.

The research already done indicates the sorts of factors which may be considered significant in the process, in more detail. They may be sub-categorized as "informal" and "formal" influences in the adjustment process, and grouped as follows:

1. *Informal influences on* (a) (examples of differentiating variables that research has shown to be significant are given in brackets).

   Family. (Economic level; social class; sibling pressure; family tradition; degree of parental aspiration for young people.)

   Neighbourhood. (Type of residential area and house; stability of residence.)

   School. (Type; area; attitude of teaching staff to pupils as individuals and as group members; school culture.)

   Peer Group. (Ages; occupations if any; social backgrounds; activities.)

2. *Informal influences on* (b)

   Part-time jobs.
   Industrial visits.
   Observations of industrial life.

3. *Informal influences on* (c)

   Communications media.
   Political/religious affiliation.

4. *Dimensions of attitudes and expectations* (d)

   Expectations of life as a worker. (Positive/negative; hopeful/pessimistic; realistic/unrealistic aspirations.)

   Attitude to old life as school pupil. (Positive/negative.)

   "*Core*" *attitude.* (Intrinsic—work valued for itself; extrinsic—work valued as a means to an end; career—work as a status provider.)

5. *Informal influences on* (f)

   Work situation. (Content of work done; conditions; payment; hours; training; relations with authority; relations with other workers.)

   Home situation. (Relations with parents; saving; possessions.)

   Leisure situation. (Friendship patterns and activities; spending; relations with opposite sex.)

Formal influences may be more briefly listed. Complementary to (a) *The socialization of the young person, through* (c) *Wider social influences*, affecting (d) *The formulation of a set of attitudes towards, and expectations about, work* are the school Careers Master with the provision of careers literature, and the Youth Employment Service in its placement function. Affecting (f) *Experiences as a worker* are the firm's personnel department, the trade union, and the Youth Employment Service in its follow-up function. In the broadest terms, the whole process takes place within the context of the labour market, taking account of the number and variety of jobs available and also of the numbers in and qualifications of the youth labour force.[21]

To set out the factors involved in this way gives the impression of a time scale, but it should be remembered that one set of factors does not necessarily cease to operate at a later period. Thus, the influence of, for example, the neighbourhood does not cease when young people actually start work. The continuing influence of the home will be illustrated below.

The influence of the factors in Group 1 affects the amount and nature of previous work experience and access to wider social influences. The interaction of all these factors produces attitudes towards, and expectations about, work, which may or may not influence actual job entry. For example, a young person might derive from previous social influences, the mass media say, a strong desire for a particular satisfaction in work. It does not follow that he will possess the necessary skills to set about translating his desire into reality, in which case his job entry will conform to the usual pattern of the social group from which he comes. The use of the term job "entry" rather than the more usual job "choice" is intentional. The latter has connotations of rational assessment of abilities and opportunities which do not seem to be a general characteristic of those seeking work.[22] Experiences as a worker test the predispositions and attitudes of the new entrant and in turn interact with home and leisure behaviour, resulting, in adjustment or non-adjustment, however it is measured. Additionally, this adjustment process takes place in the context of a labour market situation which differs markedly from area to area and at different periods in time, a situation in which the young person may be in competition with other young people and sometimes with adults. Even such a brief discussion of the process of job adjustment indicates how over-simplified it is to consider only the nature of the work undertaken.[23]

It is not intended, nor would it be possible within the scope of an article to justify in detail all the factors given significance. The identification of such factors is easier than measuring the effects in actual work situations, a problem which is rooted in general difficulties of methodology in the social sciences, nor does it suggest that all are equally important. There is too much research which asks informants to rank money, friends, or a chance to get on, in order of relevance to job satisfaction or depends on questions such as, "Do you like your job?" Such research has the advantage of presenting easily measured indicators of "satisfaction" but it does not do justice to the complexity of the influences and experiences involved; many of the problem areas indicated by the present approach are as yet hardly investigated. Nevertheless it is of value to consider some of them. The examples chosen are, the influence of the home, the school, the formal vocational guidance institutions, attitudes to work, and the general work situation for the new entrant.

THE INFLUENCE OF THE HOME (GROUPS 1 AND 5)

The importance of the home environment in discussing the process of adjustment cannot be over-estimated. In general terms, the recent study by Douglas demonstrates the marked effects of different types of social background on the school performance and the sociomedical histories of individuals.[(24)] This national sample is being followed through into working life. The work of Bernstein has shown that there is a relationship between the forms of language learning and thinking, and the different methods of upbringing of working and middle class groups, so that it is no surprise to find that the social class of parents influences the type and length of education open to and received by their children.[(25)] It follows from this that, since education and occupation are linked, such characteristics as social class and economic level of the family will have a marked influence on the attitudes to and expectations about work, as well as on the type of job entered.[(26)] It is more difficult to identify and describe the processes which result in such attitudes and expectations.

Carter gives the clearest picture of the way in which the process happens for some working class children: visits to the father's place of work, the talk at home about wages and hours, the relief that the working day is over, all convey to the young person the way in which his parents, siblings and relatives—often the people he admires and relies upon most—regard the world of work. From this he will accumulate general impressions of "good" and "bad" jobs, and work which is appropriate for him when the time comes to leave school.[(27)] Reynolds and Shister, in a study of adult workers, suggest that home and neighbourhood experiences make for the development of job "horizons" beyond which few individuals look. As a result, actual job selection often seems casual; it is not an assessment of the market possibilities but an apparently unthinking acceptance of the suggestions and recommendations of relatives and friends.[(28)] However, job horizons may be defined broadly as well as narrowly; there are homes where work is discussed more formally, where parents explore with their children the full range of possibilities and instil career aspirations. It would be valuable to have a more precise analysis of these processes, particularly as it seems that social class divisions are too broad to be more than general predictors of their occurrence. The work of Kahl in the United States and of Swift in this country are important reminders of the complexity of the development of value systems which result in various educational and occupational aspirations.[(29)]

This qualification apart, parental occupation has a general importance both for aspirations and for job entry. There is some evidence to suggest that before taking a job the occupational goals of many young people are higher than their father's occupational level, for example, more boys want skilled manual work than have fathers in skilled manual work, and fewer whose fathers are unskilled want unskilled work for themselves.[30] These aspirations are still connected with parental occupation though; the more ambitious sons of semiskilled or unskilled workers aspire, not to professional jobs, but to skilled trades.[31] Although there is not an absolute relationship between the occupational status of fathers and sons, there is an association, stronger in some groups than others. And even where there are changes in occupation level between father and son, the sons tend to be fairly close to their fathers' level in the occupational hierarchy.[32]

The home background provides continuity when the young person enters work, and again the work of Carter, and of Ferguson and Cunnison, describes its influence. Some families disapprove of job changing, for example, others rarely discuss such decisions; both attitudes are likely to influence the young person's approach to his work. In some circumstances the features of the home influence job performance, particularly in terms of job change, work lost and extent of unemployment.[33] It is also at this time that the long term effects of home background become evident, as Venables has shown in her demonstration of the depressant effect of working class and secondary modern school background on the verbal intelligence of day-release apprentices.[34] However, the continuity of the home influence does not mean that the young person's position within it remains unchanged. A full discussion of the interaction of the young worker and the family group is beyond the scope of this article, but some brief comments may be made. The young persons' wages bring benefits to the family,[35] but economic independence may also be a way of achieving emancipation from the authority of home and family.[36] This may lead to more or less overt parent/child conflict, expressed in disputes about use of money and leisure time, conflict which some research suggests is more frequent in middle class than working class homes.[37] Within working class groups, work in educational sociology would lead us to predict that conflict is more likely where parental and filial aspirations are at variance.[38] But on the whole, even in financial terms, the changes in the home appear to be gradual.[39] Where a home breaks up, however, the effect on working life may be very marked. Ferguson and Cunnison's study indicates a high correlation between broken homes and job change.[40]

THE INFLUENCE OF THE SCHOOL (GROUP 1)

While schools obviously differ from most work situations in their age composition, there may be other important respects in which they are not dissimilar. Current discussions of the educational system have tended to stress its importance as an avenue of social mobility and the barriers impeding the achievement of this. It is also necessary to consider schools as, in many cases, reinforcing the informal patterns of home and neighbourhood. Carter, studying Sheffield school leavers, relates the attitudes found in the five schools he investigated to the predominant attitudes of the populations from which they drew their pupils, a finding reinforced by Coleman's study in the Chicago area.[41] This latter draws attention to the importance of the informal social groupings which develop among school children. Webb, in an impressionistic study of his experiences in a British secondary modern school, argues that the classroom situation contains many elements of informal co-operation among the children, who are as a group in conflict with the teacher. Many industrial situations are similar.[42] Sociologists have stressed the importance of informal groupings in some industrial situations, and such schools are likely to provide good preparation for this aspect of industrial life. This kind of school, usually in slum buildings in decaying city centres, with inadequate facilities and high teacher turnover, is still very common in this country.[43] The dichotomous "us"–"them" view of society characteristic of industrial workers is strengthened by such situations.[44] In addition, both Carter and Webb stress that for this group of young people, which must make up a significant proportion of the urban population, the last year at school is seen as a waste of time, imposed by impersonal social forces, interfering with what the young people feel is the real continuity in their lives—moving from home to work.

In contrast to the implication of Miller and Form's approach, and whatever the children themselves may feel, the school situation can be seen not only as the antithesis of the industrial situation, but also as one where experience helping the adjustment to working life may be gained, and where attitudes easing the transition to industry are developed. Much more research on the inter-relationship between home, school and industry is required.

THE INFLUENCE OF FORMAL INSTITUTIONS (GROUPS 6 AND 7)

The formal aid given to young people in the process of adjustment to working life by the schools and the Youth Employment Service should be briefly considered. The range and content of vocational instruction in schools varies, but suffers from a view held by many school teachers that their job is to provide a "general education", an aim absolving them from any responsibility for the details of the mundane problems of their children's vocational prospects; from the fact that few teachers have had any experience of work either in factory, office or shop, and often disparage such work; and from the fact that few have any knowledge of the occupational range of the local community. Literature about schools' career services is slight. Some schools have a careers' master who has a stock, large or small, of pamphlets; in others the Headmaster gives a talk to leavers. In a few, various representatives of firms are asked to visit, and take the opportunity of recruiting. There are organized works visits in some schools, which give a general impression of factory atmosphere, but it is not clear whether these do more than reinforce the attitudes, positive or negative, which young people already have towards industrial life.[45]

The Youth Employment Officer visits the school at least twice, once for a general discussion with leavers, and the second time in the term before leaving, for an interview with each child. In theory he has for this meeting all the details of the child's career to hand, but some schools do not co-operate.[46] In others, teachers are present at the interview and inhibit the child's responses.[47] In theory, the function of the Youth Employment Service is three fold: to ascertain a child's abilities and inclinations; to provide the child with a knowledge of a range of occupations compatible with these, and to give some idea of the content of and prospects in the work that would be done; finally, to offer some suggestions for placement.[48] However, Carter's and Jahoda's work has shown that, for many young people, regardless of social background, only the latter function is considered. The Youth Employment Service is seen merely as a means of getting a job if one has not already been fixed up. The follow-up procedures seem to be even less effective. The structural problems of the Youth Employment Service are discussed elsewhere.[49] As part of the process of adjustment to working life, these formal agencies are relatively ineffective in comparison with informal influences.

ATTITUDES TOWARDS WORK (GROUP 4)

Informal and formal background features of the types described above create general attitudes towards, and expectations of work, and some studies of these attitudes, both among schoolchildren and adult workers have been undertaken, mainly in the United States. In these studies, three basic or "core" attitudes to work are distinguishable, each itself capable of subdivision: an "intrinsic" or vocational attitude, in which work, and/or elements of the work situation are valued in themselves; an "extrinsic" or instrumental one in which work is seen as a means of providing external satisfaction, whether financial, or in terms of status, such as adultness; and a "career-orientated" one, in which work is seen in terms of social mobility for the individual.[55] Since the range of experience in socialization is so broad, it is likely that elements of all three attitudes are to be found in the majority of people, but certain types of background experience will tend to reinforce some at the expense of others. It is clear that any discussion of work satisfaction which ignores these variations in attitude is inadequate.[51] It is also probably important to distinguish another "core" attitude which cannot really be subsumed under the other three—a desire for security. This manifests itself particularly in conditions of unemployment.[52] Some sociologists have also argued that it is a feature of bureaucratization.[53] It appears among young people in Britain today in expressions such as "having something to fall back on" and "having a trade in one's hands." Such an attitude is partly instrumental, in that it springs from a fear of not being able to maintain accepted living standards, but it may be useful to treat it separately.[(54)]

Irrespective of parental occupational background, there is some evidence that most young people enter working life with elements of an intrinsic orientation.[(55)] Thus the Eppels remark in their article, "Moral Beliefs of Young Workers":

> "There is at this stage a considerable amount of potential personal identification with work, and a fairly strong feeling of personal responsibility to complete what has been undertaken. The current stereotypes of adolescents tend to under-estimate the extent to which this is true, and unfortunately the conditions in industry often facilitate the dissipation of this potential sentiment, and its substitution by apathy or discontent."[(56)]

Their evidence is based on studies of day-release apprentices. A study of those in unskilled occupations might lead to a modification of the generalization. If the view presented here, of work adjustment as a process, is correct, a great deal of social selection had occurred prior to the entry into apprenticeship. Ginzberg also found the same attitudes, which he says, change with age, tending towards a greater instrumentality, both in young workers, and in those still at school. The same qualification applies, as his samples were weighted in favour of middle class groups.[(57)]

The relevance of this conceptualization of attitudes towards work lies in the possibility of conflict between the attitudes developed in the young person, and the work situation he enters, either in the terms of attitudes of other workers or of the nature of the job. To take a hypothetical example, a boy who has developed an intrinsic attitude towards work as a result of influences from, say, school and peer groups, but whose home persuaded him to take a piece-rate job with the possibility of high pay, might find himself in a work situation in which his desires were continually thwarted by his experience. On the other hand, the attitudes of the young person may coincide more or less completely with those of his fellow workers. Much more work on the distribution of attitudes between different social groups needs to be done.

THE GENERAL WORK SITUATION FOR THE NEW ENTRANT ADJUSTMENT (GROUP 5 AND (g))

Detailed information about the general conditions in which the adjustment takes place is not given here. The numbers and distribution of young people can be obtained from *Census Reports* and the occupational level and types of jobs entered are described in the annual article in the May issue of the *Ministry of Labour Gazette*. There is also some transfer during the first years of working life from small to large firms, a feature applying more to boys than to girls, and most especially to boy apprentices.[(58)] Such features set limits to the range of possibilities open and may even underlie what appears to be an individual decision to change a job.

As mentioned above, the majority of fifteen year old male leavers either go into apprenticeships or some form of unskilled work; almost all male clerks have at least one year's further schooling. For girls there are few apprenticeships, so that most go into clerical or unskilled work in factories or shops. Some girls classified as unskilled do have several months' training in some firms in the hosiery and shoe industries. But for the majority of unskilled boys and girls, induction consists of a brief interview, being taken to the place of work, and handed over to the chargehand or foreman, who either shows what is to be done, or assigns the entrant to another worker for the same purpose. Many of these young people will remain in that job, or type of job, for the remainder of their working lives, and will have no further training.(59) Many young entrants do not even get shown over their firm.(60)

Among other groups of employees, opportunities for formal training are not uniform. Apprentices fall into two groups—those who go into firms willing and able to give them formal training, and those who do not receive such training. Actual procedure has grown up as a response to pressures from craft unions to maintain the exlusiveness of their craft, from employers for cheap labour, and from technological demand.(61) Apprenticeships last five years for the most part, and have no certification other than the right to hold a union card on the completion of time, in some cases.

Boys who enter large-scale modern engineering works often get at least one year's formal training of a very high standard, coupled with at least three years' day or block release at technical college, which is semi-compulsory. Many of these firms are now demanding "O" levels, i.e. an extra year at school, from their recruits. Some other industries such as printing make large scale use of day-release facilities. But those who enter small firms often have neither any formal training from the firm, nor are they allowed or encouraged to take day or block release. Their apprenticeship is as mate to another worker, who "shows them the ropes". An in-between group struggles—with marked lack of success as the *Crowther Report* shows—at evening courses.(62) Among clerical and shop workers the situation in respect of induction and particularly training is, if anything, worse—a situation documented in a recent book on commercial apprenticeships.(63)

Thus the multiplicity of training procedures, the variations in their standard, and their uneven availability are all potential sources of dissatisfaction. Many more can be postulated from the examples given in the scheme, such as payment, hours worked, and relations with authority, but the above suffices to indicate the range of variables within the work situation. It is in the light of this discussion that some studies of adjustment to work should be considered. At first it seems working life is very attractive compared with school. Young people mention especially the lack of formal discipline and the fact of earning. The demands made by the job are not too arduous. There is a general feeling of satisfaction.(64) In terms of the whole process of adjustment to working life, the negative attitudes of young people towards their last year at school assume importance as a possible explanation.

But for those whose aspirations are not fulfilled, or whose grasp of the demand their work will make is inaccurate, the feeling of satisfaction may be ephemeral. Also for some it may be that further experience gained at work induces consideration of a range of alternative occupations now closed to the young person because of the work he has entered.(65) In confirmation of this, where there is dissatisfaction, it appears to increase with length of work experience. In Tenen's study of unskilled young workers:

> "It soon became evident that the most prevalent attitude to work and the work authority among the adolescents in these factories was that of dissatisfaction, even resentment. Neither youth nor sex was found to be the decisive factor in shaping these attitudes. On the contrary, among both sexes the average number of complaints increased with age."(66)

In a Glasgow study of day-release apprentices, the Eppels also found that dissatisfaction as measured by dislike of jobs, and frequency of changes, increased with age.(67) Kelchner, in pre-war Germany, found that it was after two years of work experience that worries about unemployment and complaints about jobs reached their peak.(68) In Austria, Lazarsfeld found in a pioneer study that dissatisfaction with work was expressed by one quarter of the group studied in the year after leaving school, but by three-fifths after seven years' work experience.(69) Vollmer and Kinney report an increase of dissatisfaction in an all age sample in U.S. ordnance factories until the age of thirty, after which it declines.(70)

It is clear then, that while there is no evidence that the transition between the institutions of school and work leads to any kind of sudden traumatic experience, some evidence exists that for a minority at least there is a delayed realization that work may have more frustrations than were expected by the school leaver. This only begins the explanation. It is essential to be able to specify which social groups and which work situations are in conflict and, equally importantly, which coincide.

CONCLUSION

The above examples, tentative and partial as they are, reveal the gaps in our knowledge of the process of moving into working life. On the one hand much of the literature is concerned with the aspirations of schoolchildren, who are, of course, much easier to contact. On the other, general studies of adolescence are overwhelmingly concerned with biological and sexual development, and the major social changes of the adolescent period are either ignored or discussed quite briefly and speculatively.(71) The theories of Miller and Form and de Maupeou have certain defects as approaches to the problem of working life. It is hoped that the present approach will serve students of the field both by establishing a framework for the interpretation of previous work, and by generating problems for solution. The complexity of the inter-relationships involved is apparent, but a recognition of their existence as opposed to the accumulation of more or less *ad hoc* correlations must contribute to more fruitful research. The subject like most in industrial sociology is a very open one. Whatever the specific value of the approach outlined, the authors are convinced that it is only by attempting to integrate on-going and future research within some such general framework that the fragmentary state of existing work can be superseded.

REFERENCES

1. The expressions "adjustment" and "non-adjustment" refer to the variety of attitudes and behaviour of young people in the work situation. This may be measured in many ways, indices ranging, for example, from expressions of satisfaction and dissatisfaction, through absenteeism, to job change. By the use of the term "adjustment", the authors in no way wish to imply that there should be any one-way adaptation of the young worker to whatever situation he may find himself in.
2. *Statistics of Education*, 1964, part 1, Table 2, H.M.S.O.
3. *Ministry of Labour Gazette*, May 1965, 208. Unskilled and semiskilled includes some jobs with unspecified "planned training".
4. A paraphrase of the Report of the Departmental Committee of the Board of Education, 1916, Juvenile Education in Relation to Employment after the War, by P. I. Kitchen, in *From Learning to Earning*, Faber, 1944, 12. German literature on the subject is more extensive than British, and much more thorough. Studies date back even earlier, e.g. K. Frankenstein: Die Lage der Fabrikarbeiterinnen in der Deutschen Großstadt, *Schmollers Jahrbuch*, 1888, cited in G. Wurzbacher *et al.*: *Die Junge Arbeiterin*, Munich, Juventa, 1960.
5. For a discussion, see Kitchen: *op. cit.*, 51–58.
6. Central Advisory Council for Education—England. (*The Crowther Report*) "*15–18*", **1**, 143, H.M.S.O., 1959.
7. Carter, M. P. (1962) *Home, School and Work*, Pergamon; *Crowther Report*, *op. cit.*; Veness, T. (1962) *School Leavers*, Methuen.
8. The approach developed here is relevant to the study of occupational choice. Theories of occupational choice have been developed by: Ginzberg, E., *et. al.* (1951) *Occupational Choice*, London, and Jaide, W. (1961) *Die Berufswahl*, Munich, Juventa.
9. As examples of a general type see: Crow, L. D., and Crow, A. (1956) *Adolescent Development and Adjustment*, McGraw-Hill, Ch. 16, Vocational Adjustment; and Lean, W. (1960) Work Problems of Young Factory Employees, *Personnel Practice Bulletin*, **16**, 26–30.
10. For a general comparison of the problems of the adolescent in advanced as opposed to undeveloped societies, see: Davis, K. (1944) Adolescence and the Social Structure, *Annals of the American Academy of Political and Social Science*, **236**, 8–16, and Mead, M. (1944) *Coming of Age in Samoa*, Pelican.
11. For example: Dansereau, H. (1961) Work and the Teenager, *Annals of the American Academy of Political and Social Sciences*, **338**, 44–52; Harris, D. (1957) Psychological Aspects of the Rôle of Work in Adolescent Development, *The American Child*, **39**; Kitchen, *op. cit.*, 10; Brew, J. MacAlistair (1957) *Youth and Youth Groups*, Faber, 15f. For a similar French view see: Rousselet, J. (1961) *L'Adolescent en Apprentissage*, Paris, Presses Universitaires de France.

12. MILLER, D. C., and FORM, W. H. (1951) *Industrial Sociology*, New York, Harper, ed., Chs. XV–XVIII.
13. MILLER and FORM: *op. cit.*, 622. Miller and Form do consider adjustmen tto work as part of a socilization process. But their main emphasis is on the clash of values between pre-work and work experience. They devote only six out of almost 200 pages to socialization within the home and school (523–529).
14. BELL, H. M. (1938) *Youth Tell their Story*, American Council on Education, Washington D. C. Cited in Miller and Form: *op. cit.*, 592.
15. MAUPEOU, N. DE (1960) Le Jeune Ouvrier dans l'Industrie—Une Situation de Minorité, *Sociologie du Travail*, **2**, 39–51.
16. Among others: STEPHENSON, R. (1957) Mobility Orientation and Stratification of 1000 Ninth Graders, *Am. Soc. Rev.*, **22**, 204–212.
17. LAZARSFELD, P. (1931) Jugend und Beruf, *Quellen und Studien zur Jugendkunde*, **8**, Jena, Gustav Fischer; Veness: *op. cit.*, 93f.
18. LIVERSEDGE, W. (1962) Life Chances, *Soc. Rev.*, **10**, 24.
19. Among many studies the following are particularly interesting: HOOD, H. B. (1951) Occupational Preferences of Secondary Modern School-children, *Educational Rev.*, **4**, 55f; JAHODA, G. (1953) Social Class Attitudes and Levels of Occupational Aspiration in Secondary Modern School Leavers, *Br. J. Psy.*, **44**, 95–107; PALLISTER, H. (1938) Vocational Preferences of School Leavers in a Scottish Industrial Area, *Br. J. Psy.*, **29**, 144–166; VENESS: *op. cit.*; WILSON, M. D. (1953) The Vocational Preferences of Secondary Modern School-children, *Br. J. Ed. Psy.*, **23**, 97–113, and 163–179. See also: MORLAND, J. K. (1960) Educational and Occupational Aspirations of Mill and Town Schoolchildren in a Southern Community, *Social Forces*, **39**, 169f.
20. This is based on a memorandum, *Young Workers in Modern Industrial Society. Types of Behaviour: an Interpretation.* (Unpublished), which Madame de Maupeou has sent us, but see also: MAUPEOU, N. DE (1961) Le Jeune Ouvrier ..., *op. cit.*; and her Pour Une Sociologie des Jéunes dans La Societé Industrielle, *Annales Economies-Societes-Civilisations*, **1**; Niveau d'Aspiration, Statut Professionel et Revenue, *Sociologie du Travail*, **4**, 1962, 15–33.
21. For examples of similar approaches, see: GORDON, C. W. (1957) *The Social System of the High School*, Glencoe, Free Press; CAMPBELL, A. *et al.* (1960) *The American Voter*, New York, Wiley.
22. GREEN, B., KEIL, T., and RIDDELL, D. *Occupational Choice—the Social Setting*, forthcoming.
23. FRIEDMANN might be criticised on this score. See FRIEDMANN, G. (1955) *Industrial Society*, Glencoe, Ill., Free Press.
24. DOUGLAS, J. W. B. (1964) *The Home and the School*, McGibbon and Kee.
25. BERNSTEIN, B. Social Class and Linguistic Development: A Theory of Social Learning, in HALSEY, A. H. *et al.* (eds.) (1961) *Education, Economy and Society*, Glencoe, Ill., Free Press, 288–314.
26. Central Advisory Council for Education (England): *Early Leaving*, H.M.S.O., 1954; *Crowther Report*: *op. cit.*; Carter: *op. cit.*
27. CARTER: *op. cit.*, 45, 53.
28. REYNOLDS, L., and SHISTER, J. (1949) *Job Horizons*, New York, Harper, Ch. 6.
29. KAHL, J. Common Man Boys, in *Education, Economy and Society*, *op. cit.*, 348–366. The whole of part 4, on social factors in educational achievement, is relevant. SWIFT, D. "Who Passes the 11 + ?", *New Society*, 5/3/64, 6–10.
30. FERGUSON, T., and CUNNISON, J. (1951) *The Young Wage Earner*, O.U.P., 110.
31. See reference 19, and DUFTY, N. F. (1961) The Relationship between Paternal Occupation and Occupational Choice, *Int. J. Comp. Soc.*, **2**, 81–87; SAMSON, R., and STEFFLRE, B. Like Father ... Like Son, *Personnel Guidance J.*, **31**, No. 1, October 1952;

JENSON, P., and KIRCHNER, W. (1955) A National Answer to the Question, "Do Sons Follow their Fathers' Occupations?", *J. App. Psy.*, **39**, 419–421.

32. GLASS, D., and HALL, J. (1954) Social Mobility in Britain: A Study of Intergeneration Change in Status, in D. Glass (ed.): *Social Mobility in Britain*, Routledge, 177.
33. CARTER: *op. cit.*, 190; FERGUSON and CUNNISON: *op. cit.* 25, 30.
34. VENABLES, E. The Reserve of Ability in Part-time Technical Courses, *Universities Quarterly*, **17**, 1962, 60–75.
35. ZWEIG, F. *Labour, Life and Poverty*, Gollancz, 1949.
36. CONNEL, W. F. *et al. Growing Up in an Australian City*, Melbourne, 1957.
37. EPPEL, E., and EPPEL, M. (1953) Young Workers at a County College, *Br. J. Ed. Psy.*, **23**, 29–44, 87–96, especially the second part; KOSKAS, R. (1949) L'Adolescent et sa Famille, *Enfance*, **2**, 68–71; PITTS, J. (1961) The Family and Peer Groups, in N. Bell and E. Vogel: *A Reader on the Family*, Routledge, Ch. 21.
38. For example, HOGGART, R. (1958) *The Uses of Literacy*, Pelican; JACKSON, B., and MARSDEN, D. (1962) *Education and the Working Class*, Routledge.
39. There are few studies of the actual amounts earned and money spent amongst young wage earners. Mark Abrams in his study, *The Teenage Consumer*, Press Exchange Papers, 1959, defines the teenage group in such a way as to include unmarried people up to 25 years old, giving a very distorted impression of the amount of money available to the young person between 15 and 18. See the tables in Carter: *op. cit.*, 152, and Ferguson and Cunnison: *op. cit.*, 100.
40. FERGUSON and CUNNISON: *op. cit.*, 31. See also the interesting table in SCHULZ, E. (1960) *Elternhaus und Lehrling*, Institut für Berufserziehung an der Universität Köln, 19, showing that a father's death has a noticeable effect on occupational choice, and FRIEND, J. G. (1948) Work Adjustment in Relation to Family Background, *J. Social Casework*, **29**, 89–93.
41. CARTER: *op. cit.*, Ch. 3, and COLEMAN, J. S. (1961) *The Adolescent Society*, Glencoe, Ill., Free Press.
42. WEBB, J. (1962) The Sociology of a School, *Br. J. Soc.*, **13**, 264–272. See also Carter: *op. cit.* Ch. 4.
43. Central Advisory Council for Education (England), *The Newsom Report; Half Our Future*, H.M.S.O., 1963; National Union of Teachers, *The State of our Schools*, 1964; Government White Paper, *The School Building Survey*, 1962, H.M.S.O., 1965.
44. See GOLDTHORPE, J., and LOCKWOOD, D. (1963) Affluence and the British Class Structure, *Soc. Rev.*, **11**, 133–163.
45. A study of Lancashire school leavers makes some comment about these topics: JAHODA, G. (1952) Job Attitudes and Job Choice among Secondary Modern School Leavers, *Occup. Psy.*, **26**, 125–140, 206–224, especially the latter part.
46. JAHODA, G., and CHALMERS, A. (1964) The Youth Employment Service, A Consumer Perspective, *Occup. Psy.*, **37**, 20 f.
47. CARTER: *op. cit.*, 117–118.
48. FRANCE, G. (1962) The Youth Employment Service: A look from Within, *Technical Education*, **4**, No. 3, 20–23, and No. 5, 37–40.
49. See the latter part of GREEN, KEIL and RIDDELL: *op cit.*
50. The authors have drawn, among others, on the work of FRIEDMANN, G., *op. cit.*; HERZBERG, F. *et al.* (1959) *The Motivation to Work*, Chapman & Hall; REYNOLDS and SHISTER, *op. cit.;* BOGGS, S. (1963) The Values of Laboratory Workers, *Human Organization*, **22**, 207–215.
51. For example, KLEIN, L. (1963) *Meaning in Work*, Fabian Pamphlet.
52. There were no systematic studies in Britain in the 1930's but much interesting work was done in Germany, e.g. FRANZEN-HELLERSBERG, L. (1932) *Die Jugendliche Arbeiterin*, Tübingen, Mohr; KELCHNER, M. (1929) Kummer und Trost Jugendliche Arbeiterinnen, *Forschungen zur Volkspsychologie und Soziologie*, **6**, Leipzig, Hirschfeld.

A good bibliography, especially of work relating to young female workers is contained in WURZBACHER: *op. cit.*

53. Cf. MERTON, R. (1957) *Social Theory and Social Structure*, Glencoe, Ill., Free Press, Ch. 6; WHYTE, W. H. (1957) *The Organization Man*, Jonathan Cape.
54. Other researchers have posited a "service" oriented attitude. In our terms, this would be a sub-category of "intrinsic" orientation. See SCHWARZKELLER, H. D. (1960) Values and Occupational Choice, *Social Forces*, **39**, 126–135.
55. JAHODA, G. (1960) Job Attitudes and Job Choice ..., *op. cit.* Part I; DUFTY, N. F., Vocational Choices of 13 to 14 year old Males, *Australian Journal of Education*, **4**, No. I, 38–56.
56. EPPEL, E. M. (1963) Moral Beliefs of Young Workers, *Br. J. Sociol.*, **14**, 215.
57. GINZBERG *et al.: op. cit.*
58. KEIL, E. T., RIDDELL, D. S., and TIPTON, C. (1963) The Size of Firms Entered by Young Workers, *Br. J. Ind. Rel.*, **1**, 408–411. The same situation has been reported for West Germany; see GEGLER, F., and FERBER, R., Berufsnachwuchs und Berufswechsel, *Das Arbeitsamt*, Band 2, March 1951, No. 3.
59. In the United States, only 25 per cent of young entrants get any training, according to BARTLEMAN, A. (1961) Teenagers—Industry's Hidden Asset, *Business*, **91**, No. 8, 58–60.
60. PAQUIN, J. A. (1961) An Examination of 14 Employee Induction Programmes, *Personnel Practice Bulletin*, **17**, No. 3, 38–42.
61. WILLIAMS, G. *Recruitment to Skilled Trades*, Routledge, 1957.
62. *Crowther Report: op. cit.*, 354 f. See also ASHTON, G. (1965) Enrolment and Examination Success of Day Release Students by Size of Firm, *Br. J. Ind. Rel.*, **3**, 90–94.
63. TONKINSON, E. *et al.* (1962) *Commercial Apprenticeships*, University of London Press.
64. CARTER: *op. cit.*, ch. 9.
65. LIPSET and MALM show that first job is the best predictor of subsequent career; LIPSET, S., and MALM, F., First Jobs and Career Patterns, *Am. J. of Econ. & Sociol.*, **14**, 247–261.
66. TENEN, C. (1947) The Adolescent in the Factory, *Br. J. Ed. Psy.*, **17**, 76.
67. EPPEL and EPPEL: *op. cit.*
68. KELCHNER: *op. cit.*
69. LAZARSFELD: *op. cit.*
70. VOLLMER, H., and KINNEY, J. (1955) Age, Education and Job Satisfaction, *Personnel*, **32**, No. 1, 38–43.
71. A good review of such studies is that by MUUSS, R. E.: *Theories of Adolescence*, New York, Random House, 1962. The authors looked through eighteen general textbooks of adolescence without discovering one that emphasized the new adjustments necessary to the rôle of worker.

14. *The Entry of School Leavers into Employment**

JOAN MAIZELS

IN order to select a representative sample of employers and young people for interviewing in a research study now being carried out in the borough of Willesden, it was first necessary to discover in some detail the industries and occupations in which young people were employed in the borough as well as the sizes of the employing firms. Since this information is not available from official statistics, two sources of information were used: the placements records of the local Youth Employment bureau and a direct inquiry of the employing firms. The present note summarizes the main statistical results.

THE PLACEMENTS RECORDS

Since the objective was to obtain information about the employment of those over fifteen but under eighteen years of age, the aggregate placements over the three years October 1960 to September 1963 were analysed.† It soon became evident, however, that a study of placement records in rather more detail than that required solely for the purpose of constructing a sample might yield interesting results. Accordingly, the details noted included not only the industry, occupation and size of firm, but also first or subsequent placement, placement within or without the borough, type of secondary education and the age at placement.

First Placements

Over the three year period, some 5,880 young people left school, of whom 45 per cent were placed in their first jobs by the Willesden Youth Employment Bureau (see Table 1). The proportion placed in their first employment was, however, twice as high for secondary modern school leavers (56 per cent)

* This article presents some preliminary findings from an inquiry into the employment of young people under eighteen in the borough of Willesden. The inquiry, which has been made possible by a grant from the Joseph Rowntree Memorial Trust, is being conducted under the auspices of the National Institute of Economic and Social Research.

† I am indebted to the Middlesex Education Committee for their co-operation in making the relevant records available.

(Reprinted from *British Journal of Industrial Relations*, vol. 3, No. 1, 1965, pp. 77–89, by permission of the editor and author.)

TABLE 1

SCHOOL LEAVERS AND FIRST PLACEMENTS BY THE YOUTH EMPLOYMENT SERVICE: WILLESDEN IN RELATION TO TOTAL FOR ENGLAND

	School leavers				Proportion placed by Youth Employment Service			
	Secondary modern	Technical	Grammar	Total	Secondary modern	Technical	Grammar	Total
	(No.)				(Per cent)			
Willesden (1960/61–1962/63)								
Boys	1,770	176	890	2,836	66	44	30	53
Girls	1,835	561	649	3,045	47	19	24	37
Total	3,605	737	1,539	5,881	56	25	27	45
England (1959–62)	(000's)							
Boys	646	66	136	848	39	33	28	37
Girls	609	67	120	796	41	33	23	37
Total	1,255	133	256	1,644	40	33	25	37

Sources: Annual Reports of the Willesden Youth Employment Committee, 1960–63; *The Work of the Youth Employment Service, 1959–1962*, National Youth Employment Council (London, 1962).

as for technical or grammar school leavers (25–27 per cent). These results are not too different from the corresponding figures for England* for which the proportion of all school leavers placed in their first jobs in 1959–62 was 37 per cent, while the proportion for secondary modern school leavers was above those for the technical and grammar school groups.

Willesden's placement figures differ from those for England as a whole, however, in that the proportion for boys exceeds that for girls in each educational category, particularly among secondary modern school leavers; by contrast, the percentages for boys and girls for each school leaving group in England were virtually identical. The proportion of school leavers placed by the Youth Employment Service in Willesden is somewhat higher than the national figure in every category except for technical school girls.

An examination of each year's placement figures (Table 2) shows that the proportion of first placements to the number of leavers was by no means constant. In fact, the total number of leavers increased by over 10 per cent from the first year to the third, but the proportion placed by the bureau fell by 20 percentage points. The fall was most marked for girls leaving technical and grammar school courses while, in contrast, the proportion of placements of technical school boys almost doubled over the period,

* *The Work of the Youth Employment Service, 1959–1962*, National Youth Employment Council (London, 1962).

TABLE 2
SCHOOL LEAVERS AND FIRST PLACEMENTS BY THE YOUTH EMPLOYMENT SERVICE IN WILLESDEN: EACH YEAR, 1960/61–1962/63

	School leavers (No.)				Proportion placed by Youth Employment Service[a] (Per cent)			
	Secondary modern	Technical	Grammar	Total	Secondary modern	Technical	Grammar	Total
1960/61:								
Boys	587	94	222	903	75	38	37	62
Girls	592	142	152	886	60	46	45	55
Total	1,179	236	374	1,789	67	43	40	58
1961/62:								
Boys	626	52	262	940	66	39	31	54
Girls	737	193	216	1,146	36	10	14	28
Total	1,363	245	478	2,086	50	16	23	40
1962/63:								
Boys	557	30	406	993	58	73	25	45
Girls	506	226	281	1,013	48	10	21	32
Total	1,063	256	687	2,006	53	17	24	38

Source: *Annual Reports* of the Willesden Youth Employment Committee, 1960–63.

[a] Including placements outside the borough.

though the numbers involved were relatively small. Such year-to-year differences may reflect changes in local employment conditions and the ease or difficulty with which employment is obtained; possibly, also, they reflect changes within the bureau itself, in personnel, in methods of work and in the kind of vocational help required. It is interesting to note that in the same period, the number of subsequent placements rose so that the total number of placements remained more or less stable during the three years of inquiry.

Since the majority of school leavers are from secondary modern schools, these are also the principal users of the Youth Employment Service. For England as a whole, three-quarters of all school leavers in 1959–62 were from secondary modern schools;* moreover, this group uses the Youth Employment Service more intensively than do other school leaving groups, representing a higher proportion as placements than as leavers (Table 3). Similarly in Willesden, the modern school leavers provide the majority of all leavers and use the Youth Employment Service more intensively than do others. The relatively recent extension of the Youth Employment Service to secondary grammar and technical schools may be one reason for their present less-intensive use of the Service. On the other hand, it seems more

* *Ibid.*

probable that technical and grammar school leavers have less need to use the Service than have their secondary modern contemporaries; teachers in technical schools, for example, have usually had experience in, and retained contacts with, industry and commerce, while the qualifications and relative maturity of grammar school leavers may make it easier for them to find employment by themselves.

TABLE 3

SCHOOL LEAVERS AND FIRST PLACEMENTS BY THE YOUTH EMPLOYMENT SERVICE: WILLESDEN IN RELATION TO TOTAL FOR ENGLAND

	Secondary modern	Technical	Grammar	Total	
	(Per cent of total)				(No.)
Willesden (1960/61–1962/63)					
Boys: School leavers	63	6	31	100	(2,836)
First placements[a]	78	5	17	100	(1,517)
Girls: School leavers	61	18	21	100	(3,045)
First placements[a]	76	10	14	100	(1,126)
Total: School leavers	62	12	26	100	(5,881)
First placements[a]	77	7	16	100	(2,643)
England (1959–62)					(000's)
Boys: School leavers	76	8	16	100	(848)
First placements	81	7	12	100	(312)
Girls: School leavers	77	8	15	100	(796)
First placements	84	7	9	100	(297)
Total: School leavers	76	8	16	100	(1,644)
First placements	82	7	11	100	(610)

Source: As for Table 1

[a] Including placements outside the borough.

Subsequent placements

The extent to which the work of the Youth Employment Service in the country as a whole is devoted to helping school leavers find their first employment is shown by the fact that in the three years 1959–62 rather more than half of all placements of boys and three-fifths of the placements of girls in England were of school leavers entering their first jobs.* The corresponding proportions were very similar for Willesden's placements but these conceal very sharp differences between the secondary modern group and the rest. Only two-fifths of the placements of boys from secondary modern courses relate to first employment (see Table 4) compared with over four-fifths of the placements of boys from grammar and technical courses. For girls the proportions were three-fifths and nine-tenths respectively.

The relatively high proportion of subsequent placements for secondary modern school leavers in Willesden reflects, in the main, the fact that almost

* *Ibid.*

half the placements of boys and two-fifths of the placements of girls relate to the 16–17-year-old age group. The school leavers at 15, who are predominantly from secondary modern courses, have had, generally, a longer exposure to the risk of job-change. The figures suggest that the risk of job-change may be higher for boys than for girls and very much higher for both among secondary modern school leavers than among leavers from technical and grammar schools.

At first glance, these results might appear to reflect unfavourably on the vocational guidance and placement services of the Youth Employment

TABLE 4

FIRST AND SUBSEQUENT PLACEMENTS OF SECONDARY MODERN COURSE SCHOOL-LEAVERS IN RELATION TO AGE: WILLESDEN, 1960/61–1962/63

	Boys			Girls		
	Age 15	Age 16/17 (Per cent)	Total	Age 15	Age 16/17 (Per cent)	Total
First placements[a]	65	18	42	78	23	56
Subsequent placements[a]	35	82	58	22	77	44
Total	100	100	100	100	100	100
(No.)	(1,523)	(1,493)	(3,016)	(964)	(644)	(1,608)

Source: Placements Register, Willesden Youth Employment Bureau.

[a] Including placements outside the borough.

Bureau, but this inference would not necessarily be justified. Young people presumably use the Youth Employment Service at different stages after leaving school and the second placement totals will certainly have included boys and girls with previous work experience seeking the help of the bureau for the first time. Further examination of the records would therefore be necessary to verify whether those placed in subsequent employment had also obtained their first employment through the bureau. Further scrutiny of the placements register would also be required to discover what proportion of subsequent placements relates to the same individuals. Only then would it be possible to estimate the degree of job-change occurring among young people originally placed by the bureau and the extent to which the bureau is used by newcomers seeking a change in employment.

It would be of interest to know how typical of the work of other bureaux is the ratio of first to subsequent placements of secondary modern school leavers which is apparent in Willesden. For while local conditions of full employment may make it easier for young people to change their jobs when these do not seem suitable or satisfactory for them, other factors may be important; the risk of job-change itself may be higher in some firms or in some types of employment.

Placements by occupational group

The extent to which different types of secondary courses appear to supply entrants to different occupations is shown in Table 5. A striking contrast in occupational distribution between selective and non-selective school leavers exists for both boys and girls. The secondary modern school boy placed by the bureau becomes predominantly a manual worker in unskilled or semi-skilled work, while the majority of technical and grammar school

TABLE 5

FIRST PLACEMENTS BY OCCUPATIONAL GROUP: WILLESDEN, 1960/61–1962/63

	Boys			Girls		
	Modern	Technical and Grammar	Total	Modern	Technical and Grammar	Total
		(Per cent)			(Per cent)	
Unskilled and semi-skilled manual:						
Factory	49	4	39	24	8	22
Other	22	7	19	7	—	6
Sub-total	71	11	58	31	8	28
Clerical and other non-manual	4	47	13	46	83	51
Sales assistants	12	5	11	15	4	13
Apprentices	13	37	18	8	5	8
Total	100	100	100	100	100	100
(No.)	(845)	(236)	(1,081)	(654)	(107)	(761)

Source: As for Table 4.

[a] Excluding placements outside the borough.

boys are placed either as apprentices or in clerical and other non-manual employment. The great majority of technical and grammar school girls are placed in clerical work whereas the girls from non-selective schools are placed, in the main, either in clerical work on in factories or shops.

For the secondary modern school leaver, moreover, the concentration of subsequent placements in manual work is even higher than for first placements. For boys, the proportion of placements in manual occupations rose from 71 per cent to 84 per cent from first to subsequent employment, evidently as a result of an increased incidence of placements as van boys. For girls, the corresponding proportion in manual work, mainly in factories, was almost twice as high for subsequent as for first placements (59 per cent compared with 31 per cent).

Further study would be required to discover how far the apparent shift to manual work from first to subsequent placements of secondary modern school leavers occurred mainly among those originally placed by the bureau or among newcomers. In this way it would be possible to check the number and circumstances of young people who may find themselves, a year or more after leaving school, in less skilled work than that of their immediate post-school days.

Placements by size of firm

A research note in an earlier issue of this *Journal** described the results of an inquiry made during the course of a research project in Leicester

TABLE 6

FIRST PLACEMENTS[a] BY SIZE OF FIRM: WILLESDEN COMPARED WITH LEICESTER

Size of firm (No. employed)	Willesden			Leicester		
	Boys	Girls	Total	Boys	Girls	Total
	(Per cent)					
Up to 100	62	56	60	54	34	44
101–250	13	17	15	16	17	17
251–500				19	34	26
501–1,000	4	6	5			
Over 1,000	20	21	20	11	15	13
Total	100	100	100	100	100	100
(No.)[b]	(991)	(699)	(1,690)	(2,170)	(1,990)	(4,160)

Sources: As for Table 4; List of Registered Factories & Workshops, Town Hall, Willesden; Shops Inspectorate. E. Teresa Keil, David S. Riddell and Colin B. Tipton, "A Research Note: The Entry of School Leavers into Employment", *British Journal of Industrial Relations*, vol. 1, No. 3 (Oct. 1963).

[a] For Willesden, first placements by the Youth Employment Bureau (excluding placements outside the borough); for Leicester, all school leavers entering their first employment.

[b] The Willesden totals exclude a small number of boys and girls for whom size of employing firm was not known.

into the size of firm in which young people took their first job. The note suggested that it would be of interest to know whether the tendency of young people in Leicester to start their working life in small firms was a local phenomenon or one to be found elsewhere. The Willesden analysis shows a marked tendency for school leavers placed by the bureau in employment in Willesden† to enter small firms (see Table 6); but since Willesden's placements relate to less than one-half of all school leavers, the results are not strictly comparable with those of Leicester, which were based on the city's total school-leaving population. But comparison with the size distri-

* Keil, E. Teresa, Riddell, David S., and Tipton, Colin B. "A Research Note: The Entry of School Leavers into Employment", *British Journal of Industrial Relations*, vol. 1, No. 3 (Oct. 1963).

† Just over two-thirds of all placements.

bution of firms in which young people under eighteen are actually employed (based on a direct inquiry of Willesden firms), indicated that the Leicester situation is not unique. Over one-half of boys and two-fifths of girls (see Table 7) at work in Willesden are employed in firms of 100 persons or less. In Leicester, the corresponding proportions were also one-half for boys, but one-third for girls.

Size of firm and occupation

If the size of firm entered by young people placed in their first jobs by the bureau is related to their occupation other features of the employment pattern of school leavers become evident. Not only were the great majority of boys entering unskilled or semi-skilled non-factory manual work placed in firms of 100 persons or less, but half of them began work with firms of 10 persons or less. This is partly accounted for by the boys who entered small garages, motor repair shops and building firms. The preponderance of small retail units in the borough also accounts for the majority of boys who became sales assistants entering units employing 10 or fewer persons. It is also of interest to note that though nearly one in three of the secondary modern school boys starting work as apprentices were placed with firms of 10 persons or less, the reverse tendency is apparent for boys from selective schools. Less than one-fifth of the latter were placed with firms of 100 persons or less and nearly one-half with firms employing over 1,000 persons. Presumably this asymmetry reflects the discrimination of the larger firm in favour of applicants for apprenticeships who have attended grammar or technical courses up to the age of sixteen, and have secured some "O" level passes in G.C.E. It implies, in view of the difficulties associated with training facilities in the small firm, that boys who have already obtained selective education, are more likely to receive favourable training opportunities, including that of day release, which the large firm can more usually provide.

A substantial proportion of girls (two-fifths) taking up clerical work were placed in the largest firms of 1,000 or more, and girls more frequently than boys were placed in the larger retail chain store. The concentration of girl apprentices in the very small unit is accounted for by the fact that the majority of them entered the hairdressing trade. There appeared to be no marked difference between girls from selective and non-selective schools in regard to the size of firm entered. There was, however, a tendency for second placements of all school leavers to be more highly concentrated, than were first placements, in the smaller firms.

THE DIRECT INQUIRY OF EMPLOYING FIRMS

Since the placements made by the bureau relate mainly to young people living in the borough and to only a proportion of the total number of young people under eighteen working in the borough, it was necessary to discover, for the purpose of constructing a satisfactory sample, the total numbers of young people at work and in what type of occupation and firm they were to be found. Because this information was not available from official statistics except in regard to shops, some 720 firms, including factories, offices, hospitals, transport services and other employing units were circulated with a questionnaire. This asked whether or not young persons under eighteen were employed and, if so, their number and occupation.

After allowing for firms which had closed down, had left the area, or were merely trading names, it was found that the total number of separate firms covered was 650. Of these, returns were received from 416, representing a response rate of 64 per cent. In the course of the inquiry, a telephone "follow-up" was made of all firms employing 25 or more persons, and of a sample of smaller firms, which had not replied at that time. As a result of this, the response rate reached 95 per cent for firms employing over 100 persons. The non-responding firms were mainly small ones, employing fewer than 25 persons.

On the basis of the replies, estimates were made of the employment of young persons under eighteen by the non-responding firms. This was done by sub-dividing all firms in the borough into size and industry groups* and assuming that for each sub-group, the average employment of young people per firm was the same for the non-respondents as for the respondents. In a few cases, where there were no comparable respondent firms, the most nearly comparable were used as the basis of estimation, e.g. those in the adjacent size group. Since the average number of young persons employed is much higher in the large than in the small firms, the degree of estimation involved represents a relatively small proportion of their total employment. Thus, firms making returns employed 881 boys and 678 girls; allowing for the non-respondents, the totals are estimated at 1,085 boys and 845 girls. It is of interest to note that 44 per cent of responding firms employed no young people under eighteen, but most of these employed fewer than 25 persons. Allowing for the numbers employed in shops and other establishments as recorded by the Shops Inspectorate, total employment of under-eighteens in the borough in June 1964 is estimated at 1,250 boys and 1,070 girls. The total of 2,320 compares closely with an official estimate of 2,400 for June 1960.†

Table 7 summarizes the estimates of the numbers at work in June 1964 by size of employing firm and compares these with the distributions of first placements made by the Youth Employment Bureau. There is a marked

* Six size groups and twenty-two industry groups were used.

† This corresponds to 3 per cent of the total male and to 5·6 per cent of the total female employed population in Willesden. These proportions are somewhat lower than those for England and Wales (5·3 per cent and 9·8 per cent respectively). The 1938 *Annual Report* of the Juvenile Employment Sub-Committee in Willesden contained an estimate of 10,000 under-eighteens out of a total employed population of 60,000.

difference between placements and total employment in regard to their size-of-firm distribution. For boys, little more than one-half actually work in small firms employing 100 or fewer persons, whereas three-fifths of the bureau's placements are in this group (and three-quarters of the placements of secondary modern school leavers). For girls, the difference is not so marked though still appreciable; about 40 per cent actually work in firms

TABLE 7
FIRST PLACEMENTS AND TOTAL WORKING POPULATION UNDER 18 IN RELATION TO SIZE OF FIRM: WILLESDEN

Size of firm (No. employed)	Boys			Girls		
	Placements[a]		Total at work	Placements[a]		Total at work
	Modern only	Total		Modern only	Total	
	(Per cent)			(Per cent)		
Under 11	35	29	23	26	25	18
11–25	14	12	9	10	11	4
26–100	25	21	22	23	20	20
Sub-total	74	62	54	59	56	42
101–500	12	13	16	17	17	17
501–1,000	3	4	8	6	6	10
Over 1,000	11	21	22	18	21	31
Total	100	100	100	100	100	100
(No.)[b]	(757)	(991)	(1,240)	(603)	(699)	(1,065)

Sources: 1. Placements Register, Willesden Youth Employment Bureau.
2. List of Registered Factories & Workshops, Town Hall, Willesden.
3. Shops Inspectorate.
4. Survey of employment of under-eighteens in Willesden.

[a] Excluding placements outside the borough.
[b] Excluding boys and girls for whom size of employing firm was not known.

employing not more than 100 persons, compared with over one-half of first placements in this size of firm. Conversely, the proportions of girls at work in large firms considerably exceeds that for placements.

The average size of firm in which young persons are actually at work, though considerably larger than the average size for placements, is still smaller than the average size for the total employed population in Willesden (including adults). Only 25 per cent of males aged fifteen and over are employed in firms of 100 persons or less, compared with 54 per cent of all employed boys under eighteen. For females, the difference, 35 per cent compared with 42 per cent, respectively, is relatively small. Similar differences were indicated in the Leicester study, and in both areas it would seem that though school leavers, particularly boys, enter industry predominantly through the small firm, they must eventually move to the larger firm, leaving their former jobs to be taken up by a fresh generation of school leavers.

The analysis of the size distribution of firms in which young people work, and that of first placements, for each of the main occupational groups, shows that for boys the difference is greatest for manual factory work, which is considerably more concentrated in the small firm for placements than for the total employed; the reverse position holds for clerical, etc., work, one half of the boys being placed in large firms (over 500), whereas only one quarter actually work in this size group. For girls, the principal difference once again is in manual factory work, where the differences between the size-of-firm distributions of placements and totals at work is greater than for the boys (see Table 8).

TABLE 8

PLACEMENTS[a] AND TOTAL WORKING POPULATION UNDER 18 IN RELATION TO OCCUPATION AND SIZE OF FIRM: WILLESDEN

		Boys				Girls			
		Size of firm (No. of persons employed)							
		Up to 100	101 to 500	Over 500	Total	Up to 100	101 to 500	Over 500	Total
		(Per cent)				(Per cent)			
Unskilled and semi-skilled manual:									
Factory	Placements	62	17	21	100	53	36	11	100
	At work	48	13	39	100	23	18	59	100
Other	Placements	81	8	11	100	84	9	7	100
	At work	76	7	17	100	62	38	—	100
Clerical and other non-manual:									
	Placements	30	18	52	100	36	16	48	100
	At work	40	37	23	100	25	22	53	100
Sales Assistants:									
	Placements	100	—	—	100	100	—	—	100
	At work	100	—	—	100	100	—	—	100
Apprentices:									
	Placements	47	14	39	100	100	—	—	100
	At work	42	20	38	100	100	—	—	100

Sources: As for Table 7.

[a] First placements only, excluding placements outside the borough.

Comparison of the total occupational distribution of placements with that of all under-eighteens employed in the borough (Table 9), shows that there is a tendency for the placements of boys to be considerably more concentrated in unskilled and semi-skilled manual work, particularly among secondary modern leavers, and less concentrated in apprenticeships, than applies in the total at work. Indeed, the fact that only one-fifth of all placements of boys were in apprenticeships, compared with one-third of those at work who were in this category, suggests that the demand for and supply of apprentices in Willesden is met largely outside the direct placing service of the Youth Employment Bureau.

The differences between the placements of girls by occupation and the corresponding distribution of the total at work are not so marked as for boys, though secondary modern school leavers tend to be less represented in clerical employment and more represented in factory work.

TABLE 9

FIRST PLACEMENTS AND TOTAL WORKING POPULATION UNDER 18 IN RELATION TO OCCUPATIONAL GROUP: WILLESDEN

	Boys			Girls		
	Placements[a] Modern only (Per cent)	Placements[a] Total	Total at work	Placements[b] Modern only (Per cent)	Placements[b] Total	Total at work
Unskilled and semi-skilled manual:						
Factory	49	39	34	24	22	16
Other	22	19	8	7	6	4
Sub-total	71	58	42	31	28	20
Clerical and other non-manual	4	13	14	46	51	58
Sales Assistants	12	11	12	15	13	13
Apprentices	13	18	32	8	8	9
Total	100	100	100	100	100	100
(No.)	(845)	(1,081)	(1,250)	(654)	(761)	(1,070)

Source: As for Table 7.

[a] Excluding placements outside the borough.

Several points of interest emerge from these comparisons between placements and estimated numbers at work. First, it can be inferred that the majority of young persons working in Willesden were placed in their employment by the Youth Employment Service. Excluding boys and girls who had become eighteen by the end of the three-year period of analysis (1960–63), first placements in employment within the borough represent three-quarters of boys and two-thirds of girls actually at work in Willesden. This implies, since the proportions of all leavers placed by the bureau is lower than these (see Table 1), that a high proportion of the leavers who find employment other than through the bureau work outside the borough. It also implies that young people wishing to work in the borough are more likely to seek the help of the bureau.

Second, it would seem that young people who find employment in Willesden without the help of the bureau tend to enter the larger firm. Third, as a corollary, it follows that the employers who use the bureau are predominantly the smaller firms. Fourth, it would seem that vacancies registered with the bureau are relatively concentrated in unskilled and semi-skilled manual work.

It would be of considerable interest to discover why the small firm appears to use the Youth Employment Service more intensively than does the larger firm; and to know how far this relates to difficulties in finding suitable applicants, to the type of work and conditions offered, to the reputation of the firm, to its use of advertising and to its ability to attract new entrants from outside the borough.

Clearly, the placements work of any bureau is closely linked to local employment conditions and to the type of vacancy registered. It appears, however, that school leavers seeking the help of the bureau (particularly the secondary modern school leaver), and others seeking a change in employment, are more likely to be placed with the very small firm than is the young person looking for employment on his own initiative or helped by some other agency. The principal exception to this would appear to be the grammar and technical school leavers taking apprenticeships, most of whom are placed with the larger firm.

This conclusion should lead to a consideration of how favourable a beginning to a working life is provided by the small firm. There is the important question of training and the difficulties that the small firm has in offering (and its young employees have in obtaining) satisfactory training oportunities, or in implementing official recommendations for extending day release.* Moreover, the chance of a young person under eighteen working with people of the same age group is very much less if they work in a small firm. As can be seen from Table 10, the average number of under-eighteens employed by any one firm is very much higher for the large firm than for the small one. Thus, it is fairly certain that the majority of young people starting work in the very small firm will work almost exclusively with adults. This is perhaps important in terms of their adjustment to work.

There is also the question of physical working conditions. A recent survey of small factories† concluded from a limited inquiry of 48 factories, each employing 100 persons or less, and one half of them employing 10 persons or less, that:

"... the working environment in respect of sanitary arrangements, cleanliness, tidiness, lighting on stairs and passageways was considered unsatisfactory in many firms; instances of inadequate safeguards on ma-

* *Day Release:* The Report of a Committee set up by the Minister of Education• H.M.S.O. (London, 1964).

† Jefferys, Margot, and Wood, C. H., A Survey of Small Factories, *British Journal of Industrial Medicine*, Vol. XVII (1960).

TABLE 10
AVERAGE NUMBER OF YOUNG PERSONS UNDER 18 EMPLOYED IN RELATION TO SIZE OF FIRM[a]

Size of firm (No. employed)	No. of firms		Average no. of boys per firm		Average no. of girls per firm	
	Employing under 18's[b]	Total	Employing under 18's	Total	Employing under 18's	Total
Up to 11	110	330	1·4	0·5	0·3	0·1
11–25	55	105	1·5	0·8	0·3	0·2
26–100	95	125	2·7	2·0	1·9	1·4
Sub-total	260	560	1·9	0·9	0·9	0·4
101–500	41	50	4·9	4·0	4·4	3·6
501–1,000	10	10	10·4	10·4	10·7	10·7
Over 1,000	14	15	19·1	19·1	23·4	21·8
Total	325	635	3·3	1·7	2·6	1·3

Sources: 1. List of Registered Factories & Workshops, Town Hall, Willesden.
2. Shops Inspectorate.
3. Survey of employment of under-eighteens in Willesden.

[a] Excluding retail trades, etc.
[b] Rounded estimates for the 3 smallest size-groups.

chines were seen; first aid equipment was also considered to be deficient in a number of cases; many firms had not been visited by the Factory Inspector nor by his deputy during the previous year."

CONCLUSION

The records of the Willesden Youth Employment Bureau represent impressive evidence of the scale of work of the bureau over the three years covered here. They also represent a source of information which, if extensively analysed for the country as a whole, could provide a factual basis for a re-examination of some of the assumptions of the present Youth Employment Service and possibly for the re-planning of some aspects of its work. It would seem important, for instance, to discover how far the work of other bureaux is concentrated as much upon the person seeking a change of employment as upon the school leaver deciding on his first employment. If this should be a general feature of bureaux in other industrial areas, it would suggest that the present emphasis on vocational advice to the school leaver based on a formidable programme of school visits, interviews, talks and reports, requires to be balanced by an equal investment of staff, techniques and procedures for young people seeking a change of employment.

It would also seem necessary to try to discover how far the vacancies for jobs in other areas are also concentrated in particular occupations and in types of firm, and to what extent they represent the full range of employment actually available to young people in the area. It could be that the aims of the service are frustrated by the type of employment registered if, as in the case of Willesden, it more frequently represents (particularly for boys) the unskilled or semi-skilled manual work in the very small firm.

EDITORS' NOTE

Maizels has complemented this study by following up a group of secondary modern school leavers in order to ascertain the incidence of job change amongst them, reasons for the changes, and the role of the Youth Employment Service in placing the job changers. She concludes from this study that the Working Party in the Report on the Youth Employment Service (*The Future Development of the Youth Employment Service*, H.M.S.O., 1965) underestimated both the incidence and frequency of job change among school leavers and the role of the Youth Employment Service in this regard. The study raises important questions as to the order of priority of the functions of the Service. Reference: "Changes in employment among school leavers: a sample study of one cohort of secondary modern boys", *British Journal of Industrial Relations*, 1967, **5** (2), 211–221.

*15. Young Workers in their First Jobs. An Investigation of Attitudes to Work and their Correlates**

VIRGINIA C. PALMER

THE transition from school to work has been described as a period of stress, difficulty and dissatisfaction. (See Brew, 1955; Eppel and Eppel, 1953; Miller and Form, 1951; Tenen, 1947a and 1947b.) Brew, for example, after working with young people for many years, said that they were usually eager to enter full-time employment, but when they had been at work for three or four months, they became puzzled, dejected and dissatisfied. Nevertheless, one finds that there have been very few systematic, follow-up studies of the stage between leaving school and entering a full-time job.

An investigation of work attitudes and behaviour is beset with numerous problems, and one of the most important of these is the selection of relevant criterion variables. Brown and Landsberger (1960) carried out a worthwhile study of young workers by selecting only one criterion variable, namely responsibility at work, and correlating this with factors such as the conditions at work, family background and personal adjustment. Many early studies, such as those by Tenen, gave a general indication of the young workers' attitudes to being at work.

Whatever procedure has been used, there has tended to be considerable variability among the individuals; some young workers adjust readily to their new jobs, others become dissatisfied, some display responsible, others irresponsible, work behaviour. This is, of course, a common finding in the social sciences, but it is worth trying to account for such individual differences.

One of the aims of the present investigation was to examine the correlates of favourable and unfavourable attitudes to different aspects of the new jobs. Previous results suggest that the degree of association between work attitudes and other variables may depend on the nature of the variable. For instance Brown and Landsberger (1960) found significant trends between

* This paper is condensed from part of a Ph.D. thesis. The research was carried out while the author was a senior tutor in the Department of Psychology, University of Melbourne, Australia.

(Reprinted by permission of the editor and author, from *Occupational Psychology* (1964, **38**, 99–113), the quarterly journal of the N.I.I.P., 14 Welbeck St., London, W.1.)

responsibility at work and "objective" variables, such as the father's occupation and the young worker's school attainment. No significant trends were found, however, when "subjective" assessments, such as relations with the parents, were examined. Likewise, Ferguson and Cunison (1951), in a three year follow-up of school leavers from Glasgow, obtained significant relations between the stability of the fathers' and sons' job records, but no significant trends were found between the ratings of conditions in the family and any of the job indices. Tenen (1947b) attributed young workers' dissatisfactions with work to the conditions on the job and to the problems created by the change in roles from a school child to a wage earner, but not to personal maladjustments or difficulties with family relations.

One can conclude that either there were, in fact, no significant associations between the aspects of work behaviour considered and the family relations, or that there were difficulties in getting valid assessments of home adjustment.

The main aims were: to get assessments of young workers' attitudes to work over a period of six months; to see whether they differed in their attitudes to various aspects of work; to examine the correlates of favourable and unfavourable attitudes; and to see whether there was any increase or decrease in the numbers who were favourable towards work over the six months.

PROCEDURE

(i) *Subjects and Setting*

The subjects were 106 male school leavers with a mean age of 15 years 1 month. These were the boys who left school at the end of the year from the third forms of two Junior Technical Schools. One school was in an industrial, the other in a non-industrial, area. A comparison in terms of age and percentage of third form school leavers, between this sample and the general population of Junior Technical School boys in Melbourne, suggested that the school leavers studied were likely to be representative of that population.

The scholastic and general ability level of the boys studied is probably similar to that of boys from the A and B streams of Secondary Modern Schools in England. Roughly half of the 15 year old school leavers in Melbourne are from Junior Technical Schools and these schools are less selective than the boys' Technical Schools in England. The boys who enter skilled trade jobs attend Senior Technical Schools for one day per week until they complete their apprenticeship.

(ii) *Interviews*

About six weeks before they were due to leave school, the boys were interviewed separately. They were seen again in their homes after they had been working for two or three weeks. The latter was termed the first follow-up interview. Six months later, the young workers were seen again for the second follow-up interview. About the same time as the first follow-up interviews, the parents were also seen. Whenever possible, the mother was interviewed at home during the day and the father was seen for a short time in the evening. During the evening visit, the parents were usually seen together informally. The order and wording of the questions was standardised. Some of the questions were of the free response type.

(iii) *Treatment of the Data*

When relevant, content analysis was used. Guttman Scale techniques were employed to group the responses from certain questions. Chi Square, with Yates's correction, was the main test used, and the ·05 level was accepted as being significant.

(iv) *The Variables*

(a) *Criterion Variables*

Attitudes to the job were examined in terms of three main criterion variables. These were: first, the young workers' attitudes to the work performed; second, their attitudes to the bosses; and, third, the boys' attitudes to the other workers. The boys were also asked to comment on the adequacy of their pay, and to state what they considered to be the biggest problem in settling down to the new job.

(b) *Correlates of Job Attitudes*

The correlates of attitudes to work were grouped under three main headings. These were: first, all those conditions which related to the boys before they entered their jobs, for example, attitudes to school; second, those features which were an objective part of the work situation, for instance the age composition of the work group; and third, the sets of relations which formed part of the background of the whole period of the transition from school to work were examined. These latter included how the parents got along with each other and an assessment of the boys' relations with their parents.

DISCUSSION OF RESULTS

Young Workers' Attitudes to their Jobs

(i) *Attitudes to Work*

Just after their entry to work, 67 of the 106 boys were classified (assessed by splitting a 6-point Guttman Scale at the mid-point) as being favourable in attitudes towards their work. Six months later, 76 of the 106 boys were in the favourable category. A content analysis of replies to a question which asked the boys how they liked work, gave 64 satisfied at the first follow-up interview, and 72 at the second follow-up interview. These differences between the first and second interviews are not significant. When they were asked whether they would rather be at school or work, only 14 of the 106 boys said that they would prefer to be back at school. The reason given most frequently for this preference was that the boys had less supervision at work. Of the 106 boys, 33 gave replies which were classified under the heading of "less supervision". As one would expect, different indices of attitudes to work give slightly varied results, but the general trend is the same; a majority of the young workers are favourable towards their jobs and they prefer this situation to school.

(ii) *The Bosses and the Other Workers*

At the first interview, when they were asked to appraise their bosses, 70 of the 106 boys made favourable comments. For the second interview, 75 had attitudes which were classified as favourable. In their attitudes to the other workers, the same trends appeared. For the first interview, 72 of 101 boys, where other workers were employed, made favourable appraisals; while for the second interview, 78 out of 104 boys were in the favourable category.

(iii) *The Pay*

At the first interview, 71 of the 106 boys were satisfied with the wage which they received. Six months later, 63 of the 106 boys were in the satisfied category.

Of the four aspects of the job which were considered, namely, attitudes to the work, to the bosses, to the other workers, and to the pay, the last was the only one where the trend was towards there being fewer replies in the positive category for the second interview. It must be emphasized that the differences are not statistically significant. However, the trends which did occur were in the expected direction. One would expect that as the boys moved further away from their school days, and into the activities of working adolescents, their financial demands would increase.

Hence, unless there was an increase in their wage, they would be likely to see it as being less adequate for their needs. Apart from this aspect, at least for the first six months of full time employment, there is no evidence from this study to indicate that young workers become less satisfied with work the longer they remain on the job.

(iv) *Perception of Initial Problem*

When the boys were asked to name the aspect of work which created most difficulty for them, in settling down to their jobs, they tended to refer to the social relations at work. The results are shown in Table 1.

More than 50 per cent of the young workers saw the other worker, the bosses, or both, as the main source of difficulty in their early work adaptation. Almost two-thirds of these boys, however, were explicit that the difficulties tended to be resolved after periods of four to six weeks. The problems included such things as: feeling shy; that it felt unusual to be with a crowd of men instead of the boys at school; not having any friends among the other workers; being left alone at lunch-time; and not being sure of what the bosses and other workers expected in terms of general behaviour.

TABLE 1
PERCEPTION OF EARLY WORK PROBLEMS

Category	Frequency
1. Other workers	39
2. Bosses	9
3. Other workers and bosses	11
4. Work tasks	18
5. Hours	7
6. Factors outside work	4
7. Nothing	18
Total	106

One boy put this last problem aptly. He said, "You have to know all the little things that they like you to do, so as to get on well with the other fellows."

Only 18 of the 106 boys spoke of difficulties in learning the actual work or in coping with the work tasks in general.

(v) *Interrelationships in Attitudes to Different Aspects of the Job*

Generally, the number of young workers who were classified as favourable or unfavourable towards different aspects of work was relatively constant. Whatever aspect of work was examined, roughly two-thirds of the young workers were favourable to the particular aspect of the job. Moreover, the young workers who were classified as being favourable in attitude to one aspect tended to be favourable to the other aspects of the job considered. For instance, boys who liked doing the actual work task tended to like their bosses ($P < \cdot 001$, and $P < \cdot 01$, for the first and second follow-up interviews respectively). Those who were favourable towards their bosses tended to like the workers ($P < \cdot 001$ and $P < \cdot 02$). At the second, but not at the first follow-up interview, the boys who were satisfied with their pay were positive in attitude to the other workers ($P < \cdot 001$). At the first interview only, there was a significant relation ($P < \cdot 05$) between attitudes to bosses and to pay.

Some of these variables appear to be more highly associated at either the first or the second follow-up interview. There were, however, no clear statistically significant differences in the degree of association between the variables for the different interviews. In general, the boys' attitudes to their pay were not closely associated with their attitudes to other aspects of work.

An attempt was made to relate attitudes to pay to the socio-economic level of the family and also to the slight differences which did occur in the amount of pay received, but no significant relationships were found.

For some purposes it would have been preferable to combine these various criteria into an index of jobs satisfaction. In this study, however, one of the aims was to investigate the correlates of the boys' appraisals of these logically separate aspects of work.

The Correlates of Attitudes to Work

(i) *Attitudes to School*

Young workers who had favourable attitudes to school (assessed when they were at school) tended to like the work tasks ($P < \cdot 01$ and $P < \cdot 02$, for the first and second follow-up interviews respectively). The young workers who were positive towards school tended to like their bosses at work ($P < \cdot 05$, for the first follow-up interview only), and those who liked school tended also to be favourable towards the other workers ($P < \cdot 01$, and $P < \cdot 02$, first and second follow-up interviews).

These are not unexpected findings. The boys who expressed favourable comments about school were probably those who tended to accept the formal demands of that situation. One would expect them to do the same at work. It could also be expected such boys would be on reasonable terms with their bosses. As the boys were in junior positions their work relations with some of the other workers would probably not differ from their relations with those in charge. One boy said, "Who do you mean by the boss? Everyone in the place can tell me what to do".

(ii) *School Attainment*

Within the industrial area school, there was a slight trend for the boys who obtained higher marks in their final school examination to be the ones who were favourable towards work ($P < \cdot 05$, the mean examination mark for the boys who were favourable towards work was 65·56 and for those who were less favourable it was 59·75).

In the non-industrial area school, there was no significant association between attitudes to work and to school attainment. The finding of a significant relationship in one, but not in the other, school occurred only for this particular variable. The between schools difference may have resulted from a number of factors, but there were some indications that it was related to a difference in the ability level of the boys who left school from the third forms in these two schools. The boys in the higher streams (in particular the A stream) of the non-industrial area school tended to remain at school, whereas in the industrial area school they were likely to leave at 15 years, irrespective of the class placement ($P < \cdot 001$). This variable was not associated with attitudes to the bosses or the other workers.

(iii) *Popularity with School Classmates*

Boys who were popular with their school classmates tended to see their bosses in a favourable way ($P < \cdot 05$ for the first interview, and for the second interview there was a similar trend which just failed to be significant).

There are some indications, then, that the boys who liked school, and who adapted in a favourable way to school, tended to do the same at work. Nevertheless, the degree of association is not marked; there were, for instance, many boys who disliked school and liked work and also a few who were favourable towards school and dissatisfied with work.

(iv) *Job Entered was the Same as the Job Expected*

Boys who entered the jobs which they planned to enter were likely to be favourable in their attitudes towards work ($P < \cdot 05$ and $P < \cdot 01$ for the first and second follow-up interviews). Whether the boys entered the same or a different job was unrelated to their appraisals of the bosses or the other workers. If one thinks of the boys' jobs as goals towards which they have been striving, one would expect that if they reached these goals they would be more likely to feel satisfied than if they failed to attain the goals. One could also expect that the satisfaction or dissatisfaction with the work itself, in relation to its having been an anticipated goal, would not be associated with the boys' attitudes to the bosses or the other workers. There was, in fact, no significant association between the boys' attitudes to the bosses, or to the workers, and whether or not they had entered the job which they expected to enter.

(v) *Type of Work and Training*

No significant association was found between satisfaction with the job and whether or not the young workers entered skilled trades or some other type of work. But, as only 17 of the 106 boys failed to enter jobs which were officially classified as skilled trades, this finding is of limited importance. Furthermore, the young workers who had not entered skilled trades by the end of the first six months were those who seemed to prefer some other type of work. In Melbourne, if a boy is at least 15 years of age (preferably not over 16 years) and has remained at school until this time, the probability of his being able to enter a skilled trade is extremely high. No significant association was found between any of the job attitudes indices and the type of trade entered.

When the boys were asked to describe the cycle of their day's work, it appeared that, if the only tasks mentioned could be classified as unskilled (e.g. messages, cleaning tools or sweeping floors), they were likely to have unfavourable attitudes to work ($P < \cdot 001$). Of the 106 boys, only 22 saw their jobs solely in terms of unskilled routine tasks. Whether or not the young workers described their work tasks as being unskilled or skilled was unrelated to the official classification of skilled and unskilled trades. In the first months of their apprenticeships, one would expect the boys to be given some of the less attractive tasks. It could, of course, be argued that the boys who recalled the less pleasant tasks did so because they were generally dissatisfied with their jobs. It would have been desirable to have obtained independent assessments of the job cycles. In order to do this, however, it would have been necessary to have gained the co-operation of roughly a hundred firms. After they left school, nearly all of the boys went to work in different firms around Melbourne. Moreover, there were some indications from the boys' comments that these would have been less spontaneous, and perhaps less valid, had they been obtained at work instead of at home.

(vi) *Age of the Other Workers and Size of Work Groups*

If there were one or more workers in the firm whom the boys describe as being similar in age to themselves, they tended to have favourable attitudes to the other workers ($P < \cdot 01$).

TABLE 2
BOYS' ATTITUDES TO THE OTHER WORKERS AND THE PRESENCE OF YOUNG WORKERS ON THE JOB

Boys' Attitudes	Young Workers Present		
	Yes	No	Total
Favourable	47	25	72
Unfavourable	10	19	29
Total	57	44	101

$P < \cdot 01$

An inspection of Table 2 indicates that, although there is a statistically significant relationship, a large number of boys are favourable towards the other workers, even when they are not within own age range. There was no association between the age group of the other workers and the boys' attitudes to their work or the bosses. Various breakdowns were used but no significant relationships were found between the boys' reports of the number of workers in their sections and any of the job attitude indices.

(vii) *Socio-Economic Status of the Family*

There were variations in the socio-economic status of the boys' family backgrounds, as assessed by area of residence, type of dwelling and general material comfort of the home. In terms of the fathers' occupations, however, the boys studied were relatively homogeneous. Of the 106 boys, 77 had fathers who were employed in skilled, semi-skilled or unskilled work, professional and business executives were not represented. There were no significant associations between the socio-economic status of the family (assessed by a combined index which included father's occupation, area of residence and the size and type of dwelling) and any of the job variables. This finding is not unexpected. The jobs entered by the young workers were relatively similar in terms of the nature of the work and conditions. There is little evidence from other studies to suggest that socio-economic level as such is related to satisfaction with one's environment.

(viii) *Relations Between the Parents*

In families where the parents tend to agree, and where there are few arguments, the boys are not likely to be unfavourable towards their work ($P < \cdot 01$).

An inspection of Table 3 reveals that although the relationship is significant it accounts for only 65 per cent of the cases. This finding is in line with the results from many studies; namely, that family relations influence child and adolescent attitudes but other factors also play a part.

TABLE 3

BOYS' ATTITUDES TO WORK AND RELATIONS BETWEEN THE PARENTS

Relations Between Parents	Attitudes to Work		
	favourable	unfavourable	total
Agreement	34	12	46
Disagreement	22	31	53
Total	56	43	99

$P < \cdot 01$

TABLE 4

BOYS' ATTITUDES TO THE OTHER WORKERS AND RELATIONS BETWEEN THE PARENTS

Relations Between Parents	Attitudes to Other Workers		
	favourable	unfavourable	total
Agreement	40	4	44
Disagreement	33	20	53
Total	73	24	97

$P < \cdot 01$

Table 4 shows that only 4 of the 24 young workers (from the intact families) who were unfavourable in attitudes to the other workers, were from families in which the parents were classified in the "agreement" group.

The most relevant feature of both Tables 3 and 4, and a trend which appears in all the tables showing relationships between job and family variables, is the comparatively small number of cases in the top right-hand cell. This trend suggests that if a boy is from a family where the social relations are satisfactory, as defined by the criteria used, then the boy is not likely to see his work situation in an unfavourable way. On the other hand, he may still see the work situation in a positive way even though he is from an unsatisfactory home. For the second interview only, there was also a significant relationship ($P < \cdot 05$) between the boys' attitudes to their bosses and whether or not the parents appeared to get along well with each other. Again, at the second interview, the boys' attitudes to the other workers and the relations between the parents were associated ($P < \cdot 01$).

(ix) *Young Workers' Relations with their Parents*

Assessments were made of how well the young workers got along with both their mothers and fathers separately. The boys' relations with their mothers were not associated significantly with any of the job attitude measurements. It is possible to attribute this result to the inadequacy of the assessments made. The boys were very reluctant to admit that they got along badly with their mothers. It is, of course, possible that the boys' present relations with their mothers and their attitudes to work are in fact unrelated. Boys who had positive relations with their fathers tended to see their work in a favourable way ($P < \cdot 01$ for the first follow-up interview). At the second interview the relationship just fails to be significant. The boys' attitudes to the bosses and the boys' relations with their fathers were not significantly associated for either the first of the second follow-up interview.

Relations with the fathers and attitudes to the other workers were not associated at the first follow-up interview. At the second interview, boys who had positive relations with their fathers tended to have favourable attitudes towards the other workers ($P < \cdot 05$). This finding may be linked directly to the relations between the parents. There was a relatively marked association ($P < \cdot 01$) between the parents' variable and the boys' attitudes to the other workers. In families where there was lack of conflict between the parents, the young workers' relations with their fathers were favourable. One might have expected that the home influences would be stronger at the first than at the second follow-up interview. There were no definite trends, however, which showed higher association between work and family variables at the first interview.

The young workers' attitudes and behaviour before they leave school, the conditions on the job and the family relations are all factors which seem to influence attitudes to work. Some of these variables are more closely associated to specific aspects of work than others. For instance, the age composition of the work group was associated with attitudes to the other workers, but this was not directly associated with attitudes to the tasks performed. The relative importance of these sets of "independent" variables in relation to adjustment at work, and views of the job generally, would need to be worked out by means of more refined statistical techniques.

The evidence does not suggest any increase in unfavourable attitudes to work with length of time on the job. A longer follow-up period might have shown a different trend. In general, the picture is one of young workers who tend to be favourable towards their jobs and happy to be away from school. The extent to which these same trends appear in other countries, and in other types of work, is a problem for further investigation.

CONCLUSIONS

1. Approximately two-thirds of the young workers had favourable attitudes to their jobs. This figure remained fairly constant whether the attitudes were considered in relation to the work tasks, to the bosses, the other workers, or the pay.

2. Over a period of six months, there were slight variations in the proportion of boys who were favourable of unfavourable to the different aspects of work, but there were no statistically significant changes in these proportions.

3. When the young workers were asked to name their biggest problem in adjusting to the new job, more than 50 per cent referred to the social aspects of the job. They maintained, however, that the problems were of a temporary nature.

4. Boys who were favourable towards school tended to be favourable towards work. Nevertheless, the degree of association between attitudes to these two situations was not very high. There were many boys who disliked school but liked being at work.

5. For the industrial area school only, boys who were favourable towards work tended to obtain higher school marks than those who were unfavourable.

6. Boys who were popular with their school classmates tended to have positive attitudes to the bosses and the other workers on the job.

7. Young workers who entered the jobs which they planned to enter tended to like their jobs.

8. Those who described their work cycle in terms of routine, unskilled tasks were likely to be unfavourable towards work.

9. When the boys were in jobs where there were some workers of a similar age to themselves, they were likely to have favourable attitudes to the other workers.

10. When the boys were from families in which the parents were not in conflict with each other, the boys tended to be favourable towards the work, the bosses, and the other workers.

11. When the boys were on good terms with their fathers, they tended to be positive towards the work tasks and the other workers.

12. No significant associations were found between any of the job variables and whether or not the boys entered trade or non-trade employment; the size of the work group; the socio-eonomic level of the family; or the boys' attitudes to their mothers. The lack of association between some of these variables may have resulted from invalid assessments.

ACKNOWLEDGEMENTS

The author is most grateful to Dr. Paul Lafitte for his assistance and advice throughout the investigation; to Dr. K. M. Miller, for his criticisms of this manuscript; to the heads and teachers of the schools concerned; and to the parents and boys for their valuable co-operation.

REFERENCES

BEILIN, H. (1956) The pattern of postponability and its relation to social class mobility. *J. Soc. Psychol.* **44**, 33–48.

BREW, J. M. (1955) The problems of the young worker. *Personnel Management*, **37**, 26–33.

BROWN, A. W., and LANDSBERGER, H. A. (1960) The sense of responsibility among young workers. *Occup. Psychol.* **34**, 1–14.

EPPEL, E. M., and EPPEL, M. (1953) Young workers at a County College. *Brit. J. Educ. Psychol.* **23**, 29–44.

FERGUSON, T., and CUNNISON, J. (1951) *The Young Wage Earner*. London: Oxford University Press.

MILLER, D. C., and FORM, W. H. (1951) *Industrial Sociology*. New York: Harper.

TENEN, CORA (1947a) Some problems of discipline among adolescents in factories. *Occup. Psychol.* **24**, 75–81.

TENEN, CORA (1947b) The adolescent in the factory. *Brit. J. Educ. Psychol.* **17**, 72–82.

ADDITIONAL REFERENCES TO THE TRANSITION FROM SCHOOL TO WORK

AUSUBEL, D. P. (1954) *Theory and Problems of Adolescent Development*. New York, Grune & Stratton.

BERDIE, R. F., and HOOD, A. B. (1965) *Decisions for Tomorrow: Plans of High School Seniors for after Graduation*. Minneapolis, University of Minnesota Press.

CARTER, M. P. (1962) *Home, School and Work*. Oxford, Pergamon.

CARTER, M. P. (1966) *Into Work*. Harmondsworth, Penguin.

CLEMENTS, R. V. (1958) *The Choice of Careers by School Children*. Manchester, Manchester University Press.

COLEMAN, J. S. (1961) *The Adolescent Society*. New York, Free Press of Glencoe.

CROFT, M., RAYNER, J., and COHEN, L. (ed.) (1967) *Linking Home and School*. London, Longmans.

EISENSTADT, S. N. (1956) *From Generation to Generation*. Glencoe, Ill., Free Press.

FYVEL, T. R. (1963) *The Insecure Offenders*. Harmondsworth, Penguin.

HEGINBOTHAM, H. (1957) *The Youth Employment Service*. London, Methuen.

HERFORD, M. E. M. (1957) *Youth at Work*. London, Parrish.

Industrial Training Council (1961) *Co-operation Between Industry and Education*. London, The Council.

KUHLEN, R. G. (1952) *The Psychology of Adolescent Development*. New York, Harper.

LIEPMANN, K. (1960) *Apprenticeship*. London, Routledge & Kegan Paul.

Ministry of Education (1962) *Forward from School*. London, H.M.S.O.

Ministry of Education (1960) Central Advisory Council for Education. *Fifteen to Eighteen: a report*. Chairman: Sir Geffrey Crowther. 2 vols. London, H.M.S.O.

Ministry of Education (1963) Central Advisory Council for Education. *Half our Future: a report*. Chairman: J. Newsom, London, H.M.S.O.

MORSE, M. (1965) *The Unattached*. Harmondsworth, Penguin.

National Society for the Study of Education (1965) *64th Yearbook*. Part 1: Vocational Education. Chicago, University of Chicago Press.

PAUL, L. (1962) *The Transition from School to Work*. London, Industrial Welfare Society.

Scottish Education Department (1963) *From School to Further Education*. London, H.M.S.O.

SHERIF, M., and SHERIF, C. W. (ed.) (1965) *Problems of Youth*. Chicago, Aldine.

VENESS, T. (1962) *School Leavers: their Aspirations and Expectations*. London, Methuen.

WILLIAMS, G. (1963) *Apprenticeship in Europe*. London, Chapman & Hall.

CHOWN, S. M. (1959) The formation of occupational choice among grammar school pupils. *Occupational Psychology*, **32**, 171–182.

CHOWN, S. M. (1959) Personality factors in occupational choice. *British Journal of Educational Psychology*, **29**, 23–33.

GRAUBARD, S. R. (ed.) (1962) Youth, change, and challenge: ten papers by E. Erikson, B. Bettelheim, T. Parsons, S. N. Eisenstadt, *et al. Daedalus*, Winter, 1962 (whole issue).

HAVIGHURST, R. J. (1964) Youth in exploration and man emergent. In H. Borow (ed.), *Man in a World at Work*.

HILL, G. B. (1965) Choice of career by grammar school boys. *Occupational Psychology*, **39**, 279–287.

KATZ, F. (1959) Orientations of adolescents. *New Era*, **40**, 2–5.

LIPSET, S. M., BENDIX, R., and MALM, F. T. (1954/5) Job plans and entry into the labour market. *Social Forces*, **33**, 224–232.

LOGAN, R. F. L. (1953) Rising 18 in a London suburb. *British Journal of Sociology*, **4**, 323–345.

MURRAY, E. (1958) Employment service counseling for youth—yesterday and today. *Vocational Guidance Quarterly*, **7**, 3–8.

NORTON, J. L. (1953) General motives and influences in vocational development. *Journal of Genetic Psychology*, **82**, 263–278.

POWELL, M., and BLOOM, V. (1962) Development of and reasons for vocational choices of adolescents through the high school years. *Journal of Educational Research*, **56**, 126–133.

STERN, H. H. (1961) A follow-up study of adolescents' views of their personal and vocational time. *British Journal of Educational Psychology*, **31**, 170–182.

SYKES, E. G. (1953) School and work. *Sociological Review*, **1**, 29–47.

SECTION 4

The Work Experience

"The planning for which the vocational counselor can be held responsible is planning for work satisfaction from both employed and non-employed activity."

C. GILBERT WRENN

TIN'S COLLEGE OF EDUCATION
LANCASTER

THE first paper in this section asks the apparently naïve question, what is work? Unfortunately the answer is not quite as obvious as it may at first appear. Shimmin points out that although work is often regarded as a distinct and easily definable activity it is extremely difficult to find criteria by which it can be clearly distinguished from other activities. She notes, among other things, that whereas some think the dichotomy between work and play is becoming sharper, there are others who maintain that there is an increasing fusion between the two. She suggests, therefore, that it might be more appropriate to think of a work-play continuum rather than two separate and contrasting aspects of life.

In the second paper Super considers the problem of measuring vocational success. After examining the sort of criteria researchers have used as a basis for their assessments of vocational success he suggests that it may be unwise to use the term success. Because success is usually only measured in objective terms of achievement, the concept of vocational adjustment which allows greater scope for personal and subjective measures may be more appropriate. Success or adjustment should not be judged solely on the basis of performance but also on the basis of the individual's own feelings and attitudes.

Dawis, England and Lofquist describe the development of the work personality in terms of needs and abilities and refer to the process by which the individual comes to terms with his work environment as the process of work adjustment. A person may decide to leave a particular work environment because he may be unsuccessful when judged against some objective standards of performance. On the other hand he may choose to leave for more personal reasons. He may be dissatisfied with the work environment because the "reinforcers" required for his satisfaction may not exist.

Darley and Hagenah are concerned with the problem of how to measure success in life. While some men measure their lives by the power or prestige they wield, others hold service to the community as their basic criterion. Success, according to Darley and Hagenah, can have as many definitions as happiness. Since a man's working life can span forty to fifty years they feel it is important to consider what satisfactions work can offer. They suggest that there is no simple answer to this question, for some work is an end in itself whereas for others it is only a means to an end. A job may offer a hallmark of status or it may be viewed as a "cultural trap" from which escape is difficult, if not impossible. On the other hand the job might be perceived as lying somewhere along a rigidity–flexibility continuum. The individual's satisfaction may depend on whether there exists too much or insufficient freedom of action in defining and acting out the component parts of the job.

It is extremely difficult to define even the basic concept of work so it is not surprising that the concepts of occupational success, adjustment or satisfaction are difficult to measure. The final paper presents an interesting review of some of the issues involved in attempts to measure job satisfaction. Fournet, Distefano and Pryer illustrate the multitude of characteristics and dimensions involved and discuss how different methodological approaches to the study of job satisfaction can have significant effects on the results.

16. Concepts of Work*

SYLVIA SHIMMIN

PSYCHOLOGISTS are apt to take the concept of work for granted, i.e. they are more interested in people's attitudes *to* work or factors influencing their behaviour *at* work than in the meaning and significance or work itself. In general, discussion of the latter has been left to sociologists and anthropologists. Any examination of concepts of work, therefore, would be incomplete without taking account of the contributions made by other disciplines.

Work is commonly regarded as a clearly defined area of life and a distinctive activity, but it is not easy to find criteria by which it may be effectively distinguished from other activities. Some of the criteria suggested by those seeking to define work are as follows: (i) that work is purposeful activity; (ii) that it is instrumental; (iii) that it yields income; (iv) that it entails expenditure of effort, and (v) some element of obligation and/or constraint. Anderson (1961), for example, defines work as "activity to some purpose; in more direct terms, time given to a job for which one is paid." Margaret Mead (1950) describes it as "activity that is purposeful and directed towards ends that lie outside that activity" in contrast with the self-rewarding character of play. Work is often assumed to be neither pleasurable nor self-rewarding, although Firth (1948) has warned against representing it simply as something which people do not like doing. He points out that any definition of work must be arbitrary to some extent and suggests that "income-producing activity" covers general use of the terms in its occupational sense. Nevertheless, the idea that one of the distinguishing features of work is that it is not enjoyable appears to be widely held. Thus a professor of economics in a public lecture declared that "work means unpleasant effort" and proceeded to attribute many of our economic ills to the failure of industrial managers to accept the uncongenial nature of their tasks. Perhaps some support for his view is given by the manager who, in another context, defined work as "activity engaged in from economic necessity when one

* Paper given at the first annual conference of the Social Psychology Section, British Psychological Society, at Oxford, July, 1966.

(Reprinted, by permission of the editor and author, from *Occupational Psychology* (1966, **40**, 195–201), the quarterly journal of the N.I.I.P., 14 Welbeck St., London, W.1.)

would rather be doing something else". Similarly, at a week-end conference of sixth-formers one boy remarked: "if we take the physicist's view that work equals expenditure of energy to achieve a purpose then we are working now, but if we take the commonsense view that work is something unpleasant then clearly we are not." No one disputed this statement.

Unfortunately, none of the above characteristics is peculiar to work alone. Many hobbies and leisure pursuits are utilitarian activities which, though a source of interest and satisfaction in themselves, are undertaken initially for economic reasons. There is no clear line of demarcation between gardening or house-painting done from necessity and done from choice. Individual attitudes are liable to vary with circumstances such as health, the weather, pressure of other commitments, and so on, so that what is a pleasure one day becomes a compulsory and irksome chore the next. Even the most enjoyable and self-rewarding task imposes some constraint, namely the urge towards its successful completion. Hence, as Hearnshaw (1954) says, the element of obligation is not dependent on a formal contract of employment, but applies equally to "voluntary work" and work which is self-imposed, such as writing a book or mowing the lawn. Friedmann (1961) makes the same point about the coercion involved in the use of time outside normal "working" hours, observing that some duties and obligations to one's family, friends, neighbours and other groups are incurred, but are not sought or desired. The fulfilling of such duties may acquire the irksome character so often ascribed to work. Friedmann also regards other "spare-time" activities, such as evening classes, as primarily instrumental and utilitarian, and he would reject Firth's definition of work as "income-producing activity" as inadequate, on the grounds that people with small incomes tend to augment them with paying hobbies and sidelines. In this connection it could also be argued that a daily telephone call to one's stockbroker is income-producing activity, but it might not be generally perceived as "work".

Another approach to the problem is to consider whether or not work can be inferred from observed behaviour. In factories, shops, offices and similar organisations, it is usually possible to determine whether an individual is at work, i.e. at his place of paid employment, but not necessarily whether he is working—either by his own standards or those of his employer. The difficulty is even greater with those whose occupation involves irregular hours, isolation, travel or work in what to others appears a leisured context. Is the commercial traveller on the road or dining in his hotel obviously at work, or the research worker sitting at his desk and gazing out of the window? It is impossible to tell from observation alone. Likewise the amateurs and the professional players are not immediately discernible on the cricket field. In particular, merely watching another person in his occupational role gives no information as to how he perceives the situation or what activity signifies "work" to him. Thus Mr. Roy Jenkins, in an interview with *The Observer* when he was Minister of Aviation, was quoted as saying "I only regard writing as real work" in contrast with the comparatively routine nature of his Ministerial duties; sculptors and artists also frequently distinguish between their "real work" and what they do for a living.

Further evidence of the subjectively indeterminate boundaries of work comes from the study by Donald and Havighurst (1959) in which respondents were asked what meaning work and their favourite leisure activity had for them. It was found that most of the meanings ascribed to leisure were also ascribed to work, i.e. the chance to achieve something, to be creative, to serve or to benefit society, as a means of passing the time, of making contact with friends, and as a source of interest, status and self-respect. Four per cent gave "financial return" as the meaning of their favourite leisure activity as compared with twelve per cent for whom work was only meaningful as money earned. The two meanings given to leisure alone were "a welcome change from work" and "done just for the pleasure of it". Apart from showing that, both in Kansas City and New Zealand, where the investigation was carried out, there is a considerable overlap in people's concepts of work and leisure, the enquiry gives no indication as to how the meanings of work and play compare for a particular person. In the words of the authors: "The most we can say is that equivalent satisfactions may be obtained from the two forms of activity, by some people and in some situations."

The assumption that work and play can be distinguished by any one criterion has been questioned by Cohen (1953), who suggests that it is more appropriate to think of a composite play–work continuum on which a given activity can be placed according to the extent to which it displays several characteristics. He also stresses the need to consider work in its social, cultural and historical setting and not merely to regard it as a biological concept. To this end he traces the source of two traditions associated with work in Western culture, the Puritan morality of work as an ascetic discipline on the one hand and, on the other, the ideal of spontaneity, creativity and self expression envisaged by Rousseau and Ruskin. The former view, described by William James as the Gospel of Work, prevailed for the majority in Victorian England, but this century has seen an enormous change in the values placed on work and play, associated with a shift in emphasis from production to consumption and linked with technological developments leading to a shorter working week. As Cohen puts it: "In place of the notion that play is a waste of time that could better be devoted to work, play has come to be valued as an end in itself. ... This change of emphasis has been accompanied by diminution in the seriousness of work." It has not, however, diminished the importance of having a job and, whereas at one time the lady and gentleman of leisure were socially esteemed, to-day they come low in our scale of values. In *The Affluent Society*, Galbraith (1958) asserts: "to be idle is no longer considered rewarding or even entirely respectable", or, in Klein's (1963) words, "the first thing that matters about work is to have it".

Most people nowadays are conditioned quite young to the idea of "earning one's living", that is they grow up expecting to have a job which will give them a recognised place in the community. This aspect of work is perhaps as important to the individual as any other, financial security included. For to have a job confers status and self-respect. It also provides a standard by which to judge and to be judged by others. Thus, "what is his job?" or "what do you do?" are regarded as normal questions surrounding introductions, to which the expected reply is a specific occupation. The person with no job, whether he lives on private means or on National Assistance, arouses ambivalent attitudes, unless he is retired and can be accorded the social status of his former occupation.

Work, then, may be regarded as employment within the social and economic system which is perceived by the individual as his main occupation, by the title of which he is known and from which he derives his role in society. The advantage of such a definition is that it does not put emphasis on going "out" to work, nor on a contract of service or a particular form of financial reward, and thereby includes the housewife, the poet and the writer, and all those whose work does not bring them collectively to a specific place for stated hours of the day, but whose occupation has a recognised status. It is limited by the fact that titles can be misleading and by the tendency of some people to choose the most grandiloquent, presumably to enhance their status in their own estimation and that of others. Thus one finds the driver of a bread van who describes himself as a "confectionery representative" and Karsh (1959) cites the example of the dishwashers in a Chicago restaurant who were designated "utensil maintenance men". In addition, automation and increasing refinements in the division of labour have made many jobs what Wilensky (1960) calls "status-invisible" because they carry no name by which a person may be recognised. Many industrial workers, when asked "what do you do?" or "what is your job?" will answer that they work for X's, naming the company which employs them. If the question is put to them in the factory itself they will reply by giving the department where they work, e.g. "I'm on the fourth pickle floor", but the job will not be named. This is because no title can be given which is meaningful to those outside the department as, for instance, with the "back-winder", "facing tacker" or "neck-band girl". Consequently, these workers get their status and identification not from the work they do, but from the organisations for whom they work.

This aspect of industrialisation has received attention from many writers, notably as contributing to the alienation from work induced by the machine. Moore (1951), for example, contends that pride in work is impossible when a man's job has no significance for his immediate community and that what Veblen mistook for the "instinct" of workmanship is really the desire for social recognition of one's skill. Berger (1962) makes the same point and notes that "the disengagement of self from occupational role not only is more common than it once was but is increasingly regarded as *proper*". Cynicism about one's work is now fashionable at all occupational levels as is shown, for example, by the frequently used metaphor of the "rat race" and the phrase "publish or perish" so often heard in academic circles. In other words, estrangement from what is done for a living and the failure to find personal significance in work are not confined to the shopfloor, but are found throughout the social system. Berger sees this as a sign that work is no longer an important source of normative integration in society.

Perhaps this is inevitable. If Gabor (1964) is right in his book *Inventing the Future*, work as we know it is already obsolescent for the greater part of the population. "For the first time in history we are now faced with the possibility of a world in which only a minority need work, to keep the great majority in idle luxury". But, he argues, transition to this state will not be easy because the Gospel of Work is part of our cultural heritage. He therefore suggests that a period of unnecessary work and waste is needed, whereby people will be kept artificially employed in order that they may not feel socially useless—a principle already in practice in some areas. Both economically and psychologically these measures are necessary, Gabor maintains, until a generation grows up for whom there will be no sharp limit between work and play. Ultimately, however, man must be brought into equilibrium with his new environment. "He must be adapted to leisure, and his work must become *occupational therapy*. It must not only entertain him... but must keep him mentally alert, and give him the feeling that he is useful and even creative. We shall never reach this goal by merely improving pushbutton machinery."

The therapeutic value of work has long been recognised, but, except in the clinical field, it has tended to be obscured by ecomomic and social considerations. Freedman and Leavy (1961) have drawn attention to the importance of work as a partially sublimated or elevated expression of emotional needs when neurotic feelings are controlled, and Jaques (1965), in an analysis of the mental processes in work, concludes that working, and especially working for a living, can be a fundamental activity in a person's retention of his mental health. He defines work as "the application of knowledge and the exercise of discretion within externally prescribed limits to achieve an object which can be reality tested" and notes that this requires "a continuous working-through of the attendant anxiety". An individual's capacity to work, therefore, depends largely on the extent to which conscious aims and the reality content of work are consistent with the unconscious symbolic aspects of the task. The greater the consistency the greater is the interest and satisfaction found in work.

Jaques's distinction between the "prescribed" and the "discretionary" aspects of work derives from the Glacier Project and the study of what he and Brown (1965) term "employment work". The prescribed elements of a job set the limits to what a person on the job may do, the content of his work about which he is left no authorised choice; within these limits he has to use discretion and decide for himself the best course of action in a given situation. It is the discretionary content of work which determines the intensity or weight of responsibility experienced in a job and which, Jaques claims, can be measured in terms of the maximum periods of time during which a person must exercise discretion on his own account. Whether or not one agrees with the measurement of responsibility on this basis, there is no doubt that identification of these two aspects of employment work have helped to clarify much muddled thinking in this sphere, as has the Glacier distinction between occupational role, the tasks to be performed in fulfilling that role, and the effort experienced in carrying out those tasks.

It will have been noted that most of the authors cited in this paper when discussing work have also discussed leisure, whether in terms of the allocation of time, of the activities engaged in or the significance of these activities for the individual. This is partly because the activities most valued are increasingly those which occur in time not devoted to paid employment and so, it is suggested, leisure is being used to compensate for alienating work. Others are of the opinion, however, that attitudes and practices developed in one sphere of life are apt to spill over into another, so that if work is perceived as a means of "killing time" leisure is likely to be similarly regarded. Whereas some think the dichotomy between work and play is becoming sharper, there are others who maintain there is increasing fusion between the two. Whichever position is adopted there seems to be a tendency to take a gloomy view of the future and to set "the problem of leisure" alongside that of impersonal and unsatisfying work. Riesman (1950), who has at various times advocated different solutions to the problem, only to become discouraged by each in turn, finds it difficult to see the way forward: "In the present state of our knowledge of man it seems well-nigh impossible to give a 'correct' definition of work and of play—to say precisely how society in general, or any given society, should define these spheres and how it should value them."

A more practical approach is taken by Wilensky (1962) and by Cotgrove and Parker (1963) in pleading for more systematic research in this area. Wilensky thinks we need to blend a knowledge of economic institutions with an awareness of the flow of time. He points to the absence of studies in which the interrelation of attitudes and behaviour at work, in the family, and in the community at large are examined throughout the life cycle of an individual. Such studies, he maintains, would do much to elucidate the work-leisure problem within a proper time perspective. Cotgrove and Parker also draw attention to the effect of work on family life, political attitudes and involvement, community activities and the like, and the dearth of investigations in this field by social scientists. Like Wilensky, they are aware that longitudinal studies are indicated: "Satisfaction from work and the significance attached to it will depend not only on the nature of the work but also on the expectations which the individual brings to his job. These in turn will be the result of complex processes of selection and socialization, which begin at 11-plus with entry to the grammar or modern school, each of which carries its stream of children on to broad groups of occupations." The more detailed studies which have been made of factors influencing the expectations and occupational choice of school-leavers suggest that the spread of comprehensive education is not likely to invalidate this statement.

From this review of the concepts of work held by various authorities certain conclusions emerge. First, although work may be equated with "what one does for a living" in the eyes of many people, it is important for the individual to have a recognised occupation. It may be fashionable to display a cynical attitude to one's job, but employment is valued for the social status it confers. Secondly, work and leisure are connected in that the conditions and demands of the one have a determining influence on the other, as do the associated attitudes and behaviour. For this reason it seems useful to think of a work–play continuum rather than two separate and contrasting aspects of life. Thirdly, there is considerable evidence of the lingering Puritan tradition of work as a moral, as well as a productive, force which shows itself in overt and hidden fears of the increased leisure expected in the wake of automation. An investigation of the nature of these fears would not be out of place at the present time. It might do much to reveal the reasons for anxiety and would give direction to those who feel that education for leisure will be a necessary provision in the future. Finally, more attention needs to be paid to the social and cultural matrix of work. As Hearnshaw (1954) has said, "work as a mastery of technique, as control, attention and service is the lynch-pin of modern society", and he points out that work in this sense is dependent on the attitude of those who perform it. Too little is yet known about the origins of attitudes to work and how they are transmitted, but it is likely that they will differ in societies at different stages of economic development. Can we assume that continued economic growth, to which as a nation we are committed, will lead to a leisure-orientated or a consumer-orientated society, and is it this which people desire? Gabor (1964) quotes Joad as saying that "work is the only occupation yet invented which mankind has been able to endure in any but the smallest possible doses". In the age of automation it appears that the doses will get smaller, the vital question is, do we need a placebo?

REFERENCES

ANDERSON, N. (1961), *Work and Leisure*. London: Routledge & Kegan Paul.

BERGER, B. M. (1962) The Sociology of Leisure: Some Suggestions. *Industrial Relations*, **1**, 31–45.

BROWN, W. (1965) What is Work? *Glacier Project Papers*, London: Heinemann, 54–73.

COHEN, J. (1953) The Ideas of Work and Play. *Brit. J. Sociol.*, **4**, 312–322.

COTGROVE, S., and PARKER, S. (1963) Work and Non-Work. *New Society*, No. **41.**

DONALD, M. N., and HAVIGHURST, R. J. (1959) The Meanings of Leisure. *Social Forces*, **37**, 357–360.

FIRTH, R. (1948) Anthropological Background to Work. *Occup. Psychol.*, **22**, 94–102.

FREEDMAN, L. Z., and LEAVY, S. A. (1961) Psychopathology and Occupation: Part 2, Work and Competition. *Occup. Psychol.*, **35**, 93–110.

FRIEDMANN, G. (1961) *The Anatomy of Work*. London: Heinemann.

GABOR, D. (1964) *Inventing the Future*. London: Penguin Books.

GALBRAITH, J. K. (1958) *The Affluent Society*. Boston: Houghton Mifflin.

HEARNSHAW, L. S. (1954) Attitudes to Work. *Occup. Psychol.*, **28**, 129–139.

JAQUES, E. (1965) The Mental Processes in Work, in *Glacier Project Papers*. London: Heinemann.

KARSH, B. (1959) The Meaning of Work in an Age of Automation, in *Readings in Human Relations*. (Edited by Davis, K., and Scott, W. G.) New York: McGraw-Hill.

KLEIN, L. (1963) *The Meaning of Work*. London: The Fabian Society.

MEAD, M. (1950) *Male and Female*. London: Victor Gollancz.

MOORE, W. E. (1951). *Industrial Relations and the Social Order*. Revised Edition. New York: Macmillan.

RIESMAN, D. (1950) *The Lonely Crowd*. New Haven: Yale University Press.

WILENSKY, H. L. (1960) Work, Careers and Social Integration. *Intern. Soc. Sci. J.*, **12**, 543–560.

WILENSKY, H. L. (1962) Labor and Leisure: Intellectual Traditions. *Industrial Relations*, **1**, 1–12.

17. *The Criteria of Vocational Success*

DONALD E. SUPER

WHAT is attempted in seeking to promote vocational adjustment? Is it the same as personal adjustment? If not, how does it differ from personal adjustment? Answers to these questions may be derived from an analysis of the objectives of vocational guidance as they have manifested themselves in the work of vocational counselors.

One way in which the objectives of vocational guidance manifest themselves is in the criteria used in judging vocational success. If the general objective of vocational guidance is to help people to achieve success in the world of work, then its specific objectives should manifest themselves in judgments of success. These judgments are in some instances the passing judgment of observers, and hence difficult to study; but they are also made by vocational counselors in studies evaluating the effectiveness of counseling, by personnel workers making employee evaluations, and by psychologists studying the relationships between personal characteristics and success. What are these criteria, then, which have been used in judging vocational success?

CRITERIA OF VOCATIONAL SUCCESS

Back in the 1920's when vocational educators, vocational counselors, and vocational psychologists were first beginning to undertake the scientific study of civilian occupations, Walter V. Bingham[(2)] made a study of the relationship between intelligence and success in executive employment. The vocational achievements of his executives were judged by the amount of money they earned, their credit ratings, the number and types of civic organisations and social clubs they belonged to, and similar evidences of status in their work and in their communities. Bingham pioneered in vocational psychology, but this criterion of success was as comprehensive and as carefully worked out as any of the next 20 years.

EARNINGS AND OUTPUT

During the decade after World War I *earnings and output* were often used as the sole basis for judging vocational attainment. Many recent studies have used this same production criterion as an index of achievement: for

(Reprinted from *Occupations*, October 1951, pp. 5–8, by permisson of editor and author.)

example, in a study of machine book-keepers in a large Philadelphia bank[4] the index of success used was the number of entries made per hour, and in another study of factory workers in St. Louis a few years ago[7] the criterion was the number of units assembled in the course of a day's work.

During the late Twenties and early Thirties a variety of other criteria of success began to be used. *Advancement* was one, the individual's rate of progress in the company or in his occupation. Marion Bills used advancement from routine clerical work through supervisory positions to planning positions as an index of success. Here the focus is somewhat different from that used when output is the index, for the latter criterion purports to measure success in the present job, whereas in the case of advancement the aim is to judge suitability for higher grades of work. It is not necessarily the worker who is most successful in the *present* job who will make the best worker in the *next higher* job.

In the late 1930's *stability* in an occupation began to be used as a criterion. As the depression made even holding a job, let alone progressing in it, seem like more of an achievement, occupational stability became more popular as a criterion of success. The British National Institute for Industrial Psychology[1] employed this index in evaluating the effectiveness of vocational counseling with and without test data. The reasoning was that a well-placed youngster would stay in his job, while a badly placed boy or girl would in due course leave. Strong[16] used occupational stability as one of the criteria of success in the standardization and validation of his well-known interest inventory. His reasoning was that if a man remained in a field for three years he must be reasonably competent and reasonably well satisfied; here there is introduced into the criterion of success a somewhat different note, for while competence is mentioned first, satisfaction is also considered. It is not only performance that counts, according to this argument, but also how the worker feels about his work.

RELIANCE ON RATINGS

While all these means of judging occupational success were being used, there was considerable reliance also in *ratings* by supervisors.[6] They were used largely on the grounds that more objective evidence, such as output, could not be obtained in certain types of work. Teachers, for example, can hardly be judged by the number of pupils they teach nor even by the number who graduate, pass college entrance examinations, or get over some other hurdle. The job is too complex and there are too many variables at work. In keeping with the emphasis on *performance* which characterized the other popular criteria of the years after World War I, these ratings emphasized the quantity and quality of the worker's work, as shown by the very term *efficiency* rating.

Despite their low reliability, ratings have one advantage over some of the more objective criteria such as output: they provide a broader and more comprehensive estimate of achievement. That this is so is made clear by the intercorrelations of the traits or characteristics rated and by their relationship to ratings of over-all value to the organization: apparently, no matter what the supervisor is asked to rate, no matter how specific the behavior he is asked to judge, he rates on the basis of a general evaluation of the worker as a worker and as a person. In fact, it would hardly be an exaggeration to say that he rates the worker more as a *person* than as a *worker*.

MORE COMPREHENSIVE CRITERIA

Attempts to judge the success of workers in the intangibles and in the creative fields have in recent years shown some desire for more comprehensive criteria than output, advancement, stability, and efficiency ratings. A series of studies of teaching success conducted by Barr and his students at the University of Wisconsin[(14, 15)] used as their measure of teaching success the gains made by pupils on achievement tests. Judging a teacher by the progress made by her students seems at first to be a reasonably comprehensive index of success. But it assumes that pupil learning of facts and skills, such as is measured by achievement tests, is the sole objective of teaching. And most people are not really satisfied to judge teachers by that, and just by that. They are also interested in how the teacher affects the personality development of the student, the extent to which he stimulates the student to further learning (rather than just cramming him full of presently needed subject-matter), and a number of other things not measured by the usual achievement tests.

ANOTHER BROAD APPROACH

Another attempt at a more global method of judging vocational success was made by Anne Roe,[(11)] who needed to select a group of creative artists. She obtained the names of 20 men who were adjudged by established art critics to be among the most eminent in the country. But judges are no better than the criteria by which they judge, and their criteria inevitably reflect somewhat the values, prejudices, and limitations of their times; if they did not, the public would not retain them as judges. So, although Miss Roe's objective was to study a group of creative artists (her principal interest was the effect of alcohol on creativity), all that she could actually be sure of was that she had a group who had succeeded in pleasing a vocal segment of the general public.

The use of criteria such as these is in keeping with the emphasis on the objectives of vocational guidance as expressed in the official definition formulated in the 1920's by the National Vocational Guidance Association and revised several times since then.[8] It states that the aim of vocational guidance is "to assist the individual to choose, prepare for, enter upon, and progress in an occupation." The emphasis seems to be on success; on choosing a field in which one can *compete effectively*, preparing so that one can *do the work*, getting a *foothold* in the field, and doing the work so that one can *advance* in the field. Although excluded neither from the definition nor from the thinking of those who prepared it, the attitudes, values, and needs of the worker, and his satisfaction in his work, are not explicitly mentioned and hence receive no attention. Perhaps it was assumed that a person would not get a job, or at least not move ahead in it, unless it was in keeping with his values and met his needs; if so, the assumption is not warranted, as is known from many work histories and case studies. In any case the focus is still on *achievement* rather than on *adjustment*.

A NEW TERM NEEDED

Perhaps it is unwise to use the term *success*, since in American culture success is so often measured by achievement. One tends to forget that success is not only a *social* or *objective* matter, but also a *personal* or *subjective* matter. "Success," as the world judges it, is fruitless and empty unless it is also seen as success by the individual. What would wealth have been to Ghandi, or the love and respect of humble men and women to Bismarck? What use had Thoreau for prestige and status, or Theodore Roosevelt for opportunities to be alone with himself and the universe? In the eyes of each of these persons, and of some others, each of them was successful; but in the judgment of many, each of them was a failure. Individual values, and hence individual judgments, differ in such matters. Perhaps it is necessary to redefine success, to use some other term which allows more room for individual differences in standards and in objectives. Perhaps the term adjustment would be more appropriate.

ADJUSTMENT

This is no new suggestion, for the term adjustment is, if anything, too popular. In 1925, Harry D. Kitson published a book on *The Psychology of Vocational Adjustment*, and 10 years later Laurance Shaffer wrote his widely used *Psychology of Adjustment*: in 1942 the writer published a volume on *The Dynamics of Vocational Adjustment*, which was followed by McKinney's *Psychology of Personal Adjustment*, Symonds' *Dynamics of Human Adjustment*, and several other "adjustment" texts. But one reason why the term is so popular is because with an increasing understanding of the principles of mental hygiene has developed an increasing awareness of the fact that success is a personal, subjective thing best judged not solely in terms of the individual's performance, important though that is, but also by his feelings and attitudes. Look, therefore, at some of the more recent trends in the criteria of vocational success or adjustment in order to see how this awareness has affected practice.

NEW CRITERIA

The trend is revealed, for example, in the traits or types of behavior which are dealt with in current *rating scales.* Whereas many of those that were used in the earlier days stressed descriptions of the worker's application, industriousness, and output, today rating scales pay more attention to the worker's relations with his fellow employees, subordinates, superiors, and customers. Investigations such as the Hawthorne Study[12] made it clear that these factors are of vital importance in production and in job stability. Consequently both practical personnel managers and students of men and of work have paid more attention to interpersonal relations.

Another sign of this awareness of the fact that success is partly a subjective matter appears in the use of worker's *self-ratings* of satisfaction as an index of adjustment. In one of the studies[5] which was carried out in the mid-Thirties to evaluate an experiment in vocational guidance significantly named the "Adjustment Service," questionnaires to former counselees asked them to rate themselves on satisfaction with their present field of work. In England during the Thirties[1] the National Institute for Industrial Psychology asked former counselees to rate their satisfaction in their work, and these ratings were one of the criteria which were used in ascertaining whether or not test data improved the quality of vocational counseling. Parenthetically, they did!

But perhaps the most clear-cut evidence of the fact that vocational counselors and their educational and psychological colleagues have really translated their awareness of the importance of subjective reactions into practice lies in the increasing popularity of the *clinical appraisal* of an individual and of his work as a method of evaluating vocational success and adjustment. One of the best examples is the recent study by Friend and Haggard,[3] in which worker adjustment was judged on the basis of the balancing of the satisfactions which the individual sought in his work and the satisfactions which the job provided, as seen in long-term case histories.

SCHAFFER'S STUDY

Similar to this is the current study of Robert Schaffer, a personnel psychologist with the Prudential Life Insurance Company, in which the question is the extent to which agreement between the individual's picture of himself on the one hand, and opportunities to be that kind of person in his work on the other, is related to being satisfied with his work. It is Schaffer's hypothesis that, if a man or woman cannot, in his working life, find opportunities to be the kind of person he wants to be, for self-fulfillment, he will be dissatisfied with his work. In the fullest sense of the term, vocational adjustment implies that the individual has opportunity to express his interests, use his abilities, achieve his values, and meet his emotional needs.

A REDEFINITION OF VOCATIONAL GUIDANCE NEEDED

If these trends are in fact indicative of changed understanding of the nature of vocational success, then a redefinition of vocational success and of vocational guidance is called for. That which is implicit in these criteria should be made explicit. The present NVGA definition is no longer appropriate. An attempt at a redefinition will be made in a subsequent article.

BIBLIOGRAPHY

1. ALLEN, E. P., and SMITH, P. (1940) *The Value of Vocational Tests as Aids to Choice of Employment*. Birmingham, England: City of Birmingham Educational Committee.
2. BINGHAM, W. V., and DAVIS, W. T. (1924) Intelligence Test Scores and Business Success, *J. of Applied Psychology*, **VIII** 1–22.
3. FRIEND, J. G., and HAGGARD, E. A. (1948) Word Ajustment in Relation to Family Background, *Applied Psychological Monographs*, No. 16. Palo Alto: Stanford University Press.
4. HAY, E. N. (1943) Predicting Success in Machine Book-keeping, *J. of Applied Psychology*, **XXVII** 483–493.
5. HAWKINS, L. S., and FIALKIN, H. N. (1935) *Clients' Opinions of the Adjustment Service*. New York: American Association for Adult Education.
6. MAHLER, W. R. (1948) *Twenty Years of Merit Rating*. New York: The Psychological Corporation.
7. MELTZER, H. (1944) Approach of the Clinical Psychologist to Management Relationships, *J. of Consulting Psychology*, **VIII** 165–174.
8. National Vocational Guidance Association (1937). Principles and Practices of Vocational Guidance, OCCUPATIONS, **XV** 772–778.
9. PATERSON, D. G., *et al.* (1941) *The Minnesota Occupational Rating Scales*. Chicago: Science Research Associates.
10. POND, M., and BILLS, M. A. (1933) Intelligence and Clerical Jobs, *Personnel J.* **XII**, 41–56.
11. ROE, A. (fall, 1946) The Personality of Artists, *Educational and Psychological Measurement*, **VI** 401–408.
12. ROETHLISBERGER, F. J., and DICKSON, W. J. (1939) *Management and the Worker*. Cambridge: Harvard University Press.
13. ROGERS, C. R., and WALLEN, J. L. (1945) *Counseling with Returned Servicemen*. Boston: Houghton Mifflin.
14. ROLFE, J. F. (1945) The Measurement of Teaching Ability: Study Number Two, *J. of Experimental Education*, **XIV** 52–74.
15. ROSTKER, L. E. (1945) The Measurement of Teaching Ability: Study Number One, *J. of Experimental Education*, **XIV** 6–51.
16. STRONG, E. K. (1943) *Vocational Interests of Men and Women*. Stanford, Stanford University Press.

18. The Meaning of Work and Jobs

JOHN G. DARLEY and THEDA HAGENAH

A MAN'S working life spans forty to fifty years. In the main, he keeps his nose to the same kind of grindstone for that period of time. Thus it is important to consider what makes grindstones attractive—what satisfactions may be found in jobs. For the very young child, the world of work is remote and without immediate meaning. But the grand pattern of socialization of the human animal—of inducting him into the society of which he is a part—brings the world of work into focus as early as the preadolescent years. Gradually the overriding impact of work as a way of life, as a means to an end, as an end in itself, is borne in on the individual, with the enthusiastic if often misguided assistance of parents, other adults, and peers in his surroundings. The act of occupational choice becomes important; preparation for a job, entry into the ranks of the gainfully employed, and striving for some measure of success become paramount concerns. The socialization process reaches a milestone when the individual "establishes" himself in the world of work. The past is truly prologue and he and society can now assess his worth.

But it is hard to measure the success of a life. There are material standards of income and possessions to serve as possible yardsticks. Satisfaction and enjoyment inhere in varying degrees in one's job. Some men measure their lives by the power or prestige they wield. Service to others is a criterion in certain areas of our society. Success can have as many definitions as happiness.

Several questions immediately arise regarding these criteria. Who is to make the judgment? To what extent are the various criteria psychologically equivalent or interchangeable? What are the relations among the criteria that may measure life? Are the criteria patterned in some way to represent different incentives for different occupational groups? Does satisfaction in one's work wax and wane over time? When a man has given hostages to fortune, and established minimum security for his family, does he find the

(Reprinted from *Vocational Interest Measurement, Theory and Practice*, by John G. Darley and Theda Hagenah. A volume in the Minnesota Library on Student Personnel work edited by E. G. Williamson, University of Minnesota Press, Copyright 1955 by the University of Minnesota.)

same satisfactions in his job? What factors are related to occupational success? What control does the individual have over these factors?

Since we consider the development of interests as a special case of general motivational theory, it is immediately apparent that such questions must be raised. It is equally apparent that the answers move into the realm of value judgments and life styles, where incisive, categorical, and communicable answers are difficult to find.

In our own attempts over the years to work out some rational basis for vocational counseling, we have frequently speculated on the meaning of jobs and work in this particular society. These speculations provide some framework for what we shall say about vocational interest measurement in later chapters. Let us first consider one aspect of the meaning of job titles.

In a relatively mobile society such as ours, job titles and the hierarchical arrangement of jobs by perceived prestige and status levels represent the American equivalent of aristocracy. Unlike other and more rigidly structured societies, our culture says that the individual is free to ascend the occupational ladder regardless of birth and inheritance. The occupational label that an individual ultimately bears may be the hallmark of his status in the eyes of the community. The *role* of the administrator, the doctor, the lawyer, or the engineer may be acted differently by different individuals, but their *status* in society is to a marked extent defined by their membership in the groups called administrators, doctors, lawyers, or engineers. In this context, education is often perceived as the means of moving up the social and occupational ladder; this is in part true because educational attainment is either closely related to or legally requisite for the individual's ultimate vocational and professional adjustment.

Deeg and Paterson[(3)] provide interesting evidence on the stability of our hierarchical perception of job titles. They duplicated, in 1947, a 1925 study by Counts, in which respondents were asked to rank a list of occupations "in the order of their social standing." Deeg and Paterson used four subgroups of respondents: freshmen and sophomore college students; juniors, seniors, and graduate students; seniors in a vocational high school; and seniors in an academic high school. The rank ordering by these four groups showed such high intercorrelations that they were combined into a single sample of 475 cases for comparison with the results of Counts' 1925 sample of 450 cases. The resultant correlation of ranks for the two samples was ·97, leading the authors to conclude that "the social status of occupations has changed very little in the United States during the past 21 years ... the professions and 'higher' business occupations continue to receive high ranks; the skilled trades, technical occupations in the distributive field are given intermediate ranks; and the semi-skilled and unskilled occupations are given low ranks."

It is in these terms that we may understand some of the familial pressures and individual forces behind the specific vocational choices that young people make. In study after study, the vocational choices of students, in high school and early college years, cluster in the upper reaches of the occupational scales or the socioeconomic scales. Ordinarily these choices exceed the occupational status actually attained by the fathers of these students. We do not create our sons in our own image; we create them out of our dreams of the life we might have had.

It is in these terms, too, that we must understand the pressures for early and specific occupational choices which we bring to bear on our adolescents. Beginning not later than the early high school choice between the academic and vocational curriculums, the pressure grows steadily greater to "make a choice." The highly differentiated curricular offerings at the beginning university and college level represent probably the heaviest pressure point. As adults, we are anxious for our children to take their "proper" place in this hierarchy of job titles. Through education, the "proper" place should be as high as possible, in terms of the American dream. For, in that dream, the higher one's status, the greater will be one's security, satisfaction, earning power, and contribution to society. On net balance and in spite of many defects and individual failures, the dream is not too far from reality; this mobile society, with the assistance of extensive public education, has provided a good demonstration of a functional aristocracy of jobs.

Since our concern here is with vocational interests and since interests involve in part the idea of satisfaction with one's job, we must explore further the relation between satisfaction and status. We have chosen one research study to illustrate the many published studies that report a relation between occupational level and job satisfaction.

Super,[(8)] as a by-product of a pioneering investigation of avocational interests, studied job satisfaction among 273 employed men between the ages of twenty and sixty-eight; some of his findings pertain to our problem. He finds a significant but not linear relation between occupational level (or status) and job satisfaction, with some evidence that two occupational scales exist—a white-collar scale and a manual worker's scale. On the white-collar scale, his representatives of professional occupations appear most satisfied and his commercial sample least satisfied; men in skilled occupations show the greatest degree of satisfaction on the manual scale and actually exceed the degree of satisfaction shown by the commercial workers on the white-collar scale. The size of the gap between the present occupational level and the level aspired to is negatively and significantly related to job satisfaction. For the dissatisfied in his employed sample, "lack of similarity of job requirements to individual abilities and interests" is the primary reason for dissatisfaction.

As an explanation for his finding that age and job satisfaction are significantly but not linearly related, Super suggests the existence of a "satisfaction cycle" which finds younger men satisfied at the start of their careers; somewhat dissatisfied and anxious to advance more rapidly after about age twenty-five; more satisfied again in the decade beginning with age thirty-five; less satisfied in the decade beginning with forty-five when "work loses some of its attractions and other types of satisfactions have not yet been developed"; and increasingly satisfied again in the decade from fifty-five on. Job satisfaction, here and in other studies, is, as Super points out, related to the American tradition in which one must "make good".

Although we have described American society as relatively mobile along the occupational ladder, obviously it is not completely mobile—both within the individual and within the needs of the labor market limits exist on occupational movement. What does this mean for the degree of satisfaction of the individual who does not achieve the occupational level to which he aspires? Is he therefore doomed to dissatisfaction? First, we must consider how much mobility actually exists.

In Super's study, he notes that approximately 70 per cent of his sample of employed men have never changed their occupational level. In a more detailed study by Davidson and Anderson, summarized in Kuhlen and Thompson's book of readings,[(2)] a slightly higher degree of vertical mobility is found, possibly because their sample included a wider range of occupations than did Super's. Davidson and Anderson find that their "data as a whole suggest that the occupational pyramid possesses an institutional character, that its marked stratification is due in large measure to forces related to and emerging from the occupational status of fathers and family environments in which children are reared, and that these do not submit easily to other influences such as the school but tend to form certain patterns which become characteristic of the several occupational levels." In other words, people don't move up the occupational ladder as freely as the American dream indicates. Many able students are barred from higher education because of the socioeconomic and cultural backgrounds of their parents. The labor market itself dispassionately shakes down its annual entrants from secondary schools to the various levels needed to maintain our total economy, regardless of the aspiration of the individual.

A brief glance at the composition of the total civilian labor force will help to illustrate our concern with the relation between job satisfaction and job level. In his text on *The Sociology of Work*, Caplow[(1)] presents a tabular analysis of this labor force based on recent census data (see Table 1). As counselors well know, the majority of young people aspire to specific jobs that are included in the first six of the broad categories shown in the table, with the heaviest concentration of claimed choices in the first and third groups. Only at such levels do students tend to say "*that* would be an interesting job." We as adults also tend to feel that the really "interesting" jobs are to be found only in the upper categories and that many workers are doomed to tasks requiring little training, repetitive and routine activities, and rather undemanding or unchallenging work assignments. If this interpretation of our beliefs is correct, then not more than 34,476,000 out of the 58,668,000 people in the civilian labor force, or about 59 per cent of workers, are in work that is perceived as "satisfying" in some vaguely defined way. And even here, we might wonder how "satisfying" would be many of the specific jobs in groups 2, 4, 5, and 6 of Table 1!

TABLE 1
FUNCTIONAL DISTRIBUTION OF THE CIVILIAN LABOR FORCE, APRIL 1950

Major Occupation Group	Number (in thousands)			Percentage Distribution		
	Total	Male	Female	Total	Male	Female
Total employed	58,668	41,492	17,176	100·0	100·0	100·0
1. Professional and semi-professional workers	4,457	2,595	1,862	7·6	6·3	10·8
2. Farmers and farm manager	4,596	4,343	253	7·8	10·5	1·5
3. Proprietors, managers, and officials, except farm	6,379	5,438	941	10·9	13·1	5·5
4. Clerical and kindred workers	7,657	3,118	4,539	13·1	7·5	26·4
5. Salesmen and saleswomen	3,887	2,371	1,516	6·6	5·7	8·8
6. Craftsmen, foremen, and kindred workers	7,500	7,319	181	12·8	17·6	1·1
7. Operatives and kindred workers	11,930	8,715	3,215	20·3	21·0	18·7
8. Domestic service workers	1,923	152	1,771	3·3	0·4	10·3
9. Service workers, except domestic	4,773	2,605	2,168	8·1	6·3	12·6
10. Farm laborers and foremen	2,424	1,761	663	4·1	4·2	3·9
11. Laborers, except farm and mine	3,142	3,074	68	5·4	7·4	0·4

Source: Adapted from Caplow(1) (Table B, page 294), whose source was the Bureau of the Census, *Current Population Reports*, Series P-57, No. 94.

Parenthetically, we should point out here that interest measurement has been most successful in showing valid differential results primarily with occupational samples chosen from the first five categories in Table 1. Relatively few differential scoring methods have been developed for occupational groups in the sixth category, and we know of no meaningful interest measures for occupational groups in the remaining five categories of Table 1.

Despite our feelings about the amount of satisfaction in the various jobs in Table 1, this country has a highly productive economy by any economic measure such as gross national product or comparative wage level or sales figures. The workweek is short. High per-man productivity figures and efficient production lines characterize industry. It is also a restless occupational society, in terms of labor-management conflict and "fringe benefit" negotiations. And it is a busy and mobile society, as evidenced by heavy attendance figures at paid and spectator recreational events, great volume of travel, and mounting sales of "do-it-yourself" equipment in home repair and hobby activities. Are we to conclude, from our knowledge of a relation between satisfaction and occupational level, that workers in higher level jobs are "satisfied," and workers in lower level jobs are "dissatisfied" and restless? We must define sources of satisfaction more clearly.

In the various job satisfaction and morale studies, a crude division of responses appears to be related to the hierarchy of occupations. Respondents at lower occupational levels stress as sources of satisfaction economic factors, security, a chance to get ahead, a need for recognition as persons. Respondents at upper economic levels define satisfaction in terms of "interesting work", a chance to use their abilities, a chance to work independently at challenging tasks. For the former group, satisfaction derives from sources *external* to the work; for the latter group, satisfaction relates to *internal* feelings of accomplishment and involvement in work.

We may assume then that our highly productive economy has been created in such a way as to make many jobs essentially *maintenance* activities for workers, rather than intrinsically satisfying and absorbing ways of life. We know as counselors that the vocational dreams and aspirations of many of our students are doomed to go unrealized. We know that only a relatively small, though highly important, segment of our students will enter the high-status, high-income, and high-challenge occupations. But we do not need to succumb to vague worries that only the latter group will be satisfied, whereas the former group will experience a lifetime of disappointment. In our concern with "satisfaction" and "life adjustment" as goals of education, we must keep in mind that many sources of "satisfaction" exist and many different forms of "life adjustment" can be defined.

In this view of the world of work, satisfactions of an intrinsic and creative sort tend to be characteristic of workers at the higher job levels, whereas at the lower occupational levels, we postulate a situation in which routine, repetitive, easily learned tasks comprise the working life of a substantial number of workers and satisfactions derive from sources and conditions external to the working tasks. At the one extreme, work tends to be an end in itself; at the other, work is a means to an end. Vocational aspirations and dreams, once established, do not necessarily die by lack of fulfillment, nor does tragedy always follow lack of fulfillment. Dreams may live on in hopes for one's children; they may be modulated by a movement toward accepting reality; they may be transferred to non-job satisfactions or activities; and finally, they may be fulfilled by extrinsic satisfactions, which if not psychologically equivalent are at least psychologically sustaining. The measurement of interests has historically tended to concern itself with defining satisfactions of the intrinsic and creative sort—satisfactions inherent in the job itself. Since not all jobs possess such resources of stimulation and not all people are motivated to find their work an end in itself, counselors must not expect present interest inventories to yield patterns of driving interests for all students and must not assume that "satisfaction" in the world of work is psychologically identical at all levels of the occupational hierarchy.

In trying to clarify the relation between occupational status and occupational satisfaction, we are not defending the conservative position that ours is the best of all possible occupational worlds. We know that some students of ability and high interest motivation are blocked by economic factors from moving up the occupational ladder. Our society cannot afford such waste, and social action to remove the economic barrier is essential. We also observe situations in which working tasks have been split into such small units as to require far less of the worker than he is capable of giving in the way of skill, ability, or interest. Fragmentary reports show that when this trend is reversed—where some jobs are made more complex—production may increase, turnover may decrease, and worker satisfaction and interest in the job may become greater. We can see, in modern patterns of labor relations and legislation, some attempt to provide sources of satisfaction extrinsic to the job itself, such as minimum economic security, reduction in working hours, procedures for settlement of grievances, and machinery for arbitration and negotiation of conflict situations. More and more our society is trying to define the working situation as a setting in which the individual may find the social meaning and dignity and sense of participation that are important and basic needs of all men.

The counselor predicts that the individual's abilities, broadly defined, will lead him to a particular level of the occupational hierarchy. His claimed choices point to where he wants to go in this hierarchy. His measured interests give a closer approximation of the type of work in which he will find intrinsic satisfaction, *if* he is the kind of person who can find intrinsic satisfactions. If all three of these factors are congruent, the individual's chances of a "good adjustment" are at a maximum. But the counselor's concept of adjustment must allow for situations in which vocational aspirations may not be attainable, and in which measurement of interests may indicate that the individual will not find in his work the intrinsic satisfactions we value philosophically as motivating forces. Even though aspirations are not highly related to ability, and may not be attainable, they are none the less important. If they cannot be realized within the individual's work, the task of society is to permit their realization in other ways, and to provide incentives, rewards, or satisfactions extrinsic to the work situation. Over this latter solution the counselor has relatively little control; the social forces we have briefly described are of greater impact. But it is in the understanding of the relation of abilities and measured interest patterns, and in the relation of both of these to ultimate "success" or "satisfaction," however defined, that the counselor can be most helpful to the student.

Starting with a view of the hierarchy of job titles as a particular form of "aristocracy," and referring to the research which has related satisfaction rather closely to one's level in this scheme—one's status in the eyes of others—we have tried to redefine satisfaction in such a way as to lay the groundwork for some of the findings of interest measurement.

We have, in effect, proposed a continuum of interest factors: at one end are essentially intrinsic and self-perpetuating satisfactions (the man creatively engrossed and in love with his job); then comes a band of jobs that provide a nice balance between intrinsic and extrinsic satisfactions (the man whose job is preponderantly satisfying but who also attains outside his job other wanted ends of status, security, and a moderately satisfying life style); finally there is a large block of jobs that are admittedly highly important to the economy but provide within themselves mainly subsistence outcomes, leaving to extrinsic factors and sources the satisfactions of those needs for *social* meaning and integrity that are important to all men. This view of the world of work accounts for some of the job satisfaction findings and provides a framework for a discussion of the origin and development of interests. As we shall see, interest measurement has been most effective, in both a research and a clinical sense, in defining the first two segments of this continuum, and least effective in the differentiation or counseling of workers who engage in jobs in the third segment.

Counselors may find it interesting or provocative to look at jobs in another way. We have described the individual's occupational title as the hallmark of his status in society. Others may look up to him, or down at him, depending upon his place on the occupational ladder. But if jobs are the hallmark of status, they may also be viewed as cultural traps, from which escape s difficult if not impossible. Several examples of this come quickly to mind. For those professions in which legal requirements of training, certification, and continued licensure exist, once entry is accomplished by the individual the balance of his working life is highly predictable, regardless of changes which may occur in his interests, satisfactions, skills, or motivational patterns. Medicine and dentistry illustrate this point, law and engineering to a lesser degree since these latter professions have exits from the trap to various categories of business management positions. We know too little about the sociology of work and of the professions to trace this pattern in detail, although some writing in this area of sociology is beginning to emerge[(1)]. It seems true, however, that as an occupation takes on the characteristics of a profession, its members must perforce give up some freedom of movement in order to remain members of the group. The steps in professionalization are rather clear: a social need exists to be met; a given group is perceived as having the skills to meet the need; the group can establish its priority or monopoly of these defined skills; ethical codes are formulated and to some extent enforced; entry and training of new members are controlled with increasing rigidity; legal restrictions on the practice and use of the professional skills are ultimately obtained through appropriate political channels; indoctrination of new members becomes formalized. As these steps proceed over time, the individual is tied more closely to the group and his chances of a radical change in work or conditions of employment become minimal. He is not only under the protection of the profession; he is its captive. There are occasions when such developments have a two-edged outcome for society; professionalization is not an unmixed blessing.

Another example of trapping, recognized by those who counsel adult clients, is found in the heavy emphasis on past experience that characterizes our employment practices. For an adult to make a *major* change in his employment history is extremely difficult, since we tend to view such an attempt as evidence of instability, or dubious past performance, or immaturity, or unreality.

It is of some slight relevance that our popular literature today often deals with the period of doubt in men's careers, in the decade of their forties. The early and often costly years of training are out of the way; marriage and the raising of children—hostages to fortune—are well along; success and material well-being beyond the subsistence level are established. The pressure eases enough to permit some introspection, some stock-taking. If doubt is to supervene, this is the time. Has the trap closed forever? Do the years to come hold further advancement and material success? Has the last chance to change or progress gone by? Do these daily tasks hold the meaning and satisfaction they once held? Has the point of no return been reached?

Not all men may ask these questions; for many adults, some congruence between jobs and interest patterns has emerged, and by appropriate criteria they feel satisfied and are perceived by others as successful. We have no evidence on the numbers who are assailed by doubt and dissatisfaction; it is probable that there are many.

A preliminary study by Sarbin and Anderson[(5)] touches on this problem. A group of adult cases was carefully screened to yield a small sample of 76 men and 24 women whose primary complaint was overt dissatisfaction with their jobs. In 82 per cent of the sample of men studied, their *modal* occupation, in which they had established successful performance, was markedly at variance with their patterns of measured interests. This study is preliminary in nature of course, but it affords a glimpse at least of the personal aspects of occupational dissatisfaction, even though the individual to all outward appearances is successful in his occupational status.

What can such people do with their lives? Can they escape from the occupational trap? We may define at least four probable outcomes for such individuals:

1. They may develop socially acceptable and compensatory hobbies. However, on the basis of Super's extended study of small samples of representatives of four avocational interest groups,[(9)] we must say that hobby

development is not a panacea. In his research, hobbies were in some fields primarily extensions of the kinds of activities that were found in the components of the job by which the individual earned his daily living and in which he found basic satisfactions. Super found that "Men in vocations related to an avocation tended to make higher scores in those avocations ... suggesting that both avocational and vocational interests are generically the same" (ref. 9, page 75). He reduces the general compensatory theory of avocations to manageable proportions in this manner: "The major avocation of an employed person is apt to resemble his occupation if his employment is of a type suited to his interests and abilities, but it will be different from his occupation and like his real interests and abilities if this occupation is not one he would choose if given full freedom of choice and self-understanding or if he has an urge to use skills or express interests for which his regular occupation ... provides inadequate outlets" (ref. 9, page 113).

2. They may develop personality and behavioral conflicts at home or on the job, but still keep the job. Evidence for such a hypothesis would be hard to establish because of the multiple causality and conditionality usually associated with emotional problems.

3. They may redefine the component parts of the job and its specific duties more in line with the components of their primary interest patterns, changing the job duties thereby but leaving the job title untouched. This can be done only in certain kinds or levels of professional and executive work where a considerable degree of flexibility, independence, and worker-determination exists.

4. They may establish a sufficiently poor work record to be only marginally employable or to be ultimately separated from the job. Since re-employment is usually in line with past experience, such individuals have not really escaped the trap; they merely accumulate a work history containing many shifts of employers, but no major change in their usual occupation. There have been instances when great social forces spring the trap open for certain occupational groups. For example, during World War II, many teachers moved from their primary occupation into various wartime jobs, in and out of uniform, often achieving a much higher level of income, and possibly of satisfaction, than before. It is probable that a substantial percentage of these people did not return to the field of teaching; they had escaped from their occupational group. During the war, it was also noticeable that other kinds of jobs had to be sought by many salesman, since the government gradually became the major purchaser of goods and services in a wartime economy. We do not know systematically what readjustment these salesman made, or how many of them returned to the field of selling when the civilian economy was re-established. Other examples of the impact of social forces can be found, and might serve to illuminate some of our problems of jobs and interests, if appropriate research and case studies could be made.

We mentioned earlier that for certain levels of jobs, satisfactions are not inherent in the component tasks but have to be obtained from sources external to the job. We speculated that jobs could be so subdivided as to require less of the individual than he can and wants to give. This leads to a third way of looking at jobs. They provide an arena or field for a range of different behaviors that can be attached to the component parts, or tasks, that make up a specific job. In this view, the importance of the job title is decreased and the component tasks that represent its totality become the center of study and attention. An extreme example may illustrate this. In the motion picture *Modern Times*, Chaplin created a compellingly humorous though uncomfortable picture of an assembly-line worker tied, by increased speed, to a rigid, repetitive, and narrow range of arm-and-leg movements required to perform an astonishingly small assembly task. In our postulation of a field of behavior, this scene showed a job with tight boundaries, little freedom, great submission to the demands of the machine, and an unrelieved sameness to the contours of the little, crowded arena of action. Without any value judgment's being invoked, it is evident that many jobs are more circumscribed in a great variety of dimensions than are others. No job is entirely uncircumscribed: the doctor is not really a free agent in his profession—his night calls attest to that; the most creative scientist or artist works interdependently with others; the administrator is dependent on many specialists and on the cooperation of an entire organization.

But even with these qualifications, one can see the emergence of a rigidity-flexibility continuum as one views the hierarchical structure of jobs. For certain people, rigidity—narrow boundaries, small behavioral demands, and few component parts of the total job—is characteristic of their work; for others, flexibility—distant boundaries, many component parts, and many different behaviors—is customary.

A hint in support of this formulation may be found in the extended leadership studies conducted by Shartle and his colleagues at Ohio State.[6, 7] In their summary volume and in one article, they refer to the identification of fourteen functional components of the administrative or leadership positions in a variety of organizations. The percentage of time spent on these functions naturally differs in terms of the individual's specialized leadership status in the organization; the president divides and uses his time differently from the treasurer. But there is also some evidence in their data that two or more individuals having the same status (same hierarchical title) may distribute their time differently over the fourteen functions that make up their status; in other words, individuals may play the same role differently, and with differential effect upon their respective organizations. Such comparative freedom of action in defining and acting out the component parts of a job appears to be possible only at the higher occupational levels.

This way of looking at jobs is not particularly original with us. Truman Kelley[4] has presented a detailed theoretical and statistical treatment along these same lines, using a very broad definition of human talents. We have mentioned it here because of its possible use to counselors in focusing their attention on what is done within a job title, rather than on the title itself. Let us assume, as an example, that job X and job Y require approximately the same level of general ability, but that job X involves interest components 1, 2, 7, 8, and 15, whereas job Y involves only components 1, 2, and 7. Components 1 and 2 are intrinsically satisfying to people with primary interests of type *a*; components 8 and 15 are intrinsically satisfying to people with primary interests of type *f*; and component 7 doesn't have much intrinsic interest for anybody. In this overly simplified example, an individual of interest type *a* will be more satisfied in job Y than in job X, and an individual of interest types *a* and *f* together will be more satisfied in job X than in job Y. The presence of component 7 introduces a small amount of drudgery into both jobs, making them less than idyllic.

Counselors are accustomed to perceiving jobs as requiring different *amounts* and patterns of a finite number of abilities. This idea can be extended to include a view of jobs in which the component parts of the job tap the different *types* of intrinsic interests or satisfactions that may exist within the individual, according to the evidence from interest measurement. It would not require a major change in our systems of job analysis to produce further evidence on this possibility for the use of counselors.

This leads us to a final observation on the meaning of jobs. By some process only partially understood, representatives of various occupations seem to show characteristic ways of perceiving and reacting to situations, objects, and problems in their environment, and equally characteristic blind spots for the world around them. As we shall see later, habits of perception, personality, and value systems are not unrelated to occupational group membership. For the moment, we need only raise the question of which behavior comes first. Does participation in an occupation shape personality, values, and perception? Or do individuals of certain personality, perceptual habits, and value types characteristically seek out occupations that permit the free play of these behaviors? Our interpretation of the research on interest measurement leads us to a positive answer to this latter question. The individual's occupational interests are well determined before job experience. Interest measurement merely translates existing motivations and satisfactions into the vocabulary of the world of work.

REFERENCES

1. CAPLOW, T. (1954) *The Sociology of Work.* Minneapolis: University of Minnesota, Press.
2. DAVIDSON, P. E., and ANDERSON, H. D. (1952) Career patterns in occupational life. In R. G. Kuhlen and G. G. Thompson (eds.), *Psychological Studies of Human Development,* New York, Appleton-Century-Crofts, pp. 456–464.

3. Deeg, M. E., and Paterson, D. G. (1947) Changes in social status of occupations. *Occupations*, **25**, 205–208.
4. Kelley, T. L. (1940) *Talents and Tasks*, Harvard Education Papers, No. 1.
5. Sarbin, T. R., and Anderson, H. C. (1942) A preliminary study of the relation of measured interest patterns and occupational dissatisfaction. *Educ. psychol. Measurement*, **2**, 23–36.
6. Shartle, C. L., Leadership and executive performance. *Personnel*, March 1949, 2–12.
7. Shartle, C. L., and Stogdill, R. M. (1953) *Studies in Naval Leadership: Methods, Results and Applications—Final Technical Report*. Columbus: Ohio State University Research Foundation.
8. Super, D. E. (1939) Occupational level and job satisfaction. *J. of Applied Psychol.*, **23**, 547–564.
9. Super, D. E. (1940) *Avocational Interest Patterns*. Stanford University Press.

[This is an edited version of Chapter 1 of *Vocational Interest Measurement, Theory and Practice*.—Editors.]

19. *A Theory of Work Adjustment*

René V. Dawis, George W. England and Lloyd H. Lofquist

INTRODUCTION

Frank Parsons (1909), in his classic "bible" for guidance entitled *Choosing a Vocation*, stated a sound approach to vocational choice and subsequent work adjustment. In his well-known formula, he proposed the use of man analysis plus job analysis, and a bringing together of the two in the interest of wise vocational choice. His conceptualization of guidance centered on a matching model, and set the stage for extensive research, around a similar model, to be done by the group of psychologists identified with what we now term the trait-and-factor-centered approach to vocational psychology.

As Paterson (1938) pointed out, in his timely paper on the *Genesis of Modern Guidance*, Parsons' ideas were sound, but he found the cupboard bare when he set out to apply the man-analysis part of his formula. Parsons' approach then degenerated into the use of self study plus job analysis, which was done on a rather unsophisticated basis. Some guidance workers fixated their study and practice on occupational information alone.

After Parsons, and particularly between the two world wars, the study and understanding of man analysis progressed, largely because of the extensive interest and work in the study of individual differences, particularly in the measurement of mental traits and interests. Job analysis techniques also became considerably more sophisticated, largely through the work of the U.S. Department of Labor, and culminated in the publication of the *Dictionary of Occupational Titles* (1949). This work continues in the current efforts to revise and to considerably expand the D.O.T.

The inherent soundness of Parsons' approach has been reflected in the history of vocational psychology by such major developments as:

Viteles' (1924, 1932) work in developing the job psychograph;

Dvorak's (1935) development of occupational ability patterns and the consequent development by the United States Bureau of Employment Security of Occupational Aptitude Patterns (1958);

Strong's (1943, 1955) measurement of vocational interests and the more recent development of Clark's Minnesota Vocational Interest Inventory (1961);

(Reprinted by permission of publisher and authors from *A Theory of Work Adjustment*, Minnesota Studies in Vocational Rehabilitation, January 1964, Bulletin 38.)

The development of multi-factor tests (Dvorak, 1958), with occupational norms, such as the General Aptitude Test Battery; and

The publication of counseling tools such as the Minnesota Occupational Rating Scales (Paterson *et al.*, 1941, 1953) and the Worker Trait Requirements of 4,000 Jobs (1956), in which an attempt at integration of worker traits and job requirements is made.

With these developments and instruments (and, obviously, many others could be added) available to them, many vocational psychologists have been utilizing the Parsons approach (essentially a matching approach) in their work.

Frustrations with measurement problems and with problems of how to match abilities and educational-vocational requirements, and how to evaluate the goodness of fit, appear to have resulted in a period of little progress in understanding vocational-choice behavior and vocational adjustment. During this period, attention was directed to the importance of such matters as the counseling relationship (Rogers, 1942, 1951, 1961) and communication (Robinson, 1950) in counseling. More recently, attention has been centered on such problems as the meaning of work (Roe, 1956; Herzberg *et al.*, 1959) and the process of career development (Super *et al.*, 1957, 1960).

With the availability of more sophisticated tools and techniques for man analysis and job analysis; better understanding of relationship and communication factors in counseling; renewed realization of the importance of need satisfaction through work; and study of the developmental aspects of such concepts as vocational maturity; the time seems appropriate for a reformulation of Parsons' approach.

Brayfield (1961), in a recent appraisal of the present status of vocational counseling, has expressed our feelings in the following quotations:

"My major concern, obviously, is with the underpinnings of vocational counseling practice. Though I would not minimize the importance of an improved knowledge of the counseling process and student's behavior between interviews, I am quite convinced that the most significant contribution to vocational counseling as a professional practice will be made by those who nourish us with testable hypotheses and empirical data which help to build a science of occupational behavior. Now that vocational counseling is solidly established as an instrument of national policy, we should extend our efforts as scientists if we are to have a solid foundation for practice."

Later in his paper he states that: "We need, I believe, to re-establish or reaffirm our roots in basic psychology. Which is to say that we should be psychologists first and foremost. And, further, that at least some should be scientists first and foremost. I propose that we commit ourselves to the development, as an enterprise with the highest priority, of a science of the psychology of occupational behavior."

This Bulletin proposes a theory of work adjustment which may contribute to the development of a "science of the psychology of occupational behavior." It builds on the basic psychological concepts of stimulus, response, and reinforcement, and provides a research paradigm for the generation of testable hypotheses. While it draws on concepts related to learning theory, e.g., Skinner (1953), it is oriented toward the interests of differential and vocational psychologists.

A CONTEXT FOR THE THEORY

The proper subject matter for vocational psychology, as well as general psychology, is the *individual* as a *responding* organism. The individual as a responding organism is assumed to have a set of response potentials, the upper limits of which, with respect to range and quality, are presumably determined by heredity. The individual will respond when his response potentials make responding possible, and when the environment permits and/or stimulates responding. As the individual responds, his responding becomes associated with reinforcers in his environment. Reinforcers are environmental conditions which "maintain" responding, i.e., which are associated with the continuance of responding. Specific reinforcers in the environment become associated with specific responses of the individual. As a consequence of the interaction between individual and environment, the individual develops a wide variety of response capabilities. The responses that are utilized most frequently by the individual become identifiable as a primitive set of "abilities." At the same time the reinforcers in the environment which occur most frequently in the reinforcement of the individual's responding become identifiable as a primitive set of "needs." "Abilities" then are broad, but recognizable classes of responses generally utilized by the individual, while "needs" refer to the reinforcing properties of broad but recognizable categories of environmental conditions. The primitive set of abilities and the primitive set of needs together constitute the beginnings of the individual's work personality. (See Fig. 1.)

As the individual grows, his set of abilities and set of needs undergo change. New abilities and new needs get added to the existing sets. Some abilities are "utilized" by the individual more frequently than others. Some reinforcers occur in the reinforcement of responding more frequently than others. Some abilities and needs grow in "strength" faster than others. ("Strength" is used to describe the quantification of abilities and needs. Ability strength refers to either "speed" or "power," while need strength refers to reinforcement value.) The strength of a particular ability, relative to other abilities, will depend on the individual's response potential, previous opportunities for responding, and the relative reinforcement value(s) of the reinforcer(s) associated with his responding. The strength of a particular need, relative to the individual's other needs, will depend on the frequency with which the reinforcer has been associated with the individual's responding, and on the relative strength of the ability with which the reinforcer has been primarily associated.

The individual experiences differential utilization of his abilities because of differing social-educational requirements. This results in a set of more

Inception of the Work Personality

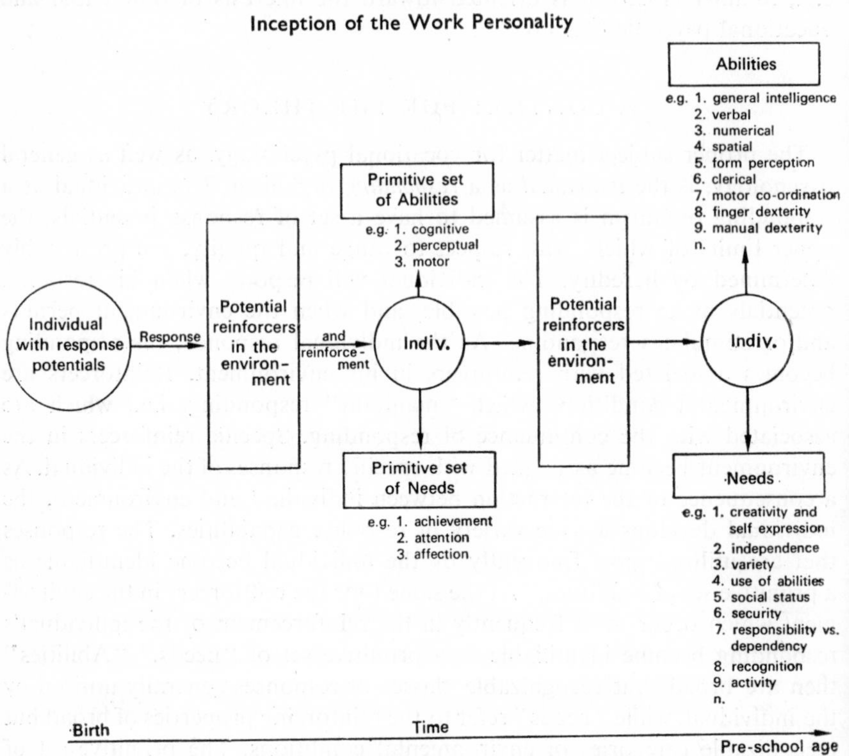

FIG. 1

specific abilities operating at different strengths. A set of more specific needs, with different needs at different strengths, also develops as a result of the individual's experiences with different social-educational reinforcer systems. The differentiation of the individual's sets of abilities and needs over time results from the varying levels of correspondence between the individual's ability and need patterns and the requirement-reinforcer systems to which the individual is exposed. The sets of abilities and needs become more specific as the individual persists in a particular "style of life," with its own relatively fixed set of requirement-reinforcer conditions. When the ability set and the need set are crystallized, successive measurements of ability and need strength will show no significant change. At this point, the individual is said to have a stable work personality. (See Fig. 2.)

The theory of work adjustment presented on the following pages is premised on the stable work personality.

Individuation of the Work Personality

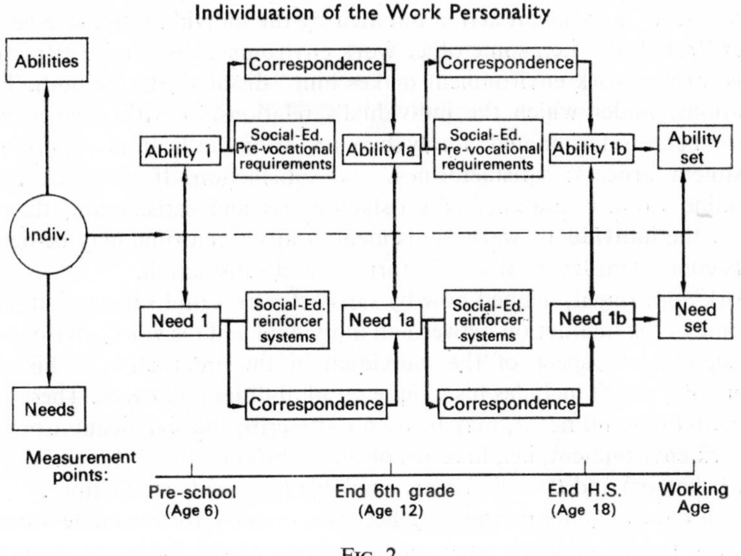

FIG. 2

A THEORY OF WORK ADJUSTMENT

Work in contemporary society is behavior which is reinforced in several ways, most characteristically by the payment of wages. This behavior takes place in a locus called the work environment. The technical terms "position," "job," and "occupation" define various limits of the work environment. The work environment may be described in terms of the behaviors which are appropriate in it and the stimuli which are potential reinforcers available to the individual in this environment. When the individual behaves in a manner appropriate to his work environment, the likelihood of his behavior being reinforced is increased. The process by which the individual (with his unique set of abilities and needs) acts, reacts, and comes to terms with his work environment is called work adjustment.

The course of an individual's work adjustment is best studied through continuous observation of the individual while he is in his work environment. Since this is not practicable at present, it becomes necessary to infer the course of work adjustment from indicators and/or outcomes of the process. The most easily observed outcome is the length of time the individual stays in a given work environment. The longer an individual stays in a given work environment, the more probable it is that the individual has arrived at some adequate adjustment with this environment. When the individual leaves a given work environment, one may infer that the adjustment was inadequate.

"Leaving the work environment" may occur because the individual is no longer "satisfactory," i.e., he no longer exhibits the "appropriate" behavior and is forced to leave. On the other hand, "leaving the work environment" may be an action initiated by the individual because he is no longer "satisfied," i.e., some other work environment is "more attractive" or his former work environment makes him "dissatisfied," or both. These conditions, under which the individual's relationship with a given work environment is terminated, imply two important indicators of the work adjustment process: satisfactoriness and satisfaction. If it is possible to determine varying amounts of satisfactoriness and satisfaction, then the state of the individual's work adjustment at any given time may be defined by his concurrent levels of satisfactoriness and satisfaction.

Work adjustment, defined now by satisfactoriness and satisfaction, is the outcome of the interaction between an individual and his work environment. The significant aspect of the individual in this interaction is his work personality, which includes his unique set of abilities and needs. These same terms, abilities and needs, may be used to describe the significant aspects of the work environment, i.e., in terms of the abilities required (for satisfactory work behavior) and the reinforcers available (for need satisfaction).

Given the foregoing premises, it becomes possible to formulate a correspondence theory of work adjustment in terms of the following definitions and propositions:

A. Definitions

1. Satisfactoriness:—Evaluation of the individual's work behavior principally in terms of the quality and quantity of task performance and/or performance outcomes (products, service). This evaluation may include other behavior dimensions, such as conformance to rules and interpersonal relations.

2. Satisfaction:—The individual's evaluation of stimulus conditions in the work environment with reference to their effectiveness in reinforcing his behavior.

3. Abilities:—Dimensions of response measurable through the application of psychological testing procedures, principally by ability and aptitude tests. These dimensions include, as examples, general intelligence, verbal ability, numerical ability, spatial ability, form perception, clerical ability, motor coordination, finger dexterity and manual dexterity. The current status of psychometrics limits the dimensions which can be included.

4. Needs:—Dimensions of reinforcement experience associated with classes of stimulus conditions which operate differentially as effective reinforcers. Some examples are: achievement, authority, creativity, economic reward, independence, and recognition. The development of need-measuring instruments has not attained the level of sophistication achieved for ability measurement.

5. *Ability requirements:*—Specifications of optimal ability ranges required for satisfactory work performance. The specifications are expressed in terms of the same dimensions as the individual's set of abilities.

6. *Reinforcer system:*—Specifications of the reinforcement values of classes of stimulus conditions. These specifications are expressed in terms of the same dimensions as the individual's set of needs.

7. *Correspondence:*—Similarity between abilities and ability requirements or between reinforcer system and needs.

8. *Tenure:*—The length of time an individual stays in a particular work environment.

B. Propositions

Proposition I. An individual's work adjustment at any point in time is defined by his concurrent levels of satisfactoriness and satisfaction.

Proposition II. Satisfactoriness is a function of the correspondence between an individual's set of abilities and the ability requirements of the work environment, provided that the individual's needs correspond with the reinforcer system of the work environment.

Given Proposition II, these corollaries follow:

Corollary IIa. Knowledge of an individual's ability set and his measured satisfactoriness permits the determination of the effective ability requirements of the work environment.

Corollary IIb. Knowledge of the ability requirements of the work environment and an individual's measured satisfactoriness permits the inference of an individual's ability set.

Proposition III. Satisfaction is a function of the correspondence between the reinforcer system of the work environment and the individual's set of needs, provided that the individual's abilities correspond with the ability requirements of the work environment.

Given Proposition III, these corollaries follow:

Corollary IIIa. Knowledge of an individual's need set and his measured satisfaction permits the determination of the effective reinforcer system of the work environment for the individual.

Corollary IIIb. Knowledge of the effective reinforcer system of the work environment and an individual's measured satisfaction permits the inference of an individual's set of needs.

Proposition IV. Satisfaction moderates the functional relationship between satisfactoriness and the correspondence of the individual's ability set with the ability requirements of the work environment.

Proposition V. Satisfactoriness moderates the functional relationship between satisfaction and the correspondence of the reinforcer system of the work environment with the individual's set of needs.

Proposition VI. The probability of an individual's being forced out of the work environment is inversely related to his measured satisfactoriness.

Proposition VII. The probability of an individual's voluntarily leaving the work environment is inversely related to his measured satisfaction.

Combining Propositions VI and VII, we have:

Proposition VIII. Tenure is a function of satisfactoriness and satisfaction.

Given Propositions II, III, and VIII, this corollary follows:

Corollary VIIIa. Tenure is a function of ability-requirement and need-reinforcer correspondence.

Proposition IX. The correspondence between the individual (abilities and needs) and the environment (ability requirements and reinforcer system) increases as a function of tenure.

(Figure 3 schematically illustrates the relationships stated above.)

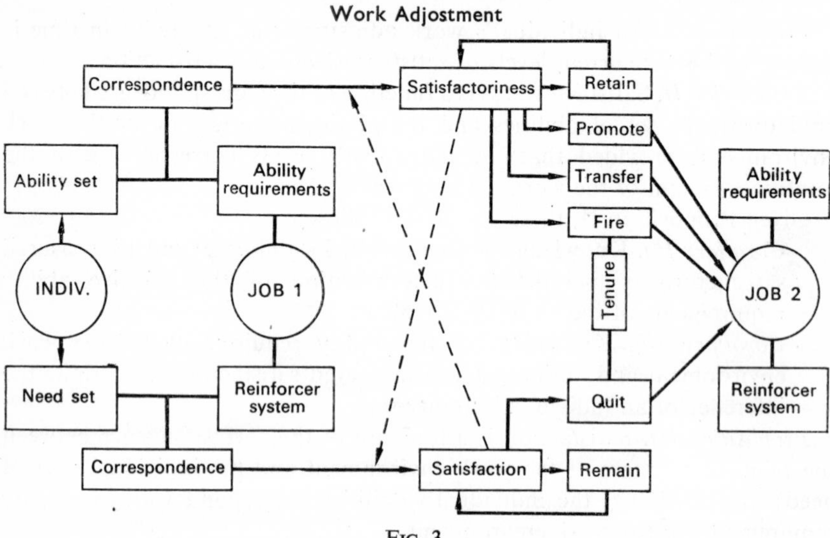

FIG. 3

If work adjustment is to be described in the terms of this theory, it becomes necessary to examine the comprehensiveness of the theory. How does the theory embrace or interpret findings or conceptualizations reported in the literature of vocational psychology, personnel psychology, and occupational sociology, as these facts and concepts relate to work adjustment?

This discussion of the literature is limited, not exhaustive, but does include some of the major concepts in vocational adjustment and vocational development literature. To avoid lengthy discussion of what is most useful or most popular in the literature, and to focus on the comprehensiveness of the theory, the following findings and concepts from the literature are presented in alphabetical order:

Adaptation (Cattell, 1957; Hahn, 1962) as it relates to work can be embraced by the theory as correspondence between the individual's set of abilities and the ability requirements of the job. "Adaptation with adjustment" adds correspondence between the set of needs and the job reinforcer system, resulting in satisfaction as well as satisfactoriness.

Hahn's (1962) "psychoevaluation," or "structured self study" entails, if one accepts the theory, exploration by the individual and the vocational psychologist of the prior development of high-strength abilities and needs.

Attitudes: Attitudes are often defined as predispositions to action. In the theory of work adjustment, needs are predispositions to effective reinforcer conditions. Since responding is a function of reinforcer conditions, needs affect response probabilities. In this sense needs are predispositions to action.

In the literature attitudes are operationally defined in yet another way, as evaluations of the environment (stimulus objects). As examples, in the work environment, one may have attitudes toward working conditions, supervision, and co-workers. In this sense, the theory would define attitudes as dimensions of employment satisfaction.

External forces: Some sociological approaches, e.g. Caplow (1954), to work theory stress such "accidents" as those of birth, sex, social class, and race as powerful external forces imposing barriers to work choice and work adjustment. "Forces," for the theory of work adjustment, are seen not only as powerful restrictions but also as opportunities, or lack of them, afforded a *particular* individual for utilization of ability and for need satisfaction in the development of a work personality and in work adjustment.

Fantasy, Tentative, Realistic Vocational-Choice Periods: Ginzberg *et al.* (1951) describe three periods in a process of occupational decision making. The fantasy period is described as a period in which the child thinks about an occupation in terms of his wish to be an adult. In the tentative period he realizes he has a problem of occupational choice and must begin to consider reality factors. In the realistic period, reality factors weigh heavily and the individual realizes he must work out a compromise. At about age 17 reality factors move into a central position.

The context for the theory of work adjustment, instead of referring to fantasy, unrealistic choice, and the wish to be an adult, assumes a period of labile, relatively uncrystallized abilities and needs when the individual may have little or no information about job requirements and job reinforcer systems. Increasing "realism" (in terms of choices more likely to maximize correspondences in both the ability-requirement and need-reinforcer dimensions) is possible as the ability set and the need set become increasingly differentiated and stable, and with increasing knowledge of available requirements and reinforcer systems. In other words, "realistic" choice is possible when a work personality has been established (there will be individual differences for the age beyond which relatively little change in abilities and needs measurement is observed). At this point an individual can make "realistic" choices. The "realism" of choices is determined, not by his description of what he feels jobs hold for him, but by the measured correspondences available to him in jobs he chooses.

Individual differences: The theory of work adjustment is predicated on the fact of individual differences, intra- as well as inter-, in abilities and needs.

Internal forces: The psychoanalytic position taken by Brill (1949) explains work adjustment in terms of powerful internal forces working themselves out in a sublimated or adjustive fashion. The theory of work adjustment describes these "forces" as high strength needs in the set of needs. Their satisfaction through work might well be achieved in many different ways, in different degrees, and in a variety of job situations.

Occupational personality: In a discussion of occupational personality, Gross (1958) states "... there is probably both a process of personality selection and one of molding for occupations. A certain type of personality may be attracted to an occupation with a higher probability than another type. But whatever the original personality, the occupation takes the person and further molds his personality until it becomes one felt to be appropriate to the occupation."

In the theory of work adjustment, some change in the ability and need sets may occur during the initial period of exposure to work. Decreasing amounts of change (increasing stability of ability and need sets) will be expected as the individual's employment experience increases. Work-oriented ability requirements may facilitate changes in the ability set. As an example, the requirement of supervising in a work setting may permit the utilization of abilities in response combinations not experienced prior to work. In a similar fashion, some needs may not be present at high strength in the set of needs at initial employment. This could be the case if pre-employment history did not include reinforcement experiences that are present almost exclusively in work settings. For example, the more exclusively work-oriented reinforcement conditions, such as receiving a paycheck, make possible the enlargement of the total number of stimulus conditions available to the individual for expression of his needs, both in work and outside of it. As a result changes in need strengths may be developed for the more exclusively work-oriented reinforcers in their own right (e.g., for continuing paychecks, raises, financial security, promotions, etc.).

Psychological discordance: Is described (Vance, Volsky, 1962) as normal distress appropriate to incompatibilities between such things as: abilities and performance, goals and internal pressures, and abilities and interests. The theory of work adjustment describes this in terms of lack of correspondence between the set of abilities and ability requirements, and/or between the set of needs and the reinforcer system. Such lack of correspondence would permit prediction of this normal distress, or discordance, and would be reflected in lack of satisfaction and/or lack of satisfactoriness.

Vance and Volsky describe "psychological discordance reduction" as aiding the individual "by adding new responses or perceptions to his repertoire, which can be used to achieve a less discordant behavior pattern in the future." The theory of work adjustment implies that, in addition to adding new responses, the individual might be assisted in psychological discordance reduction by utilizing other high strength abilities in his set of abilities and/or that he be aided in learning about the probable need satisfaction available to him in more appropriate reinforcer systems and requirements in jobs.

Self-actualization: Some theorists (Goldstein, 1939, and Rogers, 1961) postulate a self-actualization tendency in man. This is described by Rogers (1961) as "the directional trend which is evident in all organic and human life—the urge to expand, extend, develop, mature—the tendency to express and activate all the capacities of the organism, or the self." In the theory of work adjustment self-actualization is viewed only as the individual's attempts to achieve and maintain correspondences between both abilities and ability requirements, and needs and reinforcer systems.

Self-concept and vocational development: Super (1953) states that "The process of vocational development is essentially that of developing and implementing a self concept," with the individual deriving work satisfactions and life satisfactions from situations where "he can play the kind of role which his growth and exploratory experiences have led him to consider congenial and appropriate." The theory of work adjustment defines work situations which are "congenial and appropriate" in terms of preferred reinforcer systems, i.e., needs, and ability requirements that correspond to the individual's set of abilities. The context for the theory also indicates how "growth and exploratory experiences" have their effects on the development of abilities and needs, and how work satisfactions are derived from the expression of the work personality.

Vocational choice: The theory of work adjustment is not a theory of vocational choice. It seeks, however, to provide a framework for predicting the outcomes of vocactional choice.

Vocational interests: Instruments designed to measure vocational interests, such as the Strong Vocational Interest Blank (Strong, 1943), the Minnesota Vocational Interest Inventory (Clark, 1961), and the Kuder Preference Record-Vocational (Kuder, 1956), require an individual to indicate a variety of preferences. It is assumed that these preferences are based on some knowledge of the reinforcers involved, and specify conditions likely to produce satisfaction. For work adjustment, therefore, interest measurement is one possible approach to the identification of each individual's set of needs and the strengths at which these needs exist.

Vocational maturity: The theory of work adjustment focuses on the concept of the *stable* work personality instead of on vocational maturity. According to the theory, the individual's work personality is stable when he demonstrates, on repeated testings, no significant change in his set of abilities and set of needs. Stability so defined means simply that he has definitive, relatively-fixed patterns for work.

SOCIAL UTILITY OF THE THEORY OF WORK ADJUSTMENT

A. In Vocational Counseling Practice

The vocational counselor must be an expert in the measurement of abilities and needs. He also must be expert in locating and interpreting information about job ability requirements and job reinforcer systems. Utilizing his expertness in these ways, the vocational counselor can view a particular individual in terms of jobs, with their ability requirements and reinforcer systems, in order to assess the individual's potential for work (vocational diagnosis), and to specify the job conditions necessary for work adjustment (vocational prognosis).

If the vocational counselor is to operate in the manner described above, it will be necessary to make available to him additional carefully derived information about the ability-requirement and reinforcer-system characteristics of jobs representing the entire range of job families. More specifically, the counselor will require that attention be given to the empirical development of many more Occupational Aptitude Patterns (OAP's) and to the inclusion of procedures for determining and describing Occupational Reinforcer Patterns (ORP's) as a part of routine and continuous job-analysis activity.

The vocational counselor must also be expert in influencing the counselee's vocational decisions, through some form of communication or by effective manipulation of counselee experiences, so that those decisions are consonant with the ability-requirement and need-reinforcement correspondences necessary for work adjustment (individual satisfactoriness and satisfaction).

The theory should facilitate the determination of reasons for lack of satisfactoriness and lack of satisfaction. It ought also to be useful in evaluating the effects of sudden changes in the individual (physical-emotional) or in the job (changes in duties, automation, new policies, restrictions, etc.).

There are implications for counselor education, centered particularly around such subject-matter areas as occupations (the measurement and interpretation of requirements and reinforcers) and individual vocational analysis (the measurement and interpretation of abilities and needs). Perhaps less emphasis on group labels (e.g., over-dependency of counselees) and more emphasis on individual work-personality–work-adjustment relationships (utilization of assets and liabilities) is warranted.

B. In Education

It is suggested that more attention be given, in educational research, to the process of individuation of the work personality. Specifically, the theory requires attention to the identification and measurement of ability requirements and reinforcer systems in educational and social settings. In order to develop effectively, in individuals, sets of abilities and needs compatible with the realities of work environments, educators need to know how to structure stimulus situations for maximum ability utilization and optimal reinforcement. This theoretical orientation suggests, therefore, a systematic approach to problems in classroom motivation as well as to problems in work personality development.

C. In Special Problem Areas

Disability: In the theory of work adjustment, disability is viewed as a significant change in the ability set which is brought about by physical, mental, and/or emotional trauma, with or without accompanying changes in the need set. Such changes would have predictable consequences in the correspondences attainable, by the individual, with job ability requirements and reinforcer systems. Disability is viewed, therefore, in terms of its actual disruptive consequences for an individual, rather than in terms of the expectations of an observer for a particular disability class or its stereotype.

Knowledge of the measured residual set of abilities and the set of needs (after maximum medical treatment and physical restoration) should be necessary information for the vocational rehabilitation counselor in his attempts to identify jobs with the appropriate requirement-reinforcer characteristics, and which will yield maximum work adjustment. Such information would also be useful in meeting motivational problems of the physically handicapped.

The question of classifying the severity of disability, for research and case-management purposes, might be approached in terms of the measurement of the amount of disruption of ability-requirement correspondence in a previously satisfactory worker (as defined by his immediately preceding work history). Very severe disability might be so disruptive as to require considerable retraining. In this event, one would conceptualize the individual's experiences as taking place in the paradigm representing individuation of the work personality (Fig. 2). Progress in training and/or treatment might be measured in terms of ability- and need-development changes over a series of successive periodic measurements, with success in retraining and/or treatment being defined by the levels of ability and need strengths reached when the amounts of measured change become insignificant.

Automation: The effects of being technologically displaced can be viewed, in this theory, as the converse of disability. The radical change is seen as the sudden removal of the requirement-reinforcer system in which the individual has been operating. The primary problem is not one of the individual's residual ability-need characteristics, but rather is one of what other requirement-reinforcer systems are available to him after technological change has occurred.

Vocational counseling will be useful in this instance in both the search for appropriate other-job stimulus situations, and in the identification of other high-strength abilities and needs which may enable the individual to achieve work adjustment.

The problem of automation is essentially the problem of moving from one job to another, except that the move is more sudden and may be more traumatic. It is forced only from the employer side, and may occur after an individual's ability and need sets are firmly crystallized. The most promising approaches to the achievement of individual work adjustment, for the technologically displaced person with long job tenure, would appear to be those which are concerned with the requirement-reinforcer communalities which cut across a number of jobs.

Unemployment: The theory stresses the need for individualized matching of individuals and jobs. This suggests that vocational planning should be based on careful analysis of both the individual's sets of abilities and needs and the available job environments. This individualized approach would appear likely to yield more lasting solutions than programs for the retraining of unemployed workers for shortage jobs, without regard for the ability-requirement and need-reinforcer correspondences for worker and job. Solutions might be more lasting in terms of improved tenure outcomes, e.g., staying on the same job or moving across many jobs in an orderly and/or progressive fashion. Movement across several jobs having a significant number of common requirements and reinforcers would be viewed as consistent with work adjustment.

Retirement: In retirement, the theory would suggest that an individual operates in an environment composed of such ability requirements and reinforcers as those defined by his remaining job-related functions and his avocational activities. The avocational activities are regulated by the community in the sense that he must meet requirements to participate (or, even to gain acceptance of the products of his "self-regulated" hobbies). Adjustment to retirement can then be viewed in the same terms as work adjustment, i.e., matching individual abilities and needs with environmental requirement-reinforcer conditions. This requires careful environmental analysis analogous to thorough job analysis.

COMMENT

While in our definition of the term *work personality* we have focused on two sets of personality variables (abilities and needs), it should not be assumed that we feel these two sets of variables are the only ones involved. It is felt that they make the major contributions to the explanation of work adjustment. However, attention should be directed also to personality variables which characterize the individual's style of response. For example, the measurement of abilities and needs will be affected by individual differences in speed of response, perseverance in responding, response oscillation, effectiveness of schedules of reinforcement and of contingency of reinforcers to specific responses.

It also would be naïve to assume that the abilities and needs listed in Figure 1 represent the total range for an individual. One major research problem is the discovery, definition, and measurement of ability and need dimensions which will account for individual differences in responding to the full range of job requirements and reinforcer systems.

This theory of work adjustment derived from early research efforts of the Regional Vocational Rehabilitation Research Institute at the University of Minnesota and has provided a model for a continuing core research program. The research findings are reported in a bulletin series entitled *Minnesota Studies in Vocational Rehabilitation.* Of particular relevance to the present state of the theory are Bulletins X, XIII, XIV, et seq.

The authors of this theory of work adjustment regard it as a useful framework for an active research program. However, they wish to be very clear about the fact that it represents only the present stage of their thinking. Subsequent publications will reflect changes and/or additions to the theory, as dictated by additional research findings.

REFERENCES

BRAYFIELD, A. H. (1961) Vocational counseling today. In WILLIAMSON, E. G. (ed.), *Vocational counseling, a reappraisal in honor of Donald G. Paterson.* Minneapolis. University of Minnesota Press.

BRILL, A. A. (1949) *Basic principles of psychoanalysis.* New York: Doubleday.

BUREAU of Employment Security, U.S. Department of Labor. *Guide to the use of the General Aptitude Test Battery.* Section II: Norms. Washington, D.C., 1958.

CAPLOW, T. (1954) *The sociology of work.* Minneapolis: University of Minnesota Press.

CARLSON, R. E., DAWIS, R. V., ENGLAND, G. W., and LOFQUIST, L. H. (1962) The measurement of employment satisfaction. *Minnesota studies in vocational rehabilitation,* **XIII.** Minneapolis, Industrial Relations Center.

CARLSON, R. E., DAWIS, R. V., ENGLAND, G. W., and LOFQUIST, L. H. (1963) The measurement of employment satisfactoriness. *Minnesota studies in vocational rehabilitation,* **XIV**. Minneapolis, Industrial Relations Center.

CATTELL, R. B. (1957) *Personality and motivation structure and measurement.* New York: World Book.

CLARK, K. E. (1961) *The vocational interest of non-professional men.* Minneapolis: University of Minnesota Press.

DVORAK, BEATRICE J. (1935) Differential occupational ability patterns. *Bulletin of the Employment Stabilization Research Institute,* Vol. III, No. 3, February.

DVORAK, BEATRICE J. (1958) The general aptitude test battery. In Samler, J. (ed.), *The use of multifactor tests in guidance.* Washington, D.C.: American Personnel and Guidance Association.

GINZBERG, E., GINSBURG, S. W., AXELRAD, E., and HERMA, J. L. (1951) *Occupational choice, an approach to a general theory.* New York: Columbia University Press.

GOLDSTEIN, K. (1939) *The organism.* New York: American Book Co.

GROSS, E. (1958) *Work and society.* New York: Crowell.

HAHN, M. E. (1962) Forgotten people: the normal individual and professional psychology. *American Psychologist,* **17**, 700–705.

HERZBERG, F., MAUSNER, B., and SNYDERMAN, BARBARA B. (1959) *The motivation to work.* New York: Wiley.

KUDER, G. F. (1956) *Kuder Preference Record-Vocational.* Chicago: Science Research Associates.

PARSONS, F. (1909) *Choosing a vocation.* Boston: Houghton-Mifflin.

PATERSON, D. G. (1938) The genesis of modern guidance. *Educat. Record*, **19**, 36–46.

PATERSON, D. G., GERKEN, C. D'A., and HAHN, M. E. (1941) *The Minnesota occupational rating scales.* Chicago: Science Research Associates.

PATERSON, D. G., GERKEN, C. D'A., and HAHN, M. E. (1953) *Revised Minnesota occupational rating scales.* Minneapolis: University of Minnesota Press.

ROBINSON, F. P. (1950) *Principles and procedures in student counseling.* New York: Harper.

ROE, ANNE (1956) *The psychology of occupations.* New York: Wiley.

ROGERS, C. R. (1942) *Counseling and psychotherapy.* Boston: Houghton-Mifflin.

ROGERS, C. R. (1951) *Client-centered therapy.* Boston: Houghton-Mifflin.

ROGERS, C. R. (1961) *On becoming a person.* Boston: Houghton-Mifflin.

SCOTT, T. B., DAWIS, R. V., ENGLAND, G. W., LOFQUIST, L. H. (1958) A definition of work adjustment. *Minnesota studies in vocational rehabilitation*, **X.** Minneapolis: Industrial Relations Center.

SKINNER, B. F. (1953) *Science and human behavior.* New York: MacMillan.

STRONG, E. K., JR. (1943) *Vocational interests of men and women.* Stanford University Press.

STRONG, E. K., JR. (1955) *Vocational interests 18 years after college.* Minneapolis: University of Minnesota Press.

SUPER, D. E. (1953) A theory of vocational development. *American Psychologist*, **8**, 185–190.

SUPER, D., CRITES, J., HUMMEL, R., MOSER, HELEN, OVERSTREET, PHOEBE, and WARNATH, C. (1957) *Vocational development, a framework for research.* New York: Bureau of Publications, Columbia University.

SUPER, D. E., and OVERSTREET, PHOEBE (1960) *The vocational maturity of ninth-grade boys.* New York: Bureau of Publications, Columbia University,.

United States Employment Service, U.S. Department of Labor. *Dictionary of occupational titles.* Washington, D.C.: U.S. Government Printing Office, 1949.

United States Employment Service, U.S. Department of Labor. *Worker trait requirements for 4,000 jobs.* Washington, D.C.: U.S. Government Printing Office, 1956.

VANCE, F. L., and VOLSKY, T. C., JR. (1962) Counseling and psychotherapy: split personality or Siamese twins? *American Psychologist*, **17**, 565–570.

VITELES, M. S. (1924) Vocational guidance and job analysis: the psychological viewpoint. *Psych. Clin.*, **15**, 164.

VITELES, M. S. (1932) *Industrial psychology.* New York: Norton.

This is an edited version of *A Theory of Work Adjustment.*—Editor.

20. Job Satisfaction: Issues and Problems*

GLENN P. FOURNET, M. K. DISTEFANO, JR., and MARGARET W. PRYER

CONCERN for workers' attitudes, as exhibited today in the vast amount of literature on job satisfaction, is a relatively recent development in industry. Although motivation was not completely ignored by earlier writers, it nevertheless lacked the attention accorded it in today's literature.

A deeper appreciation for the worker's psychological state, as well as the motivational properties of social relationships on the job, came into prominence as a result of the now famous Hawthorne Studies (Roethlisberger and Dickson, 1939). Favorable employee attitudes and employee-centered supervision were indicated as spurs to greater production. It is in this tradition that many of the modern theories of and experiments in organizations works were formulated. The works of McGregor (1960), Viteles (1953), Argyris (1960), and Likert (1956, 1961) serve as examples of this emphasis in organization theory.

The proposed relationship between morale and production, however, has not gone unchallenged. Brayfield and Crockett (1955), in a review of the literature, concluded that the relationship is not a simple one. They proposed that high productivity and satisfaction can be expected to occur together only when productivity is perceived as a means to important goals and when these goals are achieved. In a less critical review, Herzberg *et al.* (1957) report some relationship but indicate that in many cases the correlations were positive but low.

The purpose of the present paper is to survey some of the issues and problems that have emerged from studies of job satisfaction. Although this paper is based on a rather extensive survey of the literature of the last decade, no attempt will be made to cite all of the articles that are relevant to a particular problem area. Instead, selected studies will be cited that are considered representative of the kinds of research being done in a particular area. These will be discussed under several topics: (1) methodological

* The research for this review was supported in part by Research Project 15-14-11 of the Louisiana State Department of Hospitals.

(Reprinted by permission of publisher and authors from *Personnel Psychology*, vol. 19, 1966, pp. 165–183.)

approaches, (2) factors associated with job satisfaction, (3) consequences of job satisfaction, and (4) theoretical issues and problems.

METHODOLOGICAL APPROACHES

The task of relating the findings of job satisfaction studies has become increasingly difficult because of the variety of methods employed by different investigators. As indicated by Ewen (1964), the use of single techniques in most studies leads one to question the general applicability of their findings. This problem was noted by Ash (1954), who found that the data obtained from an employee attitude inventory correlated only slightly with those obtained by the interview method.

Studies in job satisfaction have utilized different techniques of statistical analysis as well as different methods of data collection. The most frequently employed statistics have been correlations and factor analysis. The particular statistic utilized is of importance since statistical methods can influence the results as well as the labels the investigator places upon the factors which emerge. As a consequence, there is little agreement on the number or kind of factors involved, which vary from as few as three to as many as eight.

The numerous data collection techniques employed in job satisfaction studies include questionnaires, interviews, rank order studies, sentence completion tests, and critical incident inquiries.

Questionnaires

The most favored method used in studying job satisfaction is the questionnaire. However, the variety of types being used makes it extremely difficult to compare and generalize findings. Glennon *et al.* (1960) criticize the use of the questionnaire on the grounds that many questionnaires indicate only the amount of agreement with a particular item. Much more could be learned, they maintain, if the degree of importance that the worker attaches to the issue were recorded as well.

Interviews

Interviewing is seldom used alone; usually it is employed as a tool to indicate items for a questionnaire or to expand and evaluate the reliability of questionnaire data. Butler (1961), for example, used a preliminary interview, a questionnaire, and a final interview. The interview was also employed with a questionnaire in studies by Butler (1959) and Rettig and Pasamanick (1960).

The interview technique in general has come under a great deal of recent criticism because of its lack of reliability and validity. In noting this problem, Ulrich and Trumbo (1965) advocate the use of ancillary data, structuring techniques, and training for the interviewer to strengthen the interview as a tool. In view of the questionable reliability and validity of the interview, studies using this technique alone, e.g., Argyris (1959), Kilbridge (1960), and Matthews and Abu-Laban (1959), should be carefully appraised.

Rank Order Studies

Rank order studies involve the ranking of characteristics of the job in relation to their importance to satisfaction. Likert (1961) questions the use of this type of procedure, pointing out that because an item is ranked first does not mean that it is the most important factor in overall attitude. He indicates that the importance of an item can be measured only by the extent to which it correlates with total job satisfaction.

If workers are asked to make their own list of job characteristics, the procedure then has the attractive feature of gathering data which have been minimally determined by the experimenter, and the data may then be used in questionnaire development.

Sentence Completion

The use of the incomplete sentence technique (e.g., Greene and Greene, 1961; Suehr, 1962) has been a recent development in the study of worker attitudes. Essentially it is a projective approach which affords the worker an opportunity to display attitudes which may be withheld in other situations.

Critical Incidents

Herzberg *et al.* (1957, 1959) have developed a critical incidents approach to assess job satisfaction. In this technique the worker is requested, during an interview, to relate any incidents connected with a time when he felt either exceptionally good or bad about the job. Following a reply, the opposite is requested. From these data the important factors related to satisfaction and dissatisfaction are extracted.

Ewen (1964) points out that this method, when used alone, is biased since it is easy to recall incidents related to promotions, but difficult to recall those which follow no achievement. Vroom and Maier (1961) emphasize the risk of accepting descriptions by the individual as actual causes of satisfaction. There is a tendency for the individual to see causes for satisfaction within himself and hence to describe experiences involving achievement, recognition, and advancement on the job as satisfying. On the other hand, dissatisfaction may be attributed to factors in the environment rather than personal inadequacies.

FACTORS ASSOCIATED WITH JOB SATISFACTION

The factors of job satisfaction may be divided into two types: those characteristic of the individual and those characteristic of the job.

A. CHARACTERISTICS OF THE INDIVIDUAL

Many personal characteristics of workers have been chosen by researchers for study of their relation to job satisfaction. The present paper reviews the following frequently studied characteristics: individual differences, age, education, intelligence, sex, and occupational level.

Individual Differences

The existence of individual differences in reacting to situations and events increases the complexity of the study of job satisfaction since it is difficult to isolate clearly defined relationships.

Most of the studies in this area deal with the lack of congruence in the perception that an individual has of himself, his job, and the company for which he works. Foa (1957) found that sailors with authoritarian expectations are more likely to be satisfied with whatever behavior is adopted by the officers than are sailors with less authoritarian expectations. Congruent role expectations of administration and employees were found by Bidwell (1955) to be accompanied by satisfaction on the part of the employees. The importance of situational differences was also indicated by the fact that drivers, who had very little contact with their supervisors, preferred them to be authoritarian, while stock handlers, who worked continuously under the direction of the same supervisor, did not (Vroom and Mann, 1960).

Age

Herzberg *et al.* (1957) proposed that there is a significant relationship between age and job satisfaction. Specifically, they indicated that morale is high for the youthful employee immediately after employment, drops sharply after the first few years, and then begins to climb as workers continue on their jobs. In explanation of these findings the investigators proposed that early satisfaction is due to the newness of the job. Dissatisfaction sets in quite rapidly, however, due to the uncertainty and lack of seniority and security. Recent findings (Hulin and Smith, 1965) indicate that there is some question about this proposed U-shaped function.

A problem noted by the present authors in working with age as a factor in job satisfaction is that it is difficult to compare or contrast the findings of many studies because most do not give the ages of the workers used as subjects, and, when they are given, they are often given only in general terms. Therefore, what could be a young group in one study might be an older group for another. More precise descriptions of such variables should help clarify incongruous findings.

Education and Intelligence

The relationship between educational level, intelligence, and job satisfaction is very unclear. Ash (1954) found no relationship between intelligence and job satisfaction, while Suehr (1962) reported a negative relationship between IQ and morale. Similarly, Vollmer and Kinney (1955) found a negative relationship between educational level and job satisfaction, while a later study by Sinha and Sarma (1962) reported no significant relationship between these variables. Although the contradictions found in the studies relating job satisfaction and intelligence are difficult to explain, the problems encountered in studying job satisfaction as a function of educational level may be due to the fact that educational level is not a pure factor, but is contaminated with age. Because of the rising educational level in the population in general, it is likely that the young worker will be a high school graduate, while his older colleague is less likely to have completed grade school. Thus, high morale in a worker of low educational level may be a function of age rather than education. In any case, the need for simultaneous study of all three of these factors, i.e., intelligence, education, and age, appears indicated.

Sex

Hulin and Smith (1964) contend that it is not sex, *per se*, that is related to either high or low satisfaction, but rather that it is the entire constellation of factors which themselves relate to sex—such as pay, job level, and promotional opportunities. This is especially indicated in one study (Zaleznik, Christensen and Roethlisberger, 1958) in which women were more satisfied than men. The authors explained that the women in the group were receiving the same pay and also had the same social position as the men. According to Herzberg *et al.* (1957), greater variability in the attitudes of women can be attrituted to the multiple roles assumed by women when they take positions outside the home. It was further suggested that, for women, job satisfaction may depend on factors other than those for men.

Occupational Level

In any discussion of occupational levels, the difficulties involved in classifying jobs must be considered. Jobs may be classified in a number of different ways, such as by skills, length of training, amount of social responsibility, or general attitudes of society. Other complications arise as a result of the different criteria used at different levels to measure the significance of a job level.

One fact in this area that stands out above all others is that satisfaction or morale increases as job level progresses. There is some indication that different job levels allow for satisfaction of different needs. For example, Gurin, Veroff, and Feld (1960) found that people in high status jobs reported more ego satisfaction in their work than those holding lower positions. In another study, Porter (1962) found that the vertical location of management is an important factor in determining the extent to which managers feel that they can satisfy particular psychological needs. In general, those in lower management positions were more dissatisfied than managers in top-level positions. Porter reasons that higher levels of employment offer more ego satisfaction, more status, pay, and self-direction. In addition, these are enhanced by increased responsibility and authority.

B. CHARACTERISTICS OF THE JOB

Studies in this area utilize job factors as the independent variable, with satisfaction as the dependent variable. The job factors are those which traditionally have been considered important to the work situation as a result of listings made by employees, data from questionnaires, and factor analytic studies.

Some caution should be displayed when speaking of the relative importance of different factors. First, as Herzberg *et al.* (1957) have indicated, important job factors change in terms of a person's needs. When not deprived of basic needs, items such as security, recognition, and responsibility become more important. Secondly, most questionnaires arrive at a morale index and not an intensity index. That this is cause for concern is evident from the data of Youngberg *et al.* (1962) which indicated that when both satisfaction *and* importance were measured, factors emerged which were different from those related to satisfaction alone.

Important factors related to job satisfaction which have been mentioned in the literature include organization and management, immediate supervision, social environment, communication, security, monotony, and pay.

Organization and Management

Studies of this area indicate that organization and management become important to the worker when morale is low. Mann and Williams (1962) made a study of the effect on satisfaction of installing electronic data processing equipment. This disruption of the *status quo* served to raise questions for the employees concerning the interest of management in the employees. Of course, confounded with this finding is a communication problem. In another study, using a morale index on non-academic employees at a university, Brazziel (1957) found that administrative practices were directly related to the low morale of the employees.

Immediate Supervision

In a review of work done at the Institute of Social Research, Zander and Quinn (1962) point out that job satisfaction is congruent with the immediate supervisor's personal interest and support for the worker. However, employee orientation on the part of the immediate supervisor is not sufficient to insure job satisfaction, according to the findings of D. C. Pelz (1952). His study showed that a supervisor who sides with his employees tends to have a satisfied group of workers only if the supervisor has enough influence with his supervisors to make his concern for the worker profitable in terms of benefits.

Social Environment

Identification with the work group was found to be an important variable in job satisfaction by Zaleznik *et al.* (1958). People who are members of the group are more satisfied than those who are not regular members. Gurin, Veroff, and Feld (1960) maintain that the work group serves an important function in gratifying interpersonal and friendship needs, which are described as a source of job satisfaction.

Communication

As stated by Suehr (1962), communications is one of the most vital areas in the whole morale process. It is most conspicuous by its absence, and consequently it tends to be a major source of dissatisfaction.

Communications can help to aid in satisfaction provided the individuals are in positions of importance in the communication chain. As a by-product of testing the efficiency of several communication chains, Leavitt (1951) found high satisfaction among members in a group when they were in a key position in a communication network. Concurrent with this, however, he found that the remainder of the group's members were dissatisfied and did not want to continue the work. When the communication net was such that each member was allowed freedom of communication, there was greater satisfaction among all group members.

Security

Security is counted by many investigators as the most important variable in job satisfaction of employees. However, its importance is the result of its absence from a situation rather than its presence. Gurin, Veroff, and Feld (1960) discovered that concern for security occurred disproportionately among those who were dissatisfied. This fact is especially underlined in Mann and Williams' (1962) observation of the effect that the introduction of electronic data processing equipment had on employee attitudes in one company. The change brought about a general tightening of the task structure of the office, greater risks for individual jobs, greater need to understand the entire system, and a greater degree of interdependence. While the employees were more satisfied with job responsibility, variety, change in their jobs, and the opportunity to develop and learn new things, they did not express increased satisfaction with their jobs as a whole. Actually, the fear of losing their jobs was the prevailing feeling.

In an experiment involving a factor-analysis of an attitude rating scale, Crites (1961) reported that the formality of an impersonal organizational structure proves a strong source of security. This finding suggests that job security may not be as wholly dependent upon the accumulation of material goods as is commonly believed.

Monotony

There have been proposals (e.g., Kennedy and O'Neill, 1958) that expansion of jobs tends to create more satisfactory attitudes in repetitious work. However, Kilbridge (1960) found that employees preferred smaller tasks because they were less complicated. In this instance, not a single operator mentioned boredom and 84 per cent of the workers preferred the mechanical line. In a similar study, Kilbridge (1961) indicated that there was no relationship between absenteeism, turnover, and repetitive work. These findings may be interpreted to indicate that repetitiveness of work and job satisfaction are not related. Yet there appears to be a more plausible explanation of these data. According to the findings of Smith (1955), boredom is identified with personal characteristics rather than with repetition alone. Further corroboration of the importance of the personal element is found in Roy's (1959) description of the successful attempts by punch operators to overcome boredom. In summary, repetitiveness provides the opportunity for boredom. Whether the individual worker becomes bored with a repetitive job, however, depends on his resources for counteracting monotony within himself.

Pay

Contrary to the opinion of most employers, income is not ranked by employees as the most important factor in job satisfaction. In fact, Herzberg *et al.* (1957) found that, in order of frequency mentioned, pay was third; and, when factors were ordered in terms of importance to the worker, it ranked seventh. Troxell (1954) used a check list method and found that income ranked third among workers in general, but that it ranked first for laborers. The importance of pay can vary considerably from job to job. The major difficulty in assessing its relation to job satisfaction is that it is confounded with other factors, such as age, occupational level, and education.

CONSEQUENCES OF JOB SATISFACTION

In this section we are concerned with variables which are sometimes considered dependent upon job satisfaction. These are performance, absenteeism, and turnover.

Performance

The relationship between satisfaction and performance is one of the chief concerns of management, and at one time the two were assumed to be positively related. Subsequently, Brayfield and Crockett (1955) reported that such a simple relationship does not exist, while the review by Herzberg *et al.* (1957) indicated the relationship to be positive. Although these reviews seem somewhat contradictory, Katzell (1957) contends that their findings are not necessarily incompatible. In fact, the two reviews did not cover the same literature, and Brayfield and Crockett did not include absenteeism, accidents, and turnover in their review.

It is not surprising that findings in this area do not always fit together when one considers the factors involved. The first of these is the old criterion problem. What is a good measure of job success? For some positions this question may be answered rather simply, while with others no simple solutions are available. In any case, different measures will give different results. In addition to this, job performance measures have lacked homogeneity. For example, Katzell, Barrett, and Parker (1961) found that quantity of production per man-hour and profitability were correlated, but they found quality and turnover to be independent as performance measures.

Another consideration is the contamination by group pressure. Viteles (1953) very aptly makes this point. Workers tend to agree as a group as to how much should be produced, and members are punished for any display of disloyalty to the group decision. Other results (Brayfield and Crockett, 1955; Zaleznik *et al.*, 1958) supported these findings.

Brayfield and Crockett (1955) mention also that there are differences in motivation found in different strata of society. Attributing productive motives to some workers amounts to projection of a middle class trait. For some classes, increases in production may ultimately lead to exclusion from groups outside the plant. Thus, it could be that increased productivity may lead to no important goals.

The most appropriate answer to the question of the relation between production and job satisfaction appears to have been offered by Brayfield and Crockett (1955), who described it as one of concomitant variation rather than cause and effect. They assume that individuals are motivated to achieve certain goals whose achievement results in satisfaction. Productivity is seldom a goal in itself but is more commonly a means to goal attainment. High satisfaction and high production can be expected to occur together when productivity is perceived as a means to certain important goals, and when these goals are achieved. Under other conditions the relationship may be negative or there may be none at all.

Absenteeism

Absenteeism, like many of the factors discussed, is a variable of complex relationships. Most of the studies reviewed (Block *et al.*, 1964; Patchen, 1960; Talacchi, 1960; White, 1960) showed that satisfaction and absenteeism are inversely related; however, individual differences were also found. Metzner and Mann (1953) found that there was an inverse relationship with blue collar men and white collar men working at low level skills which did not hold for white collar men and women working at higher level jobs. In addition, the way a man felt about his supervisor and associates was related to absence rates, for both white and blue collar men.

Turnover

Unlike most of the findings related to job satisfaction and its consequences, the findings on turnover are generally consistent. The studies reviewed (Block *et al.*, 1964; Butler, 1961; Katzell, *et al.*, 1961; Talacchi, 1960) agree that turnover is negatively related to job satisfaction. What proves interesting is that the subjects for these studies came from different types of occupations, e.g., orderlies, nurses, life insurance agents, etc.

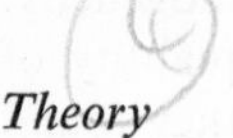

THEORETICAL ISSUES AND PROBLEMS

Theory

Possibly the most important issue in job satisfaction has been put forth by the Herzberg group (1957, 1959). These researchers present job satisfaction as a dichotomous rather than a continuous variable. Satisfaction is viewed as resulting from motivation, stemming in the challenge of the job, through such factors as achievement, responsibility, growth, advancement, work itself, and earned recognition. Dissatisfaction more often springs from factors peripheral to the task. It is hypothesized that in situations of satisfied needs, maintenance factors have relatively little influence, either as satisfiers or dissatisfiers. The removal of the opportunity for meaningful achievement sensitizes the individual to his environment, and his perception of maintenance factors then becomes colored by a readiness to find fault.

In the study of these factors, the Herzberg group employed a critical incidents technique. They asked the employee to describe a situation when he felt extremely good or bad about the job. From these data they were able to differentiate between satisfiers and dissatisfiers.

A weakness inherent in their approach is that the dichotomous nature of satisfaction, indicated by the investigators, may be an artifact of their method of study. Answers given which related to good feelings on the part of the workers were classed as satisfiers while factors related to opposite feelings were considered as dissatisfiers. It seems fallacious to assume, however, that a dichotomy exists unless these findings are corroborated by different methods. This same criticism appears to be relevant to the recent findings of Friedlander and Walton (1964) and Friedlander (1964).

As an alternative to the theoretical formulation of Herzberg *et al.* (1957, 1959) that certain job factors are either satisfiers or dissatisfiers, Smith (1963) proposes that job satisfaction is a function of the perceived characteristics of a job in relation to an individual's frame of reference. A particular job condition, on the basis of this theoretical position, can be a satisfier, dissatisfier, or irrelevant, depending on conditions in comparable jobs, conditions of other people of the same qualifications and past experience as the individual, as well as on numerous situational variables of the present job. Thus job satisfaction is not an absolute phenomenon but is relative to the alternatives available to the individual.

Other theoretical approaches, while not holding strictly to a dichotomous position, do stress in line with the Herzberg group the importance of social and psychological rewards as satisfiers. Leavitt and Bass (1964), for example, stress job enlargement as the answer for dissatisfied workers, because it provides nonmaterial stimulation. They propose that it is the expectation of rewards that attracts an individual to a job, and it is the extent to which the job actually provides rewards that maintains satisfactions. It is their contention that any theory of satisfaction should consider individual differences in perceptual responses to the same environment. While some people prefer structural job assignments, schedules, orders, and formality, they propose that others want to be free of any system.

The importance of psychological needs is also a vital part of Vroom's (1962) theoretical approach. He asserts that jobs which afford exercise of individual judgment and initiative, provide for the use and development of aptitudes, and permit some knowledge of results of a person's performance are more ego-satisfying than those which do not have these characteristics. In this same vein, Zaleznik, Christensen, and Roethlisberger (1958) indicate that the important variables related to job satisfaction involve perception, individual needs, and group membership.

Current Problems

Any outline of an area should indicate the prevalent difficulties facing researchers in that area as well as the problems being caused by the researchers themselves. It is to these that we now turn our attention.

Many of the studies of job satisfaction fail to specify the population which their subjects represent. Adding to this confusion are the vastly different populations that are used, with little attempt to compare the results from the different job areas. Some studies utilized college subjects and children, which makes the generality of their findings questionable.

As mentioned earlier, the different methods employed often tend to confound the data with their own artifacts. This could be eliminated by use of a combination of methods.

Then there is the problem of anonymity. The assumption that workers will give the same answers whether they answer the questions anonymously or not underlies most of the research in the area of job satisfaction. Dunnette and Heneman's (1956) data refute this, indicating that a threat to the employee's feelings of anonymity results in more favorable responses than when employees do not feel threatened. Hyman *et al.* (1954) distinguish between literal and psychological anonymity. This problem arises when questionnaires are unsigned but ask for department number, age, and length of work experience. These suggest to the employee, says Hyman, that special efforts are being taken to secure identifying information.

Other fallacious assumptions underlying studies of job satisfaction, pointed out by Form and Geschwender (1962), are (a) that all workers have a clear perception of the hierarchical occupational structure, (b) that they all desire to move upward, and (c) that the worker's degree of job satisfaction is a function of success in this graded occupational structure. Such assumptions ignore the satisfaction realities of urban society, such as the different experiences and aspirations of subgroups and their operation in various segments of the society. The base of all of these, which is often ignored, is individual differences. Many theories and many programs initiated to enhance job satisfaction fail to consider the differences among people.

Brayfield and Crockett (1955) point out failures to describe the specific measurement used as a criterion for productivity. In addition, they criticize the use of so many varied measuring instruments, and question whether they are measuring the same attitudes. Questionnaires are apparently accepted on face validity, and little is reported of the reliability of either the criterion or the measures of attitudes.

In brief, the literature reveals that there are many investigators working from varied theoretical positions, using numerous methods, and with different samples. As a result, much of the data appear contradictory. However, this may be due to our inadequacy at the present time to comprehend the influence of a wide range of variables, many of which are confounded.

SUMMARY

This article has attempted to survey the literature on job satisfaction published since the review by Brayfield and Crockett (1955). In doing this, a number of salient features were discussed which have substantial influence on the understanding of this important area of worker behavior.

The literature on job satisfaction has been developed by use of various experimental methods, each having some effect on the findings. Characteristics of both the individual and the job appear to be related to job satisfaction, but they are intercorrelated to such an extent that it is extremely difficult to isolate them for scientific investigation; in fact, to attempt this isolation may mean the loss of the interaction effect among variables. Similarly, it is difficult at the present time to understand how these factors are related to such behavior as performance, absenteeism, and turnover. Because of this complexity, theoretical attempts to describe job satisfaction have many shortcomings. Many of the formulations which now appear contradictory may eventually be found to be complementary. In spite of the apparent confusion and complexity in job satisfaction as an area of study, there is a large amount of literature emerging which should help to clarify the issues.

REFERENCES

Argyris, Chris. (1959) The Individual and Organization: An Empirical Test. *Administrative Science Quarterly*, **IV**, 145–167.

ARGYRIS, CHRIS. (1960) *Understanding Organizational Behavior*. Homewood, Illinois: Dorsey Press, Inc.

ASH, P. (1954) The SRA Employee Inventory—A Statistical Analysis. *Personnel Psychology*, **VII**, 337–364.

BIDWELL, C. E. (1955) The Administrative Role and Satisfaction in Teaching. *Journal of Educational Sociology*, **XXIX**, 41–47.

BLOCK, J. R., YUKER, H. E., CAMPBELL, W. J., and MELVIN, K. B. (1964) Some Correlates of Job Satisfaction among Disabled Workers. *Personnel and Guidance Journal*, **XLII**, 803–810.

BRAYFIELD, A. H., and CROCKETT, W. H. (1955) Employee Attitudes and Employee Performance. *Psychological Bulletin*, **LII**, 396–424.

BRAZZIEL, W. F., JR. (1957) Assessing Morale of Non-academic College Personnel. *Personnel Administration*, **XX** (5), 43–45.

BUTLER, W. P. (1959) Job Satisfaction among Foremen. *Personnel Practice Bulletin*, **XV**, 7–15.

BUTLER, W. P. (1961) Job Satisfaction among Foremen: Case Study No. 2. *Personnel Practice Bulletin*, **XVII**, 5–14.

CRITES, J. O. (1961) Factor Analytic Definitions of Vocational Motivation. *Journal of Applied Psychology*, **XLV**, 330–337.

DUNNETTE, M. D., and HENEMAN, H. G., JR. (1956) Influence of Scale Administrator on Employee Attitude Responses. *Journal of Applied Psychology*, **XL**, 73–77.

EWEN, R. B. (1964) Some Determinants of Job Satisfaction: A Study of the Generality of Herzberg's Theory. *Journal of Applied Psychology*, **XLVIII**, 161–163.

FOA, U. G. (1957) Relation of Worker's Expectation to Satisfaction with Supervisor. *Personnel Psychology*, **X**, 161–168.

FORM, W. H., and GESCHWENDER, J. A. (1962) Social Reference Basis of Job Satisfaction: The Case of the Manual Worker. *American Sociological Review*, **XXVII**, 228–237.

FRIEDLANDER, FRANK. (1964) Job Characteristics as Satisfiers and Dissatisfiers. *J. of Applied Psychology*, **XLVIII**, 388–392.

FRIEDLANDER, FRANK, and WALTON, EUGENE (1964) Positive and Negative Motivations toward Work. *Administrative Science Quarterly*, **IX**, 194–207.

GLENNON, J. R., OWENS, W. A., SMITH, W. J., and ALBRIGHT, L. E. (1960) New Dimension in Measuring Morale. *Harvard Business Review*, **XXXVIII** (1), 106–107.

GREENE, J. E., SR., and GREENE, J. E., JR. (1961) Illustrative Uses of the "Incomplete" Sentence Technique in Investigating Certain Attitudes of Middle Management Personnel. *Personnel Psychology*, **XIV**, 305–316.

GURIN, G., VEROFF, J., and FELD, S. (1960) *Americans View Their Mental Health*. New York: Basic Books.

HERZBERG, F., MAUSNER, B., PETERSON, R. O., and CAPWELL, D. F. (1957) *Job Attitudes: Review of Research and Opinion*. Pittsburgh: Psychological Service of Pittsburgh.

HERZBERG, F., MAUSNER, B., and SNYDERMAN, B. B. (1959) *The Motivation to Work*. New York: John Wiley and Sons, Inc.

HULIN, C. L., and SMITH, P. C. (1964) Sex Differences in Job Satisfaction. *Journal of Applied Psychology*, **XLVIII**, 88–92.

HULIN, C. L., and SMITH, P. C. (1965) A Linear Model of Job Satisfaction. *Journal of Applied Psychology*, **XLIX**, 209–216.

HYMAN, H. H., COBB, W. J., FIELDMAN, J. J., HUNT, C. W., and STEMBER, C. H. (1954) *Interviewing in Social Research*. Chicago: University of Chicago Press.

KATZELL, R. A. (1957) Industrial Psychology: In Farnsworth, P. R. and McNemar, Q. (Editors), *Annual Review of Psychology*, **VIII**, 237–268.

KATZELL, R. A. BARRETT, R. S., and PARKER, T. C. (1961) Job Satisfaction, Job Performance and Situational Characteristics. *Journal of Applied Psychology*, **XLV**, 65–72.

KENNEDY, J. E., and O'NEILL, H. E. (1958) Job Content and Workers' Opinions. *Journal of Applied Psychology*, **XLII**, 372–375.

KILBRIDGE, M. D. (1960) Do Workers Prefer Larger Jobs? *Personnel*, **XXXVII**, 45–48.

KILBRIDGE, M. D. (1961) Turnover, Absence, and Transfer Rates as Indicators of Employee Dissatisfaction with Repetitive Work. *Industrial and Labor Relations Review*, **XV**, 21–32.

LEAVITT, H. J. (1951) Some Effects of Certain Communication Patterns on Group Performance. *Journal of Abnormal and Social Psychology*, **XLVI**, 38–50.

LEAVITT, H. J., and BASS, B. M. (1964) Organizational Psychology. In Farnsworth, P. R., McNemar, O., and McNemar, Q. (Editors), *Annual Review of Psychology*, **XV**, 371–398.

LIKERT, R. (1956) Motivation and Increased Productivity. *Management Record*, **XVIII**, 128–131.

LIKERT, R. (1961) *New Patterns of Management*. New York: McGraw-Hill.

MCGREGOR, D. M. (1960) The Human Side of the Enterprise. In Rubenstein, A. H., and Haberstroh, C. J. (Editors), *Some Theories of Organization*. Homewood, Illinois: Dorsey Press, Inc., and Richard D. Irwin, Inc.

MANN, F. C., and WILLIAMS, L. K. (1962) Some Effects of the Changing Work Environment in the Office. *Journal of Social Issues*, **XVIII**, 90–101.

MATTHEWS, A. T. V., and ABU-LABAN, BAHA. (1959) Job Satisfaction and Leisure Time Activity in a Restrictive Environment. *Sociology and Social Research*, **XLIII**, 189–196.

METZNER, H., and MANN, F. (1953) Employee Attitudes and Absences. *Personnel Psychology*, **VI**, 467–485.

PATCHEN, MARTIN. (1960) Absence and Employee Feelings about Fair Treatment. *Personnel Psychology*, **XIII**, 349–360.

PELZ, D. C. (1952) Influence: A Key to Effective Leadership in the First Line Supervisor. *Personnel*, **XXIX**, 209–217.

PORTER, L. W. (1962) Job Attitudes in Management: Perceived Deficiencies in Need Fulfillment as a Function of Job Level. *Journal of Applied Psychology*, **XLVI**, 375–384.

RETTIG, S., and PASAMANICK, B. (1960) A Comparative Analysis of the Status and Job Satisfaction of State School and Public School Teachers. *American Journal of Mental Deficiency*, **LXIV**, 812–816.

ROETHLISBERGER, F. J., and DICKSON, W. J. (1939) *Management and the Worker*. Cambridge: Harvard University Press.

ROY, DONALD, F. (1959) Banana Time: Job Satisfaction and Informal Interaction. *Human Organization*, **XVIII**, 158–168.

SINHA, D., and SARMA, K. C. (1962) Union Attitudes and Job Satisfaction in Indian Workers. *Journal of Applied Psychology*, **XLVI**, 247–251.

SMITH, P. C. (1955) The Prediction of Individual Differences in Susceptibility to Industrial Monotony. *J. of Applied Psychology*, **XXXIX**, 320–329.

SMITH, P. C. (1963) Cornell Studies of Job Satisfaction: I. Strategy for the Development of a General Theory of Job Satisfaction. Unpublished Manuscript. Ithaca: Cornell University.

SUEHR, J. H. (1962) A Study of Morale in Education Utilizing Incomplete Sentences. *Journal of Educational Research*, **LVI**, 75–81.

TALACCHI, S. (1960) Organizational Size, Individual Attitudes, and Behavior: An Empirical Study. *Administrative Science Quarterly*, **V**, 399–420.

TROXELL, J. P. (1954) Elements in Job Satisfaction. *Personnel*, **XXXI**, 199–205.

ULRICH, LYNN, and TRUMBO, DON. (1965) The Selection Interview since 1949. *Psychological Bulletin*, **LXIII**, 100–116.

VITELES, M. S. (1953) *Motivation and Morale in Industry*. New York: W. W. Norton and Company.

Vollmer, H. M., and Kinney, J. A. (1955) Age, Education and Job Satisfaction. *Personnel*, **XXXII**, 38–43.

Vroom, V. H. (1962) Ego-Involvement, Job Satisfaction, and Job Performance. *Personnel Psychology*, **XV**, 159–177.

Vroom, V. H., and Maier, N. R. F. (1961) Industrial Social Psychology. In Farnsworth, P. R., McNemar, O., and McNemar, Q. (Editors), *Annual Review of Psychology*, **XII**, 413–446.

Vroom, V. H., and Mann, F. C. (1960) Leader Authoritarianism and Employee Attitudes. *Personnel Psychology*, **XIII**, 125–140.

White, B. L. (1960) Job Attitudes, Absence from Work and Labor Turnover. *Personnel Practice Bulletin*, **XVI**, 18–23.

Youngberg, C. F. X., Hedberg, R., and Baxter, B. (1962) Management Action Recommendations Based on One versus Two Dimensions of a Job Satisfaction Questionnaire. *Personnel Psychology*, **XV**, 145–150.

Zaleznik, A., Christensen, C. R., and Roethlisberger, F. J. (1958) *The Motivation, Productivity and Satisfaction of Workers*. Boston: Harvard University, Division of Research, Graduate School of Business Administration.

Zander, A., and Quinn, R. (1962) The Social Environment and Mental Health: A Review of Past Research at the Institute of Social Research. *Journal of Social Issues*, **XVIII**, 48–66.

THE WORK EXPERIENCE: FURTHER READING

Arendt, H. (1958) *The Human Condition*. University of Chicago Press.

Clark, F. Le Gros (1955) *New Jobs for Old Workers*. London, Nuffield Foundation.

Clark, F. Le Gros (1956) *The Employment Problems of Elderly Men*. London, Nuffield Foundation.

Clay, H. M. (1960) *The Older Worker and His Job*. London, H.M.S.O.

Dubin, R. (1958) *The World of Work*. Englewood Cliffs, N.J., Prentice-Hall.

Friedmann, G. (1962) *The Anatomy of Work; Labour, Leisure and the Implications of Automation*. Glencoe, Ill., Free Press.

Gross, E. (1955) *Work and Society*. New York, Thomas V. Crowell.

Heron, A. R. (1948) *Why Men Work*. Stanford, Stanford University Press.

Heron, A. (1961) *Preparation for Retirement: Solving a New Problem*. London: National Old People's Welfare Council.

Herzberg, F. (1966) *Work and the Nature of Man*. Cleveland, World Publishing Co.

Herzberg, F., Mausner, B., and Snyderman, B. (1959) *The Motivation to Work*. 2nd ed., New York, Wiley.

Hughes, E. C. (1958) *Men and Their Work*. Glencoe, Ill., Free Press.

Morse, M. (1965) *The Unattached*. Harmondsworth, Penguin Books.

Nosow, S., and Form, W. H. (eds.) (1962) *Man, Work and Society*. New York, Basic Books.

Rosenberg, M. (1957) *Occupations and Values*. Glencoe, Ill. Free Press.

Super, D. E. (1957) *The Psychology of Careers*. New York: Harper & Row.

Tilgher, A. (1931) *Work: What it has Meant to Man Through the Ages*. London, George G. Harrap.

Vroom, V. H. (1964) *Work and Motivation*. New York, J. Wiley.

Weber, M. (1958) *The Protestant Ethic and the Spirit of Capitalism*. New York, Scribner's.

Welford, A. T. (1958) *Ageing and Human Skill*. London, Oxford University Press.

Zweig, F. (1961) *The Worker in an Affluent Society*. London, Heinemann.

BRAYFIELD, A. H., and CROCKETT, W. H. (1955) Employee attitudes and employee performances. *Psychological Bulletin*, **52**, 396–424.

BROWN, A. W., and LANDSBERGER, H. A. (1960) The sense of responsibility among young workers: Part 1, Definition and measurement. *Occupational Psychology*, **34**, 1–14.

BROWN, A. W., and LANDSBERGER, H. A. (1960) The sense of responsibility among young workers: Part 2, Correlates. *Occupational Psychology*, **34**, 73–85.

CENTERS, R. (1952) Job satisfaction at various occupational levels. In R. G. Kuhlen and G. G. Thompson (eds.), *Psychological Studies of Human Development*, 470–478. New York, Appleton-Century-Crofts.

CENTERS, R., and CANTRIL, H. (1946) Income satisfaction and income aspiration. *Journal of Abnormal and Social Psychology*, **41**, 64–69.

FREEDMAN, L. Z., and LEAVY, S. A. (1961) Psychopathology and occupation: Part 2, Work and competition. *Occupational Psychology*, **35**, 93–110.

FROEHLICH, C. P., and WOLINS, L. (1960) Job satisfaction and need satisfaction. *Personnel Psychology*, **13**, 407–420.

GILLIS, J. S., and LANDSBERGER, H. A. (1963) The sense of responsibility among young workers: Part 3, Need achievement, job aspirations and life situation. *Occupational Psychology*, **37**, 101–111.

HANDYSIDE, J. D., and SPEAK, M. (1964) Job satisfaction: myths and realities. *British Journal of Industrial Relations*, **2**, 57–65.

HERON, A. (1954) Satisfaction and satisfactoriness: complementary aspects of occupational adjustment. *Occupational Psychology*, **28**, 40–56.

HERON, A., and CHOWN, S. M. (1960) Semi-skilled and over forty. *Occupational Psychology*, **34**, 264–274.

KATZELL, R. A. (1964) Personal values, job satisfaction and job behaviour. In H. Borow (ed.), *Man in a World at Work*. Boston, Houghton Mifflin.

LYMAN, E. (1958) Occupational differences in the value attached to work. *American Journal of Sociology*, **61**, 138–144.

MENNINGER, W. C. (1964) The meaning of work in western society. In H. Borow (ed.), *Man in a World at Work*, *ibid.*

MORSE, N. C., and WEISS, R. S. (1955) The function and meaning of work and the job. *American Sociological Review*, **20**, 191–198.

RIESMAN, D., and BLOOMBERG, W. (1957) Work and leisure: fusion or polarity? In C. M. Arensberg (ed.), *Research in Industrial and Human Relations*, Harper.

ROSS, I. C., and ZANDER, A. (1957) Need satisfaction and employee turnover. *Personnel Psychology*, **10**, 327–338.

SARBIN, T. R., and ANDERSON, H. C. (1942) A preliminary study of the relationship of measured interest patterns and occupational dissatisfaction. *Educational and Psychological Measurement*, **2**, 23–36.

SCHAFFER, R. H. (1953) Job satisfaction as related to need satisfaction in work. *Psychological Monographs*, No. 364, 1.

TENEN, C. (1947) The adolescent in the factory. *British Journal of Educational Psychology*, **17**, Part II, June 1947.

TURNER, A. N., and MICLETTE, A. L. (1962) Sources of satisfaction in repetitive work. *Occupational Psychology*, **36**, 215–231.

WRENN, C. G. (1964) Human values and work in American life. In H. Borow (ed.), *Man in a World at Work*, *ibid.*

WILENSKY, H. L. (1964) Varieties of work experience. In H. Borow (ed.), *Man in a World at Work*, *ibid.*

Part II. PRACTICE

"The English believe nothing to be practical until they have seen it accomplished."

R. H. TAWNEY

Introduction

INTEREST in vocational guidance has been steadily increasing for over sixty years. Ogilvie Gordon proposed a national system of Educational Information and Employment Bureaux at a meeting of the Glasgow Union of Women Workers in 1904. She suggested that the bureaux should endeavour to lead all young people "who are physically fit" towards employment that will prove congenial to them and bring them a reasonable livelihood. She also suggested that they should foster a fuller co-operation between the schools and the workshop. At about the same time people were thinking along similar lines in the United States of America. Frank Parsons became Director of the new Vocational Bureau of Boston in 1908, and, after his death, his book *Choosing a Vocation* was published in 1909.

Since then the vocational guidance movement has progressed rapidly, particularly in the United States. In America, guidance is primarily the role of the school counsellor and it is only recently that the Youth Services Program within the United States Employment Service has started to seriously expand its activities. In Britain the picture is almost completely reversed. The Youth Employment Service is charged with the responsibility of providing vocational guidance and the youth employment officers are essentially "outsiders" who visit the schools from time to time. Although the idea of having school counsellors permanently attached to a particular school is gaining support in some circles, the official policy, as expressed in the Albemarle Report (1965), and the Department of Education and Science's booklet *Careers Guidance in Schools* (1965) appears to favour the development of the "careers team". Even when a trained counsellor is available in the school he is envisaged as functioning as the school's representative within the careers team and working alongside the youth employment officers.

Teachers have traditionally held the view that vocational training must not compromise the wider aims of a basic education. Within the existing British educational structure there is a great emphasis on early specialization. To introduce vocational training into schools would only aggravate this situation. It is, however, essential not to confuse vocational *training* and vocational *guidance*. Hoyt (1965a) argues that guidance workers consider their function to be essentially one of helping people choose wisely from among the alternatives available to them. "We do this by encouraging the counselee to learn, think, consider and decide about himself and his opportunities. We don't consider it nearly so important *what* people choose as we do *that* they choose from the widest possible range of opportunities. We aren't as concerned about what the counselee decides about his opportunities as we are what he decides about *himself* in relation to these opportunities. We don't want to *make* people do things—we want to *let* them find ways of doing things. We aren't interested in the *something* they become as the *someone* they become."

The common thread among the chief recommendations in the Newsom Report (1963) is the need for a more outward looking approach to the school curriculum. These recommendations, together with the proposal to raise the minimum school leaving age to sixteen, increase enormously the scope for vocational guidance in the schools.

Given this changing environment the most urgent task is to shift the emphasis from what Super (1957) has termed last minute "crisis counselling" to a more long-term concern with the individual and his educational and vocational development. The value of last minute vocational guidance is limited as throughout an individual's school career he will have made educational decisions that will have gradually narrowed the range of occupational alternatives open to him. Its value may also be limited because the likelihood of an individual having arrived at some hierarchy of vocational preferences will increase the longer guidance and counselling is delayed, and having once made up his mind the individual is likely to be more hostile or indifferent towards new information and ideas. There is, therefore, a strong case, supported by the theories presented in Part I of this book, for vocational guidance to begin at the commencement of secondary education.

The careers teacher or school counsellor, under these circumstances, would have an even more important role to play than at present. He would, assuming he is a suitable person for the job, gradually win the trust and confidence of his students, and, therefore, be in a better position than the youth employment officer to gather valuable personal information about each individual. The youth employment officer, on the other hand, would be best fitted to accumulate detailed knowledge about the employment scene. By working as a team they would both have something useful to contribute and together they will have a vitality and competence that would transcend their individual abilities.

It must, however, be realized that the individual's need for vocational guidance is not automatically satisfied as soon as he leaves school. Entry into the world of work can be a traumatic experience, unsettling the individual for some considerable time. The progress of the young worker requires close monitoring. This follow-up is clearly a role for the youth employment officer but if he is to do it efficiently he will require more time and resources than are currently available for this sort of activity.

While it may be relatively easy to assess whether a person will be satisfactory in a particular job it is considerably more difficult to predict if he will be satisfied by that same job. It would be a less troubled world if everybody chose the right job first time. Many people choose jobs in which they are unsatisfactory, dissatisfied or both. To assume that because they have left school they will no longer be in need of guidance is obviously false. The experience of the Ministry of Labour's Occupational Guidance Units provides evidence for the fact that vocational guidance is not only necessary for the potential school leaver but that it may be required by workers, of any age, involved in occupational transition.

Hoyt (1965b) draws attention to another basic tenet behind vocational guidance when he suggests that if counsellors do not perform their duties efficiently and provide the comprehenive service required there will be a danger of increased state intervention with the possibility of undesirable consequences. He argues that Congress, in making funds available for guidance and counselling, was thinking about manpower utilization objectives and not about the individuals right to lead his own life and choose his own occupation. It is necessary, therefore, to consider whether, as Hoyt suggests, "societal needs can best be met indirectly by meeting individual needs directly ...".

In Britain, where the Youth Employment Service is responsible for almost all the vocational guidance given to young people, it is possible for Local Education Authorities to administer the Service at a local level. Nevertheless approximately three-quarters of the finance is still provided by the Central Government and therefore the Service tends to be subject to a great deal of Government direction and influence. Fortunately official policy does not compromise the individual's freedom of choice with the interests of a national manpower policy. The individuals freedom of choice is already limited by such factors as social class, educational opportunity and geographical location. It is not the role of the youth employment officer, acting in the interest of "the economy" to erect additional barriers. As Hoppock (1963) says, "The counselor is not a recruiting officer, and he should never permit himself to become one. Employers, training institutions, and professional associations can be depended upon to publicize any genuine shortage and to urge all qualified candidates to apply. The nation will survive without the counselor adding his influence. Under the seductive blandishments of the recruiters, the client needs one competent person whom he can trust to put the client's interest first and to help him to think clearly about what he wants to do. The counselor who permits any other interest to creep into his activities has ceased to be a counselor.

"The counselor need not become belligerent on this point. He can respect the convictions, the motives, and the integrity of sincere recruiters. He can help them to make accessible to his clients the factual information about supply and demand which his clients need in order to appraise their own prospects of employment. He can accept the literature which is offered and even distribute some of it. He can invite recruiting officers to answer questions in group conferences which the counselor will attend. But every time the counselor does one of these things, he assumes an obligation to find and to verify and to present to his students or clients an equal amount of pertinent data regarding the disadvantages of doing what the recruiter has proposed. Such data may include distasteful aspects of the work, earnings in the lower half of the distribution, hazards, unfavorable working conditions, and the possibility that by the time the client has completed his training, the demand for workers may have been met. ...

"... so long as we value the welfare and the freedom of the individual above the planning functions of the state, the counselor must do his counseling in terms of the needs and values of his client. ... The counselor who intentionally permits his own values or the values of a professional group or of a government agency to take precedence over the values of his client has not only done his client a disservice, he has also undermined the foundation of freedom—the right of the individual to the pursuit of happiness as he chooses to pursue it."*

REFERENCES

DEPARTMENT OF EDUCATION AND SCIENCE (1965) *Careers Guidance in Schools.* London, H.M.S.O.

HOPPOCK, R. (1963) *Occupational Information, Where to get it and how to use it in counseling and in teaching.* (2nd ed.) New York, McGraw-Hill.

HOYT, K. B. (1965a) *The Challenge of Guidance and Vocational Education.* An address at 59th Annual Vocational Convention, December 1965, Miami Beach, Florida.

HOYT, K. B. (1965b) High school guidance and the speciality oriented student research program. *Vocational Guidance Quarterly*, Summer 1965, p. 229.

MINISTRY OF EDUCATION (1963) *Half our Future—The Newsom Report.* Central Advisory Council for Education, London, H.M.S.O.

MINISTRY OF LABOUR (1965) *The Future Development of the Youth Employment Service—The Albemarle Report.* National Youth Employment Council, London, H.M.S.O.

PARSONS, F. (1909) *Choosing a Vocation.* Boston, Houghton Mifflin.

SUPER, D. E. (1957) *The Psychology of Careers.* New York, Harper and Row.

SECTION 5

The Aims of Guidance

"Guidance and Counseling:

the two words are not synonyms. Guidance, the bigger term, includes counseling as one of its 6 elements.

1. ANALYSIS: Helping the student get the facts about himself—from test results, cumulative records, and other means of identifying potentialities and interests.
2. INFORMATION: Giving him the facts about his environment—about educational and occupational opportunities and requirements.
3. ORIENTATION: Helping him to get acquainted with the school program and educational and vocational opportunities and requirements.
4. COUNSELING: Helping him to develop self-understanding and to develop his educational and occupational plans.
5. PLACEMENT: Helping him carry out those plans.
6. FOLLOW UP: Determining how his plans worked out and how effectively the educational program served him."

FRANK L. SIEVERS

THIS section is concerned with the thorny question of what we are trying to do when we give vocational guidance. The quotation of Frank Sievers which introduces this section questions the synonymous use made of the terms *guidance* and *counselling*. If we accept his definition of guidance as a general aim incorporating counselling as one of the elements in the guidance process, we then have to construct our criteria for action. Only then is it possible to assess the effectiveness of vocational guidance. It is somewhat hasty to discover that a particular programme of vocational guidance is effective, if the philosophy behind that programme is unspecified. This type of professional introspection leads rapidly to moral questions regarding the ethical responsibilities of counsellors, and practical questions concerning the skills they need to perform their functions efficiently. The following articles sample these problems and a bibliography is provided at the end of the section to enable readers interested in these basic and vitally important issues to acquaint themselves with the controversies surrounding them.

The section opens with the *Vocational Guidance Recommendation* of the International Labour Conference held in Geneva in 1949. It is fascinating to note these recommendations and to check on the progress made throughout the world almost twenty years later. The sad fact is, that for most countries, including Britain, these recommendations still appear very progressive, illustrating the painfully slow realization of the value of vocational guidance on the part of educationalists, industrialists, and governmental bodies.

Shoben, in a highly controversial article, questions the aims of many of the practitioners of vocational guidance. He claims that, wittingly or unwittingly, they attempt to transmit a universal set of values to their clients; those values about life, work, and leisure, mainly associated with the middle-classes; instead they should be encouraging individual growth and development of the "examined life", by which he means that as far as possible, counsellors should not function directly as agents of socialization. Like the best prophets, their duty should be to lay "all open to view" in terms of personal and occupational information. It is then up to the client to decide how he wishes to make use of this data.

Blocher examines some of the controversial issues to be found in counselling. He claims that some of the most discussed topics in counselling are relatively irrelevant; for example, the "directive vs. nondirective" controversy; how far should counsellors "diagnose"?; and should counselling be personal-emotional or informational-didactic? He claims that these issues are not vital in the sense that they present important alternative consequences to counsellors. The issues that are vital are more difficult to isolate, but he claims they are highly important in terms of their consequences, i.e. whether counselling is developmental-educative or remedial and therapeutic (viz. Shoben's article) and whether it is liberating or conditioning in nature.

The skills necessary to perform the guidance function effectively are examined by Hoyt. He looks at needed counsellor competencies and attitudes, and underlines the important point that as well possessing skills in counselling, the personal philosophy of the counsellor is also of vital importance. For example, he must not expect to have a life-long influence on a client's career. If he can help the client to deal with the next four or five years of his occupational life he should consider his existence justified. With the rapidly changing nature of society and the economy he can hope for nothing more.

The first fully trained counsellors entered British schools in September 1966. Their role is the subject of much heated discussion. The basic question to be answered is how much can they draw on American experiences and how much must they develop to match the peculiarities of the British educational system. Daws discusses these various possibilities and underlines the need for both therapeutic and educational–vocational counselling in the British system.

21. I.L.O. Recommendation (No. 87) Concerning Vocational Guidance

THE General Conference of the International Labour Organisation,

Having been convened at Geneva by the Governing Body of the International Labour Office, and having met in its Thirty-second Session on 8 June 1949, and

Having decided upon the adoption of certain proposals concerning vocational guidance which is the ninth item on the agenda of the session, and

Having determined that the proposals shall take the form of a Recommendation,

adopts this first day of July of the year one thousand nine hundred and forty-nine the following Recommendation, which may be cited as the Vocational Guidance Recommendation, 1949:

I. GENERAL

1. For the purpose of this Recommendation the term "vocational guidance" means assistance given to an individual in solving problems related to occupational choice and progress with due regard for the individual's characteristics and their relation to occupational opportunity.

2. Vocational guidance is based on the free and voluntary choice of the individual; its primary object is to give him full opportunity for personal development and satisfaction from work, with due regard for the most effective use of national manpower resources.

3. Vocational guidance is a continuous process, the fundamental principles of which are the same irrespective of the age of the individuals being counselled. These principles have an immediate importance for the welfare of individuals everywhere and for the prosperity of all countries.

4. Facilities for vocational guidance should be adapted to the peculiar needs of each country and be adopted progressively. Their development within each country should proceed from a widespread understanding of the purpose of vocational guidance, the establishment of an adequate administrative structure, and the provision of technically qualified personnel.

II. SCOPE

5. To the maximum possible extent consistent with national and local policy and resources, public vocational guidance facilities should be provided for all persons requiring such assistance.

6. Special provision should be made for—

(*a*) programmes suitable for young persons, including those in school, who require counselling on problems related to entering occupations or planning careers; and

(*b*) programmes suitable for all other persons who require counselling on employment and related vocational problems; such persons are referred to hereafter in this Recommendation as adults.

III. PRINCIPLES AND METHODS OF VOCATIONAL GUIDANCE FOR YOUNG PERSONS INCLUDING THOSE IN SCHOOL

7. (1) Vocational guidance policies and programmes should be determined through the co-operative efforts of the schools and other organisations and services concerned with young persons in the transition from school to work, and the representative organisations of employers and workers, to the end that each young person receiving vocational guidance may have the benefit of unified and co-ordinated assistance.

(2) These co-operative efforts should also include consultation and co-operation with the parents and guardians concerned and with associations of parents where such exist.

(3) In applying these general principles, due account should be taken of the principles of administrative organisation set forth in Part V of this Recommendation.

8. (1) During the period of general education, preliminary vocational guidance should be included within the educational programme. Such guidance should be primarily designed to make the young person aware of his aptitudes, qualifications and interests and of the various occupations and careers so as to facilitate future vocational adjustment.

(2) The preliminary vocational guidance should receive increasing emphasis at those stages of schooling at which the young person may choose to enter special vocational courses or seeks other training or employment on leaving school.

(3) The preliminary vocational guidance should include—

(*a*) the provision, in suitable form, of comprehensive occupational and industrial information;

(*b*) wherever possible in the national and local circumstances, visits, adequately supervised, to industrial and commercial establishments and other workplaces; and (*c*) counselling by means of personal interview supplemented by group discussions or talks.

9. The methods of vocational guidance for young persons set forth in Paragraphs 10 to 15 should be given particular attention and their use encouraged to the widest practicable extent.

10. (1) Each young person seeking vocational guidance should be provided with adequate opportunity for a counselling interview with a vocational guidance officer, more particularly at the time he may be able to choose specific vocational courses, or to leave school for other occupational training (including apprenticeship) or for work.

(2) Methods of interview should be continuously adapted with a view to ensuring the most complete analysis possible of individual ability in relation to occupational opportunities and requirements.

11. Records of school progress, including, as desired and as appropriate in individual cases, an evaluation of capacity, educational attainments, aptitudes and personality, should be used as may be considered appropriate for vocational guidance with due respect to the confidential character of the information contained therein.

12. (1) The facilities for the medical examination of young persons should be utilised as appropriate and developed as necessary for purposes of vocational guidance.

(2) Advice for remedial action and such other help as may be possible and useful for the purposes of vocational adjustment should be provided as needed in each individual case.

13. (1) Wherever practicable, appropriate tests of capacity and aptitude and, where so desired, other psychological tests should be made available for use in vocational guidance as appropriate to the needs of individual cases.

(2) Advice for remedial action and such other help as may be possible and useful for the purposes of vocational adjustment should be made available in individual cases.

14. (1) Suitable and reliable information regarding careers in the different occupations and industries and regarding employment and training opportunities should be made available to young persons through counselling interviews and otherwise, with due regard for the aptitudes, physical capacities, qualifications, preferences and personality of the young person concerned and the prospective needs of the economy.

(2) In this connection the competent authorities should maintain continuous co-operation with such other public and private bodies, including more particularly the representative organisations of employers and workers, as are able—

(*a*) to provide information concerning probable future openings in each industry, trade or occupation; and

(*b*) to assist with the preparation and conclusion of contracts of apprenticeship and to supervise their application.

15. Consideration should also be given to the desirability of ascertaining the aptitudes of young persons by proyiding opportunity for appropriate work experience and by other similar means.

16. Special attention should be given to the development, within the framework of the general vocational guidance services, of adequate and appropriate arrangements for the vocational guidance of young persons in rural areas.

17. Special attention should be given to the development, within the framework of the general vocational guidance services, and in co-operation with the appropriate rehabilitation services, of adequate and appropriate arrangements for the vocational guidance of young persons—

(*a*) who have physical or mental handicaps or limitations; or

(*b*) who manifest personality disorders of such a nature as to prevent or make specially difficult their vocational adjustment.

18. The competent national and local authorities should encourage full voluntary use of vocational guidance facilities, more particularly in the case of—

(*a*) young persons who may choose among several vocational courses within the school;

(*b*) young persons who are near school-leaving age;

(*c*) young persons who are entering the employment market for the first time;

(*d*) young persons who are seeking admission to apprenticeship or other vocational training;

(*e*) young persons who are unemployed, who are employed in declining industries or who are likely to become unemployed;

(*f*) young persons who have physical or mental handicaps or limitations; or

(*g*) young persons who manifest personality disorders of such a nature as to prevent or make specially difficult their vocational adjustment.

19. The competent authorities should take the necessary measures to facilitate the execution of the young persons' vocational plans wherever these are feasible; where appropriate in individual cases suggestions should be made for carrying out these plans and assistance should be provided in making the necessary contacts with other services or persons also concerned with placing the young person in training or employment in the occupation chosen by him.

20. (1) The competent authorities should take measures to organise follow-up aimed primarily at assisting in so far as possible the young person to overcome any difficulties he may be experiencing in following his vocational plans and ascertaining whether the occupation selected is proving suitable.

(2) Wherever possible, methods of follow-up should include general enquiries on a sampling basis to measure the results of vocational guidance in individual cases and to evaluate vocational guidance policy and methods. Such enquiries should permit of securing medical information in co-operation, where possible, with the medical facilities existing at workplaces.

IV. PRINCIPLES AND METHODS OF VOCATIONAL GUIDANCE FOR ADULTS (EMPLOYMENT COUNSELLING)

21. (1) Appropriate arrangements for adults should be made within the framework of the public vocational guidance services to assist any person requiring aid in choosing an occupation or in changing his occupation.

(2) The process involved in rendering this assistance is referred to in this Recommendation as employment counselling.

22. The process of employment counselling should include, as far as practicable in the national circumstances and as appropriate in individual cases—

(*a*) interview with an employment counsellor;
(*b*) examination of record of work experience;
(*c*) examination of scholastic or other records relating to education or training received;
(*d*) medical examination;
(*e*) appropriate tests of capacity and aptitude, and, where so desired, other psychological tests;
(*f*) ascertainment of aptitudes by appropriate work experience and by other similar means;
(*g*) technical trade tests, either verbal or otherwise, in all cases where such seem necessary;
(*h*) analysis of physical capacity in relation to occupational requirements;
(*i*) provision of information concerning employment and training opportunities relating to the qualifications, physical capacities, aptitudes, preferences and experience of the person concerned and to the needs of the employment market;
(*j*) follow-up on a sampling basis, aimed at discovering whether satisfactory placement in employment, training or retraining has been achieved and at evaluating employment counselling policy and methods.

23. (1) The competent national and local bodies should take all necessary measures to encourage the extended use, on a voluntary basis, of employment counselling services in the case of—

(*a*) persons entering employment for the first time;
(*b*) persons unemployed for a long period;
(*c*) persons unemployed or likely to be unemployed, as a result of declining industries or changes in the technique, structure or location of industry;
(*d*) persons living in rural areas who comprise surplus manpower in the light of current or prospective employment opportunity;
(*e*) persons desirous of benefiting from public facilities for vocational training and readjustment.

(2) All necessary and practicable measures should be taken to develop, within the framework of the general vocational guidance facilities and with the co-operation of any appropriate rehabilitation services when the person requires such assistance, specialised employment counselling for physically

disabled persons and those having personality disorders that hinder their vocational adjustment.

(3) All necessary and practicable measures should be taken to develop, within the framework of the general vocational guidance facilities, specialised employment counselling for technicians, professional workers, salaried employees and executive staff.

24. Special attention should be given, in connection with employment counselling, to the development of appropriate methods for the technical selection of workers for particular occupations and industries.

V. PRINCIPLES OF ADMINISTRATIVE ORGANISATION

25. Vocational guidance and employment counselling should be organised and co-ordinated on the basis of a comprehensive general programme, established and developed in the light of regional and local conditions and adaptable to changes in such conditions.

26. In order to encourage the development of vocational guidance and employment counselling facilities, provision should be made by the central authorities (including, where appropriate, the central authorities of the federated units of federal States) for—

(*a*) adequate financing of such facilities;
(*b*) appropriate technical assistance; and
(*c*) development of methods and materials suitable for use on a nationwide basis.

27. All necessary and desirable measures should be taken by the competent authorities to secure effective co-operation, nationally and locally, between the public and private bodies engaged in vocational guidance or employment counselling activities.

A. *Administrative Arrangements for Vocational Guidance for Young Persons, including those in School*

28. (1) The competent authorities should make appropriate arrangements for the co-ordination, nationally and locally, of policy and action in the field of vocational guidance, due regard being paid to the responsibility of the parents and to the appropriate functions of private vocational guidance bodies.

(2) These arrangements should be directed more particularly towards—

(*a*) maintaining effective public serivce to young persons, in co-operation with other interested agencies as appropriate without duplication of effort; and
(*b*) facilitating, as may be desirable and with due respect for confidential data, the exchange of information concerning—

(i) the extent and character of the need for vocational guidance services and of the facilities already available;
(ii) the young persons applying for vocational guidance;
(iii) industries, trades and occupations;
(iv) employment and training opportunities; and
(v) the preparation and use of vocational guidance materials including appropriate tests.

29. (1) National and local administrative responsibility for vocational guidance should be clearly defined.

(2) With due regard to this division of authority, primary responsibility should be entrusted either—
(*a*) jointly to the education and employment service authorities; or
(*b*) to one of these authorities working in close-co-operation with the other.

30. (1) Appropriate arrangements should be made through advisory committees for the co-operation of representatives of employers and workers in the development of vocational guidance policy.

(2) Such committees should be maintained nationally and as far as possible locally and should normally include representatives of the public and private bodies concerned with education, training (including apprenticeship), vocational guidance and other questions directly affecting the vocational adjustment of young persons.

B. *Administrative Arrangements for Vocational Guidance for Adults (Employment Counselling)*

31. (1) Administrative responsibility for employment counselling should be entrusted primarily to the public employment service, with due regard to the administrative responsibility assigned by public authority to educational or other agencies.

(2) The offices of the public employment service should include, at each administrative stage so far as practicable, specialised employment counselling units for officers.

(3) Administrative arrangements should be made to ensure, as may be necessary or desirable, co-operation by the public employment service with specialised employment counselling services maintained for special groups or persons.

32. Appropriate arrangements should be made, nationally and locally, to ensure that employment counselling is organised in close relation with—
(*a*) all other activities of the employment service;
(*b*) other vocational guidance services;
(*c*) educational and training institutions;
(*d*) the administration of unemployment insurance and assistance schemes;
(*e*) the administration of training and retraining schemes and of other plans to promote occupational or geographical mobility of labour;
(*f*) the representative organisations of employers and workers; and

(*g*) public and private organisations providing rehabilitation services to disabled persons.

VI. TRAINING OF OFFICERS

33. (1) In order to secure the efficiency of the vocational guidance services, the competent authority should ensure the employment of an adequate number of officers with suitable training, experience and other qualifications, and should organise, to the fullest possible extent and in co-operation where appropriate with other bodies concerned, specialised scientific and technical training for vocational guidance staff.

(2) The measures to be taken should include, for example:

(*a*) the establishment by the competent authority of minimum qualifications for vocational guidance officers;

(*b*) the establishment by the competent authority of regulations for the selection of officers on the basis of such qualifications;

(*c*) the organisation of specialised training courses for persons seeking to undertake the work of vocational guidance;

(*d*) the provision of supplementary training and refresher courses for all officers; and

(*e*) the maintenance by the competent authority of conditions of appointment and employment sufficiently attractive to provide an inducement to qualified persons to undertake and continue in such work.

(3) Consideration should be given to—

(*a*) the interchange of vocational guidance officers among the different branches of the services with which they are respectively concerned;

(*b*) the publication of technical material suitable for developing the professional skill of officers.

(4) Where useful, the Members should co-operate for the purposes of training staff, availing themselves of the help of the International Labour Office it they so desire.

VII. RESEARCH AND PUBLICITY

34. (1) Special measures should be taken on a co-ordinated basis, to promote public and private research and experiment in methods of vocational guidance.

(2) The public employment service should co-operate in such research.

(3) Wherever appropriate in the circumstances such research should include examination of such questions as—

(*a*) methods of interviewing;

(*b*) the analysis of the requirements of the different occupations;

(*c*) the provision of industrial and occupational information appropriate for vocational guidance;
(*d*) aptitude and other psychological testing;
(*e*) the development of model vocational guidance forms; and
(*f*) the measurement of the result of vocational guidance.

35. Systematic efforts should be made by the authorities responsible for vocational guidance in co-operation with employers' and workers' organisations and where appropriate with other bodies concerned, to promote wide public understanding of the purposes, principles and methods of vocational guidance.

22. *Guidance: Remedial Function or Social Reconstruction?*

EDWARD JOSEPH SHOBEN, JR.

THE CURRENT PUBLIC AND PROFESSIONAL STATUS OF GUIDANCE

THERE is a sense in which guidance services as a part of the American educational enterprise are in their heyday. The major policy statement about educational matters that fails to assign a prominent place to guidance is a rarity, and as an explicit beneficiary of the National Defense Education Act, along with only a tiny cluster of the currently most valued subject-matter fields, guidance has enjoyed strong financial support. According to the U.S. Office of Education, for example, nearly 8,000 people have been enrolled under N.D.E.A. auspices for short-term guidance training institutes, and more than 1,700 have been supported in regular-session institutes. In 1960, 30,000 persons were concerned with "scheduled guidance activities" in secondary schools across the nation, although only about one-third of them were functioning as full-time guidance personnel. Similarly, in the same year, the number of students studying for advanced degrees in guidance and counseling exceeded the combined total in physical education, business education, industrial arts education, and music education, and the figure closely approximated the numbers majoring in such standard programs as administration and curriculum. The American Personnel and Guidance Association has a dues-paying membership of well over 13,000, owns its own building in Washington, operates the highly successful *Personnel and Guidance Journal*, and exercises a not inconsiderable influence in the governmental and private circles where issues of policy and finance for education are decided.

At the same time, however, the pattern of ebullient expansiveness is drawn taut by tensions, criticisms, and ambiguities. Wrenn,[19] in examining the field in 1958, noted three disturbing signs of the times that still persist: (1) Among psychologists, counseling psychology enjoys the lowest prestige of all the specialties requiring the doctorate; (2) no one has yet developed an

(Reprinted from *Harvard Educational Review*, vol. 32, No. 4, 1962, pp. 430–443, by permission of editor and author.)

adequate theory of vocational choice and development; and (3) various lines of research into the learning process, including Skinner's[13, 14] make it hard to ignore the possibility that the counseling process may be so conceived as to reinforce the least integrative of the behaviors displayed by its clients. Banesh Hoffmann's recent attack[7] is only the most recent of a long series of assaults on the psychometric arsenal of guidance, and *The Brain Watchers*[5, 6] has only made highly articulate the troubled objections of many to what they regard as an invasion of the personalities and psychodynamics of the children in the school's charge. In much the same vein, Barry and Wolf[2] have documented the extent to which "myths"—assumptions and undemonstrated principles—are shot through the literature of guidance, making it less than either a firmly based discipline or a logically coherent profession.

At the very time, then, that guidance commands the greatest public favor, it is also under public fire. At the moment of its greatest expansion, it can show little in the way of solid research to demonstrate its merits or its achievements. At a peak of its influence, its basic techniques of testing and counseling evoke a marked degree of mistrust. With the best of intentions, generally if rather dimly perceived by the public and the rest of the educational fraternity, guidance is animated neither by a clear philosophy of why people should be given its special kind of service as a part of their school experience nor by a demonstrably effective core of methods by which such help can be provided.

To make this charge is by no means tantamount to a condemnation of particular guidance practices. Rather, it is a way of underscoring the place of guidance among the practical arts—in this case, the practical arts of human relationships. Pragmatically, guidance workers are undoubtedly each day doing much to assist large numbers of youngsters to cope more effectively with the business of growing up in a complex and often mystifying world. Such, at least, seems to be a reasonable article of faith, quite consonant with the common experience of those whose fate it is to visit schools and to talk frequently with the counselors and personnel officers who ply their trade there. But guidance aspires to professional status and lays claim to systematic and specialized membership within the complex educational family of occupations and disciplines. Presumably, therefore, guidance has its roots in the behavioral sciences and is watered by the springs of philosophy from which come the constant redefinitions of the role of the school in the total process of socialization. It is on this basis—the ground of its own understandable ambitions—that it is vulnerable and exposed. The gap between successes and pretensions, when one looks hard, is not only apparent; it is wide.

Nor, on reflection, is this state of affairs especially puzzling. One of the primary tensions within the guidance movement is simply a reflection of a fundamental tension in Western social thought. The societies of the West have been built essentially on the conviction that persons are free and responsible—see, for example, the whole tradition of Anglo-Saxon law.* Increasingly, however, the technique used for the investigation and reconstruction of those societies and the men who compose them has been that of science; and science carries the implication that human conduct, like any other proper object of scientific inquiry, is predictable and determined. Since this contradiction in basic assumptions has rarely been dealt with in any persuasive fashion anywhere, one cannot fairly blame guidance workers for not resolving it, but it has, for them, consequences of considerable moment. Not the least of these entailments is that of making guidance the unwitting smuggler of certain values that are not entirely explicit.

THE SMUGGLING OF VALUES

This proposition is worth examining for several reasons, one of which is its demonstration of the complexity of the guidance worker's job. In general, he supplies (or is supposed to supply) a highly individualized dimension to the pupil's experience of mass education. In contrast to the teacher, who is responsible for drawing students into the traditions of society and inviting their membership in it, the guidance worker furnishes the information, the recommendations, and the impetus that are likely to move *particular* children in *distinctive* directions on the basis of their *special* characteristics and potentialities. The business of influencing another human being is almost always touchy and edged with uneasiness, and it certainly requires justification. In the case of school guidance work, it requires justification to parents and the community at large as well as to administrators and school board members. That justification comes most readily from science—the corpus of knowledge about tests, psychological development, and the prediction of performance in college or on a job from previous experience, including academic experience. One may grant, however, the cogency and power of science in this connection and still remain impressed by two stubborn facts: (1) Guidance remains an effort to influence particular youngsters in particular directions, and (2) those directions are not given by whatever scientific data or principles that may in other ways be relevant to the enterprise.

To put the case more concretely, if a guidance counselor is attempting to help a child develop a greater sense of personal responsibility, that aim does not emerge directly from whatever psychological knowledge the counselor may have available. Behavioral science may in some fashion indicate how the

* Two instructive references here are Felix S. Cohen's *Ethical Systems and Legal Ideals* (Ithaca, N.Y.: Cornell University Press, 1959) and the popular British paperback, *Justice at Work*, by James Avery Joyce (London: Pan Books, 1957). Two books also of particular interest to educators are those by Judge Jerome Frank, *Fate and Freedom* (New York: Simon and Schuster, 1945) and *Courts on Trial* (Princeton, N.J.: Princeton University Press, 1949).

goal may be achieved; it neither defines it nor establishes its desirability. Because "responsibility" in this context is a word that carries rich positive connotations, this kind of statement of objectives is likely to evoke little opposition. But we come rapidly to more troubled waters when we discuss other such common desiderata as "spontaneity" or a "trust of one's own feelings." It seems quite probable that spontaneity and a trust of their own feelings would entail for Negro adolescents, for example, a powerful tendency to hate one's parents, to damn the school as irrelevant, and to attack society for its inequities. Despite the fact that such attitudes are by no means incomprehensible on scientific grounds, they are not likely to be encouraged by guidance workers. Even the matter of vocational choice may involve some pronounced restrictions on grounds other than those provided by psychological or sociological knowledge. Barry and Wolf (ref. 2, pp. 92–93) give an example: In Las Vegas and other gambling resorts, there is a pressing need for dealers at the gaming tables; there is even a school to train them. Pay is good, hours are short, and the working environment is, from at least one point of view, quite comfortable. For a youngster with a taste for probabilities, a suitable temperament, and an interest in games of chance, such a career may be a thoroughly "realistic" one. Yet there is ample room to doubt that any guidance counselor would condone this kind of preference, let alone raise it as an appropriate possibility.

The examples could easily be multiplied, but the point is that guidance workers, as smugglers of values, are in a position almost the reverse of that which Szasz[(16)] has recently described as the lot of psychiatrists. Taking the issue of legal abortion for therapeutic purposes as his test case, Szasz is more widely concerned with the question of how self-determined are the controls exercised over one's body. Abortions are illegal, of course, unless certain conditions obtain. While there is some variation from state to state in the nature of these conditions, mental illness is usually one of them. As a matter of fact, wherever such therapeutic abortions are legally performed in large numbers, justification is given most frequently on psychiatric grounds. At the Mt. Sinai Hospital in New York, for example, 39 per cent of legal abortions since 1952 have been done on the basis of psychiatric judgment as against only 10 per cent because of malignancies and only 11 per cent because of cardio-renal disease. But for Szasz, himself, a psychiatrist of some prominence, mental illnesses are not diseases at all. Far from being entities like tuberculosis or hypertension, they are simply strategies for coping with life that have consequences which include quite genuine misery.[(17)] The misery, however, is not like that of medically defined pain; it is the suffering associated with anxiety and interpersonal ineptness. In short, it is a *moral* suffering. In consequence, the psychiatric justification for therapeutic abortion is a moral justification, used to circumvent a legal restriction on the right of the individual to exercise whatever controls he wishes over his own body. In this sense, the psychiatrist is the bootlegger of certain moral values (mercy and self-determination) under the guise of a medical diagnosis in order to circumvent the limits set on these values under the social sanctions of law. While the psychiatric judgment here may have the appearance of science, it is in reality a camouflaged vehicle for the implementing of an inarticulate moral choice at variance with the codified rules.

In the case of the guidance worker, the appeal to science is equally in evidence, but the smuggled values are those of the dominant middle class, those that tend to reduce individual variability and autonomy rather than increase it. Viewed from one angle of regard, this state of affairs is not at all shocking. The school is, after all, a social agency, charged with the preservation of society through the transmission of the culture. Certain of its ends, therefore, are inherently and necessarily conservative, and conservatism—even in a pluralistic social context— always puts a premium on a degree of homogenization, a fitting of particular cases to the modal pattern. Perhaps the most straightforward pronouncement on this score is that of Robert Maynard Hutchins:

> I do not ignore [the argument that the most important thing about men is that they are different]; I deny it. I do not deny the fact of individual differences; I deny that it is the most important fact about men or the one on which an education system should be erected.*

One need not be a subscriber to Hutchins's doctrines to find a certain descriptive accuracy in his statement. Whatever else it does, the school—of which guidance activities are an integral part—must as a societal institution build commonalities among people. It must lead them into a common tradition, equip them with common skills, and disseminate among them a core of common standards. While the construction of commonality is not all that the school does, this task is one that is cannot neglect. Indeed, in the eyes of acute foreign observers like Denis Brogan,[4] the effectiveness of the school at turning a huge and diverse population—the children of immigrants, children from strikingly different regions, children of divergent familial backgrounds, etc.—into recognizable Americans is one of the chief glories of our educational system. It would be immensely difficult and possibly immensely disruptive for guidance *not* to participate in this fundamentally conservative responsibility which schools in the United States must carry.

But there is another factor somewhat more covertly at work here. School personnel are overwhelmingly middle class in their status. If they do not derive from middle-class origins, they have achieved middle-class membership through upward mobility and are vigorous in the consolidation of their new social position.† There is strong evidence that such teachers—and

* John Maynard Hutchins. *The Conflict in Education* (New York: Harper, 1953), p. 89.

† On such scales as the Warner Index of Status Characteristics, teachers are almost without exception and, indeed, almost by definition members of the American middle class. For an interesting example of studies of teacher–pupil perceptions, see Hilde T. Himmelweit, Socioeconomic Background and Personality, *Internatl. Soc. Sci. Bull.*, 1955, 7, 29–35.

guidance workers have almost universally come out of the classroom—perceive youngsters of lower-class status as sullen, defiant, dirty, aggressive, given to the erotic and the overtly sexual in their language and manner, intellectually inferior, and inadequately and improperly oriented to books and study. Children so perceived are unrewarding to work with, and the probability of their being rejected is high. Hollingshead[8] and Opstad* have even shown that the distribution of low and failing grades among lower class youth is substantially greater than would be predicted from indices of intelligence.

Perhaps a significant kind of light is cast on these observations by still another finding. A great deal of attention has been paid recently to the notion of "creativity," a term endowed with highly positive connotations. Surely, there can be no argument about the degree to which we want our youngsters to be creative! Yet Torrance[18] it not the only investigator to document the fact that creative children are by no means well liked by teachers and other school officials. By definition, creative pupils challenge some of the basic rules, resist the pressure toward commonality, and behave in unpredicted and idiosyncratic ways. Such a pattern of response not only puts a strain on the corporate structure of the school; it frustrates in some degree one of its fundamental purposes. In consequence, even though the notion of increased creativity as an educational objective is an appealing one, it is not without its own sources of conflict and disturbance.

What all this means is that the school provides a setting which necessarily defines a significant part of the frame of reference within which guidance workers must operate. If the tendency is less now than it was in former years for school people to regard nonconformity, aggression, and individual self-assertiveness as "the most serious behavior problem a child can have",[3] they still view with mistrust and irritation any youngster or any event that departs from the orderly, the "nice," or the "healthy" as one segment of society defines the healthy. To the extent that a guidance worker accepts as referrals those children who are perceived by teachers as disruptive, disorderly, or discordant with the classroom group, he accepts in some degree the definition of his job as that of fitting children to the dominant patterns of the school. This task may be an essential one, and on occasion, it may be quite harmonious with that of aiding an individual child to actualize his distinctive potentialities. The fact remains that there are other times when the two enterprises are certainly different and may be in opposition to each other. Even more important is the institutional derivation of the guidance counselor's objectives; they come less from a particular corpus of knowledge or from the independent point of view of an autonomous profession than from the particularities and immediacies of the school in which he works. To make this observation is not necessarily to utter a negative criticism; it

* Quoted in Boyd R. McCandless, *Children and Adolescents* (New York: Holt, Rinehart and Winston, 1961), p. 469.

is simply to underscore a state of affairs which is usually quite inexplicit and which could productively be made the direct focus of more articulate discussion and study.

FACILITATING THE EXAMINED LIFE—THE FAILURE OF SCHOOL AND GUIDANCE

One of the problems on which discussion and study of this sort could usefully concentrate is that of specialization in education generally and in guidance particularly. The present growth of knowledge is, as we have now been often reminded, no less than awesome. In the natural sciences, knowledge doubles in slightly more than a decade; in the behavioral sciences, it doubles about every thirty years. The mass of information and the complexities of its application to modern society force specialization and therefore a narrowness that is incompatible with the basic educational aim of producing an informed and responsibly participant citizen in a democratic community. In education, teachers must specialize in one or another domain of subject matter. In guidance, most workers are inclined to think of themselves as specialists of one type or another—in testing, in counseling, in the development and utilization of occupational information, etc. Yet there is a sense in which the guidance movement arose as an effort to combat the tendency of mass education, interacting with the inevitable demands of specialization, to become impersonal and confining, to lose sight of the individual and his significant role in the free state. The result is the paradox of guidance workers becoming specialists in the overcoming of specializations' undesirable effects.

Paradoxical or not, this emphasis on individual growth and on helping individual students to find socially appropriate ways for the expression of their distinctiveness is one of the primary wellsprings of the guidance enterprise. One way to conceptualize this aspect of things is an attempt to facilitate an active search for values among students. So conceived, guidance is the systematic encouragement of students to live what Socrates called the examined life. The examined life is one in which values are constantly being made articulate, subjected to criticism, and revised in the light of experience and thought. At one level, this process is sophisticated and intellectual; at another, it may be naive and both unenlightened and unencumbered by a tradition of ideas. At all levels, however, it can be authentic. The constant defining and redefining of one's self in relation to one's work and one's family, for example, entails nothing less than an on-going appraisal of one's aspirations and obligations, of the progress made by one human being in the human search for contentment and self-esteem. So presented, the examined life is as serious and as possible—even as necessary—for the plumber or the gardener as for the physicist or philosopher. Knowledge is deeply relevant to it, but a clarity about values and an ability to think of oneself in valuational terms is still more so.

To what extent does the school, including its guidance services, contribute to the cultivation of the examined life? There is a wealth of evidence* that suggests the somewhat wry and grim answer of "Not much" to be the appropriate one. Leaving aside the happy exceptions, the main conclusion that offers itself is that our schools and colleges serve, first, to consolidate middle-class students in their middle-class ways and, second, to provide a route to the acceptance of middle-class norms for about one-fourth of the lower-class children who originally enroll. About 75 per cent of lower-class pupils in the first grade, including those whose class membership is related to ethnic status, drop out before finishing high school, most of them before beginning their eleventh year. Aside from these observations, there is little in the way of a systematic or persuasive demonstration that education in the United States concerns itself methodically and effectively with the development of values in its charges.

THE CONCEPT OF INSTITUTIONAL POTENCY

This state of affairs is a strange one in the light of our strong consensus that the schools, at least through the secondary years, *should* be occupied with such matters as citizenship, character, moral development, and social growth. While there may be dissent, often of a heated kind, over the priorities to be given to such objectives in relation to more intellectual and academic ones, there is little doubt about their appropriateness. The teaching of plastic bits of protoplasm to become contributory and integral members of a viable community *requires* a concern for values and the non-intellective side of the child's progress toward adulthood.

But the over-all lack of evidence of success in studies of the school and college as agents of attitudinal and characterological change is relieved occasionally by signs that particular institutions seem to possess what Philip Jacob(9) has called a "peculiar potency" on this score. Although the directions of change vary from school to school, attendance at these "potent" institutions seems to matter, to result in graduates who are different people from what they were at the time of their first enrollment, to entail some jarring of original values and some re-examination and reformulation of them during one's time in residence.

The nature of institutional potency, however, has proved elusive and hard to identify. Yet it is possible that some insight into its basic dimensions can be obtained by looking freshly at an educational tradition somewhat different from our own. In the process, we may win some helpful collateral

* I have reviewed a good deal of this material in a chapter on "Education and Personality Change" to appear in a volume edited by Philip Worchel and Donn Byrne under the title of *Personality Change* that is now in preparation.—EJS.

perspectives on the American system and on the potentialities of guidance within it.

To begin with, we would expect the American "whole-child" outlook in education, reflecting the humanitarian and egalitarian themes in our history (which, incidentally, provide undergirding for the guidance movement itself), to contrast sharply with, for example, the ideas bound up with such institutions as the select and elite "public" schools of Britain. It is quite true, of course, that the English public schools were and are primarily concerned with the development of leaders, not with providing a universal pattern of education. It is equally true that their curricula were and are centered on subject matter—predominantly the classics and mathematics—rather than on children. But so observant and critical an interpreter of British life as J. D. Scott puts it this way: "The *real* object of the English public school is not to teach you Latin and Greek, but to turn you ... into a true-blue Church-of-England country gentleman."* The point is underscored by the famous passage in Thomas Hughes's insightful old novel where Squire Brown is musing on sending his son Tom to Thomas Arnold's Rugby:

> "Shall I tell him to mind his work and say he's sent to school to make himself a good scholar? Well, but he isn't sent to school for that . ... I don't care a straw for Greek particles or the digamma, no more does his mother. ... If he'll only turn out a brave, helpful. truth-telling Englishman, and a gentleman and a Christian, that's all I want," thought the Squire.†

Let us acknowledge at once that this conception of how the school may develop leaders through dealing with the whole personality had a corrupt and brutal side. The harshness of bullying, flogging, cold dormitories, bad food, and a compulsory indiscriminate participation in games has often been documented, perhaps most dramatically in George Orwell's essay, "Such, Such Were the Joys".(11) But as the oft criticized educators of the United States have only too much reason to know, one can hardly judge a total enterprise by its perverted examples. The rational, sensible element in the British system included and still includes, in Scott's words,

> the setting of spoilt, rich mothers' darlings to make tea and clean football boots for their fag masters, and the idea that for the average boy to be hounded out to run for a few miles, even on a sleety winter afternoon, was fortifying. And one of the things which made public schoolboys easier to work for ... than the products of most ruling-class systems of education was the fact that they had at least had a glimpse of hardship, a menial position, and "unfairness."
>
> The value set upon the public school system is that it produces leaders, but *leaders who are responsible and humane* [italics added]. ... And there is a great deal in this. The Victorian and Edwardian public schools *did* produce out of their material a reasonable proportion of young men of character and principles, accustomed to the idea of leadership and so taking it unfussily, fair-minded, not too painfully serious, but with

* J. D. Scott, *Life in Britain* (New York: William Morrow, 1956), p. 171.

† Thomas Hughes, *Tom Brown's School-Days* (London: Macmillan, 1875), p. 141.

an idea about serving their country and a contempt for money-grubbing and pot-hunting. Commonly, they had high-spirited good manners which pleased most people who were capable of being pleased.*

There is more than ample room here, of course, for those of a systematic and empirical turn of mind to wonder about the adequacy of this evaluation. Nevertheless, strong suggestions have recently appeared in the research literature† that those American independent schools that are cut from English cloth in their purposes and program have more of an impact on the personalities of their students—possess more "potency"—than do the majority of our public schools. In what does that potency consist?

One can only raise hypotheses here, but it seems quite possible that two broad factors account for much of an institution's power to evoke change of a valuational sort in youngsters. The first has to do with the frequency and intimacy of contacts that pupils enjoy with both older students and with teachers whom they perceive as "omnicompetent" in Fritz Redl's[(12)] terms. School children, as Allinsmith and Goethals[(1)] have shown, are active in their search for character models, and there is every reason to suspect that this kind of quest, like most other forms of behavior, is strengthened by reinforcement and weakened by neglect or non-reward. What is proposed here is that the child who, regarding a particular adult as able and admirable, not only encounters him in the classroom, but also on the tennis or basket-ball court, at tea in the older person's home, and in the relatively frequent context of informal talks on a campus bench, is being much more intensively exposed to a model than when the relationship is limited to the classroom or counselor's office.

Similarly, if he must deal with older youngsters, more senior than he in the school's status system, then he forms a clearer sense of just what behavior patterns, attitudes and values are expected of him as he develops under the school's tuition. Obviously, this arrangement need not imply any form of coercion into a fully predetermined and restrictive mould. Self-reliance, critical thought, and initiative can be authentic objectives in this context just as readily as other-direction or the acceptance of definite and imposed norms. The central point is that the process of self-exploration and the cultivation of the examined life are likely to be facilitated by the child's relatively intimate exposure to a variety of models; the opportunity, provided by the school, to identify with several relatively diverse persons, or with some composite that he may create from their diversity, may have much to do with the flexible development of a distinctive life-style.

The second large factor that may contribute to a school's potency may be its character as a community. Assume that teachers, administrators, and

* Scott, *op. cit.*, p. 173.

† This material is well reviewed in an unpublished research report by David Winter, Richard Alpert, and David McClelland of the Department of Social Relations, Harvard University, under the title of "The Classic Personal Style."

guidance workers share common educational aims which are genuinely operative in their work, and that they represent differences in other domains like politics and aesthetics—differences that can be openly discussed with enjoyment in the presence of and with students. Then it is probable that the child, holding a membership proper to his age and development in the community, will be responsive to its values, will interiorize its ideals, and will form the habit of reflecting on the relevance and importance of diversity among people who still participate in the attainment of other broad goals that they pursue in concert. The main question is one of whether a school has a distinctive climate within which a boy or girl virtually breathes healthful expectancies.

To the extent that these two sets of variables, the accessibility of suitable models and the degree of actual community represented by a school, account for educational potency, it is clear that the effectiveness of the educational enterprise is based bluntly in the quality of the adults participating in it and in the character of a school's or college's *de facto* social organization. In the worry about present-day priorities in education and in the discussion of changing curricular structures and a newly developing educational technology, it may be well to keep these possibilities in mind. Lip-service and teaching machines will hardly be sufficient if it truly turns out that potency is dependent, after all, on these fundamental human elements in the educational adventure.*

MORE POWERFUL FUNCTIONS FOR GUIDANCE

And what place does guidance distinctively occupy in this conception of the potent school? The position taken here suggests a radically different and more important one than the traditional role of the counselor of the obstreperous, the adviser on college selection and vocational matters, and the purveyor of tests and occupational information. It is not that these functions are irrelevant or lacking in vital merit. It is only that they are subordinate to something else. That something else is twofold in its nature: First, it is a human feedback mechanism by which the impact of the school is assessed and made available for the consideration of its official personnel; second, it is a catalyst for the clarification of the character of the school as a community and as a source of appropriate models for developing youngsters. The task may be a delicate one; it is not one to be avoided lightly.

With respect to the feedback function of the guidance worker as it is envisioned here, it must be noted that counselors, far more than either teachers or administrators, have an opportunity to hear from children themselves the extent to which their schools are disappointing or lack cogency for them. Obviously, youngsters rarely possess the fluency and insight to state their

* In this discussion of educational potency, I have drawn heavily on my editorial on Potency in the Schools in the *Teachers College Record* for April, 1962, **63**, 548–550.—EJS.

cases in terms that are immediately useful to those responsible for a school's program. But by virtue of their special training, guidance officers know, at least in some significant degree, how to elicit and to interpret the necessary material to form relevant hypotheses. If they so structure their jobs as to see a relatively large number of reasonably representative children, they have an opportunity to evaluate if not test those hypotheses. What is important is that the hypotheses be less concerned with the personalities of the pupils and more concerned with the functioning realities of the school. Are sufficient opportunities being provided for students to identify with an adequate range of useful adult models? Are children developing any sense of what it means to be a person as a result of their acquaintance with their teachers? Are they getting any conception of an ego-ideal from the curriculum?* Do they have any awareness of the diversity within the faculty or of the way that individuality of a responsible sort is prized in the adult society? Are they evolving any such concept through their contact with student leaders and the exemplars in their peer group? Have they any sense of participant membership in a community that is valuable to them and that is supportive of them even while it makes demands on them?

If the guidance worker's hypotheses are pertinent to questions of this kind, and if they are based on the poignant realities of interviews and supplemented by the inventive use of analogues to the industrial morale survey and sociometric assessments, then he can feed his information helpfully into the school's over-all operations and provide a vigorous leadership in promoting the kinds of functioning that contribute to increased potency. In other words, the guidance counselor functions less as a remedial resource than as a prime agent in the continuous reconstruction of the school culture. Basic to this notion is a lesson recently learned from the administration of mental hospitals.[10, 15]

When mental hospitals are examined as microcosmic cultures, they frequently are found to operate as social structures that are all but explicitly designed to reinforce pathological behavior. Professional personnel are relatively inaccessible; the day-to-day emphasis in management, exercised primarily through nurses and attendants, is on docility and the avoidance of behavior that would be disruptive of routines. Opportunities for privacy are curtailed at the same time that much of intramural living—meals, recreation, occupational therapy, etc.—is stringently regimented and dominated by the group. Because expectancies are low, few chances are provided for achievement and fewer still for the evolution of a distinctive life-style that could be

* One of the major justifications of the classical curriculum was the degree to which it held up to the student a model of desirable and commendable manhood. The same idea animates the study of literature today and the introduction of much of the biographical and historical material that enters the school program in other disciplines. A striking oddity of our educational life is that this plausible assumption has neither been systematically exploited nor intensively studied!

generalized to the world outside the institution. The "good patient" is essentially one who adapts to this milieu, becoming a chronic but bland and unobtrusive psychotic. If the hospital is to fulfill its rehabilitative purpose, however, it is less important for it to provide more psychotherapeutic hours (although this provision is far from of no consequence) than to restructure itself as a community. In such a restructuring, a prime consideration is that of making available relatively enduring and intimate relationships. In their context, the patients can generate functional new concepts of what it means to be "normal"; they can be confronted with expectancies which they are encouraged to meet with courageous efforts and confidence in their ultimate success, and they can examine their lives productively in a quest for new meaning and new directions for the future. There is no reason to anticipate miracles, of course, and the cost of this kind of cultural revision is occasionally high. Patients at times test their new freedom in destructive ways, abuse their physical environment in a fashion that can be expensive, and put heavy strains on the people who serve them. Nevertheless, these tendencies have their positive aspects as efforts toward the rediscovery and reassertion of meaningful selfhood, and they are worth tolerating for the gains that can be registered in humane terms when the mental hospital reconceives itself as a therapeutic culture.

The problems of the school, of course, are quite different from those of the psychiatric hospital, but there are important areas of overlap. Some basic principles—the fundamental utility of the human model, the developmental value of diverse relationships of some intimacy and intensity, the stimulus to growth of membership in a genuine community, and the facilitation of the examined life through explicit forms of encouragement and example—apply in common to both. Willy-nilly, the school represents a society-in-little. The challenge before it is whether it can transform itself into a developmentally productive one on an articulate and informed basis and, by a regular and planful process of self-appraisal, maintain itself as a true growth-enhancing community. In such an effort to sharpen the impact of the school and to give it greater cogency for individual students, guidance workers can play a key role, forging, in the course of it, a genuine new profession for themselves. To reconstruct the school as an integrated and humanly significant little culture requires that creative consideration be given to a number of topics—the grouping of pupils, the contributions of the academic curriculum to the encouragement of the examined life, the diversification of teacher load, the ways in which student government can be meaningfully related to the specific objectives of the school, and a host of others—but leadership can properly be expected from guidance workers. Because of their grounding in behavioral science, their familiarity with the techniques of testing and counseling as ways of identifying human needs, and their orientation toward the individual pupil, they have the opportunity to define new horizons in our educational aspirations and to explore novel ways of approaching them. The task, attempted in a setting of universal education and the widest possible range of individual differences, will hardly be an easy one. But part of the American educational tradition has entailed finding ways to do for the many what other nations have done only for the few.

REFERENCES

1. ALLINSMITH, WESLEY, and GOETHALS, GEORGE (1962) *The Role of the Schools in Mental Health.* New York: Basic Books.
2. BARRY, RUTH E., and WOLF, BEVERLY (1962) *Epitaph for Vocational Guidance.* New York: Teachers College, Columbia University, Bureau of Publications.
3. BEILIN, HARRY (1959) Teachers' and Clinicians' Attitudes toward the Behavior Problems of Children: A Reappraisal, *Child Develpm.*, **30**, 9–26.
4. BROGAN, DENIS (1960) *America in the Modern World.* New Brunswick: Rutgers University Press, pp. 64–86.
5. DOLLARD, JOHN (1962) Answers Unproved, *New York Times Book Review*, October 21, p. 6.
6. GROSS, MARTIN (1962) *The Brain Watchers.* New York: Random House.
7. HOFFMANN, BANESH (1962) *The Tyranny of Testing.* New York: Crowell.
8. HOLLINGSHEAD, A. B. (1949) *Elmtown's Youth.* New York: John Wiley.
9. JACOB, PHILLIP (1957) *Changing Values in College.* New York: Harper.
10. JONES, MAXWELL (1953) *The Therapeutic Community.* New York: Basic Books.
11. ORWELL, GEORGE (1954) *A Collection of Essays.* Garden City: Doubleday, pp. 9–54.
12. REDL, FRITZ (1955) What do Children Expect of Teachers? Address to the Bank Street College of Education. New York, N.Y.
13. SKINNER, B. F. (1957) *Verbal Behavior.* New York: Appleton-Century-Crofts.
14. SKINNER, B. F. (1953) *Science and Human Behavior.* New York: Macmillan.
15. STANTON, A. H., and SCHWARTZ, M. S. (1954) *The Mental Hospital.* New York: Basic Books.
16. SZASZ, THOMAS. Bootlegging Humanistic Values Through Psychiatry, *Antioch Rev.*, **22**, 341–349.
17. SZASZ, THOMAS (1961) *The Myth of Mental Illness.* New York: Harper.
18. TORRANCE, E. PAUL (1959) *Explorations in Creative Thinking in the Early School Years.* Minneapolis: Bureau of Educ. Res., University of Minnesota.
19. WRENN, C. GILBERT (1958) Editorial Comment, *J. Counsel. Psych.*, **5**, 242.

23. *Issues in Counseling: Elusive and Illusional*

DONALD H. BLOCHER

AN examination of the questions which continue to command attention in most discussions of counseling theory, practice, and research seems to reveal an interesting dichotomy. The first set of these questions comprises a group that are frequently discussed, often elicit considerable emotion, and are generally quite unproductive in terms of the consequences which they generate. These questions can well be called illusions in counseling. The second set of issues are frequently avoided in discussions of counseling; they are extremely difficult to frame clearly but have very important consequences. They are indeed elusive in character.

ILLUSIONS IN COUNSELING

It is perhaps easier to begin by demolishing illusions than by attempting to trap the elusive. One of the foremost illusions in counseling concerns the old question of should counseling be "directive" or "non-directive." This is one of the oldest, most decrepit, and least productive arguments in the field of counseling. Part of its feebleness is drawn from the fact that as an issue it is not even clear in meaning. Two kinds of questions are involved. The first concerns whether or not the counselor influences his client. The answer to this question is really no longer at issue. Writers as different in orientation as Williamson (1958) and Patterson (1958) agree that counselors do, should, and cannot avoid influencing clients. The relevant questions which survive around this part of the issue concern only directions and degrees of influence.

The second aspect of this sterile controversy over "directive vs. non-directive" counseling concerns the distribution of responsibility for the content of the interview or the nature of the counseling process as apart from its outcomes. Research by Robinson (1950) and others of the so-called "communications" school of counseling has indicated rather clearly that division of responsibility for the content of the counseling interview is one and only one of a number of relevant dimensions in the counseling process. This research suggests that virtually all counselors vary their behavior along

(Reprinted by permission of publisher and author from *Personnel and Guidance Journal*, vol. 43, 1965, pp. 796–800.)

this continuum from client to client or from one point to another in the counseling process. No counselors completely abdicate responsibility for the nature of the interview. For example, many so-called non-directive counselors use formal structuring techniques at the beginning of counseling which are quite "directive" in one sense. Decisions to respond to affect or content, to clarify, to accept, all require some degree of responsibility on the part of the counselor.

Again, the relevant questions which survive in this issue are merely how much and in what directions should counselor responsibility be exerted.

A second rather moribund question is whether or not counselors should diagnose. This is illusion number two. The term diagnosis has been an emotionally loaded word in the counseling vocabulary for some years. Two basic reasons seem to account for this fact. First, the term diagnosis was largely borrowed from medicine, and to many counselors it carries a strong flavor of telling clients what is wrong with them. This connotation does violence to values which many counselors hold concerning building on the assets of clients, distinguishing between counseling and psychotherapy, and so forth.

A second reason for this emotional reaction is the connection which many counselors see between diagnosis and the use of tests. Many counselors, apparently feel that if they do not use tests, they also do not diagnose.

Most of the thinking surrounding both of these reactions to diagnosis is fallacious. The only philosophical assumption that really affects the question of diagnostic activity is whether or not the counselor views one of his tasks in the counseling process as that of understanding the counselee. Diagnostic activities are merely those activities which have as one of their purposes helping the counselor understand his client. Research on the nature of this kind of activity by Koester (1954), McArthur (1954), and Parker (1958) has indicated that for many counselors this activity resembles a hypothesis-testing process. The Pepinskys (1954) have called attention to the counselor as a scientist-practitioner and have described the process of observation and inference by which the counselor builds a hypothetical model through which to understand his client.

The question again is not whether or not to diagnose. All counselors who attempt to understand their clients are engaged in diagnosis. The degree to which a particular counselor is committed to differential treatment for different clients may influence the nature and extent of his diagnostic activities. The counselor with a strong client-centered approach may not vary treatment processes from one client to another to as great a degree as one who considers himself eclectic. The difference in diagnostic activity between the two refers to differential diagnosis rather than to the process of diagnosis itself, however.

Diagnosis also has nothing to do with the use of tests. Tests are merely samples of behavior from which other behavior is inferred. The moment that the counselor makes inferences about behavior from any source; he is diagnosing.

From what we know about diagnostic processes now, we must conclude that all counselors do diagnose but that diagnostic activities contribute most when they are *continuous*, *tentative*, and *testable*. Diagnosis in this sense is a continuous process that is integrated into the total counseling. It is always tentative and subject to revision as further behavior samples become available. Finally, it is testable in the sense that diagnostic constructs or hypotheses are rooted in behavior and are operationally defined so that they may be confirmed or rejected through prediction.

A third illusion revolves around the question of whether counseling is personal-emotional or informational-didactic in nature. This question is another which has generated more heat than light in recent years. When either side of this issue is explained thoroughly, it can be reduced to one of patent absurdities.

First, examine the didactic-informational side. The logical extensions of this position are:

1. Counseling is impersonal.
2. Counseling is teaching occupational information to a class of one.
3. Only sick people have emotions.
4. The affective and intellectual functions of human beings can be separated and treated as self-contained entities.

These are obvious absurdities. A look at the opposite side of the coin, however, reveals some equally indefensible propositions.

1. Human behavior is not mediated by rational-intellectual problem-solving processes. (How did the client get to the counselor in the first place?)
2. The counseling interview is characterized by primarily verbal communication processes, but it is still an entirely emotional rather than an intellectual exchange.
3. All problems arise out of emotional conflicts rather than vice versa.
4. Personal problem-solving is not an important matter for counseling. People can solve all personal problems readily once their deep-seated emotional conflicts are removed.

These propositions seem equally absurd. If counseling is a process which helps whole human beings cope with total life situations, it seems clear that both affective and intellectual aspects of life will have to be considered.

Three illusions in counseling which have commanded research time and energy from counselors have been discussed and hopefully disposed of.

ELUSIVE ISSUES

The second set of issues which are dubbed elusive in character are naturally more difficult to discuss than those mentioned previously. These issues are important, have vital consequences, and are exceedingly difficult to resolve. The first of these is set up in terms of the following guestion, "Is counseling developmental-educative-preventive, or is it remediating-adjustive-therapeutic?"

It seems better to deal with this issue in terms of goals rather than in terms of methodologies. Efforts to distinguish between counseling and psychotherapy have dealt largely with methodologies and their applications. The intensity of the process, its level of impact upon the client or patient, the setting in which it is done all have been used as distinguishing criteria. Writers such as Perry (1955) and Brammer and Shostrom (1960) have characterized human personality in terms of a sort of onion-skin analogy, with the counselor busy peeling away the outer layers of skin while the therapist penetrates to the inner and apparently more pungent layers of the onion core. Presumably, every counselor should stop at whatever point his eyes begin to water.

None of these kinds of distinctions seem particularly useful. Counseling and psychotherapy are processes that are aimed at changing human behavior. If any real differences exist between the two processes, they must involve the kinds of outcomes which are specified for each, and possibly with the underlying assumptions which translate such outcomes into goals.

It seems to this writer that when the usual outcomes for counseling and psychotherapy are pooled and an impromptu factor analysis performed, two rather diminant clusters of goals appear. These can be characterized as (1) developmental-educative-preventive goals, and (2) remediating-adjustive-therapeutic outcomes.

It may be worth while examining these two clusters for a moment. One part of the first cluster deals with developmental goals. An underlying assumption here is that human personality grows or unfolds in terms of a largely healthy interaction between the growing organism itself and the culture or environment. From this point of view, development is seen as a reasonably ordered and patterned process of change moving in directions which are typically desirable for both the individual and society. The function of counseling in such a framework is to facilitate normal development. The outcomes may be stated in terms of mastering developmental tasks or moving from one stage of development to another.

The whole concept of development is closely tied to education, obviously. As part of this cluster, one may then include understanding of self, understanding of environment (world of work, for example), development of problem-solving skills, etc. Also associated with this cluster are preventive mental hygiene outcomes such as preventing too great frustrations, anxieties, or stresses; avoiding unhealthy relationships or experiences; etc.

The second cluster of outcomes can be described by labels such as remediative, adjustive, and therapeutic. These outcomes are generally characterized by goals that involve breaking down and replacing defenses; learning new adjustments to particular situations which may be familial, institutional, or societal; and removing conflicts in personality organization. These goals cluster around concepts of removing pathological components, adjusting people to environmental demands, and restoring mental health.

When the processes which are familiarly called counseling and psychotherapy are examined in the light of these two presumed clusters of outcomes, reasons for confusion in terms become apparent. Much of what is attempted in the name of counseling has been as remediative and adjustive in purpose as anything attempted in the name of psychotherapy. Counselors have attempted to "adjust" youngsters to the demands of schools and teachers. They have attempted to remediate and remove presumed pathological elements, for example, "laziness," "negativism," "aggression," and so forth.

One important issue facing counseling is whether distinctions on the basis of the kinds of clustering that have been described will be strengthened or whether they will be further broken down and no valid differences will exist between counseling and therapy. Perhaps, of course, writers such as Rogers (1957) and Arbuckle (1961) believe this has already happened.

A second elusive issue which faces counseling today is not unrelated to the first. It can be stated in its strongest terms in this question: Is counseling liberating or conditioning in nature? Modern psychology has generally tended to look upon man, as Allport (1962) says, as a reactive being or at best a reactive being in depth. Personality or learning theories based upon such a view tend to search for a set of uniform variables to which all behavior is subject. In a sense, such a system is closed. It tends to produce models based upon homeostatic principles and to view the human being functioning in a mechanistic-deterministic environment. Changing behavior in terms of this model, whether in counseling, therapy, or whatever, involves primarily identifying and controlling these variables.

The philosophical background from which counseling and guidance has emerged is not one in which formulations of this kind are comfortable. Instead, as Beck (1963) points out, these philosophical antecedents place great emphasis upon terms like individualism, responsibility, independence, personal freedom, etc. The philosophical frame of reference and American behavioristic *Zeitgeist* have now collided. This collision has become disturbingly clear in the controversies between those who term themselves existential psychologists such as May (1961), Rogers (1957), and Allport (1962), and the radical behaviorists best exemplified by Skinner (1957) and represented in the guidance literature by writers such as Michael and Meyerson (1962).

Two rather distinctly alternative directions seem to open before counseling. The existentialist position seems a philosophically attractive but scientifically unclear path. The Skinnerian-behavioristic road is scientifically rigorous, but philosophically frightening. Can or should counselors specify the outcomes of counseling in rigorous behavioral terms and proceed to shape them by conditioning processes? Do they instead deal in such quasi-behavioral commodities as self-awareness, immediate experience, and self-actualization? If counseling takes the latter course, what is its eventual relationship to a behaviorist psychology? If counseling takes the path of conditioning, what becomes its commitment in a philosophical sense?

These issues are elusive but vital in terms of their consequences. Counselors above all need to spend less time and energy tilting at the illusional windmills of the past and more time in resolving the elusive but inescapable issues that will shape the future.

REFERENCES

ALLPORT, G. W. (1962) Psychological models for guidance. *Harvard educ. Rev.*, **32** (4), 373–381.

ARBUCKLE, D. S. (1961) *Counseling: an introduction.* Boston: Allyn and Bacon.

BECK, C. (1963) *Philosophical foundations of guidance.* Englewood Cliffs, N. J.: Prentice-Hall.

BRAMMER, L., and SHOSTROM, E. (1960) *Therapeutic psychology: fundamentals of counseling and psychotherapy.* Englewood Cliffs, N. J.: Prentice-Hall.

KOESTER, G. A. (1954) A study of the diagnostic process. *Educ. psychol. Measmt.*, **14**, 473–486.

MAY, R. (Ed.) (1961) *Existential psychology.* New York: Random House.

MCARTHUR, C. (1954) Analyzing the clinical process. *J. counsel. Psychol.*, **1**, 203–208.

MICHAEL, J., and MEYERSON, L. (1962) A behavioral approach to counseling and guidance. *Harvard educ. Rev.*, **32** (4), 382–401.

PARKER, C. (1958) As a clinician thinks. *J. counsel. Psychol.*, **5** (4), 253–262.

PATTERSON, C. H. (1958) The place of values in counseling and psychotherapy. *J. counsel. Psychol.*, **5**, 216–233.

PEPINSKY and PEPINSKY (1954) *Counseling: theory and practice.* New York: Ronald Press.

PERRY, W. G. (1955) On the relation of psychotherapy and counseling. *Annals of the New York Academy of Sciences*, **63**, 396–407.

ROBINSON, F. P. (1950) *Principles and procedures in student counseling.* New York: Harper.

ROGERS, C. R. (1957) *Client-centered therapy.* Boston: Houghton-Mifflin.

SKINNER, B. F. (1957) *Verbal behavior.* New York: Appleton-Century-Crofts.

WILLIAMSON, E. G. (1958) Value orientation in counseling. *Personnel guid. J.*, **36**, 520–528.

24. *Needed Counselor Competencies in Vocational Aspects of Counseling and Guidance**

KENNETH B. HOYT

INTRODUCTION

What skills, knowledges, and attitudes do school counselors need to possess in order to perform the vocational guidance function in an effective manner? That is the basic question implied in the title of this paper. Here, an attempt will be made to provide an answer to this question which will hopefully hold action implications for counselor educators, guidance supervisors, and practicing school counselors.

The probabilities of making productive pronouncements with respect to a value laden problem such as this appear slight. In the first place, there is far from universal agreement among counselor educators with respect to *any* need for special counselor competencies in *vocational* aspects of guidance and counseling. Second, it would be both fallacious and foolish to pretend that *all* practicing school counselors need competencies in this area in order to function effectively in their positions. Third, to concentrate attention as is done here on competencies needed by school counselors ignores the more general—and, in many ways, more pressing—question currently facing counselor education with respect to competencies needed by all counselors regardless of the setting in which they function. Finally, the equally important problem of levels of counselor competency is also ignored when a generalized answer to this question is formulated. In hopes of raising probabilities for productivity, brief comments with respect to each of these four problems appear to be in order here.

It is certainly true that many of the competencies prerequisite for success in vocational aspects of guidance and counseling are just as essential to success in other aspects of the counselor's work. No attempt will be made here to isolate or identify certain competencies as though each applies only to vocational guidance aspects. This is true in spite of the fact that some do. That the school counselor's job is much broader than vocational guidance is readily apparent to all. To recognize that this is so in no way invalidates the assertion that vocational aspects of counseling and guidance represent

*This article first appeared in *Vocational Aspects of Counselor Education*, edited by Carl Mc Daniels. Report of a conference at Airlie House, Warrenton, Virginia, Dec, 12–15, 1965.

a major area of concern and responsibility for the school counselor. It will be treated as such here.

Similarly, only minimal thought is required to recognize that no one can legitimately speak of needed counselor competencies as though they applied or should apply to all practicing school counselors. Specialization in counselor job function has always been more pronounced than specialization in counselor education programs. One cannot help but wonder why some who belong to the guidance movement (predicated on the basis of individual differences) appear righteously indignant when others make statements concerning counselor competencies. To recognize that individual differences do exist in counselor role and function in no way precludes the desirability of making generalized statements regarding counselor competencies which should apply to a *majority* of counselors in a *majority* of school settings. This paper proceeds from such an assumption.

In these times, there are great pressures both from within and from sources external to the guidance movement to recognize the content of counselor education programs as appropriate for meeting needs of counselors in a variety of settings. Counselor competencies required for success in one setting are not mutually exclusive from those required for counselor success in other settings. This does not preclude the possibility that substantial variation in emphasis on particular competencies may exist. This paper is written particularly from the standpoint of needed counselor competencies in the secondary school setting. It is hoped that some applicability to other settings may be found, but that is not why this paper has been written.

COMPETENCIES RELATED TO COUNSELOR ATTITUDES AND POINT OF VIEW

It is pointless to think of competencies related to particular job activities prior to considering personal competencies of those who are to perform such activities. Therefore, this discussion of needed competencies in vocational aspects of guidance and counseling begins with consideration of certain attitudes and points of view which are believed to be necessary for those who would perform the vocational guidance function in the secondary school setting. Such attitudes and points of view are rightfully pictured as competencies in and of themselves because they relate to qualifications required for successful performance of the job.

Specification of desired counselor attitudes and points of view *prior* to specification of those related to particular job activities serves yet another function. That is, these attitudes and points of view delineated here represent the rationale for picturing competencies related to job activities. In the absence of clearcut evidence regarding efficacy of one guidance approach over another, one is forced to rely on such bases for the rationale presented. This, of course, is not to say that the attitudes and points of view presented have been developed totally in the absence of knowledge, but only that our knowledge remains highly incomplete. If prospective counselors are to acquire such attitudes, it is essential that they, too, acquire the basic knowledge we have leading to the kinds of understandings which form the basis for certain of these attitudes. Unless they do so, personal acceptance of such attitudes on the part of counselors seems unlikely. Without such personal acceptance, the words are empty phrases devoid of meaning and value.

ATTITUDES AND POINTS OF VIEW REGARDING THE VOCATIONAL GUIDANCE FUNCTION

There are certain counselor attitudes with respect to the vocational guidance function in the secondary school which should be a part of those counselors who purport to perform this function. It is particularly those attitudes associated with concepts of vocational development with which we are concerned here. Certain of these attitudes can be stated in specific form:

Counselors must recognize that their influence on the total life of any given individual is relatively small. Whatever rightful claims school counselors have to productive influence must be predicated on the kinds of recognized humility implied in this statement. Counselors need to understand the guidance function as one part of that aspect of our culture we call "education". More important, they need to understand education as representing only one of many influences on youth. In this connection, counselors need to be knowledgeable regarding other aspects of any given individual's culture—including the home and family, the community, and both peer and adult role models in the community—aspects which often serve as powerful influences in vocational choice and development. Progress toward professionalization demands this kind of perspective.

An essential part of this humility involves recognition of the vocational guidance function in the secondary school as only part of a broader process of vocational development. The time is past when we can legitimately view the process of vocational choice as something which will or should occur only once in the lives of most individuals. Both the nature and the rate of occupational change need to be understood by counselors as relevant factors here. Relationships between such factors and level of occupational choice also need to be understood. That is, it may be appropriate to visit with certain students contemplating entry into high level professional occupations in terms of career dimensions carrying through many years. With a majority of high school students, such long range career planning is neither appropriate nor defensible in terms of specific plans. If, with most students, the school counselor can help the student formulate tentative plans for as much as from five to eight years after high school, he should consider he has done well.

Differences between vocational choice and vocational development must take on operational meaning to the practicing school counselor. Such perspective is essential if counselors are to realistically assume responsibilities for vocational guidance and fairly evaluate the degree to which they have successfully met these responsibilities. It is also necessary for development of truly professional and productive working relationships with other counselors.

It is equally important that counselors recognize the importance of vocational guidance in the secondary school. Because the counselor's influence may be small in no way implies it is not of vital importance. If the process of vocational choice is to be experienced for most students more than once after leaving the secondary school, it is essential that students learn a model for carrying through this process. The model provided by the counselor holds great potential for transfer value. Secondary school and immediate post secondary school experiences are powerful influences on self perceptions of students. If the counselor can help a student begin movement toward entry into our occupational society in a positive and constructive manner, the student will be in a better position to continue such movement after he leaves the secondary school. The transfer value of knowledge regarding the process of occupational choice will be particularly important for those most likely to experience it more than once. With this segment of the high school population, the counselor's influence may be even more pervasive and vital than with those least likely to change occupations.

Finally, it is important that counselors recognize and implement concepts related to the risk function as a basic and essential part of the vocational guidance function. It is vitally important that the vocational guidance function not be pictured as one of helping individuals "play it safe"—of making decisions which hold high probabilities for successful implementation. Rather, the vocational guidance function must be pictured as involving helping individuals make decisions which take a risk factor into account as one of several elements entering into decision making. So long and to the extent that counselors consider their function as one of helping individuals "play it safe", counselors will be rightfully accused of contributing to under-development and under-utilization of talent in our society.

Counselor attitudes involved here include recognition of the fact that counselor success cannot realistically be measured by recording the proportion of individuals who successfully implemented decisions reached in counseling. Rather, the counselor needs attitudes which, while recognizing the importance of the risk function, also recognize that there are other important factors—including personal motivations of the individual and willingness of the individual to accept risk—which also need to be considered in evaluating the "goodness" of decisions reached in vocational guidance.

ATTITUDES AND POINTS OF VIEW REGARDING VOCATIONAL GUIDANCE FOR ALL STUDENTS

To *seek* to serve is not necessarily *to* serve. To say that guidance should be available to *all* students is not to say that guidance is appropriate for *all* students. To say that all students *could* profit from guidance is not to say that they *will*. There are several counselor attitudes growing out of recognition of facts such as these which are essential to successful vocational guidance practices in the secondary school setting. Most of these involve acceptance of an assumption that there are individuals in our total society whose value systems are different from those held by most counselors. We have recognized this in an academic sense for some time. It is now time to implement this assumption in an operational sense.

The first way in which this assumption should be implemented is by having counselors recognize the necessity of devoting concentrated attention to students who choose to do something other than attend a college or university after leaving the secondary school. Counselors cannot become effective change agents in our society if they accept general societal biases as they popularly exist. The current popular notion that the "best" thing students could do would be to attend college is one that counselors should be actively seeking to change. There is no hope of effectively accomplishing this goal unless practicing counselors internally accept it as a goal for them. For this to happen requires that counselors learn what can and does happen to students who choose not to attend college. Too little such knowledge is now available. It must rapidly become available and become known to counselors. One bias cannot be effectively countered by another. If a particular bias is to be overcome, knowledge must be substituted for belief, facts for faith, and truth for prejudice. Until counselors have achieved this, the odds of effectively implementing this desirable counselor attitude seem small.

Second, counselors must recognize the significance of the personal values of those individuals who could profit from vocational guidance. Guidance, like all of formal education, has constructed its basic operational approach around certain assumptions regarding elements of the personal value systems of those it seeks to serve. There are certain basic human values which are intimately tied to our rationale for contending that the guidance process exists for and has potential for helping all students. These values include: (1) A belief in self-responsibility—acceptance of responsibility for personal decision-making (this assumes the individual does have some control over his own destiny); (2) A basic belief in oneself as a worthwhile person; and (3) A desire for self-improvement—for becoming "better" in terms of criteria meaningful to the individual and (some would say) acceptable to society. Unless we assume these as basic human values, we cannot defend our claims of "guidance for all".

In addition, there are more specific values tied to that aspect of guidance we call vocational guidance—such values as a desire to work, a desire for more education, a desire to plan for the future, and a desire to be economically self-sufficient. When we offer vocational guidance as a process of helping an individual (a) better understand himself and his environmental opportunities, (b) make choices, decisions, and adjustments based on these understandings, (c) accept personal responsibility for decisions he has reached, and (d) formulate a course of action for implementing his decisions, we are often assuming that the individuals to whom it is offered have or should have the kinds of personal values mentioned above.

In this regard, it is essential to recognize that these are essentially "middle class" and certainly American values which do not and cannot logically be expected to exist within all of those who are students in our secondary schools. Is guidance for *all* students? Is formal secondary education for *all* students? If these questions are to be answered affirmatively, then a part of guidance and a part of formal education must be represented by conscious attempts to impose personal values such as outlined above on those students who do not hold them. An essential part of needed counselor competencies in vocational aspects of guidance will be those competencies required to make certain students ready for and amenable to the process of vocational guidance as pictured above. If we mean that guidance is an essentially permissive field of endeavor, then we must accept the notion that it will not be for *all* students. If guidance is to be pictured as something permissive for those whose values are consistent with ours and as involving imposing our values on those who are different from counselors, then we should say so in our definitions and lists of objectives.

One way out of this quandary which might represent a desirable counselor attitude would be to recognize that, while guidance is for all, perhaps *vocational* guidance is not. That is, the specific values underlying vocational guidance need not be a part of any individual who could profit from the total set of services school counselors have to offer. At the same time, if the school counselor is to offer vocational guidance as defined earlier, then these kinds of specific personal values must either be a part or be made a part of those individuals who can profit from vocational guidance.

One point of view would say that the imposition of such specific values may very well be a part of the total complex of activities called "education", but it is not a part of needed counselor competencies in vocational aspects of guidance. A second point of view would say that vocational guidance is an important part of the school counselor's job and that, to do this job, the counselor needs certain competencies which will help him impose such values on those students who do not hold them when they come to the secondary school. My own personal preference would be to give counselors both points of view along with an adequate basis for making personal decisions with respect to which they will adopt in practice. This is not so much a gesture of extending freedom to the counselor as it is an admission that I have not yet resolved this dilemma for myself.

COMPETENCIES RELATED TO JOB ACTIVITIES OF COUNSELORS

It seems that there is a perpetual and inevitable gap between what is taught in counselor education courses and what school counselors need to know in order to function effectively on the job. While some of what counselors are taught is recognizably useful to them, other material appears not to be. There are problems they face in their day-to-day operations which were never a part of their formal education. These things were true when I was a school counselor seventeen years ago and they seem no less true today. In 1949, as a practicing school counselor, I appeared on a program at the Council of Guidance and Personnel Associations meetings entitled "What's Wrong With Counselor Preparation?" and devoted my entire presentation to these kinds of discrepancies. There must be thousands of practicing school counselors today who would be most willing to repeat my performance.

This gap between specific course content and needed competencies is something to be applauded—not deplored. If there were no gaps, counselors would truly be technicians carrying out specific job functions in specific ways in which they had been taught to do so. If school counseling is ever to become a profession, one of the essential distinguishing features of that profession will be a requirement that its practitioners are called upon to learn how to do things other than those they were trained to do. That is, while the overall task can be taught in terms of general procedural guidelines, variation in employment environments and opportunities can always be expected to produce variations and innovations needed to make the general task a specific operating procedure in a specific setting.

Counselor education can truly succeed only if it resists temptations to teach prospective counselors a "how-to-do-it", "cookbook" approach to job functions. The "pot of gold" at the end of the counselor education "rainbow" is the presence of an intelligent basis for counselor innovation but not a set of specific techniques and procedures to be applied mechanically by practicing counselors on the job.

This is not to say that practicing counselors should see no direct relationships between what they have been taught and what they perceive needs to be done on the job. To create such a situation would make a mockery of counselor education and would impede professionalization of the school counselor just as surely as would a "techniques" approach to counselor education. What is needed, then, is a view of needed counselor competencies in vocational aspects of guidance which represents a band somewhere between these two extremes. It is this kind of picture which hopefully will emerge here.

It is, then, a blend of understanding and knowledge—of why something needs to be done and how it can be done in a specific work situation—which counselors need as competencies. This basic point has been elaborated in this introduction for two basic reasons which appear to have temporal, if not continuing, pertinence. First, if school counseling is to become a profession, than counselors must learn to become professionally responsible—to take that which they have learned and make thoughtful, rational, and innovative applications to the school and community setting in which they are employed. The second reason for elaborating on this point is to provide the beginning of a skeletal outline which might help justify counselor education as graduate education Both of these matters are of operational concern to the entire guidance and counseling movement in these times.

COUNSELOR COMPETENCIES IN VOCATIONAL INFORMATION

The counselor needs competence in utilizing and modifying a general perspective regarding the occupational world. There are certain substantive questions which the practicing school counselor should be able to answer intelligently for himself and communicate to others. Included among these are: (1) What distinctions are to be drawn among jobs, occupations, and careers? (2) How may occupations be classified so that both their relationships and their major differences become clear? (3) What major trends exist with respect to the changing nature of our occupational structure? (4) What major trends exist with respect to entry into occupations? and (5) How can practicing school counselors be kept up to date on changes in occupations and occupational patterns? The practicing school counselor who cannot give reasonably accurate definitive answers to questions such as these is ill prepared to perform the vocational guidance function in effective ways.

The counselor needs competence in understanding the psychological, sociological, and economic variables contributing to changing concepts of work as a part of society. What does "work" mean to those in various subcultures of our society? Why do people work? How are concepts regarding work currently changing in our society? Why is some work more highly respected than others to most members of society? How do concepts of work in American society differ from those in other parts of the world and those from different cultures than ours? Again, these are not academic questions for the school counselor who *understands* what he is doing in vocational guidance and why he does what he does. Answers to such questions form an essential part of the total rationale underlying the vocational guidance function.

The counselor needs competence in understanding the process of vocational development. What kinds of factors affect occupational choice? How is an occupational choice made? What kinds of occupational choices are typically expected of students at various grade levels from various kinds of socioeconomic backgrounds? With what kinds of vocational choice theories does the practicing counselor feel comfortable as he seeks to understand occupational choices made by his students? Where are most high school students expected to be in vocational development by the time they leave the secondary school and what are the most likely sources of variation involved?

The counselor needs competence in collecting, organizing, and disseminating vocational information. What are the commonly available sources of vocational information? How should a given piece of vocational information be evaluated in terms of its appropriateness for use in high school guidance? What are the advantages and disadvantages of various ways of filing vocational information in terms of meaningfulness to counselors and usefulness to students? How can vocational information be meaningfully communicated to students in groups? To individuals? What are the advantages and disadvantages of keeping vocational information in the guidance offices as opposed to other parts of the school? When, if ever, and how can vocational information be usefully disseminated through teachers? Should students be allowed to take vocational information home? Should students buy certain kinds of vocational information? How can students be encouraged to broaden their occupational horizons by studying occupational information without becoming bored, disillusioned, or discouraged? These are "hardware" questions which the practicing school counselor must somehow answer for himself as he seeks to operate a guidance program. The counselor education program which does not concentrate direct attention on helping prospective counselors develop such answers has not fulfilled its mission.

COUNSELOR COMPETENCIES IN EDUCATIONAL OPPORTUNITIES

It seems appropriate to say that the most glaring gap in counselor education programs lies in providing prospective counselors with needed competencies in respect to educational opportunities which should be discussed as an integral part of vocational guidance. It is becoming increasingly clear that to visit with high school students about vocational opportunities without also discussing training required for entry into various occupations is unrealistic, unfair, and unethical. A great majority of students leaving our secondary schools must plan to secure some additional education and/or training if they are to compete successfully in today's labor market. The need for counselors to become knowledgeable regarding training opportunities in addition to vocational opportunities was recognized and discussed in the 1949 U.S. Office of Education manual entitled *Counselor Competencies in Occupational Information*. This need has not been generally recognized in the content and structure of counselor education programs. It is hoped that specification of such counselor needs for competency here may serve to stimulate some needed changes in counselor education. The time for change in this area occurred several years ago. Implementation of such needed changes should be ignored no longer.

Counselors need competency in obtaining and implementing proper perspective with respect to total offerings in the secondary school curriculum. The counselor who expresses disinterest in the nature of the curriculum is untrue to his employer. The counselor who does not believe that there are many "best" patterns of courses in the secondary school is untrue to the students he serves. The counselor who does not see himself as one instrument of change in the nature of curricular offerings is untrue to himself. How many kinds of curricular offerings are needed by students in this school? How can a general education emphasis be made meaningful to all secondary school students? How can appropriate vocational education courses be provided for that minority of students who will seek immediate employment upon leaving the secondary school? How can the "vocational" and "academic" portions of the curriculum *and* faculty be brought into more harmonious and productive working relationships? What is a workable rationale and operational procedure for work-study programs in this school utilizing opportunities provided both through vocational education and through the Neighborhood Youth Corps? These kinds of questions are not among those in which practicing school counselors should express disinterest, lack of knowledge, or lack of responsibility for helping to answer. The fact that curriculum specialists and school administrators are interested in some of the same questions represents more, not less, reason why counselors should become competent in this area. These competencies are directly related to vocational aspects of guidance. It is difficult to understand how counselors who are knowledgeable regarding vocational development and the changing occupational society, committed to the welfare of students, and deserving of recognition as a part of the team of professional educators serving students can ignore their needs for competence and action in this area.

Counselors need competence in communicating information to students concerning post high school training opportunities. There is no doubt that "catalogue" counseling has led to academic catastrophe for many students. Counselors need to learn how to treat concepts of "good" and "poor" schools in terms of needs of individual students at least as much as in terms of needs of accrediting bodies. They need to learn how to help students decide *why* they want to be in a particular institution at least as much as they help students decide *how* to obtain admission to the institution. To do this, counselors need to know at least as much about students who attend the institution as they do about the institutional offerings. Who are the students? What happens to them while in school? What happens to them following training? Is this a "good" school for this student? It is difficult to even raise questions such as these now because the kinds of basic knowledge which could conceivably be made a part of counselor education are still largely unavailable. Yet, in terms of competencies needed by today's counselors, these questions must be raised.

Counselors need competence in helping students broaden their perspective regarding post high school training opportunities. School counselors need competence in helping students combat geographic discrimination in both educational and vocational decisions students make. Concepts involved here are inextrically tied to both those involved with local control of education and to education as part of society. Hopefully, the counselor will have learned in his counselor education program that his primary commitment is to the students he serves and that he has secondary but related commitments to the school district he serves and to society in general. If counselors understand this primary commitment to students, they will be neither "in favor of" nor "against" any particular kind of post high school educational opportunity in a generic sense. While they should be well acquainted with both educational and vocational opportunities at the local level, no practicing school counselor can consider his conversations with students limited to such opportunities. *If the counselor is to be viewed as a "recruiter", it must be as a recruiter of educational opportunities for students and not vice versa.*

Where are training opportunities for students who wish to learn watch repair? heavy equipment operation? court stenography? jet aircraft mechanics? How can a counselor tell a legitimate educational opportunity from one which is not? What sources of financial aid exist for the needy student? Illustrative questions listed here refer primarily to students seeking training opportunities in settings other than a college or university. This is done purposely in order to illustrate the currently greater need for counselor competence in this area. This in no way is meant to indicate that counselors do not also need competence—and more than many now possess—in helping students planning to attend college. Somewhere in counselor education, the kinds of basic research data required to answer questions such as these must be accumulated and then made a part of counselor education curricula throughout the country.

COUNSELOR COMPETENCIES IN BUSINESS–LABOR–INDUSTRIAL RELATIONSHIPS

To many counselors, "industry" is still thought of as a trait to be rated on a report card, "business" as something unethical, and "labor" as something illegal. The educational and experiential backgrounds of many school counselors have not equipped them with even minimal competencies required with respect to these concepts as applied to vocational aspects of guidance.

Counselors need competence in understanding basic principles of business and industrial management. Why is on-the-job training given in certain places and not in others? What is a selection ratio? What is a first line supervisor? How are pay scales determined? What kinds of education are employers looking for in entry workers—and why? How do employers view school counselors? By what means can school counselors secure actual work experience in private business and industrial settings? These are only illustrative of the kinds of pertinent questions regarding the business and industrial setting which practicing school counselors should be able to answer. While, to be sure, many specific answers can be expected to result from contacts counselors make with employers while they are working in a school, the basic principles of business and industrial management and the motivation to make these kinds of employer contacts should be a part of the counselor education program.

Counselors need competence in understanding the nature, basic structure, and operational rationale of the labor union movement. What and why is the "closed shop"? What is a union steward? Where are sources of information about specific unions? What does a new worker have to do in order to join a union? In what ways are the union and apprenticeship movements in the United States related to each other? What advantages does a union offer to the new worker? What worker handicaps are associated with the union movement? The practicing counselor will recognize these and many related questions as ones which are frequently asked by high school students. If the counselor is to supply students with more than superficial answers to questions such as these, it is essential that the counselor have made some serious study of the labor union movement.

Counselors need competence in utilizing the talents and services of the business–labor–industrial community in performing the vocational guidance function. Students who are isolated from the real working world cannot be well prepared to become a part of it. What kinds of vocational information can counselors expect to receive from representatives of business, labor, and industry? What means have counselors found successful in conducting local community occupational surveys? In conducting student visits to business–industrial settings and to labor union quarters? Under what circumstances should business–labor–industrial representatives be invited to consult with students in the school? What kinds of student work experience programs might be worked out with the business world? That practicing counselors have not always established any working relationships with the business–labor–industrial community is obvious to all who work with them. It is equally obvious that counselor cooperation with this community holds high potential for better meeting the vocational guidance needs of students. If counselors need competence in this area, who is to say provisions for acquiring such competence should not appear somewhere in the total counselor education program?

CONCLUDING REMARKS

This entire presentation has been severely handicapped by the fact that it was prepared by a person who is not today a practicing school counselor. It would be foolish to deny that concerns regarding counselor education and the entire school guidance movement have been as influential in determining content as has direct concern with school counselor activities. It is hoped that currently employed school counselors, guidance supervisors, and counselor educators will each find small portions of this paper helpful to them as we all work together in attempting to meet the vocational guidance needs of today's youth.

25. *What Will the School Counsellor Do?*

PETER P. DAWS

IT is still too early to see the answer to this question in actual school practice. The first trained counsellors emerged only last summer from the Universities of Keele and Reading, and are therefore only now finding their feet again on the teaching scene they left for their year's training. They must inevitably be unsure still of what they will be able to do, however clear they may be in their own minds about what they would like to do. For the shape of their developing role will be decided largely by what their colleagues permit them to do, or ask of them. The uncertainties that surround their novel role must continue for some time to be a source of anxiety to school counsellors.

They will be aware that few teachers have shown much enthusiasm for the idea of the school counsellor. Some see him as a foreign product, possibly well suited to transatlantic needs but quite inappropriate to the English scene. Some see him as a personal and professional threat, a specialist who will arrogate certain treasured aspects of their own role, an intimate personal concern for the individual child; someone, moreover, who while claiming to be a colleague will also claim privileged exemption from the chore of class teaching. Yet others fear that he will over-zealously develop the careers teacher's function and thereby secure for vocational matters an excessive influence upon curriculum content and choice. And other teachers—and not a few psychiatrists and psychologists—fear that he will undertake therapeutic tasks beyond his competence with disturbed and troubled children.

Little wonder that those who have launched the school counselling service in a mere handful of schools with no precedent to guide them, and with little prospect of clear, unequivocal situational support are earnestly searching for a viable definition of their function. What kind of service may they most usefully and acceptably provide? What needs may their contribution most effectively meet? Above all, they need to anticipate how best they may "sell" themselves to their fellow teachers, including their Heads. For if they

(Reprinted from *Educational Research*, 1967, vol. 9, No. 2, by permission of the editor and author. *Educational Research*, is published for the National Foundation for Educational Research by Newnes Educational Publishing Co.)

fail to convince their colleagues that they have a worthwhile service to offer the school, that they can significantly further the wider purposes of education, the very tentative interest that some head teachers and administrators are currently showing will flag, and the new ventures in counsellor training will wither from an increasingly unsympathetic shift in the climate of educational thinking.

When one discusses these matters with those responsible for the present training of school counsellors, one is well aware how seriously they have pondered these issues. Their judgements and inspired guesses are reflected in the first counsellors who have begun with some sharpened idea of their role and with certain skills with which to play it. It is also clear that the training that each has received is sufficiently flexible to permit his personal feelings and temperamental inclinations to play some part in deciding the style of his preferred role, and to allow him some choice in the selection of areas of need to which he may devote his time and energy. In short, his training has given him some elbow room to allow him, on re-entry, to adapt and define himself in personally congenial ways. Such flexibility and adaptability is of crucial importance to the pioneer. To win acceptance must be his first concern. For only then can he secure the necessary conditions for purposeful development, and be in a position to judge with confidence the best directions for growth, both for himself and for the school. That he will meet cold winds is certain; which way they will blow is uncertain. At all costs, he must be quick to discern which way the wind blows in order to bend and adjust his role appropriately. Only then will he have a fair chance of survival.

Sociologists in recent years have made increasingly clear the consequences in institutional disorganization and personal distress of our failure to define roles clearly. Incumbants need to understand the purposes they are expected to serve and the forms of behaviour and skill they must use to fulfil them. Only then can they satisfy the expectations of those whose roles are reciprocal to their own, and with whom, therefore, they will frequently interact (Cottrell, 1942; Gross, Mason and McEarchern, 1964; Ivey and Robin, 1966). The cultural anthropologists, too, have commented upon the frequent inadequacy of our social arrangements for defining roles and providing opportunities for training and rehearsal, compared with the provisions of simpler cultures (Benedict, 1938). Social and institutional change creates special problems of role definition and performance, for new roles arise and old ones gradually change under the pressure of new need and changing values. One gropes one's tentative way from the familiar to the unfamiliar. The school counsellor's role is a new one. Initially, it must be flexible, exploratory, and sensitive to need whatever form it may take. Nonetheless, some of the stress and inefficiency of an unqualified trial and error approach might be avoided by an attempt to foresee the tensions and difficulties that await the counsellor. One can explore the kinds of role that are available to him and assess the likely consequences of his trying them out. Eysenck (1961) has defined psychotherapy as:

"an unidentified technique applied to unspecified problems with unpredictable outcomes. For this technique we recommend rigorous training."

That someone may be tempted to say the same of counselling is a challenge we should prepare ourselves to meet.

PERSONAL COUNSELLING (U.S.A.)

It is appropriate to begin with an American definition of the school counsellor, for it has been shaped by many years of practice in the American High School and is to-day supported by theoretical and conceptual structures of an impressive order of refinement. Since American theorists have been able to profit from the evidence of counselling practice, we would be wise to consider what they have to say even though the answers and principles they find appropriate to American culture may not be so readily applicable to ours. Furthermore, it is likely that what emerges after years of trial and error and proves suitable for a culture where counselling has become an integral part of the school and college system may be too ambitious a practice to begin *ab initio*—too demanding for the counsellors themselves who would be wiser to walk before they run, and too sophisticated and unfamiliar to gain the understanding and co-operation of teachers. As both of the Universities that have begun to train school counsellors were able to attract eminent American theorists to spend some time with their students (Gilbert Wrenn to Keele and Gilbert Moore to Reading), the first English counsellors have a good understanding of the American conception of counselling and have some enthusiasm for it.

It is an over-simplification to talk of *the* American view of counselling, and to assume that its practice in the American high schools closely reflects theoretical ideals in every school in every State. There are, however, some basic ideas that recur throughout the writings of such influential theorists as C. G. Wrenn (1962), D. E. Super (1957), R. Mathewson (1962) and Leona E. Tyler (1961), and many of these shared ideas and assumptions can, in their turn, be traced to the very original thinking of Carl. R. Rogers (1942, 1951) in the field of psychotherapy.

1. Continuity of Concern

In a school system where teachers may not stay in one place long enough really to get to know their pupils, and where even the long stay teacher may find his classes changed annually, and where even during, say, one year his contact with any particular child is merely brief, intermittent and concerned only with a specific aspect of education, the child lacks any single figure with whom to maintain any enduring personal relationship and to whom he can easily turn for help. Such persistence of relationship is indispensable to the adult who wishes to provide such help and without it the child would not in any case volunteer his personal difficulties and problems. It is the counsellor's function to provide such continuity of concern so that he may achieve genuine developmental insight into the life of the child and more readily establish a relationship that the young person will willingly use. The importance of "continuity of concern" has been clearly recognized recently in discussions about child care work in this country (Lomax-Simpson, 1963). In England, we have traditionally relied upon the form master and the house master to provide such continuity. Their teacher role, however, has often limited their pastoral and counselling effectiveness.

2. Globality of Concern

The specialist referral services that are available to deal with specific sorts of problem that children are prone to all share the weakness of being partial approaches to the total personality and situation of the child. Other than parents (and some school psychologists), the counsellor alone is concerned with the whole person. It is true that the best teachers, too, seek a global understanding of their pupils. Unfortunately, the conditions in which they work all too frequently defeat their ideal intentions, and most have to resign themselves to a much more partial view of their function. It is never either possible, or desirable to try, to resolve personal problems by isolating them from the total personality that must deal with them. A similar argument has recently been levelled in this country against clinics for the provision of contraceptive information and materials to adolescents. The individual, asserts Wrenn, is indivisible; and on another occasion, arguing against purely vocational counselling: "Counselling is for life, not for a living" (Wrenn, 1962, 1966). The counsellor's strength, therefore, is that he takes a total, global view of his client and his socio-cultural predicament. Counselling is always personal *and* educational *and* vocational *and* whatever.

Asserting the globality principle, many Americans have questioned the counsellor's right to limit his help to specific sorts of problem or issue, and, thus, his right to qualify his counsellor title with such limiting adjectives as "vocational" or "moral" (see Doleys, 1961). Others, however, see no contradiction in insisting both, that all counselling deals with the whole person, and that there *are* different kinds of counselling. Defending the term "vocational counselling", for example, Patterson (1964) writes:

> "First, it is well to recognize the desirability of focussing upon a particular area, or problem, in an individual's life. This does not mean that other areas are ignored, or that the counsellor does not deal with a whole human being. Second, an adequate concept of vocational counselling should not rule out consideration of attitudinal and emotional factors in vocational development and choice. Third, such a concept recognizes that many individuals have problems in the area of vocational choice that

are not symptoms of a general maladjustment or emotional disturbance. Fourth, the concept is useful in that it indicates distinctions between the handling of vocational problems and the handling of other kinds of problems."

Such points of controversy over the counsellor's right to attend only or mainly to specific sorts of concern in the client's life should not obscure the general consensus that *any* problem or decision that confronts a child requires the counsellor to appraise and understand the total life predicament and personality of that child, and to help the child, too, toward such understanding, if he is to succeed in his counselling objectives.

3. Active Client Participation

The counsellor is *not* an adviser. It is true that the outcome of counselling is evident in resolutions that the client makes about how he shall conduct his life and perhaps also in decisions and choices demanded by personal problems. But it is not the counsellor's function to grasp the client's dilemmas and problems, and in his wisdom to advise the client on the wisest course of action. He must be, in Carl Roger's phrase, non-directive (Rogers, 1951). He must avoid exercising a direct influence on the client's choices and decisions; his role is that of ensuring that the client is aware of all the factors that must be weighed in seeking a decision, and of ensuring that the client then makes the decision himself. This point is sometimes made by stressing that it is the counselling process that is important and not the outcome of the process evidenced in a decision. If the outcome alone were important or even the main issue, then this could be better done by mechanical and impersonal procedures. Suppose the client needs to choose a career. If he simply wants an "expert" to advise him which occupation would most congenially fit his spectrum of talents, weaknesses, needs and aversions, a computer which stored all the known information about occupations—their skill demands and the satisfactions they offer—would quickest and most accurately provide an answer (Hull, 1925). Counselling would be superfluous. If, however, one accepts that the counselling process helps the client to reach his own particular decisions and at the same time develops his general capacity for decision taking, it is clearly a function quite distinct from mechanical evaluation processes that might safely be left to computers or punched card systems. In short, the aim of the counsellor is to promote the development of his client, to help him become mature, independent and autonomous, and both able and skilled in handling the crises that life confronts him with and which demand choices, decisions and action. The adviser who provides a client with ready-made answers is impeding that individual's maturational development by encouraging dependency and the attitude of shifting the onus of decision in crises on to the counsellor's shoulders. The client who say "What must I do to be saved?" needs counselling and the process will be beneficial. He should not be given an answer.

Not all American school counsellors subscribe to such an extreme non-directive, client-centred view of their role, but all are agreed that the client must be strongly encouraged and helped to think out his problems and to make his own decisions as far as is reasonably possible. Jones (1963) expresses a common view when he defines counselling as follows, though he prefers the term "guidance":

> "Guidance is the assistance given to individuals in making intelligent choices and adjustments. ... Guidance does not make choices for individuals; it helps them make their own choices in such a way as to promote or stimulate the gradual development of the ability to make decisions independently without assistance from others."

This viewpoint has led to a clear separation of the roles of counsellor and teacher. Extremists argue that the relationship between the counsellor and his client—high permissive, client-centred, non-directive and non-evaluative—is strikingly different from the teacher's relation to his pupils, which they see as essentially impersonal, pedagogic and authoritarian. More moderate opinion recognizes that these are caricatures of the two roles, and that good teachers often make use of counselling techniques and that counsellors need occasionally to use instructive procedures. There is little support, however, for the view that one person can undertake both the teacher and the counsellor roles (as distinct from their techniques) in the same school without seriously confusing the child's expectations (Mathewson, 1962, Chap. 7).

4. Preventive Orientation

The counsellor is not primarily concerned to deal with crises (Mathewson, 1962; Tyler, 1961). He is not someone only to be searched out when difficulties and dangers loom and the client feels unable to cope. He is not solely nor mainly a psycho-clinician skilled in diagnosis, nor is his role (as we have seen) an essentially prescriptive or recommendatory one. Rather, the counsellor begins when the child is young so that he may be helped to anticipate crises or avoid them, or be ready and able to cope with them when they do arise. To take again an example from the field of vocational guidance: if we do nothing (counsellor or client) until the child is about to leave school and then recognize that the need to choose an occupation is imminent and pressing, then we do have a crisis. If, however, appropriate counselling begins many years before the end of schooling, so that over a long period the client is alerted to the issues he must consider, is given suitable occupational information, and is given or enabled to acquire information about himself, his needs and abilities, an occupational preference will gradually crystallize and the person finds himself able to make a choice when necessary on the basis of a thorough preparatory process. A crisis has been anticipated and averted; and the outcome will be sounder than what would emerge from a hasty eleventh hour crisis-based interview (Super, 1957). Such a preventive conception of counselling has the merit that the counsellor will be able to foresee and anticipate some potential crises, including those of personal distress and personality disturbance, and will therefore be able to help the child to cope with the situation before it has become overwhelming. It is this preventive function that distinguishes counselling clearly from psychotherapy and underlines its service to normal, as distinct from disturbed, young people.

Wrenn (1962) states a commonly accepted principle when he recommends that:

> "primary emphasis in counselling students be placed on the developmental needs and decision points in the lives of the total range of students rather than upon the remedial needs and crisis points in the lives of a few students, with the major goal of counselling being that of increased self responsibility and an increased maturity in decision making on the part of the student."

5. Co-ordination of School Activities

The school counsellor is well placed to help co-ordinate the work of his colleagues by identifying in individual children where the collective school effort is failing, and the forms of such failure. He can readily harness the resources of the school to rescue the child in need. In the absence of a counsellor, only the head teacher could exercise this co-ordinative function. He, however, is invariably denied the close contact with individual pupils that would reveal the occasion and the need to harness the resources of his school. His role makes it difficult in more than one sense for pupils to open their souls to him. The counsellor, on the other hand, does not share those formal characteristics that attach to the roles of teacher and Head of School that make pupils hesitate to disclose certain kinds of problem. He, contrarily, is seen by them primarily as a source of aid, as a person outside the disciplinary system, as a dependable repository of confidences, and as a sympathetic listener who will at all times try and understand the pupil's point of view and predicament (Tyler, 1961, p. 98). It is the counsellor, too, who has responsibility for keeping a cumulative school record for each child, on which he enters psychometric data, scholastic achievement, curriculum choices, and the comments of every teacher that has had charge of the child.

When he has identified a problem or need that requires action outside the counselling relationship, the counsellor can instigate such action, whether it involves colleagues, such as teachers, house masters or school social workers, or more remote figures, such as parents or specialists in relevant referral agencies. A teacher is never so happily placed to mediate such co-ordinative action, as Mathewson (1962) clearly sees:

> "... most teachers can give only incidental and episodic attention to more complicated problems of adjustment, orientation, and development.

They simply do not have the time nor the training to make the necessary personal appraisals, gather the essential data, evaluate the person-in-situation, and reach conclusions ...

"The fact is, that no one teacher is in contact with the pupil for more than a short time in the total span of a pupil's career in a given school. The teacher sees only a part of the total picture, a cross-sectional view, and that largely in terms of classroom experiences and academic learning processes."

This brief account of the American conception of school counselling may be summarized even more briefly as a continuous concern throughout the child's school life to monitor and promote his personal, social, and educational development, and to anticipate and see him through life's hazards, not by steering or advising him, but by helping him to develop and harness his own resources of character sufficiently to deal with them himself. The counsellor will be aware of his own limitations and prompt to call upon the help of his colleagues and of specialist referral services when these are necessary. Primarily, he is concerned with health and not with breakdown. His ultimate purpose is to ensure that his clients grow up psychologically unscarred, aware of their own talents, limitations and needs, and with a sound capacity to face the challenge of crises and able to resolve them successfully. Above all, they will define and explore the shape of their own uniqueness, acquire respect for it, and exploit it creatively. All of which implies a model of healthy maturity strikingly similar to that evident in the writings of psychotherapists.

Practitioners aspire with varying degrees of inadequacy to fulfil the exacting requirements of theory, and there is often a depressing gulf between school practice and precept (see Thompson, 1964). Many counsellors spend more time in educational counselling than in either personal counselling or in more limited vocational counselling. This is partly because the curricular choices available to the pupil are more numerous than our children are accustomed to (though our comprehensive schools are able to offer a rich variety of fare) and partly because American children delay their entry into working life much longer than our children. Whereas less than 10 per cent of English children have still to begin work at 18, little more than 10 per cent of American children at that age are "drop-outs" from full-time schooling. Wise educational choices, therefore, inevitably preoccupy young Americans more continuously than do career decisions. The commonest complaint of counsellors is of the excessive demand on their time of peripheral, non-counselling duties. "In many schools, much more work is done on paper than on pupils" (Mathewson, 1962, p. 200).

American counselling represents a laudable statement of objectives that defines high expectations of counsellors. It reveals an imaginative grasp of the developmental problems that confront anyone growing up and striving to discover and define himself in a complex industrial society. But it is, perhaps, too ambitious a model for the English counsellor to take, however useful he may find it as a source of inspiration and a guide to goals and priorities. Though reluctantly, and perhaps only temporarily, he will be compelled for various reasons to set himself a more modest level of aspiration.

Firstly, it is impossible to train a teacher, however suitable and enthusiastic personally, for such a role in one year, despite the excellent resources at Keele and Reading. Mathewson selects only trained teachers who also have an M.Ed. degree (containing a considerable amount of psychological training) and provides 18 months training. Wrenn has suggested that a psychology Ph.D. is desirable, even though he stresses that personal qualities are more important than academic standing. Tyler (1961) recommends that student counsellors be of at least Master's degree standing. However, one is encouraged to find the University of Keele providing additional in-service training and support for its own students.

Secondly, we do not have adequate specialist referral services at the disposal of counsellors, and even in those areas that are more generously provided for, it is unlikely that they could cope with the volume of work that a conscientious counsellor would uncover. To compare the referral agency provision available to schools in England and America is difficult. Inter-State variations in America are greater than between the different regions of England. Furthermore, America is less "welfare-state" minded than we are. She lacks, for example, a nation-wide equivalent of our Youth Employment Service, and in consequence many counsellors undertake placement work. Nonetheless, counsellors working in the wealthier States do have readier access to more specialist services than our own counsellors can look forward to. In addition, the American counsellor can more effectively handle a heavy "caseload" because he enjoys testing and clerical facilities more generous than our own counsellors can expect for some time.

Thirdly, the role is too unfamiliar and novel in conception to attract initially the necessary enthusiasm and co-operation of teaching colleagues. They may suspect the counsellor of "empire building". Status anxieties would then seriously impede the co-operative relationship upon which the counsellor's work so crucially depends.

Fourthly, few of our first counsellors will be able (or find it politic) to avoid undertaking some class teaching. This will reduce the time available to them for counselling. More seriously, since the roles of *personal* counsellor and teacher are so distinct (even though they may occasionally make use of each other's techniques) a regular alternation between teaching and counselling might well impair a man's competence in both, and additionally confuse the counsellor's "image" in the child's mind. The child who has been chastized in the classroom, for example, will not easily accept that he can confess to minor delinquencies in confidence to the same man with impunity in the privacy of the counsellor's room, and that he will listen sympathetically and non-evaluatively.

Inevitably, some form of compromise will be necessary for our counsellors—initially, at least, while their profession becomes understood and accepted. Two attractive alternatives to the ambitious and demanding American model are Therapeutic Counselling, and Educational and Vocational Counselling, but they are very different roles with quite distinct purposes.

THERAPEUTIC COUNSELLING

The therapeutic counsellor would concern himself only with those children and young people who show evidence of stress and disturbance: the persistently truanting child, the overtly aggressive child, the silent, withdrawn child, the delinquent, the bereaved, the "new boy", the under-achiever, the sexual offender, the rejected child and the child disturbed at the prospect of examinations. There would be no shortage of clients, but as they will be a relatively small proportion of the total school population at any one time, and as he will refer the more serious cases elsewhere, his caseload should allow him to devote more time to each child than would be available to a personal counsellor.

His first task when a child is brought to his notice would be to exercise his diagnostic skill in discriminating what is essentially healthy disturbance—a *normal* reaction to a situation of stress—from that which betrays underlying morbidity, perhaps due to long-standing exposure to a high level of stress. The disturbed normal child will become his client; the severely disturbed child he will refer with a report to the school psychological service who in turn can make use of the child guidance clinic or the child psychiatry unit (B.P.S., 1962). He may also expect some diagnostic help from the visiting school medical officer, and from the school psychological service, where one exists. Such a role would ensure that seriously disturbed children are identified and referred for specialist attention earlier than usual and that many who would ultimately have deteriorated to a level necessitating psychiatric attention will be identified in good time and helped to cope with their difficulties and to survive them without damage. Such a therapeutic role would involve the counsellor's working with the parents no less than the child to help them play a significant part in the therapeutic process, and with such home-directed counselling he will find a valuable ally in the school social worker if the school is fortunate enough to have one. Regrettably, such social workers, like counsellors, will be thin on the ground for some time.

Such a counsellor would be ideally placed to gain insight into the coping and adjustment problems that beset normal, healthy young people to-day, and the knowledge he would gain would prove valuable to those working in the mental health services who are concerned with preventive techniques. We still know much less than we ought about, for example, the school child's reaction to losing a parent, or the conscientious but dull child's fear of disappointing parental scholastic expectations. Our endeavours to understand childhood development have been disproportionately directed toward the pre-school child, and we consequently remain much less well-informed of the factors critical to the mental health of the school child. If we had learned more about the adjustment difficulties of school children, our educational purposes might already reflect a stronger concern for the pupil's personal development as distinct from his scholastic progress. We still too readily assume that the causes of breakdown during the school years are to be sought in developmental mishaps in the pre-school years.

The therapeutic counsellor contrasts with the personal counsellor in many respects. He does not concern himself with all children, nor in a manner than answers the Continuity of Concern principle. But for those he does elect to help, his concern will be "global" because mental health is a function of the whole individual. He will, of course, be crisis orientated and he will be concerned with diagnoses, even though he may use the personal counsellor's non-directive techniques to help the child harness his own therapeutic resources and coping skills. He will also undertake to alter the child's social environment in appropriate ways by recruiting and co-ordinating the efforts of his colleagues and by securing, either alone or with the aid of social workers, the co-operation of the parents.

Like the personal counsellor, the therapeutic counsellor would uncover an unsuspectedly large degree of serious need that might over-tax the resources of available referral services. But equally his own timely interventions would often be sufficient to rescue a disturbed child before his distress had reached psychiatric proportions. It is, in any event, preferable that a disturbed child, who must wait his turn for an over-strained psychotherapeutic service, should meanwhile find help and support from a counsellor who is not himself swamped by the full volume of non-therapeutic demand from a healthy school population. It is a role that seems likely to engage the sympathies and co-operation of teachers far more readily than that of the personal counsellor. But will our school counsellors have learned sufficient psychology and psycho-pathology (particularly that related to child development) to undertake such a role; and will they find such a role attractive?

EDUCATIONAL AND VOCATIONAL COUNSELLING

The educational and vocational counsellor (hereafter E-V) would specialize in matters of scholastic development and vocational thinking. He would have two clear goals: firstly, to ensure the fullest development of the child's capacities in school by guiding him on curriculum choice, and secondly, to help the school child to choose a career—possibly after further education elsewhere—that promises to give him what he wants out of his working life and offers him an opportunity to develop and use his talents.

The justification for such a role arises from recognizing that vocational guidance provided at the end of schooling comes too late, partly because other contingent and non-professional sources have already influenced young people's career thinking and preferences and partly because, having virtually completed his educational programme, the school leaver's occupational opportunities are now relatively limited and fixed. Such limitations inherent in eleventh hour vocational guidance [contemptuously termed "crisis counselling" by Super (1957)] can be avoided only by bringing professional influences to bear on the choice process many years before the necessity for choice arises (thereby avoiding crisis) and by insisting that vocational considerations are not neglected when educational decisions are made. Since occupational choice is the outcome of a developmental process that has extended over many years, vocational guidance can be really effective only if it, too, is spread over those same years. Furthermore, since vocational opportunity is closely determined by educational achievement, both in kind and amount, the counsellor must make clear what educational paths lead to the occupational goals for which the child has shown some interest.

What a young person primarily needs when thinking about his occupational future is information—about jobs, about entry qualifications, about skills required and satisfactions offered, and about the various forms of higher and further education and their occupational relevance. Above all, he needs information about himself, his abilities, aptitudes, and limitations. The counsellor would give him this information and make sure he understood it. He would rely upon his own cumulative record cards which would record scholastic progress, the comments of class teachers, and psychological test results. He would need to be familiar with at least a few of the environments in which working life is lived and able to command either in memory or at his finger tips a large store of occupational information. He would have some skill in the use and interpretation of psychological tests to enable him when necessary to probe his clients more fully in occupationally relevant respects. He would also understand our educational system thoroughly and the relevance of particular courses to particular vocational ends.

He would, of course, be a counsellor and not merely a source of information, for he would frequently take the initiative in telling young people of career possibilities they may not have heard of let alone considered, and he would often need non-directively to aid the vocational thinking of his clients by asking such questions as "How do you think you will feel about a naval officer's life when you are married?" or "How much patience would you suppose teaching the physically handicapped would require?"

Though he would serve every child who passed through the school, the more intensive counselling that is so time-consuming would be needed only by a minority of confused and immature pupils. A careers teacher could free more of the counsellor's time for such specialized work by relieving him of some of the more straightforward careers work. It would be in such complex case-work that the E-V counsellor's role would approach closest that of the therapeutic counsellor.

The most important referral service available to the E-V counsellor would be the Youth Employment Service whose officers have the statutory obligation to give vocational guidance to school leavers. These officers would keep him informed of local employment opportunities and become counsellors to young people once they had begun their working lives (see Ministry of Labour, 1965). The E-V counsellor, also, would work occasionally with the child's parents, particularly if he felt that their influence on the child's vocational thinking was misguided. He might need, for example, to explain to parents the advantages to their child of his remaining at school for a year or two longer.

Because the degree of inter-personal involvement between the E-V counsellor and the majority of his clients would be much less than that to which the personal counsellor and the therapeutic counsellor are committed, he could more easily undertake class teaching alongside his counselling activities. He could usefully complement his counselling work by teaching a range of topics falling generally within the sphere of "social studies" or "civics", such as, the growth and practice of trades unionism.

The English educational tradition has never properly faced the full implication of recognizing that paid employment is an important part of the adult life for which education is a preparation. We have rightly resisted the persuasion to incorporate vocational training extensively in school curricula, accepting only that it is to some degree suitable for our less bright children. Unfortunately, our resistance to such pressures has had some undesirable consequences. Vocational training is one matter. Vocational thinking and planning for adult life is quite another matter, and our children pursue such activities whether we encourage them at school or not, as the Newsom Report (Ministry of Education, 1963) correctly recognizes. They are surely signs of maturity. If a child of 16 has resolved to become, say, a lawyer, he has a right to be told whether the school programme that confronts him (and about which he may have had little choice) will enable him to achieve his vocational aspiration or not. Or whether, indeed, an alternative course of secondary and higher education would be more appropriate. We could safely entrust such matters to a counsellor without compromising or diluting the non-vocational purposes of education. Furthermore, we should in this way do much to ensure that young people find a career that offers them personal fulfilment and the fullest use of their talent. Quite apart from the persuasion of humanitarian arguments, there are now pressing economic arguments for insisting that the latent ability in our population be fully developed and occupationally distributed to best effect. We have entered an era of increasing manpower scarcity (Ministry of Labour, 1964). Our national prosperity will depend upon our ability to balance, in the education and training of our labour force, quantitative deficiencies with qualitative efficiency.

CONCLUSION

Though the school counsellor is a newcomer to our educational scene, counselling itself is not. The good teacher has always been alive to those pupil needs that are best served by individual counselling, and many show an impressive untutored counselling ability. Such people are often recruited to posts like the house master and the tutor, or find their way into special remedial work where a personal, individual approach is especially needed. Counselling ability remains an indispensable skill to the teacher and his need of it will grow rather than diminish with the advent of the school counsellor.

Why, then do we need the school counsellor? First, because the volume of need for counselling in one form or another goes far beyond what is reasonable to ask teachers to meet. Second, because the demand can be most economically met by a professionally trained specialist that the teacher can all upon for help. Third, because children are increasingly postponing their departure from school and the personal development of young adults responds particularly well to counselling. Fourth, the new forms of organization of secondary education have brought new needs for counselling. The comprehensive school, for example, has a student population larger and socially more heterogeneous than pupils have been accustomed to, and such differences will tax the pupil's ability to establish satisfactory interpersonal relationships—particularly if the school is also co-educational. The comprehensive school also offers a much wider choice of curriculum than more traditional forms of secondary school, and will, therefore, particularly need the E-V counsellor's skill.

One over-simplifies, of course, in saying that there are only three counselling roles available for our first practitioners to choose. The personal counsellor, if he aspires to meet American theoretical demands, will ambitiously combine the functions of the therapeutic counsellor and the E-V counsellor, *and* monitor the personal development of healthy children as well. There are cogent reasons (as we have seen) why our own counsellors for some time will need to accept a more modest definition of their role.

The roles of therapeutic counsellor and E-V counsellor identify the two major forms of need that are likely to appeal to our counsellors, but each is susceptible of considerable variation and elaboration. Counsellors may wish, for example, to explore the value of group counselling to help pupils with adjustment difficulties, particularly those that spring from cross-sexed relationships. And their work, whatever their specific objectives, will undoubtedly reflect the values and style of the personal counsellor, for much of their training comes from transatlantic sources.

It would be convenient if one could make a clear case for stressing the priority need for either therapeutic counselling or for E-V counselling. One cannot. Both are needed with equal urgency. The need for therapeutic counselling is the more dramatically insistent, but the need for E-V counselling is apparent for *all* children, and it too, if less obviously, will make a significant contribution to the mental health of this country in the long run. It is the role that will appear most familiar to teachers, who will see it as an ambitious extension of the career teacher role. It is the role, too, for which present training courses appear to be the more relevant—but only marginally so. What the counsellor will do in fact is likely to be a compromise between what he would prefer to do, what he is permitted to do, and what is asked of him. James Gill, who has responsibility for the training of counsellors at Keele University, has proposed a definition of the school counsellor. To his teaching colleagues, he suggests, he is a specialist to whom they may send their problem children. To the specialist referral agencies, however, he is a general practitioner whose purpose is to refer to them those children who need their specialist attention. This definition has the merit of stressing that the counsellor will be the servant of his teaching colleagues and of the specialist referral agencies no less than of his clients.

REFERENCES

BENEDICT, R. (1938) Continuities and discontinuities in cultural conditioning. *Psychiatry*, **1**, 161–167.

BOROW, H., ed. (1964) *Man in a World at Work*. Boston: Houghton Mifflin, for the National Vocational Guidance Association.

BRITISH PSYCHOLOGICAL SOCIETY (1962) *The School Psychological Service*. London: British Psychological Society.

COTTRELL, L. S. (1942) The adjustment of the individual to his age and sex roles. *American Sociological Review*, **7**, 617–620.

DOLEYS, E. J. (1961) Are there "kinds" of counsellors? *Counselling News and Views*, **12**, 5–9.

EYSENCK, H. J. (1961). The effects of psycho-therapy. In: EYSENCK, H. J., ed., *Handbook of Abnormal Psychology*. New York: Basic Books.

GROSS, N., MASON, W. S., and MCEARCHERN, A. W. (1964) *Explorations in Role Analysis*. New York: Wiley.

HULL, C. L. (1925) An automatic machine for making multiple aptitude forecasts. *Jnl. Educ. Psychol.*, **16**, 593–598.

IVEY, A. E., and ROBIN, S. S. (1966) Role theory, role conflict and counseling: a conceptual framework. *Jnl. of Counseling Psychology*, **13**, 29–36.

JONES, A. J. (1963) *Principles of Guidance*. 5th Edition. London: McGraw-Hill.

LOMAX-SIMPSON, J. (1963) Continuity of concern. In: *An A.B.C. of Social Problems and Therapy*. London: Residential Child Care Association Magazine, Vol 11, 25-30.

MATHEWSON, R. (1962) *Guidance Policy and Practice*. 3rd Edition. New York: Harper.

MINISTRY OF EDUCATION (1963) *Half our Future* (The Newsom Report). London: H.M.S.O.

MINISTRY OF LABOUR (1964) *The Pattern of the Future—Manpower Studies No.* 1. London: H.M.S.O.

Ministry of Labour (1965) *The Future Development of the Youth Employment Service* (The Albemarle Report). London: H.M.S.O.

Patterson, C. H. (1964) Counseling: self-clarification and the helping relationship. In: Borow, H., ed., *Man in a World at Work*. Boston: Houghton Mifflin.

Rogers, C. R. (1942) *Counseling and Psychotherapy*. Boston: Houghton Mifflin.

Rogers, C. R. (1951) *Client-centred Therapy*. New York: Houghton Mifflin.

Super, D. E. (1957) *The Psychology of Careers*. New York: Harper.

Thompson, A. S. (1964) School settings for vocational guidance. In: Borow, H., ed., *Man in a World at Work*. Boston: Houghton Mifflin.

Tyler, L. E. (1961) *The Work of the Counsellor*. New York: Appleton-Century-Croft.

Wrenn, C. G. (1962) *The Counsellor in a Changing World*. Washington, D. C.: American Personnel & Guidance Association.

Wrenn, C. G. (1966) Introductory address to the International Round Table of Educational and Vocational Counselling, Neuchâtel, Switzerland, January, 1966.

SUGGESTED FURTHER READING

Adams, J. F., ed. (1965). *Counselling and Guidance*. New York: MacMillian.

Farwell, G. F., and Peters, H. J. (1960) *Guidance Readings for Counsellors*. Chicago: Rand McNally.

Shertzer, B., and Stone, S. C. (1966) *Fundamentals of Guidance*. Boston: Houghton Mifflin.

Stefflre, B., ed. (1965) *Theories of Counseling*. London: McGraw-Hill.

Williamson, E. G., ed. (1961) *Vocational Counseling: A Re-appraisal in Honour of Donald G. Paterson*. Minneapolis: University of Minnesota Press.

ADDITIONAL REFERENCES ON THE AIMS OF GUIDANCE AND COUNSELLING AND THE MORAL RESPONSIBILITY OF THE COUNSELLOR

Adams, J. F. (1962) *Problems in Counseling: A Case Study Approach*. New York, Macmillan.

Arbuckle, D. S. (1961) *Counseling: An Introduction*. Boston, Allyn & Bacon.

Blocher, D. H. (1966) *Developmental Counseling*. New York, Ronald Press.

Bordin, E. S. (1955) *Psychological Counseling*. New York, Appleton-Century Crofts.

Brewer, J. M. (1942) *History of Vocational Guidance*. New York, Harper.

Daws, P. P. (1968) *A Good Start in Life*. Careers Research and Advisory Centre, Cambridge.

Gustad, J. W. (1953) The definition of counseling. In R. F. Berdie (ed.), *Roles and Relationships in Counseling*, Minnesota Studies in Student Personnel Work, No. 3.

Hahn, M. E., and Maclean, M. S. (1955) *Counseling Psychology*. New York, McGraw-Hill.

McDaniel, H. B. (1956) *Guidance in the Modern School*. New York, Holt, Rinehart & Winston.

McGowan, J. F., and Schmidt, L. D. (1962) *Counseling: Readings in Theory and Practice*, New York, Holt, Rinehart & Winston.

Mathewson, R. H. (1955) *Guidance Policy and Practice*. New York, Harper.

Ohlsen, M. E. (1955) *Guidance*. New York, Harcourt, Brace & World.

Patterson, C. H. (1959) *Counseling and Psychotherapy*. New York, Harper.

Robinson, F. P. (1959) *Principles and Practices in Student Counseling*. New York, Harper.

Rogers, C. R. (1951) *Client-Centered Therapy*. Boston, Houghton-Mifflin.

STEFFLRE, B. (ed.) (1965) *Theories of Counseling*. New York, McGraw-Hill.

TYLER, L. E. (1961) *The Work of the Counselor* (2nd ed.) New York, Appleton.

VITELES, M. S., BRAYFIELD, A. H., and TYLER, L. E. (1961) *Vocational Counseling: A Reappraisal in Honor of Donald G. Patterson*. Minnesota Studies in Student Personnel Work, No. 11, University of Minnesota Press.

WARTERS, J. (1964) *Techniques of Counseling* (2nd. ed.). New York, McGraw-Hill.

WILLIAMSON, E. G. (1965) *Vocational Counseling*. New York, McGraw-Hill.

WRENN, C. G. (1962) *The Counselor in a Changing World*. Washington, American Personnel and Guidance Association.

AMERICAN PSYCHOLOGICAL ASSOCIATION (1956) Committee of Definition, Division of Counseling Psychology, Counseling psychology as a speciality. *American Psychologist*, **11**, 282–285.

BERDIE, R. F. (1959) Counseling principles and presumptions. *J. of Counseling Psychology*, **6**, 175–182.

BOWLES, F. H. (1959) The nature of guidance. *Personnel and Guidance J.*, **37**, 112–120.

CALLIS, R. (1960) Toward an integrated theory of counseling. *J. of College Student Personnel*, **1**, 2–9.

CRIBBIN, J. J. (1955) Critique of the philosophy of modern guidance. *Catholic Educational Review*, **53**, 73–91.

CURRAN, C. L. (1960) Some ethical and scientific values in the counseling psychotherapeutic process. *Personnel and Guidance J.*, **39**, 15–24.

FAILOR, C. W. (1957) Current problems in vocational guidance. *Educational Outlook*, **31**, 129–135.

FARWELL, G. F., and PETERS, H. J. (1957) Guidance: a longitudinal and a differential view. *Elementary School J.*, **57**, 442–445.

GOLDMAN, L. (1964) The process of vocational assessment. In H. Borow (ed.), *Man in a World at Work*, *ibid.*

HOBBS, N. (1952) Some notions about guidance. *Peabody Journal of Education*, **29**, 229–231.

IVEY, A. E. (1962) Role conflict in counseling: its effects on college student attitudes. *J. of Counseling Psychology*, **9**, 139–143.

LOWE, C. M. (1959) Value orientations—an ethical dilemma. *American Psychologist*, **14**, 687–693.

McDAID, E. W. (1956) Implications of a guidance and counseling program. *Arithmetic Teacher*, **3**, 49–54.

MURPHY, G. (1955) The cultural context of guidance. *Personnel and Guidance J.*, **34**, 4–9.

PATTERSON, C. H. (1964) Counseling: self-classification and the helping relationship. In H. Borow (ed.), *Man in a World at Work*, *ibid.*

SAMLER, J. (1960) Change in values: a goal in counseling. *J. of Counseling Psychology*, **7**, 32–39.

SCHMIDT, L. G., and RUTH, J. (1956) Is guidance suppressing individualism? *Phi Delta Kappan*, **38**, 93–95.

SEELEY, J. R. (1956) Guidance: a plea for abandonment. *Personnel and Guidance J.*, **34**, 528–535.

SHOBEN, E. J. Jr. (1962) The counselor's theory as personal trait. *Personnel and Guidance J.*, **40**, 617–621.

SUPER, D. E. (1949) Group techniques in the guidance program. *Educational and Psychological Measurement*, **9**, 495–510.

SUPER, D. E. (1955) Transition: from vocational guidance to counseling psychology. *J. of Counseling Psychology*, **2**, 3–9.

SYMPOSIUM (1958): E. J. Shoben, O. H. Mowrer, G. Kimble, C. R. Rogers, J. G. Miller. Behaviour theories and a counseling case. *J. of Counseling Psyehology*, **5**, 3–10.

THOMPSON, A. S. (1960) Personality dynamics and vocational counseling. *Personnel and Guidance J.*, **78**, 350–357.

THOMPSON, A. S. (1964) Counseling and the ages of man. *J. of Counseling Psychology*, **11**, 221–229.

THORNE, F. C. (1948) Principles of directive counseling and psychotherapy. *American Psychologist*, **3**, 160–165.

TYLER, L. E. (1958) Theoretical principles underlying the counseling process. *J. of Counseling Psychology*, **5**, 3–10.

WALKER, D. E., and PEIFFER, H. C. Jr. (1957) The goals of counseling. *J. of Counseling Psychology*, **4**, 204–210.

WALTON, L. E. (1957) The scope and function of vocational guidance. *Educational Outloock*, **31**, 119–128.

WRENN, C. G. (1958) Psychology, religion, and values for the counselor. *Personnel and Guidance J.*, **36**, 331–334.

WRIGHT, E. W. (1959) Multiple counseling: why, when, how? *Personnel and Guidance J.*, **37**, 551–557.

SECTION 6

Guidance in Practice

"Take my counsel, happy man; Act upon it, if you can!"

W. S. GILBERT, *The Gondoliers*

BEFORE the Second World War there was considerable activity and interest in vocational guidance in Britain as evidenced by the work of Burt, Earle, Hunt, Macrae, Rodger and Smith to name but a few, but since the war and until quite recently momentum appeared to wane.

The content of this section has been chosen to illustrate developments in practice that have affected or might in the future affect the British scene. The emphasis at the beginning of the section is on early developments in practice and the remaining papers deal with ideas which may improve vocational guidance techniques. Special sections in the bibliography consider specific areas that merit attention by those concerned with vocational guidance. They are industrial training, occupational classification and vocational guidance for the handicapped.

The section opens with a paper presented by Percival Smith to the British Association in 1950 in which he reports that during the 1920's the Birmingham Education Committee, after several years experience of advising school leavers about employment, began to appreciate the potential value and importance of vocational guidance. Two officers were sent to the National Institute of Industrial Psychology to acquaint themselves with psychological tests and to be trained in the latest techniques. On their return to Birmingham they began investigating the practical possibilities of including scientific vocational guidance as an integral part of the work of the Youth Employment Service. Their findings established that the use of tests considerably improved the advice that could be given to young people leaving school. They were also forced to the conclusion that vocational guidance could not easily be separated from educational guidance. It became necessary therefore to consider the teacher, when appropriately trained, as a key member of the careers team. Smith's paper reviews the results and recommendations derived from the Birmingham experiments.

During the Birmingham Education Committee's investigations Smith reported that a comprehensive analysis of each child was made by collecting and classifying information under the seven headings: circumstances, physical make-up, general intelligence, special aptitudes, attainments, disposition and interests. This system of assessment was devised by Alec Rodger and is described in the Seven-Point Plan.

McKenzie argues that some form of occupational search list which could provide worthwhile job suggestions within a clients capabilities and aspirations would be of immense value. With this end in view he evaluates various classificatory dimensions including those used in the seven-point plan.

Those readers who are particularly interested in the work of the Youth Employment Service may like to read Joan Maizels' paper "The Entry of

School Leavers into Employment" included in Section 3 of this book and to consult some of the references to be found in this section's bibliography. For example the work of Jahoda and Chalmers suggests that very few school leavers and their parents perceive the Y.E.O. as a source of guidance. The great majority look upon the Y.E.O. as a placement officer. Cavanagh, Drake and Taylor have also published some interesting research on the evaluation of Youth Employment Service Interviews.

Hopson presents a discussion on some important aspects of careers work in the school. He examines the philosophy behind a careers course and stresses the need for it to provide experience of a variety of occupations. After suggesting that one way of acquiring this is through occupational visits he considers how the role of visits has been defined in the past. He also considers the importance of designing the careers course around a logical occupational classification if this end is to be achieved.

Vocational guidance must not be thought of as a service only to be provided for those about to face the transition from school to work. The Ministry of Labour's Occupational Guidance Units are busily providing guidance to workers of all ages. Nor must it be thought that vocational guidance should only be given to "normal" individuals. Daws considers the relevance of guidance for unscholarly children and illustrates some of the problems associated with this group.

Loughary, Friesen and Hurst's paper "Autocoun: A Computer-based Automated Counseling Simulation System" demonstrates the feasibility of an automated information system capable of direct interaction with students. Although counselling may never be fully computerized there may be great benefits to be derived from counsellors specializing on certain counselling functions and delegating others to the computer.

26. *Twenty-Five Years of Research in Vocational Guidance*

PERCIVAL SMITH

IT is now twenty-five years since the Birmingham Education Committee began its research into the practical possibility of using psychological methods in giving vocational guidance to boys and girls leaving school. The Committee had then recently accepted full responsibility for dealing with employment matters affecting young people under eighteen years of age, for it was in April, 1924, that following the recommendations contained in the Chelmsford Report the Government had given such powers to Local Education Authorities. The Birmingham Education Committee even then were not inexperienced in vocational guidance procedures. For many years they had held the opinion very strongly that the authority responsible for providing education and training should also have the responsibility of advising such children in the choice of their careers and of helping them to find suitable employment. For some twelve years prior to 1924 they had to the best of their ability co-operated with the local employment exchanges of the Ministry of Labour, their own officers giving advice to school leavers and the employment exchange officers giving their attention to the placing of the children in employment. For several years the Committee's officers had been holding "choice of employment" conferences in all schools at which advice was given individually to each child leaving school. The experience gained in this way had convinced the Committee of the value and importance of vocational guidance; they had indeed formed the opinion that vocational guidance was of more fundamental importance than placing work and that in any youth employment scheme every effort must be made to improve the technique of studying the child and advising him as to his future.

The Committee had been following with considerable interest the progress being made by scientific bodies in the preparation and the use of psychological tests, and in particular the experimental work recently begun by the National Institute of Industrial Psychology in certain London schools; and they arranged for two of their officers to have a specially planned course

(Reprinted from *Occupational Psychology*, 1951, **25**, 35–43, by permission of the editor and author. *Occupational Psychology* is the quarterly journal of the National Institute of Industrial Psychology, 14 Welbeck St., London, W.1.)

of training at the National Institute. At the end of the course these two officers were allowed for a short time to assist in the London experiment and on their return to Birmingham the Committee began their own enquiries. These were aimed in the first place at seeking ways of improving the guidance given to school leavers and, secondly, at investigating the practical possibilities of including scientific vocational guidance as an integral part of the routine work of a Youth Employment Service administered by a Local Education Authority.

Six reports[1-6] have been published by the Birmingham Education Committee, and in them is set out very fully the evidence collected during the investigations. Three of the reports deal with vocational guidance given to boys and girls ceasing school attendance; and the other three deal with the vocational selection of boys for skilled engineering work.

The first vocational guidance report gives particulars of research work concerned with some 328 boys and girls who left three elementary schools in 1927 and 1928 at the age of fourteen years. The object of the enquiry was to find out whether certain tests known to be of value in estimating aptitudes and qualities required in industry could be put to practical use in advising boys and girls in their choice of carrees. The procedure adopted in this small experiment closely followed the plan of the enquiry which was being conducted in London by the National Institute of Industrial Psychology. It was felt that, apart from the intrinsic value, such research in Birmingham would serve as a useful comparison with the London experiment. It was also felt that there would be an additional advantage in Birmingham, as the one Authority would be responsible for the whole procedure involved—the organization of the schools, the conduct of the experiment, and the finding of the situations for the children concerned. In effect, it was a definite effort to explore the possibility of including vocational tests as a regular part of the routine of a Juvenile Employment Department.

All the children leaving these three schools were divided into two unselected groups—tested and control. Each child in the tested group while still at school was given a series of tests by the two investigators; each child's home was visited in order to interest the parents and to obtain some knowledge of the child's home environment; a temperament rating chart for each child was completed independently by the respective head teacher and by each of the two investigators; each child was specially examined by the school medical officer and a report containing contra-industrial indications was provided. In addition the usual school report was supplied by the head teacher. All the information collected in this way was carefully considered; vocational advice was decided upon; and the advice was discussed with the child and the parents at the choice of employment conference held at the school before the leaving date. So far as the control group was concerned each child's home was visited and each child was given vocational advice along the customary lines by a juvenile employment officer and one of the investigators. Subject to the parents' consent efforts were then made to find employment for both the tested and the control children along the suggested lines.

Contact was maintained with all the children both in the tested and in control group for a period of two years and data were obtained to show the number of posts each child held during this period; the duration of the different posts; the reasons for leaving posts; the views of the employers as to the efficiency of the children and the opinions of the children themselves as to the suitability of the posts. Taking each of these criteria separately into consideration common evidence was found to show that children whose vocational guidance was determined by a scientific procedure, including the application of tests, and who entered posts in accordance with the guidance given, were more satisfactorily placed in employment than children who were given guidance after the scientific procedure but who did not follow the advice given; and were also more satisfactorily placed than children in the control group who were given advice without the aid of tests and the other special procedure.

The results of this small experiment confirmed the results of the experiment in London conducted by the National Institute of Industrial Psychology, and the Birmingham Education Committee decided to continue their research by conducting an enquiry on a much larger scale.

In the earlier experiment the application of all the tests and all the other special work, apart from the medical examinations, was undertaken by the two investigators. It was realized that the application of tests to a much larger group of children selected from many schools could not be undertaken without additional help. Indeed, an important part of the research was to investigate the possibility of putting the scientific procedure into general use.

It was, therefore, decided to enlist the co-operation of teachers who had been taking a considerable interest in the investigations and of other members of the staff of the Juvenile Employment Department. It was appreciated that before these teachers and officers could take a share in the work, they should receive training in the special technique required. Comprehensive training courses, each part-time and extending over an academic year, were organized and conducted by the two investigators and at the conclusion of each course a theoretical and practical examination was arranged by the National Institute of Industrial Psychology. Each teacher and juvenile employment officer who took part in the investigations had succeeded in obtaining a certificate stating that he or she had received the requisite training and was competent to undertake the work.

Five training courses were held in connection with this larger investigation, and certificates were awarded to 74 teachers and 10 juvenile employment officers. At the conclusion of each course, the teachers began work in their own schools. The procedure adopted was for each teacher to be responsible, under the direction of the investigators, for testing the children at his school and for collecting all the required information. Before the choice of employment conference, the head teacher, the teacher responsible for the testing, the appropriate juvenile employment officer and the investigators met and considered all the pertinent data and decided upon the vocational guidance to be given. This guidance was later passed to the child and the parent by the juvenile employment officer at the choice of employment conference. In general, the plan of this larger investigation followed the plan of the previous enquiry but there were certain variations in order to judge the relative value of the medical report and of the home visit.

In the earlier experiment all the children were followed-up for a period of two years. It was hoped in this larger experiment to extend the follow-up period for all children to four years, but unfortunately the Second World War in 1939 made it increasingly difficult to continue the investigations. However, 1,639 children were followed-up for two years and 608 for four years.

The analysis of the data followed the earlier plan. The special variants (the medical examination and the home visit) were found to be of value but they did not appreciably affect the statistical data. As in the earlier experiment the children were divided into four groups, namely:

Group A: Tested children in "accordance" posts (that is, in posts in accordance with the conclusions reached by the advisers)
Group B: Tested children in "non-accordance" posts
Group C: Control children in "accordance" posts
Group D: Control children in "non-accordance" posts.

The evidence collected is set out in considerable detail in the published reports and is even more convincing than that obtained earlier. From whatever point of view the evidence was studied the children in the tested group who followed the advice given to them were more satisfactorily placed in employment than the children in any of the three other groups.

A special examination was made of the sequence of transference between posts. In the tested group 77 per cent, and in the control group 64 per cent, began their careers in posts in accordance with the guidance that had been given to them. The tested children showed a preference for changing from non-accordance to accordance posts, and at the end of the two-year period 89 per cent of these children were in accordance posts. The control children showed a trend in the opposite direction, and at the end of two years only 44 per cent of them were in accordance posts.

The same distinctive trends were seen in the four-year follow-up period. 80 per cent of the children with whom contact was maintained for four years began their careers in accordance posts, and at the end of the period 95 per cent were in accordance posts. Of the control children 63 per cent first entered accordance posts, but at the end of four years only 42 per cent were in such posts.

The published report states that this larger enquiry produced definite evidence for the following statements:

(*a*) That the adoption of scientific methods in vocational guidance improves very considerably the advice that can be given to children leaving school. Children given vocational guidance by these methods and who follow the advice are much more happily placed in employment, are more permanently settled, and are of greater value to their employers than children who are specially guided but who do not follow the advice and also than children who are given vocational guidance in the usual way.

(*b*) That it is possible to give scientific vocational guidance to all children leaving school provided there are available on the staffs of all schools trained teachers competent to apply psychological tests and to collect the required data, and trained juvenile employment officers competent to interpret the results and to give appropriate vocational guidance to the children.

Arising from these statements, the investigators made certain recommendations for future procedure, but before dealing with these I must refer to other research work which the investigators were undertaking simultaneously with the vocational guidance enquiries and covering which the other three reports have been published. The object of this research was to ascertain the practical value of a series of tests for selecting boys for those branches of the engineering trades requiring skilled apprentices.

In the first instance, certain tests were given to a group of apprentices at the Central Technical College in order to assess their validity, and the tests were then given to boys leaving a technical school in order to compare the ranking of the boys in engineering ability as shown by the tests with the ranking given by the school instructors. It was found that by use of the tests it was possible to arrange boys in their order of engineering ability with an 80 per cent agreement with the order given by the school instructors. Furthermore, it was shown that temperamental factors were of importance and should not be ignored in selecting boys as skilled apprentices.

The research was continued by giving the tests to the boys on admission to the technical school and comparing the results with the order of the boys in the entrance examination to the school (this examination being of the academic type) and also with the order of success of the boys in engineering subjects at the end of the two-year course. The evidence produced by this lengthy and comprehensive enquiry showed that: (1) the tests were more satisfactory than the academic entrance examination in selecting boys suitable for engineering training; and (2) it was possible to predict with considerable confidence from a boy's test results his success at the end of the two years' engineering course. The investigations were continued by following-up the careers of the boys after leaving the technical school, and again it was found that the tests given on entrance to the school were satisfactory in predicting which boys could with success enter engin eering work.

During the course of these investigations the same series of tests was also given to groups of boys of 14 years of age and 16 years of age at a grammar school and at a commercial school, in order to obtain information on the performance of boys of comparable ages who were receiving different types of education. One immediate result of these investigations was that the Birmingham Education Committee amended the entrance examination to the technical schools by the inclusion of four special aptitude tests, and this procedure has been continued during the last fifteen years.

The third vocational guidance report, to which I have already referred, was published very shortly after the passing of the Education Act of 1944; and it was natural that, in making the recommendations for the future development of vocational guidance which were included in the report, the investigators should have had in mind the plan of educational development envisaged in the Act. Taking account particularly of the requirement that Local Education Authorities should provide in their areas sufficient secondary school accommodation, and "the schools available for an area shall not be deemed to be sufficient unless they are sufficient in number, character and equipment to afford for all pupils opportunities for education offering such variety of instruction and training as may be desirable in view of their *different ages, abilities and aptitudes*, and of the different periods for which they may be expected to remain at school, including practical *instruction and training appropriate to their respective needs*", the investigators made the following recommendations:

(1) That steps should be taken to arrange training courses for selected teachers in secondary schools with a view to ensuring that there shall be on the staff of each school at least one teacher competent to apply psychological tests and trained in the collection of relevant data. Arrangements should also be made to give the necessary training to all juvenile employment officers.

(2) That these specially trained teachers should work for this purpose in close co-operation with an officer who is specially qualified to supervise the selection, application and interpretation of psychological tests and methods. These teachers should be required to give selected tests at appropriate stages in each child's school life, and to record the data on cumulative record cards with other information regarding the child's progress, attainments and history.

(3) That these records should be used from time to time to enable decisions to be reached as to the course of instruction each child should receive.

(4) That towards the end of the child's school life the juvenile employment officer should study these records, co-operate with the head and with the trained teacher and give vocational guidance.

The Birmingham Education Committee began their research work into the use of vocational tests with the object of improving their methods of giving vocational guidance to children leaving school, but during the course of the investigations it has been made clear that *vocational* guidance cannot easily, and indeed should not, be separated from *educational* guidance. When a child is directed into an educational stream of a particular type, it is inevitable that there should be a bias in that direction, and the decision made may well influence his vocational choice later and may indeed affect his whole career. It is not within my province to discuss secondary school organization, but certain questions naturally arise as a result of all this research work. Local Education Authorities and educationists generally are persevering with the development and the increased use of the "cumulative" school report but the practice continues of "creaming off" the more intelligent children at the age of eleven for a grammar school course. Are we satisfied that this procedure is in the best interests of all children? Additional secondary technical school accommodation is certainly being provided as well as additional grammar school accommodation, but improved methods must be found for assessing the abilities and aptitudes of the children and for using these assessments in school organization. The evidence collected during the course of these investigations must be of considerable help in this work. There can be no doubt that the cumulative school report completed by specially trained teachers must be of increasing importance.

And what of *vocational* guidance? Within recent years a real effort has been made to develop a comprehensive National Youth Employment Service; and the Employment and Training Act of 1948 makes provision for all schools to be required to furnish, to the Youth Employment Service, particulars relating to the health, ability, educational attainments and aptitudes of all children leaving school so that all children may be given adequate advice and assistance. The majority of Local Education Authorities have recognized that the Employment and Training Act is a natural development of the Education Act of 1944 and are including vocational guidance and youth employment administration as an integral part of their educational reconstruction.

When the Birmingham Education Committee began their research work twenty-five years ago the investigations, as I have shown, involved the extensive use of psychological tests. Their experience and the experience of other investigators in this field have shown that while valuable assessments in certain directions can be obtained by the use of tests, what is really needed is a comprehensive analytical study of each child. Some sixteen years ago, the school report drawn up for the Birmingham experiments was divided into seven sections, covering family circumstances, physical make-up, intelligence, special aptitudes, attainments, personal trends and interests. These seven headings have now been adopted on a national basis. It must, of course, be kept in mind that this analytical study of the child is only the first part of a vocational guidance plan. In a complementary way, we must also have a study of all occupations conducted in the same analytical manner, following the same seven-point plan. Industrial surveys have been an important part of the work of the youth employment officers for some years and every effort is being made to obtain the information needed. This industrial study must go on continuously and must always be regarded as part of the day-to-day work of a youth employment office.

The Birmingham Education Committee gave their general approval to the four recommendations contained in the final report, to which I have referred, and the plan suggested in those recommendations is now being followed in the Birmingham schools. Teachers' training courses are now being held regularly. Already some sixty teachers have been trained in this way during the last year or two and it is the intention of the Committee to continue until at least one specially qualified teacher is on the staff of every secondary school in the city. These teachers become responsible for the collection in their schools of all the data required concerning the children. They complete the cumulative records for the boys and girls, which will, it is hoped, be increasingly used in the school for school purposes. During the last year of school life the youth employment officers, who are, of course, also specially trained, will consult with the trained teachers and give vocational guidance.

I have spoken almost entirely of the work that has been proceeding during twenty-five years in Birmingham, but as I have said the evidence obtained in Birmingham has confirmed evidence obtained elsewhere. I have spoken of the development of the Youth Employment Service in Birmingham, but you will understand that developments are proceeding along very similar lines in other areas. Other Local Education Authorities are also arranging training courses for teachers and are giving vocational guidance to school leavers on a scientific basis following very closely the plan which I have outlined. I venture to think that there will be general agreement that the Birmingham Education Committee showed very great initiative and foresight and that the investigations which have steadily proceeded during twenty-five years have to some degree had their influence on national developments.

Local Education Authorities are entrusted with a great responsibility—the task of providing instruction and training suitable for the differing ages, abilities and aptitudes of all children. If they are to perform this duty efficiently and to the utmost benefit of all the children in their care—as, of course, they are determined to do—it is important that no steps which assist towards a better understanding of the children and a more exact assessment of their potential capabilities should be omitted. Much investigation and research still remain to be done and many are engaged on this work. But it is equally important that all this work in the schools should be closely associated with the Youth Employment Service which is now being developed on national and scientific lines. Educational guidance and vocational guidance cannot be dealt with separately. The one is the basis of the other. Every child leaving school must be given the best advice and guidance that is possible, and this advice and guidance can only be of real value if the preparatory work is tackled in a systematic and scientific manner.

REFERENCES

1. ALLEN, E. P., and SMITH, P. (1932) *The Value of Vocational Tests as Aids to Choice of Employment*. Birmingham Education Committee.
2. HUNT, E. P., and SMITH, P. (1940) *The Value of Vocational Tests as Aids to Choice of Employment*. Second Report of Research. Birmingham Education Committee.
3. HUNT, E. P., and SMITH, P. (1944) *The Value of Vocational Tests as Aids to Choice of Employment*. Final Report of Research. Birmingham Education Committee.
4. ALLEN, E. P., and SMITH, P. (1931) *Selection of Skilled Apprentices for the Engineering Trades*. Birmingham Education Committee.
5. ALLEN, E. P., and SMITH, P. (1934) *Selection of Skilled Apprentices for the Engineering Trades*. Second Report of Research. Birmingham Education Committee.
6. ALLEN, E. P., and SMITH, P. (1939) *Selection of Skilled Apprentices for the Engineering Trades*. Third Report of Research. Birmingham Education Committee.

27. The Seven Point Plan

ALEC RODGER

MANY of us are often faced with the task of summing up the employment potentialities of other people. Frequently, perhaps, we have to consider the suitability of a candidate for a certain vacancy. Occasionally, may be, we have to give somebody advice about his career. The Seven-Point Plan is meant to help us to do such jobs as these in a competent fashion. It aims at providing us with a simple but scientifically-defensible assessment "system".

The plan consists of a series of questions gathered together under seven headings. It should be regarded as a short list of items that seem to deserve consideration in any comprehensive investigation of a person's occupational assets and liabilities. As we shall see later, the items have been chosen for their general usefulness.

Before the reader studies the plan's headings and questions in detail he should have his attention drawn to some of the limitations of the scheme as a whole, and to certain other relevant matters.

SOME OF ITS LIMITATIONS

First let us note that the plan is not put forward as the only reasonable assessment system for employment purposes. It is not even claimed that it is an exceptionally good one. There are others with similar aims and similar contents, including the schedule produced by Sir Cyril Burt[(1)] from which the present scheme was derived in the years between the wars. But the Seven-Point Plan seems to have an advantage over most others, in that experience has shown it to be a popular "utility" article. There is evidence that it is being used for many assessment purposes by many people in many places.[(2, 3, 4)]

Secondly, we must not let the apparent tidiness of the plan tempt us into imagining that the device of splitting a person's attributes and circumstances into seven "segments" is anything better than a rather regrettable

(*The Seven Point Plan*, N.I.I.P. Paper No. 1, was written by Professor Alec Rodger and is published by the National Institute of Industrial Psychology, 14 Welbeck Street, London, W.1., with whose permission it is reproduced.)

necessity. The divisions we make are for convenience. We must freely admit that a shortcoming of any scheme of this sort is to be found in the fact that it may encourage us to think of an individual as a mere bundle of "qualities". Of course, this is not an argument for disdaining the use of such a plan: it is an argument for using it sensibly.

Nor, thirdly, must we allow its cross-sectional pattern to blind us, even momentarily, to the fact that everyone's attributes and circumstances are continuously changing. It is particularly important that we should remember this when we are summing up young workers and school-leavers. Accordingly, we must do our best, despite the difficulty of the task, to see them not only as they are now but also as they have been in the past. In no other way can we judge the trends of their development; and in all employment interviewing the appreciation of such trends is necessary, for the simple reason that our problem is essentially one of forecasting.

Fourthly, we must recognise that neither the Seven-Point Plan nor any other is likely to turn a bad judge of people into a good one. Thoughtful and frequent use of it may make him less bad than he was before, but beyond that it cannot be expected to take him. On the other hand, although it may seem of doubtful value to a person who is already a good judge, possibly even he may gain a little from occasional reflection on its contents. They may perhaps remind him of the danger of neglecting what is more important than he sometimes imagines, or of emphasising things that may not really matter very much.

THE CASE FOR NOT CHANGING IT YET

These and other limitations of the plan have led some users of it to suggest changes—the addition of a question here, the omission of one there, the alteration of the wording of several, and perhaps even the recasting of the whole scheme. A number of their proposals seem to have had considerable merit. The system as it stands is admittedly far from perfect, even within its acknowledged limitations, and it would be surprising if valuable critical and constructive comments were not sometimes made about it. But the potential improver of the plan must realise that changes—piecemeal, local, temporary changes particularly—carry important disadvantages as well as possible advantages.

In the first place, it is only by close adherence to the plan as it stands that we can benefit properly from the experience of other people who use it. Let us consider the use of the system in the investigation of the "requirements" of occupations. Such investigation is needed in both personnel selection and vocational guidance, for both involve the matching of people and work. Now, if the matching is to be done satisfactorily, the requirements of an occupation must be described in the same terms as the attributes of the people who are being considered for it. Suppose, then, that we privately alter the Seven-Point Plan: what happens? The chief result is that we are unable to make full use of information about occupational requirements that has been collected by others who have adopted the scheme in its existing form.

But there is a more fundamental—and more technical—reason for leaving the plan alone. It springs from the fact that our object in devising an arrangement of this kind at all is to have at our disposal a generally-useful system based on scientific enquiry into the attributes and circumstances that most commonly influence occupational success and failure. Indeed, we are seeking to compile a short-list of "influences" (or "conditions", or "determinants") which, in our personnel selection and vocational guidance activities particularly, we shall neglect at our peril, because thorough enquiry has shown them to be the most generally important.

This means that our listed items in our Seven-Point Plan should conform to four criteria. (1) They should be relevant, in that they should pin-point influences commonly and demonstrably connected with occupational success and failure. (2) They should be independent, in that they should be sufficiently separable from one another to enable us to avoid overlapping assessments that would be wasteful. (3) They should be assessable in the circumstances in which the assessments have usually to be made. (4) They should be few enough to keep the risk of hasty, superficial judgment to a minimum, but numerous enough to cover the ground adequately.

It follows from this that what is needed for the improvement of the plan is not private tinkering but a series of substantial researches directed to four ends. First must come the clarification of our ideas about the nature of occupational success and failure. Secondly, we must identify, according to these ideas, groups of successes and failures in occupations of different types and levels. Thirdly, there must be a detailed comparative study of these groups of successes and failures, which will take account of all manner of information about their attributes and circumstances, and will "quantify" it appropriately, in order to make it amenable to statistical treatment. Fourthly will come the statistical analysis of the data thus obtained, which will have the object of isolating the chief influences we are looking for, and learning how to describe and assess them in such a way that we shall be better able than we are now to forecast success and failure.

However, it is not inconsistent with this argument to say that there can be no objection to the addition of items to the standard list, where this seems desirable for special purposes. For example, in the use of the plan in the selection of management trainees, there may be a case for adding to the interests and disposition sections. What should be avoided is the changing or omission of existing items, and provided this need is observed others can be put in. Even if the new ones make an attempt to break an existing item into component parts, they can reasonably be added, provided that the parent item remains.

CAUTIONS TO BE OBSERVED IN THE USE OF THE PLAN

There are three cautions to be observed in the use of the plan. First, it must be understood that the order in which the headings appear is not meant to carry any implications whatever about the order of their importance. The weight to be attached to a particular heading, or to a particular item under a heading, will depend to a considerable extent on the nature of the employment or training for which an applicant is being considered, and on the nature of the other information assembled about him.

Secondly, it is not intended that any attempt should be made to deal with the seven sections of the plan in the order in which they appear on the paper. We must be ready to take our facts, and to form our opinions, as opportunity offers, after the manner of a sorter in a post office. We must do our mental pigeon-holing, with our seven "boxes" in front of us, while we are interviewing, while we are studying application forms, reports and testimonials while we are talking to people who know the applicant, and indeed at any other convenient time.

Thirdly, it must be realised that the questions under the seven headings are not meant to be put directly to the applicant by his assessor. They are questions for the assessor to ask himself about the applicant. It is true that some of them can be put directly in some cases, but others cannot and should not. In general, they are to be regarded as queries for the guidance of the questioner. It is safe to say incidentally that the questioner who, in the interview situation, keeps them all firmly in mind is not likely to be greatly troubled by the unmethodical assessor's problem: What shall I ask him next?

HOMUNCULUS OLDFIELDIANUS

An idea of substantial value to the user of the plan, both as a supplement to it and as a reminder of the second and third limitations already noted, has been outlined by Oldfield.[5] "The interviewer after the interview (and in general any person after an encounter with another) possesses and carries about with him a kind of homunculuslike representation of the candidate. This is essentially a 'working model', a 'living image'; and when occasion demands it can, so to speak, be taken out of its box and be made to perform. It is by placing this creature in imagined circumstances, and watching its behaviour, that the interviewer is enabled to make predictions about the candidate's probable behaviour in those circumstances."

He adds: "The homunculus ... is essentially a 'going concern' ... (It) is not constructed as a corpse in the first instance, and then infused with the breath of life." Nevertheless, as Wilson[6] has indicated, in the building up of his working model the assessor can very profitably employ headings of the sort used in the Seven-Point Plan. Oldfield's notion is, of course, a useful extension of the thought in many people's minds when they say, for example,

I can't see him doing that, or, I can easily picture him being very good at so-and-so.

CRUCIAL ACTIVITIES AND SITUATIONS

We can go even farther, and argue[7, 8] that in assembling our knowledge of an occupation for personnel selection or vocational guidance purposes we should aim primarily at having at our disposal, in our mind's eye, a series of pictures of the activities and situations involved in that occupation. As we construct our working model of the applicant with the aid of the Seven-Point Plan, we can pitch it into one activity after another, and one situation after another, and observe its performance. And if we accept what has already been said in this pamphlet about the importance of studying successes and failures, we shall, in fashioning our pictures, pay special attention to the activities and situations that appear to be crucial, in that those who fail in them are likely to become (as the Americans say) "separated" from the occupation.[9, 10]

There are, of course, some differences to be observed in the application of this notion to a personnel selection problem and its application to vocational guidance. For instance, in dealing with the former we may be able to make use of a set of fairly specific occupational "pictures," derived from a detailed study of the work which will in fact have to be done by the chosen applicant. In dealing with the latter, at least in the early stages of the formulation of our advice, we shall have to think, for example, not of a particular clerical post but of work of a clerical "type".

This is one of the main reasons why the problems of the vocational adviser are often trickier than those of the personnel selector. Associated with it is the much greater difficulty the vocational adviser experiences in making allowance for his inability to judge how well a person will "fit in" with the people with whom he will in fact have to work. But once again we have to note that the snags created by unknown factors of this kind do not provide us with an excuse for being casual about the relatively known factors which can be taken into account.

THE SEVEN POINTS

Now let us consider the seven headings, one by one, and the questions that go with them, bearing in mind the explanations and cautions already given. We shall, where it is appropriate, look not only at the interpretations which are meant to be placed on the words used, but also at the occupational relevance of the items they describe and at some main source of information about them. We may note in passing that the plan as a whole is based roughly on a series of old-fashioned dichotomies familiar to psychologists. There is a primary split between external influences (or conditions, or determinants) on which an individual's occupational success may depend, and influences that can be regarded as internal, as personal, as belonging to him, as part of his equipment. The former are here called his circumstances, the latter his attributes. His attributes (or characteristics, or qualities) are split into the mainly physical and the mainly psychological; the psychological into the mainly cognitive and the mainly non-cognitive; and these two into the natural and the acquired. We must, of course, recognise that schematisation of this sort has many limitations, and that both practical and theoretical objections can be raised to it: it has, however, the inestimable scientific advantage of encouraging observance of the principle of parsimony, and for that reason we need not hesitate to adopt it.

1. Physical Make-up

Has he any defects of health or physique that may be of occupational importance? The sooner this question is dealt with the better, because the answer to it may make further consideration of a person's suitability for a particular vacancy, or type of work, a waste of time. But there are three points to be noted. First, satisfactory conclusions about the occupational implications of a poor health record, or of a physical defect or disability, cannot usually be reached without medical aid of a properly informed kind. Secondly, the difficulties experienced in occupational life by people handicapped in health or physique are frequently far less serious than is commonly imagined, even by doctors and potential employers. It is indeed surprising what a man with one hand or arm or leg can do with suitable tools and training and a determination not to be defeated. Thirdly, it must be realised that many of the occupational restrictions imposed on people with defects of health or physique arise, not so much from the impossibility of their meeting the demands of the work contemplated for them, as from the unwillingness of employers to take on workers who might be doubtful superannuation "risks", or who might prove unacceptable to those with whom they would have to work.

How agreeable are his appearance, his bearing and his speech? These quasi-physical attributes are more conveniently housed under this heading than anywhere else. Their importance is generally greatest in occupations that involve frequent direct contact with people—for example, customers or clients—on whose favourable attitude the future of the enterprise largely depends. It is intended that attention should be given primarily to what may be regarded as the more enduring aspects of the trio. That is, for example, a remediable carelessness or eccentricity of dress is to be given less weight, in the assessment of appearance, than markedly unprepossessing physique or lack of "good looks". In the assessment of bearing, consideration is to be given to smartness and vigour rather than to such characteristics as friendliness, which belong to the section on disposition. In the assessment of speech, attention should be devoted to its physical quality, not to its fluency, which belongs to the section on special aptitudes. The separation of judgments of these three attributes is sometimes best achieved through questions of the kind: What would I think of his occupational worth, if all the knowledge I had of him had been gained from a glance at a photograph, or from passing him in the street, or from hearing him on the telephone?

Here we may note that the assessment of these and other characteristics raises the question: What are we to take as "the average" for appearance, for bearing, for speech, and the rest? In personnel selection, it is sometimes convenient to take the average for applicants who present themselves for consideration. In vocational guidance, however, the most suitable average is often the average for people of that age, sex and type of education. Thus, on a five-step rating scale used to record judgments of the appearance of girls leaving secondary grammar schools at the age of sixteen, A might conveniently represent membership of the top ten per cent; B, of the next twenty per cent; C, of the middle forty per cent; D, of the next twenty per cent; and E, of the bottom ten per cent of that particular group.

On this basis, when we say that X is of average appearance, we mean that we would place him somewhere in the middle forty per cent of the group with which we are comparing him. An A assessment would mean that we would put him in the top ten per cent, a B assessment that we consider him to belong to the sub-group that comprise the next twenty per cent. Let us note that there is nothing right or wrong about such definitions of standards: it is a matter of convention. It is nevertheless important, for sound assessments on scales of this sort demand close adherence to whatever conventions are agreed upon. Let us note also that such rating scales are not to be regarded as "tests" that produce jugdments for us: they are merely devices for recording judgments.

2. *Attainments*

What type of education has he had? How well has he done educationally? Did he finish his schooling at a secondary grammar, secondary technical or secondary modern school, or somewhere else? What evidence is there of the general standard of his scholastic achievements, compared with the average we have agreed to adopt? If he has taken the General Certificate of Education, or a School or Higher School Certificate, what indication do the results give of the general and specific nature and quality of his attainments, account being taken of the age at which he obtained them, and of any examination failures? What appear to be the school subjects in which he was stronger than other people, weaker than other people? Whether his actual levels were high or low, compared with those of others, what were his best and worst subjects? Did he win any scholarships or prizes? Did he display any occupationally ominous weaknesses in, for example, English, mathematics or science? If he has had any further education, at a university or elsewhere, what has been its nature, and how well has he done in it?

These are some of the most useful questions a selector or adviser can ask himself about an applicant's educational attainments. Obviously, where he can conveniently do so, it is desirable for him to seek his evidence in part from other people—especially teachers or parents—who should be able to provide it. There are, however, two things to be noted. First, the amount of detail required will vary according to the nature of the work or training under consideration, and according to the keenness of the competition for it. Secondly, under this same heading should be gathered information about anything else the applicant has accomplished during the period of his ordinary schooling, and indeed later, provided it does not overlap wastefully with information collected in answer to the next question on the list. His membership of teams, clubs, societies, pre-Service organisations and the like should be considered; and his positions of authority and responsibility in them—and in the school itself, as a prefect, may be—should be taken into account. So should his achievements of other kinds, whether or not they have involved membership of a group, and whether or not they have been directly concerned with his school life. In short, this question about his attainments should not be interpreted in a narrow classroom sense. It should yield all sorts of information about what he has learned and accomplished already outside the occupational field.

What occupational training and experience has he had already? How well has he done occupationally? It is important to deal here with all kinds of occupational training, from high-grade to low-grade, from theoretical to practical, from full-time to part-time, from residential to postal; and with all kinds of occupational experience. The assessor should constantly have in mind the question, What clues can I find in this individual's occupational record that will help me to make a really satisfactory prediction of his suitability for the work I have in mind for him? What does he know? What does he not know that he should know by now? What has he done? What has he not done that he should have done by now? Clearly, if the assessor is to aim at answering questions like these, he cannot be content with surface enquiries about the names of the various jobs his applicant has had, how much pay he received in them, how long he had them, and why he left. These are not unimportant, but they provide a starting-place only.

Three other points should be noted. First, although reports and testimonials sometimes have their uses in the assessment of occupational training and experience, they so often err on the side of sketchiness, leniency and equivocation that they cannot usually be regarded as of great help. However, their deficiencies can frequently be made good to an appreciable extent by the applicant himself, through careful questioning of the kind advocated above: that is, through well-conducted enquiry into what exactly he had to do in his various jobs, how he heard about them, how he was selected and trained for them (and by whom), what he found hard about them, what he disliked about them, what complaints he and his employers made about each other, to whom he was responsible, who took over his work when he was away, what kind of promotion or transfer had come to the people he replaced or worked with, and so on.

Secondly, in the course of such an enquiry much evidence can be accumulated on matters arising under most of the other headings of the Seven-Point Plan. Indeed, there is often a good deal to be said for anchoring the whole assessment procedure to the investigation of attainments, to the study of knowledge already gained and skills already acquired, educationally, occupationally and in other ways; and to aim at gathering incidentally the needed information on the other points. Thirdly, it is evident that an assessor's competence in handling his exploration of his applicant's attainments will depend to a great extent on his own knowledge of the educational and occupational fields, and of common leisure activities. He cannot hope to acquire this without well-directed effort along a variety of paths.

3. General Intelligence

How much general intelligence can he display? Many faulty forecasts by selectors and advisers are traceable to failure to distinguish between a person's attainments, which show his knowledge and skill, and his general intelligence, which is his fundamental general intellectual capacity[11, 12]. It is true that the distinction is easier to make in theory than in practice, and that it is difficult to assess an individual's general intelligence except by seeing what he does with it; but this does not mean that we are reduced to judging it merely by a survey of his attainments, though this is what is often done. Rather, we must estimate it by what he manages to do with it when it is fully stretched.

The object of a general intelligence test—whether it is a group test or an individual test, whether it is verbal or non-verbal—is to provide suitable conditions for obtaining such an estimate. Carefully devised problems are presented in a carefully devised way, and the applicant's competence in tackling them is compared with the competence displayed by others in the same tasks presented in a similar way. The value of such tests for many selection and guidance purposes is now beyond dispute, except among the ignorant. There is, therefore, justification for their use in the occupational field, provided they are employed by people who are appropriately informed about the principles involved and the procedures entailed.

There are, of course, other ways of assessing a person's general intelligence—for example, by keeping an eye open for the peaks in the record of his educational achievements, not least in mathematics and classics—but they are on the whole inferior. Nobody with sense would claim infallibility for general intelligence test results, but a good test used properly is likely to produce far fewer and far less serious mistakes than any other method of assessing fundamental general intellectual capacity. A "good" test of general intelligence is, from the standpoint of the personnel selector and vocational adviser, one that gives a better prediction of maximum learning performance, over a wide range of activity and over a long period of time, than some other assessment procedure that might have to be used in its place.

How much general intelligence does he ordinarily display? In everyday life we recognise the fact that some people do not often use their general intelligence to the best advantage. We say, So-and-so has a good head, but he doesn't use it; or, conversely, He's not very bright, but he makes admirable use of what brains he's got. The distinction indicated by such remarks is sound and important: we must differentiate between the ceiling of a person's general intelligence and the level at which he commonly employs it, for he may tend to use it either effectively or ineffectively.

Unfortunately, tests of general intelligence do not help us here, unless they are badly given and show what a person has done in them in poorly regulated conditions rather than what he is capable of doing in conditions specially contrived to stretch him to the full(13). We must instead depend mainly on interview estimates based on a careful study of discrepancies between his attainments, his results in general intelligence tests properly given, and the nature, range and depth of his interests; and on our appreciation of the maturity of his judgments, the realism of his aims, the precision with which he lights on main issues in a discussion, and the shrewdness with which he makes generalisations. Wilson's paper(6) offers useful comments on this problem.

4. Special Aptitudes

Has he any marked mechanical aptitude, manual dexterity, facility in the use of words of figures, talent for drawing or music? When we say that a person has a high degree of mechanical aptitude, or mechanical "sense", we do not mean simply that he is better than most people at understanding mechanical things. He may be superior in this respect to many others, not because he has more mechanical aptitude, but because he has more general intelligence, or because he has had more opportunities for becoming interested in mechanical problems and learning how to tackle them. In fact, "special aptitude", as we use the term here, does not mean "unusual competence", which should be assessed under the attainments heading of the plan: it means, rather, "specialised capacity". It is, indeed, convenient to regard all special aptitudes as talents supplementary to general intelligence in certain restricted fields: they are available to "help" the general capacity when material of a particular kind—mechanical, manual, words, figures, drawing, music—is being handled. They are rather like auxiliary engines, whose usefulness really depends on the extent to which the main engine is powerful and effective. Where the main engine is good, the scope for the use of auxiliaries is poor.

This auxiliary role of special aptitudes is not widely appreciated. In consequence, they tend to be given more prominence than they deserve. Broadly, we are entitled to say that their occupational value is greatest in a person whose other assets are low; and their occupational importance on the whole is not comparable with the importance of general intelligence. We can rarely, if ever, claim that a certain special aptitude is "needed" in an occupation. All we can say, usually, is that *if*, in that occupation, special competence is required in understanding mechanical things, in manipulative operations, in using words, in handling figures, in drawing or in music, *then* the possession of relevant special aptitudes will help to make up deficiencies of other kinds, especially in general intelligence.

It should be noted that mechanical aptitude is most satisfactorily regarded as a specialised capacity which helps in the solution of practical-constructional problems, whether or not they are manifestly "mechanical" in nature. Manual dexterity is a separate capacity, or cluster of capactities, which is displayed in smooth and well-timed manipulation. Facility with words may find expression in either speech or writing. Facility with figures is displayed in straightforward figurework rather than in advanced mathematics, success in which is more closely related to general intelligence. Talent for drawing is shown in freehand rather than in machine drawing. Musical talent may be evident in critical appreciation as much as in executive performance.

Tests for special aptitudes abound. The most useful are for mechanical aptitude, and for facilities with words and figures; but even these are on the whole of far less value, in guidance and selection, than tests of general intelligence coupled with satisfactory assessments of attainments and interests. But whether or not he is using tests in his enquiries, the assessor should always remember that mere competence in a special field—mechanical, manual, words, figures, drawing, music, all these particularly—is not a necessary sign of the presence of a special aptitude. The competence may have other origins. Therefore, he must repeatedly ask himself the question, Is this person better at these things than most people of similar age, similar general intelligence, similar interest, similar opportunities? Only if the answer has to be, Yes, can he reasonably argue for the existence of a special aptitude.

5. *Interests*

To what extent are his interests intellectual? practical-constructional? physically-active? social? artistic? One of the commonest mistakes made in selection and guidance is to jump from a person's statement that he is interested in a thing to the conclusion that he will be good at it. He may be: he may not. The flaws in such an argument are several. In the first place, his declared interests may not tally with the interests shown by his actual behaviour. Secondly, even his genuine enthusiasms—say, for entry to a particular occupation—may be rooted in false or inadequate ideas. Thirdly, even interests that are both genuine and based on sound ideas may prove to be too short-lived to be of practical use. Fourthly, an interest may be compensatory, and indicative of a refusal to admit lack of competence[14]: it is as if someone were to say, People tell me I'm no good at this, but I'll show them! Anyway, even if a person is both good at a certain activity and interested in it, and *could* do it for a living, we are not bound to conclude that he *should*. He may be wise to keep it as a leisure pursuit, particularly if it does not easily fit in with other accomplishments and interests he might cultivate occupationally.

Despite these pitfalls, and many more, it is to his interests that we must look for indications of the directions in which his other attributes might best be employed. How shall we list them for systematic study? Should we take some catalogue of basic interests, of the kind often labelled "instincts", and try to assess the strength of such allegedly inborn characteristics as assertiveness, gregariousness, and curiosity? Or should we adopt some other list of "drives", of a seemingly more relevant kind, such as those towards security, independence, doing good, making money, being a centre of attraction, variety, and travel? The latter of these alternatives would be the preferable, but in practice neither would be satisfactory for general—as against, specific—purposes, because what we need, at least to start with, is a "utility" list.

The method employed here is to classify interests according to a provisional fivefold classification of occupation intended for use with the Seven-Point Plan. This groups occupations into (1) those involving mainly intellectual ("mental") processes, such as clerical work; (2) those of a mainly practical-constructional sort, such as engineering; (3) those of a mainly physically-active sort, such as farming; (4) those involving, essentially, some relationship with other people, such as salesmanship; and (5) those of a mainly artistic kind.

With this classification to guide us, our problem becomes largely one of investigating a person's interests—his preferred activities—to discover those that are likely to persist, whatever their origins may be; and of sorting them out according to their relevance to the main types of work available. It lays no restrictions on the range or depth or machinery of our enquiries, which can be suited to the circumstances in which our assessment has to be made: nor is it incompatible with the use of a supplementary list of "drives" such as that given above.

6. Disposition

How acceptable does he make himself to other people? Does he influence others? Is he steady and dependable? Is he self-reliant? Here we consider certain attributes frequently grouped under such headings as personality, temperament, and character. We have expressly avoided these words, because of the diversity and incompatibility of the interpretations often placed upon them, and their consequent tendency to make for confusion rather than clarity. The word "disposition" covers well enough most of the characteristics we need to take into account for this purpose. We do in fact speak of a person as having, for example, a cheerful or retiring or calm or managing disposition, when we mean that he shows a persisting inclination to behave in these ways in circumstances in which many people would behave otherwise.

The number of adjectives we might use for this purpose is, of course, very large;[(15)] but, as we have seen, for most selection and guidance procedures only a few can be chosen. The problem we face is, therefore, to decide on a short list of items of this kind that are relevant to the largest number of selection and guidance situations; that are sufficiently independent of one another to enable us to avoid the waste of time that would result if they turned out to be closely associated; and that are assessable with reasonable accuracy and consistency in the circumstances in which the assessments have usually to be made.

The four given here were listed at the end of an extensive study of the qualities of disposition most frequently taken into account by a group of experienced psychologists. For certain purposes—for example, the selection of management trainees—the list may need to be lengthened, or one or more of its items split into component parts; but it seems unlikely that any of them could safely be dropped from any assessment scheme that claimed to be comprehensive.

The first item of the four invites us to consider, How do other people take to him? How well does he "fit in"? Does he make a good member of a group? The second, Do others take notice of what he says or does? Do his opinions carry weight? Is he good at getting people to do what he would like them to do? The third, Is his behaviour fairly predictable? Is he the sort of person of whom we might confidently say, He wouldn't do a thing like that, or, conversely, You never know what he'll do next? Does he go for long-range objectives in a determined way? The fourth, Can he stand on his own feet? Does he work things out for himself, or does he have to have somebody beside him to tell him what to do next? Does he have to be watched all the time?

It will be noticed that we have avoided the use of abstract nouns commonly employed in the study of disposition. Some of these—for example, sociability and leadership—are of doubtful value because of their lack of definiteness; but all of them are dangerous, because they have a way of encouraging unwarranted generalisation from slender evidence. The questions we have used are so worded as to fasten our attention on available facts. With these four in mind we shall be fairly well equipped for most of our assessment tasks.

7. *Circumstances*

What are his domestic circumstances? What do the other members of the family do for a living? Are there any special openings available for him? So far we have been considering our applicant's personal attributes. Now we must take account of his circumstances; that is, his background and his opportunities. Practical difficulties in the way of our doing this are, of course, very often great. In personnel selection, enquiries on these matters are often regarded as irrelevant, and are resented. In vocational guidance they are similarly viewed by some people. Clearly, however, they are not irrelevant; for it is only by looking at a person's attributes in the light of his social and economic background, and in the light of the opportunities he has already had and is likely to have in the future, that we can hope to evaluate satisfactorily his past performance and make good forecasts about him.

The first question, on domestic circumstances, is essentially concerned with finance and mobility. What can he afford to do, if, for example, outlay on training or some other form of capital expenditure is needed; and how tied is he to a particular place? The second question, on the occupations of the rest of the family, is valuable, not only because it often provides a useful short-cut to relevant information about the economic, social and cultural background of the applicant, and therefore helps in the interpretation of data about his attainments, interests, and disposition; but also because in the guidance field, it may enable the adviser to steer clear of recommendations that might, for one reason or another, precipitate family conflicts. The third question, on special openings, is desirable in vocational guidance work, if only because very many people do in fact find employment in this way, regardless of other relevant considerations; and it would be foolish to ignore the fact.

A FINAL COMMENT

The aim of the Seven-Point Plan is to provide a rough sketch of a scientifically-defensible "system" for the assessment of occupational potentialities. It is intended for both personnel selection and vocational guidance purposes. It is hoped that any improvements that may be made in it, or any scheme that replaces it, will be based on solid research rather than on private fancy. Until that research has been done, those who use the plan at all in their day-to-day work will do best if they use it as it stands, and as extensively as possible.

REFERENCES

1. Burt, C. (1925) *The Young Delinquent*. London: University of London Press.
2. Fraser, J. M. (1950) *A Handbook of Employment Interviewing*. London: Macdonald and Evans.
3. Swinden, J. B. (1949) *Careers in Local Government*. London: National Association of Local Government Officers.
4. Heginbotham, H. (1951) *The Youth Employment Service*. London: Methuen.
5. Oldfield, R. C. (1941) *The Psychology of the Interview*. London: Methuen.

6. WILSON, N. A. B. (1945) Interviewing Candidates for Technical Appointments or Training. *Occupational Psychology*, October, **XIX**, 4.
7. RODGER, A. (1939) The Work of the Vocational Adviser, in *The Study of Society*, edited by F. C. Bartlett *et al*. London: Kegan Paul.
8. RODGER, A., and DAVIES, J. G. W. (1950) Vocational Guidance and Training, in *Chambers's Encyclopaedia*. London: Newnes.
9. RODGER, A. (1945) On the Selection of Business Executives. *Labour Management*, April–May.
10. FLANAGAN, J. C. (1949) Job Requirements, in *Current Trends in Industrial Psychology*. Pittsburgh: University of Pittsburgh Press.
11. KNIGHT, R. (1933) *Intelligence and Intelligence Tests*. London. Methuen.
12. BURT, C. (1935) *The Subnormal Mind*. London: Oxford University Press.
13. RODGER, A. (1939) The Use of Tests in Vocational Guidance. *Occupational Psychology*, July, **XIII**, 3.
14. DAVIES, J. G. W. (1939) The Place of Interests in Vocational Adjustment. *Occupational Psychology*, January, **XIII**, 1.
15. ALLPORT, G. W. (1937) *Personality*. New York: Henry Holt.

28. *An Occupational Classification for Use in Vocational Guidance*

R. M. McKenzie

INTRODUCTORY

Theoretically in giving vocational guidance one could assess the characteristics of a "client" and then match them one by one or as a pattern against those needed in various jobs to find the best fit. But jobs are so many, the characteristics of people so diverse, that this is impracticable. Our approach, on which a preliminary note has appeared elsewhere (McKenzie, 1952), is to select certain important characteristics of people actually in jobs, and on these base our grouping of jobs. Assessing the client in similar terms leads one to the relevant area of classification, so reducing choice to jobs that are definitely feasible for him. Within this range, choice will then depend on other factors, including such local considerations as which jobs are actually available in the district, what kind of workmates he will meet, idiosyncrasies of firms, and even of foremen, and so on.

Thus the first aim is to make a "Search List" which provides worthwhile job suggestions all within the client's range. It must be easy to use, it must narrow the search without blinkering the user, it must be psychologically sound. It must aim not at solutions, but suggestions. At the same time it should fit into or be easily adapted to existing vocational guidance methods so as to make the fullest use of all the material available.

CHOOSING CLASSIFICATORY "DIMENSIONS"

There is some agreement on characteristics that differentiate people in a way useful in guidance. Thus Rodger's seven main points (1939, p. 259; 1952), Bingham's nine points (1942, p. 94), and Super's "psychological" facts and "social" facts (1949, pp. 6–7), all cover much the same ground. The headings are roughly: intelligence, educational attainments, aptitudes, interests, personality traits and attitudes, general "circumstances" (resources, responsibilities, ambitions, family and cultural background, etc.), and physique. In selecting "dimensions" from these for our basic grouping of jobs, six criteria are suggested. Each "dimension" should:

(Reprinted, by permission of the editor and author, from *Occupational Psychology*, **28**, 1954, 108–117), the quarterly journal of the N.I.I.P., 14 Welbeck St., London, W.1.)

1. Have a precise, easily communicable definition.
2. Be reliably and economically measurable in clients.
3. Be similarly measurable in people in various jobs. If a test is used, it must (a) be easily administered to groups of people in different jobs, often under primitive conditions, and (b) be comparable with tests of the same dimensions used elsewhere, so as to build up occupational norms.
4. Differentiate people in different jobs or groups of jobs.
5. Be relevant to satisfactory job performance or stipulated for entry.
6. Persist in the client, unless needed only for entry.

These criteria raise problems we have space only to mention, such as the familiar one of criterion of "satisfactory" performance; and the possibility that success depends on similar basic qualities in many different jobs; or that it may depend less on the man than on his relationship with his work-mates, or his supervisor, for perhaps in peace, as in war, there are no bad regiments, only bad officers. Leaving these on one side, however, we may now go on to check possible dimensions, somewhat summarily perhaps, against our criteria. (See Table 1 below.)

General Intelligence

1. This can be suitably defined and forms a continuum.
2. It can for our purpose be reliably and cheaply measured in clients.
3. It can be measured in the field, too; some occupational scores are already available.
4. Intelligence test scores differentiate between groups or levels of jobs, less well between individual jobs. Mean scores of occupational samples do fall into a hierarchy (*e.g.*, Cattell, 1934; Super, 1949), but may differ from one another by very little. Thus 15 points of raw score (test maximum 60) can cover the means of 17 occupational samples (Lingwood, 1952). Also, scores in a single job may range as widely as from the 20th to the 90th percentile (Vernon, 1949), so that ranges, even inter-quartiles, overlap/considerably (Cattell, 1934). These wide ranges might be due to grouping scores of people who nominally do the same job, but actually have different scope, responsibilities, or degrees of skill. They occur so regularly, however, that the hypothesis is doubtful. At the moment, certainly, intelligence test scores do not differentiate jobs so precisely that a client's score can do more than point to a fairly wide area of jobs.
5. Correlations between intelligence and training criteria are often high (Vernon and Parry, 1949). Sometimes this simply shows how much theoretical or abstract material is included in the training (Jenkins, 1946); relevance of intelligence to the actual work is hard to prove. Thus, although Wyatt (1929) showed that while the more intelligent girls of his group disliked certain repetitive work and the less intelligent liked the same work, yet output of the brighter stayed above the average, that of the duller stayed below. It can be argued that if a person's score is much higher than the

job requires he will need other incentives like promotion prospects, high pay, etc., to prevent his becoming so dissatisfied that he leaves. The argument for "streams" in schools has some similarities. This consideration would imply a relevant upper limit of intelligence, not so much for doing the job as for staying in it. On the other hand, as Super (1949, p. 103) points out, a score above a certain minimum for the job does not necessarily pay corresponding dividends in the form of better performance.

It may be supposed too that a person will "adjust" best where the mean score of fellows resembles that of his own, but evidence outside school is scarce. If the score is far below the occupational mean he may find it hard to compete for promotion, perhaps even to do the job. But the occupational mean found is not necessarily the optimal nor the minimal score for the job. Unger and Burr (1931) showed that many jobs can come within the reach of girls of the lowest intelligence. If they are suitably trained and have no personality difficulties, girls with a mental age of six years, for instance, can successfully do light factory or domestic work. In any case the range of intelligence found in many jobs is so wide, and often reaches so low that clearly intelligence is at best only one factor in success. Super (1949, p. 103), commenting on the lack of research into the relation between intelligence and success in higher professions, in skilled trades and in unskilled occupations, suggests there would be a positive relation in the first two and none in the last, but says "this is still an unverified hypothesis".

6. Tested intelligence is relatively constant over the ages involved, *i.e.*, from 15 years onwards.

Summing up, intelligence can be suitably defined, and assessed reliably and cheaply. It differentiates groups of jobs; a certain minimum for the job may be a factor in success, especially in intellectual work, or where training is intensive; intelligence persists. Some occupational data already exist; they show intelligence found. Minimum intelligence *required* is usually a function of the time available for training. Fuller validation is possible. General intelligence, then, is a possible basic dimension, if used cautiously and along with others.

Educational Attainments

1. The general level of attainment can be usefully defined by certificates won, type of curriculum, duration of schooling, consistency of progress, scores on attainment tests, or by combinations of these, and can be made into some kind of continuum.

2 and 3. In such terms it can be assessed in clients and in the field.

4. Attainments required differentiate between groups of jobs, less well between individual jobs. Use of standardised tests can improve this (*e.g.*, Lingwood, 1952).

5. Attainments are believed relevant in many jobs, subjects or groups of them being quoted as important; relevance to the actual work of scores on

standardised tests can be validated (Vernon and Parry, 1949). What is critical in guidance, however, is quite often the entry level stipulated or accepted, even if this serves simply to raise the status of the job, or to limit entry, without being related to the actual work at all.

6. A certificate gained is gained for ever, but "residual ability" in terms of attainment test scores may change considerably after leaving school (Wall, 1944). With reference, then, to jobs where "nominal level" only is involved, attainment level persists; where "residual ability" is involved it may not persist.

Summing up, general level of attainments seems useful as a basic dimension; it is already used as a main criterion in many fields of selection.

Special Aptitudes

1. "Aptitudes" can be clearly defined only as test scores.
2. "Tested" aptitudes can be reliably assessed. Being so specific, however, several tests may be needed, adding to time and cost.
3. Assessment in the field is costly; few useful data are ready to hand.
4. Some, especially the *v:ed* and *k:m* groups, do differentiate jobs usefully (Vernon, 1950). As Vernon remarks, others are too specific for vocational guidance, though useful in selection.
5. Some are known to be associated with success in jobs, but wider validation is needed. Apparent relevance suggested through "naming" may be spurious.
6. "Aptitudes" persist well enough for our purpose.

Summing up, many aptitudes are very specific; occupational validation in this country is scarce. Aptitudes cannot yet offer a basic classification, but may be useful within classes or levels, or to confirm eventual choice.

Interests

This word is used to mean so many different things, and the notion in general is so closely connected with such factors as abilities, environment, education and emotional needs, that any full discussion would be lengthy.

1. "Interest" as a psychological concept is hard to define (Berlyne, 1949; Vernon, 1953). We may perhaps confine ourselves to "interests" as usually spoken of in vocational guidance. Here interests in the sense of "specific interests" can simply be indicated—woodwork, cycling, etc. Taken singly, however, these rarely have direct counterparts in jobs; moreover a person's specific interests are often limited by experience and opportunity, while their actual content may mean less to him than the friends, status, etc., involved. Specific interests, in short, may not show "what he is really after". As a result stress is usually laid instead on his underlying pattern or type of interests. Such "types" can be identified on *a priori* grounds. Various "interest factors" have also been statistically isolated, e.g., "scientific", "system", etc. (Super, 1949, p. 381; Eysenck, 1953), but naming of these

has to be very tentative. In any case, the interest "type", "pattern", etc., of a client, and also the "types" of interest involved in jobs, are difficult to identify except in terms of an agreed test. Strong (1943) makes his approach to this by showing that people in different jobs make characteristically different patterns of responses to items on his Vocational Interest Blank. A particular client's pattern of responses may then be typified as resembling that of dentists bankers, etc.; the actual "interests" or "types of interest" need not be named at all.

2 and 3. One may assess interests (Super, 1949) as *Expressed*—"he likes, dislikes, or is indifferent to" a given activity; as *Manifest*—inferred from how he actually spends his time; as *Tested*—achievement in, or knowledge about, various activities; as *Inventoried*—the pattern found from a standardised and validated questionnaire (Strong, 1943; Kuder, 1949). (Sometimes, too, Expressed, Manifest and Tested aspects are taken as a continuum of *degree* of interest.) Expressed specific interests tend to the unstable, although giving interview leads, while it is hard to tell how far a Manifest interest is a function of opportunity, parents' income, etc., *i.e.*, how far it shows what a person would be interested in if he had a wider choice. Similarly Tested interest is a function of intelligence, education and opportunity. "Inventoried interests", however, can be reliably assessed. Unfortunately some Inventories are laborious to score, except by machine; material is expensive; no such Inventory has been validated in Britain.*

4. "Inventoried interests" do differentiate jobs, in that responses of people in different jobs differ. Interests assessed in other terms look as if they *must* differentiate, but validation is hard to find. In differentiating jobs by the type of activity involved (rather than by the interests of people in them) so as to link with the type of interests the client has, various difficulties arise. One is how to limit the number of possible groups; another is how to decide—"from the outside"—what the main activity is in jobs which involve several. Some jobs, too, seem to call for different interests at different stages; an engineer may at first do practical work, advance to drawing office and technical studies, graduate to costing and estimating, and finally, as a manager, handle many human problems. Thus the Committee on Education for Management (1947, p. 20) found in one survey of professional associations that 70 per cent of men who originally qualified as engineers or accountants engage later in some managerial function. Another difficulty in *a priori* grouping is seen in a study by Thurstone (1932) who analyzed 18 of Strong's occupational scales (each built on the responses of people in the given occupation). He found four factors which he named interest in science, language, people and business. Taking only three of the scales the loadings were: Doctors: science +.71, language +.33, people −.26, business −.09. Teachers: +.36, +.15, +.68, −.22. Psychologists:

* See Hopson, p. 489.—Eds.

+.77, +.47, −.04, −.28. *Prima facie*, all these jobs involve a marked interest in people, but evidently not in the same terms.

5. As for relevance of interests to jobs, it would have to be shown that entrants with certain interests do the work better and/or enjoy it more than entrants with other interests, and also that they do certain jobs better than they do other jobs. Evidence of this kind is obviously scarce. Strong, however, finds a relation between inventoried interests and success (1943). There are signs too (Strong, 1952) that the more closely a person's pattern of responses resembles that of a given occupation, the more likely he is eventually to be engaged in it.

6. Specific interests may be unstable, specially in adolescence. Inventoried interests too may be unreliable below the age of 17 (Strong, 1943). From that age onwards, however, inventoried interests do seem to persist. Thus the correlation between scores on Strong's "engineer" scale, taken at the university, with scores one year later is 0.91, with re-test nine years later 0.77, and nineteen years later 0.76 (Strong, 1952). Even so, the older a person is at first test, the more likely are test and re-test to agree (Strong, 1951).

Summing up, interests are hard to define and objective measures in this country few. Even when using occupationally validated inventories extrapolation beyond validated jobs must be cautious. Interest in the sense of drives and emotional needs is clearly important, but just as hard to validate occupationally. Lacking validated instruments interests cannot be used for basic classification, though offering useful leads later on.

"*Personality*"

1. This can be variously defined. To exclude aspects like cognitive abilities, physical characteristics, etc., is artificial but useful, but to separate, say, "Interests" from "Personality" is barely possible. Even so, what remains has many dimensions. Operational definition of some is possible, *e.g.*, Eysenck's two "main dimensions" of general neuroticism and "introversion-extraversion" (1947), or Vernon's "dependability" and "extraversion-introversion" (1953). Some traits discussed in guidance are in line with these, *e.g.*, "steadiness or reliability". Others are less easy to define, *e.g.*, "influence over others", "initiative".

2. As for assessment in a client, even the agreed important dimensions involve using several tests, few of which are yet in general use in Britain. Other methods of assessing traits tend to be unreliable. A group of people can be reliably compared with each other, but it is less easy to rate a single client reliably unless against an actual job.

3. Measuring personality dimensions of good and bad workers in jobs is even harder.

4. It may be that people in certain jobs differ characteristically from those in others in respect to some dimensions of personality, *e.g.*, on the face of things, extraversion-introversion, but this awaits validation. One feels too

that some of the subjectively defined and assessed traits *must* differentiate jobs, but again validation is needed.

5. Aspects of personality (as in 1 above) are believed to be relevant to success in many jobs, *e.g.*, as accounting for some variance beyond intelligence, etc., but it is not clear how much of which aspect is needed in which jobs. Certain traits do appear relevant to success. Some unfortunately seem relevant to all jobs, *i.e.*, do not differentiate; Vernon's "dependability" would *sound* like an example. Behaviour too depends partly on the context; *e.g.*, on group pressure to arbitrary norms of output; the impact of the group in shaping attitudes and motivations; the type of supervision; lack of definition of one's role or status; implications for behaviour of the technological process; and so on. Performance in any job depends not only on the person's traits, and of course his intelligence, aptitudes, etc., but on the interaction of these with the characteristics of the situation, the role he is given etc. Considering how unreliable is the assessment of many traits validation of their differential relevance to jobs is bound to be especially difficult.

6. Aspects of personality do persist. Since, however, behaviour is partly determined by actual job conditions, the range of prediction is clearly limited.

Summing up, personality, even in our restricted use here, has in itself many dimensions. Objective measurement of some is possible, and occupational studies have started (*e.g.*, Heron, 1951). At present, however, we cannot make a basic classification of occupations in terms of personality traits.

Circumstances

This refers to a person's "general context"; points that arise include: How long training, or even delay in picking a job, can he afford? How important will his wages be? Will his family back him up? Encourage him through his apprenticeship or classes? Will they worry about status? Will tensions in the family upset his work? What are the jobs of relatives and friends and their attitudes towards them? What are their ambitions, values, standards? It is clear that many factors are involved, acting upon one another counter-balancing one another in complex ways.

1. For our purpose these factors are important in so far as they affect choice of job. It may be possible to consider them as a single complex "dimension", in such terms as "Background Support"—how much, or how little, he can rely on outside of himself. Points on a scale may be sufficiently clearly indicated by general statements combined with examples.

2. Some aspects of the "dimension" can be reliably assessed, *e.g.*, economic ones. Others, like stability of the family group, parents' values and standards, involve difficulties, yet are familiar and in fact regularly assessed for various purposes. The more time available, however, the more chance there is of reliable assessment.

3. Similarly this "dimension" is hard to measure in people in jobs, although certain aspects can be reliably assessed.

4. The "dimension" does differentiate broad groups of occupations. The economic aspect is often critical, though losing its importance in many jobs. It remains true, however, that entrants need better Background Support in some jobs than in others.

5. "Background Support" is often relevant to satisfactory work, to judge from statements by foremen and others; its importance, in one form or another, is stressed by various authorities (*e.g.*, Wilson, 1945). In guidance it is certainly relevant; often a single aspect may make it critical, *e.g.*, cash for living costs while training. On the whole it is most often relevant to entry into, or during training for, a job.

6. Some aspects persist or can be predicted; others are unpredictable.

Summing up, the "dimension" Background Support is difficult to validate occupationally, but seems to differentiate broad groups of jobs, and is usually persistent enough for our purpose. In our society its relevance to guidance, if not to performance, is hard to dispute; this alone probably makes it an essential dimension.

Physique

1. Physical measurements can be precise (height, weight), but are rarely relevant. Operational definitions of "physique" are unwiedly and often impracticable—*e.g.*, "can lift x lbs. through y feet z times a day". "General health" too is hard to define except as lack of apparent disabilities "Unfitness" can be defined by specific disabilities; these may exclude or "bar" particular jobs, *e.g.*, "not fit to stand all day", rather than lead to positive suggestions.

2. A general estimate of a client's health can be made and disabilities noted as "bars".

3. Similarly workers in jobs can be assessed physically in rather general terms and disabilities associated with low success noted. Emphasis is usually on negative statements.

4. Physique sometimes differentiates jobs, but most need moderately active, healthy people. Some "bars" do differentiate; *e.g.*, colour blindness does not debar from all jobs.

5. In a few jobs general physique is relevant; single elements may be critical, *e.g.*, height for a policeman. Some disabilities too are critical, but "bars" must be carefully validated; a bus conductor would seem to need all his fingers, yet one with a total of five missing is known to be doing well.

6. Physique in general terms persists; disabilities may be temporary.

On the whole, physique is not a convenient "dimension" for basic classification. On occasion, of course, even a single aspect of it may be critical in guidance. Because stress is so often on negative statements—on "ruling out"—it is simpler to consider physical characteristics after reaching a "short list" of jobs.

TABLE 1

	Intelligence	Attainments	Aptitudes	Interests	Personality	Circumstances	Physique
1. Precise definition	Yes	Yes	Yes, as factors	Only by inventory	A few traits have	Cumbrous	Negatively
2. Assessed reliably, cheaply, in clients	Yes	Yes	Reliably; not cheap	Yes, by inventory. Not cheap	Not yet	Some aspects, others difficult	Negatively
3. Assessed reliably, cheaply, in the field	Yes	Yes	Reliably; not cheap	Yes, by inventory. Not cheap	Not yet	Some aspects, others difficult	Negatively
4. Differentiate jobs	Broad levels only	Broad levels only	Most too specific	*A priori* exc. by inventory	Not yet	Broad groups only	A few
5. Relevant to success	In some jobs, especially to training	In some, especially to entry	Hard to validate	*A priori* mainly	Not yet	Relevant to guidance	Sometimes
6. Persists	Yes	"Nominal" yes; "residual" may	Yes	Inventory yes, over 17 years	Aspects do	Some aspects only	Yes
Useful later	Possibly	Yes, *e.g.* specific subjects	Yes	As "leads"	Yes	Yes, in detail	Yes, bars may be critical

Characteristics of people checked against six criteria to select dimensions for a basic classification of occupations for vocational guidance purposes.

SUMMING UP

Our list probably includes those dimensions about which most is at present known for vocational guidance. Of these, Intelligence, Attainments and Background Support most nearly meet the criteria, as Table 1 shows. With fuller occupational validation Aptitudes might come higher on the list; already the *v:ed* and *k:m* dichotomy, used cautiously, is valuable. Interests and Personality come some way behind, while Physique, however important, does not give *positive* leads. All through, however, relevance to actual job requirements is still in question, even for instance in the case of intelligence. The danger lies in stressing characteristics, less because they are essentially relevant, than because they are conveniently measurable. With these provisos in mind, however, it seems possible to use Intelligence, Attainments and Background Support, or a combination of them, to make a basic classification fit for our purpose, *i.e.*, to produce in a limited time reasonably sound job suggestions. Though these three measures probably correlate with one another over large samples, in individual cases (our main concern here) each is likely to add something new to the assessment of the client.

It is not our aim, however, simply to say how jobs *might* be classified. We must go on to the next step, which is to find the Intelligence, Attainments and Background Support actually required in different jobs. We can then rate each job, by rating people in it, in terms of these. Jobs of similar ratings can then be grouped together. Rating a client in corresponding terms lead us to a group of jobs all needing basic abilities at his level. To decide which of the jobs *of his general level* should be further considered, we must turn to other characteristics including aptitudes, interests, traits, and to our local knowledge. Such considerations need differentiate only within that level. Eventual choice thus demands more detailed study both of the client and of the job suggestions that arise. Our present discussion suggests a definite order of priority in collecting information for job descriptions and the limits of weight that can safely be put on the information thus obtained. It is hoped in a later article to describe the actual construction of a Search List in these terms, and to outline its uses.*

REFERENCES

BINGHAM, W. V. (1942) *Aptitudes and Aptitude Testing.* London: Harper Bros.

BERLYNE, D. E. (1949) Interest as a Psychological Concept. *British Journal of Psychology* (*General Section*), **39**, 184–195.

CATTELL, R. B. (1934) Occupational Norms of Intelligence and Standardisation of an Adult Intelligence Test. *British Journal Psychology* (*General Section*), **25**, 1–28.

COMMITTEE ON EDUCATION FOR MANAGEMENT (1947) *Education for Management.* Report of a special Committee; Ministry of Education. London: HMSO.

EYSENCK, H. J. (1947) *Dimensions of Personality.* London: Routledge & Kegan Paul.

EYSENCK, H. J. (1953) *The Structure of Human Personality.* London: Methuen.

HERON, A. (1951) *A Psychological Study of Occupational Adjustment.* Ph.D. Thesis London: University of London Library.

JENKINS, J. G. (1946) Validity for What? *Journal of Consulting Psychology*, **10**, 93–98.

KUDER, G. F. (1949) *Examiner Manual for the Kuder Preference Record.* Chicago: Science Research Associates.

LINGWOOD, JOAN (1952) Test Performances of A.T.S. Recruits from Certain Civilian Occupations. *Occupational Psychology*, **26**, 35–46.

MCKENZIE, R. M. (1952) Occupational Classification in Vocational Guidance. *British Psychological Society Quarterly Bulletin*, **3**, 88–90.

* *Occupational Psychology*, **28**, 1954, 197–208.—Eds.

RODGER, A. (1939) The Work of the Vocational Adviser, in *The Study of Society*. F. C. Bartlett *et al.* London: Routledge & Kegan Paul.

RODGER, A. (1952) *The Seven-Point Plan*. Paper Number One. London: National Institute of Industrial Psychology.

STRONG, E. K. (1943) *Vocational Interests of Men and Women*. London: Oxford University Press.

STRONG, E. K. (1951) Permanence of Interest Scores over 22 years. *Journal of Applied Psychology*, **35**, 89–91.

STRONG, E. K. (1952) Nineteen-Year Follow-Up of Engineer Interests. *Journal of Applied Psychology*, **36**, 64–74.

SUPER, D. E. (1949) *Appraising Vocational Fitness*. New York: Harper Bros.

THURSTONE, L. L. (1932) A Multiple Factor Study of Vocational Interests. *Personnel Journal*, **10**, 198–205.

UNGER, EDNA W., and BURR, EMILY T. (1931) *Minimum Mental Age Levels of Achievement*. Albany: New York State Department of Education.

VERNON, P. E. (1949) Occupational Norms for the 20-minute Progressive Matrices Test. *Occupational Psychology*, **23**, 58–59.

VERNON, P. E. (1950) *The Structure of Human Abilities*. London: Methuen.

VERNON, P. E. (1953) *Personality Tests and Assessments*. London: Methuen.

VERNON, P. E., and PARRY, J. B. (1949) *Personnel Selection in the British Forces*. London: University of London Press.

WALL, W. D. (1944) The Decay of Educational Attainments among Adolescents after Leaving School. *British Journal of Educational Psychology*, **14**, 19–34.

WILSON, N. A. B. (1945) Interviewing Candidates for Technical Appointments or Training. *Occupational Psychology*, **19**, 161–179.

WYATT, S., FRAZER, J. A., and STOCK, F. G. L. (1929) *The Effects of Monotony in Work*. Industrial Health Research Board Report 56. London: HMSO.

29. *The Functions and Forms of Occupational Visits**

BARRIE HOPSON

AN increasing amount of time is spent in secondary education on visits to places of work by leavers or potential school-leavers. Educational journals reflect a variety of attitudes on all aspects of education—subject matter, methods of teaching, even administration. One aspect of the school curriculum which is rarely discussed, however, is that of careers teaching, i.e. the dissemination of occupational information, and guidance for the individual child. This subject is of increasing importance whether defined by the curriculum time taken or by its potential effects upon the personality and life-orientation of pupils. Recognition of this has led to the appearance recently of the booklet by the Department of Education and Science *Careers Guidance in Schools* (1965). This publication underlines the need for second ary education in this country to recog nizeexplicitly the existence of this trend, and to make it the subject of an ongoing educational debate as is found in mathematics, English, and all the other "recognized" subjects.

Now that the Youth Employment Service is taking an increasingly active role in the schools, it is appropriate to ask it to offer guidance to careers teachers on the organization of careers programmes, on the provision of suitable outside speakers, and on organising visits to industry. On all three issues, the Youth Employment officer has a vast reservoir of local experience and information to contribute.

Although this trend has been evident now for some time, its acceleration is slow. Too many schools still provide only an haphazard introduction for their pupils to the issues of choosing a job. It often takes the form of rare industrial visits (non-industrial occupational visits are even rarer), and talks from occasional and some times badly chosen speakers. At times these activities take place outside usual school hours and sometimes are presented as part of mathematics, geography, history, religious instruction, and even physical education courses.

The acknowledgement that better provision should be made is often a lone protest from one member of staff who undertakes to shake his colleagues out of their complacency. Too commonly, however, this impetus

* Based on an article which appeared in *Youth Employment*, Spring, 1967.

results only in an increasing number of occupational visits, and these tend to be chosen according to the interests and knowledge of a particular teacher. Furthermore, they often remain casual, ill-arranged ventures, vaguely prescribed to enable pupils to wander around a particular work environment. Similarly, a temporary enthusiasm for more outside speakers is inadequate in itself to guarantee the value of what they have to say or to ensure the comprehensiveness and accuracy of their knowledge of the working world. Even when a speaker satisfies both of these criteria it is difficult without prior knowledge of his lecturing ability to assess the worth of his addition to a careers programme. The local youth employment officer, however, should be able to provide this detailed knowledge to the teachers. That the youth employment officer is not a teacher nor the teacher a youth employment officer is clear, but they have a complementary function in the implementation of careers work in schools. The teacher can teach and he knows his pupils; the youth employment officer knows the world of work, and the conditions of demand and supply in the local labour market. Without the co-operation of teacher and youth employment officer, careers work in schools will not prosper.

In assisting the teacher to plan a careers programme one of the important functions of the youth employment officer is to advise on the organisation of occupational visits. However, before the youth employment officer gives any advice on this question he must first put his own house in order. He himself sometimes does not always have a clear idea of what he is attempting to do when he begins the task of organising a series of visits for a school. Too often his aims are not made explicit to the school and no one knows exactly why these visits are being carried out. Youth employment officers as a body must be clear about the aims of occupational visits. Careers work is an important aspect of a child's education and like all educational topics should have proposed aims, or else there can be nothing to debate, and the educational process must always be a centre for debate.

Occupational visits as organised by youth employment officers take one of the following three major forms:

A. *Opportunist Visiting*

The idea here is that as many pupils as possible should visit as many firms as possible to give them an idea of what different sorts of work are like. Choice of firm and industry tends to depend upon the willingness of local firms to co-operate, and to be guided by what type of work-place the youth employment officer thinks the pupils will find interesting. Summed up, the youth employment officer allows local conditions and the assumed preferences of pupils to determine his action. Choice of firms to visit is anarchic; any firm which is favourable to visits is included. A pupil could go on half a dozen visits and see the same type of working environment each time.

B. *Vocational Visiting*

The assumption that underlies this form of visiting is that a pupil should only visit a place of work when there is a real possibility of his choosing that type of work as a career; the implication being that visits other than these are a "waste of time". This idea is most current in the grammar school, but examples in other schools are not hard to find. This view sees visits primarily as a recruiting or placement device, i.e. not strictly educational.

C. *Programmed Educational Visiting*

This takes the form of a planned series of visits spread out over at least a year, during which time each child visits a representative sample of all the occupational fields theoretically open to him. Bearing in mind that in any work-place the pupil will see a large number of jobs, what is important is that he should sample as many different types of "work atmospheres" as possible. In the absence of any scheme of actual work experience, it is not possible to aquaint the pupil with the full realities of the work situation, such as the interpersonal relationships involved, the relationships between workers and management, etc. It is possible, however, to give them experience of what a place of work smells, feels, and sounds like. The aim of such a series of visits is distinctly educational. It creates in pupils an awareness of how different sections of the public spend their working lives. It should encourage the development of an understanding of the working problems of people in occupations with which pupils may not in the future have any contact.

Before initiating any scheme of visits all work must be classified by some relevant criterion. If a scheme of visits is to sample all "work atmospheres", as it must to fulfill the criterion of "programming", then a classification of occupations has to be compiled which covers the entire range of occupational possibilities in this country. If a school wants eight occupational visits as part of its career programme it is important that these eight visits should sample as many types of work as possible. Such a classification might be on the basis of socio-economic levels of labour, e.g. unskilled, semi-skilled, skilled, managerial and supervisory, etc. However, any one place of work often contains all of these levels, and each class can contain widely different "work atmospheres", so that this form of classification is unsatisfactory. What is needed is a form of classification that takes into account the different sorts of interest that are satisfied by different occupations. An example of this classification system is that of Rothwell and Miller (1966): outdoor, practical, mechanical, social service, aesthetic, computational, literary, musical, personal contact, scientific, and medical. A visits programme could take an example of each of these interests as expressed by a particular job, e.g. visiting a bank to see types of work likely to satisfy

TABLE 1

MOSER, DUBIN, AND SHELSKY'S MODIFICATION OF ROE'S CLASSIFICATION OF OCCUPATIONS*

Focus of Activity	I Service	II Business Contact	III Business Organization	IV Technology	V Outdoor	VI Science	VII General Culture	VIII Arts and Entertainments
1. Professional and Managerial (Higher)	Research Scientist (Social)	Sales Director	Principal Civil Servant, Company Chairman, Stockbroker	Research Scientist (Engineering)	Research Engineer (Mining)	Research Scientist (Physics, Chemistry)	Judge, Professor (History Maths, etc.), Chief Education Officer	Orchestra Conductor, T.V. Director
2. Professional and Managerial (Regular)	Probation Officer, Police Superintendent Matron (Hospital)	Personnel Manager, Area Sales Manager	Bank Manager, Company Secretary	Pilot, Civil Engineer	Geologist, Conservation Officer	Chemist, Veterinarian, Physicist	Clergyman, Editor, Headmaster	Architect, Critic
3. Semi-Professional and Managerial	Police Inspector, Nurse (S.R.N.)	Insurance Broker, Sales Representative, Estate Agent	Accountant, Owner (small grocery)	Building Contractor, Mechanical Engineer	Farmer (small, ind. owner)	Chiropodist, Physiotherapist	School Teacher, Librarian	Commercial Artist, Textile Designer, Photographer

4. Skilled	Hairdresser, Chef, Head Waiter	Salesman (Shop), Market-Research Interviewer	Shorthand Typist, Statistical Clerk	Carpenter, Electrician, Decorator, Dressmaker	Landscape Gardener, Farm Mechanic	Laboratory Assistant	Nursery Teacher	Window Dresser
5. Semiskilled	Chauffeur, Cook, Fireman	Sales Assistant, Van Salesman (Ice Cream)	Cashier, Clerk (File), Telephonist	Crane Operator, Fitter's Mate, Lorry Driver	Fisherman, Gardener	Laboratory Steward	Library Attendant	Clothes Model
6. Unskilled	Watchman, Roadsweeper, Office Cleaner	Newspaper Boy	Messenger	Foundry Labourer	Farm Labourer, Animal Tender			Stagehand

* Job titles more relevant to Britain have been substituted.

people with predominantly computational interests. The difficulty here is that no account of level is taken, so that if a careers master has eight visits to plan, for any one interest the job to be chosen may not represent all possible levels, e.g. a visit to a mechanic's shop can show mechanical work up to the skilled level but probably no higher, i.e. not a mechanical engineer. To circumvent this, a well planned follow-up back in school is necessary, when, amongst other things, different levels in any occupation or group of occupations may be discussed thoroughly, and the teacher can discuss the different methods of entry at these levels. A visit could then be planned at a level commensurate with the ability range of the pupils involved without falling into the trap of the advocates of "vocational visiting".

A suitable classification scheme that originated in the U.S.A. is the modification of the Roe Occupational Classification (1954) proposed by Moser, Dubin and Shelsky (1956). Occupations are classified according to three main principles:

1. The modal level of skill and training most usually required for entering the job.
2. The activity at work in which the worker spends the major portion of his time.
3. Jobs whose functions are derived from the work of a second occupation are placed in the group to which they are ancillary, e.g. a stagehand is placed not in the Technology category but under Arts and Entertainment.

In Table 1 examples of this classification are given. In the vertical column are the levels of occupational activity, in the horizontal row are the foci of activities. A full discussion of the categories may be found in the article by Moser *et al.* (1956). This classificatory system has been found to be very reliable. There is a high degree of agreement between judges in categorising occupations by this system. Using such a system an occupational visits programme could sample each of the 8 activity foci at whichever level was most appropriate. Though it may be used in its entirety as a basis for a visits programme, each youth employment officer should decide what sort of scheme is best suited to the needs of the school populations in his area and which best reflects the opportunities offered by the local and national work environments.

FORMS OF VISITS

The visits discussed above can all be varied in a number of different ways:

Size of Party

This is the most important source of variation. Diverse points of view exist on this issue, none of which can claim any objective support. The three most commonly encountered forms are:

(a) Teacher accompanied large group visit (15–25).
(b) Teacher accompanied small group visit (5–10).
(c) Unaccompanied small group visit (below 8).

In recent time, support has grown for the unaccompanied small group visit. Arguments in its favour take one or more of the following forms:

(i) Pupils behave in a more adult fashion without the presence of a teacher.
(ii) They will interact more with workers, asking more questions, without the inhibiting presence of a teacher.
(iii) Supporters of this form of visit usually also support the notion that the group itself arranges the visit, or that it is at least under the impression that it arranged the visit, again encouraging a sense of responsibility.
(iv) The size of group encourages group cohesion and thereby instructive discussion amongst its members.
(v) Workers will react more favourably to a small group of well behaved, interested pupils.
(vi) The pupils will all feel that they have to ask questions and that the onus is on each one of them to participate fully because the party is a small one.
(vii) They will thus obtain and retain more actual job information.

At the Vocational Guidance Research Unit we sought objective evidence for some of these points.*

The study involved thirty-one fourth year boys in a secondary modern school, who were separated into two groups: Group A consisted of sixteen boys, and Group B, fifteen boys. Group B was further divided into three groups of five boys each. All groups had a separate briefing session five days before the visit. Group A had a normal school visit, arranged by a teacher, while the small B groups had to confirm the arrangement with the firm concerned. This involved the informal election of a group spokesman. All four groups went to the same firm and had the same tour. Group A was accompanied by the teacher and two guides and each of the B groups was accompanied by one of the guides.

Each group was given a questionnaire the day after the visit. They were compared on measures of:

1. The occupational information retained.
2. Their ability to assess the qualities and qualifications necessary to do a particular job.
3. Their rating of how the guides and workers acted towards them.
4. Their reactions to the visit as a whole.

* Grateful appreciation is due to Paul Atkinson of Leeds Youth Employment Service for his invaluable assistance in the administration and organisation of this study.

All groups were assessed by the guides and workers on the degree of interest exhibited and on their general behaviour.

When the results were analysed for statistical significance, there were small overall differences but these were not significant, even at the 10 per cent level of probability.

Only on one of the above criteria was there a difference, viz. their reactions to the visits as a whole. The small unaccompanied groups were much more enthusiastic in their reaction to their visits than was the large group. This could of course reflect the novelty value, although having talked to all group members we think this unlikely.

Thus, we did not find corroborative evidence for some of the hypotheses in favour of unaccompanied small group visits. However, we are of the opinion that the overall effect on, for example, the increased sense of responsibility cannot be measured at the stage at which we collected our information. It would be difficult to find significant results for something which is, or should be, only one part of a total careers programme. There certainly do not appear to be significant differences in occupational information retained, in the behaviour displayed by the boys during the visits, or in ability to assess realistically the qualities necessary for success in a job. Boys do appear to enjoy the unaccompanied visits more as they feel more "grown-up" and find it easier to converse with the teacher absent. They did in fact ask more questions per boy than Group A, although there was no difference overall between the numbers of questions asked between the two Groups A and B, as certain boys in Group A tended to dominate and ask a large number of questions.

Many firms, when questioned about small group unaccompanied visits, felt that very small groups, i.e. five or less, took up too much of the time of workers who acted as guides or of their personnel managers. They were in favour of the unaccompanied visit, but of parties of around 8–10 people, feeling that pupils were often deterred by the teacher's presence from asking questions.

Duration of Visit

Visits usually tend to take 2–4 hours depending upon the size of the firm and the enthusiasm of the personnel manager. One idea which is worthy of mention, assuming the aim of a visit to be mainly to allow sampling of the work "atmosphere", is to arrange that a visit end just before lunch, or begin just afterwards, in either case the pupils being invited to lunch in the works canteen.

Day-long visits, beginning at the time a normal worker begins work, and ending when he ends work, are becoming more common, though this often develops into a work-experience scheme, which is outside the scope of this discussion.

WHAT USE DO VISITS SERVE?

Occupational visits can play a very valuable role in a careers course, as part of the overall educational programme. Even where no course exists, a programme of visits can help to provide information which will help to smooth the very important transition from school to work, from pupil status to adult status, that occurs at some point in every child's life. Some of the dangers of a visits programme have already been outlined; some suggestions have been made. However, there has been criticism that questions the basic function of occupational visits as part of the school curriculum. For example:

1. *Pupils may be "scared off" an occupation to which they are suited by interest and ability because of exposure to a work atmosphere which at first is unpleasant, but to which people quickly become accustomed.* This danger, if it exists, should be virtually eliminated by adequate preparation for the visits and follow-up, by a more extended visit such as has been described, and by representative work atmosphere sampling which encourages a sense of realism.
2. *Many visits are used merely as recruitment devices, as profit making concerns cannot be expected to be disinterested.* Firstly, this overlooks the fact that many firms do feel a responsibility to the community and try to help where they can. Secondly, although there can be no doubt that some firms bombard pupils with glossy literature, and give them V.I.P. treatment in the hope of ensnaring the gullible, adquate preparation and follow-up for the visit and representative sampling should make students much less credulous.
3. *Pupils merely regard visits as an excuse to get away from formal lessons and because of this "bank holiday" attitude, obtain little knowledge or benefit from visits.* This undoubtedly is true for some occupational visits. The fault, however, does not lie in the practice of visiting itself but in the organization of visits in a particular school, and in the general school ethos and attitudes towards careers teaching and occupational visits. If the school emphasizes the educational importance of visits both by the introduction of a visits programme in a fully organised careers syllabus, and by the positive attitude of the teaching staff towards these activities as a genuine part of a child's education, then pupils will realise themselves that this is a part of their education. If they are prepared beforehand and know that afterwads they will be expected to know many details of a work place they have visited, the occupational opportunities open to them in such work, and the kind of person best fitted to do a particular job in the firm, then they will have little time for "larking about" and considerably less inclination to do so.

This discussion has explored a number of major points relating to occupational visits and has led to certain conclusions. Firstly, that unless visiting is programmed many of the criticisms of occupational visits will be upheld, e.g. they may be "a waste of time", seen as a "lark" by pupils, teachers may act as unpaid recruitment agents, and pupils may make a non-rational choice of occupation due to biased sampling. However, with a system of programmed educational visits as previously defined, occupational visits can help the pupil enlarge his knowledge of occupations whilst promoting self-knowledge, aiding in a more realistic occupational choice, and helping emotionally in the transition from school to work.

There appears to be some evidence, though small, that the unaccompanied small group visit would be preferred by pupils and by some managements, although occupational information retained appears no greater than follows from other forms of visits. Preparation and follow-up of visits are, of course, essential. Often groups are prepared, but not followed-up. All too often, neither occurs.

For follow-up, some form of self-assessment questionnaire is very useful. To make a realistic occupational or educational choice a pupil has to know himself: his interests, capacities, aptitudes, values, and personality characteristics. One method of encouraging self-awareness is to provide a questionnaire which has to be filled in after each visit. Each pupil might fill in two or three such questionnaires after each visit. They would commence by answering questions about what sort of person would be best fitted to do such jobs as they have seen, i.e. personality characteristics, interests, capacities, qualifications, etc. The next section of the questionnaire would require the pupils to fit themselves to the jobs, asking themselves in fact, "Am I the sort of person who would be happy doing this type of work in this type of atmosphere?" As part of their careers course they should already have filled in questionnaires about themselves so as to promote self-understanding. Many schools and youth employment officers already use such questionnaires and one of these could be used or the youth employment officer and careers teacher could construct one of their own.

When visits are extended to include, for example a canteen meal, they become closer to work experience with an educational motive not a job placement role. Such an extended scheme would provide a much greater opportunity to discover the very important psycho-social aspects of work. For a discussion of the importance of psycho-social factors in work see Samler (1961) and Hayes (1967). Such schemes would still have to be subject to principles outlined in the discussion on programmed educational visits.

One can appreciate the difficulties that face any youth employment officer who tries to obtain co-operation for a full sampling range of industrial and commercial concerns, and even, in a particular occupational field, to sample the different atmospheres and environment. This must remain, however, the priority need in any scheme for occupational visits. Separate visits for groups of teachers might also be encouraged, for, as the Newsom Report (1963) points out (paras. 238, 239), it is essential for the pupil that teachers gain some familiarity with industry. If the unaccompanied small group visit continues to grow in popularity, even this small opportunity of industrial experience could be lost to the teacher, although it would be hoped that no teacher would take a follow-up or preparation session in a careers course without at some time having visited the firm.

It must be stressed also that visits to colleges of further and higher education should be an important part of any careers programme. Much of the mystique and attitude of "them's alright for others but not for us", could well be countered by intelligently organised college visits.

One final thought on this vital question of programming, if any school finds that large numbers of school-leavers enter a firm to which there has been a visit, provided there are no unusual local employment conditions there may well be something very wrong with the school's sampling system of occupational visits. The success of the visits programme is certainly not to be measured in this way.

REFERENCES

DEPT. OF EDUCATION AND SCIENCE (1965) *Careers Guidance in Schools*. London, H.M.S.O.

HAYES, J. (1967) The role of occupational information in careers guidance. *Educational Research*, **9**, No. 3.

MILLER, K. (1966) *Manual: Rothwell-Miller Interest Blank*. N.F.E.R.

Newsom Report, MINISTRY OF EDUCATION (1963), *Half our Future*. London, H.M.S.O.

MOSER, H., DUBIN, W., and SCHELSKY, I. (1956) Proposed modification of the Roe Occupational Classification. *J. of Counseling Psychology*, **3**, 27–31.

ROE, ANNE (1954) A new classification of occupations. *J. of Counseling Psychology*, **1**, 215–220.

SAMLER, J. (1961) Psycho-social aspects of work: a critique of occupational information. *Personnel and Guidance Journal*, **34**, 458–465.

they will gain some familiarity with industry. If the [illegible] about [illegible] from the small proportion of industrial experience [illegible] the teacher. Although it would be hoped that the teacher [illegible] courses [illegible]

[illegible] colleges of further and higher education [illegible] of the [illegible] college visits.

[illegible]

REFERENCES

[illegible]

30. *Vocational Guidance for the Unscholarly Child*

PETER P. DAWS

ROUGHLY half our school leavers seek their first job without the aid of formal qualifications. They search hopefully for a good job or a good firm, conscious that they have no assets to boast of or bargain with because they lack pieces of paper to testify to skills achieved. They may feel, too, that vocational guidance is a pretentious irrelevance and that the Youth Employment Officer's placement function is his only significant one for them. Such feelings are pessimistic and unrealistic. Vocational guidance offers help to understand the full range of occupations that are accessible, the demands they make upon the learning and performance capacities of the young worker, and what they have to offer him, both in the short and the long term, in return for his labour. Guidance also provides help in thinking through the problem of choice and help in settling to the demands of a strange environment when working life begins. The unscholarly child's need of such a service is no less than that of his scholastically more accomplished brother and sister.

THE EARLY LEAVER'S PROSPECTS

Most of our formally unqualified school leavers lack a social background that fosters a taste for scholastic endeavour and identification with the goals and achievements of school life. Accordingly, they escape into adult working life as soon as the law permits, usually with parental and peer group approval. Many of them are bright children who reveal their wits in various non-scholastic ways. They remain a challenge and a reproach to our school system. They are the "under achievers". Such children often prove more willing to apply their talents in a work setting. It is one of the functions of guidance to discriminate children with impressive untapped resources from those less able children who, with the best will in the world, learn only slowly and with difficulty.

For each unscholarly child there waits an unskilled job. Does *this* certainty seriously diminish the promise of vocational guidance? Again, emphatically not. For just as the "unscholarly child" defines a category of variedly talented children with richly diverse needs, aspirations, and promise, so does the "unskilled job" denote a rich diversity of occupations. Indeed, the label is *never* accurate. All jobs have to be learned and all therefore require some skill. Neither the pick nor the shovel will yield its mysteries in a day. The skills of the unskilled job are usually (but not always) a little less complex than others. The unskilled worker is not, therefore, denied the possibility of pride in a skilled and efficient performance, nor is he denied the absorbing satisfaction of learning and mastering a job. To secure these ends is in practice a relative matter. Capacity and willingness must be challenged and stretched, but not over-stretched, and appropriate satisfactions must be continuously forthcoming to sustain application and performance. Even the most undemanding job, a simple, repetitive task, will challenge the wits of a subnormal child and thus provide a sense of achievement and contentment freshly renewed each day in adequate performance (O'Connor and Tizard, 1956). Bright people too readily assume that jobs that would bore them to distraction must necessarily have the same effect upon everyone else, forgetting that pride and contentment in a job is related to the effort it has cost to master it.

Wherever people differ, and wherever the jobs from which they must choose differ, there is a role for vocational guidance. A humanitarian justification for that role has been recognised for a long time. Today there is added an economic argument. We can no longer afford to misuse or neglect the talents of our working population, for the labour market needs all that there are. Because of the need to anticipate accurately trends of change in the demand for occupational skill, and because the rate of change of demand for different forms of skill is accelerating, the Ministry of Labour created in 1963 its Manpower Research Unit. Initial results (Ministry of Labour, 1964) have suggested that, throughout the foreseeable future, and despite temporary recessions, a scarcity of manpower will threaten the maintenance of a desirable rate of economic growth. Mechanisation and automation will help to alleviate this scarcity, but only marginally so. Salvation can be sought confidently only in the more efficient use of the manpower we have, and as it has turned out in the years since the M.R.U.'s first Report, most public and governmental attention has been directed to Training and Redeployment (rather than to other equally promising factors) as ways of increasing the efficiency of the labour force. The Selective Employment Tax (1966) was clearly intended to influence the movement of labour toward areas of demand that could show the greater economic profit from it, and has achieved at best only a very limited success. Of more relevance to the vocational guidance of early school leavers was the Industrial Training Act (1964) which promised financial rewards to those firms with adequate training arrangements and threatened financial penalties to those with unsatisfactory arrangements, the money levied to be used to provide good training facilities elsewhere. It is already clear than an important outcome of the Act has been—and will be increasingly—to help the less talented school leaver to achieve levels of occupational skill that the more primitive training arrangements previously so common (such as, "Sitting-next-to-Nellie") had kept effectively beyond his grasp. The total field of occupations that are within the ability range of the unscholarly school leaver will, therefore, continue to increase as training techniques are improved in different industries and the talented "under achiever" will benefit particularly from this.

The early school leaver has never really had it so good. Because so many of his coevals are choosing to remain at school, the luxury of abundant choice welcomes him in most areas of the country. But this idyllic picture is unlikely to last. The simpler jobs traditionally labelled unskilled and semi-skilled are gradually being lost to mechanisation and automation. To offer a strong right arm and a minimal capacity and inclination to learn will become increasingly insufficient to attract a wage. The future labour force will be more highly skilled. For the unscholarly child to find a place in such a force will require that school leaving be deferred until an adequate foundation of basic educational skill has been achieved upon which it is possible to build a complicated structure of occupational skill. The sounder the foundation, the more ambitious the skill structures one may reasonably attempt to superimpose—even for those whose learning rate is slow. When considering the predicament of the unscholarly child we must consider not merely the contemporary scene but the trends of change and the new situation of labour demand that will be upon us all too soon.

THE EARLY LEAVER'S IMMATURITY

Perhaps the early school leaver's gravest handicap to a successful choice of occupation is his youth. He is insufficiently practised in vocational thinking, has had little opportunity to explore and judge the adult world around him, and his immaturity sets severe limits to the competence with which he confronts the task of choosing an occupation. It is indeed a weighty and complex decision he must make if it is to be done properly and not merely perfunctorily or impulsively, over-swayed by the whims and enthusiasms of others ever ready to give advice. It requires a considerable grasp of information, about jobs and about oneself; it demands insight into the different sorts of lives that different occupations commit one to, and the maturity to assess with confidence which occupation will suit (and which not) the adult one will become in course of time.

After all, a young person on the threshold of adult life does not so much choose a particular job merely as an attractive way of earning a living for half a century. He chooses, rather, a way of life and *a path of vocational development* of which he may see clearly only the job that defines the first step. More distant stages, offering perhaps the challenge of learning, high performance, and examinations, may take him through a sequence of jobs that removes him skill-wise very far from his initial job and into circumstances that radically alter his way of life. Can we fairly ask a 15-year-old child to undertake a decision-making task of such fearsome magnitude; or, having asked him (if only by implication, since we permit him to begin his full-time working life at 15), can we seriously expect that his decision will be appropriately rooted in experience and informed deliberation? Super and Overstreet (1960) are quite satisfied from their research involving 14-year-old New York boys that although at that age they are sufficiently mature to undertake the evaluation of occupational information, they are far from ready to undertake the task of choice. It is implausible to suppose that English boys are significantly more precocious. Is there anything about our educational system, for example, that might provide grounds for hoping that they might be so?

This stubborn fact that the unscholarly child usually chooses to begin his working life at an age when he is too immature to profit fully from professional help when deciding his future provides the biggest challenge to our traditional conception of vocational guidance. To survey his talents (however limited) and provide information about occupations that make a plausible match does nothing to overcome his immaturity and nothing to help him make an informed decision. Neither does it help him to gain awareness of the developing shape of his own life, nor increase his competence to play an active part in fashioning its course in accordance with his own deliberated choice. To be of such help, there are three strategies open to us: (1) we can try to persuade him to remain at school until he is sufficiently mature to undertake a choice that has benefited from the shrewd weighing of all relevant factors, or (2) we can attempt to accelerate the processes of his personal and vocational development by appropriate curriculum interventions and modifications during his compulsory school years, or (3) we can attempt through an ambitious after-care service to help him succeed in his choice or rescue him from an unworkable one before he becomes disturbed, demoralised and maladjusted.

1. Postponement of School Leaving

Of the three proposed aims, this promises to be the easiest to secure. In 1972 the school leaving age will rise to 16. But already there is a notable population trend towards postponement of school leaving which is evident at all ages (from 15 through to the postgraduate years) and in both working class and middle class children. A clear cultural shift in estimation of the value of education is clearly in progress. The sceptic is recommended to compare the current Department of Education and Science Educational Statistics relating to leaving rates with those of a decade ago.

In the post-war years, the early leaver—particularly the potentially talented early leaver—has excited much social concern largely because it had been hoped that the Education Act of 1944 and the 11 plus system of grammar school allocation that was one of its consequences would identify talent in whatever unpromising quarter it lay and ensure its development through 5th and 6th form achievement. The Central Advisory Council for Education's Report on *Early Leaving* (1954) gave depressing figures of national talent lost through early school-leaving, and the C.A.C.E.'s later report on secondary education (the *Crowther Report*, 1960) re-confirmed the general picture. However, the Crowther Report did note an improvement in school-leaving rates and commented that when attractive 5th form provision is made it does not go unused. It noted, too, the effect of the comprehensive school in increasing readiness to remain at school. Comment on this issue in the 1960's has shown a clear shift from expressions of disquiet to a note of cheerful optimism well founded and sustained in each year's education statistics.

If the present trend continues (as seems likely), the 1970's will relieve us of the frustrating task of guiding with indecent brevity the job choices of children too immature to benefit properly from the service we have to offer. Instead, our labours will be in the main more leisurely spread with young adults whose extra years of maturity will enable our guidance provision to make psychological sense.

2. Accelerating Vocational Maturity

An emerging theme in educational thinking in the 1960's is to consider education from the point of view of the pupil's developmental needs rather than in terms of what it is thought he should be taught. The claims on curricular time of other than purely scholastic matters are being extensively debated. More and more teachers are showing concern for the personal and social development of their pupils in addition to their scholastic needs, and their view of the nature of scholastic requirements has been modified by consideration of other pupil needs. It originated in an insistence that education should be child-centred rather than subject-centred, and a reminder that we should teach children, not subjects. The theme is similar to what was intended by an earlier generation of American theorists who argued for the "personalisation" of education.

An early stimulus to this movement originated in the schools being asked to provide sex education. It is now quite clear that an essentially scholastic and physiological understanding of this need fails to meet it. A more recent stimulus and a very influential one has been the Newsom Report on the education of the unscholarly child (C.A.C.E., 1963). It is a cogent criticism of the failure of traditional curricula to harness the wits and interests of such children, and a plea for a fresh approach that is rooted in an understanding of their major needs and which aims to prepare them for the demands of work and leisure time in the adult world that awaits them. To bring the adult world more tangibly into the classroom and to take pupils from school into the surrounding community to learn at first hand its structure and its ways—these are proving valuable ways of reviving the jaded interests of "non-examinable" secondary pupils. Two gains are hoped for: that the increased pupil enthusiasm will result in measurable improvements in attainment in all the basic curricular subjects, and that the outward-looking adult life orientation of the Newsom programme will ensure that pupils will undertake the transition from school to work with more maturity and a better understanding of their total predicament.

Understandably, careers work has assumed a prominent, and sometimes a central, role in Newsom inspired courses. Thus, a continuous stimulus to vocational thinking has been introduced early in the secondary school period instead of being delayed until the final term or two. A planned series of occupational visits, each one well prepared in advance and followed up with discussion and written exercises is a common feature of such courses. Occupational literature is brought explicitly into class work, and carefully selected speakers are invited from local firms to give a disinterested and accurate picture of their working lives. The planning of such courses has always relied heavily on the help and enthusiasm of the local Y.E.O. who has usually established excellent co-operative relations with the careers teacher. Together, they have ensured that pupils extract the maximum personal relevance from such vicarious careers experiences by helping them to explore the dimensions of human variability and through this to understand aspects (particularly occupationally relevant aspects) of their own individuality.

After such a systematic and protracted preparation, the early school leaver is better placed to make a well considered choice of occupation than he would otherwise be.

All this requires an ambitious development of the role of the careers teacher. His normal teaching load has been lightened (though often less than he would wish) to free him to plan and control an elaborate careers programme, and to work out with his colleagues the details of their participation in the total programme. He may, too, have been fortunate to secure secondment to a D.E.S. full-time course for careers teachers, and will certainly have profited from the D.E.S. (1965) booklet on careers guidance and perhaps also from the Schools Council (1967) working paper on curricula for the young school leaver.

Even more recent evidence of concern for the pupil's personal and social and vocational development is the appearance of the school counsellor (Fuller, 1967). Though they will be thin on the ground for a good many years, they will undoubtedly help alongside trained and enthusiastic careers staff and Y.E.O.'s to form a team whose co-operative endeavours will effectively accelerate the vocational development of secondary school pupils. One's only regret is that the spread of these ideas and practices, though steady, is infuriatingly slow.

3. After-care and Second Thoughts

One must regret that we do not have a climate of public opinion favourable to occupational exploration and experimentation in the early years of adult life, for there is clearly no better basis for the choice of an occupation than to have tasted in realistic fashion the different working environments that are available and to have seen for oneself at close quarters the kinds of adult that people these environments. The quality of the vocational guidance offered in the years of immaturity would cease to be a matter of crucial importance if young workers were permitted to regard their initial choices as tentative, exploratory and revokable without prejudice. Unfortunately, the young worker who fails in his job (whether voluntarily or involuntarily) often finds the experience so disturbing that he is unable to achieve a balanced and accurate understanding of the causes of his failure. Some, perhaps, respond with defiance and allocate the blame exclusively elsewhere; others suffer so great a blow to their self esteem that they come to live with permanently reduced conceptions of their capacities and settle for more modest levels of aspiration. Either way, there is some personality damage and some loss of talent to the community. Nor is the person's distress helped by evidence that he is suspected of instability and of "not knowing his own mind" by the second employer he approaches. It is not known how many young lives are marred, temporarily or permanently, by occupational failure, nor conversely, how many are able to learn constructively from such an experience and gain something in personal insight and maturity. In the absence of facts we would be wiser, perhaps, to fear the worst and plan our after-care services accordingly (see Maizels, 1965).

We do not have an adequate after-care service to supplement and carry through the vocational guidance we provide for our school leavers. We barely have the rudiments of such a service. The Youth Employment Service recognises its obligation to conduct a Review of Progress by follow-up of all school leavers, but the service is so overstrained by its responsibilities to school children that its work with young workers suffers, as the recent Albemarle Report on the Y.E.S. recognizes (Ministry of Labour, 1965). The full requirements of a satisfactory after-care service have never, in any case, been spelled out in a sufficiently ambitious way. Nonetheless, after-care remains an important final safety net to rescue the immature from the worst consequences of an ill-considered occupational choice, either by guiding them speedily to a more congenial alternative or by supporting them through the worst difficulties of adjustment to the choice they have made and which they wish to see succeed.

We sometimes overlook that not all occupational failure reflects either inadequate guidance or immaturity of choice. Good guidance and carefully considered choice are sometimes wrecked by matters that are the responsibility of the employer—poor training, clumsy supervision, lack of communication, imprecise definition of duties, conflicting role expectancies. The list could be continued. After-care, therefore, has an invaluable advisory and educational contribution to offer the employer on his induction arrangements. The Y.E.O. could become as useful and as familiar a figure "dropping in" on the firm as the Appointed Factory Doctor or the Factory Inspector. His potential contribution to industrial efficiency and human contentment is certainly not less than theirs.

The person who will stand to gain most, perhaps, from such an after-care service will be he whose wits are so limited that he learns only slowly and after considerable effort. Such people achieve impressive levels of skill in the long run provided the employer understands how much time they will need and is patient. Because of the personal effort they must invest in learning it is imperative that their task be aided by competent training procedures, and that the skill they acquire with so much effort is not wasted by job failure or job redundancy.

REFERENCES

Central Advisory Council for Education (1954) *Early Leaving: A Report.* Ministry of Education, London, H.M.S.O.

Central Advisory Council for Education (1960) *15 to 18: The Crowther Report.* Ministry of Education, London, H.M.S.O.

Central Advisory Council for Education (1963) *Half Our Future—The Newsom Report.* Ministry of Education, London, H.M.S.O.

Department of Education and Science (1965) *Careers Guidance in Schools.* London, H.M.S.O.

Fuller, J. A. (1967) School counselling: a first enquiry. *Educational Research*, **9**, 135–136.

Maizels, Joan (1965) The entry of school leavers into employment. *British Journal of Industrial Relations*, **3**, 77–89.

Ministry of Labour (1964) *The Pattern of the Future.* Manpower Studies No. 1. London, H.M.S.O.

Ministry of Labour (1965) *The Future Development of the Youth Employment Service.* The Albemarle Report. London, H.M.S.O.

O'Connor, N., and Tizard, J. (1956) *The Social Problem of Mental Deficiency.* London, Pergamon Press.

Schools Council (1967) *Society and the Young School Leaver*—Working Paper No. 11. London, H.M.S.O.

Super, D. E., and Overstreet, P. L. (1960) *The Vocational Maturity of Ninth Grade Boys.* N.Y., Bureau of Publications, Teachers College, Columbia University.

31. *Autocoun: A Computer-based Automated Counseling Simulation System*

JOHN W. LOUGHARY, DELOSS FRIESEN and ROBERT HURST

AUTOCOUN is an attempt to simulate with a computer selected aspects of the counseling behavior of an expert counselor. The testing of an automated counseling system in March, 1965, stemmed from work begun in 1959 on a related but different problem. The intervening activities represent a series of changes in interest and conceptualizations of counseling processes and outcomes.

Therefore, before reporting some results of testing autocoun, we will briefly describe its evolution. In some respects, the latter is more important than the system itself, particularly in regard to an understanding of counseling processes. The objectives of the project can be stated as follows: (1) determine which aspect of a counselor's pre-interview and interview behavior can be automated; (2) determine counselee attitudes towards an automated counseling system; (3) further test a method for analyzing counseling behavior; and (4) obtain guidelines for further exploration of the use of computers in counseling and related areas.

Our initial interest was not in simulation, but rather in applying system analysis concepts and procedures to school guidance programs. Specifically, we sought to locate and correct weaknesses in guidance programs by conceptualizing them in terms of their components, thus making it possible to improve a total guidance program by treating only its malfunctioning components, rather than attempting to overhaul the total system, many components of which were functioning adequately. We are still in this activity, attempting to refine our analysis procedures.

As would be expected, we frequently found that systems broke down due to weak "people" components. Often, there were poorly trained clerical persons, and teachers inadequately oriented to the purposes and functions of guidance programs. Of more basic importance, however, were weaknesses in counselors themselves. We were reminded that many counselors who qualify professionally in regard to masters' degrees and state certification frequently lack the behavioral competencies to achieve many of

(Reprinted by permission of publisher and authors from *Personnel and Guidance Journal*, vol. 45, No. 1, 1966, pp. 6–15.)

their stated objectives with counselees. This should not be news to the initiated.

After reviewing what we had experienced and read about counselor education, we concluded that counselor education programs in general place much greater emphasis on theory (counseling and otherwise) than on developing a wide variety of behaviors useful in counseling. With regard to the latter, most attention is given to program development skills, and relatively unprogrammed practicums where the aspiring counselor learns to say "Hmmmm," "you feel," and "tell me more than that," in a convincing manner.

Let it be clear that we have no desire for mechanical counselors with one technique for each counselee needed, but it does seem reasonable to maintain that *a counselor should have the ability to employ a particular technique or procedure in regard to a particular counselee's needs, with reasonable confidence that the procedure is more apt to produce the desired counselee behavior than would alternative procedures.* In order to teach counselors such procedures, one must know what they are. While we had our own biases about counseling competencies and many textbooks treat this subject, we rejected both sources. The first, for obvious reasons, and the second because they seldom specify the counselor *behaviors* involved.

We turned to another source, the counselor himself, and hypothesized that if we carefully observed the work of an expert counselor it should be possible to describe his behavior. Given such descriptions, we could then consider devising methods of teaching these behaviors.

The still-unresolved problem concerned the validity of our counseling behavior descriptions. We would unavoidably abstract and select certain behaviors and delete others. How could we be sure that the counselor behaviors selected were actually the behaviors that made a difference in counselee behavior?

One method of testing the validity of the counselor behavior identified would be to teach someone, or something, to act like a counselor and then compare the outcomes with those obtained by a "real" counselor. We decided to attempt simulating counselor behavior on a computer system. If the general validity criterion for counselor behavior is resultant counselee behavior, then a counseling simulation system is valid if it results in counselee behavior similar to that effected by a human counselor. A not infrequent reaction to this scheme is that you simply cannot program a computer to behave like a counselor. That is, it is impossible to program acceptance, support, empathy, sensitivity to nonverbal communication, and all those other qualities attributed to counselors, in a computer. Nor can a computer communicate dynamically with a counselee, as a counselor is supposed to do. Perhaps not.

At the same time, it is clear that a computer can be programmed to simulate some behavior performed by counselors, such as adding grade points, looking up scores, converting scores, reporting scores, and even making predictions regarding a counselee's chances for surviving or achieving in various school and occupational environments.

Because we were not at all certain as to where to draw the line in regard to what behavior could be simulated, we decided to take a relatively simple counseling situation, viz., educational planning interviews with ninth-grade pupils, and attempt to determine how much and what aspect of the counselor's behavior could be simulated.

PRELIMINARY FIELD WORK

The initial decision was to model the automated system on the behavior of "expert" counselors, and one of the first tasks was to obtain a clear description of how expert counselors actually behave in educational counseling sessions with ninth-grade counselees. Specifically, we wanted to understand (1) the procedures they use; (2) the systems they employ in using the procedures; and (3) the specific rules they use in making decisions, recommendations, and in guiding their own behavior with a counselee.

In order to secure the data needed to answer these questions, counselor educators and supervisors in nationally recognized training programs and school systems were asked to supply the names of counselors whom they felt were among the best five per cent of all the counselors they had observed. The definition of "best" was left to them.

Twenty-five such counselors from a variety of school districts throughout the United States were identified and asked to tape-record two things: (1) verbalizations of their thoughts as they examined a counselee's cumulative folder in preparation for an educational planning session, and (2) an interview with the pupil. The counselors were visited by members of the research group, and contents of cumulative folders were noted at the time of the recordings.

The recordings were analyzed in two ways. First, the procedures followed by a counselor were flow-charted in order to provide a conceptualization of his counseling as a system. Second, the flow-charts were inspected and recordings replayed in an attempt to identify each counselor's rules.

It became apparent that such analysis was feasible and that rules which the counselors were using were readily identified. However, a great variation in the kind of rules used from counselor to counselor was discovered. These rules were specifically related to such things as a counselor's school district; i.e., regulations relating to transfer and articulation; the kinds of tests used in a district testing program; the grading system of a school district; and the counselor's own personal orientation to counseling. Some of the counselors were found to be highly manipulative, i.e., felt that they knew the right thing to do for or with a certain student and acted with little hesitancy on these feelings. Others were more "client-centered," for lack of a better term, allowing a counselee to decide pretty much for himself with only an interpretive kind of guidance to initiate and stimulate planning. On the basis of these differences it was decided that it would be more fruitful for purposes of developing an automated system to model the behavior of a single counselor.

COUNSELOR MODEL

A counselor was selected from Cubberley High School in Palo Alto, California, as the model counselor. As indicated, the counseling function was educational counseling with ninth-grade students for course planning purposes. Twenty-five ninth-grade students unknown to the counselor were selected. The counselor then recorded: (1) his "talking out loud" as he studied each cumulative folder, and (2) an educational planning interview with each pupil.

Recordings were analyzed as described above. The analysis was done in pursuit of two kinds of outcomes: (1) the pre-interview behavior, where we wanted to simulate the counselor's planning and preparation for an interview, and (2) the simulation of the interview itself. Cogswell and Estavan at System Development Corporation (SDC) took primary responsibility for the former, and those of us at Oregon for the latter.

A flow-chart was developed for each interview, and a composite flow-chart was developed as a framework around which to build the program logic. Intensive examination of the flow-charts and of the typescripts was made by the researchers to discover the rules being used by the counselor in making decisions or recommendations about students. The rules took such forms as: "In order to take five solids in the tenth grade a student should have an overall B average in his previous year's work," and "Firm scheduling decisions in grades 11 and 12 can be made only on the basis of the student's performance in grades 10 and 11."

In order to allay as much as possible the preoccupation of the student with the machinery being used, the interview format followed by the counselor was maintained wherever possible within the limits of machine capabilities.

In brief, analysis of 25 pre-interview and interview recordings led to the logic for developing (1) a pre-interview program which simulates the pupil appraisal and other interview preparatory work done by the counselor, and (2) an actual interview program aimed at securing the counselee's decisions regarding the high school courses he would include in his schedule.

We should like to turn now to a more detailed and systematic account of the total automated counseling system.

THE AUTOMATED COUNSELING SYSTEM

The Automated Counseling System was constructed to produce two general outcomes. The first is an analysis of certain pupil appraisal data commonly found in cumulative folders. The analysis results in a number of predictive statements regarding a student's probable performance in high school and college courses (local district high school courses and six types of colleges and universities). The logic for the pupil appraisal analysis and a description of its workings has been described in detail by Cogswell and Estavan (1965) and will not be repeated here. Suffice it to say that the program causes the computer to calculate a pupil's grade-point average (GPA), look up his high school scholastic aptitude scores, and then select expectancies from prediction tables based on local norms. Expectancies then serve as rules for calculating the goodness of the pupil course choices and for determining which messages will be conveyed to him from the computer's repertoire of statements.

The second outcome is a list of specific courses which the student has decided to take in grade 10, and a tentative choice for courses in grades 11 and 12. An additional outcome is a print-out to counselors identifying students needing additional help, including certain diagnostic information regarding the problems involved.

The automated counseling system can be conceptualized as consisting of the following seven components:

1. Appraisal data regarding pupils (grades, test scores, and family socio-economic data), stored on tape.
2. Prediction or experience tables for Palo Alto schools.
3. The curricular offerings of a particular high school.
4. A set of instructions and rules for deciding what to say to pupils and for determining what to report to counselors.
5. A repertoire of statements which the computer can make to the pupil.
6. A set of instructions for data analysis and synthesis.
7. The computer and related input/output devices.

The experience tables were developed through the research division of the Palo Alto Unified School District (Yabroff, 1964) and indicate the probability (in chances out of 10) that a student with a known GPA in grade nine and a known scholastic aptitude measure will receive either an A, B, C+, C, or below C grade average in his course work during high school. Similar tables have been developed to indicate the probability (in chances out of 10) that a student with a projected high school average of A, B, C+, C, or below C will be accepted at various kinds of colleges. The kinds of colleges include Ivy League colleges, "other" colleges and universities, California State colleges, junior colleges, and technical-vocational schools. The curriculum offerings at Cubberley High School were obtained and organized on a chart for student use during the automated interview.

The computer used in the automated interview is an IBM, Q-32, a large experimental computer with a time-sharing system allowing for the simultaneous use of its capacities by a number of remote stations. Input and output to pupils is via a TWX Model 31.

Perhaps the clearest way to describe how autocoun operates is to present excerpts from an actual interview print-out.

The pupil is seated at a TWX (teletype) keyboard, and told to type his student number and then the carriage return key. He does this and the following dialogue takes place:

You are about to participate in an interview with an automated counselor.

The computer will help you plan what you want to do in high school and in later life.

But first, just to let the computer know you are there, please type the latter A and a carriage return (CR) (red key on the right-hand side of the keyboard).

**** A

Good.

The most important key is the CR key (red key on the right).

You will use it to let the computer know that you have made an answer.

Just for practice, type the letter B and a CR key (red key).

**** B

OK ...

Sometimes you will be asked to answer a yes or no question.

When you are, just type YES or NO and a CR, don't forget the CR.

Let's try it.

Here is a question ... please type YES or NO.

**** Yes

Fine ...

Many other people are using this computer right now.

Once in a while the computer will have to take care of their urgent needs.

When you have read this, type OK and a CR.

**** OK

Good.

By now, you have noticed that before you type an answer, the typewriter types stars like this:

****

This is to let you know that it is time for you to type something.

You should never type anything until after the stars are typed out by the computer.

Do you understand?

Please type YES or NO.

**** Yes

Another very important key is the / or "slash" key.

It is the green key on the bottom right of the keyboard.

Look for the / key (green key).

When you find it, type / and a CR.

**** /

Sometimes you will have to type more than one line and the computer cannot tell in advance how many lines you will type.

In such a case, you will let the computer know that you have finished by typing a / and a CR.
What you type will look something like this:
**** 1
**** 2
**** /
Let's try it.
Type 1 and a CR, 2 and a CR, and a / and a CR.
(Wait for the stars).
**** 11
Now, now.
Look up at the example and try again.
... and so forth.

This orientation sequence takes about eight minutes. The counseling then begins as follows:

Please type your ID number and a CR.
**** 17
Is your name John Jones?
**** Yes
According to my records this is how you did last semester.

Code	Course	Grade
1	P.E.	B
2	English 1	C
3	General Science	C
4	European History	A
5	Algebra	C
6	Spanish 1	B
7	Typing	B

Is this correct?
If so, type YES; if not, type NO.
**** Yes
Are you having any problems with any of these courses? Please type YES or NO.
**** Yes
Type the number of each course that is giving you trouble.
Type a CR after each number.
When you are all through, type a / and a CR.
**** 5/
What kind of problem do you have with Algebra?
Please type in the nature of the problem. A few words will be OK.
When you are all finished, type a / and a CR.
**** Don't like Arithmetic problems/
I see ...

If you would like to discuss this problem further, make an appointment with your counselor.
Would you like to continue with this interview at this time, or would you like to discuss you problems with your counselor before you continue?
Type GO if you'd like to continue. Type STOP if you'd like to stop.
**** Go
Do you plan to continue your formal education beyond high school?
**** Yes
Which of the following is most like the school you plan to attend?
1. Ivy League College
2. Other College or University
3. California State College
4. Junior College
5. Business or Vocational School
6. I have not yet decided

Type the appropriate code.
**** 3
Do you intend to major in Engineering or one of the Sciences?
**** Yes
Here are some areas of Science and some examples.

Code	Area	Examples
1	Physical Sciences	Geology, Chemistry, Physics
2	Biological Sciences	Biology, Pre-Med, Pre-Nursing, etc.
3	Social Sciences	Psychology, Sociology, Anthropology
4	Mathematics	Math, Statistics, Computer Programming, etc.
5	Engineering	Architecture, Drafting, Electronics, etc.

Please type the code number of the kind of science you intend to major in.
**** 3
All right. Let's see if we can pinpoint your area.
1 Psychology
2 Sociology
3 Anthropology
4 Social Work

Type the appropriate code.
**** 1
OK ...
The grades you get in high school largely determine the type of college you will be able to attend.
Let's just take a look at your projected high school grades based on your present performance.
Students who got grades like yours in junior high, did as follows at Cubberley:
50 per cent earned B

40 per cent earned C+
10 per cent earned C

On the basis of your projected grades, your present college choice indicates that you are shooting pretty high.

The fact that you are thinking about what you are going to do after school is a good sign.

The important thing is to have some ideas and be thinking about them, and what you might eventually do.

(You ought to acquaint yourself with college entrance requirements at the schools you consider)

... and so on until the interview is completed.

The total interview can take from approximately 8 to 30 minutes, depending upon the appropriateness, the complexity, and the specificity of the pupil's planning, and upon the pace which he sets for interacting with the computer.

TESTING AUTOCOUN

The initial test in a real school environment was concerned with (1) determining the validity of the system, and (2) securing a measure of counselee attitudes toward the system.

The basic validity criterion was the similarity of pupil appraisal data and course decisions generated by the two counseling modes. Our aim was to simulate counseling to the extent that students would make the same kinds of educational decisions with the computer's help as they made with that of a human counselor. The question of which mode produces the *best* results was not the concern of this study.

A sample of 40 ninth-grade students, 23 boys and 17 girls, was drawn at random from Wilbur Junior High School in Palo Alto, California. Students ranged in ability from the third to the 98th percentile on the School and College Ability Test. The sample mean score was at the 65th percentile on national norms.

The sample of students was randomly divided into two groups of 20 each. One group was interviewed by the model counselor and the automated counseling system, and the second group was interviewed by a second counselor and the automated counseling system. As a precaution to offset the effects of order, each of the two groups was divided into two further sub-groups. The order of interview modes was alternated for each of the sub-groups.

Statements and answers to questions relating to pupil appraisal were obtained from the model counselor, the second counselor, and the automated system. The results of the educational planning interview (that is, the courses selected for high school and the degree of completeness of course planning) and data relating to limitations of the counselor-based system, were also collected.

Data from subjects regarding limitations of the computer-based counseling system were gathered from the machine out-put, and from a structured interview following the completion of both counseling interviews. The attitude scale was administered after the two interviews had been completed.

RESULTS

The machine system agreed with the human counselor on approximately 75 per cent of the appraisal statements. The following differences were significant at the ·05 level:

1. The automated counseling system predicted a significantly higher GPA for pupils than did the model counselor.
2. In pre-interview appraisal the automated system predicted more students as potential dropouts than did the human counselor.
3. The automated system encouraged more students to explore widely in academic areas than did the human counselor.
4. The automated system predicted more students as getting better grades than would be predicted on the basis of their aptitude scores than did the human counselor.
5. The automated system identified more students as having a discrepancy between aptitude and achievement great enough to suspect the aptitude test results than did the human counselor.

Results regarding completeness and content of course programs selected by students include the following:

1. The automated counseling system and the human counselor had 65 per cent agreement regarding tenth-grade course plans, 65 per cent agreement regarding eleventh-grade course plans, and 53 per cent agreement regarding twelfth-grade course plans. The differences were statistically significant at the ·05 level for grades 10 and 12, but not for grade 11.
2. There were no significant differences regarding completeness of course plans between counseling modes for grade 10 and 11. There was a significant difference for completeness of course plans between counseling modes for grade 12. All students seeing the counselor made at least a partial course plan for grade 12, while 60 per cent counseled by the machine made no course plans for grade 12.
3. A significantly greater number of pupils indicated having problems with courses to the computer than they did to the human counselor.
4. The machine system had closer agreement with the second counselor than with the model counselor, but these differences were not significant. Essentially, the two counselors were quite similar in regard to the criteria used in the study.
5. In general there was no order or interaction effect when the model counselor and the machine, and the second counselor and the machine, respectively, were compared.

6. There was no significant difference between the counselor and the machine system regarding the number of students making total course plans.

7. Students' final tenth-grade course selections, made approximately two weeks after the test was completed, were obtained and compared with decisions made by students at the end of the two experimental treatments. The analysis produced the following results:

a. There was a statistically significant difference between the computer-selected plans and the final course plans.
b. There was not a significant difference between the counselor-selected plans and the final course plans.

8. The differences between the course selections made with the automated system and the final selections fell into one of three classifications:

a. Change from a special unit to another special unit (for example, from one math course to another math course).
b. Changes from one elective to another elective (defined generally as non-homework courses).
c. Changes from an elective to no course.

Over 50 per cent of the changes from the computer-assisted selections to the final selections involved changing one course to another in the same field.

A detailed analysis of this aspect of the project is available (Friesen, 1965). Less work has been done on analysis of attitude data, but the following general reactions can be reported:

1. Nearly all students had a favorable attitude toward both counseling modes, but were more positive toward the human than the automated counseling system.

2. Pupils felt that the human counselor had a greater *amount* of information than the automated counseling system.

3. Pupils felt that the human counselor would know more about their interests and personality than the automated counseling system.

4. Pupils felt that the machine had more *specific* and *factual* information than the human counselor regarding such things as GPA and college requirements.

5. Thirty-eight out of the 40 pupils indicated that they would like to see the machine system used regularly in the school, but in conjunction with human counselors.

DISCUSSION

We have essentially two kinds of validation data consisting of (1) measures of similarity between the automated counseling system and human counselors regarding pre- and post-interview pupil appraisal, and (2) measures of similarity regarding interview out-put, i.e., course selections. In addition, there are data that at least hint at the generalizability of Autocoun and its single counselor model. Finally, there is some indication of how pupils feel about using the computer-based system.

This paper will conclude with a brief comment regarding each of these kinds of data. Let it be restated first, however, that during the Autocoun test we were not concerned with comparing the goodness of the two counseling modes.

In regard to pupil appraisal, we believe that the basic shortcoming of Autocoun is that it lacks certain data possessed or possessable by the human counselors. Autocoun deals strictly in terms of probability, working from an expectancy table, using the rules that the model counselor agreed that he uses. Apparently, a counselor is able to better the predictive data (or contaminate it, as you wish) with his feelings and impressions made about the counselee during an interview. We believe that some of these additional data and rules used by a counselor could be identified and built into Autocoun, and thus, in regard to extent of simulation, increase its validity. Other data, such as non-verbal cues and general impressions, and probably some rules, defy automation.

As to agreement between counseling modes regarding course selections, we feel that for its initial counseling experience, Autocoun did well in hitting 66 per cent of the courses selected with the aid of human counselors. Two points need mentioning here. First, Autocoun had an advantage in the scoring procedure in this comparison, in that the method used was to compare Autocoun course selections with the human counselor selections, using only positive comparisons. Thus, for example, if the counselor interview resulted in selecting courses A, B, and C, and Autocoun resulted in selecting courses A, B, C, D, and F, a perfect score was recorded since Autocoun matched A, B, and C. Courses D and F were not considered.

On the other hand, it was immediately apparent after the test that we should have been more precise regarding prerequisites for enrollment in number of the courses. This problem could easily be corrected by reprogramming Autocoun to generate more messages to students regarding illegal selections.

Other differences in course selections can be accounted for by Autocoun's relatively limited communications ability (that is, its repertoire of statements). For example, the difference in taking French as compared to German, or A Cappella in contrast to Girl's Glee, is probably a function of providing the student with a small amount of information such as the differences regarding the probable function of foreign languages in college or a vocation (essentially the counselors' professional opinions), or information about the activities engaged in by each of the two performing classes. Further study could identify a number of these kinds of information which could be programmed in Autocoun.

Contrary to the notion developed during our earlier pilot work, the two counselors were found to be very similar in terms of the criteria employed. The second counselor worked in the test junior high school and knew all of the subjects. The model counselor was from the high school to which the test junior high sends students. Consequently, the model counselor worked only from cumulative records and whatever in-interview assessment he made, while the second counselor supplemented cumulative folder data with a personal knowledge of students.

While the output of the two counselors were more similar to each other than to that of the machine, the second counselor's statements and student decisions were more like the machine than were the model counselor's. One explanation for this seemingly inconsistent finding concerns the nature or validity of the extra—or noncumulative folder—data available to each counselor. Apparently both counselors attempted to better the actuarial data with additional appraisal data for each student. The second counselor's additional data, while much different in nature than the prediction tables, were based on a knowledge of the pupils, and were probably reasonably reliable and valid, and thus in the final analysis consistent with the actuarial information.

The model counselor's additional data, in contrast, were based on a single brief contact with students and probably in many cases were unreliable. As a result, the second counselor's additional data probably contaminated the actuarial prediction less than did the model counselor's.

Five of the second counselor's interview recordings had been analyzed earlier in the study, and his counseling style was found to be much more difficult to depict in flow-chart form than was the model counselor's. If one accepts this as a valid assertion, then the findings suggest that counseling style was not especially significant in regard to the criteria used. Importance of style to other kinds of counseling outcomes is a topic that we would like to investigate in future versions of Autocoun.

Pupils had few problems using Autocoun, and in general enjoyed interacting with the computer. While this may be attributed to the novelty of the situation, it does demonstrate that the computer-based system poses no particular threat to pupils.

In conclusion, the current version of Autocoun will not replace school counselors. It does demonstrate, however, the operational feasibility and suggests the potential value of a computer-based pupil information system, capable of direct interaction with students. We may never counsel—in the current definition of counseling—by computer. But, and this is entirely our own speculation, we may assign certain counseling functions to machines, and others to counselors. When this happens, counseling as we know it will be quite a different concept, and we hope its usefulness to man will be increased. There seems little if any question whether man-machine systems will emerge in counseling, teaching, and other essentially personal-relationship professions. The important questions are, rather, how will they emerge, what form will they take, and who will monitor and control their development? In our judgment, it is of the utmost importance that those of us who have assumed the responsibilities and privilege of helping others with their personal problems and aspirations become well enough informed regarding man-machine systems to participate intelligently and sensitively in their development. It is only in this way that we can assure that automated systems contribute to, rather than inhibit, the freedom of the individual.

REFERENCES

COGSWELL, J., and ESTAVAN, D. (1965) Explorations in computer assisted counseling. *Technical Memorandum* 2582. Santa Monica, Calif.: System Development Corp., August 6.

FRIESEN, D. D. (1965) The validation of an automated counseling system. Unpublished doctoral thesis. Univ. Oregon.

YABROFF, W. W. (1964) *Design for decision, a handbook of relevant information for plans and decisions in the ninth grade*. Palo Alto (Calif.) Unified School District.

GUIDANCE IN PRACTICE: FURTHER READING

ANDREW, D. C., and WILLEY, R. D. (1958) *Administration and Organisation of the Guidance Program*. New York, Harper.

BENNET, M. E. (1955) *Guidance in Groups*. New York, McGraw-Hill.

CHRISTENSEN, T. E., and MOOSEY, E. R. (eds.) (1966) *A Guidance and Curriculum Guide for Junior High School Grade Nine General Occupations Program*. Worcester, Massachusetts Public Schools.

DEPARTMENT OF EDUCATION AND SCIENCE (1965) *Careers Guidance in Schools*, London, H.M.S.O.

EARLE, F. M. (1931) *Methods of Choosing a Career*. London, Harrap.

HEGINBOTHAM, H. (1951) *The Youth Employment Service*. London, Methuen.

INTERNATIONAL BUREAU OF EDUCATION (1967) *The Organization of Educational and Vocational Guidance*, 26th International Conference on Public Education, Geneva 1963. Publication 254, Unesco, Paris. (It provides a comparative study of the organization of educational and vocational guidance in 73 countries.—Eds.)

INTERNATIONAL LABOUR OFFICE (1964) *The I.L.O. and Youth*. I.L.O., Geneva.

INSTITUTE OF YOUTH EMPLOYMENT OFFICERS (1964) *Preparation of Young People for Employment*.

INSTITUTE OF YOUTH EMPLOYMENT OFFICERS (1966) *First Survey of Recent Research Relevant to a Careers Service for Young People*.

JOHNSTON, E. G., PETERS, M., and EVRAIFF, W. (1959) *The Role of the Teacher in Guidance*. New Jersey, Prentice-Hall.

LOFQUIST, L. H., and ENGLAND, G. W. (1961) *Problems in Vocational Counseling*. Dubuque, Iowa, W. C. Brown.

LOUGHARY, J. W. (ed.) (1966) *Man Machine Systems in Education*. New York, Harper & Row.

MILLER, G. D., and SWANSON, E. O. (eds.) (1964) *Automation: the Threat and the Promise. The Role of the Counselor in the Manpower Revolution*. National Vocational Guidance Association, Washington.

MINISTRY OF EDUCATION (1963) *Half our Future—The Newsom Report*. Central Advisory Council for Education, London, H.M.S.O.

MINISTRY OF LABOUR (1945) *Report of the Committee on the Juvenile Employment Service—The Ince Report*. London, H.M.S.O.

MINISTRY OF LABOUR (1965) *The Work of the Youth Employment Service 1962–1965*. National Youth Employment Council, London, H.M.S.O.

Ministry of Labour (1965) *The Future Development of the Youth Employment Service—The Albemarle Report.* National Youth Employment Council, London, H.M.S.O.

Palmer, V. C. (1965) *Student Guidance.* London, Longmans.

Stoops, E. (ed.) (1959) *Guidance Services: Organisation and Administration.* New York, McGraw-Hill.

Strong, E. K. (1955) *Vocational Interests 18 Years After College.* Minneapolis, University of Minnesota, Press.

Avent, C. (1964) A careers advisory service for technical institutions. *A.T.I. Paper*, June 1964.

Calderwood, B. (1959) Group methods of giving careers information. *Youth Employment*, **12**, 41–46.

Cavanagh, P., Drake, R. I., and Taylor, K. F. (1963) Youth Employment Service interviews: Part 2, Differences between interviews. *Occupational Psychology*, **36**, 132–139.

Cavanagh, P., Drake, R. I., and Taylor, K. F. (1963) Youth Employment Service interviews: Part 3, Interview performance and individual differences. *Occupational Psychology*, **37**, 122–129.

Floud, J., and Halsey, A. H. (1961) English secondary schools and the supply of labour. In A. H. Halsey, J. Floud and C. A. Anderson (eds.), *Education Economy and Society*, Glencoe, Ill., Free Press.

Froehlich, C. P. (1949) *Evaluating guidance procedures: a review of the literature.* Misc. 3310. Washington, D.C.: Federal Security Agency, Office of Education.

Hart, J. D., and Lifton, W. M. (1958) Of things to come: automation and counseling. *Personnel and Guidance Journal*, **37**, 282.

Hoyt, K. B. (1963) A challenge to vocational guidance: the speciality oriented student. *Vocational Guidance Quarterly*, 192–198.

Hunt, E. P., and Smith, P. (1945) Vocational psychology and choice of employment, *Occupational Psychology*, **19**, 109–116.

Jahoda, G., and Chalmers, A. D. (1963) The Youth Employment Service, a consumer perspective. *Occupational Psychology*, **37**, 20–43.

Jahoda, G., and Chalmers, A. D. (1963) School leavers' recall of the interview with the youth employment officer. *Occupational Psychology*, **37**, 112–121.

Lifton, W. M. (1964/5) Counseling theory and the use of educational media. *Vocational Guidance Quarterly*, **13**, 77–82.

Loughary, J. W. (1967) Can teachers survive the educational revolution? *Phi Delta Kappan*, January 1967.

Loughary, J. W. (1966) Will counseling be eliminated in the cybernation revolution? Paper presented at the College Entrance Board Invitational Conference on Preparation of School Counselors, Chicago. February 25th, 1966.

Moynihan, D. P. (1964) Morality of work and immorality of opportunity. *Vocational Guidance Quarterly*, **12**, 229–236.

Nelson, D. M. (1964) Studying the employment and training of a national sample of 17-year olds. *Occupational Psychology*, **38**, 183–190.

Rodger, A. (1939) A follow-up of vocationally advised cases. *Human Factor*, **11**, 16–26.

Rodger, A. (1955) The effective use of manpower. Presidential address, section J. British Association for the Advancement of Science, *Journal for the Advancement of Science*, **12**, 237–249.

Rodger, A. (1962) Arranging jobs for the young. *New Society*, December 6th, 1962, 21–23.

Stone, H. (1948) Are vocational orientation courses worth their salt? *Educational and Psychological Measurement*, **8**, 161.

Torode, J. A. (1965) How the Youth Employment Service should change. *New Society*, No. 131, 1st April 1965.

WINTMAN, C. (1961) There's much to be said for career work. *Vocational Guidance Quarterly*, Spring 1961, 215.

YATES, A. (1959) Guidance services in the United States (Educational Guidance—1). *Educational Research* **1**, 37–48.

INDUSTRIAL TRAINING

Everyone concerned with vocational guidance must, at least to some extent, be concerned with the industrial training of young workers. These few references will provide an introduction to the pertinent literature.

INDUSTRIAL TRAINING COUNCIL (1960) *Training Boys in Industry—The Non-Apprentices.* London, Industrial Training Council.

LIEPMANN, K. (1960) *Apprenticeship—an enquiry into its adequacy under modern conditions.* London, Routledge & Kegan Paul.

WELLENS, J. (1963) *The Training Revolution.* London, Evans Bros.

WILLIAMS, G. (1957) *Recruitment to Skilled Trades.* London, Routledge & Kegan Paul.

YOUNG, J. T. (1965) *Technicians To-day and To-morrow.* London, Pitman.

B.A.C.I.E. (1962) Industrial training—whose responsibility? B.A.C.I.E. Spring Conference, May 1962.

MACQUEEN, W. M. (1963) Training and education for industry. *The Vocational Aspect*, **15**, 154.

VENABLES, E. C. (1961) The further education of the young worker. *Educational Review*, **13**, 202.

OCCUPATIONAL CLASSIFICATION

The problem of occupational classification is a vexed one that has troubled administrators, economists, psychologists, and sociologists for many years. Occupations tend to be classified according to the purpose for which the classification is desired.

As illustrated by Hopson's article, the problem of classifying jobs is one which presents itself to anyone who is concerned with giving vocational guidance. The world of work, to be understood meaningfully, must be split up into compartments that can be handled separately. The reader will undoubtedly need guidance as to the forms of classification that exist already so that he can decide if one of them will fulfil his purpose, and if not, to glean ideas from the work of others. The following bibliography is an attempt to present examples of the wide ranging approaches to occupational classification that exist.

Socio-economic classificatory systems:

CENTRAL STATISTICAL OFFICE (1958) *Standard Industrial Classification.* London, H.M.S.O.

ECKERSON, A. B. (1963) The new Dictionary of Occupational Titles. *Vocational Guidance Quarterly*, **12**, 40–42.

GENERAL REGISTER OFFICE (1960) *Classification of Occupations.* London, H.M.S.O.

INTERNATIONAL LABOUR OFFICE (1958) *International Standard Classification of Occupations.* Geneva.

U.S. Bureau of the Budget (1957) Division of Statistical Standards, *Standard Industrial Classification.* Washington, Government Printing Office.

U.S. Department of Labour (1944) *Dictionary of Occupational Titles,* Second Edition, Vol. 1 (1949), *Definitions of Titles*; Vol. II (1949), *Occupational Classification*; (Part III no longer in use); Part IV, *Entry—Occupational Classification.* Washington, Government Printing Office.

Socio-psychological classificatory systems:

Ghiselli, E. E. (1966) *The Validity of Occupational Aptitude Tests.* New York, Wiley.

Rosenberg, M. (1957) *Occupations and Values.* Glencoe, Ill., Free Press.

Shartle, C. L. (1959) *Occupational Information.* Englewood Cliffs, N.J., Prentice-Hall.

Super, D. E. (1957) *Psychology of Careers.* New York, Harper.

Fine, S. A., and Heinz, C. A. (1958) The functional occupational classification structure. *Personnel and Guidance Journal,* **37,** 180–192.

Glick, P. (1964) Preliminary trial of a three dimensional classification of occupations. *Journal of Counseling Psychology,* **11,** 95–97.

Gonyea, G. G. (1963) Job perceptions in relation to vocational preference. *Journal of Counseling Psychology,* **10,** 20–26.

Holt, P. (1950) Occupation and social stratification. *American Journal of Sociology,* **55,** 533–543.

Holland, J. L., Krause, A. H., Nixon, M. E., and Trembath, M. F. (1953) The classification of occupations by means of Kuder interest profiles: 1. The development of interest groups. *Journal of Applied Psychology,* **37,** 263–269.

Holland, J. L. (1959) A classification for occupations in terms of personality and intelligence. *American Psychologist,* **14,** 376.

Holland, J. L. (1966) A psychological classification scheme for vocations and major fields. *Journal of Counseling Psychology,* **13,** 278–288.

Nelson, D. (1964) Studying the employment and training of a national sample of 17-year olds. *Occupational Psychology,* **38,** 183–190.

Reeb, M. (1959) How people see jobs; a multidimensional analysis. *Occupational Psychology,* **33,** 1–17.

Remstad, R., and Rothney, J. W. M. (1958) Occupational classification and research results. *Personnel and Guidance Journal,* **36,** 465–472.

Roe, A. (1954) A new classification of occupations. *Journal of Counseling Psychology,* **1,** 215–220.

Shartle, C. L. (1964) Occupational analysis, worker characteristics, and occupational classification systems. In H. Borrow (ed.) *Man in a World at Work.*

Tyler, L. E. (1961) Research explorations in the realm of choice. *Journal of Counseling Psychology,* **8,** 195–201.

Vernon, P. E. (1949) Classifying high-grade occupational interests. *Journal of Abnormal and Social Psychology,* **44,** 85–96.

Walther, R. H. (1960) The functional classification project: a critical appraisal. *Personnel and Guidance Journal,* **39,** 698–706.

VOCATIONAL GUIDANCE FOR THE HANDICAPPED

By ensuring employment opportunities for a large proportion of Britain's handicapped population, the Disabled Persons (Employment) Act of 1944 may have helped to disguise the extent of their problem. The choice of careers open to a handicapped individual can be severely restricted, and there is relatively little being done to ensure that they are placed in jobs where they will be able to achieve a high level of satisfaction. Vocational guidance is important for the normal individual who can easily change jobs if he is dissatisfied. It is even more important for the handicapped who find it extremely difficult to change jobs at any time.

This short bibliography may provide a useful introduction for those who wish to investigate this area in more detail:

DREWRY, R. R. (1958) *The Deaf School Leaver in Northern England.* Nuffield Foundation, London. (Mimeo.)

HAMILTON, K. W. (1950) *Counseling the Handicapped.* New York, Ronald Press.

LOFQUIST, L. H. (1957) *Vocational Counseling with the Physically Handicapped.* New York, Appleton-Century-Crofts.

MONTGOMERY, G. W. G. (1967) *Vocational Guidance for the Deaf.* Livingstone, Edinburgh.

RATCHICK, IRVING, and KOENIG (1963) *Guidance and the Physically Handicapped Child.* Chicago Science Research Associates.

COLVILLE, T. R. (1962) Providing for the handicapped child. *N.U.T. Annual Guide to Careers for Young People*, March 1962.

DUNCAN, W. (1957) The vocational guidance and employment of handicapped and disabled young people. *Occupational Psychology*, **25**, 57–63.

MCANDREW, H. (1948) Rigidity and isolation: a study of the deaf and the blind. *Journal of Abnormal and Social Psychology*, **43**, 476.

MONTGOMERY, G. W. G. (1965) Vocational guidance of deaf adolescents. Paper presented to a meeting of the *British Psychological Society*, October 15th, 1965.

WEINBERG, E. (1962) The effects of technology and automation on employment of the handicapped. Paper presented before the Mountain States Regional Meeting of the President's Committee on the Employment of the Handicapped, Pueblo, Colo., June 1962, U.S. Department of Lab. Bureau of Lab. Statistics. (Mimeo.)

WILSON, J. (1964) Vocational preparation for dull and backward pupils. *Youth Employment*, **16**, 20–21.

SECTION 7

Occupational Information

"Examination of the training of counselors strongly suggest that they are taught a good deal more about the pegs than about the holes."

JERRY R. HOLLEMAN

A LARGE proportion of the papers included in Part I of this book discuss the need to assist the individual develop an awareness of the self. This emphasis on the psychological factors in vocational guidance underlines the importance of orienting guidance to meet the needs of the individual. Consequently, when occupational information is used in the guidance context it should be tailored to fit the individual's requirements.

In 1948 Brayfield argued that while there were many contributions to the American literature on occupational information about specific media and material, "discussions of the basic principles underlying their application were conspicuous by their absence". In Britain, nearly twenty years later, such discussions are still "conspicuous by their absence". It was with this in mind that papers included in this section were selected.

Christensen advances a number of points which he feels may provide a useful guide to those concerned with using occupational information. He emphasizes the need for individual diagnosis in order to determine how occupational information should be used in the counseling process. He then goes on to distinguish between the instructional, instrumental, distributional and therapeutic uses of information. Readers may also like to refer to Arthur H. Brayfield's classic paper "Putting Occupational Information Across" (see section bibliography) in which he deplores the dissemination of occupational information to large groups without due regard for their individual needs. Like Christensen he also proclaims the need for individual diagnosis to precede the use of occupational information and he identifies several different ways in which information can be used in the counseling process.

Hayes suggests that the majority of British school leavers receive insufficient information about jobs before they are forced to arrive at an occupational decision. Much of the information they do have is inappropriate and the number of fundamentally different occupations they are aware of is often very limited. He argues, therefore, in favour of a careers course that would provide a more adequate framework of information. Given this basis to work on the Youth Employment Officer might then be able to provide information and guidance more fitted to the individual's needs. The organization of a careers course around a representative sample of occupations is also discussed as are the dangers of providing occupational literature without any system for guidance and discussion.

The value of work experience is being widely debated in Britain. Those interested may like to refer to Rusalem's article (see section bibliography) where it is argued that passive techniques for acquiring occupational information (through reading and films) are less satisfactory than active techniques such as actual work experience.

The final paper in this section is a searching contribution by Samler, "Psycho-social Aspects of work: A Critique of Occupational Information". This paper attacks some of the basic assumptions often made by those who publish occupational literature about the sort of information job seekers require. The image presented by occupational information today is one of the Economic Man; information that would characterize the Psychological Man at work is deficient or non-existent. Samler argues that literature dealing only with the Economic Man is only dealing with one aspect of the man at work and while this is important, there is evidence that it is inadequate.

32. *Functions of Occupational Information in Counseling*

THOMAS E. CHRISTENSEN

THE occupational adjustment of the individual is dependent not only on physical, psychological, sociological, and economic factors, but also on occupational information. Occupational information* is herein considered as accurate, usable information about jobs and occupations. It includes facts about occupational trends, the supply and demand of labor, and training facilities.

Writers on vocational guidance have paid little attention to the employment of occupational information in counseling. Carter,† in a 10-year review of published articles on vocational interests and job orientation, reported only two studies which dealt with the uses of occupational information for this purpose.

This article will discuss several functions of occupational information in the counseling process. The discussion assumes that the counselor who uses occupational information in counseling is trained in the techniques of locating, collecting, and classifying occupational information. Occupational information cannot be used in counseling unless it is accessible. This means that an adequate occupational library must be available for the use of the counselor and the client.

DIAGNOSIS COMES FIRST

Diagnosis comes first in determining how occupational information should be employed in the counseling process. Williamson‡ has described the making of a diagnosis as

> ... a process in logical thinking or the "teasing out" from a mass of relevant and irrelevant facts, of a consistent pattern of meaning and understanding of the student's assets and

* C. L. Shartle, *Occupational Information* (New York: Prentice-Hall, Inc., 1946), p. 1.

† H. D. Carter, *Vocational Interests and Job Orientation* (Stanford University Press, 1944).

‡ E. G. Williamson, *How to Counsel Students* (New York: McGraw-Hill, 1939), p. 102.

(Reprinted from *Occupations*, October 1949, pp. 11–14, by permission of publisher and author.)

liabilities together with a prognosis or judgment of the significance of this pattern for future adjustment to be made by the student ... a cooperative undertaking with the student participating in the understanding of himself in so far as he is intellectually and emotionally willing to do so.

It is clear that the counselor and the client (subject to Williamson's restrictions) should have answers to questions such as the following: Has the client any vocational preferences? Are his choices dictated by emotion, glamour, or romance? Have parents or others dominated his occupational selections? Is it a personality problem, lack of occupational information, or both, which is responsible for his inappropriate choice? Does he require occupational information in order to judge whether his choice is good? Will occupational information help him to develop confidence so that he can succeed in an occupation? Does he know about job family relationships? Is he aware of the trends in the occupation which he is considering? Is he prepared to shift his plans in order to meet changed employment conditions? Does he know the lines of progress in his chosen field? Does he know how to secure additional occupational information when he requires it?

Diagnosis is only preliminary. It must be followed by the other components of the counseling process. We shall confine our discussion to the use of occupational information in this process. The several functions of occupational information in counseling may be classified as (1) instructional, (2) instrumental, (3) distributional, (4) therapeutic. The counselor must consider the client as a whole person. All that can be done here is to formulate general suggestions for the use of occupational information in counseling. Hence, the classifications employed should not be viewed as mutually exclusive.

INSTRUCTIONAL FUNCTION

The writer does not hold the non-directive point of view* which implies that the giving of information should not be properly considered a function of the counseling process. For as Hoppock† has well stated:

> Even the non-directive counselor is not relieved of the responsibility of helping his client to check his insight against the cold hard realities of employment opportunity. Effective vocational guidance requires both insight and foresight, as plenty of disillusioned clients can now testify by hindsight.

One counselee may require occupational information in order to plan his progress within an occupation. Another may need data concerning job relationships in order to change positions advantageously. If the results of

* William Snyder, The Present Status of Psychotherapeutic Counseling, *Psychological Bulletin*, Vol. XLIV (July, 1947).

† Robert Hoppock, A Check List of Facts about Jobs for Use in Vocational Guidance, *The American Psychologist* (September, 1948).

interest inventories and aptitude tests suggest several equally appropriate choices, occupational information may assist the client to resolve those choices.

A client who has made an inappropriate occupational choice on the basis of insufficient or inaccurate occupational data needs instruction in how to evaluate occupational information. The counselee who is planning to enter an occupation protected by licenses, examinations, union rules, etc., should be informed about the requirements which he must meet in order to gain admission into the occupation. When desired occupational information is not available in printed form, the counselor must instruct the client regarding methods of securing the necessary data: correspondence with trade and/or professional organizations, conferences with individuals who possess the requisite information.

The use of occupational information to stimulate the client to further activity may be termed "instrumental". Counselors are familiar with students who are unconcerned about vocational planning and who assume that it is the function of the counselor to tell them what vocation to choose. A properly selected pamphlet or book may be "instrumental" in convincing them of the need for occupational planning.

Another group of clients to whom the instrumental function of occupational information applies is composed of talented individuals who are unaware of the occupations open to them. An undergraduate student who is very successful in the study of physics often does not recognize the occupational significance of this fact. Information concerning the functional specialization of physicists and the favorable employment outlook for qualified scientists in this field might be instrumental in stimulating him to plan graduate training in physics—training which would lead to a position as research physicist.

DISTRIBUTIONAL FUNCTION

The distributional function refers to the use of occupational information by the counselor to assist in the occupational adjustment of the client in a *particular* job. Friend and Haggard* point out that the counselor is in an especially strategic position to use occupational information in the distribution of people among appropriate employment situations in which they will not experience occupational frustrations.

Symonds† defines frustration as the "blocking or interference of the satisfaction of an aroused need through some barrier or obstruction." He cites four types of frustrations which adults may meet in connection with

* J. G. Friend and E. A. Haggard, Work Adjustment in Relation to Family Background, *Psychological Monographs*, Vol. XVI (June, 1948), 139.

† P. Symonds, *The Dynamics of Human Adjustment* (New York: D. Appleton-Century Company, 1946), 68.

their work: (1) function—a vigorous, athletic person forced to do sedentary office work; (2) conviction—the physician forced to practice in a hospital where the professional standards are below those which he would like to observe; (3) ambition—a man works at a lower level than he would like to work or a student attends a school which is not rated as high scholastically as he would like it to be; (4) response—a person feels that his superiors are unjust and unfair in requirements or in evaluations.

In non-psychological terms we may say that job satisfaction is frequently related to the specific conditions of employment. In many cases it is more important to choose one's employer wisely than one's occupation. A person may be vocationally maladjusted because he is a round peg in a square place of employment rather than because he is a round peg in a square occupation.

Occupational information which is of use for distributional purposes is difficult to obtain in printed form. It may be secured from (1) correspondence and conversations with clients who have been placed in various positions, (2) visits and conversations with employers, and (3) contacts with other counselors.

THERAPEUTIC FUNCTION

The counselor often has to deal with clients with low ability but high ambitions. In counseling these individuals he must use occupational information therapeutically in order to assist them in scaling down their ambitions without losing face. Such persons may be asked to secure information about the occupation of their preference and then to compare the educational requirements with their school marks and scores on scholastic aptitude tests. The counselor should point out alternative occupations which lie within the same occupational field as do the occupations originally selected. Occupational information used in this way fulfills a therapeutic function.

When occupational choices are dictated by emotion, glamour, or romance, occupational information may again serve a therapeutic function. Some undergraduate students labor under the delusion that they will be successful as personnel workers because they have majored in psychology and like working with people. The editor of School and College Placement in response to numerous requests from members of this group for advice on how to secure positions in personnel work found it necessary to issue an editorial on the subject.* The gist of his statement is that data released by the Occupational Outlook Service of the United States Department of Labor indicate that employment opportunities for newcomers in personnel work will be limited. Graduate study is becoming increasingly necessary in order to secure an entry job in this field. No further discussion is required in order to demonstrate how this statement may be used to enlighten undergraduate

* Editorial, *School and College Placement*, IX (December, 1948), 68.

students who think they are interested in personnel work but who lack the necessary qualifications for success in graduate courses.

Other things being equal, it is usually sound practice to assist the client to choose an occupation or occupational field in harmony with his previous experiences. Thus, occupational information may function therapeutically in counseling older workers who wish to break entirely with the past and start new careers. The retired mathematics teacher who would like to become a department store buyer may need to be furnished with occupational information which will indicate the difficulties involved in achieving this goal and the possibilities for utilizing his previous experiences in the clerical field.

Occupational information may also play a role in supportive therapy. The student who is considering leaving school because of an emotional problem may report regularly upon reading in assigned occupational literature, ostensibly for the purpose of assisting him in making an occupational choice. This may be one means to support his ego until he arrives at a satisfactory solution to his problem. Occupational research in this instance may represent but one of a series of tasks to be executed. The counselor may assign additional tasks such as the taking of tests, conferring with other personnel workers, groups, conferences, etc., for the same general purpose.

GENERAL PRINCIPLES

The effective use of occupational information in counseling is contingent on the counselor's adherence to three general principles which may be stated as follows:

1. In assisting the client to solve his problems, the counselor should direct him to specific occupational information sources. Browsing in the occupational library, while highly desirable for other purposes, does not serve a useful function in counseling. It is likely to confuse rather than to help.
2. The counselor should ask the client to report his reactions to the assigned sources of occupational information. In most instances these reports will be oral and will form a part of a discussion with the counselor in which the counselor assists the client to evaluate the obtained information in light of the client's aptitudes, interests, and personality traits.
3. Other things being equal, the more capable the client is, the less attention he needs to pay to the economic, social, and political factors which affect employment. The less capable he is, the more attention he should give to these factors. When a field becomes overcrowded, members of the second group will experience difficulty in competing successfully for jobs.

33. *The Role of Occupational Information in Careers Guidance*

JOHN HAYES

THIS year 641,000 young people will leave school and enter the world of work. Each school leaver will be faced, probably for the first time in his life, with a decision that may determine his daily routine for a number of months, years or even until he retires. He has to decide which job he will do. This is a decision that he must make. Other people may help him, may push him even, but in the end the decision is his.

What are the factors that will determine the type of occupation he will choose? In America, a considerable amount of time and effort has been devoted to examining the determinants of occupational choice and a number of interesting theories have been advanced. Many theorists, notably Super (1953, 1963), Stefflre (1966), Holland (1959) and Tiedeman (1961), present apparently different models but they all, at least implicitly, suggest that the individual develops a self concept on the basis of which the *persona* he wishes to present at work is formed. It is, therefore, this particular aspect of the self concept, the occupational self concept, that determines the sort of job the individual will aspire to.

OCCUPATIONAL HORIZONS

The discovery of an occupational self concept is not sufficient. The individual has to find a job where this can be satisfied and this in turn depends upon the individual's knowledge of occupational opportunities. The fewer jobs the individual is familiar with, the less likely it is that he will be able to find a job which will provide him with the opportunity of adequately expressing his occupational self concept. It is not the absolute *number* of jobs with which the individual is familiar that is important, but the *range* of jobs. He might possess quite extensive knowledge about occupational opportunities in the wool textile industry because his father is an

(Reprinted from *Educational Research,* vol. 9, No. 3, 1967, by permission of editor and author. *Educational Research* is published for the National Foundation for Educational Research by Newnes Educational Publishing Co. Ltd.)

overlooker, his uncle and the next door neighbour are warehousemen, his mother is a mender and his sister works in spinning, but at the same time he might be completely ignorant of the multitude of alternative opportunities in engineering, baking, selling, transport or office work.

The individual's socio-economic background is one of the major determinants of the occupational information he will possess, and where the work experience of his family, peer group and other regular contacts is limited, then his occupational horizon or knowledge of various career possibilities may also be severely restricted. The impact of early socio-economic background on a person's occupational thinking is often apparent even among university undergraduates. Recent conversations with University Appointments Board Officers have indicated that undergraduates from working class environments tend to be much less adventurous in their occupational explorations than undergraduates with predominantly middle class backgrounds. When the undergraduate comes from a working class environment where few, if any, of his family or friends have had much experience of professional and managerial jobs, then he might, when faced with the possibility of choosing one of these "middle class" occupations, opt for the one with which he is most familiar—and therefore choose teaching (see Jackson and Marsden, 1965).

THE QUALITY OF OCCUPATIONAL INFORMATION

Popular magazines, television and the cinema have done a great deal to influence the average school child's awareness of job opportunities, but at the same time the mass media have contributed to the wildly inappropriate occupational role expectations which many young people have of certain jobs; for example, the "Emergency Ward 10" image of nursing or, through television "commercials", the over-glamourized image of the life of a soldier or air hostess.

Recruitment literature that misleads likely candidates into thinking a job is something different from what it really is, may prove very costly to the firm in the long run, when—after expensive training—disenchanted employees leave to find alternative work. Realistic occupational information will not, as many employers fear, necessarily make a job unattractive, but it will go a long way to ensuring that only the right sort of people are attracted in the first place, and that unsuitable candidates will be disillusioned before they commit themselves.

A recent occupational survey in the Leeds area asked employers to state what they thought were the most common reasons why young people changed jobs. On analysis it was found that, while better pay and prospects were important, these were not the dominant reasons. A group of closely related comments often made by employers such as "he felt the job did not suit him", "he wanted a more interesting job" or "the work was not what he expected" suggested that over 50 per cent of all job changes among young people resulted from the job not matching expectations.

If school children are armed with realistic and accurate information about a wider variety of occupations and if, on the basis of this knowledge, they are able to develop realistic work-role expectations, then the necessity for many of them to force an unsatisfactory compromise between their occupational self concept and a limited range of jobs will be obviated.

OCCUPATIONAL INFORMATION GIVEN TO SCHOOL CHILDREN

It has already been stressed that in many cases if the child is left to gather his own occupational information he is not likely to consider a very wide range of jobs and much of the information he does acquire may be incorrect, or at best incomplete. There is a need, therefore, to encourage and guide the accumulation of occupational information. Unfortunately, the only assistance many school children receive is the Youth Employment Officer's school talk and interview. Because the Service is under-staffed, it is frequently impossible to provide more than this statutory minimum of guidance. The twenty-minute interview is often devoted simply to introducing the potential school leaver to occupational information of a very superficial kind. The child wants a job, the Youth Employment Officer attempts to assess what kind of job would be suitable and then, in the time still available, he attempts to familiarize the school leaver with the appropriate employment opportunities and refer him to relevant occupational literature. It must be frustrating for the Youth Employment Officers who realize how inadequate the assistance they give can be, especially when they are aware of the quality of work which—given sufficient time—they could do.

The effectiveness of the guidance and placement services offered by the Youth Employment Service could be greatly increased if a careers course were introduced into the school prior to the final interview. In some areas, where the Youth Employment Service has the available resources, Youth Employment Officers do valuable work providing careers information either directly, by organizing visits and speakers, or indirectly through assisting teachers to arrange their own careers programme.

If every school were to organize a balanced careers course, then by the time the child reached the leaving interview he would have digested a considerable amount of occupational information. He would at least be acquainted with a number of jobs and he would be in a better position to discuss his employment prospects with the Youth Employment Officer. In turn the Youth Employment Officer would be less concerned with "disseminating" occupational information and would be in a position to provide information and guidance more fitted to the individual's needs.

THE CAREERS COURSE

Where the home provides only a limited experience of the world of work, the school, through its careers programme, can broaden the individual's occupational outlook.

Since one of the major aims of any careers course is to widen occupational horizons, great care is necessary to avoid considering only a narrow range of related occupations. It is often suggested that the employment patterns of past leavers is a reliable guide to those occupations that the school-leaver should study. Such an approach is typical of much of the current loose thinking in careers guidance. Past leavers are just as, if not more, likely to have suffered from a restricted view of occupational opportunities as next year's potential leavers. In many cases the chief value of such a study will be merely to furnish evidence of how limited occupational horizons have actually been in the past.

What the school leaver requires is a course that will introduce him to a wide variety of different occupations. It is important to use a good basic occupational classification and to avoid designing the course around the major local industries. To consider twenty different jobs would be of little value if they were all jobs in the textile industry. Opportunities in shops, hospitals, the armed forces and offices, to name only a few, should not be ignored. The occupational classification used is probably best left to the individual careers teacher, but some modification of the occupational interest, in the Rothwell-Miller Interest Blank (1966) may provide a guide. For example, occupations could be classified into Outdoor, Personal Contact, Social Service, Medical and Scientific, Mechanical, Artistic, Computational and Clerical [see Hopson (1967) for a discussion of some alternative classifications]. The careers teacher may feel, however, that such a classification is unnecessarily sophisticated and he may wish to design his own system. If he does, he must be very careful to produce a classification which will introduce school children to the full variety of work available.

Not only must care be taken in deciding the occupational areas to be studied but careful consideration is also necessary when choosing the levels of jobs to be included in the programme. It is all too easy to ignore the children who aspire to jobs at a higher or lower level than the average. It is particularly important that jobs for the less able children be accommodated into the course, even though this may be difficult in view of the fact that most occupational material is aimed at jobs requiring some degree of skill.

After deciding which occupational areas are to be studied, it will be necessary to consider in more detail exactly how the course should be organized. Again there will be ample scope for individual differences but the time available will impose some limit on the number of jobs which can be studied. Because of this limitation, occupations that are to some extent representative of the different occupational areas might be chosen.

A number of varied teaching methods can be employed. Some teachers may prefer to teach the subject along traditionally formal lines whereas others may prefer a more class-centred approach. Small groups might elect to undertake some research into particular occupations and then report back to the class on their findings. This could provide a valuable incentive for the class to use the careers library and if, throughout the course, the groups have to study a number of jobs, each in different occupational areas then, in a round-about way, their reading of careers literature would be subject to some degree of guidance. Group reports might be used to introduce a general discussion about particular occupations or they may precede a film or works visit. Speakers may be invited along to address the class—as may ex-pupils, who will be able to relate their experiences of some occupation either to the class as a whole or, more informally, to small groups over tea and biscuits. Rusalem (1954) argues that the "Careers team" should help the students to become ego-involved in the search for vocational information. He suggests that the greatest degree of personal involvement occurs when the student directly experiences the job at first hand and is given every opportunity to test his self concept in the reality of the world at work. Consequently he argues that passive techniques for acquiring occupational information—such as reading, films and even occupational visits—are less satisfactory than the more active techniques that involve work experience.

Some of these varied activities will not only add interest to the course but they will also facilitate the communication of those aspects of jobs that cannot easily, or are not usually, included in careers literature. As yet little is known about the effectiveness of the different aspects of careers work but there is great scope for detailed research into teaching methods, especially with a view to finding which methods are of particular value with different types of children.

Irrespective of exactly how a careers course is organized, occupational literature will form a valuable source of information; and in the absence of formal course arrangements, occupational literature is of vital importance.

THE CAREERS LIBRARY

Many schools pay lip service to the idea of careers work, but few do much more than appoint a teacher as careers master whose chief duty is to supervise a careers library. A careers library is only a tool and is of little use if the children are not taught how to use it; but before moving on to consider exactly how a careers library can be utilized, it will be profitable to evaluate the usefulness of the occupational literature contained in it.

Most occupational literature is concerned with describing the "economic man" at work. In 1940 the National Vocational Guidance Association of the U.S.A. first published a basic outline for the content of what they described as a good occupational monograph. Briefly summarized, they suggested that it should contain details on:

1. The history of the occupation.
2. The importance of the occupation and its relevance to society.
3. The number of workers engaged in the occupation.
4. Anticipated supply and demand trends for workers.
5. Duties.
6. Qualifications.
7. Methods of entry.
8. Length of training.
9. Opportunities for advancement.
10. Related occupations to which training may lead.
11. Earnings.
12. Hours.
13. Regularity of employment.
14. Health and accident hazards.
15. Employers associations, trade unions and other organizations.
16. Description of a typical place of employment.
17. Sources of additional information.

A quick appraisal of most "good" careers literature should be sufficient to satisfy the reader that these are the sort of topics that are normally covered to a greater or lesser extent. What must be considered, however, is the degree to which these traditional information areas, as indicated by the National Vocational Guidance Association's "Basic Outline", provide the school leaver with the knowledge he requires so as to appreciate fully what will be involved in certain occupational roles.

Unfortunately his knowledge from such literature is unlikely to be adequate, and usually it is not until he actually starts work that he will begin to appreciate fully which of his personality needs will be satisfied in his chosen job. There will be considerations of occupational status, group inter-action, work-family relationships and many other psycho-social factors that are important but not even hinted at in the "Basic Outline", or in the content of most traditionally-presented occupational literature (see Samler, 1961). Much of this sort of information cannot easily be committed to paper, but there is a great deal that could be, but often is not, included in careers pamphlets. For example, although the public often attribute special status to the policeman, this can have many irksome implications. Society expects a police officer to exhibit exemplary conduct both while he is on and off duty. Consequently a young constable may become frustrated and dissatisfied because he feels that his social and family life is circumscribed by too many restrictions.

The publishers of recruitment literature are often very much aware of these psycho-social factors and design many of their pamphlets in such a way as to capitilize on them. Unfortunately, because employers often try to "sell" the opportunities they have to offer, the information they publish may be biased to show only the attractive aspects of the job. They may glamourize the work and over-emphasize the status it commands. A number of people concerned with vocational guidance argue, for example, that much of the recruiting material published by the Army tends to glamourize the life and underplay such points as the discipline, hazards and work-family relationships. Nevertheless, the fact that many of those concerned with recruitment design their literature around psycho-social factors, such as status, is a possible indication of their importance. It might be useful, therefore, if the publishers of disinterested careers literature, as opposed to recruitment literature, while still presenting information on both the attractive and unattractive aspects of particular jobs, were to look at their own publications with an eye to the treatment of psycho-social factors.

Young people often find recruitment literature more attractive than unbiased careers literature because of its more interesting and readable appearance. This can be particularly dangerous because, as has already been mentioned, recruitment literature tends to emphasize only the attractive points about work. Avis Oxhandler (1950) points out that in any file on any occupation, some pamphlets will be well thumbed and dog-eared while others will still look new and unused. She questions what makes one pamphlet on the same subject more popular than another, and notes that some pamphlets are not read even though they provide the best coverage of the subject. After analysing the results of her research on the popularity of a selected group of pamphlets about one occupation, she was able to arrive at a number of interesting conclusions.

The more popular pamphlets were distinguished from the less popular by a number of features:

(*a*) They had fewer words per heading. There was more outlining of the subject matter, and information was presented so as to be more easily usable.

(*b*) They had higher Flesch Human Interest-Scores (Flesch, 1948). The use of more "personal" words and sentences of the type measured by this particular readability formula was associated with the better-liked pamphlets.

(*c*) They had more pictures; although it was found at the same time these pictures took up a smaller proportion of the total space.

(*d*) Their score on "density of appearance of type" was lower. In the better-liked pamphlets, the type was larger and there was more "white space" between lines and paragraphs. This finding received added confirmation from a comparison of the total number of words and pages in the pamphlets: in general, the better-liked pamphlets had fewer words and more pages.

These results, along with those of Brayfield and Reed (1950), even though they are derived from American experience, suggest that there is probably great scope for valuable research into careers literature, not only from the point of view of content, but also with regard to readability and attractiveness.

It has been suggested that the average child tends to have a restricted occupational outlook. This state of affairs could be remedied to some extent if there were bigger incentives for children to make better use of careers literature. Those who do bother to use a careers library usually only read about the jobs with which they are already familiar. For many, one look at the host of closely-typed, dry-looking pamphlets is enough to put them off careers literature for the rest of their school-lives. If the non-directed reading of careers literature is seen as being the most desirable way of introducing children to occupational information, then the literature must be attractively presented in such a form that one rapid flip through a pamphlet will, from paragraph headings, photographs and layout, enable the reader to ascertain the essential characteristics of the occupation. Much of the best literature published to-day contains valuable information, but is not designed so as to facilitate a quick appraisal of content. The effort required to read occupational material is a factor which serves to reinforce the tendency for children (other than those who are exceptional or highly motivated) to read the literature about occupations with which they are already familiar.

HOW SHOULD A CAREERS LIBRARY BE USED?

Where the school provides a careers library for all to use without any form of supervision, then the attractiveness and readability of the contents will be an important factor determining which material will be read. If some of the reading is more directed, as for example when it forms an integral part of a careers course, then the attractiveness and readability of the literature will not determine whether it will be read or not, although it may influence the quantity and quality of information retained. Where the pupil is completely free to choose the material he will read there is a danger that only recruitment publications will be read and consequently that misconceptions about the work involved may be fostered. There will also be the danger, already stressed, that only literature dealing with familiar occupations will be used. There is therefore a strong case, supported by the find ings of Speer and Jasker (1949), for providing some direction to the study of careers literature. Such guidance will introduce children to occupations they might never have considered and there will be less danger of their obtaining biased or grossly incomplete information, especially if the careers course incorporates some form of feed-back.

A well organized careers course will go a long way towards helping the school leaver find the sort of job in which he is most likely to be happy. A great deal of job dissatisfaction may well be due to inappropriate occupational decisions made on the basis of incomplete and inaccurate information about a narrow range of jobs. Even where the school recognizes the need for occupational information and provides occupational library facilities, these will probably be inefficiently used if the structured guidance and supplementary information which a careers programme could provide are not available.

REFERENCES

BRAYFIELD, A. H., and REED, PATRICIA, A. (1950). How readable are occupation booklets? *Journal of Applied Psychol.* xxxiv (1950), 325–328.

FLESCH, R. (1948). A new readability yardstick, *Journal of Applied Psychol.* xxxii (June 1948), 221–233.

HOLLAND, J. L. (1959). A theory of vocational choice, *Journal of Counseling Psychol.*, vol. 6, No. 1 (1959), 35–45.

HOPSON, B. (1967). Occupational visits—education, recruitment, or a lark, *Youth Employment Journal*, Spring 1967.

JACKSON, B., and MARSDEN, D. (1965). *Education and the Working Class.* (Pelican A811.) Harmondsworth: Penguin Books.

NATIONAL VOCATIONAL GUIDANCE ASSOCIATION (1940). Contents of a good occupational monograph, the basic outline, *Occupations*, October 1940, 23–30.

OXHANDLER, AVIS (1950). What makes an occupational information pamphlet popular? *Occupations*, October 1950, 26–29.

ROTHWELL-MILLER. Interest Blank (1966). Manual, N.F.E.R.

RUSALEM. H. (1954). New insights on the role of occupational information in counseling, *Journal of Counseling Psychol.*, vol. 1, no. 2, 1954.

SAMLER, J. (1961). Psycho-social aspects of work: a critique of occupational information, *Personnel and Guidance Journal*, vol. 34, no. 6, 458–465.

SPEER, G. S., and JASKER, L. (1949). The influence of occupational information on occupational goals, *Occupations*, October, 28, 15–17.

STEFFLRE, B. (1966). Vocational developments: ten propositions in search of a theory, *Personnel and Guidance Journal*, Feb. 1966.

SUPER, D. E. (1953). A theory of vocational development, *American Psychologist*, vol. 8, no. 4, 185–190.

SUPER, D. E. *et al.* (1963). Career development: self concept theory. College Entrance Examination Board, New York.

TIEDEMAN, D. V. (1961). Decision and vocational development: a paradigm and its implications, *Personnel and Guidance Journal*, vol. 40, 15–20.

34. *Psycho-Social Aspects of Work: A Critique of Occupational Information*

JOSEPH SAMLER

OUR brief history in vocational guidance reveals a period extending through the thirties of what may be termed a trait-centered approach in matching men and jobs. Perhaps it was Rogers' great impact, perhaps it was the revival of psychoanalytic thought after its lapse in the twenties, perhaps it was our growing curiosity concerning our own behavior that led to what many have termed a clinical approach in vocational counseling. It is strange that we had to wait so long since Frank Parsons and Clifford Beers set the benchmarks, respectively, of the vocational guidance and mental hygiene movements in precisely the same year. It is strange that for more than 30 years the two influential streams of thought traveled parallel but separate courses.

The influence of personality theory on the work of the vocational counselor is well known. Indeed, hindsight, always 20-20, reveals that the correction to a limited approach of "true reasoning" concerning matching interests, abilities, and aptitudes with job demands may have gone too far. Nothing was clearer and more disconcerting than the pecking order which emerged with the white-coated psychiatrist at the top of the status hierarchy, followed by the similarly attired clinical psychologist, with the guidance worker bringing up an uncomfortable rear. The preferred activity in many guidance offices became personality analysis, and the quest for help in occupational choice was seen as a masked symptom of personality disorder.

Perhaps the pendulum had to swing to its end before it could settle to its own more limited orbit. Only in current literature are we beginning to see the conceptualization of an approach which delimits the appropriate roles of counseling and clinical psychologists.

Nevertheless the progress made in enriching counselor consideration of his client as a dynamic entity is indubitable and most rewarding. In the new

This paper was presented at the symposium "A Broadened Frame of Reference in Vocational Counseling", American Personnel and Guidance Association Convention, Philadelphia, April 1960.

(Reprinted from *Personnel and Guidance Journal* February 1961, pp. 458–465, by permission of publisher and author.)

perception of the counselor, the client became invested with feelings, aspirations, conflicts, problems, relationships with significant people in his life, and these, for the counselors who were not embarrassed at helping with occupational decisions, enriched and made vital the client's problem in occupational development.

The motivation for this paper, however, came into being as a result of the continuing observation that desirable though personality oriented vocational guidance is, it is a one-sided development and that for critical other aspects of the process, we are about where we were at early stages in our professional development. For examination here is not the nature of the counselor–client relationship but the counselor's consideration of that world which the client with his unique picture of himself, his particular identity, must enter: the world of work.

THE REALITY OF OCCUPATIONAL INFORMATION

It is demonstrable that resources in occupational information have remained relatively insulated. I am concerned here with the nature of occupational information available to counselor and client. The pertinent questions have to do with the reality of the picture that emerges for the client after available information is studied, with its deficiencies, and the extent to which the picture is distorted because of its shortcomings.

The point should not be mistaken. It is not that trend data are not current, earnings are reported inaccurately, or that the reality of union organization is slighted. As far as is known, there is increasing adherence to the NVGA Standards for Use in Preparing and Evaluating Occupational Literature.[7] It is even believed that counselors are increasingly competent at catching the omissions in such information and are properly suspicious of the handout with an axe to grind.

What concerns me and my co-workers is that the same kind of rich consideration of personality dynamics that now dramatizes assessment and understanding of the client is not available in considering the role and function of work. We look in vain for a dynamic appreciation of work in terms of the individual's role, his self-concept or identity, the exercise of his attitudes and fulfillment of his values, status consideration, and other related factors.

And yet there is no longer any serious question that work is much more than a means of paying the supermarket cashier or of meeting mortgage payments. Caplow,[3] Super,[13] and Roe[8] have established the point that work is a way of life, that it affects the way we think of ourselves, the neighborhood we live in, the kind of clothes we wear, our leisure time activities, the friends we make, the values we hew to—the list is endless.

Although systematic research has still to validate it, there seems reason for thinking that occupational adjustment, the complex we identify as job satisfaction, may be much more dependent upon psychodynamic aspects than upon wages, duties, hours of work, physical conditions, and so on.

Such psychological factors are not completely lacking in the available materials. The NVGA Outline, for instance, with reference to worker qualifications, states in item VC "Special physical, mental, social, and personal qualifications, excluding those obviously necessary for success in all types of work." But this is the only such sub-item in 16 major categories of items. The Functional Occupational Classification Project takes into account a number of interest and temperament factors. An occasional reference in the standard leaflet or brochure discusses personality attributes necessary for competent performance on the job. But even these limited provisions are in themselves inadequate. The references to personality factors are in generalized terms; they are likely to have moralistic overtones; and they are cast in terms of job qualifications as against needs satisfactions.

Thus a paragraph from the *Outlook* discussion of School Counselors states:

> It is especially important for counselors to be well adjusted, even tempered, and able to inspire the confidence of students. In a recent survey, school principals given a list of qualifications indicated that they considered the following items most important in selecting counselors: (a) personality factors, such as emotional stability, (b) successful teaching experience before entry into counseling, and (c) graduate study in guidance.[(1)]

The usual coverage of the by now standard occupational information release is revealed by its outline. The highly useful *Occupational Outlook Handbook* comprehends each of its presentations under the six-part outline: Nature of Work, Where Employed, Training and Other Qualifications, Employment Outlook, Earnings and Working Conditions, and Where to Go for Other Information. Spot checking of various issues from SRA, Chronicle Press, Bellman, B'nai B'rith, Personnel Services, and the others, reveals treatment under a variable outline which contains more areas than does the Outlook outline, but the approach is much the same.

THE ECONOMIC MAN; THE PSYCHOLOGICAL MAN

It should be crystal clear that the picture occupational information presents today is one of the Economic Man. It is a one-dimensional portrayal of man who, contrary to the soundest of folk wisdom, lives by bread alone. There is no question of the need for a common framework of economic considerations, wages, competitive conditions of training and education, the duties performed in payment for wages received, the lines of advancement, the certification and union membership conditions, and so on. But the skeleton, like all such structures, lacks individuality, character, and uniqueness. For the central orientation of the economic man, the technique of choice for occupational information is job analysis and indeed as the nature of occupational information is revealed, this is precisely how such data are gathered.

This is true for the capsules in the DOT, for the studies underlying the FOCP, for the descriptive material in the *Occupational Outlook Handbook* and for their large following of commercial publications of occupational information.

It seems a fair statement that as far as present resources in occupational literature are concerned, information that would characterize the Psychological Man at work is deficient or nonexistent. It is a conclusion, however, that each of us can check for ourselves. In the Outlook Handbook, from page 45 to page 758, embodying the occupational descriptions and outlook statements, I was able to identify 35 paragraphs of the type presented before, in some way concerned with attributes of the kind looked for. This must not be regarded as criticism of the Handbook, however, since it reflects the best available thinking in the field as to the essentials of occupational information.

It is quite interesting that the greatest contribution in this area seems to be made not by the text but the occasional picture which typically reveals by the expression on the face of the worker, his posture, his inferred relationship with the person interacting, something of important relationships.

It is tempting to say that as against the concept of the Economic Man we must postulate the concept of the Psychological Man, but this would not be correct. Rather, we are concerned with both concepts in the utilization of insights and understandings of man at work. Since, however, we have a *good* understanding of the first, our emphasis, as a corrective, will be on the second.

But we must agree on what we're talking about when we refer to the Psychological Man. We refer here to the worker's role, his ability to work at a task that is congruent with his identity, the exercise of his values and attitudes, considerations of status, ways of meeting anxiety, patterns of interaction with others, out-of-work style of life, and totally, the way in which his personality needs will be met. They are all the considerations that deal with personality dynamics not infrequently so well taken into account in assessing the counseling client.

THREE ILLUSTRATIONS

Some will accept the need for such information as self-evident. For others the point needs to be reinforced and perhaps can be done best by example.

In the available descriptions of registered professional nurses, duties are described, specialties presented, training is outlined, costs are given, there is occasional reference to desired personality characteristics, the employment outlook is discussed, and there is considerable attention to earnings and working conditions. The pattern is taken from the Outlook Handbook but with some variation it is the same for other briefs describing this occupation. It is a picture as indicated before of the Economic Man (or in this case, obviously, of the Economic Woman). Contrast it with only a paragraph from Thorner:

It will be recalled that the nurse is faced with the problem of achieving a compromise between the functionally specific impersonality of her role and the therapeutically beneficial expression of interest, warmth, kindness, and sympathy elicited both by the condition of the patient and his expectations of what constitutes proper feminine conduct. The nurse, however, cannot allow herself to become emotionally involved without paying a penalty. Patients are often irritating, demanding, and unreasonable; they suffer intensely, weeping and moaning; they die. If she were to take these things to heart, if she were to bring her professional cares home with her, the nurse would collapse under the strain. Although impersonality is the norm, deviating reactions to a serious case sometimes occur. These, however, are very largely confined to private duty nursing, since regular staff nurses have too many patients to allow the development of emotional attachments. This condition facilitates the operation of functionally specific impersonality. A private duty nurse on occasion may identify with the patient to such a degree that she will suffer with the patient and, if he dies, she may mourn. The other reaction is quite different. The nurse identifies and suffers with the patient up to a certain degree of intensity of suffering on his part. Beyond that, she becomes extremely detached; the patient becomes "it." Should "it" die, however, the nurse may collapse in a nervous breakdown.[(15)]

Similarly we can contrast the information on the job of the union business agent as presented in the available literature with a more psychologically oriented presentation. SRA Occupational Brief No. 255, *Industrial and Labor Relations Workers*, offers the following as part its discussion of the field of work:

Practically every union officer, regardless of his job, performs labor relations work in his everyday duties. The main job of the business agent is to see that employer–union agreement is being lived up to and to settle grievances and misunderstandings. In some companies that operate under union agreements, grievances of employees are handled through the shop stewards who are elected for each department. In a large concern, there is a steward for each department. Stewards are employees of the company, but are allowed time off for their grievance work.

One of the important labor relations tasks of a union officer is negotiating agreements with employers. He draws up, negotiates, and interprets union contracts. He supervises picketing, strike benefits, and presents the union's case at arbitration meetings.

Consider the contribution however made by the following paragraphs, part of a more extensive discussion.

As a result of these time demands, opportunities for activities beyond the union sphere (home, family, friends, etc.) were severely limited during the work week and sometimes during the weekends as well. The weekends provided the business agents with a chance to "catch up" or sometimes were filled with meetings that either could not be fitted into the five-day week or were of an emergency nature. The job demanded all, and any reluctance to give unsparingly was viewed critically by others in the organization. Consequently, considerable psychological, as well as physical, isolation from family and friends occurred. The lack of interest in, or understanding of, the business agents' problems shown by these groups also enhanced the agents' isolation. The psychological and physical anchoring points for the union business agents had to be, and literally were, in the job.

Although they were operating under constant tension, they could not afford to show it. In all but exceptional situations, they were expected to keep their tempers and be diplomatic with management, to keep a respectfully factual attitude with arbitrators, to maintain a sympathetic attitude toward the rank and file, to support and teach their subordinate union officers, and to be helpfully constructive with their peers. They were expected to approach problems with enthusiasm, and to devote untold energy to each phase of their work. They had to be tireless, ever-enthusiastic, emotionally involved, yet intellectually calm.

The business agents, then, were operating in an environment that demanded their time and energy to the exclusion of normal social intercourse with other groups. They were constantly faced with problems of others and were responsible for taking over such burdens. They were confronted with situations that negated the advisability of being open, of sharing, or of taking the word of either antagonist or protagonist. They were always expected to be ready to take on new responsibilities with enthusiasm and grace, and to encounter aggression and hostility in others with tact and diplomacy. They lived and worked for and with others, but could not share with them.[10]

In the same way we can contrast references to secondary school teachers. If we select from a standard reference (*Occupational Outlook Handbook*) those paragraphs that come closest to a psychological view of work, we find the following:

Secondary school teachers—those employed in junior and senior high schools—usually specialize in a subject-matter field such as English, history, mathematics, or science. They teach several classes every day either in their main field only or in that field and one or two related subjects. The most frequent combinations are English and history or other social science subjects; mathematics and general science; and chemistry and biology or general science. Teachers in fields such as home economics, agriculture, commercial subjects, driver education, music, art, and industrial arts are less likely to have classes in other subjects.

Besides giving classroom instruction from 20 to 30 hours each week, secondary school teachers also develop and plan teaching materials, develop and correct tests, keep records, make out reports, consult with parents, and perform other duties. Many of them supervise student extra-class activities—sometimes after regular school hours. Maintenance of good relations with parents, the community, and fellow teachers is an important aspect of their jobs.

But consider the insight Crambs gives us about the teacher as a member of a minority group:

The behavior of teachers as members of a minority group is an outgrowth of other aspects of the role of the teacher in the community. The teacher in the small community is conspicuous. Everyone knows who the teacher is; children are everywhere, and seem to be countless little spies reporting on what the teacher is doing. The typical reaction is that of the young teacher who remarked, "I feel as if I lived in a goldfish bowl." Although neighbors and friends observe each other casually in their daily routines, teachers are subjected to many more such observations, since their range of acquaintances is wider than for most others in the community. All 500 children of a school will eventually know Miss Smith, the fifth-grade teacher; many of the parents will know her. What she wears, what she does, and whom she is seen with are commented on by many people. It is no wonder that Miss Smith feels conspicuous. This sort of conspicuousness is, in some respects, similar to that felt by the Negro; wherever he goes he is immediately "seen."

The teacher likewise is always recognized as "teacher." And recognition in the context of the American Puritan tradition also implies judgment. To be known is flattering if one is of high status, otherwise it is hardly to be desired.[(4)]

Or two paragraphs from Becker's discussion of teacher–pupil relationship.

Discipline is the second of the teacher's major problems with her students. Willard Waller points to its basis when he wrote that "Teacher and pupil confront each other in the school with an original conflict of desires, and however much that conflict may be reduced in amount, or however much it may be hidden, it still remains." We must recognize that conflict, either actual or potential, is ever present in the teacher–pupil relationship, the teacher attempting to maintain her control against the children's efforts to break it. The conflict is felt even with those children who present least difficulty; a teacher who considered her pupils models of good behavior nevertheless said:

> But there's tension all the time. Between you and the students. It's hard on the nerves. Teaching is fun, if you enjoy your subject but it's the discipline that keeps your nerves on edge, you know what I mean? There's always that tension. Sometimes people say "Oh, you teach school. That's an easy job, just sitting around all day long." They don't know what it's really like. It's hard on your nerves![(2)]

These are excerpts only, of course, and while they are believed, to be representative of this type of literature, they cannot be offered as such. Nevertheless, the manner in which the worker's personality needs will be met becomes much clearer through this type of discussion. It leaps to the eye that even in these brief paragraphs the occupation comes alive. The workers live and breathe and interact. Accordingly the message they give is all the more alive and meaningful.

THE AVAILABLE MATERIALS

The point to be made here is that the type of occupational information literature available to the counselor does not reflect the ideas and insights suggested as essential for man at work. Further that, as is evident, there *is* such a literature, but it does not happen to be in the sources generally used by the counselor. It does not *happen* to be there because the basic orientation of present occupational literature is toward job analysis and the Economic Man. We must look, therefore, to the psychological and sociological sources.

Here we find a fertile area. As a reasonably good sample, every issue of the *American Sociological Review* and the *American Journal of Sociology* for 1956, 1957 and 1958 was checked. This is a total of 36 issues for both publications. Material relating to style of life in work, status, role, personality needs were found in 49 articles in 27 issues. It is scarcely necessary to remind ourselves of the widespread contributions by sociologists in their studies of the factory worker, white-collar worker, nurses, student-physicians, psychiatrists, and other occupations.

That this should not be news to counselors is indicated in the articles carried in the *Personnel and Guidance Journal* by Danskin in the November,

1955, and October, 1957, issues. In the second of these Danskin lists 70 references to pertinent literature of the type discussed.

THE ESSENTIAL RESEARCH

One useful area of activity, it seems clear, is attention by writers of occupational information to this area of information and its integration within the occupational picture presented. While this would greatly enrich occupational information literature, in itself it is not enough. This is because we will be taking material that happens to be available. What is available is not necessarily best suited for us, changing with the changing sociology of the occupation, or sufficiently comprehensive to meet our needs for the large array of information necessary in considering a spread of occupations in counseling.

It should be quite clear by now that we require a systematic approach in securing the information we need. The problem is to identify as best we can with available techniques, and better as new theory evolves and more sensitive instruments are developed, those psychological and sociological aspects of occupations that may make the difference for the particular individual between sound choice and poor choice, between the ability to meet the expectations the individual establishes in accordance with his identity and their frustration, between the exercise of attitudes and values to the advantage of the worker and his unhappiness in functioning in a situation and in a way contrary to his basic behavior choices, between patterns of interaction with others that are rewarding and those that annoy and frustrate him; totally the problem is one of meeting his personality needs or of thwarting them.

How should this be done? The beginning of such a work is available. In 1959, reviewing the literature on personality needs in occupations, Gray annotates 22 specific investigations dealing with personality variables in occupations or student groups pursuing different courses of study.[5] In their reviews of the sociology and psychology of work, Caplow,[3] Super,[13] and Roe,[8] among others, refer to various studies in this area.

The need for additional descriptive materials of the cultural systems or subsystems of the job, occupation, industry, plant, shop, office, is self-evident. Theory must be built upon such descriptive data. It is a task that must involve the counseling psychologist as well as the social psychologist and sociologist. This is because the needs of the client and his counselor constitute a charter for such investigations.

We will need to develop the techniques and instruments to identify and assess the ideas central in this discussion. For instance, role aspiration will require definition and clarification as a personality manifestation and as a potential in given working situations. We shall have to come to terms with assessment of values in the function of personality and the possibility for their fulfillment at work. We shall have to sharpen constructs like "self-concept" and "identity" because they are totalities and probably not amenable to ready assessment or measurement in the individual or situation. Theory and techniques now available for assessing patterns of interaction with others probably could be utilized with little difficulty in this task. Our greatest need, of course, in this as in other areas, is for a sound and comprehensive theory of personality on which to build necessary structures of personality needs and their satisfaction. Work, after all, is only another setting for functioning of personality.

While working along these lines, we will have to consider a question raised by thoughtful observers. While Super feels that we need a great deal more information about the satisfaction of personality needs in occupations, he points out not only that there are many patterns of interaction in the same occupation, that different personality needs are satisfied, but that the job or occupation itself may lead to changes in attitude and values on the part of workers. There is a reciprocal effect in other words, worker to job, and job to worker.(13) Roe also points to the possibility that individual jobs have their own personality requirements.(9) In a paper delivered in 1959 Gustad raises the same issue.(6)

The idea of a sociology and psychology not of occupations or industry but of individual jobs or positions is likely to prove so complex as to make such an approach fall of its own weight. But probably the truth in this as in so many problems, lies somewhere in between, leaving room for an approach of the kind urged in this paper. While it is obvious, as Gustad points out, that medicine accommodates the "country-clubbing, extrovertive individual, it also makes room for the shy retiring individual." Medicine as a whole, and other occupations or sub-occupational groups may require at least common denominators in personality investment and social functioning capable of identification and description.

Indeed in reviewing research in their monograph *Scientific Careers—Vocational Development Theory*, Super and Bachrach state:

> ... there are sometimes advantages in working with more refined occupational categories such as creative researchers and routine assistants, pediatricians and surgeons, perhaps electrical engineers and sales engineers. Differentiating interest patterns which predict occupational choice and occupational stability have been identified for both occupations and specialties. In view of the failure to identify any clearcut personality patterns for occupations, and the success of preliminary personality studies of specialty groups, it would be worth ascertaining whether or not there are distinctive personality patterns for specialties (of both field and level) within a given occupation. It seems altogether likely that, once adequate designs and instruments are used, the differing role expectations of specialties will result in the finding of occupational personality patterns.(14)

In coming closer to the task we cannot wait for the availability of competent personality theory or for the perfection of instruments or other assessment techniques, even though it is indisputable that 10 years from now we will know more than we know now and 25 years from now we will be even more skillful. At any given point in time, psychological functioning can best be assessed by the best methods then available. While there are a great many instruments, especially in personality assessment, that are worth just about the few cents they cost, there are others that are soundly based and sophisticated in their standardization and use.

Thus the TAT and the instruments based on that conceptually respectable instrument, *e.g.*, the Edwards Personality Profile Schedule, offers an obvious resource for our purpose and indeed Cleveland has addressed himself to this problem with promising results in terms of identification of the differential needs of dietitians, nurses, and other groups. Similarly other investigators have used other instruments, *e.g.*, the Allport-Vernon Studies of Values, and obtained differentiating patterns for different occupational groups. Other approaches, *e.g.*, using the Strong Vocational Interest Blank, have been referred to earlier in this paper.

ONE CLEAR APPROACH

There is one approach, however, which holds enough promise for identifying the Psychological Man at work to warrant brief description here. This is not, of course, the only method we can follow but illustrates what is possible. It is based on Murray's constructs for classifying psychogenic needs and consists of two parallel instruments for assessing the individual's needs and the need-related characteristics of a given situation.

This work is part of the research program of the Psychological Research Center at Syracuse University.[11] The two instruments consist of:*

1. The Stern Activities Index which consists of a list designed to reflect preference in interaction and therefore capable of being analyzed in terms of psychogenic needs.

The Activities Index identifies 42 needs as distinguishable patterns of manifest behavior.

Psychodiagnostic interpretations of individual profiles are based on a clinical appraisal of the relation between the various needs. The measures are quantified and have been subject to sophisticated statistical analysis.

2. Accompanying the Activities Index is another instrument, The College Characteristic Index.

"In this case the purpose is to develop a measure of situational press as distinguished from individual needs."

The College Index has been constructed as a direct complement to the Activities Index. Corresponding to each Needs Scale of the Activities Index is a scale describing aspects of a college environment which would tend to satisfy, support, reward, or reinforce an individual who is characterized by the need in question.

* The statements following are drawn from or are paraphrased from the Preliminary Manual referenced in item 11 in the Reference list.

Findings even thus far are most interesting:

1. Differences between faculty and student responses *within* an institution were found to be very much smaller than the difference in scores *between* institutions.
2. Each college appeared to be characterized by a distinctive press profile.

It is obvious that this approach is designed to assess differential needs satisfied by different colleges but it leaps to the eye that what we have here is a means of assessing in terms of psychogenic needs a particular social system, in this case a college setting. With different items descriptive of work settings, the approach could be precisely the same in assessing the press of the occupation or the work situation. Indeed Stern, Stein, and Bloom[(12)] report that a limited number of just such investigations using the present College Characteristic Index have been accomplished with most promising results.

The prospect of a new field of investigation in order to come to terms with the psychological realities of work is, of course, threatening. However, determination of the dimensions of the Psychological Man at work is a task that the counselor confronts every day in his work, only he does it, so to speak, off the cuff, on the basis of feel and personal experiences. Here too there is a parallel with the systematization of knowledge and technique in the work of the counselor. Assessment of interest, academic aptitude, personality traits are all cases in point; previously accomplished on the basis at best of the counselor's own experience, they have been rationalized so that at best we can we use scientific method and the findings of disciplined inquiry.

In any case we are up against it and in the self-respecting exercise of our function, have no choice. To deal only with the Economic Man at work is to deal only with one part of the worker's functioning, and while this is important, the evidence on every hand points to its inadequacy. Using available theory and methodology we must begin to assess the Psychological Man at work and put what we find to use in our counseling.

REFERENCES

1. Bureau of Labor Statistics, U.S. Department of Labor. *Occupational outlook handbook*, 1959 ed. Washington, D.C.: GPO, Bull. No. 1255.
2. Becker, H. S. (1952) Social-class variations in the teacher-pupil relationship. *J. educ. Sociol.* **25**, 8, 451–465.
3. Caplow, Theodore (1954) *Sociology of work*. Minneapolis: University of Minnesota Press.
4. Crambs, J. D. (1949) Teachers as a minority group. *J. educ. Sociol.* **22**, 403–408.
5. Gray, J. T. (1959) Personality needs in occupations: a review of the literature. *IB 22–25*. Vocational Rehabilitation and Education Service, Department of Veterans Benefits, Veterans Administration. Oct. 16.
6. Gustad, J. W. (1959) Problems and implications for counseling practice. *IB 22–25*. Vocational Rehabilitation and Education Service, Department of Veterans Benefits, Veterans Administration. Oct. 16.
7. *NVGA bibliography of current occupational literature*, 1959 rev. Washington, D.C.: American Personnel and Guidance Association.

8. ROE, ANNE (1956) *Psychology of occupations.* New York: John Wiley & Sons.
9. ROE, ANNE (1958) Implications of vocational interest theory for vocational counseling. Paper presented at Eighth Annual Conference of College and University Counseling Directors, University of Minnesota. Oct. 27–29.
10. ROSEN, HJALMAR, and ROSEN, R. A. HUDSON (1957) Personality variables and role in a union business agent group. *J. appl. Psychol.* **41**, 2, 131–136.
11. STERN, G. G. *Preliminary manual, activities index, college characteristic index.* Syracuse, N.Y.: Psychological Research Center, Syracuse University, 1958.
12. STERN, G. G., STEIN, M. L., and BLOOM, B. S. (1956) *Methods in personality assessment.* Glencoe, Ill.: Free Press.
13. SUPER, D. E. (1957) *Psychology of careers.* New York: Harper & Bros.
14. SUPER, D. E., and BACHRACH, P. B. (1957) *Scientific careers: vocational development theory.* New York: Teachers College, Columbia University.
15. THORNER, ISIDOR (1955) Nursing: the functional significance of an institutional pattern, *Amer. sociol. Rev.* **20**, 531–534.

OCCUPATIONAL INFORMATION: FURTHER READING

BAER, M. F., and ROEBER, E. C. (1958) *Occupational Information: The Dynamics of its Nature and Use*, 3rd ed. Science Research Associates Inc., Chicago.

BARRY, R., and WOLF, B. (1962) *An Epitaph for Vocational Guidance*, ch. 4. Teachers College, Columbia University.

GREENLEAF, W. J. (1954) *Occupations: A Basic Course for Counselors.* Washington D.C., Government Printing Office.

HOPPOCK, R. (1967) *Occupational Information: Where to get it and how to use it in counseling and in teaching*, 3rd ed. McGraw-Hill, New York.

HUNT, D. (1957) *Work Experience Education Programs in American Schools.* Government Printing Office, Washington.

IVINS, W. H., and RUNGE, W. B. (1951) *Work Experience in High School.* New York, Ronald Press Co.

MAHONEY, H. J. (1952) *Occupational Information for Counselors.* New York, World Book Company.

MINISTRY OF LABOUR (1964) *The Pattern of the Future.* Manpower Studies No. 1, London, H.M.S.O.

NORRIS, W., ZERAN, F. R., and HATCH, R. N. (1960) *The Information Service in Guidance.* Chicago, Rand McNally.

SHARTLE, C. L. (1952) *Occupational Information*, 2nd ed. Englewood Cliffs, N.J., Prentice-Hall.

TYLER, L. E. (1961) *The Work of the Counselor*, 2nd ed., Ch. 8. Appleton-Century-Crofts, New York.

U.S. DEPT. OF LABOUR (1963) *Occupational Outlook Handbook.* Washington, Government Printing Office.

U.S. DEPT. OF LABOUR (1965) *Dictionary of Occupational Titles*, 3rd ed. Washington, Government Printing Office.

WEAVERS, G. L. (1955) *How, When and Where to Provide Occupational Information.* Chicago, Science Research Associates Inc.

BRAYFIELD, A. (1948) Putting occupational information across. *Educational and Psychological Measurement*, **8**, 485–495.

BRAYFIELD, A., and MICKELSON, G. T. (1951) Disparties in occupational information coverage. *Occupations*, April 1951, 506–508.

BRAYFIELD, A., and REED, P. A. (1950) How readable are occupation information booklets? *Journal of Applied Psychology*, **34**, 325–328.

BURKE, C. (1957) Occupational information: pawn or panacea. *Vocational Guidance Quarterly*, Autumn 1957, 31–34.

CHERVENIK, C. (1953) Tempting students to sample occupational information. *Vocational Guidance Quarterly*, Winter 1953, 39.

DIENER, T. F., and KACZKOWSKI, H. R. (1960) Readability of occupational information. *Vocational Guidance Quarterly*, Winter 1960, 87.

DOBBERSTEIN, W. F. (1963) Free occupational information—how much? how good? *Vocational Guidance Quarterly*, **11**, 141–142.

DÖÖS, STEN-OLÖF (1962) Forecasting manpower requirements by occupational categories. In Parnes H. S. (ed.), *Planning Education For Economic and Social Development*. O.E.C.D.

FEDERAL SECURITY AGENCY, Office of Ed., Div. of Voc. Ed. (1949) Counselor Competencies in Occupational Information. One of a series of reports on counselor preparation. Washington D.C.: U.S. Office of Education.

GOLDSTEIN, H. (1948) Estimate of occupational replacement needs. *Occupations*, **26**, 397–402.

GRELL, L. A. (1960) How much occupational information in the elementary school? *Vocational Guidance Quarterly*, Autumn 1960, 48.

HEATHCOTE, J., and HAYTER, R. (1964) The Carter Lodge Experiment in extended visits to industry. *Youth Employment*, **16**, 12–14.

HENDERSON, H. L. (1954) Occupational information through assignment, small group discussion, and role-playing. *Vocational Guidance Quarterly*, Winter 1954, 44–56.

HOPKE, W. (1966) A new look at occupational literature. *Vocational Guidance Quarterly*, September 1966, 18–25.

HOYT, D. P. (1955) An evaluation of group and individual programs in vocational guidance. *Journal of Applied Psychology*, February 1955, 26–30.

JOLLES, I. (1946) An experiment in group guidance. *Journal of Social Psychology*, February 1946, 55.

KABACK, G. R. (1960) Occupational information in elementary education. *Vocational Guidance Quarterly*, Autumn 1960, 55.

KIRK, B. A., and MICHELS, M. E. (1950) A study of counselee reading of occupational materials. *Occupations*, April 1950, 446–450.

MILLER, R. A. (1953) Teaching occupations using films and field trips. *Personnel and Guidance Journal*, March 1953, 373–375.

NATIONAL VOCATIONAL GUIDANCE ASSOCIATION (1964) Guide lines for preparing and evaluating occupational materials. *Vocational Guidance Quarterly*, **12**, 217–227.

NELSON, R. C. (1963) Knowledge and interests concerning sixteen occupations among elementary and secondary school students. *Educational and Psychological Measurement*, **23**, 741–754.

PARNES, H. S. (1962) Relation of occupation to educational qualification. In Parnes, H. S. (ed.), *Planning Education for Economic and Social Development*. O.E.C.D.

RUSALEM, H. (1954) New insights on the role of occupational information in counseling. *Journal of Counseling Psychology*, **1**, 84–88.

WOLFBEIN, S. L. (1964) Labour trends, manpower and automation. In *Man in a World at Work*, 460–486. H. Borow, ed. Houghton-Mifflin.

Occupational Information is published in Britain by the Central Youth Employment Executive, Bryant House, Tottenham Court Road, London, W.1.; C.R.A.C., Bateman Street, Cambridge; and many private publishers and employers.

SECTION 8

The Use of Psychological Tests in Vocational Guidance

"Examinations are formidable even to the best prepared, for the greatest fool may ask more than the wisest man can answer."

CHARLES CALEB COLTON

THE role of tests in education in Britain has been sadly misunderstood. Both psychometric ignorance and practical misuse of these aids have contributed to a hearty distrust of them. This is especially ironic in relation to the use of tests in vocational guidance, as it was British psychologists who pioneered the use of tests for this purpose, at the same time providing empirical evidence for their effectiveness (see Chapter 26). It is to America, however, that we must now look for the advances in this area, where *test usage*, as well as *test construction*, is developing its own discipline.

The major part of this section consists of an attempt by Hopson to acquaint those unfamiliar with *test usage* with the major concepts to be found in this area. The abuses current in test usage are discussed, along with the functions of tests in vocational guidance, the types of tests available, and a review of research issues relevant to test selection and administration in the guidance process. This discussion concludes with an appeal for more widespread training of test users enabling greater restrictions to be made regarding who can and who cannot use tests.

Lister and McKenzie provide a most valuable framework, within which test interpretation is examined. *Test interpretation* is one of the three major skills in test usage, the other two being *test selection*, and *test administration*. They discuss the most frequent counsellor errors in presenting test results to clients, claiming that often, test results are given too soon, interpreted without reference to clearly defined criteria, the topic of validity of the results is often passed over, and the results are not presented in terms that the student can understand.

35. *Key Concepts in the Use of Psychological Tests in Vocational Guidance*

BARRIE HOPSON

THE current position in the U.S.A. concerning the number and the variety of tests available and the use made of them, may be likened to the operation of a supermarket, with the vast array of tests available and their ready accessability; the equivalent situation in Britain resembles the small shop on the corner. However, it may be assumed that educationalists in this country will increasingly take advantage of the tests available, in a similar way to the American experience. It is, therefore, essential to clarify many important points concerning the use of tests in educational and vocational guidance.

Numerous textbooks exist which deal with the *facts about tests*—their construction, reliability, validity, describing what information a test can give about an individual, axioms of test theory, etc.; but there has been little emphasis on the *uses* to which tests can be put, the role of the test user, and the operations involved in using tests. More tests are produced every year, so that the potential test user is increasingly bewildered as to which tests to use for what purposes, and consequently is more in need than ever of guidance in test selection and the philosophy of test usage. This latter observation is apparent to anyone in close contact with schools and other institutions where the misuse of tests is appalling.

Super and Crites (1962) distinguish four major types of error made by test users in counselling:

1. A neglect of other methods of appraisal.
2. Overemphasis on appraisal with the resulting tendency to neglect counselling.
3. Failure to take into account the specific validity of the tests used.
4. Neglecting other methods of guidance which should normally accompany appraisal and counselling.

These are criticisms of the use made of tests in guidance. More staggering is the evidence for gross errors made in all phases of the testing operation (Goldman, 1961)—in the selection of tests, in their administration and

(This article is taken from the monograph *The use of Psychological Tests in Educational and Vocational Counselling*, by Barrie Hopson, Vocational Guidance Research Unit, University of Leeds, Yorkshire, England, 1968.)

scoring, and in the interpretation and reporting of scores. Perhaps the simplest of all the operations in a testing programme is scoring, yet Durost (1954) reports that in handling hundreds of thousands of teacher-scored tests he found that between $\frac{1}{4}$ to $\frac{1}{3}$ of them had to be completely rescored or re-interpreted. He also found that between 10 to 50 per cent of answer sheets due for the I.B.M. Testing Scoring service, had to be remarked and cleaned up before acurate scoring was possible.

Frequently there are misunderstandings about the nature of test results, as is witnessed by the alarming tyranny exercised by numbers over the minds of testers. The tester will often assume that a test score has a degree of precision that simply does not exist. Jimmy has an I.Q. of 120 at eleven, and is assumed still to have the same I.Q. at fifteen, and consequently is ranked higher at fifteen than Mary with an I.Q. of 118 at eleven, and lower than Bob who had an I.Q. of 125 at eleven. No allowance is made for (a) the standard error of measurement of the test, which could mean that there was no real qualitative difference between the three children, or (b) the inconstancy of the I.Q. as demonstrated time and again (Honzik, Macfarlane and Allen, 1948; Nisbet, 1957; Bradway and Thompson, 1962; Clarke, 1965).

Misunderstanding of the use of tests is evident in a question such as: "what is a good test of English for eleven year olds?" asked by someone who should know that one must first ask other questions about the kind of goals aimed at by the English course, and the purposes of existing English tests.

Goldman (1961) concludes that "many, if not most, of the tests currently in use are either wasted or, even worse, used in such a way as to misinform and mislead". An example of the latter is the practice of sending home to parents a report card which might include test results with no explanation to help the parents understand the significance of these results. Perhaps it is not too extreme to suggest that one of the reasons for this is that school staff themselves may not fully understand the significance of the results.

Barry and Wolf (1962) single out the greatest abuse of measurement as *purposeless testing*: "A test should be given only for a good and sufficient reason: because it provides information obtainable in no other way; because it describes, within reasonable limits of accuracy, some facet of the individual; because it provides information more efficiently than other methods; because it most effectively implements the purposes of the educational process". Too often tests are given in vocational and educational guidance solely out of curiosity to see what the results will be. The same authors also point out the danger of *imitation* in test use. The mere fact that a test is used in one school is no justification for its use in all schools. The only justification for use is a well thought out question that can be answered by a reliable and valid test.

The advantages of well-kept cumulative record systems are now beginning to be appreciated in Britain (Hopson, 1968). A trap into which teachers and counsellor's must not fall, and which has caught out many American practitioners, is purposeless testing resulting from a *desire for completely filled cumulative records*. If the test information is never to be used by a teacher or counsellor then it should not be obtained. One exception is the use of testing early in a school career as a preparatory step for later testing (this is discussed under the purposes of testing).

Perhaps no area in counselling is more value laden than *test interpretation* (viz. Lister and McKenzie, Chapter 47). To quote Barry and Wolf again: "Unfortunately for counselors, the test interpretation interview provides an opportunity to meet many of their own personal needs: for displaying their knowledge of the subject, for being the authority, for appearing omnipotent, for impressing the student, and for justifying the judgements they feel obligated to give". Too often, a passable ability in the administration of tests is assumed to mean also that that person is capable of interpreting a test in a way that will be most helpful to the child, i.e. to aid his self-understanding. As Rodger and Cavanagh (1964) have emphasized, "There is no point in providing instruction in the giving and scoring of tests without providing instruction in the interpretation of test results". The tester must be fully cognizant with the possible effects on the client of different form of interpretation. The client is bound to be anxious about certain test results even if he is aware that knowing them will render decision-making easier for him. The client is likely to judge himself very harshly in terms of his scores, and the tester must be trained in the process of helping the student to temper his own judgement of their implications for him.

Errors of test administration range from the failure to use a stopwatch in a timed test, to a failure to recognize the multiple use of a single test, thereby incurring unnecessary duplication of test activities (Weitz *et al.*, 1955).

It is within this context of abuse and misunderstanding that one must view the polarization of opinion held by the general public and educationalists on the topic of the value of tests in education. At one extreme are those who think that the results of testing are almost infallible measurements of a persons abilities and aptitudes and should be accepted above all other available information. Psychologists can be fairly accused of selling the principle of testing only too well. This is demonstrated vividly by an investigation of Stagner (1958). He showed that half of a group of personnel managers were ready to accept as accurate descriptions of themselves, a set of generalizations taken from dream books and astrology charts, but presented to them as individualized interpretations of a personality inventory which they had completed.

The other extreme consists of people who discredit all tests as being unreliable and almost useless in understanding and predicting human performance and behaviour. In Britain this attitude has increased over the past few years due to the antagonism aroused by "eleven-plus" selection using objective tests. As this technique of selection has fallen into disrepute, so a general antipathy towards the use of all tests in schools has grown. The confused thinking surrounding this subject manifests itself in two glaring misunderstandings:

(a) Eleven-plus selection by objective test has been proven to be the most efficient and fairest form of selection possible when compared with any form of subjective assessment (N.F.E.R., 1963). What is to be criticized is not the tests but the concept of educational pigeonholing at eleven into different forms of education, and it is this that has been illustrated to be an enormous source of talent wastage. (Vernon, 1957; Crowther Report, 1959, p. 119; Robbins Report, 1963, Appendix 1, p. 42; Douglas, 1964; Little and Westergaard, 1964).

(b) The notion that all tests must be used for some form of selection, or what Cronbach and Gleser (1965) call "institutional decision-making". This view completely overlooks the value of tests as a diagnostic tool to promote self-understanding in the child and insights for the teacher into the childs school performance. Cronbach and Gleser describe this latter use of tests as an "individual decision-making" function. (This dichotomous function of tests is discussed fully under "Purposes of Tests".)

Neither of these extreme points of view is defensible and each exists due to incorrect information about the psychometric *facts of tests* and about the various *uses of tests*. A test, essentially, is intended to sample a persons performance or behaviour. This means that tests are designed or constructed to measure representative performances or behaviour from which the whole, within reasonable limits, can be inferred. To discover the extent of a child's ability in mathematics, he would have to be given every possible mathematical problem. This is obviously impossible, so the next best thing is to sample the total field of mathematical problems by asking him a reprentative problem from each area of mathematics. This is essentially what a test does whether applied to intelligence, attainments, aptitudes, or interests and personality characteristics. Cronbach (1961) defines another important use of a test as a "systematic procedure for comparing the behaviour of two or more persons". Having sampled the mathematical ability of the child, his teacher may wish to compare his ability with other children in the class. A fully standardized test enables the teacher not only to compare the child with other children in the class, but also with all children of his own age and other ages in that country.

Too many tests are on the market whose value is dubious due to poor reliability, but much more commonly, poor validation. Test users all too often assume that if a test is produced and sold, therefore it must serve its stated function efficiently, and consequently they do not read the test manual thoroughly to decide for themselves if the test is reliable and valid.

However, the most valid test may not necessarily help to solve a particular selection or guidance problem; the important factor is the nature of the question that is asked.

Finally, tests in and of themselves are far from being perfect measuring instruments. A test can often fail in its function as an efficient sampler of an area of behaviour due to factors out of its control, such as the attitude and motivation of the testee or the conditions under which the test is given. MacMinn (1960) neatly sums up the dilemma, replying to some of the critics of tests and to the overzealous defenders of tests by paraphrasing a remark of Lincoln's, "It's not so much the use of a bad thing, but the abuse of a good one". Most tests are well designed and constructed and when used wisely for the purposes intended are instruments which can help to reduce substantially the guess work in understanding and predicting human behaviour and performance.

THE PURPOSES OF TESTS

Much of the current criticism of testing in schools that is evident in Britain stems from a narrow understanding of the uses of tests. Certain educationalists and administrators, conditioned to the use of tests in educational selection programmes, and having revolted against this practice, fail to take into account the non-selection uses of tests in education. Their hostility towards this use of tests for selection purposes has generalized to the level of an ideological crusade against the use of any tests in schools. Their confusion could well be clarified by studying Cronbach and Gleser's (1965) dichotomy of decision-making. Discussing tests in terms of decision theory, they examine how well a test result will aid in a particular decision-making situation. They distinguish between two main types of decision:

Institutional decisions, which are made by individuals acting for an institution who choose or reject people according to the expressed needs of the institution. Examples of these are: ability streaming in schools, selection or rejection for courses, schools, universities, etc. In the typical institutional decision, a single person makes a large number of comparable decisions.

Individual decisions are ones where the choice confronting the decision maker will rarely or never recur. The best course of action here is determined by the individual's value system and varies from one individual to another. Examples would be: choice of curriculum, occupational choice, marital choice, etc.

Until recently the use of tests in institutional decision-making situations has overshadowed their value for individual decision-making. One of the reasons is that institutional decisions lend themselves to rigid mathematical and statistical treatment, making generalization possible, whereas this is more difficult for individual decisions. But the chief cause undoubtedly has been the success of tests in personnel selection programmes and the strong desire of most institutions to classify or select their members in an efficient way. To take a test has thus, especially in Britain, developed into a test *for* something which will either be beneficial or detrimental to the testee. It is synonymous with examinations. The designation "test" itself gives away its function. The testing situation has indeed become a "testing" (trying) situation. In any classification of the purposes of tests, this dichotomy in terms of the nature of the decision at hand, is a very useful one.

Goldman (1961) defines his own dichotomy of test usage in terms of the counselling and non-counselling uses of tests, which cut across Cronbach and Gleser's decision situations. The remainder of this section will discuss the varied purposes of tests within a modified version of Goldman's framework, as this out of all other existing classifications, would appear to have most relevance to vocational guidance and is perhaps the most comprehensive treatment of the subject.

NON-COUNSELLING USES OF TESTS

1. Selection of Candidates for the Institution

In Britain, selection for educational institutions has existed since these institutions first became public bodies. Selection is still common in all spheres of education. It can take the form of written examinations, verbal interviews, teachers or headmasters reports, or complicated quota systems like the Thorne experiment. (For a review of techniques used for secondary allocation, see N.F.E.R. 1963.) It may involve institutional decision-making on the basis of attainments such as English and Mathematics for secondary selection, or grades in public examinations like the General Certificate of Education for University entrance. Ability or scholastic aptitude tests are used at all levels, and increasingly used for University selection with a corresponding decrease for secondary selection. Personality and interest tests have been experimented with at all levels but their results, predictably, have not been rewarding for the adminstrators.

2. Placement of Individuals within Institutions

This procedure is often called *classification* (Cronbach, 1961; Camp, 1960). It involves the grouping of pupils on the basis of mental abilities, attainments, or previous school record. In Britain, "ability streaming" often begins very early in the primary school, at 7 or 8 and is often executed by reference to a child's reading age compared with those of his year group (Douglas, 1964). Numerous tests of reading ability are readily available for this procedure. This is rarely found at universities, apart from the system of classifying people to read for an honours, general, or pass degree at some stage prior to or during an individuals university career. The only classification that is universal in universities is the final one of degree grading. But the essential difference between this form of classification and streaming is that streaming effects a deliberate change in the form of instruction for the individual.

A sharp distinction between *classification decisions* and *selection decisions* is required because a test which is useful in making one type of decision may not help with the other (Cronbach and Gleser, 1965). A test may be excellent at predicting grammer school success (selection), but might not help at all in diagnosing pupils likely to encounter difficulties of one sort or another within the grammar school (diagnosis is a form of classification).

3. Adaptation of Institutional Practices to Meet the Needs and Characteristics of Individuals

Camp (1960) and others commonly refer to *identification* as an example of this use of tests. Standardized tests may be used, along with other data, to identify high and low ability students. This feedback to the teacher means that he can adapt his teaching methods accordingly. If, for example, a slow-learner is identified, he can be provided with individual help, and poor readers can be provided with special reading materials. All remedial work can benefit from the use of tests as a screening device. In its broadest sense, this category includes every use of test data that could help teachers to understand a pupil, and if the information results in increased understanding, it might then be possible to make better use of the institution's resources for more effective learning and development.

4. Development of Institutional Practices to Meet the Needs of Students as a Group

This refers mainly to the organization of the curriculum. Through the use of test results a class average may be compared with the averages of preceding classes in order to determine whether changes in the methods of instruction are having a desirable effect. Camp (1960) calls this function *evaluation*. Standardized tests enable one school to compare its progress and the nature of its pupil population with other schools. Seashore (1951) showed how a school's curriculum could be more adequately planned if information on students' occupational aptitudes were available. An aptitude survey would provide at least one basis for judging the relative proportion of vocational bias to introduce in secondary education. How often are children in this country asked at the age of 13 or 14 years whether they would like to opt for a commercial or technical course at school when they have as their only bases for decision—expressed interest, the choices of their friends, the inclinations of their home, and the administrative strait-jacket of the school system that *wants* a particular percentage choice split? By testing their pupils much earlier schools might be in a better position to plan their curriculae accordingly.

Tyler (1951) describes another contribution of testing as that of formulating clear instructional objectives. As pointed out earlier in this article, a test should not be used in a school unless the question that it will help to answer is clearly defined. The use of tests in schools is likely to force teachers into classifying their own objectives, to discover if using tests will measure the attributes that they wish to teach.

COUNSELLING USES OF TESTS

A. For Informational Purposes

Goldman, adapting schemes developed by Super (1957b) and Bordin (1955), arranges the information to be sought into three categories:

1. Precounselling diagnostic information. This is intended to help the counsellor decide if he is in a position to help the client. It may be a separate preliminary step or may be merged with the actual counselling session. The counsellor at this stage is asking questions about the nature of the counselling problem. Does the student really want information on his probabilities of success as a computor programmer, or has he a much deeper problem? Perhaps he feels that circumstances are pushing him towards this area of employment when we would really feel happier in some sort of social work, yet he feels helpless in not being able to stop the process. The counsellor must try to decide at this stage whether the student's problem is one of personality adjustment, financial or health problems, simply a need for occupational information, or for personal data to be used in making educational and vocational decisions. The absence of an efficient referral service in vocational guidance in this country is apparent to all practitioners. Youth employment officers are only too aware of the persistent job changer who they can never satisfy, primarily because his problems are not those of occupational adjustment but of personal adjustment. They are not psychotherapists and so attempt to do what they can, but there is no clear cut referral procedure for such cases, and no body of practising psychologists or social workers large enough or with enough time to deal with these cases.

Information of this kind is usually obtained from interviews, records, and questionnaires rather than from tests, but personality inventories and interest tests can be used for diagnosing severity of disturbance, along with problem check-lists. If the counsellor decides that he is the person best fitted to deal with this problem he then moves on to seek the information discussed below.

2. Information for the Counselling Process itself. The counsellor quickly has to decide what information he wants from the client, how he might best obtain it, and what services he can offer to the client after having obtained the information. Some classification system is essential for the counsellor to organize the information he receives in an orderly manner. It will also serve as a guide to him as to what information to try to obtain. Two examples of such a system are:

The Seven-Point Plan—developed by Rodger (1951) at the N.I.I.P. (described fully in Chapter 36), by which information is collected under the headings of physical characteristics, attainments, general intelligence, specialized aptitudes, interests, disposition, and circumstances. The first four account for capacities, the next two for inclinations, while "circumstances" and "opportunities" are virtually synonymous. Standardized tests can of course provide useful data under attainments, aptitudes, interests, intelligence, and to some extent dispositions. McKenzie (1954) provides a useful analysis of how tests can be applied to the Seven-Point Plan, along with his own suggested scheme for obtaining information quickly for routine vocational guidance (Chapter 37).

Bordin's Diagnostic System (*1946*). This differs from the Seven-Point Plan in that it is concerned with classifying the clients problem, whereas the Seven-Point Plan is concerned mainly with gathering personal information about the client. This system is considered by many to be the most well-developed, and has been modified and tested in research by Pepinsky (1948). This system includes the categories: Dependence, Lack of Information, Self-Conflict, Choice-Anxiety, and Lack of Assurance. This kind of information is usually obtained from non-test data from interviews and questionnaires, although personality inventories and sometimes other kinds of test are useful, for example, using an I.Q. test to diagnose under- or over-aspiration. Bordin also refers to a use of tests to aid the client in developing more realistic expectations about counselling. He sees this as especially useful in cases in which:

(a) Clients are overdependent upon tests to solve their problems.
(b) Clients try to escape from their real problems by focusing their attention on tests.

An economical counsellor should try to clarify a client's real needs without tests, but, failing this, he may find it expedient to give the client actual experience in learning the inadequacies of test results alone in satisfying his real needs. Goldman calls this a *negative information* use of tests, as the counsellor intends the client to realize that the information he seeks, i.e. test data, will *not* provide him with the help he needs.

3. Information Relating to the Client's Postcounselling Decisions. This is the major use of tests in counselling, as counselling is, in the final analysis, concerned with decisions, plans, *and* their implementation. Tests can serve an invaluable function in presenting the client with facts about himself that will help him to rationally make his own decisions, whilst also providing him with facts about an occupation or educational course. This is where the compromise process described by Super (1953) (Chapter 1), if it is not developing spontaneously, is best encouraged by laying out all variables to view.

Goldman (1961) claims that the information-seeking by the client at this stage has three dimensions to it:

(a) The *degree of affect*, by which he means the emotional involvement with the outcome of the information seeking process. One pupil may not be particularly bothered whether he takes engineering or mathematics at university and will choose whichever appears to be more appropriate to his abilities and interests. For another student, his heart may be set on reading mathematics so that it is vitally important for him that his predisposition be reinforced.

(b) The *degree of superficiality* of the clients stated need for information. By this is meant to what extent is the presented problem the true source of the client's need for counselling. Bordin (1955) and Super (1957b) both point out that it is sometimes necessary, and even desirable, to begin to work with the client at the more superficial level. Helping him to solve a small problem successfully could well encourage him to disclose a larger problem.

(c) The *degree of realism* of the alternatives being considered and of the request for information. For example it is clearly unrealistic if a low ability child enquires sincerely about how good an engineer he will make, when he will be fortunate to obtain a Certificate of Secondary Education in any subject yet alone a university degree.

These three dimensions can all be clarified for the counsellor and for the client by the intelligent use of tests. If a test serves no function other than helping to clarify the individual's self-concept then it has more than justified its administration.

Tyler (1961) outlines a number of specific functions of tests in this stage, which Camp (1960) would call the "*planning* function":

1. They rule out areas of decision-making that will not be profitable for that individual to consider. *It is useful to note in relation to this, that low scores on a test are usually more predictive than high ones.* A bright student is more likely to achieve less than was predicted for him, due to extraneous circumstances, lack of motivation, etc., than a dull student is to achieve more.

2. An intelligence test can predict the educational level a child is likely to reach—an essential for any educational or vocational counselling. It can also discover special abilities that need to be developed.

3. Attainment tests show his present level of functioning—necessary when considering his suitability for a specialized course.

4. They can also provide information on specific aptitudes.

Traxler and North (1966) provide an additional function of tests at this stage:

5. They can provide objective information for parents on the progress of their child. However, this is only useful if the parents are informed about the significance of the scores. Such information can aid a teacher in persuading parents of the necessity of a particular educational decision for their child.

Perhaps the most important point relating to the efficacy of tests in guidance, is that for the results to be really meaningful to the child he must be to some extent emotionally involved in the situation. Goldman stresses the importance of there being some opportunity to relate the test information to other aspects of the individual's experience, to his school work, leisure-time activities, or family and neighbourhood values. "Without these elements, self-concept development through information about himself is likely to be superficial and lacking in real impact on the individual".

This emphasis on self-concept development and self-understanding is described by Mathewson (1962) as the *developmental* approach to guidance, and it is the *problem-oriented* approach (akin to Super's "crisis counselling" (1957a)) which has received so much more attention both in the literature and in practice. In fact, in Britain, almost all the vocational guidance that is carried out by the Youth Employment Service, schools, and private agencies, is problem-oriented. Yet, as Mathewson points out, it is the more positive, developmental and preventative approach which in the long run seems likely to be of help to the largest number of people. To know oneself is an essential ability for the maturing person, and here tests have something to offer everyone.

B. Non-Informational Purposes

1. Stimulation of Interest in Areas Not Previously Considered. Interest tests—the Rothwell-Miller Blank is a good example—can be used to stimulate further thinking about the world of work and to widen the horizons of the children completing the blank. From his test interpretation, a client can learn about educational potentialities or of jobs of which he had little awareness or had never considered.

With the rapid technological and social changes of the modern economy talent wastage becomes an even greater problem than formerly. Wolfle (1958) in the U.S.A. calculated that their needs for skilled, technical, and professional workers can be met only by increased upward mobility of those in under-privileged groups who lack not only the money but also the conscious interests and the motivation to seek out advanced education and training. Beilin (1956) states that counsellors, armed with valid and reliable tests, can contribute to the stimulation of interests and to the development of altered self-concepts. The economic situation is no less acute in Britain, and the wastage of talent is enormous, as illustrated earlier in this article. An equal responsibility lies upon teachers and the growing body of school counsellors in this country (still less than two hundred) for widening the educational and occupational horizons of the lower income groups.

2. Laying the Groundwork for Later Counselling. This is taking the *developmental* approach to guidance one step further. Tests are given to children in primary and junior schools simply to prepare them for the more important tests which they will receive later in their school careers. However, any counsellor or teacher worth his salt would opt for a test that will serve some useful diagnostic function as well as providing anticipatory socialization for the pupils.

3. Learning Experiences in Decision-Making. Tiedeman's (1966) current research programme includes teaching decision-making to school children. This underlines the important fact that a person *can* be trained to make decisions more quickly and efficiently than he would if it was left for him to develop his own strategems. In guidance sessions, too many clients want decisions to be made for them, and it is all too tempting to fall into the trap and try to assist them directly when they are so obviously begging for the counsellor's help. The counsellor who resists these temptations can look forward only to the occasional reward of the realization that a client has made an appropriate decision. Providing a client with test data about himself forces him to think of its relevance to his self-concept and to his future educational and vocational prospects. By giving him a choice as to what information he wishes to obtain, i.e. allowing him to choose the tests he will take (after their purposes have been individually explained), he is forced to make decisions as to what is important to him in life. As Goldman says, "the tests selected are not nearly so important as the *manner* in which they are selected, and the manner in which the counsellor later helps his client to learn from the experience".

Many British readers by this stage will be wondering what all of this has to do with the situation here, where to see a test used in a school at all is not common. However, this discussion would appear to be glibly pursuing the purposes of, if not altogether *aimless testing*, at least testing of a secondary importance compared with what needs to be done in our schools. Two points should be borne in mind in relation to this:

(a) The use of tests in schools must be viewed against a comprehensive framework of test usage theory, whether this is currently practicable or not. And

(b) the educational system has to make its own decision whether to opt for developmental guidance or problem-oriented guidance.

If it opts for the former then such a decision carries all the implications discussed above under Goldman's framework. If it opts for problem-oriented guidance, then tests can only have the limited uses as aids to institutional decision-making as at present, and to provide clients with data about themselves which, unless they are trained how to handle and use it in relation to their self-concepts, will hardly justify the cost of the test administration.

THE ADMINISTRATION OF TESTS

Having decided that tests may be useful in a school, how does one begin to organize a testing programme, and what are the important issues surrounding test administration?

Reppert, Campbell, and Kirk (1965) formulate five questions basic to the introduction of a school testing programme: these are the *why*, *when*, *where*, *how* and *which* questions of the testing programme.

1. *Why* are tests to be used at all?
2. *When* should they be given?
3. *Where* should they be given?
4. *How* are the results to be used?
5. *Which* tests are to be used?

1. The objectives of the school curriculum for each subject must be fully worked out, so that it is possible to decide if tests can provide information on the pupils progress in each subject (the *why* of testing). If intelligence, aptitudes or personality tests are to be used, all the staff, parents and, as far as sophistication allows, pupils, must be aware of the uses to which the results will be put. "Tests can never be more than a tool to collect the information needed to carry out other functions in the school programme" (Wellman, 1960). One person should have ultimate responsibility for the tests used in the school, and it is imperative that he have sufficient understanding of psychometrics so that he can best determine the possibility of having the objectives elicited by the philosophy of the programme met by its functioning.

2. There are four basic approaches to *when* the testing should take place:

Saturation Testing

The counsellor administers to one or a group of pupils a battery of tests selected to cover everything that is likely to be of importance for counselling; it could include general intelligence, spatial visualization, perceptual speed, mechanical comprehension, an interest blank, various personality traits, etc. In the U.S.A. the typical procedure is to score the tests, plot a profile of the results, present it to the student, and then discuss their significance with him. The assumption is that most abilities and interests are of some importance, and the best way to take them into account is to test them all at once and transmit the information to the pupil.

Disadvantages. Inappropriate and unnecessary testing, no client participation, difficulty of arousing client motivation.

Advantages. Economy of time and administration.

Individualized Battery Testing

Each pupil takes all his tests in a group, but they are not necessarily the same tests as those being taken by others in the group. Private vocational guidance agencies often use this approach.

Disadvantages. Testing is still separated from counselling, with the consequent dangers of lack of client participation and motivation.

Advantages. It is tailored to the individuals needs, characteristics, and expressed goals.

Preliminary Screening Battery

Cronbach (1955) provides the theoretical rationale for this. He begins with the assumption that "... the value of test information should be judged by how much it improves decisions over the best possible decisions made without the test, whereas the conventional validity coefficient reports how much better test decisions are than *chance* decisions". He concludes that it may be wiser to use imperfect tests of important objectives that are hard to measure, such as creativity or attitudes, than to use highly valid tests that merely supplement nontest data. He suggests a programme of *sequential measurement* (Cronbach and Gleser, 1965) which would mean in practice that a short test would, firstly, be given to all. For some pupils this might provide enough information to make whatever decision it is that needs to be made (selection, classification, etc.) For the remainder, there is a continuous process of narrowing-down, each person dropping out of the testing programme at the point at which a decision can be made. The entire testing procedure would be terminated at the point where added value of further testing is less than its cost. This approach is illustrated by the *Lee–Thorpe Occupational Interest Inventory*, which samples six fields (such as Mechanical and Personal-Social) and then each field is analysed more fully; that is, a person scoring heavily on Personal-Social would take a further test in that area but not in the other areas.

For many teachers and counsellors, interviews and records serve as informal screening devices to narrow down the choice of test.

Disadvantages. The same as for all group testing.

Advantages. Economical use of time and materials, and individually tailored.

Precision Testing

Tests are given within the counselling process, to encourage client participation and to further develop rapport. As discussion of a pupil's problems make it clear that certain specific data should be considered, counsellor and pupil together obtain and evaluate the needed data. Thus a test may be given, scored, interpreted, and discussed during the course of one interview. Further tests may then be planned, or not, depending upon the needs defined by further interviewing.

Disadvantages. This form of testing is the most time-consuming.

Advantages. Client participation and motivation; the tests actually encourage counselling rapport rather than act as a barrier between counsellor and pupil, which is what is predicted by Rogers (1946); tests fall into the perspective of *reality-testing devices*, a function suggested by Bordin (1955).

3. *Where* the tests should be administered is partly covered by the last question. However, the physical conditions accompanying testing are of vital importance. Common sense dictates that tests should be administered in well-lighted rooms, with suitable writing surfaces, and with a minimum

of noise and other distractions. However, if conditions in a school are not good this should not necessarily rule out testing for that school. Little research has been done on the physical conditions of testing, but what has been done suggests that the nature of the physical conditions are probably not as important as the attitudes and motivation of the testee.

4. *How* the results are to be used depends upon the original reasons for the setting up of the testing programme; mainly, whether the results are to be used for *institutional* or *individual* decision-making. If they are to be used for *individual* decision-making, then the problems of test interpretation are uppermost (see Chapter 47). The methods and materials of interpretation have to be decided, as well as the rationale of the counselling procedure. Some training in psychometrics and test interpretation is especially essential at this stage of the testing programme.

5. The question of *what* tests are to be used again presupposes a thorough knowledge of the tests available and the differences, if any, between them. If a teacher does not possess this knowledge he could consult his local educational psychologist who should be able to assist him.*

RELEVANT ISSUES TO TEST ADMINISTRATION

Coaching and Practice

This factor is of most concern when tests are to be used for *institutional decision-making*. However, if tests do not reflect exactly what they are supposed to reflect, this factor is important for the use of tests in vocational guidance. Gibson (1954—reported in Vernon, 1957) has described the misery that can be caused by firm parental belief in the efficacy of coaching for I.Q. tests. It is, therefore, essential to examine the evidence on what could be an important limiting agent on the validity of tests.

The short answer to this problem is that, to date, research indicates the noticeable but limited values of coaching for tests. It may be effective in raising scores of people who have not had recent experience in taking tests of that general type, and who have not had recent experience with the subject matter of that particular test. Vernon (1952) estimated the average rise after a single practice on an I.Q. test at about 5 points, but further practice brought progressively smaller increases, totalling about 10 points, and scores tended to fluctuate irregularly or even to drop after five or six practice tests. Coaching then, could make a total difference of 12 to 15 points, but its maximum effectiveness seems to be reached in two to three hours. Yates (1953) reports other work showing considerably smaller effects and even how uninstructed practice was more effective than coaching. However, these discrepancies can be explained by the fact that the pupils tested were

* Traxler and North (1966, chapter 9) provide a useful example of a step by step procedure in planning and and conducting a testing programme.

sophisticated to varying degrees, and because coaching was not uniform in all the investigations. Wiseman and Wrigley (1953) demonstrated that coaching seemed to have more pronounced effects at the lower end of the I.Q. range, whereas practice was more effective at the upper end of the range. Other studies suggest the same conclusion of the very limited effectiveness of coaching and practice, (Peel, 1952 and 1953; Dyer, 1953; Longstaff, 1954; Maxwell, 1954; French and Dear, 1959).

Vernon (1957) concludes that, "Coaching by parents or teachers from published books of intelligence test items, or from other, more or less dissimilar, tests, is singularly ineffective, particularly when it does not include doing a complete parallel test under timed examination conditions". Obviously, to establish equality, a minimum amount of coaching should be given to all candidates for a selective intelligence test (James, 1953). When individuals are tested rather than groups, it could be desirable to give two different forms of the same test if they exist. This factor, however, will be of maximal importance in intelligence and attainment tests, to a lesser extent in aptitude tests, and hardly at all in personality tests.

Response Sets

A response set is a tendency to perceive questions and to answer them in a particular way, regardless of the test item. For example, Tyler (1964), illustrating the development of interests in children, showed that young children tend to have positive attitudes towards test items, and that only with increased maturity would they answer an item negatively. It is, therefore, essential to ensure that tests do not favour people who have a tendency, or set, to respond positively to most questions, and vice versa. A test has to be answered by people as diverse as Fanny Hill and Grumpy of the seven dwarfs! Much research on response sets has been inspired by Cronbach's (1950) review of the literature and his statement that these sets sometimes operate to reduce the validity of tests. Cronbach suggested that they were more frequent on tests with ambiguous instructions and on tests which are really too difficult for the person taking them. Both of these situations encourage indiscriminate answering, which leads directly to the operation of response sets.

Fredericsen and Messick (1959) classify some of the most commonly occurring response sets as follows:

1. *Acquiescence*. Tending to accept any personality statement as applying positively to oneself, or alternatively to reject all items. This often reflects immaturity (viz. Tyler, 1964), lack of motivation, or may represent a genuine personality factor.

2. *Evasiveness*. Giving many *Doubtful* or *Indifferent* responses. This response can be very useful diagnostically. It could mean that the client is not motivated sufficiently to take the test, which signifies either the irrelevance of that particular test from the clients viewpoint, a misunderstanding

of its function by the client, or genuine uncertainty which could reflect immaturity or underlying personal problems. Which is the correct explanation depends upon the diagnosing skill of the counsellor.

3. *Extremeness.* Giving a preponderance of *Strongly Agree* or *Strongly Disagree* rather than intermediate responses. For example, Asch (1958) studied a "negative response bias" which appeared on a "Speed of Decision" test. Operating on the premise that, in the American culture at least, people tend to agree rather than disagree when in doubt, he found some support for his hypothesis that a negative response set is associated with a tendency to be neurotic or maladjusted, and in particular to have obsessive-compulsive symptoms. These results are not conclusive, but such a response set obviously is a source of hypotheses for the counsellor giving guidance.

4. *Inclusiveness.* When the potential number of a particular response (e.g. Agree's) is unspecified, giving a large proportion of these. Its opposite could be *criticalness* in accepting words, phrases etc., as adequate or as equivalent. Fredericsen and Messick (1959) investigated criticalness in evaluating the similarity or acceptability of words and phrases, hoping to find its personality correlates. It proved to be a fairly reliable and generalized tendency, independent of accuracy of discrimination. Vernon (1960) suggests that this response trait would be largely affected by educational background, in particular, the standards of equivalence to which clients had become habituated from their own school work. It is of value to the counsellor to realize that such individual differences do exist, that they are a product of differential educational environment, and not necessarily symptomatic of any great personality disorder.

5. *Social Desirability.* This is the tendency to try to portray oneself via a personality inventory in a manner that the client thinks is most acceptable to his culture and to the tester who is a representive of that culture. Even in the counselling situation where a client should realize that candidness is to his benefit, the temptation to present a socially acceptable image of oneself is often overwhelming. Many self-report tests are very easy to falsify to one's advantage (see William H. Whyte (1960) and Huff (1964) for practical tips on how to present the "right" image for job selection purposes). Apart from deliberate distortion many people do not know themselves well enough to answer factually, and are likely to produce unwitting self-deceptions or rationalizations in the direction of social conformity. As Vernon (1938) noted, not everyone aims merely to display a favourable self-picture. Some are more suggestible and tend to exaggerate their defects, e.g. neurotic patients, or extraverted students attempting to appear introverted and neurotic as this is the socially acceptable thing to be. Highly educated persons are often self-analytic and introspective and might be more self-depreciatory than non-academics.

Many test constructors have introduced devices to counteract this defensive or self-deprecatory response set. Edwards, in his *Personal Prefer-*

ence Schedule (EPPS), uses the forced choice approach, in which one must choose between two statements the one which is most nearly true of him, the two statements having been matched for social desirability (Edwards, 1957). This is a promising approach, although the reliability of the matching process is hotly debated. Some tests, like the *Minnesota Multiphasic Personality Inventory* (MMPI), *Kuder Preference Record*, and *Eysenck Personality Inventory* (EPI), incorporate consistency checks, or lie scales, which shed light on the validity of the final scores. A more recent device is the *adjective check list*, in which the client chooses one adjective from a group which is most descriptive of him, and one which is the least descriptive. All adjectives are in the group because they have been judged approximately equal in social desirability (Dunnette and Kirchner, 1960). It is important for counselling purposes to diagnose if someone is lying as this can give much information about the client's problems. If the counsellor cannot use an inventory that has a consistency *gauge* of some kind then he must try to reduce this response set in the client by establishing an atmosphere of trust and concern for the clients well-being.

6. *Cautiousness*. For example, omitting difficult items in an ability test. The opposite to this is a set to *guess* whenever in doubt rather than to omit. The study of Swineford and Miller (1953) suggests that (1) the directions given to testees as to whether they should guess makes some difference in the amount of guessing that occurs; (2) there are individual differences in that some people will guess under any circumstances, others being always hesitant to guess; (3) there may be a relationship between readiness to guess and certain personality characteristics. (For example, Eysenck's findings on the differential approaches to tests of extraverts and intraverts, 1967b.) Anyone who has administered personality tests can comment on differences between the *guesser* or *non-guesser*. The former is often more aggressive, self-assured, or prepared to accept a greater probability of failure in decision-making as long as the reward is high. A readiness or non-readiness to guess could also mean motivational differences or a lack of concern about doing well. Very little research has been done on this question, although Sherriffs and Boomer (1954) did find that students low in self-esteem tended to omit more items than did other students.

The counsellor, therefore, must be aware of the possibility that the set to guess freely or vice-versa may raise or lower an individual's score on a test. Inspection of answer sheets can provide a clue here, and the results of this inspection may then be related to what one knows of the client already.

7. *Speed*. People respond to items at different speeds. The person who checks and re-checks his answers is obviously bound to be handicapped on a timed test. In a "within-counselling" testing situation, the tester can spot if a person has this set and can either give an untimed ability test, or deviate from the standardized instructions for administration and allow the client unlimited time (after noting the number of items completed at the prescribed

time limit). In either case, the difference between the two scores will give an estimate of the degree of this response set. Mollenkopf (1950) reported results suggesting that additional time for slow test-takers is more likely to result in score increases when the type of item requires problem solving of items like verbal antonyms.

The problem of the prevention and control of irrelevant response sets is basically a problem for the *test constructor*. However, the implications for the *test user*, as illustrated, are of the utmost importance. The counsellor must be alert to these and other response sets that may be interfering with the validity of test scores and thereby will impair the information that a counsellor obtains about a client.

MOTIVATIONAL FACTORS IN THE TESTING SITUATION

Response sets are the more permanent idiosyncratic influences at work on test performance. Other factors operate to determine the attitude of the client towards a particular testing session. Many of these depend directly upon the success of the counsellor in establishing a good rapport with the client, and in explaining the purposes and nature of the tests. If the counsellor does not succeed in this, various undesirable results may ensue, such as faking, anxiety, and lack of effort.

Faking

This has already been illustrated by the social desirability response set. Client participation in test selection and *precision* testing should help to reduce the reasons for faking considerably. Group administration makes this kind of rapport much more difficult, and counsellors using test results obtained from group testing sessions should be more cautious in accepting the resulting profiles as accurate reflections of interests and traits. It is not always possible to establish good rapport, whatever the qualities of the counsellor, in which case tests should be selected that are either resistant to distortion (like the forced choice inventories) or have built in lie-detectors.

Anxiety

The amount of tension experienced during test-taking usually depends upon the purpose of the testing session, so that it is greatest in an institutional decision-making situation. But anxiety is present also in testing for counselling. The issue is not at all clear as to what the effects of anxiety and tension actually are, and whether they are at all deletarious. Sears (1943) reported that a wide variety of emotional disturbances, even neuroses and psychoses, did not have consistent or uniform effects upon test scores. This would appear to support the view that tension does not aid test performance. Sarason has initiated a large number of studies, unfortunately using small samples and resulting in nonsignificant findings, but the tentative conclusions are that test anxiety *can* be measured and that extreme amounts can interfere with test performance especially in a clients first efforts in a new test situation (Sarason, 1950; Mandler and Craighill, 1952). Sarason and Mandler (1952) found that social class was related to test anxiety, with upper middle classes having higher test anxiety scores than those above or below this level. They suggest that this is due to the high pressure to achieve educationally at this status level. Interestingly, Sarason *et al.* (1960) comparing English and American elementary school children, found greater test anxiety in the English sample. This was predicted due to the 11 plus examination used for secondary school selection in England. They concluded that the influence of anxiety varied according to the degree of threat which the child saw in a test. The effects of anxiety were more apparent in verbal than in nonverbal tests; this they suggest resulted from the fact that school children and parents place more emphasis on verbal tests.

The suggestion has been made (Martin and McGowan, 1955) that test anxiety is a response set in itself, i.e. it is simply a manifestation of general anxiety. Other studies have not supported this however (Gordon and Sarason, 1955; Sarason *et al.*, 1960; Sinick, 1956b), so that test anxiety reduction remains a real aim for the counsellor.

One of the seeming contradictions related to this question is the evidence showing that a high level of anxiety although generally resulting in an impaired performance, occasionally causes improvement (Sinick, 1956a). Sinick (1953) discussing the reason for this claims that people react differently to anxiety, and some anxious people exhibit exceptional mental alertness while others "... seem to have their minds temporarily in deep freeze". This could well be related to different styles of decision-making.

What is the counsellor to learn from all of this? Goldman concludes that until much more is known about the variables involved, counsellors "... will probably be wise to seek to encourage only a moderate amount of tension enough so that most subjects will be alert and ready to work". In pursuit of this aim group testing is likely to be less successful than individual testing, as standardized conditions of test administration do not guarantee a uniform emotional response from all the testees. Instruments such as Sarason's scales and the *Taylor Manifest Anxiety Scale* could well be experimented with as "blanket tests" so that all future test results could be interpreted in the light of a person's measured test-anxiety.

An interesting technique used with an achievement test by McKeachie, Pollie and Speisman (1955) gave the testees space on the answer sheet to comment on the test items. This led to higher scores than did the conventional answer sheet, as this reduced the threat situation and created a channel for the release of anxiety.

Effort Put Into Test Situation

Lack of effort may be directly due to lack of interest, ignorance as to what to do, lack of expectation that the test has anything to offer, anxiety which renders the client jellylike, or perception of the test as a threat (Sarason *et al.*, 1960). Flanagan (1955) has developed an "index of examinee motivation" because of the vast importance to the counsellor of knowing the motivation of his client. The counsellor must not assume that a client's performance on a test is typical unless he has investigated the importance of these other factors too.

TYPES OF TEST AVAILABLE

Tests may be classified in two ways—according to their *function*, i.e. what they test and according to the *testing procedure* used:

FUNCTIONAL CLASSIFICATION

Boyle's diagram (p. 484) illustrates the logical inter-relationships between the various types of test. Tests may be readily thought of under five headings—general mental ability, attainment, aptitude, interests, and personality.

General Mental Ability Tests

These tests are also known variously as *scholastic aptitude* tests, *mental ability*, or *intelligence* tests. In Britain, as mentioned earlier, these tests have a misleading image based upon their role as a selection agent for secondary schools. They provide an estimate of an individual's ability to learn by requiring him to perform certain mental activities, which emphasize in particular his knowledge of vocabulary and his ability to reason. Some intelligence tests yield a single total score (*Stanford-Binet*, *Wechsler*) while others provide a profile so that different abilities can be compared (*Thurstone's Primary Mental Abilities*). Diagnostically the profile is more useful, where as for purposes of institutional decision-making the single score is more convenient, for administrators. The simplest profile is that obtained by giving one or two tests, as required, in order to obtain a verbal and a non-verbal score. The verbal score is the most heavily influenced environmentally (Clarke, 1965; Bernstein, 1960) and the non-verbal score is least influenced. This is why social class is very highly correlated with verbal ability and correlates much less with nonverbal ability. Much of the abuse associated with intelligence tests over the years stems from their purported function as an estimator of innate potential. This had led to many inaccurate and unjust institutional decisions. The tendency over recent years has been to abandon the concept of a fixed, genetically determined intelligence, because not only is it non-measurable due to environmetal influences, but it also encourages

A Heuristic Classification of Psychological Tests*

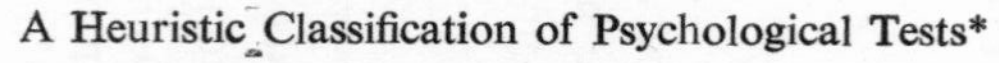

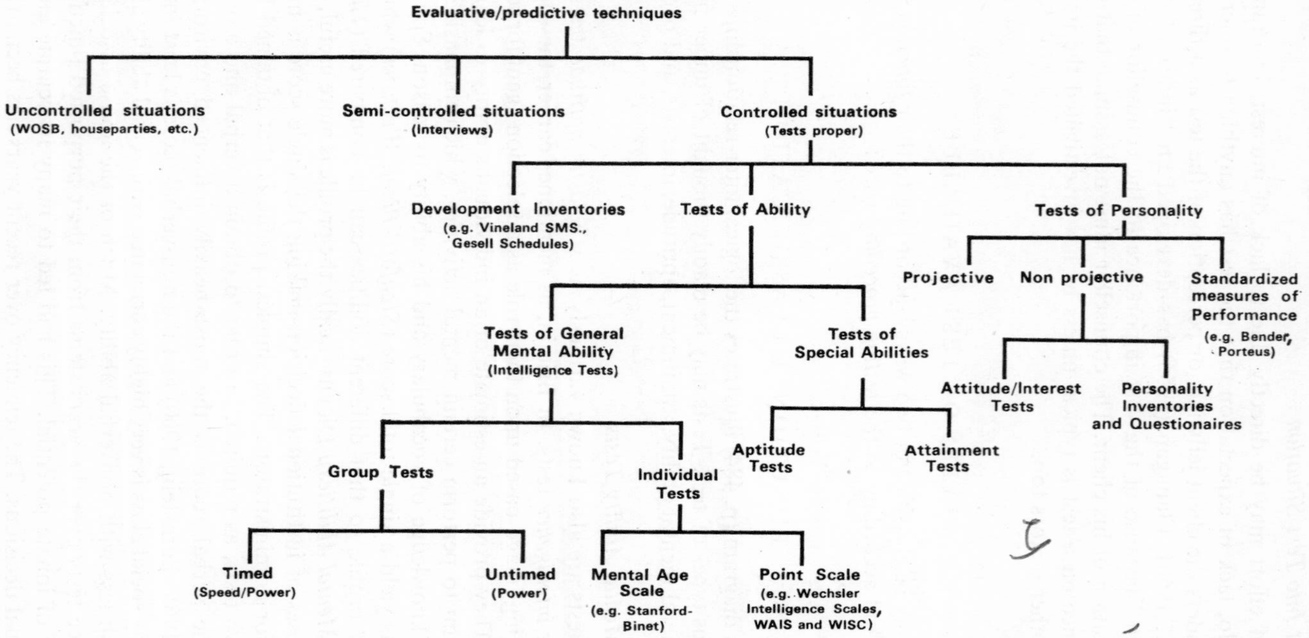

* This format was designed by D. G. Boyle of the Dept. of Psychology, University of Leeds, and is reproduced with his kind permission.

the notion of a "pool of ability" which itself leads to a stultifying definition of inviolable limits of development. Hunt (1961) in an exhaustive review of research pertaining to this concept, concluded that intellectual development and the explanatory construct, intelligence, grows from the interaction of the child with his environment. In this context, a counsellor must use intelligence tests not to attempt to measure some artificially defined set of limits on development, but to help determine the kinds of environmental situations that will best facilitate the optimal development of this interaction.

Two typical vocational guidance problems are found with the underaspirer and overaspirer. *Underaspirers*, commonly from lower income bracket homes, are found with a verbal score one or more percentiles behind their non-verbal score. For practical purposes it is often correct to suppose that such a child is capable of performing better than he has done until then, given encouragement and good teaching. *Overaspirers*, commonly from higher income brackets, present the reverse profile—high on verbal and lower on non-verbal. Typically, they are highly motivated educationally, attending grammar school, but the going gets tougher and tougher until by the time of the G.C.E. examinations they are often close to complete breakdown. Their high verbal abilities have carried them through their early educational careers and it is only with the more taxing work demanding higher level reasoning and comprehension that their verbal abilities no longer will suffice. These cases are amongst the most difficult in vocational guidance. To inform someone that he is capable of doing much better is far less traumatic than informing him, *and* his parents, that he is probably aiming too high. Both individuals have to readjust their self-concept, but for the overaspirer it too often signifies failure and ignominy and demands extraordinary parental understanding.

General ability tests in themselves are only very broad predictors of occupational satisfactoriness as occupations typically encompass large ranges of ability so that occupational differentiation on this basis becomes very difficult (Vernon, 1960, p. 189). Tyler's (1961) dictate should again be recalled: that low scores are always better predictors than high scores, as high scores cannot take into account numerous attitudinal factors. Feldt (1959) sums up the predictive potential of intelligence tests thus: "It may be expected that future research will lead to critical minimum values below which a disproportionately large number of workers fail, but only in clerical and related white-collar fields have such minimums been tentatively derived at this time."

Attainment Tests

Also called *achievement* tests, they measure the amount of progress made in a particular subject. Being standardized they provide an excellent evaluation of one child with another, one group with another, and feedback as to whether the objectives of the course are being met. Few devices provide a more objective and valid means by which parents may be brought to adopt reasonable standards of performance for their children.

Some attainment tests are called *diagnostic* tests, as their function is to enable a teacher or counsellor to determine a pupil's specific strengths or weaknesses in subjects like English and Arithmetic. Test items are grouped according to the skill they are supposed to measure. Frequency of errors in groups of test items identify the learning needs of the pupil.

Attainment tests, like all tests, have been abused in practice, and one of the dangers of attainment tests is that they encourage the so-called "back-wash" effect on teaching; that is, the nature of tests mould the teaching syllabus and consequently restricts a teacher's freedom. They have also been used to encourage unhealthy competition among classes and pupils, and have been unfairly used to judge the competence of teaching personnel. Again, it must be emphasized that these are mainly abuses of *test usage*. However, the tests do have certain inadequacies in themselves. It is debatable if any adequate techniques have yet been developed which permit sufficiently objective measurement of the ability to write effectively and creatively (Wiseman, 1961; Schools Council, 1964 and 1966).

Feldt (1959) sees the chief weakness of attainment tests as that "... to too great a degree they elicit from the student skills and knowledge which rapidly lose significance outside the classroom". Undoubtedly there is some truth in this, but their value for educational and vocational guidance remains unquestionable.

Aptitude Tests

These are used in estimating future success of a person in various occupations or further education. They attempt to measure certain stable, unitary, and relatively independent psychological characteristics of a person which are believed to be necessary for success on a job or in further education. Memory, spatial perception, manual dexterity, reaction time, perceptual speed, word fluency, are all examples of aptitudes.

Some aptitude tests, for example, those for clerical, mechanical, musical, and computer programming aptitudes, attempt to measure the combinations of traits or specific aptitudes discovered by empirical research to be associated with them; e.g. mechanical aptitudes is believed to include, among others, spatial perception and mechanical reasoning ability.

It would be very time-consuming to administer large numbers of individually standardized aptitude tests so as to cover a large range of aptitudes, also, technical differences among tests and the differences among group norms cloud the picture of a client's strengths and weaknesses. Thus, over the past fifteen years, batteries of tests (*multifactor tests*) have been developed which provide a broad screening of the basic abilities required in many occupational families. The client obtains a profile which can then be compared with profiles obtained from large numbers of occupational and educational groups. There are numerous tests of this nature in the U.S.A., for example, the *General Aptitude Test Battery* (GATB), *Scholastic Aptitude Test* (SAT), *Differential Aptitude Tests* (DAT). In Britain, the only major test battery to be developed is Morrisby's *Differential Test Battery* (DTB), but not nearly enough validity studies have been carried out with this potentially very useful test.

Aptitude tests have come in for much criticism as regards their logical *raison d'être* and empirically in relation to their usefulness. Blocher (1966) makes the point that aptitudes can never be measured directly. Only performances can be directly observed. "In designing so-called aptitude tests, therefore, we contrive to observe a *performance* that is always *learned or achieved*, and we then *infer aptitude*. We measure achievement and infer aptitude" (Blocher, 1966, p. 134). The important assumption here, often overlooked, is that this inference is only reasonable if all subjects on whom observations are made have had equal opportunity to learn or achieve the measured performance.

This pessimistic view of the nature of aptitudes is unfortunately reinforced by the empirical evidence for their validity in predicting occupational and educational success. Ghiselli's (1966) exhaustive survey of the literature highlighted some disturbing facts:

(a) That correlations between all varieties of aptitude tests and the criteria they might be expected to predict, on the average, are rather low;
(b) These correlations differ greatly from study to study;
(c) Correlations with training criteria are not related to correlations with proficiency criteria for the same test;
(d) The correlations with training criteria were consistently higher than those with proficiency criteria. Thorndike and Hagen (1959) also failed to demonstrate much correlation between aptitude measures and occupational criteria in their follow-up of Air Force personnel. Tyler (1962) comments that the implications of this for the counsellor is that," any given test predicts a criterion inaccurately if at all, that whether a person's score is significant or not depends upon the situation he gets into in the unpredictable future, and that if a high score forecasts success in a training program it does not have anything to say about his success in the work to which training leads".

Does this mean that aptitude testing is a complete waste of time? This need not be the case for two reasons:

(a) Most of the reported studies indicate that many occupations can be *differentiated* from one another on the basis of measured aptitudes; what cannot be predicted is the *degree of success* within an occupation, as this depends upon so many other factors not measured by aptitude tests. There could well be *aptitudinal thresholds* for occupations below which a person may not be capable of functioning, similar to that suggested earlier for intelligence differences between occupations. Much more research is needed to determine these limits, if they exist, and they could then serve a very important function in vocational guidance.

(b) Aptitude measures might well suggest new occupational possibilities for the client that had been previously ignored or simply not known about. They would also help to structure the choice situation for him and so assist decision-making. For the counsellor, the use of specific aptitude tests e.g. for typing, clerical work, computor programming, and engineering, may still be profitably used, again remembering the dictum that low scores are more accurate predictors than high scores, a fact that itself lends more support to a concept of occupational aptitude thresholds.

Interest Inventories

These are designed to permit an individual to record in a structured manner his likes and dislikes in different situations. They usually take the form of choosing between activities, occupations, or reactions to events or people. For vocational guidance purposes an individual's interest profile is often compared with profiles obtained for different occupations to ascertain whether there are any correlations. If there are similarities between an individual's profile and an occupational group's profile, the assumption is made that the individual should be satisfied with that kind of work, other situational and motivational factors held constant.

An inventory can also be scored to indicate a larger interest area, such as computational, mechanical, aesthetic, etc., to enable counselling to take place within the context of the profile. Interest scores are, of course, no indicator of ability, although a logical relationship exists, in that a person may well have a greater chance of success in work which he enjoys doing. Research suggests that there is considerable stability of interests after 16 or 17 years of age (Strong, 1943, p. 657; Schmidt and Rothney, 1955). If inventories are used before this age, it must be remembered that interests may be subject to rapid change (O'Hara and Tiedeman, 1959). There is evidence to suggest that before the age of 16–18, inventoried interests are more reliable than expressed interests (McArthur and Stevens, 1955) and so would provide valuable information for counselling purposes. But after 18, with students certainly, there would appear to be little advantage in using an inventory as opposed to asking after their interests. Counsellors would still probably benefit from using inventories with less educated clients over the age of eighteen.

A mistake that is consistently made in giving vocational guidance is to infer vocational interests from avocational interests (leisure-based hobbies and pastimes). Super (1940) found that a vocational pursuit often compensated for occupational disatisfaction. He found that satisfied workers tended to have hobbies akin to their work interests; dissatisfied workers had outside interests much removed from anything connected with their work. Counsellors should not assume that because a child underlines a hobby such as *cycling*, on a questionnaire, that this necessarily means an interest in outdoor activities. He could enjoy it because there is an active social club and he enjoys meeting people, or because he enjoys tinkering with the bicycle, taking it to pieces, reassembling it, etc., none of which signify in themselves an outdoor interest.

One of the outstanding uses of an interest inventory is not in matching a client to an occupation, but as a diagnostic device, whose profile and individual items serve as the basis for a counselling discussion with the aim of defining the clients self and occupational self-concepts.

Numerous interest inventories exist (Strong, Kuder, Lee-Thorpe, Thurstone, etc.) but the one main developed for the British population, the Rothwell-Miller Interest Blank, is an Australian test revised on the basis of British studies. Counsellors could well use American tests, but their value as predictors of occupational success cannot be assumed to be consistent with American findings. Again, their best use is probably as diagnostic counselling devices.

A basic question for counsellors, is how far do they accept a client's interest profile for what it is, or how far do they encourage changes of interests in directions that, on the basis of other information, would seem more helpful to the client?

Further research will gradually assess the value of interest inventories. For the present, the counsellor will feel himself justified in using them to encourage clients to consider occupational fields in which they show unusually strong interest, and in discouraging clients from embarking on careers in which they evidence a marked disinterest.

Personality Tests

In recent years more basic research has been devoted to the measurement of personality than to any other of the previously discussed areas, yet more criticism has been directed at personality tests than at any other type of instrument. Feldt (1959) defines three main uses of these tests for counsellors:

(a) to obtain a useful self-portrait of new students;
(b) to identify students with normal problems that may be effectively handled via group or individual counselling;
(c) to screen out cases of serious maladjustment for referral to the proper psychological and welfare services.

They have been experimented with as secondary education selection devices, but with little success (see Vernon, 1957, and Walker, 1955, for reviews of the use of personality tests as selection agents in Britain). They have also been used as talent matching devices for occupations and individuals, but obtaining personality profiles to differentiate between occupations is even more difficult than using interest profiles for this purpose. (See Super and Crites (1962) for a review of these attempts).

The main function of these tests for the counsellor is in providing information so that he is able to assist in helping the client classify his self and occupational self concepts. They are best used in conjunction with cumulative school records, but the basic question, always to be asked, is whether the test contributes more to the thinking of the counsellor and client than do alternative methods of obtaining the same information.

Many of the worst vocational guidance cases are suffering from some form of personality maladjustment, and it is therefore, vital to ensure whether an occupational failure *is* due to an unwise occupational choice or poor employment conditions, or whether it is symptomatic of a more deep rooted personality disorder. Personality tests can often assist here, though again, whether they can provide more information than a skilled counsellor would obtain is questionable. It is only too apparent, however, that many counsellors are not skilled enough to "tune in" to every client's wavelength, and in such cases these tests can be of use. Such a troubled person may be recommended for clinical treatment, or placed in a situation in which his "liabilities" are turned into assets, or are at least minimized, e.g. the nonconformist, weird-dressing, avant-garde individual often fits to his own satisfaction into artistic pursuits such as commercial art and textile design, or working in "boutiques", record shops, or small bookshops.

A personality test could well have a function as a screening device for response sets seated in personality differences. One of the earliest findings relating to extraversion-introversion was that extraverts opt for speed, introverts for accuracy, when there is a choice in the carrying out of an experimental task (Eysenck, 1947). Jenson (1964) and Farley (1966) found similar evidence regarding intelligence testing, i.e., extraverts are faster and make more errors when conditions are such that the test is administered without stress on speed. It is, therefore, essential for the counsellor to give explicit instructions, as if the test is untimed, extraverts will be handicapped due to their natural tendency to opt for speed and not accuracy. But in speed testing, Eysenck (1967) quotes much evidence to support the view that introverts also perform better than extraverts, as the extraverts are much the slowest since they tend naturally to have a lower drive level (Eysenck, 1967b). These findings lead Eysenck to stipulate that personality variables such as neuroticism and extraversion should always be included in studies of intellectual functioning. The point for debate among counsellors which emanates from this research is the usefulness of screening everyone with a personality test so that these response sets to power and speed tests, rooted in personality differences, can be considered during test interpretation.

CLASSIFICATION OF TESTS BY TESTING PROCEDURE

Performance vs. Paper-Pencil Tests.

Performance tests require the testee to manipulate objects, for example, to assemble mechanical parts, place pegs in holes, perform on a typewriter etc. *Paper-pencil* tests involve writing words or sentences or making an answer sheet. *Performance* tests are more expensive to administer and difficult to administer to large groups. They have the advantage of providing an opportunity to observe the subjects behaviour in approaching the task, solving problems, etc. Insights thus obtained can sometimes be more valuable to a counsellor than the actual quantitative scores. They are also useful for clients who feel uncomfortable with paper and pencil, perhaps because of inexperience in their use. This happened especially in the area of mechanical and manual occupations, for which some performance tests of, for example, mechanical comprehension and spatial ability, are available.

Individual vs. Group Tests

Individual tests are administered by a qualified tester to one testee at a time. The tester records the answers and observes the testee while he is responding to oral questions or performing the tasks assigned. Examples: Stanford-Binet Scale, Wechsler Intelligence Scales, Rorschach, Thematic Apperception Test. *Group* tests are administered to more than one person at a time.

There is an erroneous assumption that individual tests for all purposes are superior to group tests. For most purposes group tests of mental abilities are better established as predictors of educational and occupational success. Analysis of differential aptitudes and abilities is better accomplished through the multifactor group tests developed for this purpose. The research literature provides little evidence even for the *diagnostic superiority* of individual tests, e.g. for diagnosing neuroses, psychoses, and character disorders.

Individual tests are very useful for testing handicapped clients, and where it is important to carefully observe client responses.

Objective vs. Subjective Tests

Objective tests require the testee to check one from a number of possible answers, or write in a word or phrase next to the question. There is no equivocation regarding the correctness of an answer—it is either right or wrong. This makes for very high scoring reliability. A large amount of subject matter can be sampled in a very short period. *Subjective* tests require a considerable exercise of evaluation on the part of the scorer. Oral and essay examinations are examples of subjective tests.

Objective tests are commonly lauded for their reliability but criticized for their lack of validity. It is often assumed that they cannot be used for diagnostic purposes. This is not so; for example, an objective attainment test can pinpoint very quickly the areas of a subject that are weak for a student. Interest, personality, and intelligence tests are commonly objective in structure, and as such, do fail to obtain more than a rough blueprint of any individual, hence the recent plea for less structured intelligence tests that do not strait-jacket a persons mental abilities in "unnatural" ways. For counselling purposes, subjectively obtained information is of the greatest use wherever vocational guidance is seen as something more than a matching-process of jobs and clients. But even here, an objective test, for example the Kudor Preference Record, can provide the framework for discussion by which the way the client has marked individual items is used to discover more about the client's self-concept and life values.

Standardized vs. Teacher-Made Tests

A *standardized* test is administrated and scored according to specific instruction. Norms and age-correction tables are available to convert the raw scores into scores that are comparable with the rest of the population and/or various subgroups. *Teacher-made* tests are constructed by a teacher, usually for his own use in evaluating progress in his own subject. These tests of attainment provide the teacher with feedback relating to the effectiveness of his teaching in a way that standardized tests cannot do. His tests evaluate how far he has achieved his aims. A standardized test examines how well his students have done compared with other students on proficiency criteria defined by the test constructor. Both sorts of test provide essential information for counselling and should be used widely.

Speed vs. Power Tests

Speed tests require the testee to complete as many test items as possible in a specified time. If the test was not timed, the testee could complete all the items. The main purpose is to determine how rapidly the responses can be made. *Power* tests examine the extent of the testee's knowledge or depth of his understanding with the time factor eliminated as much as possible. There is, of course, a practical time limit determined, in the case of a standardized test, by the amount of time required by most of the examinees in the standardized population on whom the test was tried out. Questions are presented in the *order of difficulty*, from easy to hard. Thus power tests are not completely untimed, but are at the further end of the continuum that has speed tests at its opposite end. Speed tests rarely occur in areas of interest and personality evaluation.

TEST READABILITY

At this point, a short note is relevant regarding the extent to which a reading deficiency can interfere with test performance not intended to measure reading abilities. In theory all that is called for from the counsellor's viewpoint is to discover a client's reading level and then assign tests whose reading difficulty is within that range of reading ability. Unfortunately, all reading tests do not measure the same qualities. Some emphasize vocabulary level, others the use of personal pronouns, and others comprehension. One of the disadvantages of using American tests in Britain is that for equivalent age-groups, the American tests assume a vocabulary range not characteristic of the average British child.

It has been shown that a *reading age of at least nine years* is necessary for the reading and understanding of verbal items in a typical intelligence or verbal reasoning test for eleven year old children. Similarly, many arithmetic tests are equally dependent upon reading ability. Where a child's poor reading level is suspected of being responsible for a low score on an intelligence test a performance test should be used rather than a paper-and-pencil test.

WHO SHOULD USE TESTS?

One of the major factors preventing a much wider usage of tests in Britain has been the lack of a clearly defined policy from a central authority stating the qualifications necessary in order to administer tests. Under the present anarchic structure, tests are available in this country from a large number of private publishers, from the National Foundation for Educational Research, and Moray House in Edinburgh. In practice there is little, if any, control over the distribution of tests by private publishers. Anyone can ring or write and order an intelligence test or any other form of test. People may administer them to their own children, to school classes, to work-people, etc., whether they know anything about test administration or not. There is far more to test administration than understanding how to operate a stopwatch. The tester must realize that the instructions in the test manual must be followed to the letter. He must also be skilled in establishing rapport between the testee and himself. He must know how to put the testee at his ease, and the best way of achieving this is to be able to dispel the client's apprehension about the function of the test. This can only be done when the tester has had sufficient training, not only in *test usage*, but in the *facts* about tests. How many people have administered an intelligence test themselves believing that the result will be a once for all estimate of a pupils potential? Only training can dispel these notions. The suggestion of training people just to administer tests, in itself, is highly dangerous. They must know why they are doing it; and they must have a reason for wanting to use tests. A training in test administration will do nothing to provide essential knowledge on these questions. Test usage, by definition, implies more complex skills than the ability to hand out, collect, and score tests (Rodger and Cavanagh, 1964).

The *National Institute of Industrial Psychology* develops tests but mainly for their own research activities, although certain arrangements are made with local education authorities in whom they have the confidence that qualified people exist who can administer their tests.

The *National Foundation for Educational Research* classify their tests into three levels according to the qualifications demanded of the test user:

(a) Tests requiring the minimum amount of technical knowledge for their administration and interpretation.

(b) Tests which can only be used by a person qualified by successful attendance at a course of training in test administration and interpretation which is acceptable to the *N.F.E.R. Test Agency*, or by a person who can produce evidence of experience in the use of tests (under the guidance of someone qualified by training), which the Test Agency may recognize as equivalent.

(c) Tests which can only be used by a qualified psychologist, i.e. a degree in psychology or Associate Membership of the British Psychological Society.

This, undoubtedly, is a valiant attempt to prevent the misuse of N.F.E.R. tests and the large number of American tests that are also distributed through their Test Agency. However, whilst providing the necessary restrictions, it has done little to provide facilities by which individuals could be trained and thereby be able to make use of their tests. Even these restrictions, however, must be questioned. The one large assumption, which is largely unfounded, is that anyone with a psychology degree is qualified to administer tests. University courses in psychology differ enormously, and one of the topics on which emphasis differs is psychometrics. It is perhaps not unjust to suggest that the majority of graduates in psychology are not trained to use psychological tests, and, therefore, are just as likely to commit the same errors in test selection, administration, and interpretation, as most other untrained people.

Test abuse was examined earlier in this article and the danger of untrained persons using tests in vocational guidance must be apparent to all. The only conclusion must be that all potential test users must have their credentials examined, including psychologists, and that all tests should be encouraged to be published by a central body like the B.P.S. or N.F.E.R., and that any psychologist who publishes a test privately, be faced with "excommunication" from the B.P.S. In this way distribution can be clearly controlled. This will sound very authoritarian but the dangers of test misuse are great enough to warrant such a step.

However, as one of the most pressing problems in this country is that tests are not used enough, a step like that suggested would ensure that even fewer tests were used. Therefore, much more training in the use of tests must be initiated, bearing in mind that such training *must* include:

aspects of test selection, including the facts of tests,
test administration,
test interpretation.

This training could take any, and preferably all, of the following forms:

1. B.P.S. authorized options in psychometrics at Universities and Colleges of Education (at present most teachers' knowledge of tests is abysmal).
2. B.P.S. authorized courses (4 weeks would be a theoretically preferred minimum length) for careers teachers and departmental heads.

3. N.F.E.R. and N.I.I.P. organized courses for industrialists and educationalists, again under the auspices of the B.P.S.
4. B.P.S. authorized courses for youth employment officers (a) as part of their introductory training, and (b) as in-service training for older members.

It is good to hear that the B.P.S. now have a working party to consider this whole question.

The predictive value of tests in vocational guidance is proven (Smith, 1951) and the diagnostic value of tests as agents in the development of the self and occupational self-concepts has much evidence in its favour from the U.S.A. Looking at the state of affairs in Britain today regarding the application of scientific advances to vocational guidance procedures, is, to quote Daws (1963), "... rather like finding a chemist who uses the tip of his elbow to measure the temperature of liquids or a builder who determines distance by pacing it out with his feet". Tests are here to be used, but used wisely. Their potential value both to teacher and counsellor is enormous.

REFERENCES

ASCH, M. J. (1958) Negative response bias and personality adjustment. *Journal of Counseling Psychology*, **5**, 206–210.

BARRY, R., and WOLF, B. (1962) *Epitaph for Vocational Guidance*. New York, Teachers College, Columbia University.

BEILIN, H. (1956) The utilization of high level talent in lower socioeconomic groups. *Personnel and Guidance Journal*, **35**, 175–178.

BERNSTEIN, B. (1960) Language and social class. *British Journal of Sociology*, **9**, 271–276.

BLOCHER, D. H. (1966) *Developmental Counseling*. New York, Ronald Press.

BORDIN, E. S. (1946) Diagnosis in counseling and psychotherapy. *Educational and Psychological Measurement*, **5**, 169–184.

BORDIN, E. S. (1955) *Psychological Counseling*. New York, Appleton-Century-Crofts.

BRADWAY, U. P., and THOMPSON, C. W. (1962) Intelligence at adulthood: a twenty-five year follow up. *Journal of Educational Psychology*, **53**, 1–14.

CAMP, D. (1960) Uses of tests. In *Understanding Testing*, ed. K. F. Mclaughlin, U.S. Department of Health, Education, and Welfare. Washington, U.S. Government Printing Office.

CLARKE, A. D. B. (1965) The measurement of intelligence: its validity and reliability. In *Mental Deficiency* (2nd ed.), Ann M. Clarke and A. D. B. Clarke eds. London, Methuen.

CRONBACH, L. J. (1950) Further evidence on response sets and test design. *Education and Psychological Measurement*, **10**, 3–31.

CRONBACH, L. J. (1955) New light on test strategy from decision theory. *Proceedings, 1954 Invitational Conference on Testing Problems*, 30–36. Princeton, N.J., Educational Testing Service.

CRONBACH, L. J. (1961) *Essentials of Psychological Testing*, 2nd ed. New York, Harper.

CRONBACH, L. J. and GLESER, G. C. (1965) *Psychological Tests and Personnel Decisions*, 2nd ed. Urbana, University of Illinois Press.

CROWTHER REPORT (1959/60) *Fifteen to Eighteen*. 2 vols. Ministry of Education. Central Advisory Council for Education, London, H.M.S.O.

DAWS, P. P. (1963) Scientific aids to vocational guidance and selection. In *Report of the Third Annual Conference of Employers and Teachers*. Grantley Hall, Ripon, West Riding County Council—Youth Employment Service. (Mimeo.)

DOUGLAS, J. N. B. (1964) *The Home and the School*. MacGibbon & Kee, London.

DUNNETTE, M. D., and KIRCHNER, W. K. (1960) Psychological test differences between industrial salesmen and retail salesmen. *Journal of Applied Psychology*, **44**, 121–125.

DUROST, W. N. (1954) Present progress and needed improvements in school evaluation programs. *Educational and Psychological Measurement*, **14**, 247–254.

DYER, H. S. (1953) Does coaching help? *College Board Review*, **19**, 331–375.

EDWARDS, A. L. (1957) *The Social Desirability Variable in Personality Research*. New York, Dryden Press.

EYSENCK, H. J. (1947) *Dimensions of Personality*. London, Routledge & Kegan Paul.

EYSENCK, H. J. (1953) *Uses and Abuses of Psychology*. London, Pelican.

EYSENCK, H. J. (1962) Response set authoritarianism and personality questionnaires. *British Journal of Social and Clinical Psychology*, **1**, 20–24.

EYSENCK, H. J. (1967a) *The Biological Basis of Personality*. New York, C. C. Thomas.

EYSENCK, H. J. (1967b) Intelligence assessment: a theoretical and experimental approach. *British Journal of Educational Psychology*, **37**, 81–98.

FARLEY, F. H. (1966) Individual differences in solution time in error-free problem solving. *British Journal of Social and Clinical Psychology*, **5**, 306–308.

FELDT, L. S. (1959) The role of testing in guidance. *Educational Forum*, **23**, 293–301.

FLANAGAN, J. C. (1955) The development of an index of examinee motivation. *Educational and Psychological Measurement*, **15**, 144–151.

FREDERICSEN, N., and GILBERT, C. F. (1960) Replication of a study of differential predictability. *Educational and Psychological Measurement*, **20**, 759–767.

FREDERICSEN, N., and MELVILLE, S. D. (1954) Differential predictability in the use of test scores. *Educational and Psychological Measurement*, **14**, 656–657.

FREDERICSEN, N., and MESSICK, S. (1959) Response set as a measure of personality. *Education and Psychological Measurement*, **19**, 137–157.

FRENCH, J. W., and DEAR, R. E. (1959) Effect of coaching on an aptitude test. *Education and Psychological Measurement*, **19**, 319–330.

FURNEAUX, W. D. (1960) Intellectual abilities and problem solving behaviour. In H. J. Eysenck (ed.) *Handbook of Abnormal Psychology*. London, Pitman.

GHISELLI, E. E. (1960) Differentiation of tests in terms of the accuracy with which they predict for a given individual. *Education and Psychological Measurement*, **20**, 675–684.

GHISELLI, E. E. (1966) *The Validity of Occupational Aptitude Tests*. New York, Wiley.

GIBSON, G. (1954) *An Enquiry into the Incidence of Coaching for the 11 Plus Examination*. M.Ed. Thesis, University of Manchester.

GOLDMAN, L. (1961) *Using Tests in Counseling*. New York, Appleton-Century-Crofts.

GORDON, E. M., and SARASON, S. B. (1955) The relationship between "test-anxiety" and "other anxieties". *Journal of Personality*, **23**, 317–323.

HENDERSON, M. T., CREWS, A., and BARLOW, J. (1945) A study of the effect of music distraction on reading efficiency. *Journal of Applied Psychology*, **29**, 313–317.

HONZIK, M. P., MACFARLANE, J. W., and ALLEN, C. (1948) The stability of mental test performance between two and eighteen years. *Journal of Experimental Education*, **17**, 309–324.

HOPSON, B. (1968) *The Uses of School Record Systems*. Vocational Guidance Research Unit, Leeds University, Yorkshire.

HUFF, D. (1964) *Score: Strategy of Taking Tests*. Harmondsworth Penguin, Books.

HUNT, J. M. (1961) *Intelligence and Experience*. New York, Basic Books.

JAMES, W. S. (1953) Symposium on the effects of coaching and practice in intelligence tests. II, Coaching for all recommended. *British Journal of Educational Psychology*, **23**, 155–162.

JENSON, A. R. (1964) *Individual Differences in Learning: Interference Factors.* U.S. Department of Health, Education and Welfare, Co-op Project No. 1867.

LITTLE, A., and WESTERGAARD, J. (1964) The trend of class differentials in educational opportunity in England and Wales. *British Journal of Sociology,* **15,** 310.

LONGSTAFF, H. P. (1954) Practice effects on the Minnesota Vocational Test for Clerical Workers. *Journal of Applied Psychology,* **32,** 360–369.

MCARTHUR, C., and STEVENS, L. B. (1955) The validation of expressed interests as compared with inventoried interests: a fourteen-year follow-up. *Journal of Applied Psychology,* **39,** 184–189.

MCKEACHIE, W. J., POLLIE, D., and SPEISMAN, J. (1955) Relieving anxiety in classroom examinations. *Journal of Abnormal and Social Psychology,* **50,** 93–98.

MCKENZIE, R. M. (1954) An occupational classification for use in vocational guidance. *Occupational Psychology,* **28,** 108–117.

MACMINN, P. (1960) A few basic facts about tests. In *Understanding Testing,* K. F. McLaughlin (ed.), U.S. Dept. of Health, Education and Welfare, Washington, U.S. Government Printing Office.

MANDLER, G., and SARASON, S. B. (1952) A study of anxiety and learning. *Journal of Abnormal and Social Psychology,* **47,** 166–173.

MARTIN, B., and MCGOWAN, B. (1955) Some evidence on the validity of the Sarason Test Anxiety Scale. *Journal of Consulting Psychology,* **19,** 468.

MATHEWSON, R. H. (1962) *Guidance Policy and Practice,* 3rd ed. New York, Harper.

MAXWELL, J. (1954) Educational psychology. *Annual Review of Psychology,* **5,** 357–376.

MELTON, A. W. (ed.) (1947) *Apparatus Tests.* Washington, Government Printing Office.

MOLLENKOPF, W. G. (1950) Slow—but how sure? *College Board Review,* No. 11, 147–151.

NATIONAL FOUNDATION FOR EDUCATIONAL RESEARCH (1963) *Procedures for the Allocation of Pupils in Secondary Education.* London.

NISBET, J. D. (1957) Contribution to intelligence testing and the theory of intelligence. IV. Intelligence and age: retesting with twenty-four years interval. *British Journal of Educational Psychology,* **27,** 190–198.

O'HARA, R. P., and TIEDEMAN, D. V. (1959) Vocational self-concept in adolescence. *Journal of Counseling Psychology,* **6,** 292–301.

PEEL, E. A. (1952) Practice effects between three consecutive tests of intelligence. *British Journal of Educational Psychology,* **22,** 196–199.

PEEL, E. A. (1953) Footnote on above. *British Journal of Educational Psychology,* **23,** 126.

PEPINSKY, H. B. (1948) The selection and use of diagnostic categories in clinical counseling. *Applied Psychology Monographs,* No. 15.

REPPERT, H. C., CAMPBELL, J. P., and KIRK, O. R. (1965) The management and supervision of a testing program. In T. F. Adams (ed.), *Counseling and Guidance.* New York, Macmillan.

ROBBINS REPORT (1963) *Higher Education.* Ministry of Education, London, H.M.S.O.

RODGER, A. (1951) *The Seven-Point Plan.* Paper No. 1. London, National Institute of Industrial Psychology.

RODGER, A., and CAVANAGH, P. (1964) Tests in vocational guidance. *Journal of the Careers Research and Advisory Centre,* **1,** 21–26.

ROETHLISBERGER, F. J., and DICKSON, W. J. (1940) *Management and the Worker.* Cambridge, Harvard University Press.

ROGERS, C. R. (1946) Psychometric tests and client-centered counseling. *Educational and Psychological Measurement,* **6,** 139–144.

SARASON, S. B. (1950) The test-situation and the problem of prediction. *Journal of Clinical Psychology,* **6,** 387–392.

SARASON, S. B., DAVIDSON, K. S., LIGHTHALL, F. F., WAITE, R. R., and RUEBUSH, B. K. (1960) *Anxiety in Elementary School Children.* New York, Wiley.

SARASON, S. B., and GORDON, E. M. (1953) The test-anxiety questionnaire: scoring norms. *Journal of Abnormal and Social Psychology*, **48**, 447–448.

SARASON, S. B., MANDLER, G., and CRAIGHILL, P. G. (1952) The effect of differential instructions on anxiety and learning. *Journal Abnormal and Social Psychology*, **47**, 561–565.

SARASON, S. B., and MANDLER, G. (1952) Some correlates of test anxiety. *Journal of Abnormal and Clinical Psychology*, **47**, 810–817.

SCHMIDT, J. L., and ROTHNEY, J. W. M. (1955) Variability of vocational choices of high school students. *Personnel and Guidance Journal*, **34**, 142–146.

SCHOOLS COUNCIL (1964) *An Introduction to Objective-Type Examinations*. London, H.M.S.O.

SCHOOLS COUNCIL (1966) *Multiple Marking of English Compositions*. London, H.M.S.O.

SEARS, R. (1943) Motivational factors in aptitude testing. *American Journal of Orthopsychiatry*, **13**, 468–492.

SEASHORE, H. G. (1951) Human resources and the aptitude inventory. *Test Services Bulletin* (Psychological Corp.), No. 41.

SHERRIFFS, A. C., and BOOMER, D. S. (1954) Who is penalized by the penalty for guessing? *Journal of Educational Psychology*, **45**, 81–90.

SINICK, D. (1953) Anxiety in the testing situation. *Personnel and Guidance Journal*, **31**, 384–387.

SINICK, D. (1956a) Encouragement, anxiety, and test performance. *Journal of Applied Psychology*, **40**, 315–318.

SINICK, D. (1956b) Two anxiety scales correlated and examined for sex differences. *Journal of Clinical Psychology*, **12**, 394–395.

SMITH, P. (1957) Twenty-five years of research in vocational guidance. *Occupational Psychology*, **25**, 35–43.

STAGNER, R. (1958) The gullibility of personnel managers. *Personnel Psychology*, **11**, 347–352.

STRONG, E. K., Jr. (1943) *Vocational Interests of Men and Women*. Stanford, Stanford University Press.

SUPER, D. E. (1940) *Avocational Interest Patterns: A study in the Psychology of Avocations*. Stanford, Stanford University Press.

SUPER, D. E. (1950) Testing and using test results in counseling. *Occupations*, **29**, 95–97.

SUPER, D. E. (1953) A theory of vocational development. *American Psychologist*, **8**, 185–190.

SUPER, D. E. (1957a) The preliminary appraisal in vocational counseling. *Personnel and Guidance Journal*, **36**, 154–161.

SUPER, D. E. (1957b) *The Psychology of Careers*. New York, Harper.

SUPER, D. E., and CRITES, J. O. (1962) *Appraising Vocational Fitness* (rev. ed.). New York, Harper.

SWINEFORD, F., and MILLER, P. M. (1953) Effects of directions regarding guessing on item statistics of a multiple-choice vocabulary test. *Journal of Educational Psychology*, **44**, 129–139.

TIEDEMAN, D. V. (1966) An information system for vocational decisions (ISVD): Cultivating the possibility for career through operations. Paper read at Panel, Significant Research Findings from Section 4(c) Projects, Annual Meeting, American Vocational Association, Denver, 7th December, 1966.

THORNDIKE, R. L., and HAGEN, E. (1959) *10,000 Careers*. New York, Wiley.

TRAXLER, A. E., and NORTH, R. D. (1966) *Techniques of Guidance*, 3rd ed. New York, Harper.

TYLER, L. E. (1961) *The Work of the Counselor* (2nd. ed.) New York, Appleton-Century-Crofts.

TYLER, L. E. (1964) The antecedents of 2 varieties of vocational interests. *Genetic Psychology Monographs*, **70**, 177–227.

TYLER, R. W. (1951) The functions of measurement in improving instruction. In E. F. Lindquist (ed)., *Educational Measurement*. Washington, American Council on Education.

VERNON, P. E. (1938) The assessment of psychological qualities by verbal methods. *Industrial Health Research Board Report*, No. 83. London, H.M.S.O.

VERNON, P. E. (1952) *Intelligence Testing*. London, Times Publishing Company.

VERNON, P. E. (ed.) (1957) *Secondary School Selection*. London, Methuen.

VERNON, P. E. (1960) *Intelligence and Attainment Tests*. London, London University Press.

WALKER, A. S. (1955) *Pupils School Records*. London, Newnes.

WEITZ, H., COLVER, R. M., and SOUTHERN, J. A. (1955) Evaluating a measurement project. *Personnel and Guidance Journal*, **33**, 400–403.

WELLMAN, F. E. (1960) Administration of the testing program. In K. F. McLaughlin (ed.), *Understanding Testing*, *ibid.*

WHYTE, W. H. (1960) *The Organization Man*. Harmondsworth, Penguin Books.

WISEMAN, S. (1961) *Examinations and English Education*. Manchester, Manchester University Press.

WISEMAN, S., and WRIGLEY, J. (1953) The comparative effects of coaching and practice on the results of verbal intelligence tests. *British Journal of Educational Psychology*, **44**, 83–94.

WOLFLE, D. (1958) Guidance and educational strategy. *Personnel and Guidance Journal*, **37**, 17–25.

YATES, A. (1953) Symposium on the effects of coaching and practice in intelligence tests. I. An analysis of some recent investigations. *British Journal of Educational Psychology*, **23**, 147–154.

36. A Framework for the Improvement of Test Interpretation in Counseling

JAMES L. LISTER and DONALD H. MCKENZIE

THE interpretation of tests in counseling has become well established as a means for improving student self-understanding (Goldman, 1961; Ohlsen, 1963; Lister and Ohlsen, 1965). This use of test interpretation is designed to provide the student with information that will enable him to behave more effectively. Such information is best presented within a conceptual framework dealing directly with problems of test validity and evaluation of interpretation effectiveness. This article suggests such a framework. It outlines interpretive errors that limit student self-understanding; conditions are proposed for eliminating such errors; and a framework for studying test interpretation effectiveness is presented.

SOURCES OF ERROR

Errors in student self-understanding frequently result from the following types of counselor error: premature interpretation, interpretation involving undefined criteria, interpretation based on unknown validity, and interpretation that the student does not understand.

1. *Premature interpretation.* Tests are often interpreted without first determining what the student wants to learn. When the counselor interprets tests "on request," or when he schedules "routine" interpretation interviews, the student often does not want or is not ready for the information tests provide. If the counselor assumes both desire and readiness for test interpretation, he risks introducing unwanted, possibly threatening, information. Although most students apparently want to know their test results (Lister and Ohlsen, 1965), this interest can stem from needs and concerns of which a student is not clearly aware. Early compliance with the student's request for his test scores risks failing to determine his more important reasons for such requests.

(Reprinted from *Personnel and Guidance Journal*, vol. 45, No. 1, 1966, pp. 61–66, by permission of editor and authors.)

2. *Interpretations involving undefined criteria.* Even when the student wants test results, his questions are often stated so imprecisely that the counselor cannot determine whether the results will be helpful. Both student and counselor often fail to define what they mean by "ability," "interest," or "success." When a student asks how he did on a particular test, he may want to know whether he has the background for advanced work in a particular field; he may wonder whether he has the ability to complete a degree; or he may simply want to know whether he surpassed his room-mate on the test. Until the student can say what he means in behavioral terms, the counselor cannot provide a useful interpretation.

3. *Interpretations based on unknown validity.* Tests are often interpreted to students as if they bear a relationship to a particular criterion when such a relationship has in fact not been demonstrated. The counselor often assumes a test is valid because it possesses other desirable attributes such as a reputable publisher, relevant item content, large standardization group, or high reliability. In presenting an interpretation based on assumed validity, he typically presents the student's standing in comparison with a particular norm group and the degree of confidence that can be placed in that standing. For example, the counselor may in effect tell a student that compared with other freshmen, the chances are roughly two out of three that his true score is between the 20th and 28th percentiles. This is essentially a *reliability* interpretation which conveys nothing about the relationship between test performance and the criterion. Such an interpretation erroneously implies that the student is also higher than 20 to 28 per cent of these freshmen on the criterion.

4. *Interpretations the student does not understand.* The most accurate interpretation is of little value when it leaves the student confused. Test information is not likely to result in modified behavior unless it is understood. Interpretations couched in statistical terms or psychological jargon may impress the student but provide him with little usable information.

ESSENTIAL CONDITIONS

If the following conditions are satisfied, test interpretation should facilitate student self-understanding.

1. *The student experiences a need for information.* The need for information is defined in terms of the student's perceptions. It is not enough for the counselor to believe the student can benefit from knowing his test results; the student himself must feel such a need. The counselor may believe every ninth-grader should understand his interests and abilities, but until each ninth-grader can experience a need for such information, test results will not be useful, no matter how accurately presented.

2. *The student's questions are translated into operational terms acceptable to him.* To provide meaningful information to an individual, the inter-

pretation must be made in terms of the criterion of importance to him. Until a student can approach operational statement of his questions, test interpretation remains generalized and of limited value to the individual.

In the course of counseling with a student about higher education, the student might successively ask the following questions:

What are my chances of getting into college?

What are my chances of finishing the first two years of college?

What are my chances of graduating from college?

What are my chances of succeeding in the engineering curriculum at the state university?

What are my chances of graduating from medical school?

These questions are all related to plans for higher education, but when one tries to answer them using test results it becomes apparent that each question places different demands upon the test as a predictive instrument. Before test results can be used meaningfully, a more precise statement of the student's questions is required. Any student could almost certainly be accepted by *some* college, but the question of completing the first two years or graduating would depend upon the school entered, course of study elected, and many other factors. "Success" in the engineering curriculum would have to be more specifically defined before test results could apply. Likewise, the probability of graduating from medical school would vary, depending upon school entered, course of specialization, etc. Until the student can say what he means in behavioral terms, the counselor cannot provide a useful interpretation.

3. *There is a relationship between test results and the criterion performance.* Translating a student's test results into a statement about some probable behavior takes specific evidence of a relationship between his scores and that behavior. The counselor should not make intuitive or "clinical" interpretations without empirical support, however plausible they may seem. As Levy (1963, p. 234) pointed out, the logical consistency of any interpretation can be determined through reference to a theory or to the interpretive process itself, but the validity, of any particular application of test results rests upon independent criteria outside the interpretive system. Plausibility does not guarantee validity.

It would be *logical* to tell a student who scored above the 95th percentile on need-for-change on the Edwards Personal Preference Schedule that he might be bored working as a librarian. Although logically consistent, this interpretation would be justified only when based on empirical evidence of a negative relationship between need-for-change scores and satisfaction as a librarian.

4. *The information is clearly communicated to the student.* The most accurate interpretation is useless to the student unless he understands it. Even when the counselor presents simple probability statements, he should often supply related information which the student does not request but

which is essential for adequate understanding. When a student asks, "What are my chances of graduating from college?" the counselor may tell him that 40 per cent of entering freshmen graduate. Before the student is allowed to conclude from this statement that he stands six chances out of 10 of becoming a college dropout, he should be told the factors that distinguish dropouts from graduates in the college he is considering. Few students would independently request such essential information, but most would readily understand it.

EVALUATION OF EFFECTIVENESS

Research on test interpretation has relied heavily upon student self-estimates as evidence of improved self-understanding. Pre- and post-counseling estimates of test performance have been compared with actual test scores. Increased agreement between self-estimates and test scores has been taken as evidence of test interpretation effectiveness (Dressel and Matteson, 1950; Johnson, 1953; Singer and Stefflre, 1954; Froehlich and Moser, 1954; Rogers, 1954; Adamek, 1961; Lister and Ohlsen 1965). Within this framework, however, other evidence is required. It has been emphasized that interpretations should be stated in terms of validity; evaluation of effectiveness should be conducted within the same framework. A student who can accurately recall his aptitude test results after interpretation may not know his predicted college grades or probable success in apprenticeship training. Furthermore, what a student reports learning about himself is not always reflected in his behavior. For these reasons, the writers suggest that recall of information alone provides limited evidence of test interpretation effectiveness unless also associated with meaningful behavior change. As Berdie noted, "the extent to which a person's self-knowledge has increased can be determined only through observations of behavior change, and increased self-knowledge is a sterile end unless it is accompanied by such change" (1963, p. 128).

Interpretation is effective when independent observations of a student's behavior in relevant areas indicate that he understands the probability statement. A student could understand an interpretation without accepting it. He might continue a course of study with low probability of success. His understanding of the interpretation (without acceptance) could be reflected in several ways: he might enroll in "insurance" courses in a non-major curriculum; he might try to change the prediction by taking more courses, by doing remedial work, or by getting related work experiences; he might try to strengthen abilities not tapped by the tests interpreted to him.

A student who both understood and accepted an interpretation would "play the odds." He would maintain a course with high chances of payoff; he would abandon goals with slight chance of achievement.

Test interpretation, then, is considered effective when a student's behavior indicates that he understands the interpretation. Evidence should be based on independent observations of behavior rather than on self-report, these observations should be made in areas sensitive to change as a result of the interpretation; and they should focus on the student's understanding of the validity statement, not upon his recall of his scores or normative standing.

DISCUSSION

Test interpretation should give probability statements relevant to the student's questions rather than generalizations from test labels and theoretical principles. Most interpretations that counselors make are actually of a probability nature, whether they realize it or not. When a student is told that he scored much higher on a mechanical aptitude test than most high school students in the standardization group, he usually assumes he can expect higher grades in mechanics courses or perform mechanical work better than those who scored below him. As noted, such an interpretation is based solely on test reliability and the *assumption* of validity. The principles suggested here preclude the interpretation of *any* test without evidence of empirical validity *in terms of the student's questions*. The accumulation of a variety of validity data is essential to the application of this approach. Computer measurement systems, however, will make feasible the gathering of probability data relating to many student questions (Cooley, 1964) and will remove many of the current limitations to this approach.

A counselor who cannot tolerate ambiguity will be quick to translate a student's questions into operational terms. Operational statement is required before test data can apply, but premature operational statement risks dealing with superficial questions. Test data are easily applied to questions stated in terms of intermediate, specific criteria. As the student's questions are stated in more personal terms, however, probability statements become less applicable. A girl might ask, "Do my grades and test scores show that I could earn a degree in electrical engineering at the state university?" The counselor could give the student a probability statement that would indicate her chances of getting the engineering degree. But if further counseling revealed that the girl is trying to compensate for inferiority feelings by competing against men, success in engineering would no longer be relevant. The important question would be that of achieving personal adequacy through competition—a question to which test data clearly do not apply. It is difficult for the counselor to resist stating questions at the level at which tests are most applicable. In so doing, however, he may remain insensitive to the student's most central concerns, where probability statements are less easily applied, if at all. Only a courageous counselor can facilitate the emergence of questions for which he has inadequate data.

It is finally the student who interprets his tests. Unless the counselor wishes to influence the student in a particular direction, interpretation is complete when the student clearly understands the probability statement. The student then becomes his own interpreter, choosing what he will do with the information. For example, when the counselor describes the student's predicted performance as the *average* for persons with his score, the student may accept the prediction or he may modify his self-expectation in a direction more in line with his own self-evaluation. If the counselor has clearly described the group from which the validity data were obtained, and if he has made it clear that probability statements are more accurate for groups than for individuals, then the student has some basis for deciding whether a particular interpretation fits him.

A counselor's particular use of this interpretive framework will depend upon his theoretical orientation and professional role concept. Some counselors will induce the student to select a course of action with high probability of success; others will reinforce movement toward choices which meet a social, economic, or national defense need; others will restrict themselves to helping the student explore the meanings the information holds for him. Counselors will likewise differ in their screening of students for test interpretation. Some will interpret tests only to those students who already want the information; others will try to create desire and readiness through persuasion, reinforcement, or through sensitivity to unexpressed needs.

The counselor who views himself as a dispenser of infallible information will find it difficult to act on these principles of interpretation. If he acknowledges the degree of error present in each prediction, he cannot view his information as infallible. His focus becomes that of helping students understand and confront the uncertainties inherent in probability data. Test information is introduced into the counseling interview to describe the probability of outcomes, not their desirability. It requires a sensitive and insightful counselor to help students perceive their central questions, state them clearly, and face the inevitable uncertainties.

The research strategy for studying outcomes of test interpretation should examine changes in the student's behavior in terms of *validity* interpretations. The researcher will need to obtain independent measures of behavior change on dimensions that are likely to change as information is presented. For example, researchers might determine the percentage of students whose stated vocational goal, following counseling, has changed in directions with higher probability of success. When appropriate behavior change is the criterion of effective test interpretation, whether the student can recall (or ever knew) his scores is unimportant. What is important is the meaning scores have for the student in terms of his questions and purposes.

Recall of test results is a questionable index of interpretation effectiveness because scores are raw data until related to some criterion. There are, in fact, as many possible interpretations as there are criteria. A student who recalls his test results may be unaware or unconcerned with his relative standing on any external criterion. When results are only recalled, it cannot be determined whether they have been accepted or rejected. A student may remember one year after interpretation that he scored within the 16–24 percentile band total score on the SCAT while continuing in a pre-med curriculum without compensating efforts. This student recalls his scores, but the interpretation can hardly be considered effective. More appropriate criteria would include recall and understanding of validity interpretations as well as independently observed behavior change. These criteria consider whether students remember and understand information and whether it leads to more effective behavior. When both of these outcomes can be clearly demonstrated, the effectiveness of test interpretation through counseling will have acquired sound empirical support.

REFERENCES

ADAMEK, E. G. (1961) The effects of testing and test interpretation on selected self-perceptions. Unpublished doctoral dissertation, Univ. Illinois.

BERDIE, R. F. (1963) Testing programs and counseling in the schools. In *The impact and improvement of school testing programs.* The Sixty-Second Yearbook of the National Society for the Study of Education. Chicago: Univ. Chicago Press.

COOLEY, W. W. (1964) A computer-measurement system for guidance. *Harvard Educational Review*, **34**, 559–572.

DRESSEL, P., and MATTESON, R. W. (1950) The effects of client participation in test interpretation. *Educational and Psychological Measurement*, **10**, 693–706.

FROEHLICH, C. P., and MOSER, W. E. (1954) Do counselees remember test scores? *Journal of Counseling Psychology*, **1**, 149–152.

GOLDMAN, L. (1961) *Using tests in counseling.* New York: Appleton-Century-Crofts.

JOHNSON, D. G. (1953) Effect of vocational counseling on self-knowledge. *Educational and Psychological Measurement*, **13**, 330–338.

LEVY, L. H. (1963) *Psychological interpretation.* New York: Holt, Rinehart & Winston.

LISTER, J. L., and OHLSEN, M. M. (1965) The improvement of self-understanding through test interpretation. *Personnel and Guidance Journal*, **43**, 804–810.

OHLSEN, M. M. (1963) Interpretation of test scores. In *The impact and improvement of school testing programs.* The Sixty-Second Yearbook of the National Society for the Study of Education. Chicago: Univ. Chicago Press.

ROGERS, L. B. (1954) A comparison of two kinds of test interpretation interview. *Journal of Counseling Psychology*, **1**, 224–231.

SINGER, S. L., and STEFFLRE, B. (1954) Analysis of the self-estimate in the evaluation of counseling. *Journal of Counseling Psychology*, **1**, 252–255.

ADDITIONAL REFERENCES TO TEST INTERPRETATION

For research findings and implications for vocational guidance:

BENNETT, G. K., SEASHORE, H. G., and WESMAN, A. G. (1951) *Counseling from Profiles.* New York, Psychological Corporation.

EDUCATIONAL RECORDS BUREAU (1964) *Parents Guide to Understanding Tests.* New York.

GOLDMAN, L. (1961) *Using Tests in Counseling*, chapters 7, 11, 12, 13, 14. New York, Appleton-Century-Crofts.

LINDBALL, C. M. (1961) *Testing and Evaluation*. New York, Harcourt, Brace & World.

LYMAN, H. B. (1963) *Test Scores and What They Mean*. Englewood Cliffs, N.J., Prentice-Hall.

MCLAUGHLIN, K. F. (1964) *Interpretation of Test Results*. Washington, D.C., Superintendent of Documents.

ROTHNEY, J. W. M., DANIELSON, P. J., and HEIMANN, R. A. (1959) *Measurement for Guidance*. New York, Harper.

SUPER, D. E., and CRITES, J. O. (1962) *Appraising Vocational Fitness* (2nd. ed.), chapters 20, 21, 22. New York, Harper.

TYLER, L. E. (1961) *The Work of the Counselor* (2nd ed.), chapters 6 and 7. New York, Appleton-Century-Crofts.

BERG, J. A. (1956) Test score interpretation and client confusions. *Personnel Guidance Journal*, **34**, 576–578.

BIXLER, R. H., and BIXLER, V. H. (1946) Test intepretation in vocational counseling. *Educational and Psychological Measurement*, **6**, 145–155.

BORDIN, E. S., and BIXLER, R. H. (1946) Test selection: a process of counseling. *Educational and Psychological Measurement*, **6**, 361–373.

BOWMAN, H. A. (1952) Techniques for graphical representation of pupil personnel data to indicate individual deviates and to provide a basis for more adequate guidance. *Educational and Psychological Measurement*, **12**, 490–502.

COPLAND, R. E. (1966) School reports. *Educational Research*, **3**, 196–208.

DAVIS, F. B. (1959) Interpretation of differences among averages and individual test scores. *Journal of Educational Psychology*, **50**, 162–170.

DUMAS, F. E. (1953) Quick methods for the analysis of the shape, elevation, and scatter of profiles. *Journal of Clinical Psychology*, **9**, 345–348.

ENGELHART, M. D. (1956) Testing and use of test results. *Review of Educational Research*, **26**, 5–13.

GUSTAD, J. W. (1951) Test information and learning in the counseling process. *Educational and Psychological Measurement*, **11**, 788–795.

GUSTAD, J. W. (1956) Helping students understand test information. *Proceedings of the 1955 Invitational Conference on Testing Problems*. Princeton, N.J., Educational Testing Service.

GUSTAD, J. W., and TUMA, A. H. (1957) The effects of different methods of test introduction and interpretation on client learning in counseling. *Journal of Counseling Psychology*. **4**, 313–317.

HOLMES, J. E. (1964) The presentation of test information to college freshmen. *Journal of Counseling Psychology*, **11**, 54–58.

KIRK, B. (1952) Individualizing of test interpretation. *Occupations*, **30**, 500–505.

LUNDY, C. P., and SHERTZER, B. (1963) Making test data useful. *Personnel and Guidance Journal*, **42**, 62–63.

MCCABE, G. E. (1957) Test interpretation in the high school guidance program. *Personnel Guidance Journal*, **35**, 449–451.

MCCAULEY, J. H. (1962) Reporting results of the standardized testing program to parents. *Personnel and Guidance Journal*, **41**, 56–57.

OHLSEN, M. (1963) Interpretation of test scores. In W. G. Findley (ed.), *The Impact and Improvement of School Testing Programs*. 62nd Year Book of the National Society for the Study of Education. Chicago, University of Chicago Press.

PATTERSON, C. H. (1955) The interpretation of the standard error of measurement. *Journal of Experimental Education*, **23**, 247–252.

RICKS, J. H. JR. (1959) On telling parents about test results. *Test Services Bulletin*, No. 54. Psychological Corporation.

ROGERS, C. R. (1946) Psychometric tests and client-centered counseling. *Educational and Psychological Measurement*, **6**, 139–144.

ROTHNEY, J. W. M. (1952) Interpreting test scores to counselees. *Personnel and Guidance Journal*, **30**, 320–322.

RUDIKOFF, L. C., and KIRK, B. A. (1959) Test interpretation in counseling. *Journal of Counseling Psychology*, **6**, 223–229.

SEASHORE, H. G. (1955) Methods of expressing test scores. *Test Services Bulletin*, No. 48.

SEEMEN, J. (1948) A study of client self-selection of tests in vocational counseling. *Educational and Psychological Measurement*, **8**, 327–346.

SEIGLE, W. F. (1953) The teacher reports test scores to parents. *Journal of Educational Research*, **46**, 543–549.

ADDITIONAL REFERENCES TO THE USE OF TESTS IN VOCATIONAL GUIDANCE

For information on the *facts* about tests:

ANASTASI, A. (1954) *Psychological Testing*. New York, Macmillan.

CRONBACH, L. J. (1961) *Essentials of Psychological Testing* (2nd ed.). New York, Harper.

SUPER, D. E., and CRITES, J. O. (1962) *Appraising Vocational Fitness* (2nd ed.). New York, Harper.

THORNDIKE, R. L., and HAGEN, E. (1960) *Measurement and Evaluation in Psychology, and Education* (2nd ed.). New York, Wiley.

VERNON, P. E. (1956) *The Measurement of Abilities* (2nd, ed.). Univ. of London Press.

VERNON, P. E. (1960) *Intelligence and Attainment Tests*. London University Press.

VERNON, P. E. (1964) *Personality Assessment*. London, Methuen.

For information on the *uses* of tests: Always consult

BUROS, O. K. (ed.) (1965) *The Sixth Mental Measurements Yearbook*. Highland Park, N.J., Gryphon Press. [This is a "consumer's view" of all tests on the market, an invaluable handbook. Its only drawback is that the reviews are written by different people from different philosophical backgrounds, and it is not always easy to compare a review of one test with that of another. However, this still does not detract from its fundamental role as an aid to the counsellor.]

Further useful books and articles are:

BERDIE, R. F., LAYTON, W. L., SWANSON, E. O., and HAGENAH, T. (1963) *Testing in Guidance and Counseling*. New York, McGraw-Hill.

CRONBACH, L. J., and GLESER, G. C. (1965) *Psychological Tests and Personnel Decisions* (2nd ed.). Urbana, University of Illinois.

FINDLEY, W. G. (ed.) (1963) *The Impact and Improvement of School Testing Programs*, 62nd Yearbook of the National Society for the Study of Education. Chicago, University of Chicago Press.

GOLDMAN, L. (1961) *Using Tests in Counseling*. New York, Appleton-Century-Crofts.

GOLDMAN, L. (1964) The process of vocational assessment. In H. Borow (ed.) *Man in a World at Work*. Boston, Houghton Mifflin.

MEEHL, P. E. (1954) *Clinical vs. Statistical Prediction*. Minneapolis, University of Minnesota Press.

REMMERS, H. H., and RUMMEL, J. F. (1960) *A Practical Introduction to Evaluation*. New York, Harper & Row.

TYLER, L. E. (1963) *Tests and Measurements*. Englewood Cliffs, N.J., Prentice-Hall.

Author Index

Subject Index

Printed in Germany – III/18/203